Warfare in England, 1066-1189

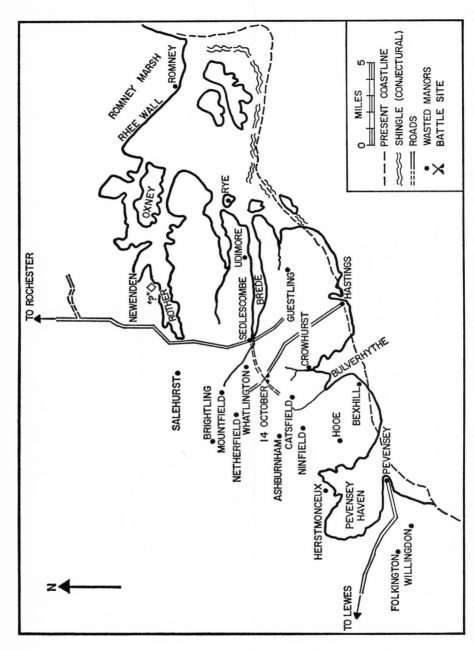

The Invasion Coast, 1066

(The reconstruction of the coastline is necessarily approximate.)

WARFARE IN ENGLAND 1066-1189

JOHN BEELER
Professor of History
The University of North Carolina at Greensboro
Captain CA USAR (Retired)

CORNELL UNIVERSITY PRESS
ITHACA, NEW YORK

CORNELL UNIVERSITY PRESS

First published 1966

Library of Congress Catalog Card Number: 66–16896

Printed and bound in the United States of America

By Kingsport Press, Inc.

To Anne

Preface

THIS study had its inception a number of years ago in a doctoral dissertation prepared under the direction of the late Professor Carl Stephenson at Cornell University. The dissertation, which fortunately was never published, was concerned with the role of the castle in the military history of England from the Conquest to the end of the reign of Henry II. But I soon found that the castle, though probably the most important military innovation of the Normans, could not be studied intelligently without reference to other military developments. So the scope of my inquiry was eventually broadened to include the whole history of warfare in England from the landing of Duke William in September 1066 to the death of Henry II in July 1189. It had long been suspected that the old notion of an "age of cavalry," at least as it applied to England, needed modification, and the work of C. Warren Hollister, Michael Powicke, Robert S. Hoyt, and others has confirmed this suspicion. But these scholars have confined their efforts largely to the institutional aspect of military history—to the means by which English kings raised their armies, rather than to the uses made of the troops once they had been mustered. In fact, no such survey exists, and in the current debate over the history of English and Anglo-Norman military institutions, a detailed examination of warfare in the Norman and early Angevin periods might help to clear the air. Much to my regret, Professor C. Warren Hollister's *The Military Organization of Norman England* was published too late to be taken into consideration; but it is gratifying to note that we are of the same mind on many a controversial issue.

It seems almost invidious to single out individuals for acknowledgment when so many have contributed to whatever merit this work may possess. My debt is greatest to Professor Stephenson, who introduced me to the fascinating Norman period, and whose rigorous but just and kindly criticism encouraged me to persevere in what has seemed at times an endless endeavor. Grateful acknowledgment must also go to the late Professor Sidney Painter of The Johns Hopkins University, Professor C. Warren Hollister of the University of California at Santa Barbara, and Professor Archibald Lewis of the University of Texas, for suggestions that have enabled me to avoid numerous pitfalls. To D. J. C. King, F.S.A., I am deeply indebted for helpful comments and for permission to quote from his invariably interesting and informative letters. The errors that remain, and interpretations of fact, are solely my own, and for them I take full responsibility.

I wish to thank the editors of *The Journal of British Studies, Military Review,* and *Speculum* for permission to use material from articles of mine that have appeared previously in their pages. I must also thank the officials of the British Museum and especially the personnel of the Map Room for their generous assistance. I am likewise grateful to the reference staff of the University of North Carolina at Greensboro, and particularly to Miss Sue Vernon Williams, Miss Mary Robert Seawell, and Mrs. Elizabeth Holder for their unending patience in procuring for me obscure books and periodicals on interlibrary loan. To Professor Norman W. Schul of the Department of Geography of the University of North Carolina at Greensboro I am enormously indebted for his assistance in preparing the maps; their accuracy is due largely to him.

Acknowledgment must also be made to the Southern Fellowships Fund for the grant-in-aid which made possible a summer of study in England, and to the Superintendent of the Royal Greenwich Observatory and the Director of the Tidal Institute and Observatory of the University of Liverpool for their generosity in providing me with meteorological and tidal data that have contributed not a little to the reconstruction of the events of September and October 1066. To Mrs. Harold Luce, who typed the final draft so expertly, and to the Research Fund of the University of North Carolina at Greensboro, whose generous grant provided for the typing of the manuscript and for reproducing the maps, my thanks are also due.

To my wife's parents, Mr. and Mrs. C. W. Boise, I am indebted not only for the comfortable and hospitable base of operations

which their Kentish home provided, but for a thousand pleasant
memories of two summers spent in the English countryside. And
finally it would be impossible to express my debt to my wife
Anne, who has encouraged me through all the ups and downs of
research and writing, and who has cheerfully put up with Pipe
Rolls and chronicles, charters and calendars, for lo these many
years.

JOHN BEELER

Greensboro, North Carolina
Saint Wilfrid's Day, 1965

Contents

Maps

Warfare in England, 1066-1189

Introduction

ON many points, earlier students of the military history of medieval England may now be accused of misinterpretation, distortion of evidence, ignorance, or any combination of the three. Attacks on the work of Sir Charles W. C. Oman have been particularly frequent, all the way from Cairo to California.[1] Such a synthesis as Oman's is especially vulnerable because its vastness of scope has served to discourage any attempt to supplant the only comprehensive work in English on medieval warfare. On a narrower front, Round and his followers have also come under fire, and the whole concept of a feudal age dominated by the ill-disciplined squadrons of heavy horse has been seriously questioned. The apostles of revision now have an extensive literature of their own, and it is perhaps time for an attempt to draw up a balance sheet, at least as it applies to warfare in England from the Norman invasion to the death of Henry II.

That the heavy-cavalry thesis stands in need of revision is no longer open to doubt. All supposition that the mounted knight was the dominating factor on the battlefield is to be discarded as unsupported by the evidence. Even though Oman himself cited example after example in which the role of infantry was of major significance—battle after battle in which the Norman knight got off his horse and fought as an infantryman—he refused to abandon the thesis that the charge of the mailed horseman was the major, if not the only tactical expedient of the day, and insisted that whatever happened to the contrary was exceptional, or accidental.[2] It is now quite generally recognized that Oman's

1

concept must be considerably modified, and that "the men who fought on foot had not, as is so often stated, lost their importance in war."[3] Although Hollister's statement that the *fyrd* and the mercenaries existed "alongside" the feudal host betrays an unfamiliarity with military terminology, it is certainly true that the cavalry did not dominate the battlefield to the degree once thought.[4] At Hastings, at the Standard, and at Lincoln I, the role of the infantryman was important, if not decisive; in 1075, 1088, 1101, and 1102 the English *fyrd* was called out, and there is no indication that it was considered a less reliable element than the feudal contingents. Accounts of the wars of Stephen's time contain numerous references to the employment of infantry. And yet a word of caution must be interjected. There were cavalry fights. Stephen's defeat at Wilton in 1142 was one such, and the slaughter of the earl of Leicester's Flemings at Fornham in 1173 was an instance of the rout of professional infantry by cavalry charges. And if the knight on horseback did not dominate the battlefield in the literal sense after 1066, it was still the knight, invariably of Norman or continental extraction, who exercised the dominant role in warfare. No Englishman—with the single exception of the turncoat Wulfstan of Worcester—even by adopting the military customs of the conquerors, ever rose to a position of command after 1066. To assert that the disappearance of a whole social and military class within the space of a single generation—or that years of war, turmoil, and bloodshed—do not constitute a revolution, is practically to invent a new definition of the term.[5] One of the most telling arguments against Glover's proposition that the old English army had cavalry capabilities is its complete inability to offer any effective resistance to the Norman advance. It would seem unlikely that all Englishmen capable of waging cavalry warfare perished at Hastings. Although lack of inspired leadership and the absence of fortified bases made for the easy occupation of England, it is also probable that the inability of the English to put a cavalry force into the field was an important element in the Norman success. A mounted army does not necessarily fight mounted, and Glover's ingenious arguments on this score will not bear close scrutiny.[6] Dragoon tactics have had a long history, and even within the last century battles have been won by soldiers who rode to battle and dismounted to fight.[7] There is nothing at all incongruous in assigning a similar role to the *huscarles,* or the elite elements of the *fyrd,* especially when the only near-contemporary account of an English mounted action relates that it ended in a complete fiasco. Since there was little or no difference between Englishman and Norman so far as arms and equipment went, the superiority of the Normans can be explained only in terms of their ability to fight mounted. But the Norman soldier could—and did—fight dismounted, and all the evidence supports the thesis that the Normans were able to combine the virtues of the Norman and the English systems into a workable combination of horse and foot, including missile weapons, which represented a degree of military efficiency superior to anything known at the time in western Europe. This combination had made possible the Norman Conquest in the first place. Combined with the English *fyrd,* and augmented when the situation required by continental mercenaries, the feudal contingents were nevertheless the most important elements in the feudal army; and from their ranks came the military leadership of the Norman and early Angevin period. Occasionally a talented mercenary such as William of Ypres rose to a position of command, but the *fyrd* provided no such exceptions. This combination of the mounted and infantry arms enabled William and his sons to repress revolts by tenants whose only resort was to shut themselves up in their castles; by skillful use of cavalry and infantry the politically inept Stephen was able to maintain himself as king for nearly two decades; and the improbable "Angevin Empire" owed its half-century of existence as much to the superior military organization developed by the Anglo-Norman kings as to the restless energy and ability of Henry II. It should be no surprise that in the Palestinian campaigns of the succeeding reign Richard I should have been so successful in his combination of cavalry and missile-bearing infantry. This was no innovation, nor was it adopted on the advice of old Palestine hands; it was simply a century-old tactical system employed by a first-rate captain. The heavy-cavalry thesis is a myth, at least as applied to Anglo-Norman warfare in the eleventh and twelfth centuries. It would be most unwise, however, to state that because it can be demonstrated from the evidence that the wars in England during this period the Normans did much of their fighting on foot, the whole traditional concept of an "age of cavalry" can be swept onto the ashheap of discarded theories. To do so would be to disregard the testimony of one of the keenest military observers of the twelfth century. Giraldus Cambrensis criticized the king of England for paying too much attention to the advice of continental "experts" in planning his Welsh campaigns. He said, in so many words, that Europeans were accustomed to fighting in dense squadrons on open, level ground, and had no notion of what was involved in a campaign amongst the mountains and forests of Wales.[8]

Nor can Oman be upheld in his contention that most medieval generals were incompetent dolts. The charge may be true in some instances; but it is unlikely that inept generals were any more numerous in the Middle Ages than they have been since. It seems only fair to concede that the medieval military mind was at least as flexible as that of more recent times. War, for the upper classes of the Middle Ages, was far more a way of life than it is for any but professional soldiers today, and to assert that medieval commanders never thought about the problems of war is arrant nonsense. When it can be demonstrated that second-raters like the men who commanded the Yorkshire host at the Battle of the Standard— men who, so far as the record shows, never again exercised independent command—could come up with a rather novel tactical formation, one thing is clear: These men were thinking about how best to repel the anticipated Scottish attack with the material that they had at hand; in other words, they were thinking about how to win a battle, not about whether it was a breach of dignity or of class discipline for a knight to get off his horse and fight on foot beside a peasant. William the Conqueror was a first-rate general as well as a statesman; Stephen was certainly a better than average commander; and William II and the two Henrys were at least adequate. In campaign after campaign, each of these men exhibited an awareness of strategic considerations in dealing either with foreign invasions or with internal rebellions. Tactics were simple, to be sure, but to say that western Europeans "were accustomed to only one development of tactics—the shock tactics of heavily-armed cavalry," is more than a little inaccurate, and does less than justice to many a competent commander.[9] King David of Scotland, a Norman in tastes and training, established an order of battle at the Standard in 1138 that is more than a little reminiscent of that developed by the great Theban general Epaminondas at Leuctra in 371 B.C.[10] By concentrating his striking power on one wing he should have achieved victory over the none-too-imaginative Yorkshiremen. It was the king's indecisiveness in committing his reserve—a tactical device which belies Oman on yet another point—that cost the Scots the day.[11] What ought to be recognized is that medieval commanders were professionals in the truest sense of the word. Their military establishments were simple and not always reliable, but they were prepared to utilize them whenever necessary. They were not bound by conditions of terrain or of weather—as the winter campaigns of William I and Stephen, and the campaigns on the Welsh marches prove. The study of military history has too long been inhibited by the belief that there is nothing to be learned from the martial exploits of the Middle Ages. In reality, much of interest and value is revealed by a detailed study of how the commanders of medieval Europe dealt with their often very complex military problems, using imperfect and frequently unsatisfactory means.

Turning to the Norman Conquest and problems more particularly English, it must always be kept in mind that William's invasion was a gamble on a grand scale. In western Europe an amphibious operation of this magnitude had perhaps not been attempted since classical times. However it might have been dressed up for propaganda purposes—and never let it be forgotten that effective propaganda played an important role in the outcome of that gamble—the whole project was aggressive. Once William had secured a foothold in England, feudalism there was bound to develop as it did because during its formative years—the decade after Hastings—England was essentially a military frontier and its government that of a military occupation. Stenton has grasped the truth of the matter, but it has nowhere been given proper emphasis.[12]

To go on endlessly debating whether this or that feature of English feudalism was an outgrowth of old English practice, or whether the Normans really introduced anything new, is to beg the question. The cold truth is that William and his followers were foreign invaders, and the odds were that they would not be able to retain what they had seized.[13] They had to make do with whatever happened to be at hand. That William introduced knight service into England certainly cannot be doubted; it was the only system of military service he and his followers knew. That it followed the Norman pattern precisely would be most unlikely; that it consciously imitated English practices to a significant degree would be equally improbable. Ecclesiastical lands survived the Conquest as units to a far greater extent than did lay lands, and administrative machinery existed at monastic and episcopal centers to a degree which cannot have been possible at the *curiae* of even the most powerful of the lay tenants-in-chief. Bishops and abbots might very well have adapted to the raising of their *servitia debita* procedures which antedated the conquest. This might account for the apparent survival of the five-hide unit in, for example, the diocese of Worcester; but to believe that there was a conscious preservation of the old English system requires an undue exercise of imagination. The first years of the Conqueror's reign, when quotas for knight service were established and arrangements for castle-guard were worked out, were years of improvisation; and that Wulfstan of Worcester or Lanfranc of Canterbury used existing means or personnel to meet the new military demands does not constitute proof that the same was true elsewhere. The success of the whole enterprise hung in the balance, and any device used by an individual tenant to put into the field the requisite number of armed men doubtless had the tacit approval of William. Moreover, it has been clearly and repeatedly shown that William made use of the old English system —and however badly Harold had used it in the Hastings campaign, it had been a working system—and that he continued to do so, as did the successors who were thus enabled to offset the monopoly on military service which might otherwise have been established by the knightly caste. The tradition that the free man, whatever his condition, had a right to bear arms was never forgotten in England. That English *cnihten* found their way into the lower ranks of the feudal hierarchy is doubtless true; that they were accustomed to fight on horseback before 1066 is doubtful in the extreme, but at least they knew how to ride, and the whole argument about them is irrelevant, for they must soon have absorbed the attitudes of the class into which they were being assimilated.[14] The point that is important, and that has not hitherto received proper attention, is that William and his successors, the Normans who had to make military decisions in the field, could have had little concern over where the men came from so long as there were enough of them, in the modern phrase, to accomplish the mission. Whether they could fight on foot, on horseback, or both, must have mattered very little so long as they could fight effectively. It was a substandard performance that brought down the royal wrath on the head of Archbishop Anselm.

Since the history of the first years of the Norman Conquest is military history, and since the government was in all essential respects a military government, these conditions determined the kind of relation between the crown and the tenants-in-chief that was to endure, with few exceptions, until Stephen's day. Because of the constant need to be ready for armed intervention anywhere in the kingdom, William's subordinates submitted to a measure of control which would have been unthinkable elsewhere in western Europe, even in Normandy; and they in turn exercised a self-restraint that contrasts strikingly with their own conduct when on the Norman side of the Narrow Seas. All were in danger; each had to support the others against the ever-present threat of native rising or Norse invasion. The Norman kings could not count on the customary procedures of continental warfare. They had to improvise with what means were available. Hence the complexity of Anglo-Norman military history. It fit no pattern because there was none to fit, and students of social and institutional history might better occupy their time than with whether five hides might after all be three and a half or six and a half hides. William and his sons used feudal troops, the old English militia, mercenaries—whatever forces could be got up to meet each emergency as it arose.[15]

Were the results of the Norman Conquest revolutionary? In spite of attempts to show that there was more of continuity than change, Round's basic premise has withstood the attacks of critics no less staunchly than Arnulf de Montgomery's castle at Pembroke withstood the assaults of the Welsh. As noted earlier, the disappearance within a generation of the whole upper class of English society, lay and ecclesiastical—always with the exception of the opportunistic Bishop Wulfstan of Worcester—and its replacement by foreigners can be adequately described as nothing less than revolutionary. Knight service was an innovation, and the attempts thus far to prove that *huscarles,* thegns, *cnihten,* or *drengs* were horse cavalry have been singularly unconvincing. That the *fyrd* was regarded as a component of the total military power of the realm, sufficiently refutes the assertion that it was substantially the same as the feudal heavy horse. If it had been, the *fyrd* would have been amalgamated into or absorbed by the feudal element, and no more would have been heard of it. The skillful integration of the feudal and nonfeudal elements—the *fyrd* and the stipendiary troops—into an efficient military force is but another facet of the Norman genius for organization. This genius was expressed also in the development of a vast, mutually supporting network of fortresses for the defense of the realm, and in providing garrisons for them in time of peace and war.[16] The castle was undoubtedly the most significant of the Normans' military innovations, and the association of castle-guard with knight service was so close as to make one conclusion inescapable —that they were of common origin, and were introduced into England simultaneously. The combination of royal and baronial castles, and the introduction of the castlery or rudimentary frontier military district, again testify to the remarkable creative ability of the Normans.

When the period of danger was over, when the military occupation had become a true settlement and all attempts to reverse the outcome of Hastings or to restore Cnut's northern empire had been abandoned, the military character of the Norman upper classes began to soften. This provided Henry I and his grandson Henry II with the opportunity to concentrate more and more military authority in their own hands. The development of scutage and the commutation of garrison duty for fixed payments provided the kings with the money to hire mercenaries who were better trained and more reliable than the feudal levy, and who were willing to fight at any time or any place for pay. These developments, traceable at least to the reign of Henry I, though held somewhat in abeyance during the troubled years of Stephen's reign, were accelerated rapidly during that of the second Henry. By 1189 the military power structure had altered significantly, and from this time forward the great tenants-in-chief played a dwindling role in providing the armed forces on which the crown depended for the defense of the realm and the implementation of its foreign policy. Only on the marches of Wales, and to a lesser extent on the northern frontier, did the old feudal spirit survive to provide trouble in the generations to come.

Chapter 1

The Hastings Campaign, September-December 1066

THROUGHOUT the month of September 1066 the winds in the English Channel had blown steadily from the north and west. Finally, on the twenty-sixth or twenty-seventh, the breeze came around to the south and thereby forever altered the course of English history. This shift in the wind was the signal for a great burst of activity in a military encampment at St. Valerie, a small port on the Somme estuary, where an army under the command of William, duke of Normandy, had waited, imploring heaven for a favorable wind.[1] For months the duke had been making ready this amphibious operation in order to lay claim to the crown of England. He had assembled what was, for western Europe in the eleventh century, an army of unusual size, and a quite unprecedented navy. All this cost money, the more since William, a strict disciplinarian, had issued orders against indiscriminate foraging— and seen that those orders were enforced.[2] It would be of great interest to know how such a body had been mustered and maintained on foot for so long a time. Providing the necessary rations for perhaps 7,000 fighting men, plus the inevitable camp followers, was a formidable problem in logistics, but one that appears to have been satisfactorily solved.[3] Factors such as supply, discipline, and morale must have been complicated by the diverse composition of the army William had assembled. Although its nucleus consisted of the duke's own Norman tenants, significant numbers came also from Brittany and Flanders. Smaller contingents had been attracted from Champagne, from the county of Boulogne, and from places as remote as Apulia. Many of these

11

recruits can only be described as mercenaries.[4] Even allowing for some exaggeration on the part of biased chroniclers, all the evidence suggests that both the material resources of Normandy, and its communications network were adequate to support and supply an extraordinary concentration of troops for at least a limited period.

With the change of wind came the long-awaited order to embark.[5] It may be supposed that many of the stores and much of the impedimenta had already been stowed aboard, but to load perhaps 7,000 men and as many as 3,000 horses was a feat of no mean proportions. Enshipment must have begun early on the twenty-seventh, if not before, since high water at St. Valerie occurred at about 4:00 P.M., and the first ships should have been ready to weigh anchor when the tide turned.[6] Before midnight the entire invasion fleet had slipped down the Somme and into the open sea, and were headed for the shores of England, some seventy miles away.[7] Just how many ships were used in the expedition will never be known, although Wace's figure of 696 may not be very far wrong; certainly the 3,000 proposed by William of Jumièges is impossible. Modern estimates vary from William Corbett's 700 down to General Fuller's 450.[8]

The expedition's flagship, the *Mora,* with Duke William aboard, had a lantern affixed to the masthead to guide the fleet through the hours of darkness.[9] During the night the ducal vessel so outsailed the rest that when dawn broke William found his ship alone, with nothing visible but sea and sky.[10] The separation was temporary, however, for during that same Thursday morning the fleet entered Pevensey Haven and the expeditionary force began to disembark. The statement of Guy of Amiens, that the landing was completed by 9 o'clock, is much to be doubted. For one thing, high water at Pevensey on the morning of the twenty-eighth was at 4:35 G.M.T., and the tide was on the ebb until approximately 11:20.[11] Second, and more to the point, even had the tide been favorable, there would simply not have been time enough to debark so large an army by that early hour. The first phase of the campaign—the successful transfer of a striking force across the Channel—had been a spectacular success, a tribute to the energy, resourcefulness, and above all the leadership of Duke

William. That the enterprise was unopposed in no way detracts from its magnitude. Had it been Harold rather than William who won the ensuing battle, the latter's amphibious campaign would still stand to refute those who maintain that medieval warfare as a whole was sterile, accidental, and devoid of imagination.[12]

All modern accounts of the opening phases of the campaign on English soil relate that William disembarked his army at Pevensey, fortified and garrisoned the derelict Roman fort of Anderida, and then marched eastward down the coast to Hastings.[13] Contemporary and near-contemporary sources support this account.[14] But there is one flaw in this traditionally accepted version: So far as can now be determined, there was no way in which an army could be moved eastward from Pevensey by land. A Roman road ran westward from Pevensey to Lewes and from thence to London, but there is no indication that Anderida had any direct communication with points to the east.[15] Moreover, in the eleventh century the Pevensey Levels were an extensive tidal lagoon extending four miles inland.[16] This was scarcely an auspicious place in which to debark an army, its horses, and impedimenta. That the surrounding terrain was difficult is clearly indicated by the statement of William of Poitiers, that after debarkation the duke in person led out a reconnaissance party of twenty-five mounted men, but that they returned on foot because the trackways were too difficult.[17] As long ago as 1928, G. H. Rudkin suggested that the Norman landing must have been made at several points around the perimeter of Pevensey Haven; Williamson speculates that it was made on the eastern side of the bay.[18] More recently, Colonel Lemmon has proposed that the Pevensey landing might have been made by a small force which fortified the shell of the Roman fort, detailed a garrison, and rejoined the main body.[19] The fleet would then have coasted eastward to the vicinity of Hastings, where the entire army would then have disembarked. This explanation, however attractive, presents certain difficulties, the chief being that it does not square with the most reliable sources. The Bayeux Tapestry and the principal narrative accounts state that the army landed at Pevensey and moved overland to Hastings.[20] It is possible but unlikely that an operation such as Colonel Lemmon suggests would have escaped the notice of contemporaries. It must then be

conjectured that landings were made in the Pevensey area as
suggested by Rudkin and Williamson, and that the army made its
way across country, perhaps following local trails, to Hastings,
where another position was taken up and fortified by the inevitable earth and timber castle.[21] The port of Hastings was admirably
suited to William's needs. It provided a haven for his fleet and a
sure means of communication with Normandy. Moreover, it could
be easily defended. In the eleventh century Hastings was located
at the base of a small peninsula. The eastern and western flanks of
the position were covered by the tidal estuary of the river Brede
and the Bulverhythe lagoon, and the narrow neck of the peninsula
could have been held by a small detaining force were evacuation
of the main body to have become necessary.[22] The movement of
the army overland from Pevensey to Hastings must have involved
considerable disorder, and it was fortunate for the Normans that
the march was unopposed.

For the next two weeks William seems to have remained idle in
his camp. This inactivity has been criticized by Colonel Burne,
who asserts that William should, like Caesar, have pushed inland
at once.[23] Such a course would have been unwise in the extreme,
an open invitation to disaster. As the army marched away from the
coast, its numbers would have constantly decreased, not only from
the necessity of garrisoning a line of communications to the base
at Hastings, but through the normal wear and tear of service. The
farther William advanced, the less able he would have been to
win the decisive battle. He was merely exercising normal prudence in staying within easy reach of his base until a general
action had been fought.[24] Of the activities of the Normans
between their arrival at Hastings and the eve of the battle, what is
known remains distressingly little. The Bayeux Tapestry gives
some interesting vignettes of camp life in the eleventh century,
and indicates that the soldiery foraged for at least some of their
supplies, devastating the property of the inhabitants in the
process.[25] Contemporary accounts also mention widespread destruction, while the Domesday survey implies that the damage in
the vicinity of Hastings was extensive.[26] Although there is no
evidence that William attempted much in the way of reconnaissance, or what would now be called intelligence work, since the

area of major destruction extended from ten to eleven miles north and northeast of Hastings, he does at least appear to have pushed out foraging columns in the direction from which the English might most likely be expected to approach.[27] Only one item of intelligence is recorded to have come into his hands: Robert fitz Wimarch, a Breton minister of Edward the Confessor, sent word to the Norman camp advising William to remain in his entrenchments because of the overwhelming force that Harold would bring against him.[28] Although it is hard to believe that William had no knowledge of the course of Harold's northern campaign other than fitz Wimarch's pessimistic report, there is no further evidence of the Normans' activities before 13 October, the eve of the Battle of Hastings.

On that day Norman scouts reported that the English army under the command of King Harold was advancing southward along the road from London to Hastings.[29] The news seems to have caught William by surprise, since it is recorded that a large part of his army was out foraging and had to be hastily recalled.[30] The duke now decided to risk an immediate general engagement, and gave orders that the men were to stand to arms throughout the night of 13/14 October.[31]

After a night recorded to have been spent in prayer, the Norman army moved out of its encampment on the high ground above Hastings.[32] Sunrise was at 6:48 (Local Apparent Time) on the morning of 14 October, and by that hour the advance must have begun.[33] About an hour later the head of the column reached Telham Hill, slightly less than 1,900 yards from the English front. Here a scout reported that he had sighted the enemy.[34] On receiving this information William brought the column to a halt and ordered that armor be put on; then the march was briefly resumed. Less than half a mile farther on, where the road crossed the 300-foot contour, William had his first view of the English army, drawn up to bar his further advance.[35] At this point the head of the Norman column was only 900 yards from the enemy, and the duke had an immediate decision to make. If he were to deploy from his present position, his left and part of his center division would have to negotiate the low and marshy valley of the Sandlake brook, where of necessity they would be thrown into some confusion; alignment would have been lost, and the rather complex order of battle which the duke had planned might be seriously compromised. The alternative was equally hazardous: to advance beyond the narrow saddle separating the Sandlake brook from another small stream flowing east, and from there to deploy literally in the face of the enemy.[36] Nevertheless, the decision to follow this course was quickly made. The advance continued, until at about 8 A.M. the saddle had been crossed and the Norman army began to deploy within 200 yards of the English position.[37]

This was the first of several crucial moments in the day's action. Why Harold permitted the Norman army to form up below his position unmolested will never be known. Had he issued from his lines, as did Bruce at Bannockburn, and charged down upon an enemy only half deployed, with the remainder piled up along a narrow roadway, the day might have been settled at an early hour. But he did not, and the English army stood passive on its hillside while the invading force completed its maneuvers. The Franco-Flemish division under Roger de Beaumont, which had formed the vanguard, marched across the valley and took position on the Norman right; the Breton division, commanded by Count Alan of Brittany, wheeled and deployed to the left, while the Norman division, by far the largest of the three, occupied the center.[38] Since the column was about three miles long it must have been approximately 9 A.M. before the Normans completed the change from column into line.[39] The duke probably established his command post on the north slope of Telham Hill at about the 250-foot contour, from which point he could survey the whole field.[40] As Colonel Lemmon has observed, "Harold, who had planned to surprise the Norman army was himself surprised; the penalty of attempting to concentrate his forces within striking distance of the enemy." [41]

Vast amounts of labor, and thousands of words, have gone into attempts to reconstruct the Battle of Hastings.[42] Of all the modern accounts, those of Burne and Lemmon are the most credible, and Colonel Lemmon's reconstruction may very well come as close to the truth as will ever be possible.[43] The English army that faced the Normans numbered possibly 8,000 men, drawn up some ten ranks deep on a front of about 750 yards.[44] The king had chosen the site with considerable skill. His army was deployed on rising ground about fifty yards below the crest of the ridge, directly astride the road along which William must advance if he desired to approach London by any route. And if Harold's position was chosen with tactical skill, it was also not without strategic merit. An English army on the slope at Senlac not only barred the Norman road to London, it also blocked William's egress from the peninsula on which Hastings was situated (Map 1). To get around the heads of the Brede and Rother estuaries it would be necessary to take the road across which the English army was posted. Unless they could drive the English from this position, the invaders would be penned up in the Hastings bridgehead, with no escape except by sea. Harold had established his command post somewhat higher on the ridge so that he might easily survey the entire line.[45] The general conscensus of modern authorities is that the front rank of the English host was composed of *huscarles*, perhaps the best infantry of the day, with some nine or ten ranks of the *fyrd*, or militia, behind them. A special detachment of *huscarles* supplied a guard for the king at the center of the line.[46] The English had no cavalry, and the missile arm—made up of archers—was insignificant.[47] On both sides, morale must have been very high. The English had just defeated, and all but annihilated, a Norwegian invading force at Stamford bridge.[48] The Normans, French, Flemings, and Bretons, in their turn, could anticipate rich rewards were the victory to be decisively theirs.

The army commanded by Duke William was probably equal in numbers to that of King Harold. A likely guess would give the duke 1,000 archers, 3,000 mounted men, and 4,000 infantry of various sorts.[49] It has been stated that medieval battles were hardly more than "a scuffle and scramble of men and horses over a convenient heath or hillside," with little evidence of tactical skill.[50] As related by contempories, the Battle of Hastings gives the lie to this assertion. It is evident from William's order of battle that he had worked out a tactical plan consisting of three distinct phases. The action was to be opened by the archers performing much the same mission as modern artillery—to soften

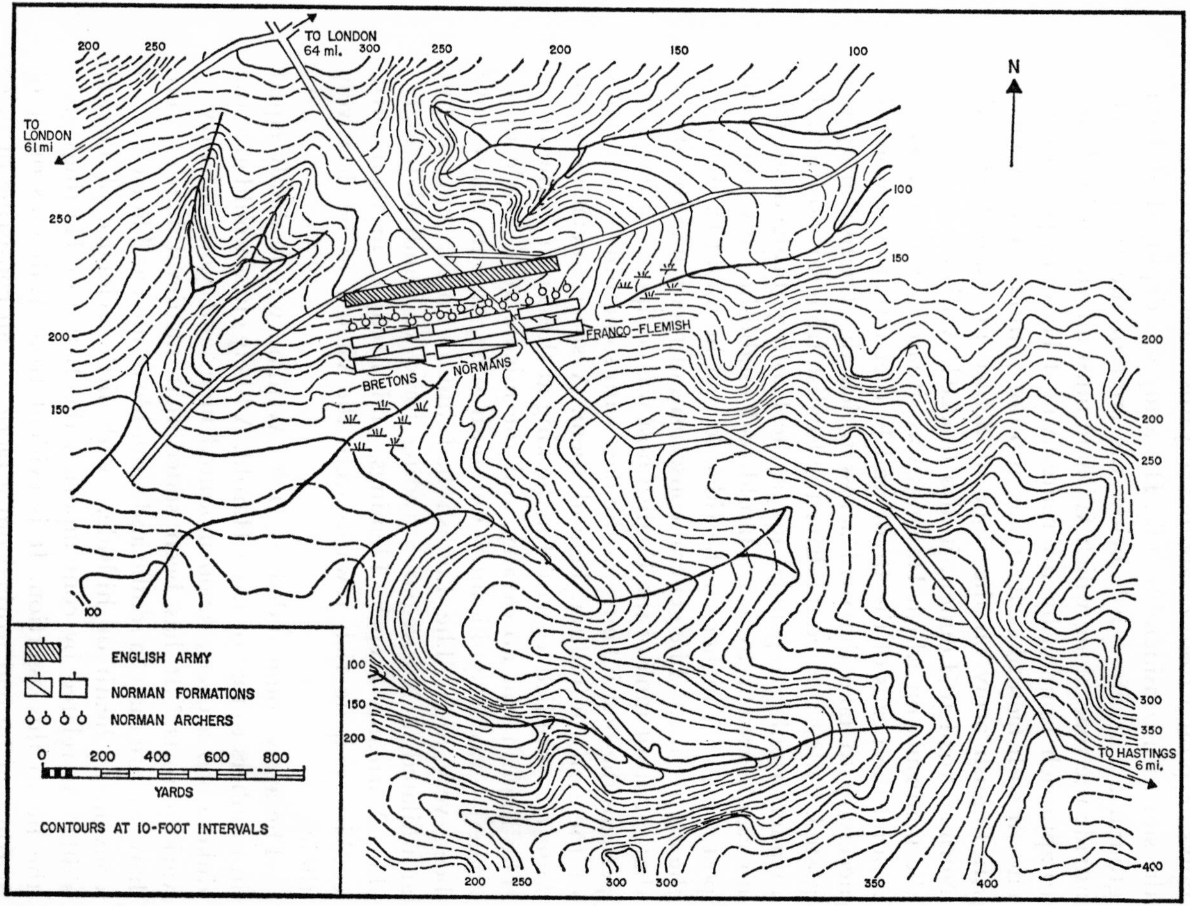

Map 1. Battle of Hastings, 14 October 1066

up the defense. After the preliminary barrage the infantry would advance and break the line; then the mounted arm would ride through and exploit the breaches, either breaking up the defense into isolated pockets of resistance, or pursuing a demoralized and broken enemy.[51] That such an operational plan should not only have been worked out but actually employed in action is a tribute both to William's imagination and to his confidence in the steadiness of the troops to whom its execution was assigned.

The action was opened by the archers who advanced to within about a hundred yards of the English line and opened fire. Since they had to shoot uphill, this attempt to soften up the position had little effect. Arrows with a flat trajectory were taken on the shields of the *huscarles;* those with a high trajectory must have passed over the heads of the defenders. Since the weakness of the English in archery meant that there were few arrows for the Normans to pick up from the ground by way of replenishment, the invaders must soon have run out of arrows. But in spite of the archers' failure to accomplish their mission, William held to his plan. He now launched the heavy infantry up the slope against the English position. As they approached the line they were met by a murderous hail of stones, clubs, stoneheaded axes, and javelins.[52] Nevertheless the Norman infantry continued to advance until they had closed with the *huscarles.* Unable to break the front, they suffered heavy casualties because their defensive armor was not proof against the blows of the two-handed Danish axes wielded by the English.

The Bretons on the left, who had the easiest slope before them, were the first to encounter the English missile barrage.[53] The advance hesitated, halted, then broke back toward the rear, carrying away the Breton knights with it. At this juncture a considerable element on the English right sallied from its position and pursued the panic-stricken Bretons down the slope. The pursuit carried archers, infantry, and cavalry all the way to the marshy bottom of the Sandlake brook. Here the cavalry bogged down, incurring numerous casualties.[54] Elsewhere the Norman baggage guard was threatened; the center division, its left flank now uncovered, began to fall back lest it be taken from the rear. The withdrawal became general, extending even to the Franco-

Flemish division on the Norman right. Duke William's army seemed just then to be on the verge of disintegration.

The withdrawal raises an interesting possibility: Was the counterstroke that piled up the Breton division in the marshy bottom simply the wild rush of undisciplined shire-levies? Such, until recently, has been the assertion made by those who have written about the battle.[55] But Colonel Lemmon remarks:

In this episode of the battle one cannot fail to notice the very strange disproportion between the alleged cause and the recorded effect. A supposed undisciplined rush of some shire-levies is said to have caused disorganization in the whole Norman army which their own chroniclers admit was little short of a debacle. There are strong reasons for supposing that the Saxons made a planned counter-attack on the Norman left, and it may even have been Harold's main counter-stroke. If the latter, it was made, of course, much too early in the day; but that would be quite in keeping with Harold's impetuous nature.[56]

At this critical moment William, who had probably been watching developments from his vantage point on Telham Hill, intervened in an attempt to restore the rapidly deteriorating situation. He was unhorsed, and the rumor spread rapidly that he had been killed. Had this rumor proved true, only disaster could have ensued. The Bayeux Tapestry illustrates this incident vividly. The Norman duke is pictured with his helmet pushed back to show his followers that he is indeed alive. With the energetic assistance of Odo, the warlike bishop of Bayeux, and of Count Eustace of Boulogne, the incipient panic in the center was halted. When the position here and on the Norman right had been stabilized, William was able to detach from the center cavalry, which could be used as a tactical reserve. This detachment was launched downhill against the exposed left flank of the counterattacking English, now fighting in the soggy bottom of the Sandlake brook. Caught by surprise, the English were all but annihilated, for only a handful managed to regain their lines.[57]

At this juncture Colonel Burne and Colonel Lemmon both speak of a pause or lull in the action.[58] There is no mention in the contemporary accounts of any such interruption, nor does it seem necessary to invent one to explain the next phase of the battle. The first two assaults had scarcely produced the effect on the

English line that William had anticipated, although he may have believed that the repulse of the English counterstroke had shaken the enemy morale. Whatever the reasoning may have been, the duke adhered to his original plan, and all along the line the knights of the third Norman echelon picked their way through the wreckage of archers and spearmen, and began to advance up the slope toward the still intact English front.[59] It could not have been a very orderly advance under the circumstances. As each group of knights came within range, it met the same reception as had greeted the earlier infantry attack—a hail of spears, rocks, and stoneheaded clubs. Through this the attackers attempted to force their "frightened and jibbing horses close enough to the Saxon line to prod at it with their lances." [60] Those who got close enough had then to face the solid rank of *huscarles* and their Danish axes, which could cut down man and horse at one blow. The knights did not readily desist, and the contest must have gone on for some time. However, as casualties began to mount, small clumps of horsemen began to give way down the slope, and finally the whole center division, composed of William's own Norman vassals, fell slowly back. Then, as earlier in the day, the English sallied from their lines in hot pursuit, pushing the Normans before them. But once again the resourceful duke was equal to the crisis. Gathering what can have been scarcely a corporal's guard of knights, he took the English in flank, inflicting heavy casualties. It is around this sequence of actions that the Norman chroniclers built their legend of the "feigned retreat," so convincingly that it has only recently been challenged.[61] Even such respected historians as Sir Frank Stenton and David C. Douglas, in *Anglo-Saxon England* and *William the Conqueror,* have perpetuated the myth.[62] Colonel Lemmon's clear exposition of the hoax would be difficult to improve upon:

According to the Norman chroniclers, the retreat of the Norman cavalry was a feint designed to draw the Saxons out, after which they wheeled about and destroyed their pursuers. Apart from the fact that no allegation of a retreat "according to plan" carries conviction, there is the serious military objection that such a manoeuvre is contrary to the principle that troops once committed to the attack cannot be made to change their direction. The impossibility of passing orders to hundreds if not thousands of individuals, all engaged in separate hand-to-hand combats; and of simultaneous timing of such an operation should also be sufficiently apparent; yet the incident of the "Feigned Retreat" has been almost universally accepted, given great prominence in all narratives as the cunning ruse whereby William won the battle, and will die hard. The reason why the chroniclers made up the story is fairly obvious: they dared not record that the Norman cavalry ran away, though they did not scruple to say that the Breton infantry did so earlier in the day.[63]

William's prompt action restored the situation, however, after what logically should have been the principal English counter-stroke. The real question is not whether the Norman retreat was feigned or compelled, but rather why there was not a general English advance instead of piecemeal sorties here and there along the line. Could it be that King Harold had ordered such a counterattack, but that for one reason or another it met the fate of Somerset's ill-fated charge at Tewkesbury in 1471?[64] This would seem to be the most logical conclusion. The opportunity was ripe; one after another, the duke's assaults had been beaten back; the flower of his army was in disordered retreat down the slope; the invading army must have trembled at the verge of demoralization. Had a general counterattack taken place, the Norman army must surely have been cut to pieces as it milled about in the hollows. It was, in essence, the very sort of situation that Bruce took advantage of to rout the English at Bannockburn.[65] At this critical moment, which seems to have gone largely unnoticed by historians, I would suggest that an order for a general advance was probably issued, but that it was not carried out as intended for precisely the same reasons that the feigned retreat could not have been undertaken—the lack, in the eleventh century, of an adequate staff and of troops sufficiently disciplined, once they had been committed, to make coordinated movements a practical expedient.[66] So the isolated counterattacks by the English were beaten back with heavy loss, and William had at least time to formulate one more plan to dislodge them from their position astride his road to London.

As a result of the piecemeal sorties, the English line had been so weakened that it was compelled to pull in its flanks and shorten the front.[67] Still it must have appeared formidable to the Norman soldiers—archers, infantry, and cavalry intermingled at the bottom of the slope. The day was growing late; by this time it must have approached midafternoon, and in a couple of hours the sun would set.[68] Whatever was done now would have to be done in a hurry. William's original plan had anticipated the disintegration of the English line by the three successive attacks of his three echelons, each fighting what amounted to a separate action. The results, after approximately six hours of fighting, were somewhat less than satisfactory from the Norman point of view. The army had suffered heavy casualties, and the English still occupied their original position, although on a shortened front.

In a final bid for victory, William now ordered a general attack in which all arms were to cooperate.[69] The archers, who presumably had replenished their supply of arrows, were ordered forward to commence the action; now, instead of aiming directly at the enemy line, they were ordered to direct a plunging fire into the ranks of the English. This furnished a covering barrage for the advance of the remainder of the army, consisting of infantry and probably a considerable number of dismounted cavalry, with the remaining mounted troops in close support. The barrage was particularly effective against the more lightly protected members of the *fyrd*, but a chance shot also struck King Harold in the eye— not a fatal wound, but one which undoubtedly spread consternation through the ranks of his army.[70] Certainly the conduct of the defense must have been seriously impaired.

Thanks to the shortening of the English line, the mounted troops were able to ascend the easier slope on the left, and to gain the ridge on which the defense was maintained. Charging in on the English right flank, the Normans were able to roll it up on the center, where the household troops were maintaining a stubborn resistance about the royal standards and the wounded king. At about the same time a mounted force commanded by Count Eustace gained the ridge at the opposite end of the line, so that both flanks of the English army were enveloped. The only course now open to the remnants was to hold out until darkness and then withdraw into the forest at the rear. Thus the *huscarles* fought on, with ever thinning ranks, until their numbers were so reduced that a band of Norman knights were able to hack their way through to King Harold's command post, where they cut him down on a spot where the high altar of Battle Abbey church was later to stand.[71] It was now dusk, and practically speaking the battle was over.[72] With the *fyrd* in total rout, the leaderless *huscarles* fell back in small groups to the sheltering forest.[73] Even though it was now nearly dark, and though his troops must have been near exhaustion from the long struggle, William detached Eustace of Boulogne to pursue the fleeing English. Some hundreds of yards to the rear of the field the pursuing cavalry were brought up short at a ravine, on the farther side of which a group of *huscarles* had rallied.[74] The count, reluctant to commit his men against the triple hazard of ditch, darkness, and the English, turned back; but William, who had come on the scene, ordered him to renew the pursuit.[75] In the ensuing fight the Normans suffered heavily—Count Eustace himself becoming a casualty—but they eventually carried the position. By this time it was quite dark, and the action at Hastings was ended. "Duke William was left on that ridge-top, lord of all he surveyed." [76]

In fact, by now William was lord of more than that, since he had garrisons at Hastings and Pevensey; but in the gloom of the October evening he could not have known that he had won a kingdom. To be sure, Harold lay dead upon the field; but there were many Englishmen who had never welcomed Harold's elevation to the throne. Only a small fraction of the potential armed strength of England had taken up arms on the battlefield. Were a leader of ability to appear, he would have no trouble in finding men.[77] And if William was indeed the commander he appears to have been, he must have made his calculations on the premise that this was at least possible. So, instead of advancing at once on London, he spent the next day on the battlefield, burying the fallen. Then he returned to the coast, so that his battered army could recuperate and await reinforcements—or stand on the defensive, if need be.[78] Most historians have failed to emphasize sufficiently that even after Hastings the Norman Conquest was not a sure thing. Though later events appeared to prove that it had been, a doubt or two must have remained in William's mind as he surveyed his host, now much battered and depleted, and awaited reinforcements and remounts under the walls of his hastily built fortifications at Hastings.

William remained at Hastings five days before proceeding to march, not directly for London, but eastward along the coast toward Dover.[79] There were sound strategic reasons for this move. The Normans' possession of the coastal towns not only would make their current position more tenable, but also would provide an avenue of retreat, should the final military decision be unfavorable. In possession of Pevensey, Hastings, and the ports to the east, William could safely land replacements and if necessary, provided he had not moved too far from the coast, escape to Normandy.

For the period between the battle on 14 October and William's coronation at London on 25 December, the narrative sources of information are meager indeed. Some scattered bits of evidence are available, but not enough even to trace the Norman line of march with perfect accuracy. Fortunately, as with the depredations around Pevensey and Hastings, the valuations in *Domesday Book* provide a supplement to the contemporary chronicles. From these it is possible to map with some certainty the route of the Norman columns as they circled and then converged on London.[80]

The first ascertainable point on William's itinerary was Romney. Here, at some time before the Battle of Hastings, the crew of a Norman ship or a party of foragers had been roughly handled by the inhabitants. Romney thus became one of the two English communities to uphold the martial reputation of their ancestors. Upon these offenders William now meted out severe punishment before proceeding via Burmarsh to Folkestone, ten miles farther east.[81] From the extensive damage in the vicinity it appears likely that William again detached a garrison from his main body, in which event the motte-and-bailey castle which stands on the ridge above the town was probably begun at that time.[82] Another march of seven miles brought William to the gates of Dover. Here a crowd of refugees seems to have gathered, trusting in the protection of the almost impregnable castle Harold had recently built.[83] But at the approach of the Norman army the garrison had lost heart, and they surrendered without standing a siege which might seriously have upset William's plans.[84] The Conqueror spent eight days at Dover, strengthening its fortifications; he detailed a garrison, and also left behind such of his troops as had not yet recovered from an outbreak of dysentery. He then turned north on the Roman road to London, with Canterbury as the immediate objective. If London was the economic and commercial center of the kingdom, and Winchester the political center so far as any existed, Canterbury was certainly its religious capital, whose possession was of considerable psychological significance. Having as one objective the restoration of England to Roman authority, the Norman army marched under a banner blessed by Pope Alexander II. The occupation of the seat of Stigand, the schismatic and simoniacal archbishop of Canterbury, would surely improve William's position. For a day or two the advance was halted by the duke's illness; then he pushed on by way of Patrixbourne and Bekesbourne.[85] At the approach of the invading column, the inhabitants of Canterbury came out and submitted to the duke.[86] Raiding parties seem to have been pushed out as far east of Canterbury as Littlebourne, Preston, Sturry, and Chislet, and the whole region from the archiepiscopal city to the southern coast was harried.[87] The Domesday entries suggest that William remained in Canterbury for only a short time—perhaps no more than a day or two—before he pushed on for London.[88]

The main body of the Norman army did not, however, pursue the obvious route—the old Roman road, or Watling Street, from Canterbury by way of Rochester. Instead, it seems to have concentrated at Lenham and then marched northwestward along the ancient trackway now known as the Pilgrim's Way–North Downs Ridgeway.[89] At Lenham William brought together his scattered detachments—the right from Ostspringe and Eastling; the center from Chilham; and the left, or possibly reinforcements from Folkestone, via Brabourne, Stelling, Crundall, and Pluckley-cum-Pevington. From this assembly area the column moved by way of Maidstone, Seal, Westerham, Limpsfield, Oxted, Tandridge, and Godstone. Occupation of the latter uncovered the road leading through the Andredsweald to the fortified Norman base at Hastings. Here a halt appears to have been made, for the devastation recorded in the vicinity was unusually severe. The reason for the delay seems obvious: namely, that the main body was awaiting the return of a "task force" which William had detached at Seal for a dash on London.[90] This command, which must have consisted entirely of cavalry, advanced by way of Cudham, Chelsfield, Orpington, Eltham, and Lewisham to Southwark.[91] Here they were attacked by a body of Londoners who sallied across the bridge, but the city militia were easily beaten off.[92] However, the Normans were not in sufficient strength to force a crossing; so, after burning Southwark, they retired to join the main body at Godstone, via Battersea, Tooting, and Merton.[93] With his army once again united, William continued his march below London. Passing in the vicinity of Ewell, he gained control of the road to Chichester, whose port the fleet seems to have seized for a base not long after the Battle of Hastings.[94] It ought not to be inferred that William depended on lines of communication in the modern sense, once he had left the immediate vicinity of the coast. Although garrisons were certainly left at Pevensey, Hastings, and Dover, and possibly at Folkestone, once the expeditionary force had left Canterbury and marched away into the interior, William was as much on his own as Major General W. T. Sherman was to be when he cut loose from his communications at Atlanta in the summer of 1865. These bases did provide useful ports of entry both for supplies—although, like Sherman, William foraged liberally off the country—and, more importantly, for reinforcements. *Had* the English rallied, and *had* the Norman army been defeated, only a remnant could have been expected to reach the protection of the coastal castles. The prospects for survival in such an eventuality became increasingly slim once the army had passed Ewell. After this, with no line possible of retreat, defeat would have meant total disaster.

After crossing the Chichester–London road, the Normans moved through Ashstead and Leatherhead, then turned west to Guildford. From Guildford the line of march extended through Compton and Wanborough, across the border into Hampshire to Basing, thence to Micheldever, and northward to Sutton Scotney and Hurstbourne. This advance had brought William to within six miles of Winchester, where it is likely that the surrender of the city occurred.[95] The importance of this event was both military and political. The submission of both the religious and the

political centers of the kingdom—Canterbury and Winchester—
gave William a considerable psychological advantage over those
Englishmen who might be tempted to oppose him. The duke
must have known a good deal about what was going on in yet
unconquered England, and he probably had grounds, political as
well as military, for pursuing this seemingly roundabout line of
march.

The Domesday entries for the vicinity of Winchester also
suggest that the Norman army was heavily reinforced through
Chichester or Portsmouth.[96] This augmentation apparently
marched through Fareham, Wickham, Bishop's Waltham, Drox-
ford, Exton, Wanford, and West and East Meon to Alresford.
Here they were met by a detachment from the main army that
had reached Alresford by way of Farnham, Hartley Maudit, and
Farringdon. These two detachments combined to form the left
wing of an army moving in two columns northward toward the
Thames.[97] No strategic inference need be drawn from this. The
division of so small an army into two, and later into three,
columns marching on separate roads was of course a violation of
what would now be called sound doctrine, but it was rendered
necessary by the problems of supply. Had the entire army
marched on a single road, the rear elements would have starved.
Wherever William concentrated his whole force for even a day or
two at a time, as at Canterbury and Godstone, the area of
devastation extended for miles in every direction.

This strong left wing now moved from Alresford westward,
skirting Winchester, then wheeled north to the west of Andover
and moved on to Lambourne in Berkshire. The right division,
which seems to have been the weaker at this time, advanced from
Hurstbourne northward to Highclere, where it divided. The
center division continued to march north to Wantage, where it
swung east to reach the Thames at Wallingford. The new right
wing marched farther east from Highclere to East Isley and then
to Wallingford. From Lambourne the left swept through the
northwestern corner of Berkshire by way of Farringdon, Sutton
Courtney south of Abingdon to Whittenham, and thence to
Wallingford.[98] Here, it is now agreed, William crossed the
Thames and established a camp on the Oxfordshire side of the

river.[99] Here also the first important defection from the English occurred: Stigand, the archbishop of Canterbury, came in and made his submission.[100] Although it is impossible to fix the chronology of William's march with any exactness, the crossing of the Thames and the submission of Archbishop Stigand cannot very well have been made before the middle of November.[101]

From Wallingford the main body of the army continued its march along the Icknield Way, keeping the Chiltern Hills as something of a shield on its right flank, to Risborough and Wendover.[102] There are some indications that a flanking column operated to the north, or on the left flank of the army, which occupied Buckingham and later joined the left division for the advance on Bedford. From Risborough and Wendover, with the shelter of the Chilterns no longer available, the Normans again reverted to movement in three columns. The center continued along the Icknield Way, while to the southward, the right division occupied the heads of the valleys of Bulbourne and Gade. The left column, apparently the strongest, struck north to Aylesbury and then rejoined the center at Luton.[103] This cut, at least temporarily, the Watling Street, and sealed off London from any reinforcement from the northwest.

The center column marched from Luton in the direction of Hertford, which perhaps had been designated as a general rendezvous, while the right wing swung east down a tributary of the Ivel and crossed it at Langford. It would appear that a detachment seized Hitchin, and that the whole column then marched south toward Hertford. The left wing diverged again from Luton and advanced north to Bedford. There it wheeled eastward to cross the Ouse, and then turned south toward Hertford while a detachment raided eastward across the Ermine Street to Cambridge. This force too turned south, moving by way of Potton.

Eventually, then, the entire army would appear to have been concentrated in the vicinity of Hertford. As Fowler has pointed out, even in the eleventh century an army could not be maintained for any length of time in a town. The Domesday evidence suggests that the troops were billeted in a circle about Hertford, the posts to the east being astride the Ermine Street, while to the southwest a garrison at St. Albans dominated the Watling

Street.[104] In effect London was now cut off from the north and northwest, the directions from which any relief might reasonably be expected.[105]

Once again there is a complete absence of chronology, but Fowler computes that the element that marched farthest—which seized Buckingham and later joined the left wing for the strike at Bedford and Cambridge—covered not more than 150 miles after leaving Wallingford.[106] If the estimate of ten miles a day is anywhere near correct, the left division, likely composed entirely of cavalry, could have reached Hertford during the first week in December. The other columns, presumably containing the infantry and impedimenta, had much shorter lines of march, and they probably began to reach the concentration area early in December. It is certainly possible, or even probable, that the Norman army was concentrated in the Hertford area by 10 December.

At about this time the English leaders in London seem to have concluded that resistance was futile, though it is difficult now to see how William could possibly have invested London with the forces at his command. Nevertheless, the chief men of the interim administration, Edgar the Atheling, Archbishop Aeldred of York, and the earls Edwin and Morcar—if they were actually in the city —with the principal men of London came out and surrendered to William at Berkhamstead.[107] The chronicle asserts that the surrender should have occurred earlier—that the English submitted after the damage to the country had been done. At any rate, hostages were given by the magnates, and William swore that he would be a faithful lord. A diehard party apparently still existed in London, however, for the English annalist complained that the Norman army continued its ravages after the surrender agreement had been made.[108] William of Poitiers, who did not mention the surrender at Berkhamstead, wrote that the city did not submit until the Norman army had come within sight of London itself.[109] Another contemporary mentioned William's preparations for a siege, his negotiations with the London commander, and a skirmish in the vicinity of Westminster.[110] A fourth account, also contemporary, described a fight between the advance guard of the Norman army and a determined band of Londoners in the central square of the city itself.[111] At all events, such resistance as was offered was soon overcome; picked men were detailed to construct a castle; and preparations were made for the entry of the Conqueror.[112] Finally, as the climax of the campaign, William was crowned king of the English by Archbishop Aeldred on Christmas day.[113] Shortly after the ceremony William withdrew to Barking, where he remained until the fortifications had been completed.[114]

This ended the initial phase of the Norman Conquest. William was now king, but he ruled in a very limited sense. His authority could be enforced only in those areas actually occupied by his troops. True, he had taken a number of important Englishmen as hostages, but this was hardly a guarantee of good faith under all circumstances. The results of the battle at the "hoar apple tree" and the long march around London had done so much toward establishing Norman military control over England, however, that it is well to offer a critique of these operations.[115]

Concerning the Battle of Hastings, the implications are clear enough. Here perished not only King Harold, the ablest military commander of his realm, but also his brothers Gyrth and Leofwine, upon whom the command might have devolved. Gyrth in particular seems to have been able, though headstrong.[116] In addition, the professional infantry of royal *huscarles,* who were the flower of the English army, suffered prohibitive losses on that October day. These, however, are only the negative aspects of the defeat. On the other hand, a mere fraction of the military potential of the kingdom had appeared on the field. For example, the northern earls, Edwin and Morcar, whose losses at Fulford in September could not as yet have been replaced, had not taken part in the action at Hastings, nor had Earl Waltheof, who held an important block of Midland shires. The levies present on 14 October were those Harold could collect in the thirteen days after he learned, while still at York, of the Norman landing, and his concentration almost literally on the battlefield itself.[117] The statement by Florence of Worcester, that Harold marched from London before half his army had assembled, may be taken literally.[118] William, able and experienced commander that he was, evidently realized that a single battle, no matter how

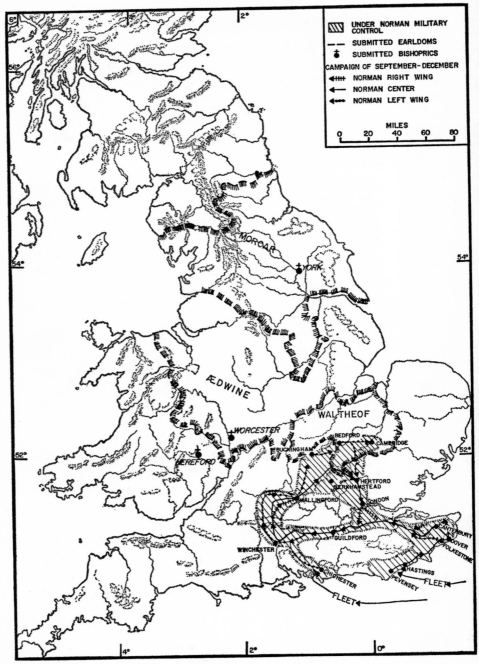

Map 2. Situation as of 25 December 1066

decisively won, need not augur success for the entire campaign. Hence the circuitous and seemingly protracted operation which culminated in December with the submission of the English leaders and the occupation of London. "Medieval warfare is not solely, nor even largely, battles and sieges. For weeks and even months at a time, it is military pressure exerted by the destruction of life, property and the means by which life is maintained." [119]

Much has been written in explanation of William's long march around London. Strategic considerations surely played a part, and the intent to isolate the metropolis was no doubt one of these.[120] But, as Baring points out, William simply did not have much time for wanton destruction. The 380-odd miles between Hastings and London could not have been covered in less than two months "if he had allowed his troops to be scattered for widespread ravage. . . . Outside the line of march the immediate effect of the conquest on the value of land in the southeast seems to have been very slight." [121]

The purpose of William's march, then, was not so much military in the ordinary sense, as it was to persuade the English that resistance was futile—that he could march unopposed wherever he wished. No community through which his army passed offered even token resistance; Dover itself, with its "modern" castle, opened its gates on summons. Nor is the oft-quoted remark of Ordericus Vitalis to be ignored—that the English, though brave and warlike, had few modern fortifications into which to retire to wear out the invader in interminable sieges.[122] The patriotic leaders in London who sought to continue resistance to the invader were not proof against the demonstration that the Norman was able to execute his purpose, in his own time. The most vulnerable of the English magnates—Stigand, the schismatical and simoniacal archbishop of Canterbury—was the first to yield, when William crossed the Thames at Wallingford; the remaining advocates of resistance had done likewise by the time William had completed three-fourths of the circuit around London. Military pressure, demonstrated by the unopposed march of the Norman army through southeastern England, had brought about a collapse of resistance that was, as events proved, more than temporary. It was in fact the end of all coordinated resistance to the Norman occupation of the kingdom.

Chapter 2

William I, 1066-1087

DURING the early months of 1067 William worked to consolidate the position he had formally assumed on Christmas day 1066. What emerged was a military government only slightly camouflaged. In the earldoms of Kent and Herefordshire formerly held by the house of Godwine, Norman military might was openly displayed. According to Ordericus, castles were put in the custody of William's henchmen, together with vast domains as an inducement to maintaining their defense.[1] Elsewhere William governed with the aid of what a later age would have called collaborators. Earls Edwin and Morcar had submitted at Berkhamstead and had given hostages as pledges of good behavior. At a somewhat later date Earl Waltheof, who controlled the important Midland shires of Bedford, Northampton, Huntingdon, and Cambridge, was won over, apparently by the promise of marriage into the Conqueror's family.[2] Finally, a group of important ecclesiastics, headed by Aeldred, the archbishop of York, and including the able and respected Wulfstan, bishop of Worcester, actively supported the policies of the new king.[3] A number of surviving charters and notifications from 1067 indicate that William was attempting to govern through the existing hierarchy, both civil and ecclesiastic. In addition to Archbishop Aeldred and Bishop Wulfstan, these English officials included Aednoth the Staller; Tofi, sheriff of Worcestershire; Maerleswegen, sheriff of Yorkshire; Swawold, sheriff of Oxfordshire; Bishop Giso of Wells; Bishop Wulfwig of Dorcester; Abbot Aegelwin of Evesham; and Abbot Wulfwold of Chertsey.[4]

35

By March 1067, after constructing a castle at Winchester, William regarded his position as secure enough to permit a return to look after his affairs in Normandy.[5] He took the precaution, however, of including in his entourage a number of hostages, the most important of whom were Archbishop Stigand and Edgar the Atheling. He sailed from Pevensey and did not return until 6 December.[6] The king left behind him as military governors his half-brother Odo, bishop of Bayeux, and one of his ablest lieutenants, William fitz Osbern, whom he had created earl of Hereford.[7] Fitz Osbern's headquarters during this period were in William's newly built castle at Winchester.[8] A Norman earl without a castle as headquarters was simply unthinkable. As Stenton aptly remarked, "The regency of William fitz Osbern and Odo of Bayeux in 1067 can have amounted to hardly more than the military government of a half-conquered land."[9] Both English and Norman chroniclers agree that William and Odo exercised their authority with great rigor. They "wrought castles widely throughout the land and oppressed the poor people; and after that it grew greatly in evil."[10]

The absence of King William in Normandy saw the first indications of general unrest, although no outbreak occurred that necessitated his return. All necessary countermeasures were taken by his lieutenants. The most serious disturbance in 1067 was in Kent, the province of the bishop of Bayeux, whom William had made its earl. The disaffected English there attempted to enlist the aid of the Danes, and this failing, finally secured a promise of support from Count Eustace of Boulogne.[11] These allies agreed to make a joint attack on the strongly situated and as strongly held fortress of Dover. However, their plans miscarried badly; although the town was captured, an assault on the castle was repulsed with heavy loss, and a sortie of the garrison led by the castellan, Hugh de Montfort, dispersed the attackers.[12]

Less serious, but equally bothersome, was a revolt that developed on the Welsh frontier. Incited by an English "patriot" named Eadric, the Welsh appear to have conducted a guerrilla campaign against the Normans in Herefordshire. For the first time since 1055, mention is made of Hereford castle by the English chronicler for the year 1067, who noted that Eadric and his Welshmen were "warring against the castle men of Hereford and doing them much harm."[13] But since such isolated flareups did not threaten the Norman hold on the part of England that had been occupied, they were no cause for concern. William was able to spend the greater part of the year ordering his affairs in Normandy, and returned to London in time for the Christmas feast.[14]

There followed three years of rebellion and invasion which, if they did not shake the hold of the Normans, must have altered profoundly the character of the new government. Tangible evidence of this change, in the form of motte-and-bailey earthworks, is still to be seen everywhere in England. Although the vast majority of these remains are impossible to date precisely, the years from 1068 to 1070 unquestionably marked the transition from a sort of partnership between the Normans and their English collaborators to outright military rule of all territory under Norman occupation. "He [King William] gave the custody of castles to some of his bravest Normans, distributing among them vast possessions as inducements to undergo cheerfully the toils and perils of defending them."[15]

The year 1068 was taken up with expeditions into widely separated parts of England and with the construction of the castles necessary to make the occupation permanent. Early in the year the town of Exeter, which seems to have been a gathering place for English malcontents, raised the standard of rebellion. William took the field in person, at the head of a mixed army of Normans and Englishmen, but a siege of eighteen days was needed to bring about the capitulation of the city.[16] As soon as Exeter had been occupied, a site within the Roman wall was chosen and the construction of a castle was begun. While the king marched westward into Cornwall—a move doubtless intended to overawe the inhabitants—Baldwin de Molis was left in Exeter with a small garrison to control the town and to supervise the completion of the castle.[17] It is likely that the appearance of a Norman army in the west of England brought about the submission at this time of Gloucester and Bristol. The campaign was a brief one, for by Easter (23 March) William was at Winchester, and he spent Whitsuntide at Westminster.[18]

The advent of summer brought another series of disturbances, in which uniform success again attended Norman arms. The most serious of these from the military point of view was the rebellion of Edwin and Morcar, the sons of Leofric and earls of York and Mercia respectively.[19] There was a sympathetic response among the Yorkshiremen, and the rebels seem to have controlled the city of York itself. William took the field against the insurgents with his usual promptness. Marching by way of Warwick and Nottingham, he ordered castles built at both places, leaving William Peverel in command at Nottingham.[20] Upon his appearance before York, the spirit of resistance suddenly collapsed, and many of the malcontents fled to Scotland. The king had a castle built within the city, and garrisoned it with specially selected troops.[21] His business at York seemingly finished, William marched southward along the Ermine Street, founding castles at Lincoln, Huntingdon, and Cambridge as he went.[22] These strongholds gave the Normans a grasp on a rudimentary line of communications to the north.

Meanwhile a piratical foray led by the illegitimate sons of King Harold who had taken refuge with the Dublin Vikings, had occurred in the area about the Bristol channel and the Severn estuary. The raiders landed at the mouth of the Avon and, after plundering the countryside, attempted to storm Bristol. Beaten off by the townsmen, they returned to their ships with their booty. From Bristol the marauders passed into Somersetshire, but were intercepted there by the local *fyrd* under the command of Aednoth the Staller. A pitched battle ensued, probably at Bleadon on the river Axe, in which Aednoth was slain; but the pirates appear to have been roughly handled, for they withdrew to their ships and returned to Ireland.[23] Such raids, though not a serious threat to the Norman hold on England, made the problem of local defense an urgent one. In the following summer (1069) the English exiles and their auxiliaries conducted another raid with a fleet of sixty-six ships, landing at the mouth of the Taw near Exeter.[24] Their march was intercepted by Brian of Brittany and William Gualdi, who "came upon them unawares, with no small force," and so severely defeated them that this time only a remnant escaped to their ships.[25]

The year 1069 opened with a serious reverse for the Normans. To extend his influence into the turbulent and as yet unconquered north, William had created Robert de Comines earl of Northumberland, and had sent him north with a small army to take possession.[26] The unfortunate baron had proceeded no farther than Durham when he was set upon by the inhabitants, and on 28 January he and his command were slain almost to a man.[27] This striking success emboldened other discontented elements north of the Humber. Edgar the Atheling and other Englishmen who had taken refuge in Scotland now appeared in Northumberland; soon, as the rebellion spread into Yorkshire, they had a respectable following. Robert fitz Richard, the governor of York, was trapped with a detachment of the garrison outside the city walls, where he was slain, and the constable of the castle, William Malet, dispatched an urgent appeal for help to the king. The Northumbrian and Yorkshire rebels concentrated before York were easily dispersed by King William, who hurried north on receiving the castellan's appeal. Although he remained in the city little more than a week, by the time he left he had added another castle to the defenses of York.[28] When the insurgents proceeded with another drive against York, they were driven off with ease by the reinforced garrison.[29]

But more serious trouble was brewing. King Sweyn of Denmark had prepared a formidable expedition in order to prosecute the Danish claim to the throne of England. Landing parties were repulsed by Norman troops at Dover and Sandwich, and at Ipswich a similar attempt was repelled by local levies. After another setback at Norwich, inflicted by Ralph de Guader, the Danish fleet made for the estuary of the Humber. Ordericus reports that a raid to the south was roughly handled by the garrison of Lincoln.[30] Following this incident the Danes were joined, early in September, by the English insurgents, among whom were Edgar the Atheling and Earl Waltheof; Earl Gospatric, Maerleswegen, the former sheriff of Yorkshire, and Siward Barn. This combination was the most serious threat yet faced by the Normans, for the Danish fleet was estimated by contemporaries at from 240 to 300 vessels; and if Stenton's supposition is accurate, in numbers the Danes were not much inferior to the army with which Harald Hardrada had invaded England in 1066.[31] Allowing for a certain amount of exaggeration, there can be no doubt that this was a major effort on the part of Sweyn to assert the claims of Cnut's heirs to the English crown.

The combined force of Englishmen and Danes now appeared before York. On 19 September the castle garrisons, instead of waiting for relief from the south, set fire to the city, made a foolhardy sortie, and were either slain or captured.[32] The city of York with its castles fell to the victors the next day, and the strongholds were razed.[33] But instead of exploiting this success, the Anglo-Danish army frittered it away within the walls of York. Only a prompt and vigorous offensive could have held out any hope of defeating the Normans.

King William was hunting in the Forest of Dean when news reached him of the disaster at York. Gathering all readily available forces, he again took the road northward. When intelligence of the king's approach reached York, the Anglo-Danish army made no attempt to hold the city or to make a stand in the open. Instead, there was a precipitate withdrawal to the Danish fleet still anchored in the Humber, followed by a crossing to the Lincoln side of the estuary and an attempt to take refuge in the fenny reaches of the Isle of Axholme. When William pursued them into the marshes, the English and their Danish allies recrossed into Yorkshire and stood on the defensive. The king made no immediate attempt to drive them out, for he was obliged to divert his attention to a serious rising in Mercia. Leaving a corps of observation under the command of counts Robert of Eu and Robert of Mortain to watch and contain the enemy, William marched rapidly to Stafford, the apparent center of the rebellion. Here he scored what seems to have been an easy victory, although no detailed account of the campaign has survived.[34] He then began the return march to Yorkshire and a final reckoning with the Anglo-Danes. But he had only reached Nottingham when the information came that the insurgents were preparing to reoccupy York. Then began a race for the city. William headed due north in a vain effort to head off the enemy, but his army was brought up short at the river Aire, where the one existing bridge had been destroyed, and the northern bank was held in force. The delay thus imposed enabled the Danes—and presumably their English allies—to reoccupy York, while for three weeks the king was held up on the line of the Aire. Finally an unguarded ford was discovered, a passage was effected, and the road to York was opened. Instead of marching directly on the city, however, William cut a wide swath of devastation to the west and north of his objective.[35] Before the isolation of the city was complete, the Danes came to terms, agreeing to evacuate on condition that they might winter in the Humber, and leaving the English rebels to make whatever peace as they could with William.[36] York was immediately reoccupied by the Normans, whereupon one of the king's first moves was to begin rebuilding the castles.

These repeated insurrections on the part of the northerners persuaded William that only the most rigorous measures would effectively and permanently subdue the region. The procedure he adopted has been severely condemned, not only by contemporary chroniclers but by succeeding historians as well. Following the defeat of the English and Danes, William resolved that Yorkshire must not again become the focal point of internal rebellion or a bridgehead for foreign invasions. Partly in retaliation, but certainly also as part of a deliberate strategy, he laid waste a broad band of the country between the Humber and the Tees. Houses and crops were systematically destroyed; the populace were either slain or ruthlessly dispossessed. The devastation was so complete that fifteen years later, when the Domesday survey was instituted, Yorkshire had not yet recovered.[37] However severe such a measure might seem, it could be justified on the grounds of military expediency. Never again were the Normans troubled by the combination of northern rising and Scandinavian invasion. Military policy is to be justified on the basis of success alone, and in his northern policy William was eminently successful. It must be noted that the tendency toward political separatism in the north was well understood by the king and his intimate advisers. Archbishop Lanfranc in defending the primacy of the see of Canterbury argued

that it was expedient for the unity and solidarity of the kingdom that all Britain should be subject to one primate; it might otherwise happen, in the king's time or that of one of his successors, that some one of the Danes, Norwegians or Scots, who used to sail up to York in their attacks on the realm, might be made king by the archbishop of York, and the fickle and treacherous Yorkshiremen, and the kingdom disturbed and divided.[38]

The king spent the Christmas of 1069 at York; early in 1070 he was again on the Tees, returning by way of Hexham. Ordericus noted that the severity of the weather imposed great hardships on the troops. Arriving at York and finding that the work on the castles had been completed, William then embarked on a campaign that has few parallels in eleventh-century warfare.[39]

While the king had been occupied with northern affairs, sporadic outbreaks in other parts of the country had been occupying his lieutenants. The English of Devonshire and Cornwall rose in arms and laid siege to Exeter, which was stoutly defended by the townsmen. A sudden sally by the embattled burgesses raised the siege, and the discomfited rebels were badly cut up by a column which the earls William (fitz Osbern?) and Brian were marching to the relief of the town.[40] Farther north and to the east, the natives of Dorsetshire and Somersetshire made an attack on Montacute but were beaten off by forces hastily levied in Winchester, Salisbury, and London, under the command of Geoffrey, bishop of Coutances.[41] In the Severn valley a more serious threat developed when the Welsh and the English of Cheshire combined to besiege "the king's castle" at Shrewsbury. They were aided in this operation by the inhabitants of Shrewsbury itself, and had the assistance of Eadric the Wild, who had earlier been harassing the Normans in Herefordshire. But though they took possession of the town, the insurgents were unable to reduce the castle, and on the approach of a relieving force under earls William and Brian, they burnt the town and retired.[42] Since these two earls also commanded the force that contributed to the relief of Exeter, it may be that the two risings were in some way connected; perhaps William and Brian even marched directly from Exeter to Shrewsbury.

The audacity of the Shrewsbury attack determined William to embark on a winter campaign, a most unusual military expedient for the eleventh century. He left York early in the new year, probably in late January or early February, marching along a line that almost certainly followed the track of the old Roman road by way of Leeds and Rastrick through the Manchester gap to Chester.[43] As described by Ordericus, the hardships of the winter march were such that the grumblings of the soldiers amounted almost to mutiny; but since the Normans came upon the Cheshire malcontents before they were aware that the enemy was in the vicinity, there was no difficulty in putting them down. At Chester, following what by now amounted to "Standard Operating Procedure," William erected a castle within the old Roman walls before he left, and garrisoned it strongly. At about the same time the king had a castle built at Stafford to prevent a recurrence of the previous summer's disturbances there.[44] This done, William returned south in time to celebrate Easter (4 April) at Winchester.[45]

However, this was not the end of military operations for the year 1070. Some of the Danes who had participated in the Yorkshire campaign had wintered in the fens, and during the spring, under the command of Earl Osbern and Bishop Christian of Aarhus, they established a camp in the Isle of Ely.[46] Here they joined forces with the irregular band of the now semi-legendary Hereward, a skilled guerrilla chieftain, with the object of raiding the wealthy monastery of Peterborough. The monks heard that the Anglo-Danish force was approaching, however, and dispatched one of their number to Stamford, where he found the newly appointed abbot, Turold, on his way to join the Peterborough community. Before the new abbot could take any effective action the raiders struck. Sailing up the river Nene, they met with only token resistance, and set fire to the town. The Danes and English irregulars then broke into the monastery and sacked it from cellar to roof, in spite of the anguished pleas of the monks.[47] It was not until several days later that Abbot Turold arrived at the head of 160 knights. The Anglo-Danish marauders, though they had possession of the walled precincts of the monastery, now showed no inclination to defend their position. The Danes desired only to get away with their plunder, and a treaty was negotiated permitting them to take it with them from England unmolested. Hereward and his English "patriots" withdrew into the watery fastnesses of the Isle of Ely to continue their resistance to the Normans.[48]

Viewed objectively, it would seem that the military operations of 1068–1070 set the seal upon the Norman conquest of England. If at any time from 1066 until the campaigns of 1070 a leader of vigor and imagination had appeared among the English, the work of Hastings might still have been undone. Fortunately for the Normans, the only Englishman so endowed, the one man who might have commanded widespread support among the native populace, was Bishop Wulfstan of Worcester; and he had gone over to the Conqueror. Thus the resistance to Norman rule was sporadic and uncoordinated, and the prompt and ruthless action taken by the Conqueror himself soon made revolt or invasion a forlorn hope—although his contemporaries were evidently not convinced, for the outbreaks continued.

In 1071 the English earls Edwin and Morcar again resorted to arms.[49] Finally Edwin, after some months of vainly soliciting aid from the Welsh, Scots, and English, was murdered by his own attendants.[50] Morcar, together with Bishop Aethelwine of Durham, and Siward Barn—who appears to have been a prominent landholder in Essex and Suffolk—then fled to the Isle of Ely. Here the party took refuge with Hereward, who was still at large in the fens.[51] The sequence and nature of the subsequent operations are not entirely clear. The one writer who had access to contemporary accounts—the compiler of the *Liber Eliensis*—is of little help.[52] But by sorting out the various episodes in his confused account of the events of 1071 and comparing them with other sources, it is possible at least to sketch the outlines of that fascinating campaign.

It seems possible that Hereward's irregular operations in the fen country had begun as early as 1068, and that the castles built at Huntingdon and Cambridge were intended to confine his depredations, or to keep him under observation.[53] His attack on Peterborough in 1070 in conjunction with the Danes had been handled well enough by Abbot Turold, but this new combination—the name of Morcar and the ability of Herward—was threatening enough to bring William himself into the field. Ely, girt with river and marshland, was not easy to assault, and the

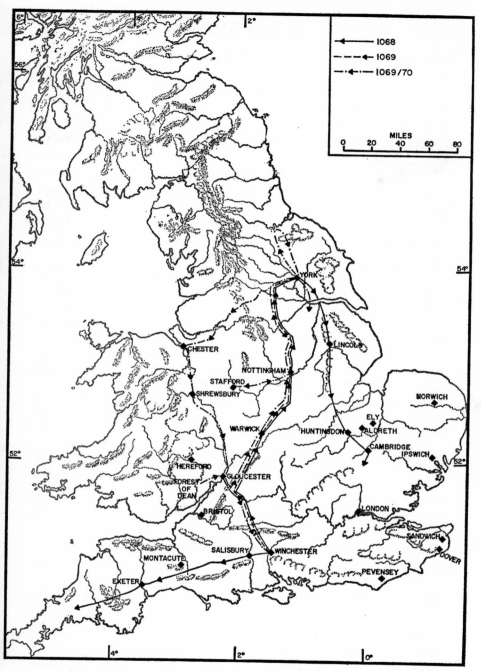

Map 3. The Campaigns of William the Conqueror, 1068–1070

king made elaborate preparations before attempting it. Both the land and sea *fyrd* were called out, since William had evidently resolved to crush this threat before the resistance could spread.[54] Presumably the naval flotilla sailed up the Ouse to blockade all seaward exits from the Isle, while the king set himself to the difficult task of bridging the fen and rounding up the elusive rebels. The exact point of the Norman attack is uncertain. Although a case can be made for an assault from the east, in the direction of Stuntney, it seems more likely that the main effort was concentrated on the west, opposite Aldreth.[55] The burden of the defense seems to have fallen on Hereward, whose actual exploits have been so embellished by popular tradition that it is impossible to disentangle the facts from the embroidery.[56]

William's first attempt to force a crossing ended in failure, but a contemporary description of the event provides a rare glimpse of eleventh-century field engineering techniques:

After bringing instruments and engines of logs and stones, and piles of all sorts, they constructed a causeway in the marsh, though it was apparently useless and narrow, near to a great river by the aforesaid place, namely Aldreth; they also put in the water very large trees and beams and bound them together, and beneath them, sheep-skins tied together, turned after flaying and inflated with air, so that the weight of men going over it might be better borne.[57]

The assault came to an abrupt end, according to the Ely chronicler, when the Norman engines and materials—possibly even the causeway itself—were fired by Hereward.[58] A second attack was successful in breaching the defenses of the Isle; a bridgehead was established at Aldreth, where a castle was built.[59] With the Normans lodged in the Isle of Ely, organized resistance soon collapsed. The monks of Ely sought the king's clemency; Morcar, Siward, and Bishop Aethelwine surrendered on discretion, and were immediately imprisoned; their subordinates suffered mutilation, and only Hereward with a small following managed to escape.[60] Ely itself was occupied, and probably a motte-and-bailey castle was erected.[61] Although Hereward remained at large, he was never again a threat serious enough to call for military action on any scale.

Not all the disorders calling for suppression were internal. Beginning in 1070, Malcolm III, king of Scots, sought to take advantage of the disturbances in England by raiding across the border.[62] Another raid in 1072 brought William north at the head of a combined land and naval expedition which ended with the submission of the Scottish king at Abernethy. The castle at Durham was apparently built on this occasion.[63] The expedition of 1072 is notable as providing the first chronicled mention of knight service and of the *servitia debita*. Abbot Aethelwig of Evesham was summoned for duty with the five knights due from the abbey, and the Ely annalist noted that on this occasion the king required military service from abbots as well as bishops.[64]

In August and September of 1079, with King William again abroad in Normandy, Malcolm sought to improve his position on the border by conducting a massive raid through Northumberland which carried to the banks of the Tyne.[65] Not until the late summer of 1080 did William's Norman affairs permit his return to England. First in the order of business after he landed seems to have been the organization of a punitive expedition against the Scots.[66] The king's eldest son, Robert, had accompanied his father to England, and to him was entrusted the command of the northern expedition. Although the composition and size of Robert's army is unknown, a number of tenants-in-chief were present, including Abbot Adelhelm of Abingdon. The Anglo-Norman army advanced northward and crossed the frontier into Lothian without opposition. At Eccles the Scots army barred any further uncontested advance. However, King Malcolm was not prepared to risk a general engagement, and in a negotiated settlement he apparently recognized the suzerainty of the king of England, agreeing to give hostages as pledges of his good faith.[67] On the return march after this bloodless triumph, Robert built a castle at the point where the main road to the north crossed the Tyne.[68] Later Robert's crude fortifications were strengthened, and under its walls a town grew up which became known as Newcastle-upon-Tyne.

In addition to controlling his northern neighbors, King William had to remain on the alert against a possible return of the Danes, whose fleets still cruised off the coasts of England during the summer months and occasionally landed raiding parties. Such incidents occurred in 1070, 1071, and 1075.[69] As late as 1085 King Cnut IV (the Saint) in alliance with Count Robert I of Flanders, prepared a great fleet for an invasion of England. This new threat led to almost feverish military preparations. The English chronicler wrote that William imported great numbers of mercenaries, horse and foot, from France and Brittany. These he quartered on his tenants-in-chief, who in their turn were ordered to put their knights on a stand-by status. The king also saw to it that a wide belt of country along the "invasion coast" was stripped of all provisions that might give subsistence to an enemy, were he to succeed in establishing a bridgehead on the island. This measure is strongly reminiscent of the devastation of Yorkshire sixteen years earlier, and suggests that the operations of 1069–1070 were not provoked by a desire for vengeance alone. Even the news that Cnut's expedition had miscarried did not cause the king to relax his vigilance. He dismissed some of the mercenaries, but retained others in service until the following year.[70] From this thorough preparation, described by a chronicler who was largely hostile to the Normans, it is clear that Norman military thinking did not lack an understanding of strategy. Here William, although on a less ruthless scale—there were no tales this time of slaughter or dispossession—repeated the process which in Yorkshire had denied vast areas to potential enemies. But by 1085 the great threat both from English risings and from Scandinavian invasions had passed, and the chief danger to the Norman kingdom was henceforth to come from its own unruly barons.

In 1075, the first such revolt occurred. The castle, which heretofore had served as a national stronghold in time of invasion or civil strife, now became the final refuge of the Norman baron, or the base from which operations might be conducted against king or neighbor. The rebellion of Roger, earl of Hereford, and Ralph, earl of Norfolk, was not in itself a serious affair. King William was again absent in Normandy at the time, and had left the direction of military operations to his justiciars, William de Warenne and Richard de Bienfaite.[71] When word of the plot by the disaffected earls to overthrow King William, and divide the spoils between them, became known to the justiciars, Roger and

Ralph fled to their castles to prepare for hostilities.[72] With commendable dispatch, Bishop Odo of Bayeux and Bishop Geoffrey of Coutances collected a mixed Anglo-Norman army and moved to intercept Earl Ralph's forces before they could join with those of Roger of Hereford. The bishops' force surprised Ralph near Beecham in Norfolk just as he was preparing to bivouac, and a skirmish took place of which no details are known, but which constrained the earl to shut himself up in Norwich castle.[73] Thereupon the king's lieutenants not only mobilized the available Norman tenants, but mustered the local *fyrd* as well for the siege of the castle.[74] Despairing of relief, Earl Ralph finally escaped by sea to the Danish court, where he vainly sought aid while the defense of the castle was left in charge of his wife. That lady, a sister to the earl of Hereford, proved a better commander than her husband, for she managed to prolong the resistance for another three months. She finally surrendered on terms which not only allowed her to retire to Brittany unmolested, but guaranteed the safety of her devoted garrison as well.[75] On the Severn front the overall command seems to have been entrusted to Bishop Wulfstan of Worcester, with Abbot Aethelwig of Evesham, along with Urse d'Abitot, sheriff of Worcestershire, and Walter de Lacy, as his chief subordinates. The royal officers, in addition to their own feudal contingents, called out the general *fyrd* for the campaign, the object of which was to hold the fords of the Severn against any attempt by Earl Roger to join his forces with those of Ralph of Norfolk. The operation was completely successful, and on the return of King William to England in the autumn, the earl of Hereford submitted tamely.[76] Thus ended the first attempt of the Norman barons to oppose the power of the crown; for the remainder of his life, with the exception of the invasion scare of 1085, William ruled England in peace.

It is not difficult to sum up the military achievements of the Conqueror. In the twenty-one years between 1066 and 1087 William had to fight but one general engagement. He subdued an often hostile population and defeated several attempts at invasion by forestalling any possibility of concentrating a force or penetrating to the interior of the island. This was done by devastating wide tracts of the countryside, as in Yorkshire, and by constructing castles on such a scale as to dominate the main lines of communication. The critical period was the four years between 1066 and 1070 while the work of conquest and consolidation was being carried out. The threat of foreign invasion and native revolt necessitated the construction of great numbers of castles for the maintenance of the conquest. It must be emphasized that the reduction of England was accomplished by armies that now appear ridiculously small. The entire *servitia debita* of Norman England may scarcely have exceeded 5,000 knights.[77] The native *fyrd* could be used but sparingly. For this reason the construction of many strong points was a prime military necessity, since the conquerors were spread thinly over a large area and local places of refuge were essential. The simplicity of a motte-and-bailey castle made it easy to throw up, and though it might be taken easily by a determined onslaught, or by an enemy in overwhelming strength, its earth and timber ramparts could usually be held until a force could be assembled to relieve it. As Douglas has noted, "the motte-and-bailey castle, in charge of a trusted lieutenant of the king, was proving itself an essential, and a highly effective, instrument by which the conquest of England might be completed." [78] The operations around York in 1068 and 1069 are illustrations of this. So long as the garrison remained inside the fortifications, the Northumbrian rebels and their Danish allies were held at bay until the king could march a relieving army up from the south. But on the occasion that the garrison rashly ventured out, not only was it cut to pieces in the open, but the undefended castle soon fell into the hands of the enemy.

It has frequently been taken for granted that the period of castle warfare is devoid of strategical or tactical interest. Oman writes, for example: "It is the number and strength of the fortified places . . . which explains the futility of so many campaigns of the period. . . . A narrow line of castles might maintain its existence for scores of years against a powerful enemy . . ." [79] Such a generalization might apply to some parts of Europe, but in no sense to eleventh-century England. It should always be borne in mind that castles in England, as elsewhere, arose to meet a specific military need, and were adapted later to the purposes of rebellion. This is no reflection on the military acumen of the

Norman conquerors who devised the system, or that of later kings who had to face the problems that grew out of it. It would be as much to the point to describe the campaigns of the Duke of Marlborough in the Low Countries as "futile" because he was never able to break through the chain of French barrier fortresses that blocked the road to Paris.

The problem that confronted William of Normandy during the first years of the occupation of England was how to maintain control of an increasingly large area with a very small army. This small force had to face not only a potentially hostile English population, but the almost annual threat of full-scale foreign intervention. There were two methods that King William might have adopted to meet these problems. He could have concentrated his available forces in a few strategic localities, where they would have been instantly available to meet either a rising of the English or an invasion from abroad. This solution, however, would have been ruled out on grounds other than military. No northern European prince of the eleventh century had sufficient financial resources to maintain several thousand troops on a permanent war footing. The only practical alternative was the system to which the Normans were already accustomed—that of local fortification on a vast scale. William's loyal followers were rewarded with the confiscated estates of the English thegnage, and on these estates the fortified residences of the Norman barons rose by the hundreds.

One question that the military historian must try to answer is whether or not there was any systematic or strategic arrangement in the castle-building of the Normans. It must be granted that there is nothing in the accounts of the time to suggest a preconceived plan of defense. But the idea of haphazard fortification does not agree with the known character and ability of the Normans who were widely respected by their contemporaries for their practicality. And there can be no doubt that the fortress-building of the Conqueror himself was done with strategic considerations in mind. These castles, according to Oman, "were placed in strategical positions which had been chosen with the general defense of the realm in view." [80] One has only to plot the location of William's castles to verify this statement. By those castles the important Channel ports were secured, the lines of the chief rivers were guarded, and the road network was protected. This, on the other hand, accounts for no more than a small fraction of the castles known to have existed during the early period of the Norman occupation. Oman was of the opinion that the castles of the barons "had for the most part a purely local significance," and Mrs. Armitage has remarked that "in England the reasons for the erection of mottes seems to have been manorial rather than military." [81] Two questions immediately arise: First, was there any pressing military need for the erection of fortifications that could not be met by the castles that had been built by the king at a few strategic places? Second, does the geographical distribution of motte-and-bailey castles bear out the contention that their chief significance was local?

As has been emphasized repeatedly, the period from 1066 to 1070 was critical for the Norman conquest of England. During these years William and the limited forces at his disposal were faced with English rebellions in the south and southwest, on the Welsh border, in the fenlands, and in the north. Piratical forays based on Dublin were a yearly occurrence. Annually, Danish fleets appeared off the coast of England—fleets which on occasion put landing parties ashore to cooperate with native insurgents. Front had to be made in all directions against these constant threats, and the financial resources of the crown were unequal to the emergency.[82] The king could encourage fortification by the baronage only on a scale that would ensure the preservation of their conquests. Thinly distributed over the greater part of England, the small garrisons commanded by individual tenants could not hope to offer successful resistance to a determined English uprising, or to halt a large-scale invasion. But if the residence of each baron were fortified, the result would be a system of mutually supporting castles which in the aggregate could prove very formidable. Even the simplest castle of earth and timber, if resolutely held, could in most instances be expected to hold out until relieved by detachments from the garrisons of neighboring castles.[83] Historians with a tendency to minimize the significance of English feudalism have almost without exception failed to understand the importance of the feudal castle and its garrison of military tenants. Although a baron holed up in his castle could—and on numerous occasions did—present a problem to the crown, it is difficult to see how the Conquest could have been achieved and maintained without him. Knight service was more than field service; it included castle-guard, and to say that "it is by no means clear that the feudal army was, as some historians have maintained, the chief military bulwark of the realm" is to ignore the service of countless knights who performed unpaid garrison duties through countless crises in the history of Norman England.[84]

"The great majority of mottes in England," Mrs. Armitage has written, "are planted either on or near Roman or other ancient roads, or on navigable rivers." She adds that where a motte is found on a river that is not navigable, its purpose was probably to defend a ford.[85] The geographical location of the majority of the motte-and-bailey castles is the real clue to their military significance. Castles located on or near roads or navigable rivers not only exercise military control over the lines of communications, but can also be easily supplied, reinforced, or relieved in the event of siege. It ought not to take a military expert to see such an obvious point. The Normans were the military experts of their day. Is there any reason to suppose that William and his lieutenants were not aware of such strategic considerations?

Professor Painter observes that although "it is, of course, possible that the crown encouraged castle building in regions which were vital to the national defense and discouraged it in others, . . . I can find no evidence to indicate such a policy."[86] But clearly the actual evidence for just such a policy is to be found simply by plotting the locations of the motte-and-bailey castles on a map. In medieval England, the communications system so vital to the exercise of military control, feudal or otherwise, radiated from two principal foci—London and Coventry. When the castles of the eleventh century are mapped, it will be found that both these centers were protected by wide bands of fortifications.[87]

The protective ring of castles about London is worth detailed examination. Within a radius of twenty miles in any direction from the city, no important castle existed save the castle of the bishop of London at Hertford.[88] But in a zone twenty miles wide,

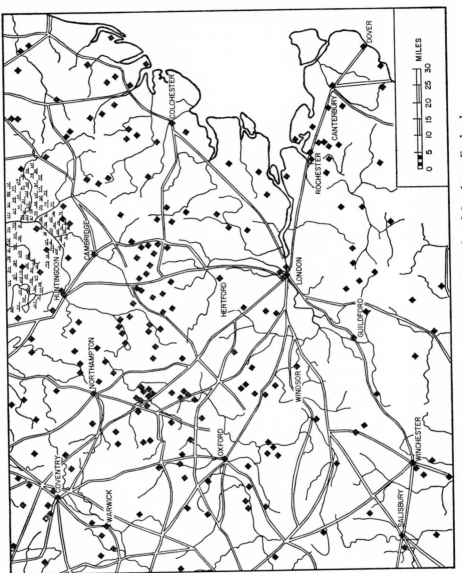

Map 4. Distribution of Castles in Central and Southeast England

at a distance of between thirty and fifty miles from the metropolis, about eighty castles were sited. Taken together, these strongholds covered every road leading into London as well as all the lateral connecting roads between. To the south, the fortresses were concentrated in the direction of Dover; on the east, the line was anchored on the important castle of Rochester, which commanded the Watling Street and the crossing of the Medway. This major thoroughfare was also covered to the northwest in the direction of Coventry and Shrewsbury. Another group of castles ensured control of the Ermine Street, which linked London with Lincoln and York. A similar but smaller system protected the roads that coverged in the neighborhood of Coventry. One can concede with Painter "the complete geographical ignorance with which the Conqueror faced his newly acquired realm," without having to suppose that ignorance prevented the Normans from constructing a system of defense to insure their control of the vital lines of communications throughout the kingdom.[89] And yet Oman has insisted that the castles of the barons were "usually isolated units with no interdependence on each other." [90]

Stenton is, in fact, the only observer who has grasped the real significance of the English castle and its place not only in the political but also in the military life of Norman England. "It was not until the death of William son of Robert of Normandy in 1128 that the Anglo-Norman monarchy at last became secure. For more than sixty years after the Conquest it had depended in the last resort on the loyalty of the barons and the knights of their honours." [91] The danger of Scandinavian invasion had not passed completely before William was faced with the first of a series of baronial revolts that utilized the defensive system of castles for a different purpose. The resources of the crown alone proved insufficient to crush this and later revolts. The support of loyal barons was always necessary if a rebellion were to be suppressed. The antagonism which would have followed a severe policy of repression would in all probability have destroyed not only the intricate defensive system on which the safety of the realm depended; it might have destroyed the monarchy itself. Vengeance was a luxury the Norman kings simply could not afford. For this reason the kings were nearly always forced to deal leniently with defeated rebels. Even so ruthless a monarch as William Rufus did not dare hang Robert de Mowbray in 1095; and Henry I permitted Robert de Bellême to retire to the Continent after his unsuccessful rebellion in 1102. Until the king was able to assume full responsibility for the defense of the realm, the barons with their castles and their garrisons remained a vital part of the military system.

The building of hundreds of castles within the limited confines of England had, in turn, a profound influence upon the strategy and tactics of the Norman period.[92] William the Conqueror had originally been able to march unhindered through the country because, with the single exception of Exeter, no fortified town chose to stand a siege. But the castles he constructed, as well as those built by the Anglo-Norman baronage with his permission, in completely changing the military geography of England, altered strategy, and, to a lesser extent, tactics. In spite of the assertion that "the Normans had very little to teach, even in the art of war," Norman castle-building constituted nothing less than a revolution in the military development of England.[93] No longer might an army of hostile intent march unchecked from London to York, with important castles barring the way at Hertford, Huntingdon, Stamford, Newark, Tickhill, and Pontefract, and with a score of smaller baronial strongholds within striking distance of the Great North Road. An enemy attempting to run this gauntlet would find himself continually harassed by these garrisons. It was the good fortune of the English kings until the time of Stephen never to be faced with a revolt that simultaneously threatened all the chief lines of communication. Either the rebels were widely dispersed, as in 1075 and 1088, or the rising was confined chiefly to a single area, as in 1095 and 1102. In the former instances the king or his lieutenants were able to crush the revolt in detail; in the latter, it was possible to isolate the insurgents and reduce their castles one by one.

Castle warfare was a warfare of position which called for special strategy and tactics. Usually the weaker side retired within its fortifications, hoping to exhaust the patience and resources of the stronger before a decision had been reached. This strategy of attrition never worked in England under the Norman kings. The two Williams and Henry I invariably succeeded in running the rebels to earth, compelling them to stand siege in their castles, and eventually forcing them to surrender. The uniform success of this method lay probably in the fact that the Norman kings understood the usefulness of infantry in siege warfare. The old English militia, the *fyrd,* was not allowed to fall into desuetude once the conquest was consolidated, but was used on numerous occasions. In the eleventh and twelfth centuries infantry seldom could stand in the open against feudal cavalry; but few medieval generals understood, as the Norman kings did, that in siege warfare the role of the foot soldier is decisive. It was this understanding of positional warfare that enabled the Conqueror and his successors to suppress baronial risings with apparent ease. If the crown had had to rely upon feudal contingents alone, the campaigns might well have resulted in military stalemate and political compromise.

Chapter 3

William II, 1087-1100, and Henry I, 1100-1135

THE death of William I, and the division of the Norman inheritance, opened a new period in the military history of England. The late king's eldest son, Robert, to whom Normandy fell, had proved incapable of maintaining the strong government of his father. Accordingly, the more unruly spirits among the Anglo-Norman baronage formed a plan to reunite England and Normandy by replacing the competent though unscrupulous William II (William Rufus), who had inherited the English kingdom, with his more pliant elder brother. Since most of the great barons held of both the duchy and the kingdom, the problem of the succession continued to vex English and Norman political life until the death without issue of William Clito, Duke Robert's son, in 1128.[1] The baronial revolts of the reigns of William II and Henry I made it clear that only a strong and able king could prevent a repetition in England of the chaotic conditions which prevailed in Normandy under the weak Duke Robert.

This became apparent within a year of the accession of William II. Where the conspiracy originated is not at all clear. Ordericus seemed to think that it began in Normandy, the English chroniclers that it began in England.[2] There is no diversity of opinion, however, as to the originator of the plot. Every finger points to Bishop Odo of Bayeux.[3] That ambitious schemer, who had been imprisoned since 1082, had gained his liberty in the general amnesty that followed the death of the old Conqueror. The earldon of Kent was restored to him, and he seems to have

59

attended William's Christmas court in 1087. The conspiracy may have had its beginning at this time; certainly it cannot have originated much later. A large number of the Anglo-Norman barons were won over to the idea—Earl Roger of Shrewsbury; Robert of Rhuddlan; Robert, earl of Northumberland; Bernard de Neuf-Marché; Hugh de Grantmesnil, sheriff of Leicester; Roger Bigod; Geoffrey, bishop of Coutances; and Bishop William of Durham all became involved.[4] The first overt action, however, was taken by the king. On 12 March 1088 the temporalities of the see of Durham were seized by royal officials from York and Lincoln.[5] The bishop's men managed to retain control of the castle at Durham. This action on William's part may have been the signal for the conspirators to declare themselves. They retired to their castles, strengthened their fortifications, increased their garrisons, and gathered "abundant supplies of food for both men and horses."[6] Actual hostilities began just after Easter (16 April), when the insurgent barons issued from their castles and began to ravage the lands of the king and his supporters.[7] The rising was widespread, ranging from Northumberland and Durham to the Channel, and from East Anglia to the Welsh marches. In Norfolk, Roger Bigod seized the castle of Norwich by surprise, and from this base harried the surrounding territory. In the Midlands, the sheriff of Leicester, Hugh de Grantmesnil, led plundering raids through Leicestershire and Northamptonshire.[8] Bishop Geoffrey of Coutances and his nephew Robert de Mowbray, earl of Northumberland, seized Bristol castle, one of the strongest in the kingdom. From it they raided far and wide, sacking Bath and ravaging Gloucestershire, Somersetshire, and Wiltshire as far as Ilchester.[9] Arundel, on the Sussex coast, a possible landing place for an expeditionary force from Normandy, was held for Roger, earl of Shrewsbury.[10] These disturbances were minor, however, and must have been dealt with by local forces, for the chronicles record nothing more about them. A more serious rising occurred in the Severn valley, where Roger de Montgomery, earl of Shrewsbury, with Bernard de Neuf-Marché, Roger de Lacy, Osberne fitz Richard, and William d'Eu joined the revolt. These marcher barons were aided by Welsh levies in addition to their own tenants, and from Shrewsbury they raided widely.[11] In the course of their depredations, Gloucester was attacked and burnt.[12] Eventually this irregular warfare developed into something like a formal attack on the town and castle of Worcester. In the absence of the sheriff the custody of the castle had been committed to the venerable Bishop Wulfstan.[13] A motley force of marchers and Welsh auxiliaries, both horse and foot, under the command of Earl Roger, appeared before the town; the rebel army was dispersed with considerable loss by a sally of the castle garrison, augmented by the knights of the bishop's household and the burgesses of Worcester, who crossed the Severn bridge and caught the attackers before they could form a line of battle.[14]

But the outcome of the rebellion was not to be determined on the marches, a fact well understood by King William. With characteristic exaggeration, William of Malmesbury wrote that "nearly all the Normans" revolted against the king; in fact, he had the support of such important tenants as Earl Hugh of Chester, William de Warenne, and Robert fitz Hamon, as well as the primate, Archbishop Lanfranc, and of the church.[15] Moreover, the kind of war that William had to fight did not depend primarily on the feudal retinues of the barons. The center of the rebellion lay in the southeast, in Bishop Odo's earldom of Kent, and in neighboring Sussex, where his brother Robert, count of Mortain, had extensive holdings. The earl-bishop had garrisoned the castles of Tonbridge and Rochester, and Pevensey on the Sussex coast was held by Count Robert.[16] From these castles the rebels conducted raids, paying particular attention to the lands of the king and the archbishop.[17] But the real menace of Bishop Odo's position was its proximity to Normandy. The port at Pevensey, where William the Conqueror had landed not a quarter century earlier, might again become the bridgehead for an invading force if Duke Robert were able to fulfill his promises of aid. Already Count Eustace of Boulogne and Robert de Bellême had crossed to England with their knights; they had been assigned by Odo to the garrison at Rochester, and the Duke Robert had agreed to levy an army to support the English rebels.[18] The latter attempted no more than scattered raids, and seem to have made no effort to organize a field army. If they were waiting the arrival of the promised support from Normandy, they merely played into the hands of King William. Since his enemies had obligingly shut themselves up in castles, he used the opportunity to root them out one by one. Basing his operations on London, he mustered the English militia in addition to the contingents of the loyal barons.[19] It does not seem necessary to explain that mobilization of the *fyrd* as a measure of desperation induced by the defection of a majority of the barons.[20] For the kind of war that William Rufus had to fight—a war of sieges—the English infantry was invaluable. It is not entirely accurate to assert that to save his crown the king was forced to rely on English troops for lack of any others. He could have employed continental mercenary infantry as his father had done in 1085; but why go to the trouble and expense when soldiers just as good might be had in England— without delay and at no cost, since the five-hide unit that sent the soldier also paid him for sixty days' service?

The king began a systematic campaign to reduce the fortresses of his uncle the bishop by marching south from London. He first invested a formidable motte-and-bailey castle at Tonbridge, into which Odo had thrown a strong garrison of knights under the command of Gilbert fitz Richard. But the defenses were inade- quate, the place was carried by storm, and the infantry was given credit for the victory.[21] William then set his forces in motion for Rochester, where Bishop Odo had his headquarters. The prelate, appraised of the king's intentions, then transferred to Pevensey, where his brother, Count Robert of Mortain, was in command; for so long as Pevensey could be held, communications with Duke Robert in Normandy would be assured.[22] When the king learned of the bishop's change of base, he immediately altered his own plans and closely invested Pevensey by land and sea, bringing up siege machinery for the purpose.[23]

In the meantime, preparations had been going on in Normandy for an invasion of England, and eventually a part of this force was dispatched across the channel. But the Norman transports were intercepted at sea by the king's ships, in an engagement that proved a disaster to the rebel cause. According to the chronicler, "the Englishmen who guarded the sea captured some of the men, and slew and drowned more than any man could tell." [24] The siege of Pevensey dragged on, though the issue could no longer be in doubt. The only event of note was the fatal wounding of William de Warenne, earl of Surrey and one of the king's principal supporters among the barons.[25] Finally, after an investment of six weeks, provisions in the beleaguered fortress gave out, and the bishop was compelled to negotiate for its surrender. The best terms he could obtain were that he quit the kingdom during the king's pleasure, and procure the capitulation of the garrison still holding out in Rochester.[26]

The bishop was sent under armed guard to deliver Rochester into the king's hands, but by a ruse a detachment of the garrison seized the whole party and liberated the wily Odo, who took refuge in the castle. The king, infuriated at this piece of duplicity, immediately marched on Rochester, at the same time issuing a summons to the English to repair to his standard. The latter "flocked in troops to the king," and Odo and his supporters were soon closely besieged in Rochester castle.[27] Although Ordericus asserts that the siege began in May, this can hardly be reconciled with the other known events of the campaign, and the siege must have begun in early June. That the fighting was heavy there can be no doubt. William erected two counter-castles, and the church of St. Andrew was damaged.[28] While the rebels waited in vain for Duke Robert to appear, an epidemic broke out in the beleaguered city and castle, and the defenders were obliged to treat for surrender. Although some of the barons sought leniency for their defeated colleagues, some of the rebel leaders suffered temporary exile and the confiscation of their English lands, and Odo was banished from England forever.[29] With the fall of Rochester, the rebellion that at first has seemed so formidable virtually collapsed. Although there are no definite dates for the end of the rising, Ordericus wrote that it was crushed by the beginning of summer, and this would seem to be confirmed by the statement of Symeon of Durham that the siege of Rochester required only a short time.[30] One piece of business had yet to be transacted. William of St. Calais, bishop of Durham, was suspected of complicity in the revolt, although the Durham chronicler attempted to clear his name. The bishop was called to stand trial as a lay baron, refused to recognize the jurisdiction of the court, and was allowed to go into exile only upon the surrender of Durham castle, an event that took place on 14 November 1088.[31]

The causes for the failure of the rebellion are not hard to find. There seems, for one thing, to have been no coordination of military activities, at least none that can be detected in the scanty sources available to the historian. Another important factor was a misplaced confidence in Duke Robert's promises of support, even though his previous record of performance was well enough known. And by holing up in their castles to await help from Normandy, the rebel leaders committed another serious blunder. Had they concentrated their forces, instead of scattering them in castles all over England, their presumed superiority in heavy cavalry might well have proved the deciding factor. As it was, their waiting strategy played directly into the king's hands.

King William had a number of advantages, and it has been seen that he made the most of them. The English church gave him all but unanimous support. Bishop William of Durham was the only holder of an English see to desert the royal cause.[32] Even more important was the support given to the king by his native subjects, which enabled him to fight the kind of a campaign necessary to put down the revolt. But the decisive factor was King William himself. He was obviously a first-rate soldier who knew his business. Had he conducted what has come to be thought of as a typically medieval war of raid and counter-raid, the rebellion might have dragged on long enough for the arrival of Duke Robert, to alter the military balance of power. But the king did no such thing. Leaving such subordinates as Bishop Wulfstan at Worcester to deal with smaller outbreaks, he mustered an army to deal with the center of rebel strength in the southeast. This army was a composite force, adequate to the mission. One by one the castles of the rebels were besieged and captured, and contemporary accounts are clear that much, if not most, of the credit for the king's victory was due to skillful use of his infantry. Again it must be noted that so far as Anglo-Norman warfare is concerned, the traditional view that heavy cavalry was the decisive factor in military operations must be modified, if not completely abandoned.

For the rest of William's reign, military activity was confined to the north and to the almost continuous operations on the Welsh frontier. Scarcely a year passed without an expedition into Wales, commanded either by the king in person or by the chief marcher barons.[33] Both Scots and Welsh were more than prone to cause disturbances when the kings of England were occupied with their continental problems. In May of 1091 King Malcolm of Scotland led one of his periodic forays into Northumberland, while William was in Normandy attempting to reduce the duchy to some kind of order. Simultaneously, trouble erupted on the Welsh border.[34] All the evidence points to a very hasty revision of plans by the king, and thus to the seriousness with which the situation was viewed in Normandy. On 18 July King William, Duke Robert, and Prince Henry are known to have been in the duchy; early in August, or perhaps even before the end of July, all three embarked for England. The king turned his attention first to the Welsh frontier, and not until the end of the summer was he able to set his forces in motion against the Scots.[35] William now seemed determined to put an end to the destructive raids from Scotland by an overwhelming display of force. Preparations for the campaign were on a much larger scale than usual, and both land and naval forces were mobilized.[36] By September the naval force had been assembled and dispatched northward, but a few days before Michaelmas (29 September) the fleet was caught in a storm and destroyed. The organization and advance of the army seems to have been even slower. The king was at Durham on 14 November, a very late date for campaigning on the border. Marching northward, the Anglo-Norman army eventually passed the Tweed into Lothian.[37] Meanwhile King Malcolm had mobilized what was described as a formidable army, and from the north he too advanced into Lothian.[38] Again, as in 1080, the two armies faced each other, and again no general engagement took place. Duke Robert, as on the previous occasion, undertook to negotiate a peaceful settlement.[39] The terms agreed upon were not dissimilar to those of eleven years earlier. Malcolm renewed his homage to the king of England, and in return was regranted his English lands. In addition—if Florence of Worcester may be credited—William Rufus agreed to pay the Scottish king an annual subsidy of twelve gold marks.[40] As C. W. David remarks, it would have been unlike William II to risk the decision of arms if his end were as readily attainable with money.[41] A settlement having been reached, the English army marched rapidly south after what must have been a very short campaign, for on 23 December Duke Robert sailed from the Isle of Wight for Normandy.[42]

The punitive expedition of 1091 did not result in peace and quiet on the border, however. The next year saw the king again in the north, this time in Cumbria, where he occupied Carlisle and directed the building of a castle in that strategic town. To ensure English domination of the newly occupied territory, numbers of peasant families and their livestock were sent north as colonists.[43] On the eastern flank of the Scottish frontier, additional security was provided at about the same time by a castle the king's favorite, Ranulph Flambard, had erected at Norham on the Tweed.[44] But in spite of the additional defenses in the north, Malcolm was across the border again in 1093. This time he fell into a trap laid by Morel of Bamborough, the steward of the crafty and unprincipled Earl Robert of Northumberland, and both Malcolm and his eldest son, Edward, were treacherously slain.[45]

The year 1094 saw the celebrated occasion on which "the king sent thither to this land, and commanded twenty thousand Englishmen to be called out to his support in Normandy; but when they came to the sea, they were ordered to return, and to give for the king's behoof, the money that they had received; that was half a pound per man; and they did so." [46]

Although William II had promptly crushed the rising of 1088, he had been fairly lenient with the rebels, and no attempt had been made to solve the basic problem of baronial allegiance. Hence it is not surprising that plots and conspiracies continued to plague both England and Normandy. One such plot erupted into open rebellion in the late spring of 1095, under circumstances which are far from clear. The participants were, for the most part, men who had rebelled once before in 1088.[47] The leading figure was Robert de Mowbray, earl of Northumberland, one of the most powerful barons in England. Unsmiling and taciturn, he was connected by marriage to leading Anglo-Norman families, and he had inherited the vast properties accumulated by his uncle, Bishop Geoffrey of Coutances.[48] Others involved in the conspiracy, or suspected of complicity, were Roger de Lacy; Gilbert fitz Richard de Clare; William, count of Eu; Odo, count of Champagne and lord of Holderness in Yorkshire; William de Merlay; Arnulf de Hesdin; Earl Roger of Shrewsbury and his son Philip.[49] This was potentially a very powerful combination, for these barons held castles in all parts of the country, posing the same sort of military problem that had faced the king in 1088. William of Eu was lord of Hastings; Gilbert fitz Richard held the castle of Clare in Suffolk; and Arnulf de Hesdin was in possession of the huge motte-and-bailey at Chipping Norton in Oxfordshire.[50] Hugh of Shrewsbury and Roger de Lacy were powerful on the Welsh marches; Odo of Champagne held Skipsea castle in Yorkshire.[51] Finally, in the north, Earl Robert was in possession of the powerful castles of Tynemouth and Bamborough, and probably Newcastle, and his ally William de Merlay held that of Morpeth on the Wansbeck.[52] The object of the conspiracy seems to have been to supplant King William with his cousin, Stephen of Aumale, the son of Odo of Champagne and Adelaide, a sister of William the Conqueror.[53] But, fortune favored the king. He must have been aware that something was in the wind, and when an opportunity presented itself, he nipped the plot before the treasonable plans of the barons could mature.

At some time, apparently in the early months of 1095, four Norwegian merchant vessels had been so unlucky as to fall into the clutches of Earl Robert, who seized everything aboard. The merchants, fortunate to escape with their skins, complained to the king, who ordered the earl to restore the cargoes to their owners. When the order was ignored, William compensated the merchants for their loss, and summoned Robert to appear before his court to answer the charges.[54] These events certainly took place before the second week in May, and it seems likely that Robert's refusal to attend the Whitsun court at Windsor (13 May) precipitated the rebellion.[55]

King William acted with his usual energy and promptness. His moves indicate an awareness that the conspiracy was widespread, and that it was possibly supported with promises of help from Normandy. Although the king had been engaged in a bitter struggle with the church, he hastily patched up his differences with Archbishop Anselm and put him in charge of the overall defense of southeastern England, the goal of any cross-Channel operation. Shortly after 10 June the primate was at his post and writing that an invasion was daily expected through the ports near Canterbury. From the same source it is also known that the king had already reached Nottingham on his northward march.[56]

From accounts of subsequent operations it is clear that some of the conspirators answered the king's summons for military service. It would also seem likely that he called out the *fyrd* to push the siege operations inevitable in any eleventh-century campaign, and probably to act as a check on the more than doubtful loyalty of the barons.[57] The surprising thing is that of all the suspected magnates, only William de Merlay seems to have joined the earl of Northumberland in open rebellion. The treasonable designs of even those barons who remained ostensibly loyal were soon revealed. At some unknown point on William's line of march to the Tyne, Gilbert fitz Richard de Clare drew the king aside, and after having obtained a promise of immunity, revealed that the royal army was marching into an ambush. He also named the other members of the conspiracy, though it is most unlikely that their identity was news to the king.[58] This timely warning enabled the king to avoid the ambush, and the advance was continued without incident as far as the Tyne.

What happened next is not entirely clear, but it is probable that Earl Robert had seized Newcastle, and that the king's initial operation was the reduction of this important fortress.[59] William then moved down the Tyne to invest Robert's castle at Tynemouth, an operation that went on for two months. When at last the castle surrendered, Robert's brother and the entire garrison were made prisoner. In the meantime the king had captured another castle, referred to by Symeon as a *munitiuncula* and by the English chronicles as a *faestene*, which the earl had garrisoned with the pick of his troops.[60] This was probably William de Merlay's castle at Morpeth, which had to be taken before the way could be opened to Robert's final refuge at Bamborough.[61]

With the earl now confined to this almost impregnable fortress on the coast, the king faced the prospect of an interminable siege. Moreover, the Welsh rising required attention, and the campaigning season was wearing on. So while part of the army stood by to repel any sortie by the garrison, the remainder was engaged in the erection of a counter-castle to which William, with grim humor, gave the name of Malveisin ("bad neighbor").[62] According to Ordericus, the erstwhile conspirators in the royal army, through either fear or shame, labored with the rest on the siege works, even though Robert, from the battlements of Bamborough, called on them by name to honor their promises to him. With Malveisin completed and an amply provisioned garrison installed, King William turned south to see what might be done about the Welsh problem. Although it was very late for such an expedition, during October he led an army into Wales, confident that his lieutenants in the north could take care of Earl Robert.[63] William's confidence was entirely justified; for the unknown commander whom he left in charge of operations in Northumberland proved to be a man of some ingenuity.

The garrison at Newcastle sent a message to Earl Robert to the effect that if the earl would come secretly, the castle would be delivered into his hands. At the same time the troops holding Malveisin were put on the alert. Mowbray fell into the trap completely. When with an escort of thirty knights he left Bamborough in darkness, his departure was noted by the garrison of the counter-castle, and a messenger was at once dispatched to Newcastle with the intelligence. The earl, thus caught between two forces, managed to take refuge in the monastery of St. Oswin at Tynemouth, which he himself had refounded in 1090.[64] Here he was able to hold out for six days, but after he had been wounded the earl and the other survivors were captured and placed in close confinement.[65] There is a professional finesse about this little action that is strongly reminiscent of Frontinus, and it would be interesting to know who was responsible for it.[66]

Returning from an unsuccessful expedition against the Welsh, King William found Bamborough castle still holding out. Upon the departure and subsequent capture of Earl Robert, the defense of the place had devolved upon the earl's wife, Mathilda de l'Aigle, and his nephew and steward Morel. It would appear, since there is no evidence that Bamborough was blockaded on the seaward side, that the siege could have dragged on indefinitely. This William had no intention of permitting to happen. Resorting to a measure commonly used in the Middle Ages to procure a surrender, "he commanded Earl Robert of Northumberland to be taken and led to Bamborough, and both his eyes to be put out unless those therein would give up the castle." [67] These terms left the defenders of the castle with little choice, and the rebellion thus came to an end, probably at some time in November.[68] The king then proceeded to punish those who had had, or were suspected of having, a part in the conspiracy. Robert de Mowbray was confined for the remaining thirty years of his life in Windsor castle, while lesser personages suffered death, mutilation, fine, forfeiture, or exile.[69]

As usual, there is a woeful lack of information on the composition of the army mustered by the king for this lengthy campaign. It is possible that the *fyrd* was summoned for duty, but this is in the realm of conjecture.[70] It is known that Gilbert fitz Richard de Clare and others of the original plotters joined the campaign, but who these others were is not specified.[71] Concerning the loyal magnates who supported the king, the records are again vague. Thomas of Bayeux, archbishop of York, and "aliis episcopis et principibus" were with the king.[72] Eudo the Dapifer witnessed two notifications issued by the king at the siege of Newcastle, and a third notification, possibly of this date, was also witnessed by Peter of Valoynes, lord of Bennington in Hertfordshire.[73] It may be assumed, finally, that Geoffrey Baynard, lord of Little Dunmow in Essex, who successfully appealed William of Eu of treason, helped in the suppression of the rebellion.[74] And this about exhausts the list.

The reign of William Rufus does not appear to have been one of widespread castle-building. Of the castles that appear for the first time in the chronicles and charters of the reign, there is reason to suspect that some at least had their origins in the reign of the first William. Most of the new references are to castles in territory recently seized from the Welsh. The names of Tynemouth and Morpeth, Carlisle and Norham, first appear in the literary remains of the second William's reign. Preston Capes in Northamptonshire and Bridgnorth are other examples. The latter castle was built in 1098/99 by Robert de Bellême on a site of great natural strength, to which he transferred the town and population of Quatford.[75] The motte-and-bailey at Quatford was probably allowed to fall into decay. King William himself instituted improvements at the Tower of London, causing some inconvenience to the Londoners by reason of the wall which was built around the castle.[76] But following the suppression of the Mowbray rebellion, there is little of military interest in the final years of William Rufus.

The events that followed the accession of Henry I in 1100 closely paralleled those of a dozen years earlier, at the beginning of the reign of William II. When a sizable fraction of the baronage plotted to place Duke Robert on the English throne, the result was civil war, whose suppression required a major effort on the part of the monarch. Actually these developments should not be considered surprising. Most of the barons involved were tenants both of the duchy and of the kingdom, and such divided allegiance could not but lead to internal discord. As William of Malmesbury put it, "Some began to fortify their dwellings, others to plunder; and the rest to look out for a new king." [77] Until England and Normandy were again united, conditions on both sides of the Channel tended to provoke the discontent of the barons.

To show his good intentions, and to allay suspicions, Henry issued in 1100 the so-called Coronation Charter, in which he promised to end the abuses current during the reign of William II; also, he imprisoned the latter's agent of extortion and oppression, Bishop Ranulf of Durham, in the Tower of London. However, signs of discontent began to appear as early as the autumn of 1100, and Henry seemed to regard the situation as critical although an invasion from Normandy, or even local insurrection, could not have been expected before the following spring or summer.[78] Then, on 3 February 1101, Bishop Ranulf escaped from the Tower and fled to Normandy.[79] This, together with the return of Duke Robert from the Crusade, brought an intensification of conspiratorial activity, with Flambard playing the part taken by Odo of Bayeux in 1088. King Henry was aware of the potential danger, and attempted to allay the discontent by reissuing his Coronation Charter and urging his subjects to remain loyal to him against all men, including his brother the duke of Normandy.[80] And the danger was indeed serious. Although William of Malmesbury's assertion that "almost all the magnates of the realm violated the fealty which they had sworn" is an exaggeration, a formidable number of the Anglo-Norman baronage were involved in the conspiracy.[81] The list included Robert de Bellême, earl of Shrewsbury; his brothers, Roger the Poitevan and Arnulf de Montgomery; William de Warenne; Walter Giffard; Ivo de Grantmesnil; and Robert, the son of Ilbert de Lacy.[82] Later William, earl of Cornwall and holder of the vast Honor of Mortain, joined the plot. This array, though imposing, represented only a fraction of the baronage, and the chronicler notes an equally impressive group who stood by the king—Count Robert of Meulan; Henry of Beaumont, earl of Warwick; Robert fitz Hamon; Richard de Redvers; and Roger Bigod.[83] Of perhaps greater importance was the support given Henry by Archbishop Anselm and the English church. With this in mind, it would appear that the chroniclers had overstated the danger, and their accounts of the king's fear and consternation do not ring quite true.[84] Nor had Henry been idle in preparing for an expected attack. On 10 March 1101 he was at Dover, where he concluded a pact with Count Robert of Flanders which had, in all probability, a bearing on the campaign that followed. In return for a yearly grant of £500, the count agreed to provide a thousand knights for the king's service to defend the kingdom of England, if necessary, saving only his allegiance to the king of France.[85] Although the treaty stipulated that these knights might be required to serve in England, it is unlikely that such an eventuality was really expected. Apart from the difficulties involved in transporting such a force to England and maintaining it there, it would seem to have been more economical to employ mercenaries directly, as the two Williams had done, and as Stephen and Henry II were to do later in the century. It seems clear that this agreement between Henry and the count of Flanders was mainly strategic—an attempt to create a diversion on Duke Robert's flank that would prevent his committing all his reosurces to the projected invasion of England. And it is quite possible, though there is no proof, that this threat had an effect on the ensuing campaign.

The king was at Winchester for Easter (21 April), and on Whitsunday (9 June) he was at St. Albans.[86] It may reasonably be supposed that during these weeks he was making the necessary military and naval preparations to meet the threatened invasion.[87] Early in June, reports reached England that Duke Robert had assembled a fleet at Treport, and that he had mustered an army of knights, archers and other infantry for the attack across the Channel.[88] At this intelligence, Henry acted with great promptness and vigor. A fleet was ordered into the Channel to intercept the invasion force, while he himself marched south at the head of an army. But then the king made a tactical blunder that nearly led to disaster. Since the Norman assembly area at Treport was not far from St. Valerie, Henry assumed that the projected landing would be in the Hastings-Pevensey area, as it had been in 1066.[89] Hence, instead of holding his main force well behind the coast until he learned the precise objective of the enemy, Henry marched directly to the coast "at midsummer" and established a camp at Pevensey.[90] Nothing very definite can be said of the size or composition of either army, although the Norman invasion fleet is said to have numbered two hundred vessels.[91] Henry's army apparently included the feudal contingents of the loyal barons and of the English clergy, plus a levy of the native militia. Poole very aptly remarks that the invasion "was frustrated, as in the previous rebellion, by the alliance of the church and the native English." [92] It should be noted that the latter component was made up of infantry. During the weeks after the establishment of the camp at Pevensey, there was time to whip the army into shape. Henry himself actively supervised the training of the English infantry, showing them how best to meet and repel a cavalry charge.[93]

But there was to be no second Battle of Hastings. At least part of Henry's squadron had been suborned, and the traitors piloted the hostile fleet to safety in Portsmouth harbor, where on 21 July the army of Duke Robert disembarked unopposed.[94] This blow put Henry at a serious disadvantage. Robert at Portsmouth was but thirty miles from Winchester, where the royal treasure was kept, and from Winchester it was less than seventy miles by road to London. The king might very well have fallen back from Pevensey to cover the metropolis. Instead, relying perhaps on the known sluggishness of his brother the duke—or perhaps having had word from the Continent of some diversion that would give the invaders pause—he broke up his camp at Pevensey and set out to head off the enemy.[95] This was a calculated risk, since by hard marching the invaders could have put themselves beyond his reach. But the king had reckoned correctly, and so canceled out his previous error.

In the meantime the duke's army advanced on Winchester as though to attack the city; but the defenses must have appeared too formidable to assault, and there was certainly no time to open a siege. Whatever idea there had been of capturing the town, if it had been entertained at all, was abandoned, and the Norman army took the London road past Alresford.[96] From Winchester their advance must have been at a snail's pace; for Henry, although he had a much greater distance to cover, managed to get ahead of his brother, and was astride the London road at Alton, just seventeen miles beyond Winchester, at some time before the end of July.[97]

From the military point of view this ended the campaign of 1101. Henry was, unwilling to move to drive Robert back to Normandy, and Robert was unwilling to risk the attempt to crush Henry and seat himself on the English throne. A hasty peace—which turned out to be little more than a truce—was made: Robert was to receive an annual subsidy of 3,000 marks—which Henry apparently had no intention of paying any longer than necessary—and those barons who had sided with Robert were to be granted an amnesty, which the king proceeded to violate as soon as he could with impunity. By the end of July it was all over; the king was conducting business as usual at Winchester, and the royal army had been dismissed. Part of the duke's army returned to Normandy, while the rest remained with him in England.[98]

It was not long after the Treaty of Alton that King Henry set about eliminating, one after another, the barons who had supported the invasion. The most powerful of these enemies was Robert de Bellême, earl of Shrewsbury, an utterly vicious and unscrupulous man who for many years had been involved in every disorder, whether in England or in Normandy. In 1098, on the death of his brother Hugh, he had acquired the English estates of the house of Montgomery, including the castles of Montgomery, Bridgnorth, Shrewsbury, Carreghofa, Arundel, and Tickhill, and had thus become the most dangerous and powerful baron in England.[99] One brother, Arnulph de Montgomery, held the castle of Pembroke; another, Roger the Poitevan, was lord of the castlery of Clitheroe in Lancashire.[100] Fortunately for the king, most of these strongholds were so widely scattered that they could not be mutually supporting.

Henry made very careful preparations before openly challenging the earl of Shrewsbury. His agents and informers kept a close watch on Robert.[101] By the spring of 1102 the king was ready to act on the basis of their reports. The earl was cited before the *curia regis,* most likely at Winchester during the Easter feast (6 April), to answer forty-five separate charges of treasonable words spoken or actions taken against the king.[102] Earl Robert, by taking refuge in his castles, tacitly admitted either that the charges were true, or that he had no confidence in the king's justice; whereupon he was declared an outlaw.[103]

The king accepted the trial at arms, but it is very difficult to reconstruct the campaign from the conflicting accounts of the chroniclers. At his strongholds in the Severn valley—Bridgnorth, Carreghofa, and Shrewsbury—Earl Robert renewed the fortifications and laid in provisions against long sieges, "carrying thither from all the district around Shrewsbury, wheat and every necessity that war requires." [104] He mustered an army composed of his Norman and Welsh tenants, and with his brother Arnulph led it on a plundering raid through Staffordshire.[105] The king's movements at the time are not so easily accounted for; but upon receiving news of Robert's defiance, he at once assembled an army, presumably at Winchester, and all authorities agree that his first move was to invest Arundel.[106]

The castle was strongly sited, and Henry constructed at least one counter-castle to keep the defenders in check. The chroniclers disagree as to what happened next, but the most likely sequence of events is that recorded by Ordericus. The siege of Arundel was pushed with vigor, but the garrison held out through May and June. In the meantime the king sent a strong detachment under the command of Robert Bloet, bishop of Lincoln, to besiege, or, more likely, to blockade Tickhill.[107] Eventually the garrison in Arundel was reduced to such straits that the commander applied to Earl Robert for either relief or permission to surrender. Late in June, unable to force the king to raise what by then had been a three-month siege, he reluctantly authorized the defenders of the castle to capitulate.[108] Henry then marched north to reinforce Bishop Robert before Tickhill. His arrival produced the desired result, for the castle garrison surrendered without further resistance.[109]

The reduction of Arundel and Tickhill now freed the king for the real business of the campaign—an attack on Earl Robert's principal strongholds on the Severn. Henry's first objective was Bridgnorth, which was immediately invested; a counter-castle was built, and "machines" were constructed.[110] At the same time the king strengthened the garrison at Stafford by the addition of two hundred men under the command of William Pantulf. This reinforcement doubtless served the double purpose of protecting the district from the raids of Earl Robert's Welsh supporters, and of rendering hazardous any attempt by the earl to withdraw toward the north or east. The king, obviously intending to press home the campaign, persisted in the siege despite the attempts of the Welsh to beat up the quarters of the army before Bridgnorth, and despite divided councils among his advisers.[111]

The Welsh were dealt with by diplomacy and bribery. Through the mediation of William Pantulf, Henry was able—by making promises that were never fulfilled—to detach Iorwerth ap Bleddyn from the earl, although Iorwerth's brothers, Cadwgan and Maredudd, remained loyal to their lord, and dispatched him to raid Shropshire.[112] The barons in the royal army feared to see one of their number completely ruined, and at least some of them attempted to dissuade the king from crushing Earl Robert. It would seem that, as in the campaign of the previous year, Henry received his strongest support from the English militia, who protested against any baronial proposal for mediation. This is the only mention of the *fyrd* in the entire campaign. Bridgnorth itself proved to be stoutly defended. On the approach of the royal army, Earl Robert had retired to Shrewsbury, entrusting the defense of the town and castle to Roger fitz Corbet, Robert de Neuville, and Ulger the Hunter. The regular garrison of the earl's tenants was augmented by eighty stipendiary men-at-arms.[113] After the siege had been under way for some time, the townsmen and Earl Robert's men, abandoning hope of victory, opened negotiations for the surrender of the place, with William Pantulf again acting as intermediary. The earl was notified, but found himself unable to relieve the town or to raise the siege, and matters seemed set for the surrender of Bridgnorth without further resistance. However, Robert's mercenaries—who had not been included in the parleys, presumably because they had no stake in prolonging hostilities— proved more loyal than his own sworn vassals. It was only with difficulty that their opposition was overcome, and they were allowed to march out with what amounted to the honors of war.[114] The siege had lasted, according to Ordericus, for three weeks, and the king was now ready to run the rebel to earth. From Bridgnorth the army began its march up the Severn toward Shrewsbury, at times constructing its own road as it went.[115] The rebel cause was now hopeless; with King Henry fast closing in upon his final refuge, Earl Robert surrendered the castle of Shrewsbury and threw himself on the king's mercy. Robert and his brothers Arnulph and Roger were banished from England, and their vast estates escheated to the crown. The army was mustered out, and by Michaelmas (29 September) the king was at Westminster.[116]

The suppression of this rebellion had its effect on the whole history of Henry's reign. For the next thirty-three years England was undisturbed by civil commotion, for the condign punishment visited upon the overweening house of Bellême served to warn the baronage of what opposition to the crown entailed. From the military point of view, the campaign is both interesting and instructive. Whether or not Henry thought in such terms, he had conducted his operations according to sound strategic principles. Fortunately for him, his enemy's strongholds, with the exception of the Severn castles, were too widely separated to lend support to one another. The reduction of Arundel and Tickhill was a necessary preliminary in the military action against the rebels. Had he moved first against Bridgnorth and Shrewsbury, the king would have had always to make provision against the possibility of harassing movements in his rear, as well as the very real danger that these castles would act as magnets, drawing to them other discontented elements among the baronage. With Tickhill in rebel hands, communications with York and the north were in jeopardy, and might have been completely interdicted were the rebellion to have spread. Arundel represented even more of a threat. It gave the rebels a line of communication to Normandy; it was also a possible bridgehead through which reinforcements might be landed to support the rising. It seems likely that this reasoning caused Henry to turn his attention first to Arundel. With this link to the Continent broken, Earl Robert was forced to rely on his English resources alone—resources that were insufficient to maintain anything like an equal contest with the crown. When the king lopped off his outlying garrisons, Robert's only hope of avoiding utter ruin lay in prolonging his resistance until Henry would accept some sort of compromise, or until lukewarm supporters of the king had persuaded him to accept a less drastic outcome than total victory. Neither of these hopes materialized, and the earl was fortunate to escape with his life.

Of the composition and strength of the royal army there is very little real information. The statements of Florence of Worcester that the king "with nearly the whole military force of England, sat down before Bridgnorth," and of the English chronicler that "with all his forces [he] went to Bridgnorth" are not very revealing.[117] The army was of sufficient strength to detach a force from the siege of Arundel for the blockade of Tickhill, and again to augment the garrison at Stafford by two hundred men. A reference by Ordericus to "tria millia pagensium militum" can only refer to the English *fyrd*, doubtless utilized for prosecution of the sieges, and probably as a counterweight to the baronial contingents. There is no mention of the use of mercenary troops by the king, although this might be inferred from the length of the campaign and from the fact that Earl Robert had some scores in his employ.[118] But whatever the means, the king disposed them well, and the conduct of this campaign did much to enhance King Henry's military reputation.

Although England was undisturbed by war or rebellion for the remainder of Henry's long reign, mention of castles continues to appear not only in the annals of the chroniclers, but in other, increasingly abundant documents. Often the only historical verification of the existence of a castle is that it had a chapel which was given to some religious house, and that the terms of the gift were embodied in a charter. For example, at Ascot d'Oilly in Oxfordshire not a trace of a castle remains, but it is known that Roger d'Oilli gave the chapel in the castle of Ascot to the canons of St. Frideswide.[119]

For the later years of the reign of Henry I, the most illuminating source concerning the castles in the king's hands is in the sole surviving Pipe Roll prior to the time of Henry II.[120] Upon the nineteen castles mentioned in this earliest extant official financial document,[121] the total amount expended was a mere £112 9s. 7d. Four of these strongholds—Kirkby Malzeard, Thirsk, Burton-in-Lonsdale, and Brinklow—were Mowbray castles in the hands of the crown, and the £25 17s. 1d. spent by the government represented the wages of watchmen and caretakers. The custodians, Robert de Woodville and Henry de Montfort, duly accounted to the exchequer for the sums expended.[122] In general the sums disbursed were small, and except at Arundel, where work on the castle amounted to £22 7s. 8d., no single expenditure exceeded twenty pounds.[123] At London £29 3s. 10d. were spent, but only £17 6d. was for construction, the remainder representing the wages of *servientes, vigilii,* and *portarii.*[124] Work on the *turris* at Gloucester cost £7 6s. 2d., and at Tickhill—which seems, like Arundel, to have remained in the hands of the crown after the rebellion of 1102—£9 2s. 8d. were spent on construction *per breve Regem.*[125] The amounts then range downward to the 20s. paid for having a door made in the tower at Salisbury, and the 7d. for repairing the gate at Bamborough.[126] None of these sums are large enough to suggest that any but maintenance work was being done on the king's castles, or that any transition to masonry structures was in progress. They give the impression of a kingdom at peace with no expectation of war, either foreign or domestic.

Chapter 4

The Troubled Time of Stephen: December 1135– September 1139

THE death of Henry I in Normandy on 1 December 1135 left behind a succession problem that was to bedevil the political life of England for almost twenty years. The late king's only son had perished some years earlier in the wreck of the White Ship, and his failure to produce a male heir by a second marriage had left his daughter Mathilda, the widow of the Emperor Henry V and now the wife of Count Geoffrey of Anjou, as his only legitimate direct descendant. Twice before his death Henry had extracted an oath from the leading barons and clergy of the kingdom that they would honor the rights of his daughter to the succession. Among the subscribers to this oath was Stephen, count of Boulogne and a prominent tenant of the English crown by reason of his possession of the vast Honor of Mortain. Stephen was a nephew of King Henry I, and a grandson of William the Conqueror. It would serve no purpose here to enter upon a discussion of the proper descent of the crown in a century which had only begun to develop a concept of definite laws of inheritance. But in the twelfth century an oath was not a thing to be regarded lightly. It is enough to say that Stephen, who was in Normandy at the time of his uncle's death, chose to disregard his own oath, and sailed for England to make a bid for the crown.[1] He landed at an undetermined port in Kent and advanced on Dover, where a garrison of Robert, earl of Gloucester, the ablest of King Henry's illegitimate sons, refused to admit him.[2] At Canterbury the castle, likewise held by the earl's men, was also barred to him. Undeterred, Stephen pushed on to London, where he was well received by the townsmen.[3] He then marched rapidly to Winchester, where Bishop Roger of Salisbury, King Henry's treasurer, delivered up the castle and the royal coffers without protest.[4] The de facto king now returned to London bent on securing the consecration that would make him king in right. He got around the problem of the oath by the convenient fiction that it had been exacted by force, and Hugh Bigod swore that Henry on his deathbed had named Stephen as his successor. On 22 December 1135 Stephen was crowned at London by William, archbishop of Canterbury.[5] He then proceeded to Reading for the burial of his predecessor, and early in the new year (1136) he went on to Oxford, attended by a respectable number of English magnates.[6]

King Stephen was apparently still at Oxford when word was brought to him that David, king of Scots, had invaded the northern counties in the interests of the Empress Mathilda. King David, who as earl of Huntingdon was also an important English tenant, had subscribed to the oath guaranteeing the succession of the king's daughter, and his own interests in the north coincided with the honoring of this obligation. At sometime during the Christmas season King David crossed the border with a formidable army, and he seized the castles of Carlisle, Wark, Alnwick, Norham, and Newcastle. Bamborough alone of all the border fortresses remained in English hands. The Scottish king was contemplating an advance on Durham when he was induced to open negotiations by the arrival of Stephen in the north at the beginning of February at the head of a considerable array. The ensuing agreement provided that all the Scottish conquests were to be restored with the exception of Carlisle, which was to remain in Scottish hands for the duration of Stephen's reign.[7] The king stayed at Durham for fifteen days before returning south by way of York, in time to celebrate Easter (22 March) at London.[8] Shortly thereafter Earl Robert of Gloucester landed in England, and the court traveled to Oxford to meet him.[9] At this time a charter of liberties, somewhat resembling the charter of Henry I but differing in the latitude of action guaranteed the church, was issued.[10]

Toward the end of April a report was widely circulated that the king had died. This became the opening signal for the series of baronial revolts which were to characterize Stephen's reign. Hugh Bigod seized the castle at Norwich, and relinquished it only when the king appeared before it in person.[11] Then rebellion flared at the opposite end of the kingdom. A minor baron, Robert of Bampton, began to terrorize the countryside in the vicinity of his heavily garrisoned Devonshire castle. King Stephen proceeded quickly against the outlaw; in June he captured the castle and exiled the garrison to Scotland.[12] Hardly had this action been concluded when more serious trouble broke out in the same region, as Baldwin de Redvers seized the town and castle of Exeter and garrisoned them against the king.[13]

With the promptness that characterized all his military endeavors, Stephen assembled an army and marched against the rebel baron. The town was quickly recaptured, but Baldwin and his garrison held out in the castle for nearly three months despite the siege engines the king is said to have constructed. Mining and mercenary slingers from abroad were also employed. In the meantime the king had detached a column to seize the neighboring castle of Plympton which had been garrisoned by Baldwin. It was surrendered without resistance and then destroyed, but a part of the garrison were permitted to join Baldwin in Exeter. Here, the capitulation of the castle was caused by a failure of the water supply, which compelled Baldwin to sue for terms.[14] On the advice of the barons, Stephen pardoned Baldwin, but in September the unrepentant baron fled to the Isle of Wight.[15] From the castle of Carisbrooke on his island stronghold, the versatile rebel now embarked on a career of piracy, and King Stephen was once again forced to lead an army against him. He marched to Southampton, where he had ordered a fleet to be assembled, possibly by way of Farnham in Hampshire.[16] The prompt action of the king gave Baldwin second thoughts about continued resistance. He submitted voluntarily and was permitted to take refuge in Anjou, where he joined forces with the empress.[17]

For the rest of the year and for most of 1137 the kingdom was undisturbed. From Lent until December the king was in Normandy, returning to hold his Christmas court at Dunstable.[18] During his absence a truce was negotiated with the king of Scots by Archbishop Thurstan of York,[19] and both Ordericus and the

Ely annalist contain vague and rather garbled accounts of a widespread conspiracy against the king.[20] This plot either involved Bishop Nigel or was detected and suppressed by him. Shortly after his return to England, Stephen had ordered Miles de Beauchamp, the constable, to deliver up the castle of Bedford.[21] When the latter refused to do so, Stephen mobilized an army and invested the place on Christmas eve (if Henry of Huntingdon is to be believed) or very shortly thereafter.[22]

Stephen's willingness to launch a campaign in midwinter is evidence at once of the seriousness with which he regarded the situation and of his qualities as a soldier. Campaigning at this time of year was not a general practice of the twelfth century. After five weeks, during which the king once again brought up a siege train, the garrison was reduced by famine and forced to capitulate.[23]

The operation against Bedford had scarcely been concluded before Stephen was forced to turn his attention to affairs in the north. Indeed, the year 1138 was one of almost continual warfare on the Scottish border. On 10 January the Scots under the command of William, a nephew of King David, crossed the frontier and attempted to capture the town and castle of Wark.[24] On this occasion the invaders were repulsed, but shortly thereafter King David, with a considerable army and a siege train, began an investment of Wark that lasted three weeks. The garrison of the castle, inspired by its commander, Jordan de Bussey, "set at naught and rendered useless all the king's endeavors." Leaving a covering force at Wark to protect his line of communications, King David pushed on into Northumberland. The main body of the Scottish army marched as far as Corbridge, almost fifty miles south of Wark, and raiding parties were dispatched in all directions. One such detachment was repulsed at Hexham, but the monastery of Tynemouth was forced to pay a ransom of twenty-seven marks. Then the raiders, crossing the Tyne, pushed south into the palatinate of Durham.[25]

By this time, however, King Stephen had finished his business at Bedford, and shortly after the beginning of February he appeared in the north at the head of a large force. King David retreated before the English advance past Wark, and concentrated at Roxburgh on the northern bank of the Tweed, where he hoped to lure Stephen into a general action on terms favorable to the Scots.[26] The English king was not to be enticed, however, and after ravaging the Lowlands he returned to England at some time after the beginning of Lent (16 February), when his supplies were exhausted.[27]

The Scottish king was not deterred by this brief invasion of his own country, for on 15 April he again crossed the border into England. The main body reached the Tyne at Newcastle, with raiding parties flung out all the way to Durham. On the other side of the island, a column commanded by the king's nephew William, and probably based on Carlisle, advanced to Craven in Yorkshire, and on 10 June defeated an English force at Clitheroe in Lancashire, seventy-nine miles south of Carlisle. The main army under King David, however, began a retreat after hearing a false report that King Stephen was advancing from the south. During this foray the bishop of Durham's town and castle of Norham were taken and destroyed, and Wark again was besieged. The king of Scots had apparently resolved on taking Wark, for the siege continued without intermission through the summer, with the Scots employing siege machinery against the walls.[28]

In late summer the strength of King David was augmented when a prominent northern English baron, Eustace fitz John, with a body of troops, defected to his standard. Even more important from the military standpoint was the fact that Eustace also transferred the castles of Alnwick in Northumberland and Malton in Yorkshire to David's allegiance. Thus encouraged, King David launched a new offensive, the third for that year, and on a far greater scale than its predecessors. Although the force collected by the king certainly did not muster the 26,000 men attributed to it by Richard of Hexham—and although even half that figure is probably too high—it was still a formidable array.[29] The army was concentrated about 22 July, and Normans, English, and Scots from all parts of the north were said to have furnished units.[30] With the siege of Wark still in progress, the king of Scots turned over its conduct to two of his "thegns" and the Norman turncoat Eustace fitz John, and moved his forces southward. Marching via Bamborough and crossing the Wansbeck in the vicinity of Mitford, the Scots passed the Tyne and halted on the Wear, while contingents from west of the Pennines came to join them. These reinforcements consisted of Picts from Galloway and of levies from Carlisle and Cumbria, the old kingdom of Strathclyde, now under Scottish control.[31] At full strength, King David's army then resumed its southward advance. It bypassed Durham, ravaging as it went, and reached the line of the Tees on the border of Yorkshire, probably about the middle of August.[32] The timing of the invasion could not have been better from the Scottish point of view. King Stephen was totally committed in the southern part of the kingdom, and could dispatch only a token force to aid the hard-pressed northerners.[33]

Word of the Scots' advance had, of course, reached York, although no mention is made of any attempt to resist the invaders or to observe their actions before they reached the line of the Tees. Indeed, the northern chronicler reported that because of mutual distrust and suspicion, and the absence of any local military leadership, it seemed as if the country north of the Humber might fall to the Scots by default.[34] The first action seems to have been taken not by a soldier but by the king's lieutenant in the north, the venerable Archbishop Thurstan of York.[35] A meeting of the local magnates summoned by that prelate to decide on a course of action was attended by Count William of Aumale, Walter de Gant, Robert Bruce and his son Adam, Roger de Mowbray, the aged Walter Espec, Ilbert de Lacy, William de Percy, Richard de Courcy, William Fossard, and Robert de Stuteville. Before the council had concluded its deliberations, Bernard de Balliol reached York at the head of a mounted contingent sent by King Stephen. Thus encouraged, and heartened by the words of the archbishop, who in effect called for a holy war against the barbarous Scots, the barons decided to fight.[36] At the conclusion of the council they departed to call out their men, and the archbishop mustered the shire-levy, whose local contingents marched under the command of the parish priests. It would also seem likely that the civic militias of York, Beverley, and Ripon were called out, each marching under the banner of its patron saint.[37]

York was the mustering place, and here it was that a motley

army assembled—the feudal contingents of the Norman barons, French and English, the levies of the countryside and the city companies, of English and Danish descent; even some Scoto-Normans, for, as Colonel Burne notes, the lines of demarcation in the first half of the twelfth century was far from clear-cut. Indeed, names that in later generations were to have a distinctly Scottish flavor—such as Bruce and Balliol—were found among the Yorkshire host. Whether a single commander was appointed seems doubtful. Archbishop Thurstan, himself far too aged and feeble to accompany the army, appointed the bishop of Orkney, Ralph Nowel, as his deputy in matters spiritual. The crusading aspect of the expedition was further heightened by the three great banners, mounted on a wagon, that flew over the host—the banners of St. Peter of York, St. John of Beverley, and St. Wilfred of Ripon.[38] The army marched about nineteen miles out of York on the Great North Road, as far as Thirsk, where it halted while one further attempt was made to negotiate a settlement with the Scottish king. Bernard de Balliol and Robert Bruce, both of whom were tenants of the crown of Scotland as well as of the king of England, were sent into the hostile lines to see whether a compromise could be reached. Although the negotiators seem to have been empowered to hold out the earldom of Northumbria as a bribe to King David if he would at least restrain his troops from atrocities, the offer was rejected—the Scots being in a fair way to acquire Northumberland by force of arms. Thereupon Bruce and Balliol renounced their fealty to the Scottish king and returned to their own lines at Thirsk. In the meantime the Yorkshire host at Thirsk was reinforced by contingents from Derbyshire and Nottinghamshire, commanded by Geoffrey Halsalin, Robert de Ferrers, and William Peverel.[39] It can be assumed that these units were the mounted military tenants of the barons.[40] More details are available concerning the preliminary moves of this campaign than for most twelfth-century operations. So far as can be determined the Yorkshiremen had conducted the opening phases in accordance with sound doctrine. They were astride the enemy's line of advance, and an engagement seemed imminent.

On 21 August the commander of the northern army, whoever he may have been, sent reconnaissance parties out from Thirsk to observe the movements of the enemy.[41] The scouts returned, probably late in the afternoon, with the intelligence that the Scots were across the Tees, some twenty-one miles away from Thirsk, and were marching south along the Great North Road. It was at once decided to intercept the enemy as soon as possible; and if Richard of Hexham is correct, a night march must have been resolved upon. Since the battle of the twenty-second began at about 6 A.M., the advance must certainly have been in progress by midnight in order to have covered the eleven miles between Thirsk and the battle site, and to have permitted time for deployment before the Scots made their first charge.[42] This hitherto unnoticed aspect of the campaign offers room for conjecture. Is it possible that the Yorkshiremen were hoping to surprise the Scottish army in bivouac? If so, they were to be disappointed, for the invaders either were themselves on the move early, or had intelligence of the English advance. At any rate, the two armies were marching toward each other through dense fog in the predawn hours, and a clash was now inevitable.[43]

Three miles beyond Northallerton, the Great North Road is flanked on the right by two hillocks about six hundred yards apart.[44] At some time before 6 o'clock on Monday morning, 22 August, the English army began to deploy to the right, and to occupy the southernmost of the two hills. How long this movement may have taken it is impossible to even guess, since there is no indication of the strength of the army. At the summit of the hill was posted the cart or wagon to which the holy standards were affixed. "In doing this their hope was that our Lord Jesus Christ by the efficacy of His body might be their leader in the contest. They also provided for their men a certain and conspicuous rallying-point, by which they might rejoin their companions in the event of their being cut off."[45] Thus spiritual and military ends were combined.

For the impending engagement, the English command decided to assume the tactical defensive; all personnel were to fight on foot, with the exception of the unit commanders and a small detail assigned to guard the horses of the knights who were to fight as infantry.[46] Up to this point modern authorities are fairly well agreed; but from here on, opinions vary greatly as to just what happened.[47] The English order of battle, for example, has been reconstructed in a number of ways. "All we know for certain," wrote Burne, ". . . is that all the troops were dismounted, that three lines were formed, that the first line consisted of archers, the second of spearmen, and the third of men-at-arms." This is also the formation suggested by Barrett.[48] Ramsey asserts that "in the front rank were placed the pick of the men-at-arms. . . . Intermingled with them as a sort of rear rank were the archers. Behind, and in support of them were massed the baronial contingents. . . . All round the barons, on flank and rear, were grouped the parish levies." [49] Finally, Oman has had a try at the formation:

They drew up their whole force in one deep line along a hillside . . . with the chariot bearing the standards in the rear of their centre. The knights all dismounted and served on foot with the shire-levies, apparently forming a mailed front line behind which the half-armed country-folk arrayed themselves. There were a considerable number of archers among the Yorkshiremen, who are said to have been "mixed" with the spearmen. Presumably they stood in the mass and shot over their friends' heads down the slope, for there is no statement that they took position either on the flank or in front of the main body. Some of the elder knights formed a sacred band in reserve around the Standard; among them stood the commanders of the host, Albemarle and L'Espec.[50]

Now some of this borders on sheer, unnecessary nonsense, for there is a very clear statement in Richard of Hexham as to how the front rank was drawn up: "The greater part of the knights, then dismounting, became foot-soldiers, a chosen body of whom, interspersed with archers, were arranged in the front rank." [51] What this says, if it says anything, is that the English front was composed of archers stiffened with dismounted men-at-arms to prevent a charge from breaking the line. Why this should require an elaborate interpretation is difficult to understand. The Hexham chronicler goes on to say that the remainder of the knights and barons were arrayed around the Standard, and that the rest of the host—presumably the shire-levies—were posted on the flanks and in the rear; and that the horses with their mounted guard were posted some distance in the rear lest they should become frightened by the din of battle.[52] This seems a reasonable and straightforward account, and if yet another interpretation may be added, the English army was ordered essentially as an oblong phalanx, the front rank composed of archers stiffened with dismounted men-at-arms, the center made up of knights afoot, and the flanks and rear ranks filled up with the shire-levies. Perhaps the alignment in Diagram 1 would represent the English formation with a fair degree of accuracy.

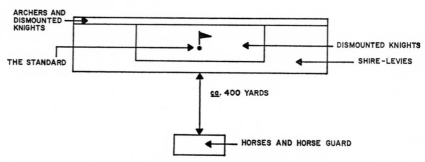

Diagram 1. Probable disposition of the English Army at the Battle of the Standard

About the Scottish order of battle there is less division of opinion. The unusual thing about it is that the commander, King David, was forced to change his dispositions on the field itself and in the presence of the enemy. His first decision was to imitate the English pattern, with dismounted knights and archers as the spearhead of the attack. When a gap had been opened in the ranks of the Yorkshire host, it was to be exploited by the less well-armed Highlanders and Picts from Galloway. This sensible plan was upset by the insistent demands of the Galwegians to be put in the front line despite their total lack of armor—a position they claimed as a matter of ancient right, and so vociferously that the king reluctantly and unwisely gave orders for the clansmen to move to the front.[53] As nearly as it can be reconstructed from the incomplete account of Richard of Hexham, and the rather confused statements of Ailred, the final Scottish order must have been more or less as follows: The Galwegians formed the center, with the two wings somewhat refused. The right wing was commanded by the king's son Henry, and seems to have been organized as the main striking force. It was composed in part of the levies from Cumbria and Teviotdale, including a large proportion of the archers, as well as the major fraction of the English and Norman knights of the Lowlands. It also seems probable that these knights remained mounted.[54] The left was made up of contingents from the Lowlands and the western Highlands, apparently all on foot. Unusual for the period was a tactical reserve, under the command of the king himself, drawn from Moray and the eastern Highlands, as well as a small bodyguard of knights, all of whom, the king included, had sent their horses to the rear and were prepared to fight on foot.[55] Oman's diagram is probably not far wrong as to the final disposition of the Scottish army.[56]

Thus the two armies were drawn up facing each other at a distance of three or four hundred yards. The Scottish army had the more flexible organization since it was divided into smaller units under subordinate commanders. Moreover, it possessed a tactical reserve which could be thrust in, were a break to be made in the English line. The Yorkshiremen, committed to the defensive, hazarded everything on being able to maintain their position against the attacks of the enemy. Tactical flexibility was certainly not provided for in their monolithic formation.[57]

The battle opened with a charge by the Galwegians against the English line, to the accompaniment of wild screams and yells. Although the archers in the front rank took a tremendous toll, the impetus of the charge carried it to the English line, and a momentary penetration was made. However, the steadiness of the dismounted knights soon restored the situation and the attack was beaten off. Again and again the unarmored men of Galloway returned to the charge, but with the same fatal results in their attempt to break into the massive English formation.[58] At this juncture, and seemingly on his own initiative—at least there is no evidence to suggest that he received an order—Prince Henry launched the Scots' right wing against the English left. The cavalry, outdistancing its infantry support, crashed into the northerners' line, and broke into the mass of the shire-levies behind the line of dismounted knights. They cut their way forward and emerged, sadly diminished in numbers, at the rear of the English left. Had the Scots reined in to take their enemy in the rear, a serious diversion might have been created, but instead they were tempted by the picketed horses some four hundred yards behind the lines. The English, undisturbed, made good the breach in their front, and hurled back the infantry who tried to exploit it. By the time Prince Henry could reorganize his squadron, the opportunity had passed, and he and his men escaped only by throwing away their insignia and mingling with their foes, from whom they were indistinguishable in arms and equipment.[59]

The day was now lost for the Scots. The Galwegians had made a final charge and were in headlong retreat, with two of their chiefs, Donald and Ulgerich, dead on the field. The Scottish left had made a single half-hearted charge, and then had broken off the action.[60] Far too late to have had any effect on the decision, King David ordered the reserve forward in an effort to retrieve the day; but the Highlanders showed no stomach for battle after having witnessed the fate of their center and right. The king soon found himself deserted but for the few English and Norman knights of his bodyguard. Seeing that the situation was hopeless, they called for their horses and retired from the field; the flight became general, and by nine o'clock the battle was over. Well it was for the Scots that the English tactical disposition was not adopted with pursuit in mind, else few of the invaders would ever have regained their homes. Many prisoners were taken, as the wrecks of the Scottish army, all semblance of organization gone, made their way back to the base at Carlisle.[61] The Yorkshiremen made no real attempt to exploit their victory. Although casualties had been small—only one man of note, a brother of Ilbert de Lacy, is said to have been killed—the army was rapidly disbanded, and the only subsequent action was that a part of the baronial component marched off to besiege the castle of Eustace fitz John at Malton.[62] It was considered enough to have turned back the Scots.

From the Scottish point of view the battle was one of lost opportunities. There were at least two occasions during the action on which the commitment of the reserve might well have changed the fortunes of the day. The first came when the initial charge of the Galwegians had shaken the center of the English line; the second occurred when Prince Henry's charge had opened a gap in the left. On neither occasion is there any sign of an attempt to utilize the reserve. To Oman and Burne, the main lesson of the battle seems to have been that charges of unarmored men against a steady line of bows and spears can never succeed.[63] But there is another, more valuable lesson to be learned from the Battle of the Standard. King David's tactical dispositions should have produced victory against the passive mass of the Yorkshire army; and the real moral of the Scottish defeat is that tactical flexibility, unless directed with firmness and promptness, is no guarantee of success. The battle provides, in addition, another demonstration that even when given a preponderance of heavy cavalry, the Normans of the eleventh and twelfth centuries were never committed to fighting on horseback.

Far to the north, the garrison at Wark had been under continuous siege since 10 June. Following his defeat at the Battle of the Standard, King David rejoined his troops in the lines before the castle. By the end of September the garrison had been reduced to severe straits. At the beginning of November their plight was so desperate that the lord of the place, Walter Espec, ordered them to surrender. Terms were secured at Martinmas (11 November) through the good offices of William, abbot of Rievaulx, and the heroic garrison were allowed to march out of the castle under arms. At the time of the surrender the provisions within Wark consisted of one live horse and one preserved in salt. A final episode in the military history of the border for 1138 was a long plundering raid led by Edgar, a bastard son of Earl Gospatric, together with Robert and Uchtred fitz Maldred. They overran Northumberland, crossed the Tyne into Durham, and returned to Scotland by way of Errington and Denton, not far from Hexham.[64] The events of 1138 show rather conclusively that the Scottish frontier was inadequately fortified. The two castles that defended the line of the Tweed were both taken and dismantled by the Scots during the course of the year. At the other end of the border, the town and castle of Carlisle were in the hands of the Scots by virtue of the treaty that King

Stephen had negotiated in 1136. This provided Scottish armies with a base for operations against the northern counties, as well as a safe refuge in case of defeat. Elsewhere along the border the defenses were equally weak. The defection of Eustace fitz John to the Scots had delivered the strong castle of Alnwick into their hands, and no doubt facilitated the invasion of August which culminated in the Battle of the Standard. The castle of Bamborough was able to resist the attacks of the Scots, but no mention is made of the other Northumbrian castles, including Morpeth, Tynemouth, and Newcastle, which are known to have been in existence at this date. Since the Scots usually passed the Tyne in the vicinity of Hexham, it may be inferred that the normal invasion route, whether from the Tweed or across the Pennines from Carlisle, avoided the castles held by loyal garrisons, and crossed the river at an undefended point.

Meanwhile, events in the south and west of England required the full attention of King Stephen. If the absence of castles in the north facilitated the invasions of the Scots, the large numbers of such strongholds in the rest of the kingdom greatly hampered Stephen's efforts to maintain the peace. On his return from the Scottish expedition, the king arrived at Northampton in Easter week.[65] The end of the Easter season was marked by the revolt of Geoffrey Talbot in Herefordshire.[66] Stephen immediately took the field against him. On 10 May he reached Gloucester, where he was cordially received by Miles the Constable, and almost at once he departed for the scene of the revolt.[67] Marching straight on Hereford, he laid siege to the castle, but finding his forces insufficient to continue the investment, he then summoned reinforcements. Talbot managed to elude Stephen, but after a siege of four or five weeks, his garrison in Hereford castle was forced to surrender, and was replaced by the king's own men. Thereupon Stephen proceeded to the reduction of the neighboring stronghold of Woebley, which Geoffrey had garrisoned against the king. By 15 June Herefordshire apparently had been reduced to order, and the king returned with his army to Oxford. The departure of Stephen from the west, however, gave the fugitive Talbot the opportunity to conduct, in reprisal, a savage raid against Hereford, during which he burned a large part of the town.[68]

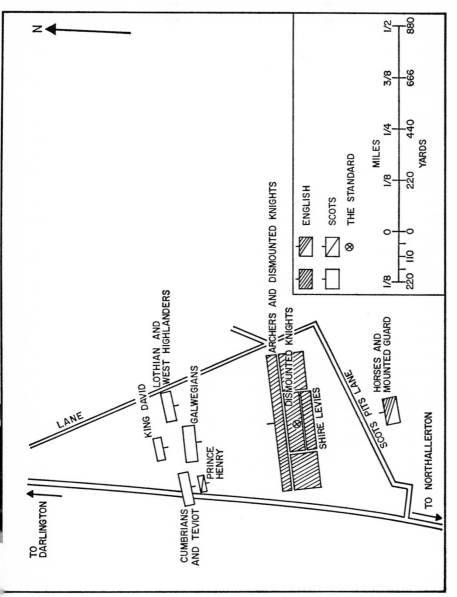

Map 6. Battle of the Standard, 22 August 1138

N

TO DARLINGTON

LANE

KING DAVID

LOTHIAN AND WEST HIGHLANDERS

GALWEGIANS

PRINCE HENRY

CUMBRIANS AND TEVIOT

ARCHERS AND DISMOUNTED KNIGHTS

DISMOUNTED KNIGHTS

SHIRE LEVIES

SCOTS PITS LANE

HORSES AND MOUNTED GUARD

TO NORTHALLERTON

ENGLISH

SCOTS

⊗ THE STANDARD

MILES

1/8   0   1/8   1/4   3/8   1/2
220   110   0   220   440   666   880
YARDS

Heretofore the outbreaks against the authority of King Stephen had been sporadic and isolated, so that he had been able to deal with each crisis as it arose. Now, however, came a general revolt which, added to the activities of the Scots, was to try the abilities of the king to the utmost. About midsummer of 1138, messengers arrived from Normandy to notify the king that the powerful earl of Gloucester had repudiated his allegiance. Stephen immediately moved to deprive him of such of his castles as he could lay hands on, and proceeded in arms against those that refused to surrender.[69] But the defection of Earl Robert brought into open rebellion many of the minor barons of the west country, where his influence was strong. As a result, the king found that the rebels held a line of castles extending from the borders of Cheshire to the Channel. Indeed, during this summer of watchful waiting, all men seemed to be preparing for the struggle to come. The Winchester annalist reported, not quite accurately, that Bishop Henry of Winchester had built or strengthened castles at Winchester (Wolvesey), Merton, Farnham, Waltham, Dunton, and Taunton; Bishop Roger of Salisbury, the castles of Salisbury, Sherborne, Devizes, and Malmesbury; the earl of Gloucester, those of Gloucester, Bath, Bristol, Dorchester, Exeter, Wimborne, Corfe, and Wareham; Brian fitz Count, Oxford and Wallingford; Bishop Alexander of Lincoln, the castle in his episcopal city; John the Marshal, Marlborough and Ludgershall; and Geoffrey de Mandeville, Rochester and the Tower of London.[70] It will be noted that most of these castles were located in the southern part of the kingdom, and that they were held for the most part by barons openly or potentially hostile to the king. Not only did the south and west appear most threatening, but Stephen was faced, in modern terminology, with a war on two fronts. In Kent, threatening the city of London and interdicting all communications with the Channel ports, were Earl Robert's important strongholds of Leeds, Canterbury, and Dover.[71]

But it was in the west, where only Bath, under the influence of Bishop Robert, is recorded to have remained loyal to the king, that the situation appeared most dangerous.[72] Gloucester, commanded by Miles the Constable, maintained a watchful neutrality; but along the borders of Cheshire four castles of William

Peverel were held against the king: Overton, Whittington, Bryn, and Ellesmere. Overton and Ellesmere, four miles apart, commanded the road from Shrewsbury to Chester. Shrewsbury, also in revolt, was held by William fitz Alan, a nephew by marriage to Earl Robert.[73] Shrewsbury castle, since it commanded a long stretch of the Severn line, was of great strategic importance. Here the Watling Street reached the river Severn and turned north to Chester. From Shrewsbury two roads ran south and southwest to Worcester and Hereford. Dudley was held against the king by Ralph Paynell; the great marcher fortress of Ludlow was in the hands of Stephen's enemies; and the castle of Usk in Monmouthshire was held by another foe, Morgan the Welshman.[74]

But the center of the revolt was Bristol. Its strong castle, nearly surrounded by two rivers, was the refuge of the discontented and the dispossessed. Thither resorted men such as Geoffrey Talbot, whom Stephen had driven from Hereford; and here plans for the rebellion were concerted, as well as for reducing the isolated royalist strongholds such as Bath, thirteen miles from Bristol.[75] To the southwest, on the Bristol Channel, stood Dunster, the castle of William de Mohun, who joined the revolt against the king. South of Bristol, William fitz John at Harptree, and in the same neighborhood Ralph Lovell at Castle Carey, had gone over to the rebels, and at the southern end of the line stood Wareham on the Dorset coast.[76] Castle Carey was of strategic importance because it stood near the Fosse Way, which cut diagonally across England from Exeter to Lincoln. Its position between Ilchester and Bath made it an important link in the line of communications which the rebels had to maintain between the Channel and their chief strongholds in the Severn valley. But still more important than Castle Carey to the cause of the empress were the town and castle of Wareham, held by Robert fitz Alured. Just as the revolt of Robert de Bellême had been doomed when Henry I reduced the castle of Arundel, so the fall of Wareham might be fatal to the rebellion of 1138, which was dependent to a great extent on the support of the Angevin party in France. However, the revolt faced by Stephen was more serious, and much more widespread, than the one that confronted Henry in 1102, and its local resources were far better able to sustain a contest with the crown. In addition to the revolt in the west and in Kent, Stephen had to make front against the hostile activities of the king of Scots and the defection of Eustace fitz John in the north as well.

Faced with this highly unfavorable situation, Stephen acted with vigor and an awareness of strategy indicating that he possessed military abilities of a high order. He had, as noted elsewhere, crushed the premature rising in Herefordshire. The invasion by the Scots he had left, of necessity, to be dealt with by the northern barons—a move that had worked out to the king's advantage, for the Scots were soundly beaten at the Battle of the Standard, and the victorious Yorkshiremen themselves took care of Eustace fitz John. Stephen was thus able to concentrate on the insurrections in Kent and the Severn valley. His queen, Mathilda, a lady of marked ability, was designated to command in Kent, while the king went west in person. On his return from the short campaign against Geoffrey Talbot, Stephen had stopped at Oxford, a central point from which he could keep an eye on the activities of the malcontents in Bristol and Gloucester, and at the same time be in a position to move in any direction should disorders develop.[77] From Oxford the king marched to Bath, where after a careful inspection he ordered the defenses of the town to be strengthened. Stephen's next move was to march straight on Bristol; but the castle was too well defended to risk an assault, and the king was not in enough strength to establish a regular siege. He then decided to reduce the minor strongholds that depended on Bristol.[78] During the ensuing operations Castle Carey fell after a short investment, and Harptree was carried by escalade in cooperation with the loyal garrison from Bath.[79] The result of the reduction of these two castles, which the king garrisoned with his own men, was to jeopardize the communications of the rebels with the Channel coast and their supporters in Anjou.

Following the capture of Harptree, Stephen turned north. Bypassing Bristol and the not-too-friendly castle of Gloucester, he marched past Dudley, ravaging the countryside but making no serious attempt to reduce the castle.[80] Then in August he appeared in front of Shrewsbury and settled down to besiege the castle. Miles of Gloucester was among the barons who joined the king for this operation.[81] William fitz Alan, the castellan, escaped with his family; but after a month's siege, the king carried the castle by storm. Following the victory Arnulf de Hesdin, the commander, and the remainder of the garrison were summarily hanged.[82] This condign punishment, remarked Ordericus, produced the hasty submission of some of the revolted barons.[83] The fall of Shrewsbury had the effect of splitting the revolt into three pockets. The four castles of William Peverel north of Shrewsbury were now isolated, and it is not improbable that they were recovered by the king at this time. Wareham, in the extreme south, had been cut off by the capture of Harptree and Castle Carey, and it was against this stronghold that the king next directed his attack.[84] The outcome of the operation is not entirely clear, but in view of subsequent developments it seems likely that Wareham also was reclaimed for King Stephen. Thus the summer campaign of 1138 had stripped the rebellion of all its strongholds, saving only the almost impregnable fortress of Bristol and the marcher castle at Ludlow—a not inconsiderable achievement.

Meanwhile the royal cause had triumphed completely in Kent. There Queen Mathilda had commenced the siege of Dover. Not only was she able to blockade the castle by land; summoning the sailors of her seaboard county of Boulogne, she invested it by sea as well. Gilbert de Clare, the loyal lord of Tonbridge, also laid siege to the castle of Leeds, "and so pressed the garrison that, at last, they surrendered." [85] Finally, upon learning of the fall of Shrewsbury, the garrison of Dover castle surrendered to the queen.[86] King Stephen, had reason, as he met with a council of the English church at London in December, to congratulate himself on the outcome of the year's campaigning. But his failure to satisfy his brother Henry, bishop of Winchester, who sought elevation to the metropolitan see of Canterbury, raised up for himself more trouble than was to be allayed by purely military victories. The disappointed bishop is believed to have begun a treasonable correspondence with the Angevin party at this time.[87] As a footnote to the military history of the year it should be recorded that the Danish king, Eric the Lamb (1137–1147), encouraged by the disorders in England, conducted a raid along the east coast, the first such Norse attack in more than half a century.[88]

The early months of 1139 saw only one incident of military interest.[89] It came after Stephen had removed—temporarily as it turned out—one of the threats to his regime by buying off the Scots. On 5 April an agreement signed at Durham granted King David's son Henry all of Northumberland with the exception of the castles of Bamborough and Newcastle.[90] The king returned south by way of Nottingham, and shortly thereafter he took the field against the remaining rebel strongholds in the west.[91] On 30 April he was in Worcester, which apparently was the king's base for operations against Ludlow. Finding his force insufficient for the task of reducing the stronghold of Joceas de Dinan, he blockaded the castle and returned through Worcester to levy reinforcements. With these he was able to carry the siege to a successful conclusion, following which he returned to Oxford via Worcester.[92] The rebellion now appeared to have been confined to the immediate vicinity of Bristol, and Stephen was apparently quite confident of the strength of his position. With his next move, however, he alienated a very important segment of that strength.

Among the men who had been raised to positions of power and affluence by the late king, none were of greater importance than the family of Roger, bishop of Salisbury. His nephew Alexander was bishop of Lincoln; another nephew, Nigel, was bishop of Ely; and his son Roger was chancellor of the kingdom. As royal officials they had the custody of a number of important castles; what is more, they had used much of the wealth which their positions brought to construct or "modernize" castles of their own. Alexander of Lincoln was in possession of the castles of Lincoln, Sleaford, and Newark, which he had built "for the defense and dignity of the bishopric." [93] Nigel of Ely was in possession of the castle in his episcopal city; Roger of Salisbury controlled the castles of Salisbury, Sherborne, Malmesbury, and Devizes, which the bishop had erected "at great and incalculable expense." [94] Throughout the early part of the year, rumors had been prevalent in England of the imminent arrival of Robert, earl of Gloucester; and the king, suspicious of the powerful churchmen, very naturally wished to put the kingdom in the best possible state of defense against such a contingency.[95] Only military necessity could have justified the step that Stephen now took. At Oxford, during a session of his council, the king seized the persons of the bishops of Salisbury and Lincoln and Roger the chancellor, and required that the castles in their possession be delivered up to him. As soon as the arrests were made, about 24 June, Stephen hastened to secure the castles. Malmesbury, Salisbury, and Sherborne yielded at the first summons to surrender.[96] Nigel of Ely, who had fled to Devizes, prepared to stand a siege in the castle. He was dissuaded, however, by the appearance of the king beneath the walls of Devizes, and his threat to starve the bishop of Salisbury to death unless the surrender of the castle were forthcoming. This produced the desired result; after a three-day investment, Devizes was occupied by the king.[97] The prompt action of the king deterred Bishop Alexander of Lincoln from offering any resistance, and his castles, Lincoln, Newark, and Sleaford, passed into the king's hands.[98] Reference to a map will show clearly how the king's military position was strengthened by the acquisition of the episcopal castles. Stephen's possession of Salisbury, Devizes, and Malmesbury cut off Bristol completely from communication with the Channel ports. In addition, his garrisons in the castles of the bishop of Lincoln ensured his own line of communication along the Great North Road to York and beyond. But the opposition engendered among the church party by this coup entirely negated the military advantages.

It was probably at this time that the king took measures to restrict the activities of William de Mohun in Dunster castle. In concert with Henry de Tracy, who held Barnstaple for the king, Stephen constructed a counter-castle in front of Dunster and placed de Tracy in charge of operations there. The chronicler noted with satisfaction that the depredations of William were henceforth on a reduced scale. Henry de Tracy was most successful with his assignment; in one engagement he is reported to have captured 104 of de Mohun's knights.[99] Then, about 1 August, Baldwin de Redvers suddenly descended on the Dorset coast and captured the castle of Corfe. Stephen, acting with his usual energy, soon appeared before Corfe at the head of an army which included a siege train; but before the castle could be reduced, events elsewhere forced him to raise the siege. Warned by

Baldwin's overt act of hostility, the king's troops nevertheless maintained a careful watch along the Channel coast in the hope of apprehending the empress or Earl Robert, should there be an attempt to land.[100] The king himself in all likelihood returned to Oxford, ready to move in any direction should the need arise.[101] In September, prompted doubtless by the defection of John the Marshal, Stephen laid siege to the castle of Marlborough.[102] In the midst of this operation Stephen was notified that his enemies had evaded the coastal watch; on 30 September the empress and Earl Robert had landed in Sussex and been given refuge in the castle of Arundel.[103] With this unwelcome news, the king's position was decidedly changed for the worse. Instead of having to deal with isolated revolts which might have been handled in detail, he had now to contend with his rival for the throne in person, together with her most able lieutenant. The strategic situation had altered almost overnight.

Chapter 5

The Troubled Time of Stephen: October 1139' December 1141

THE unwelcome news that his chief enemies, the empress Mathilda and her half-brother the earl of Gloucester, were now in England, prompted King Stephen to lift the siege of Marlborough and march to Arundel, where the pair had taken refuge. In his march the king almost intercepted Earl Robert, who immediately after his landing had set out for Bristol with a small armed retinue. The earl paused long enough at Wallingford to reach an agreement with the lord of the place, Brian fitz Count, and then continued his march.[1] King Stephen in the meantime had arrived before Arundel and prepared to invest the castle. Accounts of what followed are so at variance that it is impossible to reconstruct the actual course of events. At any rate, to his own detriment, whatever may have been the reason, the king gave the empress a safe-conduct to join her brother in Bristol.[2] With the departure of Mathilda, the siege of Arundel was abandoned.[3]

Now that both the head of the opposition and its most capable military leader were in England, the rebellion took on more of the aspect of a regular war. Stephen found that most of the previous year's campaigning was to be done over again, and in some respects his military position had deteriorated. Upon the arrival of Earl Robert a number of important tenants had renounced their allegiance to the king. Brian fitz Count, who held the important castle of Wallingford on the middle reaches of the Thames, was among the first to do so.[4] Not long after her arrival in Bristol, the cause of the empress was also joined by the able Miles of Gloucester.[5]

103

Despite these defections and the lateness of the season, the king was not idle. Following the abortive siege of Arundel he embarked on a campaign that was not without strategic merit. From the Sussex coast he marched directly upon the castle of Brian fitz Count at Wallingford and closely invested it. A counter-castle was constructed, and the intensiveness of the siege shows the value the king placed upon either reducing or neutralizing this stronghold. Wallingford threatened his line of communication from Oxford to the east and southeast. The castle was so strongly situated, however, that the king's efforts proved unavailing. Leaving a large detachment in the siege castle as a check on the activities of Brian, Stephen marched away to the west to begin the second phase of his campaign.[6] For the remainder of the year Stephen attempted to duplicate the strategy that had worked so well the year before— that is, cutting off the center of the rebellion in the Severn valley from all communication with the coast. From Wallingford he marched on Cerney, a small castle which Miles of Gloucester had built near Cirencester. It was so placed that its garrison could keep a watch on both the Fosse Way and the southern branch of the Ermine Street, which had their junction at Cirencester. Taking this castle by storm, the king placed in it a garrison of his own men. The castle at Malmesbury, strategically located on the Fosse Way between Bath and Cirencester, had been occupied by a royal garrison after its seizure from the bishop of Salisbury; but on 7 October it had been captured for the rebels by Robert fitz Hubert.[7] Here, after his success at Cerney, Stephen struck swiftly, and within a fortnight the castle was again in the king's hands.[8] From Malmesbury Stephen advanced against the castle of Humphrey de Bohun at Trowbridge. The reduction of this fortress would have severed the last direct connection between the rebels in Bristol and their port at Wareham, since the king's garrisons in Bath, Castle Carey, and Sherborne effectively controlled all other roads south from the Severn. However, Trowbridge held out stubbornly, and the lateness of the season forced Stephen to raise the siege and withdraw to his base at Oxford.[9] The garrison at Devizes was strengthened in an effort to neutralize Trowbridge, and the king retraced his steps to the Thames valley.[10]

While the king was busy campaigning against the rebel's communications, the partisans of the empress had taken advantage of Stephen's absence from the Thames valley. The removal of the empress from Bristol to Gloucester about the middle of October had transferred the center of the rebellion to that place.[11] This concentration of forces brought quick results. Late in the same month, while Stephen was unsuccessfully besieging Trowbridge, Miles of Gloucester marched rapidly on Wallingford. In a night attack he dispersed the blockading force, and then returned to Gloucester.[12] Thus Stephen's autumn campaign ended in only partial success. Round is of the opinion that the king had been deliberately lured farther and farther from his base of operations so as to make possible the relief of Wallingford.[13] This seems most unlikely. When Stephen's operations in the same area in 1138 are considered, the most reasonable explanation is that the king was carrying out a deliberate campaign against the rebel's lines of communications, trusting that his blockading force in front of Wallingford would be equal to any contingency. The expedition of Miles of Gloucester would seem to have been devised on the spur of the moment, and bore no relation to the operations that followed. In fact, these moves would have been simplified by allowing the king to remain before Trowbridge instead of falling back to the Thames valley to protect his vital interests there.

Following the relief of Wallingford, the rebels moved against the few remaining royalist strongholds in the Severn valley. On 7 November Worcester was sacked and burnt; no mention is made of the fate of the castle.[14] Winchcombe and Sudely were captured and garrisoned for the empress, and Cerney seems to have been recaptured.[15] Hereford was attacked, but the loyal garrison withdrew into the castle, where it held out against all attempts to dislodge it.[16] Its plight brought Stephen into the field again, although it was very late in the year to begin a campaign. He marched from Oxford to Worcester—an indication that the castle there was still in friendly hands—advanced to Little Hereford on the Teme, then pushed on to Leominster, ten miles north of Hereford. Before he could relieve the castle, the beginning of Advent afforded a pretext to suspend hostilities, and a truce was signed on 3 December.[17] Stephen then returned to Oxford, celebrated the Christmas feast at Salisbury, and returned to Reading on the Thames at the end of the year.[18]

The year 1139 had seen a noticeable deterioration in the king's strategic position. At its beginning the rebellion had been confined to a small area in the Severn valley, centered upon the castles of Bristol and Ludlow. In spite of skillful campaigning, the revolt had widened during the last months of the year. The partisans of the empress were now in control of the greater part of the line of the Severn, and had immobilized the garrison at Hereford which threatened their rear. In addition, their outpost at Wallingford on the middle Thames was a constant threat to the king's operations. Most important, his failure to reduce Humphrey de Bohun's castle at Trowbridge gave the rebels a free avenue of communication to Wareham on the Channel, and insured continuous and direct contact with the Angevin party on the Continent. To offset this decided advantage, the king had purchased the temporary neutrality of the Scots with the grant of the earldom of Northumberland; also, he had acquired the castles of the bishops of Salisbury, Ely, and Lincoln, at the price of alienating much of his ecclesiastical support. But the situation, though threatening, was not alarming. With the exception of Wallingford, all the castles of the south, the east, and the Midlands were in his hands or those of his supporters, and there must have been little reason to fear that the rebellion could not be suppressed or at least confined.

Late in 1139 or at the beginning of 1140, Bishop Nigel of Ely secretly returned to his cathedral city, strengthened the episcopal castles, and took a force of mercenary knights into his employ. The isolated location of the territory made military action against the bishop a difficult proposition; nevertheless, with his usual energy and skill, Stephen once again took the field. The marshy approaches to the Isle of Ely gave the operation an amphibious character. A bridge of boats covered with fascines was constructed, and along this improvised causeway the king's forces moved to the attack. A small castle held by the rebel bishop— presumably Aldreth—was captured, and the demoralized remainder of his supporters soon dispersed. Stephen now entered Ely and garrisoned its castle with his own men, while Bishop

Nigel fled to the empress at Gloucester.[19] The comparative ease with which Stephen breached the defenses of the Isle contrasts sharply with the difficulties encountered there by William the Conqueror not quite seventy years before.

The movements of the king for the remainder of the year are obscure. He was at the Tower of London for Pentecost (26 May), and in June he commanded an expedition to East Anglia, where trouble had erupted. Bungay castle was taken from Hugh Bigod on this occasion; by August, new punitive measures had to be taken against Hugh.[20] At some time during the summer King Stephen led a campaign in Cornwall, where the Angevin party had tried to establish Reginald, another of King Henry's bastards, as earl. The expedition met with considerable success. Reginald was reduced to the possession of a single castle, and Alan of Dinan, earl of Richmond and a mercenary captain, was left in charge. Although Earl Robert, with an army from Gloucester, intercepted the king's return march, he was too weak to accept the battle in the open that Stephen offered.[21] Little more can be ascertained of the king's activities until the end of the year.[22]

There was, however, a great deal of activity by the partisans of the empress. On 26 March Robert fitz Hubert captured the important castle of Devizes by a night escalade, ostensibly for the Angevin faction. Called upon to deliver the castle to Earl Robert, he refused, apparently intending to hold it independently of either party. Eventually fitz Hubert fell into the clutches of John the Marshal, the castellan for the empress at Marlborough, who handed him over to the earl of Gloucester. When fitz Hubert again refused to surrender Devizes, Earl Robert had him hanged.[23] Fitz Hubert's garrison then proceeded to sell the castle back to the king, who appointed his son-in-law, Hervey the Breton, as castellan. That baron proved such a scourge to the countryside that the peasants of the neighborhood rose and laid siege to Devizes. Hervey managed to escape with his life, and soon the castle was once again in the hands of the rebels.[24] Harptree was also recovered by Earl Robert, but an attack on the royalist garrison at Hereford at some time between 15 and 22 August led to a severe reverse, in which Geoffrey Talbot was slain.[25] Early in September, a column commanded jointly by the earl of Glouces-

ter and Ralph Paynell sacked and burnt the town of Nottingham, but there is no record of any attempt against the castle.[26]

Late in the year King Stephen paid a visit to Lincoln, but
before Christmas he had returned to London. Shortly thereafter
Lincoln castle was captured from its royal garrison, through a ruse
devised by Earl Ranulf of Chester and his brother William de
Roumare.[27] Although the exact date of the coup is not known, the
details as recorded by Ordericus Vitalis bear the stamp of
veracity. It would seem that Ranulf and William, who were
ostensibly on good terms with the king, were in Lincoln or its
immediate vicinity. On a day when the garrison were largely
dispersed—engaged in sports, according to the chronicler—the
wives of the two conspirators went to the castle to pay a courtesy
call on the wife of the commandant.[28] After a suitable interval,
Earl Ranulf, himself unarmed and attended by only three men-at-
arms, entered the castle as though to fetch the ladies. At a given
signal the four men fell upon the skeleton guard that was
maintained inside the castle, using whatever weapons came to
hand; and before the remainder of the garrison could be recalled
or rallied, the watch had been ejected, and a body of troops under
the command of William de Roumare had been admitted. Even
though the seizure of Lincoln castle was without doubt an act of
treachery, it is impossible not to admire the ingenuity and
simplicity of the plan by which it was accomplished.

Once the earl and his accomplices were in control of the castle,
they began to harass the burgesses, who were steady partisans of
the king. Dispatches from the townsmen as well as from Bishop
Alexander soon apprised Stephen of the situation; and collecting
such forces as he could on short notice, he marched north about
the middle of December. The earl's intelligence seems to have
been unreliable, for the king entered the city so unexpectedly
that nearly a score of the rebel garrison were captured in the town
with the aid of the local population.[29] On or shortly after
Christmas, Stephen invested the castle on all sides, and had siege
engines constructed to batter down the walls.[30] Earl Ranulf saw at
once that the fortress must be relieved at an early date if it were
not to fall into the king's hands through either starvation or
assault. With a small detachment he succeeded in escaping

unnoticed, probably through the postern on the west side of the enceinte, which gave access to the open field. He slipped through the royal lines and made directly for Chester, where he could raise his own retainers.[31]

Perhaps anticipating that the resources of the earldom would be insufficient to raise the siege of Lincoln, Earl Ranulf also opened communications with his father-in-law, Earl Robert of Gloucester. Even though the earl of Chester was not highly regarded by the Angevin faction because of his hitherto shifty conduct, it may be that his protests of loyalty to the empress had an effect. It seems more probable, however, that Earl Robert was motivated chiefly by concern for his daughter, shut up in Lincoln castle.[32]

Although the chroniclers speak of enormous forces raised by the two earls, the factors of time, distance, and season must have operated to keep the comital army at a modest level. No contemporary so much as hints at the actual numbers, and even the composition is not entirely clear. In addition to his Cheshire tenants, Earl Ranulf is known to have recruited a considerable number of Welsh mercenaries under the command of Cadwaladr ap Gruffydd of Gwynedd and Madog ap Maredudd of Powys.[33] The makeup of Earl Robert's column is even more obscure. The author of the *Gesta* refers to Miles of Gloucester "and all who had armed themselves against the king"; Ordericus mentions "the disinherited"—those whose lands had been declared forfeit because of their adherence to the Angevin cause; and the *Liber Eliensis* adds the names of Brian fitz Count and Baldwin de Redvers.[34]

Nor is the route followed by the two components of the rebel army known with certainty. Miss Norgate suggests, logically enough, that Earl Ranulf marched down the Watling Street while Earl Robert moved northeastward along the Fosse Way, a junction being effected at Claybrook in Leicestershire where these roads intersect.[35] The combined forces of the two earls would then have continued on the Fosse Way, passing the Trent at Newark, where there probably was a bridge, and appearing under the walls of Lincoln on the morning of 2 February.[36] Now, from the scanty facts available, it is possible to construct a very rough timetable. As noted above, Stephen began the siege of Lincoln castle late in December—certainly not before Christmas. Between this time and 2 February, Earl Ranulf escaped from the castle, got to Chester, made contact with his father-in-law and secured his aid, mustered his own tenants, recruited Welsh mercenaries, effected a juncture with the contingents from Gloucester, and got back to Lincoln—all in not more than forty days. This in itself was no mean accomplishment, but when the distances involved and the season of the year are taken into consideration, it becomes truly remarkable. Winter is usually a dank season in England, and that of 1140–1141 seems to have been no exception. William of Malmesbury mentioned the heavy rains that had swollen the streams in the vicinity of Lincoln, and the roads must have been in very bad condition. To begin with, time must be allowed for Ranulf to have covered the distance— nearly a hundred cross-country miles—between Lincoln and Chester, and to exchange messages with Earl Robert in Gloucester, more than a hundred miles to the south. Certainly not more than three weeks could have been available for the summoning and mustering of the Cheshire contingents, and not more than two weeks for those in Gloucester. From Chester to Claybrook the Cheshire column had to march about eighty-five miles, while the Gloucester contingent had some sixty miles to go. After the army had concentrated, more than sixty miles had yet to be covered before the objective was reached. The force under Earl Ranulf's command thus had to march a total distance of 150 miles; that of the earl of Gloucester, 125 miles. Considering the probable state of the roads and the presence of infantry, it is unlikely that the rate of march exceeded ten miles per day. In that event the Chester column would necessarily have gotten under way by 18 January, and the Gloucester force no later than the 20th, with the rendezvous at Claybrook taking place about the 26th. That any kind of army could have been put together on such short notice, have marched 150 miles over bad roads in the dead of winter, and yet been in condition to fight a pitched battle reflects very favorably on the system of mobilization, the resources, and above all the leadership of earls Ranulf and Robert.

Arriving in the vicinity of Lincoln on 1 February, the comital army was faced with the problem of crossing the water barriers between it and the city. The river Witham, which abruptly alters its course from north to east under the very walls of the town, is joined at this point by the Fossdyke, a canal linking the Witham with the Trent. At the point of confluence, what was known as the Brayford Pool formed a considerable obstacle at the southwestern angle of the city wall. Southwest of the city the Fossdyke was in spate, and its banks were waterlogged by recent rains. These were the hazards to be surmounted if the expedition was to raise the siege of Lincoln castle. Unfortunately, the contemporary accounts do not throw much light on the means by which the earls got their army onto the Lincoln side of the Fossdyke. Of more modern writers, Miss Norgate and Sir James Ramsey, the two who have written most extensively on the operation, disagree as to where the crossing was made, the sources being themselves somewhat contradictory. William of Malmesbury states that the army, finding the "Trent" unfordable—surely this should be read "Fossdyke"—swam across. This statement must be discounted largely, for assuming that horses and men could have been gotten over in this manner, it is hard to believe that they would have been in any condition to fight a general engagement after their midwinter dip.[37] Henry of Huntingdon wrote that the earls "boldly crossing a marsh which was almost impassable," drew up their forces in battle array.[38] The *Gesta* is somewhat more precise. One learns from it that the king had detailed a covering force to guard a ford —presumably over the Fossdyke—but that this guard was stationed on the south bank of the watercourse rather than on the north; that the rebel army charged and scattered the guard, seized the ford, and effected a crossing.[39]

On the basis of this information, Miss Norgate suggests that the comital army followed the Fosse Way across the Witham at Bracebridge, up the right bank of the river, and through the suburb of Wigford. Then, instead of trying to cross the Witham again by means of the High Bridge, the line of march bore to the left and forded the river in the area between the bridge and the eastern end of Brayford Pool—a stretch which is no more than 150 yards long.[40] What Miss Norgate apparently did not consider was that both this ford—if it actually existed—and the bridge were literally within bowshot of the city walls, so that it would have been more hazardous to attempt the ford than to cross by the bridge. It is most unlikely that a ford near Brayford Pool was the scene of the crossing.

Sir James Ramsey's reconstruction of the operation is much more convincing. He suggests that the earls left the Fosse Way just before it crossed the Witham at Bracebridge, about two miles south of Lincoln. Then, using secondary roads and lanes, he conjectures that they marched almost due north, striking the Fossdyke about 1,100 yards west of the city wall. Here they chased away Stephen's covering force and made the difficult crossing through the high water and the marshy ground on either side of the watercourse.[41] Having gained the Lincoln side of the Fossdyke without serious opposition, Ranulf and Robert presumably drew up their army in battle array, although the usual argument over precedence occurred.[42]

Meanwhile, King Stephen was taking steps to meet the threat imposed by the appearance of an enemy field force. He had received daily intelligence of the hostile advance, but its implication had been ignored. Only when he learned that the earls were within striking distance did he take the precaution of detailing a guard to watch the ford across the Fossdyke. Stephen then summoned a meeting of his principal commanders to discuss possible courses of action. The proposals aired were generally on the side of caution. Some advised the king to garrison the town strongly and then retire with the remainder of his forces until he could raise a larger army; others suggested that negotiations be opened with the commanders of the relieving force.[43] Stephen was unwilling to accept such counsel, and determined upon an immediate general engagement. He gave orders for the entire royal army to assemble—apparently not even a detachment was to be left behind to observe the garrison in the castle—and marched out to meet the enemy, who by now were forming up within sight of the city walls.[44]

The attempt to reconstruct the first Battle of Lincoln is in some respects an exercise in frustration, and the most baffling problem is the uncertainty over just where the action took place. Sir James Ramsey, citing "local tradition," insists that the battle was fought on the level heights north of the city, beyond the suburb of Newport and astride the Ermine Street.[45] This is perhaps the best site in the vicinity of Lincoln for a battle; but according to Hill, Ramsey's "tradition" is unknown to local historians.[46] Moreover, to reach this position, the earls would have had to march in column directly across the front of the royalists in Lincoln over a distance of more than a mile and a half, exposing them to attack in flank by a sally from the city.[47]

It is much more likely that the scene of the battle was on the sloping ground to the west of the city, as suggested by Miss Norgate and Sir Charles Oman.[48] Oman has admirably summed up the evidence, both factual and circumstantial, for this location of the battlefield:

In the absence of any precise indication of the battle spot, we have to put the following facts together in order to identify it. (1) The earls forded the Fossdike somewhere west of Lincoln. (2) They fought with it at their backs so that defeat meant disaster; *i.e.* they faced north or northwest [northeast?].[49] (3) The routed cavalry of Stephen's host escaped into the open country, not into the town; *i.e.* they were drawn up so as to give a free flight to the north. (4) The infantry fled into the town, which was therefore quite close. Probably the battlefield lay due west of the city, and the Royalists apparently faced south or southwest.[50]

It can be assumed, then, that Stephen marched out of Lincoln by the West Gate and occupied a position on the long slope extending from the western wall of the town down to the Fossdyke. This gave him a tactical advantage, which he attempted to exploit in his order of battle. Although it is impossible to determine the size of the royal army, the tactical disposition is quite clear. In accordance with standard twelfth-century procedure, three divisions were formed; in this instance the two wings remained mounted, while the center was composed of infantry and dismounted men-at-arms. The royalist right wing does not appear to have had an overall commander. It was made up of the numerous contingents of Hugh Bigod, earl of Norfolk; Earl William of Warenne; Earl Simon of Northampton; Earl Waleran of Meulan; and Earl Alan of Richmond, a mercenary captain.[51]

The left was under the joint command of the Flemish mercenary commander, William of Ypres—who was later to render signal services to his royal employer—and William of Aumale, who had been created earl of York for his part in the victory at the Standard.[52] The center was made up of the city levy of Lincoln, stiffened by the king's own contingents who dismounted to fight as infantry. Included in the number were Bernard de Balliol, Richard de Courcy, Roger de Mowbray, Ilbert de Lacy, and William Peverel, all veterans of the Standard campaign. The king himself, with the royal standard, took post with this center division.[53] Ordericus noted the presence of Flemish and Breton mercenaries serving under William of Ypres and Earl Alan respectively, and hinted at disloyalty among the earls, several of whom had been raised to comital dignity by Stephen himself.[54] Henry of Huntingdon states that royalists enjoyed numerical superiority in infantry, and equality in mounted troops; but Ordericus's statement that "the best knights and men-at-arms were in the king's army; but the enemy outnumbered them in infantry and the Welsh allies," seems more credible.[55] According to the archdeacon of Huntingdon, a speech by Baldwin de Clare to the royal army (oratory was not one of Stephen's strong points) was interrupted by the advance of the enemy.[56]

After their successful crossing of the Fossdyke, the rebel army settled the argument over precedence, and Earl Robert of Gloucester, by virtue of his age, rank, and connections with the royal family, assumed supreme command. The order of battle that he adopted doubtless influenced the king in making his disposition of the royalist forces. Earl Robert assigned the left wing to the "Disinherited," who retained their mounts; the center was placed under the command of the earl of Chester, whose knights dismounted to fight on foot with the infantry levies. Although no specific mention is made of Gloucester's role in the fighting, it may be assumed that he commanded the cavalry of the right wing. The Welsh, "ill-armed, but full of spirits," were thrown out in front of the right wing.[57] Having gotten into order, the rebels advanced up the slope toward the king's army, with trumpets blaring and with shouts of mutual encouragement.[58]

What happened next is not entirely clear. The most explicit

account of the opening phase of the combat is given by William of Malmesbury:

The royalists first attempted that prelude to the fight which is called jousting, for in this they were accomplished, but when they saw that the "earlists," if that expression may be allowed, were fighting not with lances at a distance, but with swords at close quarters, and charging with their banners in the van, were breaking through the king's line, then all the earls to a man sought safety in flight.[59]

This can be interpreted approximately as follows: When the royalist right wing saw the enemy left advancing up the slope, the men-at-arms lowered their lances and advanced to meet them in the approved manner of the day. In this sort of fighting, apparently, fatal casualties were not numerous, but captives to be held for ransom were many. When, however, the "Disinherited" crashed into the royal cavalry, it was clear that the rebels meant business—that they were fighting with cold steel. Whereupon this wing of the king's army, having no single commander who might even attempt to rally the panic-stricken knights, fled incontinently from the field. It was every man for himself, and the chroniclers are unanimous in their condemnation of the royalist earls.[60] On the other flank, the division commanded by Earl William and William d'Ypres had at first enjoyed greater success. Charging down the slope, it had brushed away the Welsh without difficulty and was apparently making head against the cavalry commanded by Robert of Gloucester. But having been brought to a stand, it could not hold out against the infantry of the center under Earl Ranulf, which intervened at once in aid of the rebel right. Soon the tide had turned, and the two Williams and their command had joined the rest of the royalist horse in precipitate retreat.[61]

Only the central division of Stephen's army now remained to be dealt with. Here stood the king, surrounded by his knights and the faithful burgesses of Lincoln. Although they were surrounded on all sides by the enemy, their resistance was maintained for a long time. Stephen, according to all accounts, was conspicuous for his prowess, laying about him with his sword until it snapped, and then continuing to rain blows upon his enemies with a Danish axe (a weapon evidently still used in the north, seventy-five years after

Hastings) supplied him by a burgess of Lincoln.[62] But valor alone
could not retrieve the situation, and the king, his axe shattered in
his hand, was felled by a stone cast by an unknown soldier. A
knight, William de Caimes, seized the prostrate king, who was
then constrained to surrender to Robert of Gloucester. With
Stephen were taken Bernard de Balliol, Roger de Mowbray,
Richard de Courcy, William Fossard, William Peverel, William
Clerfait, Ingelram de Sai, Baldwin fitz Gilbert de Clare, William
fitz Urse, and many others of lesser rank.[63]

With the capture of the king, all organized resistance came to
an end. If Ordericus is correct, the battle was not a bloody one.
Not more than a hundred men were slain in combat, and of these
only one, a nephew of Archbishop Geoffrey of Rouen, was
important enough to be named. In addition, Henry of Huntingdon noted that Baldwin de Clare was wounded.[64] But for the
unfortunate inhabitants of Lincoln the worst was yet to come.
The victorious rebels pursued the fleeing burgesses into the town,
which "was given up to plunder, according to the laws of war." [65]
Many were slain in the pursuit; others attempted to escape by
boat, but a panic ensued, and most of the overcrowded craft
capsized, drowning the would-be fugitives.[66] Within the city itself
churches as well as houses were plundered and burnt; those
inhabitants who remained were slaughtered indiscriminately, the
victors conducting themselves as utter barbarians. To this fright-
ful scene the king and other prisoners of war were unwilling
witnesses.[67] Earl Robert, however, soon departed with his royal
captive. By 9 February he was back in Gloucester, and shortly
thereafter Stephen was conveyed to Bristol and placed under
guard in the castle.[68]

In attempting a critique of the first Battle of Lincoln, it is
necessary to eliminate the blind prejudice that has characterized
such accounts as Ramsey's. If it is assumed that "the faint-
heartedness of Stephen's men might almost be excused for the
want of generalship that exposed them to such needless risks," it
becomes impossible to look at the campaign and battle with any
kind of objectivity.[69] Although it can be seen that Stephen was
out-generaled, it cannot be said that his defeat was a foregone
conclusion as soon as he emerged from behind the walls of

Lincoln.[70] Stephen's conduct of the campaign is indeed open to criticism, but offering battle was probably justified from the information then at his disposal. What the king did not take into consideration—and what later historians have not accorded proper weight—was the almost incredible speed shown by Ranulf of Chester and Robert of Gloucester in mobilizing an army and getting it to Lincoln under such unfavorable conditions. Although it seems quite obvious that Stephen should have accepted his intelligence reports at face value, and have taken concrete steps —such as bringing up additional troops—to meet the threat, potential or actual, the likely explanation is that he did not think it possible that his enemies could appear in such force as to raise the siege of Lincoln castle. Thus it was not until the last moment that he took even so elementary a precaution as detailing a force to guard the passage over the Fossdyke.

The energy and leadership displayed on this occasion by Earl Ranulf merit the highest praise. Although on the battlefield the earl of Gloucester exercised command, the driving force behind the relief expedition seems to have been the turbulent and often untrustworthy earl of Chester. The difficulties posed by an operation in midwinter have already been enumerated and need not be reiterated here; but it is necessary to re-emphasize that the two earls realized the importance of time, as their rapid movements show. Of the tactical disposition made on the battlefield by Earl Robert, little criticism can be made since it was good enough to procure victory, which in the final analysis is the sole criterion for any arrangement. Wisely, the earl provided for a solid mass of reliable troops on foot—apparently the most nearly homogenous force in the entire army, the Cheshire contingents, were told off for infantry duty. This provided a rallying place for either cavalry wing, should it be defeated, and also a reserve which could be thrown in to aid the mounted troops, should they require assistance.

With Stephen's decision to accept a general engagement it is difficult to quarrel. He had, as has been noted, a preponderance in men-at-arms, and a decided advantage of position. There is no reason to suppose that he did not anticipate victory. And had he followed the example of the Yorkshiremen at the Standard—had

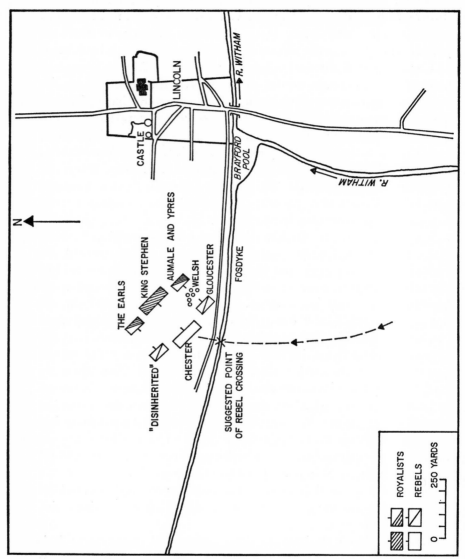

Map 4. First Battle of Lincoln, Ela

he dismounted all his men—he might well, although by no means certainly, have been right. The surprising thing about Lincoln is that so many men who were prominent in the victory at the Standard were present; all of them, with the exception of William of Aumale, fought on foot with the center division, yet they do not seem to have influenced the king in making his tactical dispositions. Stephen simply countered the line of battle chosen by his opponents. What he could not have anticipated, of course, was the disgraceful conduct of his mounted troops. Oman is correct in placing Lincoln I in the same tactical category as Tenchebrai and Bremûle—battles in which infantry and cavalry were combined—but he is certainly mistaken as to the intended role of the Welsh mercenaries. The men of Gwynedd and Powys were not archers but spearmen, and their usefulness on the battlefield hardly justified the efforts of the earl of Chester in marching them clear across England.[71] If there was a decisive moment in the battle, it came on the royalist left when William of Ypres and the earl of York, having scattered the Welsh, closed with the mounted wing led by the earl of Glouces-ter. Just what happened is a matter for conjecture; but the situation on this flank warranted the commitment of the infantry of Earl Ranulf, and it can only be concluded that Gloucester was in some sort of trouble—that the Cheshiremen not only bailed him out but drove the royalists off the field. The question remains, as it must remain, unanswered: Why did not Stephen bring the infantry under his personal command to the assistance of his beleaguered left? Was he already so engaged with the victorious "Disinherited" that he could not break off the action? At any rate, the cavalry made no attempt to rally behind the dismounted division, and the king was left to his fate.

The Angevin faction at once prepared to exploit this unex-pected windfall. Throughout England the partisans of the em-press intensified their activities, and the fainthearted or self-seeking among Stephen's erstwhile adherents sought how they might turn the situation to their own advantage. By 16 February, negotiations had been opened with Bishop Henry of Winchester, and the empress soon set out from Gloucester to reap the rewards of victory. Advancing by way of Cirencester, she was admitted to

Winchester by Bishop Henry on 3 March, and the royal castle with all it contained was surrendered into her custody.[72] Thereafter her progress was slower. By Easter (30 March), proceeding via Wilton, the empress had only reached Oxford, where she received the surrender of the castle from Robert d'Oilli, the castellan.[73] Not until the early part of May had she arrived at Reading; by the beginning of June she was at St. Alban's, negotiating with the Londoners for entry into the city.[74] Shortly before midsummer the empress entered London at the head of an impressive retinue; but her avarice and haughty conduct soon alienated the Londoners, who on 24 June rose and drove her and her entourage helter-skelter from the city. The fugitives passed through Oxford in their flight, which continued until the safety of Gloucester had been reached. Their subsequent return to Oxford was at a more leisurely pace.[75]

During these months of prosperity the empress had been lavish in the granting of lands and titles to her own partisans, and in the purchase of support from those of Stephen's followers who showed an inclination to change sides. In July of the previous year she had granted the faithful Miles of Gloucester hereditary possession of the castle of St. Briavels in Gloucestershire; now, in July 1141, she made him earl of Hereford.[76] The self-seeking Geoffrey de Mandeville was made earl of Essex, and was confirmed as hereditary constable of the Tower of London.[77] A charter to William de Beauchamp, given in July at Oxford, confirmed him in his possession of Worcester castle, and his claim to that at Tamworth was also admitted.[78] Thurstan de Montfort was granted the castle of Beldesert in Warwickshire at about the same time, and Nottingham was given as a reward to William Paynell.[79] Possession of castles bulked large indeed in the baronial ambitions of the time.

The expulsion of the empress from London as a result of her highhanded and arrogant conduct apparently gave Bishop Henry of Winchester pause. Shortly thereafter he conferred with his sister-in-law the queen at Guildford, and with amazing dexterity reversed himself to become once again the ally of his brother Stephen. The bishop vowed to do everything within his power to secure the release and restoration of the king, and lifted all ecclesiastical censures that had been imposed upon Stephen's supporters at Winchester earlier in the year.[80] It may be inferred that he began by returning to Winchester and laying siege to the royal castle, then held by an Angevin garrison.[81]

After the failure of a mission by Robert of Gloucester to induce Bishop Henry to lift the siege of the royal castle and return to the allegiance of the empress, Mathilda concentrated a large army at her base in Oxford, to attempt by force what she had been unable to accomplish by persuasion.[82] Although William of Malmesbury states that only a few magnates accompanied the empress, the author of the *Gesta* makes it quite plain that this was a major effort on the part of the Angevin faction, and that the principal men of the party took the field in person. In addition to the earl of Gloucester, who must be regarded as the commanding officer—or possibly as his half-sister's chief of staff—the major figures were King David of Scotland; Earl Miles of Hereford; Earl Roger of Warwick; William de Mohun, earl of Somerset; and Geoffrey Boterel, probably the commander of a Breton mercenary contingent. Barons of lesser rank included Brian fitz Count; John the Marshal; Robert d'Oilli; Roger de Nunant; William fitz Alan; Robert fitz Edith; William of Salisbury; and Humphrey de Bohun. Earl Ranulf of Chester, who at first threw in his lot with the royalists, changed sides during the campaign, being justifiably regarded with suspicion by the king's supporters; but his aid came too late to have any effect on the outcome.[83] Archbishop Theobald of Canterbury, along with other bishops, was also present with the Angevin army, although it is not clear whether they brought more than spiritual aid to the Angevin cause.[84] The muster at Oxford, then, indicated that the empress was determined on an all-out offensive to lift the siege of Winchester castle and bring the bishop to terms. It may be assumed that her army began its march out of Oxford on 27 or 28 July along the fifty-odd road miles to Winchester, under whose walls the hostile array appeared on 31 July.[85]

What followed is not entirely clear. The author of the *Gesta*, whose account of the whole campaign is by far the fullest and most circumstantial, suggests that the appearance of the Angevin army caught the bishop by surprise—a reflection on his intelligence service—and that as the empress was marching unopposed into the town through one gate, Bishop Henry, mounted on a fleet horse, was making his escape through another. This account is supported by the continuator of Florence of Worcester.[86] If John of Hexham and William of Malmesbury are correct, and the bishop had already commenced the siege of Winchester castle, his precipitate departure from the city is highly probable. In any event, the empress established her headquarters in the castle, and the earl of Gloucester set up a command post in the town, near the cathedral church of St. Swithin.[87] The townsmen seem to have sided largely with the Empress, although there is mention of some hostility at her entrance, and a later reference to "kinsfolk engaged in mutual hostilities." [88]

The next day, 1 August, the Angevin forces commenced hostilities against the garrisons left behind in Winchester by the bishop.[89] The *Gesta* speaks of two episcopal strongholds in the city: "the bishop's castle, which he had built in a very elegant style in the middle of the town," and "his palace, which he had fortified strongly and impregnably just like a castle." [90] There has been some argument about the nature of this episcopal palace in the center of Winchester, but almost certainly the main center of resistance of the bishop's men was his new castle of Wolvesey, located in the southeast angle of the city walls and communicating directly with the open field.[91] Wolvesey had been built as recently as 1138, and it was no doubt into this modern fortress that the bishop's garrison retreated.[92] On the second day of the investment (2 August), the defenders fired the town, doubtless intending to deny the enemy shelter and cover. A large part of the city was leveled, including the nunnery of St. Mary's in the eastern part of Winchester, although the cathedral was spared. Spreading beyond the walls, the blaze also destroyed the monastery of Hyde immediately north of the city.[93] Despite the razing of much of the city, the siege was pressed with vigor.

On the other side, Bishop Henry had not been idle since his flight from Winchester. He issued a call for all of the supporters of the captive king to rally in an effort to raise the siege of Wolvesey. In addition, the bishop engaged the services of mercenary troops, whom he later paid with spoils sifted from the ashes of Hyde abbey.[94] A royalist field army was already in being, for even at the time of the empress's triumphant entry into London, Queen Mathilda and William of Ypres with his Flemish mercenaries had been operating in Kent below London. It is more likely that their close approach to the city strengthened the resolve of the Londoners, with whom Stephen had always been popular, to rid themselves of their unwelcome guest. After the expulsion of the Angevins, the queen entered the city and immediately "by prayer or price" began to reconstitute a royalist organization.[95] At the bishop's summons, the queen, at the head of a contingent of her own Boulognese, together the Flemings under William of Ypres and his nephew Pharamus, moved at once toward Winchester.[96] Here they were eventually joined by Geoffrey de Mandeville, earl of Essex; by Earl Simon of Northampton; by Gilbert de Clare, earl of Hertford; and by Bishop Henry himself.[97] Mention is also made of the de Chesney brothers, Roger and William—who may well have been mercenaries, since they are specifically described as plain soldiers lacking in large estates, and yet they appear on the scene in command of a body "of knights and archers very ready for action." As noted above, Earl Ranulf of Chester proffered his service first to the queen, then to the empress, to the profit of neither side. A notable accession to royalist strength was a contingent of Londoners, nearly a thousand strong, whose arrival apparently gave numerical advantage to the queen.[98] Being infantry, they would be most useful in static warfare.

The royalist army was now in a position to establish an effective blockade of Winchester.[99] Communications must also have been opened with the garrison of Wolvesey castle, since it abutted on the city walls; and the queen seems to have controlled the open country beyond the municipal defenses. This in effect raised the siege of Wolvesey, and only the bishop's garrison in the center of town was still in jeopardy.[100] Thus siege and blockade were maintained through August and into September. Skirmishing was a daily occurrence, casualties were numerous, and the royal forces slowly tightened the blockade. They established roadblocks on every principal avenue leading into Winchester; raids were conducted along supply routes against convoys coming from the west, and during one of these the village of Andover was burnt.[101] By early September, rations in Winchester were running short, and the Angevin army, as well as the civilian population, was beginning to feel the pinch of hunger.[102] The royal army, on the other hand, suffered no lack of provisions, for "on the east, all the way to London, the tracks were crowded with masses of supplies" moving up to support the army engaged in the blockade.[103]

Finally, a council of war decided that a desperate attempt must be made to break the blockade. A fortified post was to be established at Wherwell abbey on the river Test, six miles north of the city. By placing a strong detachment here, it appeared possible to guard the incoming convoys in such strength that food in adequate quantities could be brought into Winchester.[104] Accordingly a detachment of three hundred knights under the joint command of John the Marshal and Robert fitz Edith was dispatched to Wherwell abbey.[105] Unfortunately, the movement of so large a body of troops could not go undetected, and a royalist force commanded by William of Ypres was soon in pursuit. He overtook the empress's troops just short of Wherwell; after a sharp fight, he drove them into the nunnery, which was then fired to drive the enemy out. The Angevin detachment was almost annihilated; John the Marshal was one of the few who remained in the blazing abbey church and eventually managed to escape.[106]

When news of the disaster at Wherwell reached Winchester, Earl Robert realized that the game was up—that the position of the army inside the city had become untenable, and that there was nothing left but to withdraw.[107] Round's suggestion that "the besieged were seized with panic" is not supported by the statements either of William of Malmesbury, that the earl of Gloucester prepared for an orderly withdrawal, or of the *Gesta,* that the impedimenta were collected and that the army withdrew from the city in a closed-up formation. Earl Robert had organized his retreat with care. An advance guard was entrusted to Earl Reginald and the faithful Brian fitz Count, and the empress rode with this column. Then followed the main body, and finally a rear guard of two hundred knights commanded by Earl Robert in person. The retreating army moved out by the West Gate on 14 September, and took the Salisbury road that crossed the Test at Stockbridge.[108] But the withdrawal had scarcely commenced when the column was attacked on all sides by a royal army with the scent of victory in its nostrils. Sweeping around the rear guard, the brunt of the attack fell on the main body; soon all semblance of order was gone, and the Angevin army degenerated into a panic-stricken mob, who fled in every direction. A hard core of the advance guard under Brian fitz Count managed to hold together and, perhaps because it was mounted on swift horses, outdistanced all pursuit, so that the empress reached Ludgershall in safety. But it was not considered safe to remain here; the flight was continued to Devizes, and eventually the empress reached Gloucester, half dead from exhaustion.[109] Of the remainder of the army, only the rear guard commanded by Robert of Gloucester maintained its organization. As the main body broke up, the pursuing army

. . . spread out all over the surrounding country to attack those of less account, and not only made prisoners of any knights it caught, but gained plunder of incalculable value which was scattered everywhere for the taking. You could have seen chargers finely shaped and goodly to look upon, here straying about after throwing their riders, there fainting from weariness and at their last gasp; sometimes shields and coats of mail and arms of every kind lying everywhere strewn on the ground; sometimes cloaks and vessels of precious metal, with other valuables flung in heaps, offering themselves to the finder on every side.[110]

Barons and knights threw away their arms and skulked off as fugitives; some fell into the hands of peasants and were severely beaten. Others hid out until they had a chance to escape, or were discovered and made prisoner. King David of Scotland was thrice captured, and twice secured his liberty by bribery. The third time he fell into the hands of his godson, David Oliphant, who let him go. But David and his chancellor, William Cumin, did not reach Durham until late in September. Earl Miles of Hereford threw away his arms and equipment, and made his way alone to Gloucester. Although little mention is made of casualties, one William de Curcell and six troopers, slain in the rout, were buried in Hyde abbey. The archbishop of Canterbury and a number of his suffragans were despoiled of clothes and horses and forced to seek places of refuge.[111]

In the meantime, the rear guard had been fighting its way

toward the crossing of the Test at Stockbridge, eight and a half miles from Winchester. Here, forced to a stand—either because of the narrowness of the bridge, or because the way was blocked with fugitives, or both—it was surrounded by elements of the royal army, including the Flemish mercenaries under the command of William de Warenne, earl of Surrey, and compelled to surrender. By all odds, the most important prisoner was Earl Robert of Gloucester. Also captured in the rout were Geoffrey Boterel, William of Salisbury, and Humphrey de Bohun.[112] While these events were taking place to the west of the city, Winchester itself was being methodically sacked by the Londoners. As troops returned from the pursuit of the beaten enemy, they joined in with a will. Houses, stores, and even churches were broken into and pillaged, and "they went away in great joy, each to his home with many spoils and countless captives." [113]

From the point of view of the military historian the Winchester campaign is one of the most interesting episodes of the twelfth century, as well as one of the most fully documented. Yet it has been entirely neglected by the students of medieval warfare. The most complete account is given by Round in *Geoffrey de Mandeville,* and from this and other sallies of his into the military sphere, one could wish that he had turned his great talents to clearing away the many obscurities concerning warfare in Norman England.[114] One thing that makes the campaign which culminated in the rout of Winchester unusual is that it was so protracted. Between the march of the empress Mathilda's army out of Oxford and its final dispersal west of Winchester, almost seven weeks elapsed.[115] Static operations of such duration are not very frequent in the history of twelfth-century warfare; and the curious "siege within a siege" seems to be unique. Another aspect worth noting is the large role played on the royalist side by the nonfeudal elements in the army. It was the London contingent that finally gave the queen numerical preponderance; and it was the Flemish mercenaries of William of Ypres who were responsible for the two decisive actions of the campaign—the destruction of John the Marshal's force at Wherwell, and the capture of Earl Robert at Stockbridge.

The campaign was distinguished by sound if not brilliant

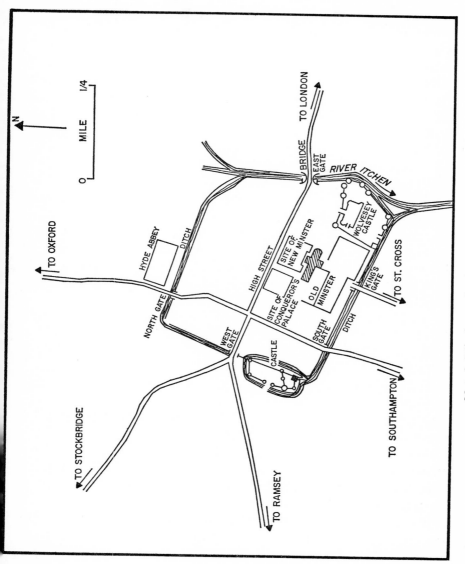

Map 8. Winchester in the Twelfth Century

tactics on the part of the royalists, and by what can only be called obstinate stupidity on the Angevin side. It may be surmised that the presence of the empress with the army had something to do with the continuation of the campaign after any real hope of success was gone. The capture of the bishop's strongholds in Winchester depended either upon surprise or upon a deliberate siege, unhampered by a relieving force. When the Angevins were unable to achieve the one, and the prompt arrival of Queen Mathilda's forces negated the other, the game was up. Once the queen had established communications with the bishop's garrison in Wolvesey, there could be no hope of reducing the castle except by storm; and it does not appear that this was attempted or even thought of. If, as Henry of Huntingdon says, the Londoners who turned the scales in favor of the royalists did not arrive at Winchester until late in the campaign, the failure of the empress to retire from a dangerous situation while there was still time appears close to folly.[116] Under conditions approaching equality, her army might have got away in good order, possibly without any fight at all. It is not difficult to see in this obstinate persistence in a hopeless operation the counsel of the haughty and imperious empress, rather than of the cautious Earl Robert. On the other hand, whatever ignominy may have attached itself to William of Ypres for his conduct at the Battle of Lincoln was certainly removed by his astute generalship at Winchester. Nothing rash was attempted; no great feats of arms were achieved. It was a campaign of pickets and outposts, of skirmishes and ambushes. The one action of note—that at Wherwell—involved but a few hundred knights all told. And all the while, as the days and weeks went by, the slow effects of this pressure began to tell. At last, with literal starvation confronting it, the blockaded army in Winchester had no choice but the desperate hazard of making a run for it in the face of a numerically superior enemy.

The capture of the earl of Gloucester destroyed at one blow all the advantages that the empress had obtained as a result of the Battle of Lincoln. Earl Robert was given into the custody of William of Ypres and carried off to Rochester, where he was imprisoned in the castle. Robert was at once the most able and the most respected leader on the Angevin side, and there was no question but that his release would have to be obtained, even at the price of returning King Stephen to full liberty. After long negotiations an even exchange was agreed upon; and early in November the king was released from confinement in Bristol castle. Earl Robert, liberated from Rochester, proceeded to join the empress at her headquarters in Oxford.[117] The king was at Westminster during the first days of December; then, to remove any stigma that might seem to be attached to his captivity, he had himself recrowned during the Christmas festivities at Canterbury.[118] This, however, did little to restore royal authority, and an uphill struggle was in prospect for Stephen as the new year began.

Chapter 6

The Troubled Time of Stephen: December 1141' December 1154

THE tasks facing King Stephen when he was set free appeared overwhelming. In the north the king of Scots, taking advantage of the king's difficulties, had advanced his influence below the Tyne to occupy the castle of Durham, where he was conniving to have one of his creatures appointed to the vacant see.[1] Earl Alan of Richmond was acting independently in Yorkshire and in the Midlands; he had erected a new castle at Sheriff-Hutton, and had seized the castle of "Galcluit"—probably Gaultney in Northamptonshire—from Stephen's protégé, William d'Albini.[2] Earl Alan was also carrying on a private war with William de Clerfrith, who held the castle of Tickhill.[3] Stephen was compelled to buy back the support of Geoffrey, earl of Essex, by confirming all the concessions previously made by the empress, and by giving him license to build an additional castle on his own lands.[4] During 1141 the king had lost possession of the important castles of Devizes and Oxford, and the rebels now had a secure hold on a broad area extending from the Welsh border to the middle Thames, and from Shropshire to the Channel coast. Only isolated garrisons, such as those at Bath and Barnstaple, remained in the king's obedience. To counter the favorable position held by his enemies, Stephen possessed one really decisive advantage; he had at his disposal a working administration, which meant that he could find the means to continue the struggle. The Exchequer was still functioning.[5]

This was the situation at the beginning of 1142 as Stephen set to work to regain what he had lost. It is impossible to trace his movements during the early part of the year with any accuracy. At some time before Easter (19 April), the king was in East Anglia with Earl Geoffrey and Earl Gilbert of Pembroke, in a campaign to reduce the Isle of Ely, where Bishop Nigel had once more returned to stir up rebellion. Still before Easter, the king was at Stamford, where he reached an agreement with Earl Ranulf of Chester and Earl William of Lincoln, which confirmed the latter in the possession of the castle of Gainsborough.[6] After Easter Stephen was at York, trying to bring an end to the feud between Alan, earl of Richmond, and Earl William of York.[7] At the time he returned south—about the end of April—the king was mustering levies for a full-scale renewal of the war; but during a halt at Northampton he was taken dangerously ill, and the contingents that had been called out were dismissed.[8]

The partisans of the empress had not permitted the debacle at Winchester to shake them from their purpose. The leading spirits of the rebellion had concentrated at Oxford, and Earl Robert, mindful of the lesson of Winchester, had carefully protected his line of communication with the Severn valley by building castles or fortified posts at Woodstock, Radcot, Bampton (Oxfordshire), and Cirencester.[9] During Lent (4 March–17 April) the empress was at Devizes conferring with her lieutenants, and a second council was held here shortly after Whitsunday (14 June).[10] On this occasion several important decisions on the conduct of the war were made. One of these was to adopt a plan that can only be called Grand Strategy. The support of Earl Geoffrey of Essex was to be purchased by the costly expedient of outbidding King Stephen. If the operation were successful, the king would then be confronted by enemies on both east and west—in other words, he would have to fight a two-front war, and his position would be desperate indeed. The results of council at Devizes were embodied in a series of charters that show the great importance of the castle in the military thinking of the twelfth century. As the price of his support, Earl Geoffrey demanded and received confirmation of his possession of the castle that Stephen had permitted him to build on the river Lea, as well as permission to build another castle wherever he liked on his own lands, and the right either to occupy or to destroy the bishop of London's castle at Stortford in

Hertfordshire. This latter stronghold interfered with the communication between the Tower and his other castles in Essex. Moreover, Geoffrey's ally, William fitz Walter, was to be hereditary castellan at Windsor.[11] A companion charter was issued at the same time to Aubrey de Vere, Geoffrey's brother-in-law, who was to be created earl of Cambridge; or, if that county were already held by the king of Scots, he might have his choice of Oxford, Berkshire, Wiltshire, or Dorsetshire. Aubrey was also granted possession of the important castle of Colchester.[12] At the same time the faithful earl of Hereford was rewarded with custody of the castle of Abergavenny in Monmouthshire.[13] Further to implement the plan, Earl Robert was to seek the active participation of the count of Anjou in a final campaign to overthrow the king and seat the empress on the throne of England. Shortly after 24 June, Earl Robert sailed from Wareham for Normandy.[14]

By this time Stephen had recovered, and was ready to embark on what was probably his most brilliant campaign.[15] Shortly after the departure of Earl Robert, the king appeared before Wareham; finding the place lightly held, he burned the town and seized the castle, thus cutting off direct communication between the Angevin faction and its supporters in Normandy and Anjou.[16] Stephen then marched north and got astride the enemy's line of communication between Oxford and the west. He took Cirencester by surprise and destroyed the castle; then he proceeded to reduce the remaining outworks of Oxford, completely isolating the empress, who was within the town. Bampton was carried by storm, and Radcot surrendered at discretion.[17] On 26 September King Stephen appeared on the Thames opposite Oxford. The rebel garrison obligingly deployed on the west bank, prepared to dispute the passage. However, an unguarded ford was discovered, and the king's army crossed the river, to fall upon the astonished enemy before he could make front in a new direction. The rout was complete, and Stephen's men, in hot pursuit, were able to enter the town with the fugitives. The city of Oxford thus fell into the king's hands, while the empress took refuge in the castle. Stephen immediately began a siege that was relentlessly maintained from late September until the end of the year.[18]

In the meantime, Earl Robert had not been able to enlist the active support of the count of Anjou. He was more successful in securing additional men, however, and he returned to England in December with between three and four hundred knights in fifty-two ships. Since Wareham was held by a royal garrison, he at first decided to land at Southampton, then thought better of it and returned to Wareham, which he captured after three weeks' siege. A short time later, he captured the castle of Lulworth and the fortified Isle of Portland.[19] But these reverses were not sufficient to lure the king from his business at Oxford; the siege was maintained, and by Christmas the plight of the garrison was desperate.[20] The forces that Earl Robert had concentrated at Cirencester and Wallingford were not strong enough to raise the siege; and Stephen, doubtless remembering his experience under similar circumstances at Lincoln, would not come out and fight.[21] At this juncture the empress succeeded in escaping from the castle. One night she was let down from a tower of the castle, dressed in white and passed undetected through the lines of the besiegers because the ground was snow-covered. She made her way on foot to Abingdon, six miles away, and from there rode to join her partisans at Wallingford. Left to its own devices, and with food supplies nearing exhaustion, the garrison of Oxford castle soon surrendered to the king, who installed a garrison of his own men.[22]

With the siege successfully brought to an end, Stephen marched south to attempt the recapture of Wareham; but the defenses of the castle had been so strengthened by Earl Robert that he had to content himself with a thorough devastation of the surrounding countryside.[23] The failure of the Wareham expedition was minor in comparison with the success obtained at Oxford. The loss of that castle with its garrison, coupled with Earl Robert's failure to obtain substantial aid from the count of Anjou, had ruined the elaborate plan drawn up at Devizes in June. Earl Geoffrey had not dared to move while the empress was immobilized at Oxford, and upon her flight to Wallingford he decided to come to terms with the king. During the year 1142 the king's supporters, encouraged by his successes, had been active in other areas. In a night attack, William Peverel scaled the rock on which Nottingham castle was built and ejected the garrison loyal to the empress.[24] Encouraged by a charter from the king, Earl Robert of Leicester is known to have recovered the castle and borough of Hereford—a development which would indicate some activity on Stephen's behalf in the far west.[25] Thus the end of 1142 saw the king in a much better military posture than he was at the beginning of the year.

The year 1143 saw comparatively little change in the relative position of the belligerents. In the north, King David of Scotland continued to push his own ambitions under the pretext of aiding the empress. His chancellor, William Cumin, held the castle and town of Durham as de facto bishop; but the barons of the palatinate, under the leadership of Roger de Conyers, built a castle at Bishopton from which they carried on a guerrilla operation on behalf of William of St. Barbara, who had been canonically elected.[26] Private warfare continued to disturb other parts of the north country. The king's supporter Earl William of York, "troubled by the hostility of Earl Ranulf of Chester and Gilbert de Gant, converted the monastery of St. Mary of Bridlington into a castle." [27]

The king himself was at London during Lent (17 February–2 April), but early in the summer he was again campaigning in the south. Late in June he was busy converting the nunnery of St. Etheldreda at Wilton into a castle [28]—probably as an observation post against Salisbury, three miles to the northeast, which at this time may have been held by the Angevins.[29] On 1 July, while Stephen was thus engaged, Robert of Gloucester appeared in force before the town. The royal army seems to have rushed out to offer battle without bothering to get into any kind of order—a rather surprising blunder, especially since the king's Flemish mercenaries, who should have known better, were present. It was an easy matter for the earl's forces to defeat each element in detail as it came out of the town, and to send it flying. The king himself barely escaped capture, and many prisoners and much booty were carried back to Bristol by the victorious Robert.[30] Among the more prominent prisoners taken was the king's cupbearer, Geoffrey Martel, who was obliged to deliver up the strategically located castle of Sherborne as the price of his freedom. This victory greatly encouraged the partisans of the empress. The author of the *Gesta,* who was much prejudiced in favor of Stephen, admitted that in the western part of the country at this time, only Henry de Tracy at Barnstaple continued to hold out for the king.[31]

That King Stephen did not appear disheartened by his recent reverses, however, is indicated by his next move. Earl Geoffrey of Essex had no doubt been regarded with suspicion ever since the discovery of his treasonable correspondence with the Angevin party, but the king bided his time until a favorable opportunity arose to take action. Finally, in September 1143, while the court sojourned at St. Albans, Stephen ordered the arrest of the earl.[32] He was carried off to London, where under threat of hanging he agreed to surrender his castles—Pleshy, Saffron Walden, and the Tower—into the king's hands.[33] Now Geoffrey was not the man to submit readily to such indignities. As soon as he had gained his liberty, he recruited a band of desperadoes, withdrew into the fen country, and embarked on a career of rapine and pillage.[34]

It was indeed fortunate for the king that his enemies, despite their recent victory at Wilton, were unable to take advantage of this diversion in his rear, for the earl soon proved himself to be a guerrilla chieftain of considerable skill. His first base of operations was at Fordham on the edge of the Cambridgeshire fens, just across the border from Suffolk. There he could draw supplies in men and material from Suffolk and northern Essex. From Fordham his next move was to occupy the Isle of Ely, some eight and a half miles to the northwest. Ely was the largest and most important "island" in the fen country. Its principal inhabitants, including the knights of the Honor of St. Etheldreda, had for some time opposed the king's authority, and were ready to welcome Geoffrey as a liberator. Very probably the Isle, with its two castles at Ely and Aldreth, came into his possession in November. This successful and apparently unopposed occupation gave Geoffrey relative security against a surprise attack by the king. His own tenants in Essex proved loyal; he was actively supported by his brother-in-law, William de Say, and the other great barons of East Anglia were benevolently neutral.[35]

Encouraged by his success, the earl soon demonstrated that he had no intention of remaining on the defensive. Striking from his protected base in the Isle of Ely, he appeared unexpectedly before Ramsey abbey on a frosty morning in December. Here he unceremoniously ejected the monks, clad just as they were, and "without the least compunction turned the place into a fortress from which he harried the surrounding districts." [36] Ramsey occupied a strategic position on the Huntingdonshire borders of the fens; moreover, its church was built of masonry an important consideration in a day when many castles were still mere earth and timber structures.[37]

Although the chroniclers state that as a result of these highly successful operations at the end of 1143, adventurers from all over England flocked to his standard, there are no sources from which the actual size and composition of Geoffrey's forces can be ascertained.[38] It is possible, however, to make some informed guesses. Mounted knights could scarcely have been of much use in the waterlogged and roadless fen country; but according to one of the most reliable contemporary accounts, he mustered "all the knights who were bound to him by faith and homage," which would have given him a nucleus of nearly a hundred heavy cavalry.[39] It would seem likely, also, that the knights—from fifty-six to eighty, depending on the interpretation of the sources—who owed service to the bishop of Ely as lord of the Honor of St. Etheldreda took service with Earl Geoffrey when the Isle was occupied. As early as 1130, the bishop's knights, who had formerly done castle-guard at Norwich, were relieved of this duty in order to perform similar service for the bishop in the Isle itself.[40] It is conceivable, therefore, that from all sources the earl may have been able to put upward of two hundred knights into the field, a very respectable force in twelfth-century terms. A cavalry commander (*princeps militum*) is referred to, in addition to the captain of the infantry (*magister peditum*), who presumably commanded the "strong force of ordinary soldiers." [41] Beyond this it is impossible to go, but it is certain that Geoffrey's was a mixed force capable of operating either in the fens or in open country.

Following the seizure of Ramsey and the installation of a garrison there, the earl set about improving his already strong position. Additional fortified posts were established at Wood Walton in Huntingdonshire, and at Benwick, four and a half miles northeast of Ramsey.[42] This completed the earl's outpost line. Its front and left flank were covered by the fens and the river

Ouse; its right at Benwick rested on the Nene, which could not readily be turned, and it was further strengthened by the advanced post at Wood Walton. Behind this line lay the citadel of the Isle of Ely, with its two castles and friendly population. Communications with his allies in East Anglia were maintained through the castle at Fordham. It was, as Round remarks, "a strategical position unrivaled for his purpose." [43]

Thus entrenched, the outlaw began a reign of terror throughout Cambridgeshire and western Essex that continued for most of 1144. The unprotected countryside was at his mercy, as he subsisted his marauders at the expense of his enemies. The anonymous author of the *Gesta Stephani* wrote that "he devoted himself with insatiable greed to the plundering of flocks and herds; everything belonging to adherents of the king's party he took away and used up, stripped and destroyed." [44] Nor did Geoffrey confine his depredations to the defenseless rural areas. Although Cambridge had been defended by a royal castle since the days of William the Conqueror, it was not immune from attack.[45] In time of war or civil disturbance, the inhabitants of a locality customarily stored their movable wealth in the churches as the safest possible repository. This expedient proved fatal to Cambridge. The town was seized by surprise and systematically plundered, churches and all; and when everything portable had been carried away, the place was given over to the flames.[46] The castle garrison apparently was not strong enough to prevent the attack or to interfere with the looting and destruction of the city.[47] In like manner St. Ives was sacked, and the surrounding countryside was thoroughly pillaged.[48]

At the earliest possible moment, presumably in the spring of 1144, King Stephen took the field in some strength. Geoffrey, wisely avoiding an encounter in the open, retired to his fenland fastnesses, where he could not be brought to bay.[49] Moreover, when the royal forces were committed to hunting the outlaw through the trackless fens, he "with his followers left the district where the king had followed him and cunningly turned away elsewhere to create a disturbance . . ." [50] The baffled king now tried constructing a series of fortified posts across his front as a means of confining the depredations of the earl. Not all of these posts can be identified with certainty, but Sapley in Huntingdon-shire, Knapwell, Rampton, Burwell, and Wisbeach in Cam-bridgeshire, Weeting in Norfolk, and Freckenham in Suffolk were probably among them. Of these, Burwell and Freckenham were sited so as to cut off or seriously impede Geoffrey's communi-cations with East Anglia—Burwell being three miles to the southwest of Fordham, and Freckenham two miles to the north-east.[51] So far as can be determined from existing remains, except for Burwell these were simple motte-and-bailey structures of earth and timber. But though "Geoffrey vigorously employed all the means at his disposal against those who had been left to harass him," the garrisons are not reported to have been seriously inconvenienced.[52]

Indeed, Stephen's expedient was proving most effective. Geoffrey's activities were hereafter largely confined to the terri-tory over which he exercised actual military control. No longer was he able to maintain his forces at the expense of his foes—and, since the fenlands were economically poor to begin with, they suf-fered terribly at his hands. In particular, the maintenance of his comparatively large mounted force must have been a severe drain on his resources. Contemporary accounts, even when dis-counted for exaggeration, offer graphic testimony as to the desperate measures taken by the earl when he was compelled to rely on the scanty means at his immediate disposal. Crops were seized without compensation; plow teams were appropriated, leaving the peasants unable to cultivate the land. Those who re-fused to collaborate with Geoffrey were held for exorbitant ransoms. The historian of Ely wrote that for a distance of twenty or thirty miles not an ox or a plow was to be seen; that many people starved to death and their corpses lay unburied in the fields, a prey to beasts and fowls.[53] At nearby Peterborough the English chron-icler reported at first hand:

Many thousands they killed with hunger . . . They laid imposts on the towns continually . . . when the wretched men had no more to give, they robbed and burned all the towns, so that you might go all a day's journey and you would never find a man sitting in a town, or the land tilled. Then was grain dear, and meat, and cheese, and butter; for there was none in the land. Wretched men died of hunger;

some went seeking alms who at one time were rich men; some fled the land . . . nor did heathen men ever do worse than they did; for everywhere at times they respected neither church nor churchyard, but took all the property that was therein, and then burned the church altogether.[54]

A more vivid picture of utter devastation would be hard to find.

By late summer Geoffrey's position had become so critical that he was forced to attempt to reopen his line of communication with East Anglia. Early in August he concentrated his forces in the vicinity of Burwell. There, while reconnoitering the approaches to the castle for a possible avenue of attack, he was careless enough to remove his helmet, and was struck in the head by a chance arrow.[55] Although the wound did not prove immediately fatal, it ended the attempt to reduce Burwell. Apparently his forces retreated unmolested by the royal garrisons in Burwell and Freckenham, through Fordham, to the abbey of Mildenhall in Suffolk, and there the once-powerful earl died about the middle of September.[56] The insurrection now began to collapse. Geoffrey's son and heir, Ernulf, held out in Ramsey for some time, but before the end of 1144 he was captured and banished from England.[57] The king's authority was restored, and for the balance of the reign peace seems to have prevailed in the fenlands.

Stephen's conduct of operations against Earl Geoffrey illustrates once again his talents as a general. The earl had shown himself to be an energetic, resourceful leader who, by training or intuition, knew how to maintain himself against an opponent whose resources were vastly superior to his own. He could not be defeated by formal methods of warfare so long as he refused to accept battle in the open, for the unwieldy formations of twelfth-century heavy cavalry were helpless in the fens, and there is no indication that Stephen used infantry against him. The turning point came when the king adopted a policy of what would now be called containment, designed to limit the area from which the rebels might draw supplies. At the same time, the cordon of fortified posts threatened Geoffrey's tenuous line of communication with his allies and sympathizers in the eastern counties, thereby reducing his available resources still further. Having exhausted the reserves in the area still under his military control, he had no

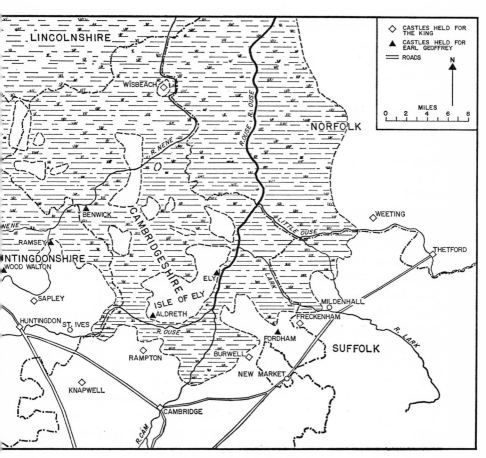

Map 9. War in the Fenland, 1143–1144

choice but to attempt to reopen his line of communication by reducing the castles in the vicinity of Fordham. Once committed to more formal warfare, he forfeited all his advantages, and since the earl could not hope to compete on equal terms with the king, the end of the rebellion became only a matter of time. The chance bow-shot of the *vilissimus sagittarius* that terminated his career merely hastened the inevitable.

The death of Earl Geoffrey ended a very formidable threat to the stability of Stephen's government. Had that threat been combined with an offensive by the western rebels, the king would have been in a perilous predicament indeed. The party of the empress, however, had not recovered from the setback brought by the loss of Oxford; even the victory at Wilton added very little real strength. The death of Earl Miles of Hereford in 1143 was a grave loss to the Angevin faction.[58] Elsewhere in England, the fighting was on a smaller scale than heretofore. The empress shifted her headquarters to Devizes, but no operations are known to have been based here.[59] The earl of Chester, still in possession of Lincoln castle, again became involved with the king, who made an unsuccessful attack on that fortress. Farther south, Robert Marmion disputed the possession of Coventry with Earl Ranulf, who held a castle in the town. To oppose him, Robert converted the parish church into a stronghold, but he was killed as he prepared to offer battle.[60] In May 1144, King David's candidate for the episcopal throne in the palatinate of Durham was driven from the city after his troops had made a vain defense of the church of St. John the Baptist at Merrington, which they had turned into a castle. On 18 October William of St. Barbara entered Durham, and comparative quiet was maintained in the north for the duration of Stephen's reign.[61] Only one other sector appears to have witnessed serious military activity. In 1144 one William of Dover, a supporter of the empress, had constructed a castle at Cricklade on the upper Thames between Malmesbury and Oxford. From this convenient location William was able continually to harass the royal garrisons in both the latter castles.[62] A rapidly moving column commanded by the king was successful in revictualing Malmesbury; the neighboring castle at Tetbury was then besieged, until the approach of a relieving column of horse and foot, including infantry levies from Bristol and Wales, under the command of Earl Robert, compelled the king to abandon the effort. He thereupon attacked the Angevin castle at Winchcomb, which was carried by storm.[63] But there is no record that William of Dover was evicted from Cricklade. The king's only real success of the year was the suppression of Earl Geoffrey's rebellion; the empress could show even less profit.

Contemporaries regarded 1145 as the year when the tide finally turned in favor of the king. Earl Geoffrey's former castle at Saffron Walden in Essex was recovered from Turgis of Avranches, and for a time East Anglia ceased to be a trouble spot. Cricklade continued to be a nuisance. Here William of Dover was succeeded as castellan by Earl Robert's son Philip, who proved no better a neighbor to the garrison at Oxford than William had been.[64] Philip also persuaded his father to build a castle at Faringdon, fifteen miles west-southwest of Oxford, to command the road between that city and Malmesbury. This threatened once again to bring the boundary of the revolt right up to the middle Thames. Stephen acted with his usual promptness. Mustering an army which included a large contingent from London—no doubt infantry for the thankless job of siege-work—he began the investment of Faringdon. A counter-castle and outworks were constructed; the siege was pressed with vigor; and with Earl Robert unable to muster sufficient strength to raise the siege, the garrison capitulated.[65]

The vigor and determination displayed by the king in the reduction of Faringdon now persuaded Earl Ranulf of Chester to make his peace with Stephen. He reduced the borough of Bedford "with great valor" and returned it to the king's obedience.[66] Later in the year, when King Stephen again undertook to reduce Wallingford, he was aided by the earl. This operation ended in failure, however; its only result was the erection of a strong counter-castle at Crowmarsh on the opposite bank of the Thames.[67] The end of 1145 saw Stephen in a much stronger position than at its beginning.

The king's arrest of this same Earl Ranulf was the most notable event of 1146. The earl's record for loyalty was little better than that of Geoffrey of Essex, and Stephen had good reason to be

suspicious of his recent professions. He was suspected of conspir-
ing with the empress, and he appeared reluctant to give up the
castles he had seized or to make a proper financial accounting to
the Exchequer.[68] Accordingly, Stephen ordered the earl into
custody at Northampton and required that certain of his castles be
surrendered as the price of his liberty.[69] Among these was the
castle of Lincoln, which the earl had held since 1140. Upon his
release, after the surrender of the castles, Ranulf at once joined
the rebels. He invested the king's garrison in Coventry castle, but
was forced to lift the siege when King Stephen approached at the
head of a relieving column. From this time onward, the earl of
Chester was the king's implacable enemy. King Stephen spent
Christmas at Lincoln, but he had scarcely departed when Earl
Ranulf appeared before the city. An attempt to storm the north
gate of the town was repulsed with heavy loss, and the earl was
compelled to retire discomfited.[70]

In 1147, for the first time since early in the reign, rebellion
flared in Kent. Gilbert fitz Richard de Clare, earl of Hertford, and
his uncle Gilbert, the earl of Pembroke, were involved, although
the circumstances are somewhat obscure. King Stephen quickly
reduced three of the earl of Hertford's castles; but a fourth,
Pevensey, held out for so long that Stephen had to be content to
leave it blockaded by land and sea.[71] Lidell, near Southampton,
was also taken by the king in 1147. The year was notable as well
for an invasion nominally led by the youthful Henry of Anjou,
accompanied by a small nmber of mercenaries. It failed to
arouse much enthusiasm among the Angevin partisans, and from a
military point of view its collapse before Burton, near Bampton,
and Cricklade—which somehow seems to have come into the
king's possession—was so complete that Henry finally had to
appeal to Stephen for funds to return to Anjou. These the king
generously granted.[72] The cause of the empress received a nearly
fatal blow in the death on 31 October of her most able and
devoted supporter, Earl Robert of Gloucester, at Bristol castle.[73]
On this occasion the castle of Sherborne was restored to the
bishopric of Salisbury, and consequently to royal control.[74] With
the death of Earl Robert the drive went out of the rebellion.

Before Lent of the following year, the empress herself left England for the Continent, never to return.[75]

This is not to suggest that peace descended upon England with the departure of the empress. Armed bickering continued in many parts of the kingdom, and Stephen had to face another attempt by Henry of Anjou to revive the fortunes of his faction. The reduced scale of the fighting was due in part to the wave of crusading fervor following the fall of Edessa in 1144 which brought the departure of some of the English barons for the Holy Land. William de Warenne, earl of Surrey, and Waleran of Meulan, earl of Worcester, were the most prominent among them; they were joined by others of lesser rank, including the infamous William of Dover and the equally notorious Philip of Gloucester.[76] Typical of the minor operations of these years were those on the Wiltshire-Hampshire borders. In 1148, when hostilities broke out between Bishop Henry of Winchester and the turncoat Earl Patrick of Salisbury, a detachment of the earl's men seized the bishop's castle of Downton, south of Salisbury.[77] From this newly won base, Earl Patrick's men plundered the surrounding district, paying no attention whatever to the excommunications hurled at them by the outraged bishop. Indeed, the chronicler records that instead of turning from their evil course, "they . . . were confirmed in it and kept on doing still worse." When Bishop Henry was summoned to Rome, he turned over the defense of the episcopal properties to the able Hugh de Puiset, later bishop of Durham. Hugh, casting aside the spiritual sword in favor of one more temporal, took the field in person at the head of a band of mercenary knights, and carried the fight to the enemy. By constructing a counter-castle in the vicinity of Downton he was able to cut off supplies from the earl's garrison, eventually compelling it to surrender.[78] This sort of private warfare, though carried on under factional banners, had little effect upon the course of the main struggle.

Operations were more serious when in 1149 Henry of Anjou landed in England for a third time.[79] The exact place and date of his arrival are unknown; certainly it could not have been later than the first part of May, and it may be surmised that he landed at the Angevin stronghold of Bristol. Taking with him Earl Roger of Hereford, among others, he made his way to Carlisle, where on 22 May he, Roger, and other young men were knighted by King David of Scotland.[80] But the gathering at Carlisle had a purpose other than the ceremonial; Ranulf, earl of Chester, was present, and here an army of Scots and English rebels was mustered for an advance on York. King Stephen, however, had been warned in advance of the hostile preparations, and had effected a concentration of his own at York. As the allied forces approached the city, the king moved out to meet them with overwhelming numbers. The chronicler notes that the rebels had mobilized very nearly their total available manpower, while King Stephen was receiving continual reinforcements. The approach of the royal army inspired sober second thoughts among the confederate commanders; they withdrew their forces "to safer positions," and eventually the prospects became so discouraging that the army broke up and the soldiers drifted back home.[81] The disintegration of the Scoto-rebel army seems to have left the young Henry of Anjou and Earl Roger of Hereford stranded far from the friendly reaches of the Severn valley. The *Gesta* gives a picturesque account of their flight to avoid capture:

Henry, too, the newly made knight, with the Earl of Hereford, stealthily leaving these regions (for he had feared lest the king might send knights after him to pursue), chose ways of return that were not familiar or commonly-used but lonely and devious, and at last, worn out with fear and exertion, arrived with his companions at the city of Hereford.[82]

But his safe arrival at Hereford did not end Henry's troubles; he still had to get back to Bristol. As soon as Stephen learned that the Angevin prince had slipped away, he set his forces in motion to intercept the fugitive. Small mounted detachments were sent in pursuit, and the king's son Eustace, who was commanding a corps of observation at Oxford, was directed to do likewise. Eustace, who seems to have possessed many of the soldierly qualities of his father, marched west rapidly and very nearly succeeded in capturing Henry at Dursley castle, southwest of Stroud in Gloucestershire, as he was making his way to Bristol. Thanks to reliable intelligence—on which he wisely acted—Henry was able to escape in a midnight flight to the sheltering walls of Bristol. In the morning Eustace, finding that his prey had flown, pursued Henry almost as far as Bristol itself, and after devastating the immediate vicinity, returned to his base at Oxford. Throughout the summer he seems to have engaged in a systematic harrying of the advanced positions of the Angevin party in Gloucestershire and Wiltshire, particularly the districts around Devizes, Marlborough, and Salisbury.[83]

After the breakup of the confederate army of Scots and dissident Englishmen, Stephen had remained at York with a part of his forces, suppressing disorders, and destroying "castles belonging to the enemy or his own adherents that were burdensome to the city," before he returned to London. He then decided, since the initiative had passed to his hands,

. . . to attack the enemy everywhere, plunder and destroy all that was in their possession, set fire to the crops and every other means of human life and let nothing remain anywhere, that under this duress, reduced to the extremity of want, they might at last be compelled to yield and surrender.[84]

To carry out this decision, the king mobilized a large army made up of stipendiary companies and feudal contingents, and moved into Wiltshire in what seems to have been three columns. The purpose was to continue with greater thoroughness the devastation that Eustace had begun. Again the neighborhoods of Salisbury, Devizes, and Marlborough were singled out for especial attention. This campaign of devastation seems to have taken place during September and October.[85]

The campaign was in full swing when Stephen received reports of a diversionary movement far to the north. Earl Ranulf of Chester had launched a surprise attack on Lincoln, and though the sturdy burgesses had beaten off the assault on the city, his forces were ravaging the environs. Leaving the operation in Wiltshire to be carried on by Eustace, the king hurried north with a portion of the army to bring relief to the harried men of Lincolnshire. The operations there can scarcely be termed successful, for Stephen was unable to dislodge the earl from his position.

Finally he "fortified a castle in the most suitable spot, and by garrisoning it adequately checked the earl's raids after this with more ease and effect." [86] The earl of Chester's diversionary operations in Lincolnshire, and the king's movement northward with a large fraction of the disposable royal forces, encouraged the Angevin partisans to become more active. Eustace is described as having to make head not only against the enemy in Wiltshire but also against hostile sorties from Bedford; Earl Hugh of Norfolk also assumed a threatening attitude and had to be held in check.[87]

While Eustace was thus occupied, Henry of Anjou, who had established field headquarters at Devizes, collected a force for a raid into Devonshire. He was joined in this venture by the earls of Gloucester and Hereford—an indication that the expedition moved in some strength. Striking southwestward from Devizes, the column crossed Devonshire and carried the town of Bridgport by storm. As a result, the commander of the castle garrison was persuaded to change his allegiance. Following this exploit, the only notable achievement of Henry's 1149 expedition, the column ravaged the lands of Henry de Tracy, King Stephen's most loyal supporter in the West Country. The wily de Tracy retired into his castle, which the Angevin raiders were not prepared to besiege. The column was on its march back to the Wiltshire base when Henry of Anjou learned that Eustace was moving in force against Devizes. Henry promptly detached a portion of his column with orders to push ahead with all speed to the threatened castle. The main body continued its march, taking unusual precautions against attack or ambush. Henry's intelligence branch served him well on this occasion, for Eustace, with commendable judgment, had determined to take advantage of Henry's absence to attempt the capture of this important fortress. It may be surmised that to make up his column, Henry had reduced the garrison at Devizes to the lowest level consistent with normal operations, and had drawn heavily on the available reserve strength of his faction. The presence of the two earls with the raiding force lends credence to this assumption. Eustace arrived before the castle and launched his assault with such determination that the bailey of the castle was carried and the garrison were driven into the keep. The buildings within the outer precincts were fired by the successful royalists. Just at this moment, the advanced detachment of Henry's column arrived on the scene, turning almost certain defeat into victory. The garrison, heartened by the unexpected arrival of reinforcements, sallied from the keep, and Eustace's men, caught between the two fires, were able to extricate themselves only after much hard fighting.[88] The unsuccessful assault on Devizes was the last episode in the campaign of 1149. Convinced by the opposition he had encountered that the time was not yet ripe for the overthrow of Stephen's regime, in January 1150 Henry embarked for Normandy.[89]

The next two years in England were comparatively quiet. In 1150 the king was again at York, where he aided the townsmen in reducing an obnoxious castle at Wheldrake.[90] Affairs in England were actually so peaceful that Eustace was posted off to France to assist King Louis VII in his struggle against the Angevins.[91] The archdeacon of Huntingdon reports expeditions in 1150 and again in 1151 against Worcester; the *Gesta* mentions only one such operation, and assigns it to 1152.[92] The lull in the military activity can be attributed in part to Stephen's successes in the preceding years, in part to the inactivity of the Angevin faction, and in part to war-weariness among even the more turbulent of the feudal magnates. Although the greater among them were virtually free from royal control, they found that their interests were better served by peace than by war. A private treaty concluded between Earl Ranulf of Chester and Robert, earl of Leicester, dated 1149/1153, illustrates both the growing desire for peace and the means taken to enforce it. It also indicates the continued importance of the castle in feudal political and military thinking:

Neither the earl of Chester, nor the earl of Leicester ought to build any new castles between Hinckley and Coventry and Donnington, nor between Donnington and Leicester, nor at Gotham, nor at Kimbolton, nor nearer, nor between Kimbolton and Belvoir, nor between Belvoir and Oakham, nor between Oakham and Rockingham, nor nearer except with the common consent of both. And if anyone shall build a castle in the aforesaid places or within the aforesaid limits, each shall aid the other without any illwill until the castle shall be destroyed.[93]

The agreement also shows quite clearly that royal control over the construction of castles was at least temporarily in abeyance. Not much is known about military operations for 1151. For the second time in the reign of Stephen, England was subjected to an attack from Scandinavia. In the spring and summer the Norse king Eystein Haraldson (1142–1157) made a wide ranging piratical foray through the North Sea. After an attack on Aberdeen he coasted south into English waters. At Hartlepool, where a landing was made, a defending force of cavalry was driven off and some shipping was seized. At Whitby, after a sharp fight, the town was put to the torch, and three other localities, so far unidentified, were attacked successfully before Eystein's return to Norway in the autumn.[94]

Then in 1152 the pace of events quickened once more. Unfortunately, the chronology for the year is obscure, but the order in which the principal events occurred can be worked out without doing violence to the scanty sources. The author of the *Gesta* states that Stephen was very active in raiding the territory of his enemies, in destroying their castles, and in building fortifications in the combat zone. He then describes the resumption of operations against Brian fitz Count's isolated castle at Wallingford. This attack occurred in 1152, on the testimony of Henry of Huntingdon and Robert of Torigni.[95] Henry of Huntingdon also states that Stephen attacked and reduced the castle of John the Marshal at Newbury, whereas the biographer of William Marshal gives a long account of the same operation, spinning it out into a two months' siege from which the king retired discomfited.[96] The former seems the more credible, and it would appear, in light of subsequent events, that the reduction of Newbury preceded the attack on Wallingford.

The force of Stephen's attack on the stronghold of Brian fitz Count would indicate that he proposed once and for all to eliminate this perpetual thorn in the flesh. The counter-castle at Crowmarsh on the opposite bank of the Thames was enormously strengthened; baronial contingents were summoned from all over England, and the levy of London again appeared in the field.[97] From what now amounted to a heavily fortified camp, the king was able to eliminate the bridgehead held by the garrison of Wallingford at the Oxfordshire end of the bridge over the Thames from the town. The organization of the defense of

Wallingford is not clear. The lord of the honor, Brian, is not mentioned in connection with the heavy fighting that took place here in 1152 and 1153; instead, Earl Roger of Hereford seems to have been in command. The one detailed source suggests that Earl Roger did not shut himself up in the castle, but kept the field.[98] Robert of Torigni states that the garrison at Wallingford destroyed Stephen's counter-castle at Brightwell, on the Berkshire side of the Thames, as well as the stronghold which the king had made at Reading abbey. Although the destruction of Brightwell might have been within the capacity of the garrison, it seems unlikely that a raid in force would have been conducted as far as Reading, some twelve miles away. More probably this latter exploit was the work of Earl Roger, and it may have been an attempt to draw the king away from the business at Wallingford.[99]

In any event, the siege of Wallingford was pressed with such vigor and determination that the earl resorted to guile and duplicity to achieve what he despaired of obtaining by force of arms. Messages were sent secretly to the king proposing that their long enmity be ended by a pact of peace and friendship. The only condition attached by Roger to the proposal was that Stephen should join him in reducing the castle of Worcester, then held by a garrison of the count of Meulan. Not only did Earl Roger's offer appear to be a break in the solid front of the Angevin faction; but if the powerful and influential earl of Hereford were to change allegiance, the whole military balance in the Severn valley, long the hard core of his enemy's strength, would be altered in Stephen's favor. Accordingly, the king accepted Roger's offer, and marched with him to Worcester, where together they opened a lengthy siege of the castle.[100] The withdrawal of the king with a large part of his army must have lessened the pressure on the garrison at Wallingford to a considerable extent—certainly one of the objectives of Earl Roger.

Needless to say, Stephen had been completely gulled. The earl of Hereford, alarmed at the strength shown by the king, kept up a steady stream of messages to Duke Henry in Normandy, reiterating that his partisans were losing ground, and urging him to return to England before the whole kingdom had submitted to Stephen. In the meantime the earl maintained the appearance of pressing the siege of Worcester until Stephen, aware at last of Roger's double-dealing, withdrew from the investment, leaving a detachment of his army there to go through the motions of continuing the operation. Then, shortly afterward, the earl made a private bargain with the garrison whereby he recovered the castle; whereupon Roger quickly renounced his pact with Stephen and once more aligned himself with the party of Duke Henry.[101] One cannot but admire the skill with which Earl Roger managed this duplicity. True, he was dealing with an opponent not distinguished for acuity, who was inclined always to take a man at his word; but in drawing Stephen away from Wallingford by luring him into a fool's errand at Worcester under the pretense of changing his allegiance, he had carried off a stroke worthy of the craftier princes of the Renaissance.

Earl Roger's advice was heeded, and in January 1153 Duke Henry crossed to England with a convoy of thirty-six ships carrying a small army of 140 knights and 3,000 infantry.[102] He landed, probably at Bristol, on 6 January or shortly thereafter, to open the final phase of the long struggle.[103] Stephen was now to be opposed by a general who was perhaps not his equal in military ability, but who had the advantages of youth and a valid claim to the throne. Henry's political campaign began almost at once as the supporters of the Angevin cause flocked in, and by means of grants and concessions he sought to buy the support of the king's adherents.[104] Such a charter, confirming the inheritance of Earl Robert of Leicester, was issued at Bristol.[105] From Bristol the course of the duke's movements can be followed with considerable accuracy, thanks to the evidence of the charters and the narrative of the *Gesta*.[106] Duke Henry apparently established his field headquarters at Devizes, the advance Angevin base in Wiltshire; here troops were concentrated for an attack on the royalist stronghold at Malmesbury, some seventeen miles to the north-northwest. He was joined here by Earl Roger of Hereford and by the earls of Cornwall and Salisbury, as well as lesser partisans.[107] The offensive against Malmesbury was launched, probably in February, under abominable conditions—cold weather with heavy snows and rain. At the approach of the ducal army the garrison of the castle, supported by the burgesses, manned the walls in an attempt to hold the town itself. But Henry ordered his mercenary infantry to make an immediate assault. While some of the professionals kept up a steady fire of arrows and missiles to keep the defenders under cover, the rest stormed the city walls with scaling ladders and soon had established a foothold in the town. The demoralized citizens fled into the abbey church for sanctuary, pursued by the victorious enemy, who ruthlessly cut them down. The regular garrison, commanded by one Jordan, retreated into the castle, which was then closely invested by Duke Henry.[108]

The king, as soon as he learned of the hostile move on Malmesbury, mustered an army and marched westward, accompanied by his son Eustace, who had returned to England on the heels of Duke Henry. He arrived before Malmesbury after the town had fallen to the duke's army. The royalists, however, were separated from the town and the enemy by the little river Avon, and although under normal circumstances it would have presented no military obstacle, at this time it had been swollen by the heavy rains to an impassable torrent. This situation played straight into Duke Henry's hands. His army was no doubt snugly quartered in Malmesbury, while Stephen's must perforce have bivouacked in the open. Unable to get at an enemy who understandably made no move to force an engagement, and running short of provisions in a district that had already been swept bare, the king resorted to negotiations. Perhaps he only hoped to save face, for certainly all the advantages lay with his opponent. Nevertheless Stephen was able to obtain surprisingly good terms: the castle at Malmesbury was to be demolished, and the royal garrison was to be withdrawn. But instead of carrying out his orders, Jordan, the castellan at Malmesbury, promptly handed over the castle intact to the duke, who confirmed him in all his possessions.[109] The king's failure to raise the siege, and the treacherous surrender of Malmesbury castle to Duke Henry, had two immediate results: Stephen's army at once began to disintegrate, and the king himself fell back on London. Even more significantly, Henry's show of strength prompted Earl Robert of Leicester, who had earlier negotiated with the duke, to side with him openly; thus thirty strong and well-provisioned castles, ac-

cording to Gervase, came into Henry's hands.[110] Indeed, many of
the king's adherents were beginning to look to the future. The
author of the *Gesta* noted that after the breakup of his army
before Malmesbury Stephen "went off with his followers gloomy
and downcast, especially because he noticed that some of his
leading barons were slack and very casual in their service and had
already sent envoys by stealth and made a compact with the
duke." [111]

Duke Henry, correspondingly encouraged, marched from Malmesbury north across the Cotswolds to Gloucester, where preparations were made for a campaign into the midlands. During the
spring months of 1153, Coventry and Dudley were occupied.[112]
During May or early June the countess of Warwick succeeded in
surrendering Warwick castle to the duke's partisans, "tricking the
royal garrison to whom it had been entrusted." [113] Henry was at
Leicester on 7 June, and at some time thereafter he was at
Warwick, where plans were concerted with Earl Robert of
Leicester for an attack on the earl of Derby's castle at Tutbury.
This stronghold, after a lengthy siege, was surrendered under an
agreement that brought the earl of Derby himself into the duke's
camp.[114] Only after he had consolidated his position in the
Midlands did Duke Henry turn his attention to the task for which
he had been summoned to England—the relief of Wallingford.
Marching south, he sacked and burned Bedford on the way, but
made no attempt to reduce the castle held by Stephen's garrison.
When he arrived in the vicinity of Wallingford late in July, in the
words of the *Gesta* he had "gained a number of towns and a good
many castles . . . and had, by force of arms, already brought
almost half of England over to his side. . . ." [115] For the relief of
Wallingford, which necessarily entailed the reduction of Stephen's
counter-castles, Henry had mobilized what must have been the
total strength of his partisans. Charter evidence reveals the
presence "apud Craumersiam in obsidione" of the earls William
of Gloucester, Roger of Hereford, Ranulf of Chester, and Reginald of Cornwall, together with Archbishop Theobald of Canterbury and such lesser figures as the constable Richard de Humez,
Philip de Columbers, Ralph Basset, Ralph the Welshman, and
Hugh de Hamslape.[116] Perhaps the series of uninterrupted suc-

cesses beginning at Malmesbury had made Henry confident of his invincibility; perhaps he hoped to clear out the royalist forces before Stephen could come to their relief. At any rate, he ordered an immediate assault on the counter-castle at Crowmarsh. The outworks were carried with a rush, and most of the defenders were driven into the keep atop its high mound, although some pockets of resistance remained in the bailey. But before the assailants could consolidate their position, a sudden sally by the garrison turned the tide, driving the duke's men entirely out of the castle.[117] After this repulse, Henry settled down to a regular siege of Crowmarsh, constructing a line of circumvallation around his own positions "so that his army had no egress but by the castle of Wallingford and the besieged had none whatever." [118]

In the meantime King Stephen had been taking measures to counter the duke's operations. A detachment of three hundred knights, presumably mercenaries, was dispatched to Oxford to assist the local tenants in harassing Henry's army. The king himself, accompanied by Eustace, marched with the royalist field army to the vicinity of Wallingford, though according to the *Gesta* he kept the Thames between himself and the duke of Normandy. Upon the arrival of the royalist army, Henry marched out of his entrenched siege lines and offered battle; but the king, after his experience at Malmesbury, probably entertained some doubts as to the trustworthiness of his own forces, and refused the challenge. Instead, negotiations took place, and a private interview between king and duke ended with a truce, whereby the siege of Crowmarsh was to be lifted by Henry, while Stephen was to demolish the castle.[119] Again having managed to avoid a showdown, the outcome of which was unpredictable, the two rivals each marched off to attend to business elsewhere. The king and Eustace began a campaign in East Anglia by laying siege to the castle of that perennial troublemaker, Hugh Bigod, earl of Norfolk, at Ipswich.[120] On 10 August Eustace is known to have ravaged the lands of St. Edmunds; he died a week later, probably in the camp before Ipswich.[121] Although Ipswich castle eventually fell to the king—probably early in September—it was poor compensation indeed for the loss of his elder son, who had recently shown real military ability, and whose death came as a severe blow to the royalist cause.[122] After the conclusion of the truce at Wallingford, Duke Henry marched north for a strike at Stephen's line of communication to Lincoln and York. He captured the town of Stamford and closely invested the castle for several weeks. The hard-pressed garrison appealed to the king for assistance, but Stephen, committed to the siege of Ipswich castle, was unable to provide the necessary relief.[123] The siege dragged on through August and was still in progress at the end of the month, but eventually the garrison was forced to capitulate.[124] Following the capture of Stamford castle, Henry put his forces in motion for the relief of Ipswich; but learning that Earl Hugh's castle had already fallen, he redirected his march to Nottingham. The town was captured and sacked, but the castle on its lofty rock was deemed too strong to attack, and was left unmolested.[125]

This was the last hostile act of a campaign which had been almost phenomenally successful for the Angevin cause. No military decision had yet been reached; but royalist strength was clearly on the wane, even though much fighting possibly remained before Henry could become king of England. Stephen was tired and disillusioned, and at nearly sixty he was by twelfth century standards an elderly man; he had suffered grievous personal losses in the deaths of his courageous queen the year before, and of his elder son in August. The latter blow seemed to have taken much of the fight out of him. Indeed, on both sides the old actors were beginning to pass from the scene. During 1153 the earls of Warwick and Northampton died, and the Angevin cause lost King David of Scotland and Earl Ranulf of Chester. War-weariness and a sense of futility made the task of the peacemakers an easier one. For once the bitter rivalry between Archbishop Theobald and Bishop Henry was submerged, and together they worked for a restoration of peace to the troubled kingdom. On 6 November Henry visited Winchester, where he approved the terms of a final settlement between himself and King Stephen. This treaty, formally ratified at Westminster before Christmas, stipulated that Stephen should remain king during his lifetime, but that Henry should succeed to the crown. It was further provided that the partisans of each should do homage to the other, and the bishops who had negotiated the agreement were to punish any who might violate its provisions. Stephen's second son, William, already a great magnate through marriage to the heiress of the earl of Surrey, was guaranteed the inheritance of his father's private estates, and was granted further property in Sussex.[126] It was also understood that all the unlicensed castles built since the death of Henry I were to be destroyed at once.[127] On the Octave of Epiphany (13 January) 1154, the magnates rendered homage to the king and duke, and the "anarchy" of Stephen's reign came to an end.[128]

In evaluating the military developments of Stephen's reign it is evident that the castle is of pivotal importance. When an action took place in the open, it was nearly always incidental to prosecuting or lifting a siege. The only exceptions were the Battle of the Standard and the rout of Wilton, and in the latter the construction of a castle had led to the action. If it is kept in mind that the warfare of the mid-twelfth century was a warfare of position, in which the castle controlled not only stretches of the countryside but vital lines of communication, the generalship of Stephen appears in a largely favorable light.[129] In current terminology, Stephen would have been considered a good corps or divisional commander. He was quick to seize the initiative, and he had an excellent appreciation not only of tactics but also of the strategical aspects of castle warfare. In all of his campaigns, the only serious mistake was in offering battle at Lincoln in 1141. This blunder was not repeated, although Stephen was to find himself in a similar situation at Oxford. The king's weakness lay in the political sphere; he never learned how to turn a victory to account.

It is very easy to criticize medieval generalship from the vantage point of the twentieth century. What is often overlooked is that in spite of the weaknesses of feudal military organization, medieval generals were not only capable of adapting their resources to meet the tactical needs of castle warfare, but were quite aware of the strategical implications as well. In 1102 Henry I struck first at the rebel lines of communications. When he isolated the rebellion by reducing Arundel and Tickhill, he showed sound strategic insight. But it was Stephen who was to provide classic examples for the history of medieval castle warfare. Stephen was handicapped politically by the attitude of a large minority of the baronage, who regarded as fraudulent both his claim to the throne and the means he had taken to assert it. Thus he had to reckon with many important magnates who supported the daughter of Henry either through self-interest or because they were convinced of the justice of her cause. That Stephen was able to maintain his position at all was due to his ability as a soldier.

The strategic problem confronting the king was that of preventing his enemies actual and potential, from combining against him simultaneously. It was also of prime importance to keep the partisans of the empress, who were strongest in the Severn valley, from direct communication with the Angevin party in northern France. Stephen's avantage lay in his being able to operate along what modern strategists would call interior lines. From a central position in the Thames valley Stephen was able, thanks to the road network radiating from London, to strike in any direction. His chief aim had to be to maintain control of the Channel ports while holding a chain of castles between the Severn estuary and the English Channel. In this he was largely successful, and his control of Wareham during a few critical months of 1142 deprived the rebels of their best chance of overthrowing the king.

Sir Charles Oman observes that in the campaign of 1214, by which John proposed to crush Philip II Augustus between the forces of the Empire and those of the English operating in southern France, "we seem to detect . . . almost for the first time in mediaeval history the project of a fine strategical combination." [130] Although the wars of Stephen's time were on a much smaller scale, the same strategic principle is to be found in the plan concerted between Robert of Gloucester and Geoffrey of Essex in the spring of 1142. Attacking from the advance base of the rebellion at Oxford, the forces of the empress were to act in coordination with those of Earl Geoffrey in Essex. The king's forces, obliged to fight a two-front war, would be crushed between them. To say that strategic combinations were unknown before the beginning of the thirteenth century is to argue against positive historical evidence to the contrary.

Stephen's response to this threat showed that he was aware of the danger; that he had time to meet it speaks well of his intelligence service. He anticipated the attack by seizing the port and castle of Wareham, which was the rebellion's sole direct link with the Angevin party in Normandy and Anjou. He then proceeded, first, to isolate the rebel fortress at Oxford, and afterward to reduce it by a lengthy siege. The surrender of Oxford castle early in 1143 was a blow from which the rebellion never recovered. It restored to the king the control of the strategic Thames valley and its network of roads. With this accomplished, Stephen no longer had to fear the insurrection of the earl of Essex; he was able to choose his own time for striking. Earl Geoffrey, deprived of his castles and driven into the fens, might wage a long and skillful guerrilla war, but the end was certain. The superior resources of the king prevailed, and Geoffrey was eventually brought to bay and slain while trying to fight his way out.

Stephen as a general has received less than his just due at the hands of historians. Faced with political problems with which he was unfitted to cope, he held his own for years against powerful and resourceful enemies. Without an understanding of the problems of castle warfare he would almost certainly have gone down before such competent commanders as Robert of Gloucester, David of Scotland, Geoffrey of Essex, Ranulf of Chester, and Miles of Hereford. By keeping his lines of communication open, by never letting his enemies combine in overwhelming strength, by isolating the rebellion with his chains of fortified posts, Stephen was able to preserve his throne. He did this through sheer military ability and in spite of political blunders that would have wrecked a less able commander. Even Stenton has missed this point. Laying particular stress upon Stephen's shortcomings as a politician, he writes: "It is impossible to read even the narrative of a writer so well disposed towards the king as the author of the *Gesta Stephani* without feeling that Stephen was chiefly responsible for his own failure." [131] The fact is that Stephen remained king until his death despite having to oppose a contender whose claim to the crown was better than his own.

Prolonged civil strife naturally had its effect on the country. Unlicensed castles, according to the chroniclers, arose on every hand, estimates of their numbers ranging from 375 to 1,500—the usual medieval exaggeration. The names and locations of only a few of these adulterine castles have survived, and the remains of even fewer have been discovered. Some of these "castles" were converted religious houses—Ramsey abbey, which was fortified by Geoffrey of Essex; Reading abbey, which was converted to military use by the king himself; and Robert Marmion's fortified church in Coventry are examples. Stenton was of the opinion that the majority of the motte-and-bailey castles were in existence before the disturbances of Stephen's time.[132] The bulk of the evidence seems to support this view. Despite the complaints of the monks about castle-building, only a few castles are known to have been deliberately destroyed at the end of the civil wars. In 1153 Stephen pulled down the castle of Drax in Yorkshire; Earl Geoffrey's castle at Saffron Walden, and six strongholds of the bishop of Winchester, including Wolvesey, were destroyed at the beginning of the next reign, but some of these were in existence prior to 1135. It seems likely that in addition to hastily converted religious houses, many of the mottes built during the Conquest, and then allowed to fall into decay during the long peace of the first Henry's reign, had been refortified to meet the emergency. This would account for the absence of remains that could definitely be assigned to the reign of Stephen. Later, during the reigns of both Henry II and John, such ancient sites were often recommissioned at times of internal strife.

Chapter 7

Henry II, 1154·1189

THE death of King Stephen in October 1154 found his successor in Normandy. Since the succession was uncontested, Henry remained on the Continent until his business there was settled, returning to England only on 8 December. Following his coronation at London on 19 December, the new king held his Christmas court at Bermondsey priory.[1] The decisions reached at this time had to do with restoring the royal authority throughout the kingdom. The Flemish mercenaries were to be dismissed; those unlicensed castles that had not yet been destroyed were to be pulled down; and all royal lands and castles that had been alienated during the nineteen years of Stephen's reign were to be surrendered to the crown.[2]

This sweeping program met with surprisingly little resistance. The Flemings caused no trouble at all, and there seems to have been no serious opposition to the destruction of unlicensed castles.[3] Tired of disorder and war, most of the English magnates cooperated with the king in restoring peace. There were some grumblings, however, over the orders to restore crown property, and early in 1155 King Henry, with sufficient force to impress the discontented, marched north to York by way of Oxford, Northampton, Peterborough, and Lincoln. After this display of power, Hugh Bigod, earl of Norfolk, and William of Aumale, earl of York, came to terms, the latter surrendering the castle of Scarborough.[4] Returning south by way of Nottingham, the king confiscated the lands of William Peverel, who at the king's approach sought refuge in a monastery and later fled overseas.[5] By early

March the king was again in London, holding a council which renewed the edict demanding the surrender of royal castles.[6]

It was now abundantly clear that the king meant business, and the new decrees provoked two of the most powerful barons of the West Country to overt defiance. Earl Roger of Hereford—whose father, Miles of Gloucester, had been one of the most steadfast supporters of the Angevin cause—held the two important castles of Hereford and Gloucester, the first as earl, the second as hereditary constable. These strongholds Earl Roger put on a war footing and provisioned with food and arms. In addition, Earl Roger persuaded Hugh Mortimer to join him in opposition to the king. Hugh, one of the most powerful marcher barons, who held not only his own castles of Cleobury and Wigmore but also the great royal castle at Bridgnorth on the Severn, now strengthened his fortresses and enlisted Welsh support.[7] As it turned out, Roger's resistance collapsed before a blow was struck: a relative, Gilbert Foliot, bishop of Hereford, convinced the disgruntled earl of the folly of challenging the king. He submitted on 13 March, two weeks before Easter; and although Henry allowed him to retain his earldom, Roger was compelled to give up the castles at Hereford and Gloucester.[8] This left Hugh Mortimer alone in his open defiance of the royal mandate. King Henry appears to have been in no hurry to suppress this contumacious marcher lord, perhaps believing that Hugh would think twice about taking on so powerful an opponent as the king, and that he would surrender voluntarily. At any rate, as late as 10 April the king was at Wallingford, where he made provisions for the succession in the event of his own death.[9] Only when this was settled does he seem to have taken any active measures against Hugh.

Once begun, however, Henry's actions were sure and relentless, and there could be but one outcome. The king must have summoned a sizable force, for he was able to dispatch separate columns to each of Mortimer's own castles, Wigmore and Cleobury, while he himself, accompanied by many important tenants, took command of the siege of Bridgnorth.[10] There are no dates for the beginning of the campaign; Ramsey has asserted that it extended through May and June,[11] but this seems rather unlikely, since the chroniclers describe the campaign as a short one.[12] King Henry at once indicated that he was in earnest by constructing a line of circumvallation around Bridgnorth, which not only protected his own installations but also cut off any possibile escape from the castle where Hugh was in command.[13] As the campaign progressed the castles of Cleobury and Wigmore were taken, although in what order is unknown; finally, in early July, Mortimer in Bridgnorth was compelled to ask for terms. On 7 July peace was made between Hugh and the king, who apparently kept Wigmore and destroyed Cleobury, while repossessing the royal fortress at Bridgnorth.[14]

Although the process of reclaiming the military resources of the kingdom was not yet complete, the surrender of Bridgnorth and the submission of Hugh Mortimer marked the end of open hostilities. Two years later the king had an opportunity to extend his authority into East Anglia, where two potentially dangerous tenants, Hugh Bigod, earl of Norfolk, and William of Blois, the son of King Stephen, count of Mortain in his own right and earl of Surrey in right of his wife, held positions of strength. Returning to England from the Continent early in April 1157, Henry held his Whitsun court (19 May) at Bury St. Edmunds.[15] This manifestation of royal authority in their very midst seems to have put the pressure on the two earls. Although William of Blois had been guaranteed possession of the castles of Norwich and Pevensey under the convention of 1153, he was now forced to relinquish them, as well as his castle of Mortain in Normandy. At the same time Earl Hugh, whose reputation for double-dealing was second to none, was forced to surrender his castles.[16]

Having disposed of this possible source of trouble, Henry was able in the same year to register an even more important victory. King David I of Scotland had died in 1153, leaving a twelve-year-old grandson, Malcolm IV, as his successor to the throne. Beset by the usual troubles of a minority, Malcolm's government had been unable to withstand the pressure of the English for the return of the three northern counties—Northumberland, Cumberland, and Westmoreland—that had been extorted from Stephen at the height of his difficulties. The young king was invited to attend Henry's court at Chester, and in return for confirmation of the English earldom of Huntingdon, Malcolm surrendered the three counties with their key fortresses of Carlisle, Bamborough, and Newcastle-upon-Tyne.[17]

Thus within three years Henry II had regained virtually all that had been lost during the preceding nineteen. This not only speaks highly of the king's ability and resourcefulness, both as a soldier and a politician; it is indicative as well of the misconceptions that have been customary concerning Stephen's reign. Had the military position of the crown been as weak as is often alleged, it would scarcely have been possible for Henry to have restored it completely within the space of three years. The military aspects of the early years of Henry's reign are only part of the evidence that the machinery of government in 1154 was still in tolerable working order.[18]

For almost twenty years England remained undisturbed by civil commotions. But though the pages of the chroniclers are silent as to military events, during this time a process of military centralization confirmed the increasing power of the crown, both political and economic. For the long reign of Henry II the Pipe Rolls are complete except for the first year, and give an accurate idea of the extent to which the defense of the realm was being taken over by the king.[19] A military historian cannot trace in detail the economic revival that occurred during the twelfth century; but it is obvious from the Pipe Rolls that the money income of the crown was increasing, and that the king could undertake projects that no tenant, or even group of tenants, could match. In earlier times the tenant of a modest fee could erect a motte-and-bailty castle as strong as any that the king might build. By the middle of the twelfth century this was no longer true. Although Hugh Bigod, the earl of Norfolk, for example, could build a strong castle of stone at Bungay by straining his resources to the limit, the king was not only spending large sums on the keep at nearby Orford, to hold the earl in check; at the same time he was strengthening his castles in other parts of the kingdom as well. It may be that one reason for the barons' revolt in 1173 was a realization that the crown no longer had to depend on them for military support.

The process by which the king took over the defense of the

realm was gradual. Henry I, in the thirty-first year of his reign, had spent £112 9s.7d. on the nineteen castles mentioned in the surviving Pipe Roll of that administration. The largest sum spent on a single castle was £22 7s.8d. at Arundel.[20] In the second year of his reign (for the first the figures are incomplete) Henry II spent only £30 9s.7d. on eight castles. This modest sum certainly did not include any important building enterprise; the £13 10s.8d. spent on a room for the king at Winchester was the largest single amount. In the following year—1156/1157—the expenditures had risen to £57 5s.10d., out of which the largest item was £20 to provision the castle at Norwich, and the most expensive building operation was on the bridge and bretasch at Southampton.[21]

With the fourth year of King Henry's reign the amounts spent on castle-building and in pay to garrisons increased to more than twice those of the preceding year. The cost of maintaining the garrison at Norwich was £51 12s., and for the first time notable sums were spent on actual building: £20 on the castle of Worcester, and a like amount at Wark.[22] Perhaps no less significant than the increased allocations for defense were the expanding interests of the crown. Heretofore the castles in the south of England and the Severn valley had occupied the attention of the king; now the royal influence began to extend into East Anglia and the Scottish march.[23] The king also served notice to the baronage that their fortresses were no longer so vital to the defense of the kingdom by approving the expenditure of £9 12s.4d. for the destruction of a castle of the late Earl Geoffrey of Essex at Saffron Walden.[24]

The fiscal year 1158/1159 saw another large increase in the sums spent for military purposes. The maintenance of the garrison at Walton in Suffolk amounted to £96 12s.8d.—a sum far in excess of any previous expenditure for such a purpose.[25] Even more indicative of the trend toward centralization was the new construction of strategic fortresses within the kingdom. The heavy expenditures involved can only mean that the new works were of masonry. Castles were strengthened in the north, where the experience of the previous reign had shown the need for greater protection. The expenditure at Wark on the Scottish border was £103 14s.3d.[26] Farther south, at Scarborough in Yorkshire, the expenses for new construction came to £134 9s.4d.[27] This was almost as much as the king had spent altogether on castles in the preceding year. Minor expenses on the castles at Carmarthen and Cambridge indicate the widening range of the building program.[28]

The Pipe Roll for 1159/1160 shows military expenses totaling £707 14s. Some of this was the cost of maintaining garrisons and providing them with rations. At Carreghova on the Welsh border of Shropshire, a paid garrison consisting of one knight, twenty sergeants, a gatekeeper, and a watchman, received £25 13s.9d. in wages, whereas the cost of provisioning the castle amounted to only £3 14s.[29] The garrison at Walton, consisting of ten knights and four sergeants, received £126, and the cost of their rations was £12 12s.1d.[30] Dover castle must have been a general depot, judging from the amount and variety of stores laid in: 4800/6400 bushels of grain, 480/640 bushels of salt, thirty salt hog carcasses, and eleven cheeses, at a cost of £13 5s.8d.[31] The continued works at Scarborough and Wark cost £94 3s.4d. and £141 4d. respectively.[32] Another major project was the keep at Chester, probably begun by Earl Ranulf in King Stephen's time, which was either finished or improved by the king at a cost of £102 7s.[33] Work on the castle at Berkhamstead amounted to £43 6s.8d.[34]

Before the outbreak of rebellion in 1173, the cost of construction and upkeep on the king's castles fluctuated widely from year to year. But the trend was toward greater expense, over a broader geographical area. In the Pipe Rolls of the first eighteen years of the reign—through the fiscal year 1171/1172—seventy-one castles are mentioned. Some of these castles are those of fees that were only temporarily in the hands of the crown, such as those of the palatine earldom of Chester in the sixth year of the reign, and of the bishopric of Lincoln in 1170.[35] Sometimes the king appears to have retained the fortresses long after the fee had passed from his hands. Thus the castle of Lydbury North (Bishop's Castle) in the bishopric of Hereford, which was first garrisoned by the crown in the thirteenth year of Henry's reign, was still in his hands in 1171/1172.[36] Three castles of the honor of William fitz Alan—Clun, Ruthin, and Whitchurch—fell into the king's hands in 1159/1160.[37] Clun and Ruthin disappeared from the Roll after

1163/1164, but Whitchurch remained, doubtless because of its strategic location near the borders of Cheshire.³⁸ The number of castles mentioned in the yearly accounts varies as greatly as the amount spent. The largest number referred to in a given year is twenty-three—in 1170/1171 and 1171/1172—whereas only seven are mentioned in the second and eleventh years of the reign— 1155/1156 and 1164/1165. As might be expected, these figures correspond to the greatest and least expenditures for maintenance. In 1155/1156, the expenditure was less than £40; in 1159/1160 it had risen sharply, to £707 14*s*. After that year the charges decreased, until in the eleventh year of Henry's reign no more than £70 5*s*.2*d*. was spent on seven castles; and of this total, £32 13*s*.4*d*. was charged to work on the castle of Eye.³⁹ In 1165/1166 the amount rose to £990, of which £660 went for work on Henry's new keep at Orford.⁴⁰ For the next four years after this initial outlay, the annual totals at Orford ran between £510 and £620. Then, in the two years preceding the outbreak of the revolt, the amounts charged to military purposes shot to unprecedented heights. In 1170/1171 the Pipe Roll shows a total military expenditure of £1,237 9*s*.6*d*.; the total for 1171/1172 amounted to £1,223 9*s*.3*d*. Since the beginning of the reign, £8,155 1*s*.5*d*. had been spent on maintaining and improving the castles in the hands of the crown; thus 30 per cent of the total was spent in the two years before the outbreak of the baronial revolt. It is obvious that Henry and his justiciar, Richard de Lucy, were anticipating trouble.

It now becomes necessary to examine closely the amounts spent for construction, and to relate the more important of these to the geographical location of the castles themselves. Of the seventy-one castles mentioned in the Pipe Rolls before 1173, a breakdown of the figures shows that actual building was done on only forty-two. But by the end of the fiscal year 1171/1172 this work amounted to £5,881 8*s*.4*d*.—about 71 per cent of all the money spent for military purposes. Of the forty-three castles for which there is some evidence of masonry construction by the time of Henry's accession, no more than fourteen were in the king's hands in 1172.⁴¹ Two—Wolvesey and Saffron Walden—had been destroyed at the beginning of the reign. Launceston, Tintagel, and Trematon were held by Earl Reginald of Cornwall, the king's uncle. St. Briavels was held by William de Neville, the custodian of the Forest of Dean.[42] Berkeley was held for the king jointly by John de Riparia and William of Worcester, whose pay as custodians seems to have been a charge on the sheriff of Gloucester.[43] Thus in time of civil disturbance, unless the ratio were changed, the king could count on holding less than half of the strongest and most "modern" castles in England. Moreover, the strategic distribution of the fortresses he did hold was poor. With the exception of the castles in Kent which barred the way to London, of Arundel in Sussex, and of Earl Reginald's Cornish castles, the stone structures under Henry's control were located in places of little strategic value, or so isolated as to render their neutralization easy. In the Midlands all the masonry castles were baronial; those of Chester, Llancillo, and Ludlow on the Welsh border were in the hands of marcher lords; and in the north the king held only Carlisle. Richmond in Yorkshire came into Henry's hands only in 1170, upon the death of the earl of Richmond.[44] It was this weakness which the castle-building of Henry II seems designed to correct.

In the years between 1155 and 1172 the Pipe Rolls indicate ten castles on which the king spent more than £200 each.[45] Of these, only for the one at Scarborough is there evidence of masonry construction before Henry became king, so that this represented new building on a very large scale. The king first turned his attention to the north. He had recovered Carlisle from the Scots in 1157, but the history of the northern countries suggests that they were poorly defended by the existing castles. Moreover, the only major strongholds on the eastern end of the frontier, those at Norham and Durham, belonged to the bishops of Durham, whose distance from the royal authority had encouraged a spirit of independence and a tendency to connive with the Scots. In the fourth year of his reign King Henry began to reconstruct the castle at Wark on the Tweed, just nine miles upstream from the episcopal castle of Norham. Here, from 1157 to 1160, he spent £382 3s.7d.[46] Meanwhile, to strengthen his position in another section of the north, the king began erecting a powerful fortress at Scarborough, not far from the monastery of Bridlington which William d'Albini had turned into a castle during the wars of

Stephen's time.[47] The total cost of the work at Scarborough, spread over an eight-year period, amounted to £656 1s.8d.[48] The completion of the castles at Wark and Scarborough made the military position of the king in the north as strong as that of any tenant. The acquisition of Richmond castle in 1170 further strengthened the central authority which, with the building of the stone keeps at Bowes in 1170–1172, and at Newcastle-upon-Tyne (1167–1172), became predominant.[49]

Elsewhere in the kingdom Henry was equally active. In 1168 work was begun on a stone keep at Bridgnorth on the river Severn, in a part of the realm notorious for its disregard of law and order.[50] In the southeast, defenses were strengthened by the erection of the keep at Chilham in Kent.[51] With the exception of Southampton and Exeter, the only stone castles to the southwest of London had been in baronial hands at the beginning of the reign. Arundel seems to have come under royal control in 1170/1171.[52] Baronial power in this direction was offset by the construction of stone keeps at Windsor and Winchester.[53] In the north Midlands, the erection in 1170–1172 of the keep at Nottingham must have increased the king's strength.[54] But it was in East Anglia, where Hugh Bigod, the turbulent earl of Norfolk, had not only a stone castle at Bungay but very probably another one at Framlingham, that the king built his most elaborate fortress. Here at Orford, the king spent £1,221 15s.10d. within a seven-year period (1165–1172).[55] Finally, the large occasional expenditures on the older stone castles indicate how Henry intended to maintain his military ascendancy.[56]

Thus, in the autumn of 1172, King Henry held a nucleus of twenty-three "up-to-date" castles around which to build a countrywide system of defense against invasion or civil commotion. In the southeast, Dover, Canterbury, Chilham, and Rochester stood between the Channel coast and the line of the Thames; Pevensey, Arundel, Southampton, and Exeter protected important harbors on the south coast; and Winchester interdicted the increasingly important road from Southampton to London. The line of the Thames was guarded along the lower third of its course by the castles at Windsor and London. Colchester, Orford, and Norwich stood on or near the old Roman road from London into East

Anglia. In the north the king held Carlisle, the terminus of the road from Chester and the south, and an entry to England from Scotland. Wark guarded the passage of the Tees, another point of invasion from the north; Newcastle stood astride the road from York to the border at the point where it crossed the Tyne; Scarborough dominated an unruly district of Yorkshire. Bowes and Richmond, recently acquired from the escheated Honor of Richmond, occupied strategic positions. Richmond stood at the entrance to Swaledale, through which ran a road to Penrith and Carlisle. Bowes, on the north bank of the Tees, dominated another road from Yorkshire to Carlisle. Since these roads were the avenues by which invaders from Scotland struck at York, the importance of these castles is at once apparent. Only in the Midlands and on the Welsh border had Henry failed to strengthen his position materially by the acquisition of older stone castles or the building of new ones. The isolated castle of the Peak in Derbyshire had apparently been constructed as a final refuge for its owner, William Peverel. It lay far from the normal lines of communication, and its strategic value was practically nil. Although the construction of the stone keep at Nottingham gave the king control of an important crossing of the Trent, the remaining masonry castles of the Midlands were in baronial hands. Bridgnorth on the east bank of the Severn was the sole stone fortress held by the king in the troublesome border area. Both St. Briavels and Berkeley lay too far away from main roads to have much strategic significance.

In addition to this nucleus of masonry castles, on the eve of the great revolt the king held a number of other strongholds which, for lack of any evidence to the contrary, must be regarded as conventional motte-and-bailey structures. In the Pipe Rolls for the two years preceding the outbreak of the rebellion, fourteen such castles are mentioned.[57] The crown either provisioned these castles or paid the castellan. Eight of the strongholds were either in the Severn valley or on the Welsh march. On the southern borders of Cheshire stood Ellesmere and Whitchurch; Ellesmere was on the Watling Street between Shrewsbury and Chester. The possession of Shrewsbury on the Severn gave Henry control not only of the important river crossing, but also of the roads radiating east, north, south, and southwest from this important junction. Seven miles above Shrewsbury, the important fortress of Shrawardine was likewise in the hands of the king. Lydbury in Herefordshire stood near the main road from Shrewsbury to Hereford; Stratton was situated between Bridgnorth and the potentially hostile castle of the Mortimers at Ludlow. Gloucester, another important river castle, was in the hands of the crown; so was Caerleon in Monmouthshire, which dominated the coastal road from Gloucester to Cardiff and the marcher lordships of Glamorgan and the west. Elsewhere, the king held the castle at Hertford on the south bank of the Lea, a position that commanded the Great North Road as it passed the river at Ware, four miles downstream from the castle. Berkhamstead was also held by Henry; it occupied a strategic position between the Watling Street and the road from London to Buckingham. Newark, one of the strongholds of the bishopric of Lincoln, was likewise in the king's hands. At Newark, where the Fosse Way intersected the Ermine Street, the castle also protected the latter highway as it crossed the Trent, and was thus of considerable military importance. Bamborough, on its rocky Northumbrian headland, was also in Henry's possession. The repeated efforts of the Scots to secure this almost impregnable fortress, as well as the determination of Stephen to retain it during his reign, show its importance to the defense of the border. In the south the king held Hastings, which strengthened his hold on the all-important Channel coast, as well as Salisbury on the important road from London to Exeter. A study of the map shows that except in the Midlands, King Henry had firm control of most of the chief lines of communication in England at the time the barons openly took up arms. The king's principal strategic handicap was that his contact with the north could be severed at any time by an outbreak in the Midland shires.

The political origins of the revolt lay in the rivalry between the house of Anjou and the Capetian dynasty in France. Louis VII was reluctant to acquiesce in the consolidation of the vast Angevin domain stretching from the Tweed to the Pyrenees; nor was he averse to stirring up discontent in Henry's immediate family in order to weaken the position of his rival. King Henry II had secured the coronation of his eldest son, Henry, but the title was insufficient to satisfy that young man's ambitions; he wanted the power—and the income—that he regarded as the true insignia of royalty. The Young King's discontent proved a fertile seed bed for the schemes of King Louis. At Christmas 1172 he lured the Young King to Paris, where designs were laid for a general revolt, involving England as well as the elder Henry's continental possessions.[58] A number of powerful Anglo-Norman tenants agreed to join it in return for the promise of a share in the spoils. King William of Scotland was to receive Northumberland, which his grandfather had held of King Stephen.[59] In East Anglia, Eye and Norwich were to fall to Hugh Bigod, the shifty earl of Norfolk.[60] Dover and Rochester were to be the reward of the count of Flanders. Earl Hugh of Chester; David, earl of Huntingdon and brother of the king of Scots; Earl Robert of Leicester; William de Ferrers, earl of Derby, and Roger de Mowbray were also involved in the conspiracy.[61]

It will be seen at once that the chief conspirators were strongest in precisely the places where the king was weakest. Huntingdon was held by Earl David; its possession by the rebels gave them command of the Ermine Street at the point where it crossed the Ouse, cutting the king's line of communication with Lincoln. Another road to the north ran from London through Northampton to Nottingham, but halfway between lay the rebel garrisons at Leicester and Mountsorrel. Tutbury and Duffield, castles of the earl of Derby, effectively cut off Nottingham from the royal strongholds in the Severn valley. Groby served as an outpost to the castle at Leicester. Roger de Mowbray's castle at Kinnardferry interdicted the Ermine Street between Lincoln and York, and his castle at Thirsk the highway between York and Newcastle-upon-Tyne. Malzeard, another Mowbray castle, stood not far from the York-to-Richmond route. In East Anglia, Earl Hugh's castle at Bungay cut off Norwich from London and Colchester, although his stronghold at Framlingham was effectively neutralized by Henry's new castle at Orford. The defection of the earl of Chester seems to have brought the whole of the palatine earldom into the rebel camp. In addition to the citadel of Chester itself, Hamo de Masci's castles at Dunham and Ullerwood, Richard de Moreville's castle of Hawarden, and the stronghold of Geoffrey de Cotentin at Stockport, were held by rebel garrisons.[62] Of these castles, only Dunham was of much strategic significance; it threatened the road from Chester to York. But the Cheshire castles constituted a standing menace to the royalists in the Severn valley, and to the tenuous line of communications with the northern countries that went by way of Shrewsbury. The revolt in the Midland countries had the effect of splitting the kingdom in two, but its only chance of success lay in maintaining this stranglehold while linking up with the two isolated outbreaks in East Anglia and Cheshire. The great strategic weakness of the revolt was that it had no direct communication with the Channel and its supporters in France; it had to maintain itself largely on its own resources in men and matériel. Only three castles in the southern part of the kingdom seem to have been connected with the revolt. Saltwood, near Hythe on the Channel coast, and Allington, near Rochester, were effectively neutralized by the network of castles that the king held in this area.[63] These, together with the castle that Gilbert Montfichet held against the king in London near the Blackfriars, can have had little more than nuisance value.[64]

The revolt began simultaneously in England and Normandy just after Easter (15 April) of 1173.[65] King Henry was in Normandy, so that the conduct of operations in England fell to the justiciar, Richard de Lucy, and the king's uncle, Earl Reginald of Cornwall. The actions of these lieutenants were prompt and vigorous. It seems probable that the garrisons of many of the royal castles had already been reinforced, and that large stores of provisions had been laid in. In addition to those the king is known to have held before the revolt began, seventeen more castles are referred to in the Pipe Roll for 1172/1173. Two of these—Brackley, on the road from Buckingham to Worcester, and Thetford, on the route from Cambridge to Norwich—were held for a short time only before they were destroyed by the king's order.[66] Kenilworth, Warwick, Northampton, and Prudhoe were the castles of tenants who remained loyal to the crown; and part, at least, of the expense of garrisoning and provisioning them was assumed by the royal authorities.[67] But there is a strong suspicion that a number of the castles that appear for the first time this year on the Roll are nothing but old motte-and-bailey structures quickly reconditioned for the emergency. This was almost certainly true of Brackley and Thetford. Although the £66 spent for reconditioning at Oxford might well indicate major repairs to a stone castle. the £31 charged to work at Cambridge can mean only that a motte castle on which nothing had been spent for fifteen years was being refortified for the crisis.[68] The castle wall that was rebuilt at Hereford at a cost of £3 6s. was certainly not of masonry.[69] The castles of the loyal barons, together with those hurriedly recommissioned, filled in some of the gaps in the royalist defenses. Notable among the former was the castle at Northampton, where a large garrison was maintained at the king's expense during the entire rebellion. In 1172/1173 the pay of the garrison amounted to £142 1s.; it increased to £416 7s.8d. in the following year.[70]

Northampton stood on the alternate route to the north from London. Its connection with the metropolis remained unbroken, providing a convenient base for operations against the rebel strongholds at Leicester and Huntingdon. Kenilworth and Warwick, near the junction of Watling Street and the Fosse Way, kept open a direct route from London to Shrewsbury and the upper Severn valley. Ellesmere, Whitchurch, and the reconditioned motte at Newcastle-under-Lyme formed a cordon that separated the rebel castles in Cheshire from those in Leicestershire. In the north, Newcastle-upon-Tyne and Odinel de Umfraville's castle of Prudhoe held the chief crossings of the Tyne. The line of the Thames was strengthened by the addition of Oxford and Wallingford to its defenses. The most significant achievement, however, was the separation of Earl Hugh in East Anglia from the rebels in the Midlands. A line of castles extending from London to the Wash prevented any outflanking of the royalist garrisons except by a crossing of the Thames below London—almost an impossibility—and a march between London and Rochester. Any army attempting to run the gauntlet would find its flanks and rear continually exposed to attacks from hostile garrisons. This line of fortresses was composed of London, Hertford, Cambridge, Haughley, Eye, Thetford, Aldreth, and Wisbeach. The last four of these, together with Cambridge, were probably refortified motte-and-bailey structures.[71] Elsewhere, York was repaired, ensuring the loyalists' control of a vital northern communications center, while the eastern approaches to London were strengthened by regarrisoning Rayleigh on the Thames estuary.[72]

Actual military operations were slow in getting under way; each side doubtless was concerned with consolidating its position before committing itself to the offensive. King Henry appears to have made a flying visit to Northampton, probably in June, since the sheriff's account for the year includes an item covering the king's expenses for a four-day period.[73] At this time plans must have been formulated for an attack on the rebel strongholds, for on 3 July Richard de Lucy appeared in front of Leicester with an army accompanied by a siege train. The town was taken and burned, but the royal army failed to capture the castle, which was promptly invested.[74] The operation had been well planned; the Pipe Roll of the year contains numerous entries covering the expenses of the siege. The sheriff of Shropshire accounted for the pay of 410 men, including archers and heavy infantry; 10,000 arrows were sent from Gloucester; the sheriff of Worcestershire furnished a hundred hoes; Warwickshire and Nottinghamshire provided 156 carpenters and a master "to make machines for the army at Leicester." [75] All this is not only indicative of the organizing ability of the justiciar, but also proof that the king's forces retained control of the vital lines of communication which enabled them to concentrate men and supplies without hindrance from the enemy. But the siege of Leicester castle was only in its fourth week when de Lucy was forced to turn his attention elsewhere. King William of Scotland had entered the conflict by crossing the frontier on 20 August with a motley, ill-equipped, and poorly led army.[76] On 28 July the justiciar felt obliged to raise the siege of Leicester and hurry north to meet the new threat.[77]

The ponderous Scots army first invested Wark, but Roger d'Estuteville, the castellan, obtained a truce which enabled him to summon help from the south.[78] Alnwick also refused to surrender. However, Bishop Hugh of Durham signed a sort of neutrality pact with King William which gave the Scots the right of passage through the bishop's lands, and Warkworth was surrendered without a struggle.[79] The Scots' advance was finally halted under the walls of Newcastle-upon-Tyne. Bypassing Prudhoe, King William then retreated westward up the valley of the Tyne, finally reaching Carlisle, which was closely invested.[80] Upon the approach of the English army, the king abandoned the siege of Carlisle and retired across the border to Roxburgh, followed by de Lucy, who burned Berwick and ravaged a small district in the Lowlands.[81] But before any clear-cut decision could be reached, de Lucy was again forced to change front to meet a new and more serious threat.

On 29 September, Earl Robert of Leicester had landed near Walton in Suffolk with a large force of French and Flemish mercenaries, chiefly foot.[82] Bypassing the king's heavily garrisoned castle at Walton, the earl had marched inland to the castle of Earl Hugh at Framlingham. Operating from this base, Earl Robert began an attempt to clear a path through the network of royal castles that separated East Anglia from the chief rebel strongholds in the Midlands. On 13 October he captured and burned the castle of Ranulf de Broc at Haughley.[83] Following this success the earl pushed on into the line of royal castles.[84] It seems likely that the rebels marched westward, intending to strike the Icknield Way just west of St. Edmundsbury. Continuing south on this road, they would then have taken the old *via Devana* at Babraham and proceeded to Leicester by way of Cambridge and Godmanchester.[85] The size of the rebel army is unknown. The more than 10,000 given by the *Gesta Regis* is clearly an impossible figure; and although the 3,000 "Flandrenses" mentioned by Ralph Diceto and the Continuator of Florence of Worcester come within the realm of possibility, the number still seems too large. What is fairly certain is that the bulk of Earl Robert's army consisted of infantry.[86]

In the meantime, apprised of the earl of Leicester's landing, de Lucy patched up a hasty truce with the Scots that was to last until 13 January 1174, and hurried south.[87] The royalist forces concentrated at St. Edmundsbury under the command of the justiciar and the constable, Humphrey de Bohun. The troops at their disposal seem to have been three hundred of the king's stipendiary horse, plus the contingents brought in by Earls Reginald of

Cornwall, William of Gloucester, and William of Arundel.[88] In addition, the justiciar and de Bohun were joined by many peasants from the surrounding countryside, armed mostly with pitchforks and flails.[89] The odds, then, do not seem to have been nearly as great as Oman insists they were, and although Arnold may have exaggerated in the other direction, it is possible that de Bohun's army was larger than that of Earl Robert.[90]

The earl, apparently well aware of the royalist concentration at St. Edmund's, swung north of the town instead of attempting to take the most direct route. On 17 October the Flemings were marching past the town in what would seem to be route order, and with what looks like an incredible want of caution. They were singing what is said to be the oldest recorded Flemish verse:

Hoppe, hoppe, Wilekin, hoppe, Wilekin
Engelond is min ant tin.[91]

In the vicinity of the church of Fornham St. Genevieve, within four miles of the north gate of the town, they were suddenly attacked by the constable's army, which had marched out under the banner of St. Edmund.[92] The precise location of the ensuing fight is unknown. Whether Leicester had forded the Lark is a matter of speculation, though there is good reason to believe that he may have been in the process of crossing when the attack took place. Arnold noted that "in the meadows near the Lark, in the Fornham parishes, the bones of men, bearing more or fewer marks of violence, have often been dug up." [93] Since Fornham St. Genevieve and Fornham St. Martin are on the east bank of the Lark, whereas Fornham All Saints is on the west bank, it is entirely possible that the opening of the battle found Earl Robert caught with part of his men on each side of the river. It is also known that the ground in the vicinity was marshy—which certainly had a bearing on the results of the fight. It may be conjectured, then, that the rebel earl was surprised with his forces divided by the river; and that his outnumbered mounted contingent was ridden down by the first charge of the constable's feudal and stipendiary horse. The Flemish infantry, unable to form up to receive a cavalry charge, fled panic-stricken into the marshy meadows of the Lark, where they were an easy prey to the flails and pitchforks of the peasants. The chroniclers are in general agreement that the engagement was short, and that Earl Robert, his wife Petronilla, and most of the Norman and French knights were taken captive. There is equal agreement that only a few of the Flemings were so fortunate—most of them perished, many by drowning.[94] Some clue as to the casualties among the rebel army may be found in a late fourteenth-century manuscript, which states that a thousand soldiers perished outside the gates of St. Edmund's within the space of an hour.[95] The victorious royalists, heartened by this almost total success, proceeded to increase the pressure on Earl Hugh by strengthening the garrisons at St. Edmund's, Colchester, and Ipswich. The earl, impressed with the strength of the royalists, negotiated a truce to last until the following Easter, and agreed to dismiss the Flemish mercenaries in his service. This ended hostilities for the year.[96]

Since the end of the fiscal year 1172/1173 coincided so nearly with the temporary halt in military operations, the amount spent by the king in the prosecution of the war can be estimated with some accuracy. Forty-seven castles are mentioned in the Pipe Roll for the year that ended at Michaelmas (29 September) 1173. Twenty-three of these had been garrisoned by the king at a total cost of £913 14s.5d.[97] At current pay scales, this represented a considerable body of men. The 330 sergeants from Shropshire who served for eight days in the army at Leicester received in wages a total of £9 13s.8d.; ten archers in the castle of Roger de Powis were paid 11s.8d. for fifteen days' service, roughly a penny a day. Knights, though more expensive, received at most only a shilling per day.[98] Twenty-five castles were provisioned by the central authority.[99] A "seam" of wheat (6/8 bushels) then cost slightly less than 3d., beans were 2 1/2d. per "seam," and a salt hog was not much over 2s., so that the £909 12s.7d. that was the total cost of provisioning the royal castles took care of a sizable consumption by their garrisons. London, Dover, and Berkhamstead, from the amount and variety of their stores, appear to have been general depots for distribution to outlying strongholds.[100]

Besides the expense of provisioning and paying the soldiers in garrison, a large amount of work apparently had to be done before many of the castles could be considered fit to stand a siege. At London repairs to the Tower cost £60; a bailey was made around the keep at Colchester; the well at Southampton and the wall at Winchester stood in need of repair.[101] Moreover, the normal building program seems scarcely to have been disturbed, although much of the money for this purpose may have been spent before the actual outbreak of hostilities in the spring of 1173. Expenses for the year of more than £100 are recorded for each of seven castles.[102] The total amount spent for work on thirty-six castles came to £2,031 16s.5d., bringing the outlay for the defensive system to £3,855 3s.5d. The cost of the abortive siege of Leicester in July came to £144 18s.11d.; that of such miscellaneous items as the maintenance of troops on the Welsh border had been £53 2s.1d.; and the military budget for the year reached the unprecedented total of £4,053 4s.5d. The king's normal yearly income before the rebellion has been estimated at less than £21,000; thus more than 20 per cent of his revenues were devoted to the prosecution of the war.[103]

After the fight at Fornham in October 1173, hostilities remained suspended until after Easter (24 March) of the following year. Then, at the end of March, King William of Scots again crossed the frontier, at the head of an army bolstered with mercenaries from Flanders.[104] Nicholas de Stuteville's border castle of Liddell was quickly captured, leaving the road open to Carlisle. When King William summoned the castle of Carlisle to surrender, William de Vaux, the king's castellan, answered that he would hand over the fortress only if assistance were not forthcoming by Michaelmas.[105] The tactical disposition of the Scottish army for the next several weeks is not clear. The only satisfactory way to account for the events that followed is to assume that the Scots were operating in two columns, one in Cumberland and Westmoreland, the other in Northumberland.[106] Following the agreement with de Vaux at Carlisle, the army under the command of King William moved up the valley of the Eden in the direction of Yorkshire. Gospatric fitz Orm, the castellan at Appleby, surrendered at the first summons, but Brough was taken only after its garrison had offered a desperate resistance.[107]

Meanwhile, the elements of the Scottish army operating in

Northumberland had been equally successful. Wark was besieged after an assault had been repulsed by the garrison, but the situation appeared serious enough for the castellan, Roger d'Estuteville, to arrange for a truce of forty days so that he could await instructions from King Henry in Normandy.[108] At about this time Bishop Hugh of Durham concluded an agreement with the Scots which gave them control of his castles of Norham and Durham.[109] From Wark the invaders pushed south, capturing both Harbottle and Warkworth.[110] From this time onward, the Scottish army seems once again to have been operating as a unit. King William soon appeared on the Tyne, and laid siege to the important castle of Prudhoe. The importance of successfully defending the line of the Tyne was fully recognized by the northern barons. Now that the bishop of Durham was collaborating with the Scots, the fall of the river line would have opened the way to an invasion of Yorkshire. An army was hastily mobilized at York and was soon marching north. The commander of the Yorkshire host, as for the Standard campaign thirty-six years earlier, is unknown; but the leading participants were Robert de Stuteville and his son William; William de Vesci; Ranulf Glanville; Ranulf de Tilli, constable of the archbishop of York; Bernard de Balliol; and Odinel de Dumfraville. King William, upon learning of the advance of a relieving army, raised the siege of Prudhoe, but withdrew only as far as Alnwick, some thirty miles to the north, where he sat down to the investment of that stronghold.[111]

For the royalists, the seriousness of the situation in the north was obvious. Seven castles had been captured by the Scots; two others were under obligation to surrender unless relieved by a specific time; a tenth was besieged; and one of the most powerful of the northern magnates, Bishop Hugh of Durham, was conniving with the enemy. In western Yorkshire and northern Lincolnshire, on the other hand, the royalist cause seemed more prosperous. The energetic action of the king's illegitimate son Geoffrey, bishop-elect of Lincoln, had resulted in the capture and destruction of Roger de Mowbray's castle at Kinnardferry, thus opening the road between Lincoln and York. Geoffrey then refortified the old motte at Topcliffe in Yorkshire, and captured another of the Mowbray castles at Malzeard.[112] From Topcliffe, the elect of

Lincoln's castellan, William d'Estuteville, was in a position to threaten Roger's remaining castle at Thirsk, as well as the bishop of Durham's reconditioned motte-and-bailey at Northallerton.[113]

The Pipe Roll for 1173/1174 shows the widening scope of the crown's military activities. The castles of Lincoln, Guildford, Malmesbury, Chichester, and Porchester appear for the first time. To Porchester the earl and countess of Leicester were carried for safekeeping after their capture at Fornham.[114] But despite the number of castles in the hands of the king's lieutenants, and the successes of the previous year's campaign, when hostilities were resumed in the Midlands in the spring of 1174, the initiative was seized by the insurgents. It was essential for them to break out of the cordon of royal fortresses that had been drawn around them. In the absence of its captive earl, the castle of Leicester was committed to his constable, Ansket Mallory. At some time after 19 May he attacked the town of Northampton and defeated the burgher militia, though he seems to have made no attempt on the castle. During the same month, Earl William of Derby made an attack on Nottingham in which the town was burned, but he too seems to have kept clear of the castle.[115] On 15 May a body of Flemish mercenaries landed at Orewell in Suffolk and marched inland to join Earl Hugh at Framlingham. A month later—on 18 June—they attacked and burned Norwich, apparently avoiding any action against the castle. Some time later, Earl Hugh's assault on Dunwich was repulsed.[116] The results of these operations were completely negative. The rebels in the Midlands had failed to break out of the encircling network of castles, and Earl Hugh had likewise failed again to establish himself on the coast. The insurgents simply did not have the military resources to operate in the open field or to conduct formal siege operations against the king's castles. Hit-and-run raids, though a nuisance, could not affect the outcome of the struggle. Once outside the walls of their own strongholds, the rebels were vulnerable to attack by the superior forces of the royal lieutenants. And as long as the royalists could maintain a stranglehold on every possible egress, the position of the rebels in the Midlands was hopeless. Only in the north, where King William of Scotland continued to besiege Alnwick, did the situation still threaten, but even there it was by no means desperate. Despite the success of King William's campaign, his army before Alnwick was less than thirty miles south of the border, and seven castles remained untaken in his rear. The garrisons of these castles were no real threat to the Scots so long as their army remained intact; but an English army was known to be advancing from the south, and in the event of defeat King William's retreating forces might have difficulty in regaining Scotland.

On 24 June the king's forces went over to the offensive. Richard de Lucy appeared before Huntingdon and immediately began the siege of the castle. Lines were drawn; a siege castle was built opposite the principal gate of the fortress, so that the operation could be maintained with a minimum of troops, and Earl Simon of Northampton was placed in command of the investment.[117] On 8 July King Henry landed at Southampton; on the 12th he performed public penance at the tomb of St. Thomas Becket at Canterbury; by nightfall of the following day he was in London.[118] The king was still in London five days later when he received word that on the 13th King William of Scotland had been captured beneath the walls of Alnwick.[119] The army from York had reached Newcastle-upon-Tyne, presumably during the second week in July. On the night of the 12th it had moved out, and the mounted element, by dint of a forced march, had reached the vicinity of Alnwick by daylight on the 13th. King William, making an early morning reconnaissance of his siege lines, mistook the advancing English column for his own troops and was captured before assistance could arrive.[120]

Now that his most dangerous enemy was removed from the field, Henry was able to proceed at once with liquidating the revolt in the Midlands and in East Anglia. The king was in the camp before Huntingdon when the castle surrendered on 21 July.[121] He advanced immediately against the strongholds of Earl Hugh, and encamped at Seleham, not far from the earl's castle at Framlingham. The king's intention to lay siege to the castle was obvious, since five hundred carpenters were summoned to Seleham for the king's service.[122] The elaborate preparation proved to have been unnecessary, for on 25 July the earl came out and surrendered the castles of Framlingham and Bungay to the king [123]

—an event that signaled the general collapse of the rebellion. King Henry returned to Northampton to negotiate for the transfer of the castles that still remained in rebel hands. On 26 July he conferred with the captive king of Scotland and with Bishop Hugh of Durham. The Scottish monarch was compelled to relinquish his conquests in the north and to pledge a number of his own castles as part of the price of his release; and the bishop of Durham was required to place the castles of Norham, Durham, and Northallerton in the king's hands unconditionally.[124] On 31 July the remainder of the rebels made their submission to the king. Earl William of Derby surrendered his castles of Duffield and Tutbury, the latter then being under siege by Rhys ap Gruffydd.[125] Thirsk was given up by Roger de Mowbray, and Ansket Mallory, the earl of Leicester's constable, turned over his lord's castles of Leicester, Groby, and Mountsorrel to the king.[126] The rebellion had been so thoroughly crushed that Henry was able to return to Normandy on 8 August, exactly a month after he had landed in England.[127]

The total outlay for military purposes during the year 1173/1174 was about £800 less than it had been the year before, but it still amounted to the not inconsiderable sum of £3,213 9s.6d. Moreover, the distribution of this amount shows a decided shift in emphasis. In 1172/1173, almost half the total expenditures were for the building and repair of castles under the king's control. In the succeeding year, two-thirds of the military budget was devoted to the maintenance of garrisons—a charge that amounted to £2,006 7s.3d. The cost of provisioning had dropped to £455 13s.3d., and the total appropriated for building purposes was only £674 16s.10d. Windsor was the sole castle on which more than £100 was spent.[128] Two of the surrendered castles—Leicester and Mountsorrel—had been garrisoned with the king's own men before the exchequer year ended.[129]

The surrender of the rebel leaders in July 1174 brought actual military operations to an end. The revolt had been put down chiefly because the king's armed forces—consisting principally of the stipendiary royal garrisons and the troops of the loyal barons —had control of the lines of communication, which permitted them to strangle the enemy. In the years immediately following this victory, King Henry used two methods of ensuring his military supremacy. He continued his building program, specifically on the keep at Newcastle-upon-Tyne, at Peak, and at Windsor.[130] By now the king was powerful enough to force the barons to admit his castellans into their fortresses. "This same year [1176] Henry, the father, king of England took into his own hand all the castles of England, whether episcopal, or baronial, or comital, and put his own custodians in them."[131] The earl of Gloucester was forced to give up his strategically placed castle at Bristol; Durham was given into the custody of the faithful Roger de Conyers; and even the king's own justiciar, Richard de Lucy, was compelled to surrender his castle of Ongar.[132] The strongholds that did not fit into the king's defensive scheme were to be ruthlessly dismantled, and the itinerant justices were charged, under Clause 8 of the Assize of Northampton, with seeing to it that these were thoroughly demolished.[133] If not, they were to be hailed before the *curia regis* on charges of contempt. The same justices were also to make inquiry into "the custody of castles, as to who owes service for them, and how much, and where. . . ."[134] The real measure of the military strength achieved by King Henry is not to be found in the record of the campaign; Stephen had often displayed equal ability. Rather, it is implicit in such routine entries of the Pipe Rolls as this: "In pay to Alnoth the engineer and carpenters and masons for destroying [*prosternendo*] the castle of Framlingham, £13 15s.11d.;[135] and for filling in the ditch, 36s.1d." "For hooks to pull down the palisades at Huntingdon, 7s.8d."[136]

Henry II had ascended an undisputed throne to rule a baronage which was evidently tired of civil disorder. Only in that traditional seat of rebellion, the Severn valley, was there any inclination to resist. Moreover, the revival of trade and commerce was gradually increasing the money revenue of the crown. The king could now embark upon a policy of military centralization; he could build castles and pay garrisons.[137] No longer would he be forced to rely heavily on the uncertain device of castle-guard to provide for the defense of the royal fortresses. This development certainly could not have taken place unobserved by the great tenants, who saw the new royal castles rising every year in every

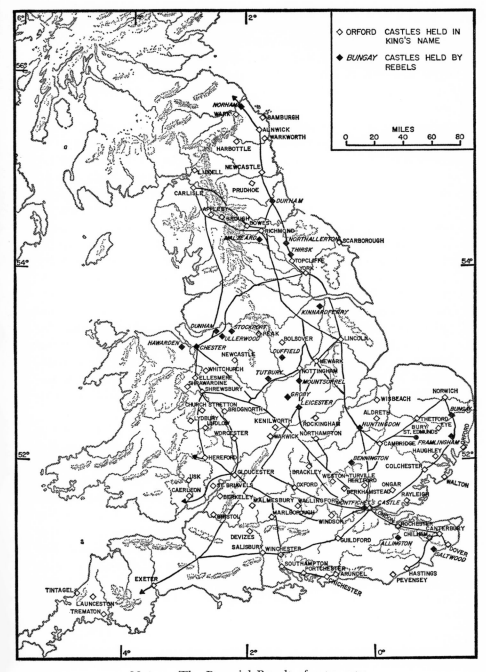

ORFORD   CASTLES HELD IN
    KING'S NAME

BUNGAY   CASTLES HELD BY
    REBELS

Map 10. The Baronial Revolt of 1173–1174

corner of the land. No one of the tenants could hope to outdo the king in this. They might improve their old strongholds; but during the entire reign of Henry II, so far as is known, only a single baronial castle was built on a new site.[138] Year by year, the military position of the crown became stronger in relation to that of the barons. Even when the rebellion of 1173–1174 broke out, it is true, the king's position was by no means secure; he required the aid of the loyal barons to suppress the revolt. But that revolt was the end of castle warfare—the last civil war fought on the old defensive principles. The royal fortresses, those of the king's supporters, and the reconditioned mottes of an earlier day, drew a ring around the castles of the rebels, cutting them off from communication with each other and with their supporters in France and Scotland. At the same time, the king's lieutenants were able to draw supplies of men and material from all parts of the kingdom. It was the old pattern, but with a difference. The large stipendiary garrisons who over long periods of time held the principal castles, both of the king and of his tenants, and who were paid by representatives of the crown, were an innovation. There was even the suggestion of warfare in the open field, unconnected with the siege of any castle. In East Anglia, Humphrey de Bohun concentrated his army not behind walls but in St. Edmundsbury, where there had never been a castle.

Thus the triumph of King Henry II over baronial factionalism marked not only the military supremacy of the crown but also the end of a phase in the military development of the English people. To preserve the integrity of the realm, the king was no longer dependent entirely upon knight service, baronial levies, or even the English militia. The paid garrisons in the castles, or the stipendiary knights who fought under the constable's banner at Fornham, could in no sense be called a national army; but they were clearly nonfeudal. A century was to elapse before an English king would rely almost entirely on stipendiary troops to fight his wars; yet the beginning of the system is to be found in the policy of the second Henry.[139] On the other hand, it would have been impossible for the king to subdue the rebellion without the support of a majority of the feudal magnates, especially those of the Midland counties. Thus the military history of the reign presents an admixture of custom and innovation characteristic of periods of transition. One thing, however, should be noted. When the barons next appeared in arms against the king, neither they nor the able John showed any inclination to shut up their major forces in castles. Although fortifications continued to play an important part in English civil commotions, the military decisions turned not on the number and location of the castles held by the contending parties but on the strength of their field armies.[140] The results of Henry's policy were seen in the filled-up ditch at Framlingham, and in an Angevin sheriff's accounting to the Exchequer for the proceeds of the sale of materials from the castle at Walton. "By the end of the century, except along the Welsh and Scotch borders, national defense had come to turn essentially on the king's own castles, and the mercenary soldiers in his service. The baronial castle had become an anachronism." [141]

The remaining years of the reign saw a continuation of these centralizing tendencies. When the lands of the rebels were returned, the castles were frequently excepted. Typical is the procedure by which the lands of the earl of Leicester were restored in 1177: ". . . But the king kept in his own hands the castle of Mountsorrel and the castle of Pascy, which alone remained standing of all his castles." Later in the same year, it is recorded that the Council of Winchester deemed it best for the king to retain control of the bishop of Durham's castles at Durham and Norham. Castellans were changed frequently, and they were drawn to a large degree from knights of the royal household whose loyalty was above suspicion.[142]

But the resources of the crown are most dramatically evident in the monetary outlay, year by year, for the military establishment. The extent of the building activity for the reign, as shown by Brown, is truly impressive, although taken alone the sums are somewhat misleading.[143] Of the £10,188 7s.8d. spent on castle-building between 1177 and 1189, at least £1,370 5s.1d. was for such facilities as halls, jails, chapels, dwellings, and gardens, which had no direct military function.[144] On the other hand, although construction was the main item in the military budget, considerable sums were spent on wages to garrisons and to custodial personnel for castles that were obviously maintained on a standby basis. Expense of this nature ranged from a low of £74 15s.6d. in 1178/1179 to £429 5s.11 1/2d. in 1184/1185. All told, during the final twelve years of Henry's reign £3,010 6s.2d. went for these purposes. An additional £236 11s.9 1/2d. must be listed under the heading of "provisions and supplies," so that the total nonconstructional military outlay for the period from 1177 to 1189 comes to £3,246 17s.11 1/2d. This gives a total figure of £13,435 1s.1 1/2d. for all military expenses, or an average of approximately £1,117 per year. Construction accounted for 76 per cent of this figure, and 24 per cent was devoted to other military purposes.[145] Thus it can be seen that a substantial part of the military budget was devoted to noncapital expenditures.

During this period, eighty-four castles are listed in the Pipe Rolls for one reason or another. As might be expected, both the number of castles mentioned and the amounts spent on them declined significantly after the suppression of the revolt. The lowest figure is for 1178/1179, when less than £500 was spent for all purposes on twenty-five castles; the highest "peacetime" expenditure was in 1184/1185, when the total came to just under £1,850. The geographical distribution of the fortresses in which the crown had an interest was as wide as the kingdom itself, but the castles on which substantial amounts were spent were, of course, less numerous than the total number recorded. The total number of castles mentioned over the twelve-year span varies from twenty-four in 1177/1178 to fifty-five in 1187/1188.[146]

Troubles in Wales during the latter years of the reign were largely responsible for this increased attention to the kingdom's fortifications. Of the fifty-five castles cited, a score were on the Welsh frontier or immediately behind it.[147] In addition, eighteen border and staging castles are mentioned in the Pipe Roll of the previous year.[148] Heretofore, trouble on the marches of Wales had called for an occasional punitive expedition commanded by the king in person—which generally had little effect.[149] Now, however, the government saw to it that border castles were repaired, garrisoned, and provisioned during periods of unrest. Thus Stenton's suggestion that the baronial castle had become obsolete everywhere except on the Welsh and Scottish borders calls for modification.[150] Even on the marches, the crown took a hand in the defense of the realm. The king's concern with maintaining that defense was becoming paramount as the twelfth century neared its close.

The last years of Henry's reign were notable also for advances in the art of fortification. Of especial interest is the vast rebuilding of Dover castle between 1180 and 1188,[151] when more than £5,900—an unprecedented sum—was expended on this single fortress.[152] This was probably the strongest castle in England at the time; Brown has stated well its importance in defending what he calls the southeastern coastal "frontier." Large sums were spent on other castles in this area exposed to invasion from the Continent, which at once provided staging areas for overseas expeditions and protected vital lines of communications to the Angevin possessions in France.[153]

Since southeastern England was strategically the most sensitive area in the kingdom, it is not surprising that during the reign of Henry II more than £7,600 were spent on the castles of the district. It might be suggested that the entire southern coastal region constituted a military frontier. As the landings of Duke Robert at Portsmouth in 1101, and of Earl Robert of Gloucester at Wareham in 1142, had both demonstrated, the danger of hostile invasion was not confined to the coasts of Kent and Sussex alone. That Henry realized this seems quite evident from the Pipe Roll statistics. Of thirty-one castles on which more than £100 was spent during the reign, eleven were south of the Thames. Of the nearly £21,500 spent on construction, more than half—£11,157 14s.9 1/2d.—was spent on castles in this area.[154]

It might be observed here that Brown's division of England into four regions is somewhat arbitrary, and that he is not very accurate in saying that "the major part of the overall expenditure remains devoted to the castles of the interior." More than half the total expenditure was devoted to the "frontier" areas as he defined them. Statistics from the Pipe Rolls could be used to prove all sorts of things, of which the most significant for a military study is not the extent of royal castle-building. The large sums spent annually on building and maintenance reveal the importance attached to military preparedness by the king and his officials, as well as the growing centralization of military power, and the

wealth that could be invested in stone and mortar without
stinting other activities of the government.[155] Again it should be
emphasized that the king's interest in fortification was wider than
the building statistics would indicate. Brown noted ninety castles
on which money was spent for construction; but in the Pipe Rolls
the names of nearly 140 fortresses are mentioned for one or
another reason.[156] This must represent a very considerable fraction of the castles then in commission, so to speak. It would be
difficult to quarrel with Brown's conclusion:

Angevin castle-building in England during the period, seen against the
disorders of Stephen's reign, represents the latent military power of a
strong centralized government, no less necessary to its success than its
other aspects of economic superiority and administrative efficiency.
Committed to the keeping of trusted officials, often the centers of local
government, at all times the impressive display of royal power, and
ready in times of emergency to be rapidly stocked and garrisoned to
encourage and enforce the loyalty of surrounding districts, the royal
castles were, in the expressive phrase of a contemporary writer, "the
bones of the kingdom." [157]

The same latent military power was further demonstrated in
1181, when the Assize of Arms was issued.[158] It followed similar
legislation issued at Le Mans late in the previous year, and marks
an attempt to establish a uniform basis for military service
throughout the Angevin dominions.[159] As in the army of the early
Roman republic, the free subjects were classified according to
their ability to find the requisite military equipment.[160]

The Assize of Arms is not a long document, but it marks a
radical departure from feudal concepts of military service. Indeed,
its very character is nonfeudal. It consists of twelve paragraphs or
articles, the first three specifying the arms and armor to be
maintained by each of three classes of the free population. Every
holder of a knight's fee, and every freeman whose chattels or rents
amounted to £10 13s.4d. (16 marks) was obliged to provide
himself with a mail shirt (*lorica*), helmet (*cassis*), shield (*cly-
peus*), and lance (*lancea*). Those whose chattels or rents were
valued at £6 13s.4d. (10 marks) were required to possess a mail
shirt (*aubergel*, presumably less expensive than the *lorica*), an
iron cap, and a lance. Lesser freemen, including burgesses, were to

have a quilted doublet (*wambasia*), an iron cap, and a lance. And a provision in the final paragraph made it explicit that none but free men might be accepted for the oath of arms: "Et praecepit rex, quod nullus reciperetur ad sacramentum armorum nisi liber homo." Those who commanded feudal contingents were responsible for maintaining equipment for the knights charged to the demesne.[161] The fourth paragraph is of interest in that it not only called on individuals of all three categories of freemen to attest that they had the required arms, but also stipulated that each subject must take an oath of loyalty to the king before 13 January 1182 (the feast of St. Hilary). This article also prohibited the alienation of arms by sale, pawning, or outright gift, and forbade a lord to deprive his men of their arms in any manner whatsoever. Paragraph five directed that military equipment was to be inherited, and that if the heir were under age his guardian was to find a man to fulfill the military obligation until such time as the heir could assume it.

Item six required that no burgess was to have in his possession more arms than were permitted by regulations; any excess was to be sold or given to someone eligible for service under the terms of the assize. In the seventh article, Jews were prohibited from possessing arms. Paragraph eight and part of paragraph twelve forbade the export of arms, ships, and shipbuilding materials. Apparently some sort of export license had to be obtained before military and naval equipment could be transported from England.

The ninth, tenth, and eleventh articles concerned the machinery for enforcing the assize. The itinerant justices were to impanel juries in the hundreds and boroughs; and the juries were to declare, under oath, who in each jurisdiction fell into each of the three categories. Afterward, all free men were to be enrolled, and to take an oath that they possessed the equipment required and would loyally support the king. Those who were missed in the first enrollment were to be listed by the justices elsewhere, or at Westminster during the octave of Michaelmas (29 September–6 October). All were to be in possession of their equipment by 13 January 1182. The penalty for delinquency was imprisonment, but was not to include forfeiture of lands and chattels.[162]

That the Assize of Arms was an innovation is certain. The contention that it was meant "to recreate the ancient 'fyrd' as an efficient force supplementary to the feudal levies" is not sustained by the evidence.[163] *Fyrd* service, as Vinogradoff long ago pointed out, and as recent scholarship has confirmed, was due from the land.[164] The Assize, on the other hand, based the military obligation upon the possession of a stated amount of individual property, which might or might not be land. It was both a new system for national defense and yet another indication of the growing authority of the central administration. Military service was now defined in terms of money rather than of land, and the obligation of every free man to perform military duty was clearly stated.[165]

Whether the innovation was a success in providing an adequate military reserve is far from clear. The militia was called out to suppress the revolt led by John in 1193, but the assertion that the Assize of Arms was intended only to provide for home defense is not proved.[166] Although it seems most unlikely that a total mobilization of the arms-bearing population ever took place, the classification and enrollment of the free men provided a pool of manpower which made possible the development of a sort of draft or selective service. In 1214, for example, the sheriff of Norfolk was ordered to select a hundred men of Dunwich to guard the coast.[167] This practice, in course of time, developed into the notorious Commissions of Array. The twelfth century witnessed a steady decline in the importance of the feudal host, and a corresponding increase in the use of nonfeudal troops of various descriptions.[168] This development in turn was bound to strengthen the position of the crown in military affairs—a situation of which Henry II was not slow to take advantage. If the baronial castle had become an anachronism by the end of the century, it may also be said that the feudal array with its unpaid baronial contingents was rapidly becoming obsolescent.

Chapter 8

Warfare on the Marches of Wales, 1066–1134

THE Welsh peninsula, jutting out into the Irish Sea, has an area of just under 7,500 square miles, slightly less than that of New Jersey; its greatest length from north to south is 132 miles, and its width varies from 92 miles in the south to less than 40 miles in the center.[1] Yet it took the English more than two centuries thoroughly to subdue the "wild Welsh," for all the great disparity between England and Wales in area, population, and resources. The failure of the Normans to reduce Wales as they did England can be partially explained by their inability to mount a sustained offensive; and that inability was due in large part to the physical characteristics of the land.

The most striking feature of Welsh geography is the huge stretch of high moorland that extends from the Berwyn range in the north to the Black Mountains in the south. In the northwest, the highlands rise to the jumbled fastnesses of Snowdonia; in the southeast, the Brecon Beacons are the salient feature. The coastal plain bordering the central massif to the south is much wider than in the north—a fact of considerable importance in Welsh history. Rising close upon the narrow northern coastal strip are mountains which in medieval times were densely forested, providing the Welsh with concealment and cover on the left flank of any force advancing westward along the coast.[2] The southern coastal plain, as it broadens into the peninsulas of Gower and southern Pembrokeshire, offered a natural avenue of approach for any invading force.

From the watershed of the central highlands, rivers flow in four directions—northward into the Irish Sea, southward into the Bristol channel, westward into the Bay of Cardigan, or eastward into England. The south of Wales was all the more vulnerable to invasion, as compared with the north, because several of the southern streams were navigable for some distance inland—the Wye at least as far as Monmouth, the Monnow to Chepstow, and the Towy to Carmarthen.[3] Along the middle marches the valleys of the Severn and Wye, in particular, aided the Norman advance. The mountainous character of the country, and the extensive bodies of water that surround it on three sides, are productive of heavy rainfall. Most of the highlands receive an average of 60 inches of rain per year, but in some areas the annual rainfall may be 80, 100, and even 150 inches.[4] The rainfall is heaviest between October and December, but it is rather consistent and uniform throughout the year. Matters are all the worse because the soil is largely of heavy clay, which retains the moisture. Vast stretches of the uplands are marshy; the atmosphere is damp, and there are frequent fogs.[5]

Given these characteristics, military operations in Wales would be difficult under optimum conditions, and these seldom obtain. Further obstacles to the Norman conquest of Wales were the lack of roads and the primitive Welsh economy, which scarcely permitted an invader to live off the country. Even during the Roman occupation, Wales was not adequately served by roads, although the extent of the Roman system there is as yet imperfectly known.[6] At any rate, the principal towns of the march—Chester, Shrewsbury, Hereford, and Monmouth—were linked to England and to each other by roads which had survived from Roman times.[7] To the west of these advanced posts, roads into Wales were few. From Chester a Roman road, following the ridge lines over high ground, ran westward to Carnarvon, but it seems fairly certain that the Norman invaders took a route nearer to the coastline.[8] Farther south, another route into Wales is said to have followed the course of a Roman road from Oswestry across the Berwyn range to the valley of the Dee, and thence by way of the valleys of Afon Tryweryn and Afon Prysor to Mur Castell in the vicinity of Trwsfynydd. The latter part is certainly Roman, but there is doubt about the section from Oswestry to the Dee valley.[9] That

South Wales was much better supplied with roads than the north, once again contributed to the earlier conquest of the south. From Hereford a road ran generally westward through Hay, Brecon, Trecastle, Llangadock, Llanderisant, and Llywel to Carmarthen. This was certainly Roman, but its continuation to Haverfordwest and St. David's may have been a later addition.[10] The southern coastal road from the Severn estuary ran through Caerleon, Cardiff, and Neath to Carmarthen, where it linked up with the Hereford route.[11] At the end of the twelfth century Archbishop Baldwin of Canterbury was able to make a complete circuit of Wales, indicating, perhaps, that much of the Roman system around the perimeter of the country was still passable.[12]

All these factors bore upon the economy of the country. Wales in the Middle Ages was a thinly populated land whose people were largely pastoral. The population as late as Tudor times has been estimated at less than 500,000.[13] A particularly vivid account of the Welsh economy in the twelfth century is given by Giraldus Cambrensis:

. . . They neither inhabit towns, villages, nor castles, but lead a solitary life in the woods, on the borders of which they do not erect sumptuous palaces, nor lofty stone buildings, but content themselves with small huts made of the boughs of trees twisted together, constructed with little labor and expense, and sufficient to endure throughout the year. They have neither orchards nor gardens . . . The greater part of their land is laid down to pasturage; little is cultivated, a very small quantity is ornamented with flowers, and a still smaller is sown.[14]

Giraldus also noted that almost all the Welsh lived on the produce of their herds; that milk, cheese, and butter were notable in their diet, and that meat rather than bread was the staple food. He added that the Welsh had no interest in commerce, shipping, or the production of goods.[15] This primitive economy was one reason the Welsh were able to maintain their independence for so long against the pressure of the relatively affluent Anglo-Normans. The conventional eleventh- or twelfth-century army could not maintain itself in "wild Wales"; when the food and forage carried in the supply train was exhausted, the only alternative to retreat was starvation, for the road system, as well as the military system, precluded the regular forwarding of supplies from an established base. Furthermore, the pastoral economy rendered the population extremely mobile. For a people with few material possessions, it was a simple matter, when invasion threatened, to round up flocks and herds and retreat into the safety of the mountain fastnesses. Their rude huts could easily be rebuilt whenever they were destroyed by the invader, for as a rule the territory that was abandoned could be reoccupied as soon as the enemy, plagued by bad weather, impassable terrain, and the harassing tactics of the natives, had retired across the border.[16]

In general, the strategy of the Welsh consisted of letting geography and the elements do their work for them, and was usually restricted to the simple expedient of moving virtually the whole people with its livestock into the remotest mountain fastnesses, there to remain until the military threat had passed.[17] The terrain and the weather combined usually forced the invader to retrace his steps, and as Morris noted, kings frequently led punitive expeditions right up to Snowdon without accomplishing anything of note.[18] Moreover, there was always a remoter refuge, far beyond the reach of any king of England before the time of Henry II: a chieftain, driven from his mountain citadel, could find refuge in Ireland, there to await a favorable time for his return, often with Irish or Danish mercenaries, to mend his fallen fortunes. Thus Wales was an extremely difficult land to conquer.[19]

The character of the terrain, and the primitive organization of Welsh society, made guerrilla-type operations the natural tactical expedient in combat. Although when they fought among themselves the Welsh frequently engaged in pitched battles, it became almost a national policy to avoid combat in the open with the better organized, far more heavily armed Anglo-Normans. Only when the odds seemed overwhelmingly in their favor did the Welsh accept the gage of battle. To conquer Wales required more than an occasional punitive expedition into the heart of the country, where it could accomplish little beyond "displaying the flag." [20] On the other hand, the same mountain barriers that made the conquest of Wales so difficult were also obstacles to unity.

Only occasionally were the princes of north, center, and south to be found fighting for a single cause under common leadership. Mutual suspicion and distrust among the numerous princely families facilitated the subjugation of Wales, particularly in the south, and tended to some extent to offset the difficulties imposed by climate and the terrain.[21]

The chief authority on Welsh fighting methods, is the twelfth-century observer Giraldus Cambrensis. His *Itinerarium Kambriae* and *Descriptio Kambriae* suggest that Giraldus was somewhat miscast as a cleric, and might well have been more successful as a general than as a churchman. "He had . . . a clear insight into the military needs of the time," and he laid down the basic lines of strategy which Edward I was to follow a century later in the conquest of Wales.[22]

Giraldus noted that the Welshman was "light and active, hardy rather than strong," and that military service was universal. "When the trumpet sounds the alarm, the husbandman rushes as eagerly from the plow as the courtier from his court." [23] According to Giraldus, the armor of the Welsh was light, so that mobility would not be impaired. It consisted of a helmet, a mail shirt, a shield, and occasionally greaves. By the end of the twelfth century the upper classes had learned to fight on horseback in the Norman style; but even then, wherever the situation warranted, they dismounted and fought on foot with the general levy. The offensive armament consisted of either bows or spears, depending on the locality. In the northern principality of Gwynedd, the main weapon was the long lance; in the south, particularly in Gwent, the bow prevailed.[24]

In combat, the Welsh relied on a single charge accompanied by wild shouts and the noise of trumpets, calculated to demoralize the enemy. When the charge was repulsed, they melted away into the forest without attempting to rally. However, if pursuit was attempted, the pursuers were likely to find themselves ambushed; and though unsuccessful in the open field, the Welsh did not readily admit defeat, but continued to harass the enemy through ambuscades and night attacks. As Giraldus put it, the Welsh were as easy to defeat in a single battle as they were difficult to overcome in a protracted campaign.[25] The obstacles to a conquest of Wales—and the process had been going on for more than a century by the time of Giraldus—led him to formulate a basic strategy for the subjugation of the land:

The prince who would wish to subdue this nation, and govern it peaceably, must use this method. He must be determined to apply a diligent and constant attention to this purpose for a year at least; for a people who with a collected force will not openly attack the enemy, nor wait to be besieged in castles, is not to be overcome at the first onset, but to be worn down by prudent delay and patience. Let him divide their strength, and by bribes and promises endeavor to stir up one against the other, knowing the spirit of hatred and envy which generally prevails among them; and in the autumn let not only the marches, but also the interior part of the country be strongly fortified with castles, provisions, and trusted families.[26]

Further, he advocated the establishment of an embargo on all supplies of food and cloth, to be enforced by a naval blockade which would prevent the importation of supplies from Ireland. Then, toward the end of winter, when the Welsh were weakened by lack of sufficient food, when the trees and undergrowth were leafless, which would reduce the chances of falling into ambush,

. . . let a body of light-armed infantry penetrate into their woods and mountainous retreats, and let these troops be supported and relieved by others; and thus by frequent changes, and replacing the men who are either fatigued or slain in battle, this nation may be ultimately subdued. Nor can it be overcome without the above precautions, nor without great danger and loss of men. Though many of the English hired troops may perish in a day of battle, money will procure as many more on the morrow for the same service; but to the Welsh, who have neither foreign nor stipendiary troops, the loss is for the time irreparable.[27]

Giraldus then emphasized the necessity of adopting the methods of the enemy to combat him successfully. The advice of the marchers, who were long accustomed to fighting the Welsh, should be listened to and followed. The heavily armored knight, accustomed to fighting in the open countryside of England or the Continent, was out of his element in the broken, forested terrain of Wales. He also urged the establishment of a military frontier district along the entire Welsh border from Chester southward to the Bristol channel, in which the entire population would be trained in the use of arms. Depots of arms and provisions should be established and inspected annually. Such a district, Giraldus continued, would not only preserve the peace of the march, but could provide the king with military resources for use elsewhere, should the need arise.[28]

Giraldus's recommendations were not adopted in his time; nearly a century passed before they were implemented by Edward I. But it is of interest to note that the militant Welshman anticipated by more than three hundred years the policy followed by the Habsburgs in establishing the military border in Croatia along similar lines.[29] The conquest of Wales, then, was to be achieved through unrelenting pressure exerted year in and year out. The extent to which this policy was followed was to measure the success of the Anglo-Norman invaders throughout the eleventh and twelfth centuries.

The Welsh had had some acquaintance with the Normans at least a decade and a half before the Norman Conquest of England. Possibly as early as 1048, a castle had been built in Herefordshire; and it is not unlikely that by 1051 three such strongholds were in existence—at Hereford, at Ewias Harold, and in the vicinity of Ludlow.[30] By 1052 there was a Norman earl in Herefordshire—Ralf, King Edward's nephew, who was the son of the count of the Vexin, and who is presumed to have built the castle at Hereford. By that same year Richard fitz Scrob had erected the stronghold near Ludlow, and Ewias Harold had probably been constructed by Osbern Pentecost.[31]

The Welsh soon learned that the Normans were more to be feared than the English had been for many years. Early in the summer of 1052, Gruffydd ap Llywelyn, the prince of Deheubarth, crossed the border into Herefordshire, plundering as he went. He had almost reached Leominster when his advance was barred by a hastily raised force of Englishmen and Normans. In the ensuing battle the Welsh were completely victorious; they inflicted many casualties on the Norman-English forces, and Gruffydd's army returned home laden with booty.[32] Three years later an even more humiliating defeat was inflicted on the inhabitants of the march. Early in the autumn of 1055, an army composed of Irish mercenaries and English malcontents, as well as Welshmen, again invaded Herefordshire under the command of Gruffydd. Earl Ralf mustered his forces at Hereford; and in an attempt to secure some sort of homogeneity among his mixed force of Normans and English, he ordered the latter, "contrary to their custom, to fight on horseback." [33] At the near approach of Gruffydd and his motley host, Earl Ralf marched out of Hereford and on 24 October intercepted the Welsh line of march some two miles from the town. Of what happened next, the chroniclers offer two versions. The English chronicler had it that "before there was any spear thrown the Englishmen fled because they were on horses"; whereas Florence of Worcester asserted that Earl Ralf and his French and Norman followers were the first to flee. The results, however, are not a matter of dispute. The Anglo-Norman army was easily defeated, and some hundreds of the fugitives were cut down. The Welsh and their allies then seized Hereford, carried the castle by storm, thoroughly looted the town, including ecclesiastical establishments, then put it to the torch, and took many of the inhabitants captive.[34] This crushing defeat brought Earl Harold Godwineson into the field. Concentrating at Gloucester, he marched into Wales, but accomplished little beyond strengthening the defenses of Hereford, which he surrounded with a "wide and deep ditch," and fortified with gates and bars. Finally a truce was concluded between Gruffydd and Harold at Billingsley.[35] Nothing more is heard of the Normans on the march until after the Conquest, and the ease with which they had been twice defeated may have led the Welsh to underestimate the fighting capabilities of the Norman adventurers.

But, as Lloyd notes, "the conquest of England by Duke William of Normandy meant far more for the Welsh than the substitution of a strong for a weak king of England . . ." [36] Instead of facing a people who were largely content to maintain the status quo along the border, the Welsh now had to contend with the foremost colonizers of the day—a pushing, grasping set of pioneers for whom the rigors of frontier warfare had no terrors. Until about 1100 the struggle was confused, and the tide line of battle, ebbing back and forth along the march, is very difficult to trace. But in time a rough balance was struck between the contending parties, and a clearer picture emerges as warfare between Norman and Welshman took on a more formal character: the Welsh began to adopt some Norman military techniques, and the Normans became more adept at irregular tactics.

The Welsh princes apparently were aware almost at once of the danger posed by the Norman Conquest. In August 1067, Bleddyn of Gwynedd and Rhiwallon of Powys cooperated with the Mercian rebel Eadric the Wild in operations "against the castle men at Hereford," which caused considerable damage.[37] At first the new Norman earl of Hereford, William fitz Osbern, one of the Conqueror's ablest lieutenants, was unable to make any headway against the combination. In the following year, the threat appeared still greater when Earl Edwin of Mercia joined the rebel alliance—although, as it turned out, the earl was not the man to provide resolute leadership, and he caved in almost at once.[38] But Eadric and his Welsh allies continued the struggle, and in 1069 a concentric attack was launched on Shrewsbury from the north, south, and west. The town itself was captured, and the royal garrison was besieged in the castle. When King William sent a relieving column to the aid of the garrison, the Welsh and English burned the town and retired westward. But the situation on the Welsh border remained critical until after a midwinter march from York at the beginning of 1070, when King William put down a hostile concentration in Cheshire and built a castle at Chester, which he strongly garrisoned. A few months later Eadric realized that further resistance was useless and made his peace with the king.[39] This ended English opposition to the new order along the march, and thenceforth the Welsh had to depend solely upon their own resources to oppose the Norman advance.

In the meantime, Earl William had been active in providing for the defense of Herefordshire against Welsh incursions. His subordinates had built a line of castles at Wigmore, Clifford, Monmouth, and Chepstow, in addition to the earlier structures at Hereford and Ewias Harold. Each of these castles became the center of a Norman settlement, with houses and a church, which was frequently given to some alien monastery.[40] In addition, to encourage Norman settlement—and this was a very important factor in the Normanization of the march—burgess rights were sometimes extended to the inhabitants. Earl William granted the "customs of Breteuil" to his burgesses at Hereford, and similar chartered boroughs were established at Wigmore and Clifford. Besides protecting the earldom against Welsh raids, Earl William pursued an aggressive policy against his western neighbors. Among these were the brothers Maredudd and Rhys ab Owain of Deheubarth, and Cadwgan ap Meurig of Morgannwg. As a result, the Welsh region of Gwent fell into Norman hands, and from bases at Monmouth and Chepstow Norman influence was advanced as far as the line of the Usk. But although he advanced Norman military and political domination beyond the old frontier, Earl William was wise enough to adopt a policy of conciliation toward the natives. Many were allowed to retain possession of their lands; local officials frequently retained their offices, and Welsh chieftains were sometimes enfeoffed with English lands to give them an interest in preserving peace along the border.[41] Lloyd has remarked of William fitz Osbern that "he effected so much in four years as to show that with longer life he might have anticipated by a couple of decades the winning of South Wales." [42]

At the end of 1070 Earl William left England, never to return. In February 1071 he fell in battle in Flanders, and the earldom of Herefordshire, with the rest of his English possessions, passed to his second son, Roger. Earl Roger was ambitious, but he lacked the ability, fidelity, and courage of his father—as his performance in the baronial revolt of 1075 was to prove. The rebellion was easily suppressed; King William, who was in Normandy at the time, did not even bother to return, and actual operations were left to his lieutenants, William de Warenne and Richard de Bienfaite. Roger of Hereford submitted without a fight, all his lands were declared forfeit, and he was imprisoned for the remainder of his life.[43] The earldom remained in abeyance until the second quarter of the twelfth century, and this lack of established authority largely accounts for the Normans' failure to continue the advance that had begun in South Wales under the leadership of Earl William.[44]

Elsewhere along the march, matters fell out quite differently. To the north, the collapse of English resistance in 1070, and the installation of a Norman earl in Cheshire, constituted a direct threat to the Welsh of Gwynedd. The earldom was virtually sovereign, and Hugh of Avranches (Hugh the Fat), the second to hold the title, for all his corpulence, pursued a relentlessly aggressive policy for more than a generation. His attempts to extend Norman domination westward were ably seconded by his cousin and chief lieutenant, Robert of Rhuddlan, whose castle, built shortly before 1075 at the mouth of the Clwyd, became a base of operations first against the Welsh of Rhos and Rhufoniog, and later against those of Anglesey and Snowdonia. During one of Robert's raids against the Welsh, King Bledynn of Gwynedd narrowly escaped capture.[45]

The Norman advance along the coast was aided by the disunity among the Welsh princes. As soon as those who had held authority at the time of the Norman Conquest passed from the stage, shortly after 1070, the usual murderous warfare broke out among their would-be successors. Some of the contenders were not above seeking Norman aid in support of their claims. On the death of Bledynn of Gwynedd in 1075, Gruffydd ap Cynan returned from exile in Ireland to Anglesey and secured aid from Robert of Rhuddlan. With a small army of Welsh, supported by sixty Normans, he led a successful raid on Lleyn which made possible his seizure of Gwynedd. Gruffydd then proved his ingratitude and duplicity by launching an attack on his erstwhile ally. Later in the same year, Rhuddlan was raided by Gruffydd, but though the bailey of the castle was carried by storm, the garrison retreated to the keep, where it managed to hold out despite heavy casualties.[46] Gruffydd's rule in Gwynedd was short-lived, however; before the end of 1075 he was again an exile in Ireland, and until 1081 the chief ruler in the north was Trahaearn ap Caradog, who proved unable to hold back the Normans. Shortly after his rise to power a great raid was made on Lleyn by Earl Hugh of Chester, accompanied by Robert of Rhuddlan, Warin of Shrewsbury, and one Walter (de Lacy?), in alliance with the Welsh of Powys, who had no love for the men of Gwynedd. Crossing the mountain passes of Eryri, a formidable array of horse and foot ravaged Lleyn for a week without encountering resistance. But such plundering raids were less of a threat to Welsh independence than the steady advance of the Normans along the coast, against which the Welsh, for the time being, had no defense. Before 1085, Robert of Rhuddlan had pushed westward as far as the Conway, where he built another castle at Degannwy to serve as a base for the eventual conquest of Gwynedd. The intervening territory of Rhos and Rhufoniog was added to his domains. The Normans' success was further aided by another round of civil strife among the Welsh princes in 1081, ending with the death of Trahaearn and a second victory by Gruffydd ap Cynan. But again Gruffydd was dogged by bad luck. He was captured by a ruse at Rug in Edeyrnion with the aid of Earl Roger of Shrewsbury, and held prisoner for many years at Chester.[47] Since there could be no stability so long as the Welsh princes refused to unite against the Norman advance, by the end of the Conqueror's reign the way seemed clear for the occupation of Gwynedd.

Between Cheshire and Herefordshire lay the third of the marcher earldoms. Here, about 1071, Roger de Montgomery was created earl of Shrewsbury, and at once initiated an aggressive policy against the Welsh on his western borders. With the aid of Ralph Mortimer, whose lands in the valley of the Teme were held directly of the king, he was intervening in Welsh affairs as early as 1072. In that year Caradog ap Gruffydd of Gwynllwg secured Norman aid in his war against Maredudd ab Owain, who was slain in battle on the banks of the river Rhymni. In 1073 and again in 1074, Earl Roger and his men crossed the mountains of Arwystli to devastate the plain of Ceredigion.[48] From such bases as Oswestry and Cause, the men of Shropshire operated against the Welsh of Powys; the Chirbury district, overrun by the Welsh in the days of Edward the Confessor, was reoccupied and nailed down by the construction of Montgomery castle, named for Roger's ancestral home in Normandy. At once it became a forward base for further encroachment on Welsh territory. By 1086 Earl Roger and his men had extended Norman domination over territory hitherto exclusively Welsh to the northwest and southwest, though without progress in the center, along the upper Severn. From the Welsh of Powys they had seized the commote of Ial (Yale); they had conquered Edeyrnion, added to Rainald the sheriff's fee of Oswestry; and the border commote of Nanheudwy seems to have been held directly of Earl Roger by the Welsh prince, Tewdwr ap Rhys Sais. In the southwest the establishment of Montgomery castle enabled Earl Roger to extend his military domination over Ceri, Cydewain, and Arwystli, which gave him control of the passes leading into Ceredigion.[49] This was of strategic importance, since a Norman conquest of Ceredigion would split Wales in two at the narrow waist and prevent any cooperation between the Welsh of Powys and Gwynedd in the north and those of Deheubarth in the south.

Before surveying the march as it stood at the death of William I, some mention must be made of the Conqueror's Welsh expedition of 1081. This, his sole incursion into Welsh territory, was interpreted in different ways by the Welsh and English chroniclers. To the Welsh it was a pilgrimage to the shrine of St. David; to the English it was an armed reconnaissance that freed many prisoners.[50] Since it seems unlikely that devotion to the patron saint of Wales would have led William to make such a journey— and in such strength—the conclusion must be that he intended primarily to impress the chieftains of South Wales with the power of the king of England.[51]

The status of the march at the death of the Conqueror is perhaps best revealed by the statistics contained in that unfailing mine of information, *Domesday Book*. Although the English chronicler boasted, surprisingly enough, that Wales was in William's power, that he built castles there and "completely ruled over that race of men," the situation was far less favorable.[52] In the north, it is true, there had been a steady expansion westward, and the earl of Chester held not only what is now the county of Cheshire, but also Flintshire and the intervening portion of Denbighshire. Much of this area, particularly that west of the Dee estuary, had been occupied by Gruffydd ap Llywelyn, although the Clwyd had been the limit of English settlement. Rhuddlan, Gruffydd's former stronghold, was now the principal seat of Robert of Rhuddlan, Earl Hugh's chief lieutenant, and by 1086 the nucleus of a Norman borough, with the laws and customs of Breteuil, had been established under the walls of Robert's castle.[53] Moreover, it is clear that Robert had ambitions which, if realized, would have made him at least the peer of his erstwhile feudal superior, Earl Hugh. All that was conquered by Robert beyond the Clwyd he held directly of the king as tenant-in-chief, and (as Lloyd convincingly argues) it was his ambition to become lord of Gwynedd. By the time of the Survey he had already conquered the cantrefs of Rhos and Rhufoniog—an indication that the castle of Degannwy was already in existence.[54] By an annual payment of £40 Robert had secured title to "Nortwales" (i.e., Gwynedd), saving only the lands of the see of Bangor.[55] All that he had to do now was to take physical possession of the principality. His position in 1086 was clearly summed up by Lloyd:

After the fall of Trahaearn and the capture of Gruffydd, the English government clearly regarded the crown of Gwynedd as having escheated to the feudal overlord, and passing over all Welsh claims, bestowed the dignity upon Robert, who thus succeeded to all its possessions.[56]

Valuable though this royal recognition was to Robert, it could not be turned at once into military power, especially if its terms were not accepted by the Welsh.

In the earldom of Shrewsbury the Norman pressure on the Welsh of Powys coincided with that of Hugh of Chester's men on Gwynedd. This led to the early establishment of a military frontier which shielded the plains of Cheshire and Shropshire.[57] The Domesday record is not very enlightening about the military dispositions in Roger of Montgomery's earldom. The castles of Shrewsbury, Montgomery, Castle Holgate, and Oswestry are mentioned, but with little revealing comment.[58] More light is thrown upon military matters in the survey of Herefordshire and the Welsh lands occupied by the followers of William fitz Osbern. Here the frontier was essentially unchanged since William's death in 1071, for there seems to have been no central direction of marcher activity after that date. Only in Ewias and Gwynllwg do the Normans seem to have maintained pressure; Radnor, Brecknock, and Glamorgan were only beginning to feel its effects.[59] In Herefordshire, Ewias, and Gwent, Domesday provides information about eight border strongholds—Chepstow, Wigmore, Monmouth, Clifford, Ewias Lacy, Caerleon, Ewias Harold, and Richard's Castle.[60] This last was held in 1086 by Osbern fitz Richard, an old "border hand" who had "gone native" to the extent of marrying a daughter of Gruffydd ap Llywelyn. He had been on the march since the days of Edward the Confessor, when he had succeeded his father, Richard fitz Scrob. His land abutted on the Welsh territory of Maelienydd. Ralph Mortimer held Wigmore of the king in chief and his lands, like those of Osbern fitz Richard, adjoined the Welsh commote of Malienydd. The castle and castlery of Clifford, held by Ralph de Toeni, figured little in border history at this period since Ralph's major interests lay elsewhere in England.[61] it was otherwise with Ewias Lacy. To these lands, with their seat at Woebley, Roger de Lacy succeeded in 1086 as heir to his father Walter.[62] An active policy of aggression pursued by the Lacys against their Welsh neighbors had brought the commote of Ewias into their hands, and the building of the castle and castlery had followed. Ewias Harold was held by Alured of Marlborough as a tenant-in-chief of the crown, an arrangement doubtless surviving from the days of the Confessor. In Gwent, land that had been exclusively Welsh before the days of Earl William, were three castles mentioned in *Domesday* —Chepstow, built by Earl William; Monmouth, likewise his foundation but given to Wihenoc the Breton on Earl Roger's forfeiture in 1075; and Caerleon, held by Turstin fitz Rolf. These represented the advanced posts of the Norman offensive against the south Welsh, a frontier that had remained virtually stationary since the death of Earl William fifteen years previously.[63] It is also likely that the rise of Rhys ap Tewdwr in Deheubarth impeded the Norman advance along the south coast. On the death of Rhys ab Owain in 1078, Rhys ap Tewdwr occupied the vacant throne of Deheubarth, from then until his death in 1093 he had some success in checking Norman encroachments. Since at the time of the Survey he held South Wales of the king at an annual rent of £40—the same amount that Robert of Rhuddlan paid for North Wales—his position as ruler of Deheubarth evidently had official recognition.[64] It is quite possible, as Lloyd suggests, that this arrangement dated to William's Welsh expedition of 1081.[65] Royal sanction of his rule in Deheubarth was no doubt helpful to Rhys in withstanding the aggressive Normans who had occupied Gwent in the short span of six years.

No military survey of the Welsh march at the end of the reign of William I would be complete without some mention of the unique system of castles that shielded the marcher earldoms against Welsh attacks and raids. As Armitage noted a half century ago, the Survey is not a catalogue of castles, and those referred to are by no means all that were in existence at the time King William's commissioners made their inquest.[66] Castles by the score existed all the way from Cheshire to the Severn estuary.[67] It would of course be impossible to prove that such a system of fortification in depth was deliberately planned; indeed, it is quite unlikely to have involved any deliberate planning. The chances are that the fortresses rose one by one in response to local military needs— except perhaps in the vicinity of Montgomery and in Ceredigion, where systematic defensive arrangements on a local scale seem to be indicated. To protect the frontier against Welsh raids a few major castles were insufficient. Many local strong points were needed, to which the Norman settlers and their dependents could repair in time of danger; and these appeared in large numbers all along the border. Frequently they were small—sometimes little more, apparently, than ramparted mottes; often they were within a few hundred yards of one another.[68] Their proximity had the advantage not only of providing mutual support, but also of making it extremely difficult for any marauding Welsh column to work its way undetected or unmolested into the relatively undefended interior. By the time a force of any size had reached the eastern edge of the frontier zone, an army drawn from the garrisons of the major castles would be there to meet it. The effectiveness of this system, if such it may be called, was proved by the relative immunity of the English side of the border from attack by the Welsh. In Herefordshire the military character of the Norman settlement is particularly clear. The earliest English charter which granted land in return for knight service was issued in Herefordshire in 1085; and it seems fairly certain that by this date the military organization of the county, a primary task after the Conquest, was complete, at least in outline. The castleries of Ewias Harold, Clifford, and Richard's Castle shielded the county on the north and west, and the south had been brought under Norman military control. As Stenton remarks, "There is no county in which the military aspect of the Norman Conquest is felt more strongly than in Herefordshire." [69] Welsh raids on Norman settlements in occupied Wales were of frequent occurrence; but along the march, where every landholder of significance must have had his castle, such raids were infrequent, and Welsh attacks, when made at all, were full-scale military ventures.[70]

By the end of the reign of William I, the Normans had consolidated their military position all along the old frontier between England and Wales. In the north they had made considerable advances against the principality of Gwynedd, and the days of its independence appeared to be numbered. Progress in the center and south had been less spectacular; but Ewias and Gwent had been subjugated, and Rhys ap Tewdwr had been able to halt the Norman advance only by accepting the overlordship of the Conqueror. The way seemed clear for further Norman penetration, and the final subjection of the Welsh might have been predicted within the space of a few years.

The reign of William II opened with the revolt of a large proportion of the Anglo-Norman baronage.[71] Although none of the fighting took place on Welsh or marcher territory, the insurrection had important repercussions there. For one thing, many of the marcher lords threw in their lot with the rebels— notably Earl Roger of Shrewsbury, Robert of Rhuddlan, Osbern fitz Richard, Bernard de Neuf-marché, Roger de Lacy, and Ralph Mortimer.[72] This formidable array of barons strengthened the fortifications of their castles, increased the garrisons to war strength, and laid in provisions for both man and beast. Nor did they wait to be attacked, but took the offensive against the king's adherents in Gloucestershire and Worcestershire.[73] Bernard de Neuf-marché was involved in an attack on Gloucester in which the town and the church of St. Peter were destroyed.[74] But the main object of the rebel offensive was the city of Worcester and its castle. The insurgents, commanded by Earl Roger, included not only Norman knights but many Welsh auxiliaries, and met a well-deserved and crushing defeat in front of the city.[75]

Although William Rufus dealt leniently with his revolted tenants, one of them, Robert of Rhuddlan, found on his return after the collapse of the rebellion that the Welsh had taken advantage of his absence to raid in the vicinity of Rhuddlan. Determined to make an end of such incursions, Robert established his headquarters at Degannwy at the mouth of the Conway; but before his preparations were complete, he was killed on 3 July 1088 in what appears to have been a frivolous skirmish with Welsh pirates.[76] Although Robert's death removed an implacable enemy of the Welsh, it did nothing to lessen the pressure on the principality of Gwynedd. Earl Hugh of Chester assumed command of the Norman advance along the north coast, and for the next six years he maintained the offensive.[77] Castles were constructed at Carnarvon in Meirionydd, at Bangor in Arfon, and at Aber Lleiniog in Anglesey.[78] As Lloyd remarks, there is much evidence that by the beginning of 1094 the conquest of North Wales by the Normans was nearly complete.[79]

But in the spring of 1094, the absence of Earl Hugh in Normandy gave the Welsh of Gwynedd their opportunity. A castle west of the Conway, otherwise unidentified, was captured, and a Norman punitive expedition dispatched to restore the situation was roughly handled by Cadwgan ap Bleddyn at Coed Yspwys.[80] In the absence of the earl of Chester, the defense of the northern frontier had fallen to the recently installed Earl Hugh of Shrewsbury, a second son of Earl Roger. He gained success over one column of Welsh insurgents, but could not prevent the Welsh from re-establishing control over Gwynedd. Marauding bands were soon terrorizing the border settlements of Cheshire and Shropshire, although William of Malmesbury's assertion that all of Chester and part of Shropshire were depopulated is doubless an exaggeration.[81] In the attendant confusion, Gruffydd ap Cynan contrived to escape from the earl of Chester, who had held him prisoner. Moving onto the already crowded stage, Gruffydd attempted an invasion of Anglesey with the aid of Godred Crowan, king of Man. The attempt failed, but the hardy Gruffydd then made a landing at Nevin in Lleyn, recruited an army of sorts, and launched another attack on Anglesey. This time he was successful. The castle at Aber Lleiniog was carried by storm, and the castellan and the garrison of 120 men-at-arms were put to the sword. This striking victory not only cleared the Normans out of

Anglesey, but also gave the North Welsh a respite of more than a year.[82]

Meanwhile the Norman advance in South Wales had been resumed, a process made easier when the Welsh fell back into their old habit of bitter internecine fighting. In 1088, and again in 1091, Rhys ap Tewdwr was compelled to devote his energy to suppressing local rivals rather than to opposing the Norman threat.[83] The offensive was renewed by Bernard de Neuf-marché, the son-in-law of Osbern fitz Richard, who began the conquest of Brycheiniog. He advanced through the gap between the Black Mountains and the Wye to the Llynfi valley, thence to that of the Usk. By 1093 he had probably occupied Talgarth, the Welsh "capital" of the district. The Welsh of Deheubarth were not unmindful of this threat to their independence, and in the spring of 1093 Rhys ap Tewdwr launched a counteroffensive against the Norman invaders of Brycheiniog. During Easter week (17–23 April) a battle was fought between the Welsh and Normans, in which Rhys was slain.[84] Bernard continued the building of the castle of Brecknock (Aberhonddu) near the scene of the battle—a crucial one indeed, for the death of Rhys had removed the symbol of legal rule, thus clearing the way for the rapid Norman occupation of much of South Wales. ". . . Force was to be henceforth the sole arbiter of the affairs of the distracted and unhappy land." [85]

By 30 April—little more than a week after the death of Rhys—the chieftains of the south were already fighting over the succession, and the Normans did not permit the opportunity to pass without profit to themselves. At the beginning of July, Earl Roger of Shrewsbury marched from his advanced base in Arwystli, crossed the mountains, and occupied Ceredigion (Cardigan). The aggressors indicated their intent to make the occupation permanent by building a castle at the mouth of the Teifi. At the time the place was called Din Geraint; later, confusingly, it was known as Aber Teifi, and as Cardigan.[86] The Norman occupation of Ceredigion exposed Dyfed to attack, and one soon followed. As early as 1091 the admirably situated castle of Pembroke—a rude stockade of earth and timber—had been built, and its custody, as well as that of the territory conquered later, was entrusted to

Arnulf, a younger son of Earl Roger of Shrewsbury. The castellan was Gerald of Windsor, who within his own lifetime was to become a legendary figure along the march.[87] Farther to the east, another Norman outpost was established by William fitz Baldwin, the sheriff of Devon, at Rhydygors, commanding a ford on the Towy, about a mile south of the old Roman fort at Carmarthen. The occupation of Ceredigion and Dyfed made untenable the position of the remaining Welsh chieftains in the south, especially those wedged in between the Normans in Dyfed and Gwent—the more since it was probably at about this time that the remainder of Brycheiniog fell to Bernard de Neuf-marché.[88]

The invasion of Glamorgan must have begun early in the reign of William II; although the precise date is unknown, the process was well advanced by 1093. The leader of this enterprise was Robert fitz Hamon, a prominent tenant in Gloucestershire and one of the king's favorites. He built the castle of Cardiff on an old Roman site, which became the *caput* of the lordship, and from which Robert and his knights pushed the Norman occupation as far as the River Tawe, thus obliterating the Welsh principality of Morgannwg.[89] Coincidentally, it would appear that the cantref of Buellt (Builth) was occupied about 1095, at which time Philip de Braose was securely established at Radnor.[90] At this juncture, when matters seemed to be prospering for the Norman adventure in South Wales, the revolt of 1094 spread from Gwynedd southward. All along the frontiers of Cheshire, Shropshire, and Herefordshire, Welsh raids brought death and devastation. In Dyfed and Ceredigion, all the Norman military posts except Pembroke and Rhydygors were swept away. Although retaliatory raids from Glamorgan and Brecknock devastated Gower, Kidwelly, and Ystrad Tywi, little was done to stem the tide of revolt.[91] The return of William Rufus to England late in 1094 had no immediate effect on the situation, for he was kept busy with the baronial unrest which culminated the following year in Robert de Mowbray's revolt. Though the military operations of 1095 were limited, they dragged on beyond the normal campaigning season, and it was not until autumn that the king was able to deal directly with the Welsh situation. He was then compelled, indeed, to take a personal hand in it. for the Welsh had mounted a successful

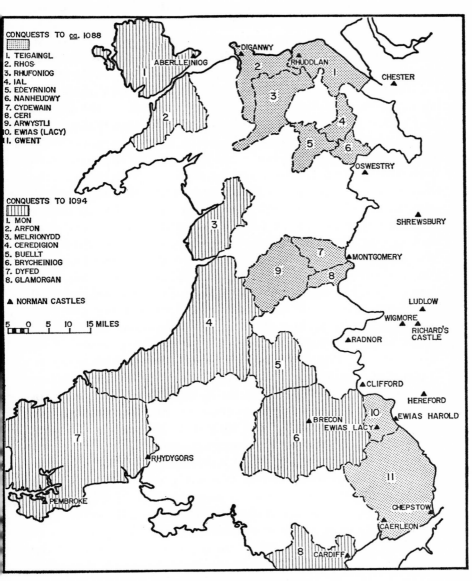

CONQUESTS TO <u>ca.</u> 1088

1. TEIGAINGL
2. RHOS
3. RHUFONIOG
4. IAL
5. EDEYRNION
6. NANHEUDWY
7. CYDEWAIN
8. CERI
9. ARWYSTLI
10. EWIAS (LACY)
11. GWENT

CONQUESTS TO 1094

1. MON
2. ARFON
3. MELRIONYDD
4. CEREDIGION
5. BUELLT
6. BRYCHEINIOG
7. DYFED
8. GLAMORGAN

▲ NORMAN CASTLES

5 0 5 10 15 MILES

ABERLLEINIOG
DIGANWY
RHUDDLAN
CHESTER
OSWESTRY
SHREWSBURY
MONTGOMERY
LUDLOW
WIGMORE
RICHARD'S
CASTLE
RADNOR
CLIFFORD
HEREFORD
BRECON
EWIAS LACY
EWIAS HAROLD
RHYDYGORS
PEMBROKE
CHEPSTOW
CAERLEON
CARDIFF

Map 11. Norman Occupation of Wales to 1094

attack on Montgomery, capturing and destroying the castle and putting the garrison to the sword.[92]

The fall of Montgomery laid much of Shropshire open to Welsh raiding parties; thus, even though the season was late, another army was mustered after the feast of St. Michael (29 September). The king himself assumed command, and the expedition, marching in several columns with orders to concentrate by the feast of All Hallows (1 November), crossed the frontier into Wales.[93] The pattern of the campaign was followed by every subsequent royal punitive expedition into Wales for the next two hundred years. With woodcutting pioneers in the advance to clear away the thickets that might hide a Welsh ambuscade, the Norman columns moved slowly forward. Concentration was effected on the appointed date at Mur y Castell in northern Ardudwy.[94] But nothing else happened. In the words of the English chronicler, "the Welsh were constantly before into mountains and moors, so that it was impossible to come at them." [95] Following their usual tactics, they had withdrawn with their livestock and personal belongings into the mountain fastnesses, and harassed the Norman advance by ambuscades. So although King William had concentrated his army in the heart of Gwynedd, the campaign was in fact ended. The problem now was not one of defeating the Welsh, but of extricating the army before the weather became impossible. William of Malmesbury noted that the causes of Rufus's failure were "the meanness of the country and the badness of the weather." [96] The king therefore retraced his steps with nothing to show for the campaign except loss of men and horses, plus whatever impression as the show of force may have had upon the Welsh.[97] It had absolutely no influence on the Welsh revolt. And though several marcher lords were implicated in de Mowbray's revolt, and though one of them, Roger de Lacy, lost his lands in consequence, neither did the baronial rising of 1095 have any noticeable effect on the military position of the Normans on the frontier.[98]

The Welsh revolt continued unchecked. With the death of William fitz Baldwin in 1096, the castle of Rhydygors was abandoned, and Pembroke was left as the only Norman outpost in Dyfed. Fortunately, since it could be supplied by sea, its existence was less precarious than might be supposed. Elsewhere in South Wales, the inhabitants of Brycheiniog, Gwynllwg, and Gwent rose in revolt. Minor victories were won but the overall effect was not great, owing largely to the failure of the Welsh to press home their attacks on Norman castles.[99] As long as the strong points remained in Norman hands, the eventual success of any revolt was unlikely. The Welsh of Gwent won a battle over the Normans of Glamorgan at Celli Carnant, "slaying not a few," and a Norman column, also from Glamorgan, was roughly handled at Aber Hech in Brycheiniog, about three miles northeast of Ystrad Gwynlais.[100] Farther west, the Welsh princes Uchtred ab Edwin and Hywel ap Gronw, aided by the "household guard" of Cadwgan ap Bleddyn, thoroughly devastated Dyfed and invested Pembroke castle.[101] Nearly a century later, a descendant and namesake of the castellan of Pembroke, Gerald of Windsor, wrote a highly dramatic account of the siege. That it was a critical event in the history of the Norman occupation of South Wales is not open to question; whether Giraldus's account of the siege can be taken at face value is another matter.[102] The effect of Gerald's numerous *ruses de guerre* on the enemy is not known; at any rate, the Welsh eventually raised the siege, returning home with the booty obtained during the campaign, and with nothing of military significance to show for their efforts.[103] What was perhaps more important, the Normans retained a base which could easily be supplied and reinforced for future offensive operations. In fact, by the beginning of 1097 Gerald was able to conduct a raid through the lands of Bishop Wilfred of St. David's in retaliation for the aid and comfort he had furnished the insurgents the previous year.[104] In the spring of the same year, King William led an army into Wales for the second time, with no more effect than the first. Although he was able to secure Welsh guides, and although he campaigned "from Midsummer almost till August, and lost much therein in men and in horses," eventually realizing "that he could there further nothing according to his will," he "returned to this land, and shortly thereafter caused castles to be made on the borders." [105] But the revolt in the south flickered out, mainly for lack of cohesion, and at the end of William's reign the Welsh retained possession only of Ceredigion and Ystrad Tywi.[106]

In the north, however, the Normans fared much less well. Earl Hugh of Chester was determined to restore Norman rule in Arfon and Anglesey, and in the summer of 1098, with Earl Hugh of Shrewsbury, a joint operation was undertaken. Their combined forces, led by Welsh guides, marched west along the coast road to Arlechwedd on the Menai straits opposite Anglesey, to which the Welsh leaders, Gruffydd ap Cynan and Cadwgan ap Bleddyn had retired. Unfortunately, Gruffydd and Cadwgan were relying on a Danish mercenary fleet to hold the straits against a Norman crossing; but the Normans had heavier purses, and bribed the Danes into changing sides, so that their own army crossed to Anglesey unmolested. Gruffydd and Cadwgan sought refuge in Ireland, and Anglesey was given over by the Normans to pillage and atrocities were committed.[107] The operation on Anglesey was proceeding according to plan when there occurred one of those historical accidents whose consequences could not have been foreseen. During the summer of 1098 King Magnus Barefoot of Norway, a true corsair, was making a great sweep through the Irish Sea. When his fleet appeared off Priestholme, a running fight developed between the Normans on the beach and the Norwegians in their ships. A chance arrow, said to have been shot by King Magnus himself, struck the earl of Shrewsbury in the eye. The wound, whether fatal or not, toppled Earl Hugh from the saddle, and his body, in its heavy armor, could not be recovered until low tide.[108] King Magnus made no attempt to force a landing; perhaps he was unaware of the advantage he had gained. He vanished into the mists of the Irish Sea as suddenly as he had appeared, leaving the Normans still in possession of Anglesey. But the sudden death of Earl Hugh had badly shaken the morale of the invaders. Thus reminded of the precariousness of their foothold in the far west of Wales, they abandoned Anglesey, carried off the booty and captives, and recrossed the Menai straits to the mainland, leaving the island to be reoccupied by the Welsh.[109] The attempt to establish control over Gwynedd had proved that the Normans did not have the strategic resources to retain a foothold in the far west. As Lloyd clearly puts it:

This development brings home the importance of sea-power as a necessary element in every scheme of conquest of the lands west of the

Conway. Without control of the sea passage to Chester, Rhuddlan, and Degannwy, the Norman holders of Anglesey were in a helpless position, at the mercy of countless foes who could bar every road by which they might expect supplies and reinforcements. The attack of King Magnus showed how real the peril was, and it was decided that the risks of campaigning in Gwynedd were too great to warrant further attempts at conquest.[110]

In the following year (1099) Gruffydd and Cadwgan returned from Ireland. Anglesey was occupied by Gruffydd, and Cadwgan was enfeoffed by the new earl of Shrewsbury, Robert de Bellême, with Ceredigion and his share of the family inheritance of Powys.[111]

Another consequence of the death of Earl Hugh was the change of regime in Shrewsbury. Hugh was succeeded by his elder brother, Robert, who earlier had inherited the family estates in Normandy. By offering the enormous relief of £3,000, he secured possession of Hugh's English lands, including the castles of Arundel and Tickhill as well as the earldom. Robert's violence and ruthlessness have become proverbial, but he was also very able. During the four years he occupied the comital office he established such amicable relations with his Welsh tenants that they willingly supported his defiance of Henry I early in the succeeding reign. The assertion of Ordericus that the earl treated the Welsh with great cruelty cannot have much foundation.[112] Robert's only recorded action on the frontier was to erect a castle at Carreghofa in 1098; but this may well have been a move to strengthen the border defenses commanding the valleys of the Tanat and Vyrnwy, rather than one of aggression against the Welsh.[113]

The first thirty-four years of the struggle between Norman and Welshman set the pattern for a conflict that was to continue for generations to come, even though the final outcome had already been decided. By 1100 the Norman hold on Glamorgan, Brecknock, and Dyfed in the south was secure; in the north, Tegeingl and Rhos had been lost to the Welsh beyond recall. On the other hand, the Normans had learned through the hard experience of the revolt of 1094 that attempts to hold such areas as Ceredigion, Anglesey, and Powys could not be made without courting disaster.

To quote Lloyd again: "North Wales, it was decreed, was to retain substantially its Welsh rulers and its independence, while most of what was best worth having in the South was to fall into the hands of the invaders." [114]

Developments of a new century and a new reign had an effect on the political and military situation along the march. On the northern front Earl Hugh of Chester, the inverterate enemy of the Welsh, died on 27 July 1101, leaving a seven-year-old boy as his heir.[115] For a time at least, Gruffydd ap Cynan, now prince of Gwynedd, could go about the work of consolidating his territory west of the Conway without interference from the Normans. The unsuccessful rebellion in 1102 of Robert de Bellême, the overpowerful earl of Shrewsbury, not only brought the fall of the house of Montgomery, but at the same time removed two of the most prominent military leaders on the border. The rebellion was significant also in that Welsh auxiliaries—or mercenaries—were involved in an English civil conflict for a second time; nor was it to be the last. Although the operations in Shropshire and elsewhere have already been discussed, the political and military effects of Robert's defeat and exile remain to be evaluated. The decision of the Welsh princes Iorwerth, Cadwgan, and Maredudd ap Bleddyn, who were tenants of Earl Robert, to support their feudal overlord against the king was, of course, a mistake. What inducements may have led them into it will never be known. With hindsight, it is easy to see that the Welsh would best have served their own interest by supporting the royal authority against the overweening Montgomerys, who in the long run would never have been anything but their enemies. As things developed, the Welsh were the real losers. During the campaign, English promises and English money were able to seduce Iorwerth from his feudal allegiance, and a deciding factor in the Shropshire campaign was the Welsh raid through the county under his command.[116] The victory of Henry I brought forfeiture and exile to all the members of the house of Montgomery; this included Earl Robert and his brother Arnulf, who had governed Pembroke (Dyfed) almost as an earldom.[117]

The banishment of Robert and Arnulf had its effect on the always precarious balance of power along the border. As in 1075 after the revolt of Roger of Hereford, the vacant earldom was not filled. This time, however, the forfeited lordship was treated as a palatine earldom rather than as an ordinry shire. Within a short time after Earl Robert's defeat, Richard of Beaumais, who had been a clerk in the earl's establishment, was appointed justiciar, a post he occupied for the next twenty-one years, although after 1108 he paradoxically combined it with the functions of bishop of London.[118] Elsewhere the former territories of the house of Montgomery and their Welsh satellites were arbitrarily distributed with an eye to strengthening the position of the crown in Wales. Although the agreement that detached Iorwerth ap Bleddyn from Earl Robert's faction had provided that the Welsh land of the Montgomerys—Powys, Ceredigion, Ystrad Tywi, Gower, and Kidwelly, plus Arnulf's half of Dyfed—should be his, King Henry had no intention of creating so powerful a Welsh principality on the borders of the march. Instead, the forfeited lands and their dependencies were broken up. In Pembroke an otherwise unknown Norman knight named Saher became custodian— an arrangement that did not last long, for by 1104 the castle was in possession of Gerald, Arnulf's heroic castellan.[119] Cadwgan ap Bleddyn was confirmed in his possession of Powys and Ceredigion; Ystrad Tywi, Gower, and Kidwelly were given to Hywel ap Gronw. Iorwerth naturally showed his resentment of these acts of royal duplicity, and in 1103 he was charged with various crimes before a royal court, convicted, and clapped into prison. Nor was the royal settlement in South Wales proof against the aggressive activities of the Norman marchers. In eastern Dyfed, Richard fitz Baldwin in 1105 challenged the authority of Hywel ap Gronw by rebuilding and garrisoning the castle at Rhydygors, abandoned since 1096.[120] This brought Norman military power again up to the Towy, which separated Dyfed from Hywel's domains in Kidwelly. That the Normans would allow the Welsh prince to rule undisturbed was hardly to be expected, and in 1106 Hywel was treacherously assassinated by a Welshman in Norman pay. Mention must also be made of the establishment by King Henry of a Flemish colony in Rhos about 1106.[121] Although Lloyd states that the Flemings did not form a military aristocracy, but were artisans and peasants, they nevertheless displaced the native Welsh and made Dyfed more secure against incursions by the latter. William of Malmesbury specifically stated that the purpose of the settlement was to erect a barrier against the Welsh and to keep them within bounds.[122]

The chief beneficiary of the shakeup following the fall of the house of Montgomery was Cadwgan ap Bleddyn. Although his character was rather weak and vacillating, from 1105 to 1111 he was the leading figure on the Welsh side of the march. According to all strategical rules, Powys had no right to primacy among the Welsh principalities. Its geographical location was against it; there was a long frontier with England that could not be easily defended, since the river valleys provided natural avenues for invasion. Nor was there any natural citadel such as Snowdonia in Gwynedd, or the inhospitable moors of Ystrad Tywi in Deheubarth, to provide a last place of refuge. More often than not in the military annals of the border, the princes of Powys were to be found arranged as allies of the invaders, or as satellites of the princes of Gwynedd. That Powys played the leading role in Welsh affairs during the first half of the reign of Henry I, is due largely to the inability of either Gwynedd or Deheubarth to assert its strength, and to the disappearance from the march of the powerful and aggressive house of Montgomery. But Cadwgan was not the man to consolidate the position of Powys; he could not even control his own turbulent relatives. His sons, brothers, and nephews kept the border in a state of constant confusion for years. Cadwgan was deposed, restored, deposed, and restored again before his assassination in 1111. The crown tried various measures to bring some kind of order, intervening directly in Welsh affairs in a manner unknown in previous reigns. A division of Cadwgan's lands among his enemies only made matters worse; in 1110 Iorwerth ap Bleddyn was released after ten years' confinement, in the vain hope that he would be more capable than his brother; but both Iorwerth and Cadwgan were murdered in 1111, and Cadwgan's hitherto wild and irresponsible son Owain came into power.[123]

Owain's career had begun inauspiciously in 1109 when he kidnaped Nest, the wife of Gerald of Pembroke, apparently with the lady's consent, from Gerald's castle of Cenarth Bychan.

Norman pride took cognizance of this insult by forcing Owain to take refuge in Ireland, and by deposing his father Cadwgan as ruler of Powys for the first time.[124] In 1110 Cadwgan was restored in Ceredigion, and Owain returned to the court of Madog ap Rhiryd, now prince of Powys. But Owain's uncle, the recently released Iorwerth ap Bleddyn, at once chased both Owain and Madog out of Powys, and Owain took refuge with his father in Ceredigion. At once he abused the hospitality he had been shown by using the cantref as a base for raids against the Normans and Flemings in Dyfed, during one of which an influential Flemish merchant was slain. For King Henry this seems to have been the final straw. Cadwgan was deposed a second time in 1110; Ceredigion was given to Gilbert fitz Richard de Clare, a member of one of the most eminent Norman families; and Owain again fled to Ireland.[125] This was the background of the prince who, after the violent deaths of Cadwgan and Iorwerth ap Bleddyn, shared Powys with Madog ap Rhiryd. But Owain, like Prince Hal, made a far better ruler than he did an heir apparent. He hired his surviving uncle Maredudd to be captain of his household troops (*penteleu*) and probably his military adviser. By 1113 Madog had been captured and blinded, thus effectively removing him from the scene.[126]

By the succeeding year King Henry had become alarmed by the increasing strength not only of Owain but of Gwynedd as well. Following the abandonment of the Norman attempt to conquer North Wales, Gruffydd ap Cynan went quietly about the business of rehabilitating his shattered realm. Unlike the princes of Powys, he had no rivals for the throne, and his most dangerous enemy had been removed when Earl Hugh of Chester died in 1101. Although his domain was limited to the seven cantrefs west of the Conway and north of the Mawddach, by 1114 Gruffydd had been so successful in rebuilding the strength and influence of Gwynedd that the king decided to direct a punitive expedition against him, as well as against his more exposed neighbor, Owain ap Cadwgan.[127] The pretext on which the invasion was launched is unknown, although Earl Richard of Chester complained that Gruffydd harbored fugitive tenants from Rhos. In any event the expedition was carefully planned and executed on a large scale. It appears likely that Henry made his headquarters at Castle Holgate in Shropshire during the planning and organizational stages of the campaign.[128] Castle Holgate was located about midway between the Dee estuary and the Bristol channel, approximately fourteen miles south-southeast of Shrewsbury, in rear of the actual frontier—an excellent location for directing so vast a project.

The expedition was to move about midsummer in three columns, converging on Mur y Castell near Trawsfynedd. The Anglo-Norman left was composed of the men of Deheubarth, reinforced by contingents from Devon and Cornwall. The center, commanded by the king in person, marched westward from Shrewsbury via the old Roman road across the Berwyn. The right, under the command of King Alexander I of Scots and the young Earl Richard of Chester, probably marched westward along the coastal road leading to the mouth of the Conway.[129] Against this overwhelming display of force the Welsh could offer little effective resistance. Maredudd ap Bleddyn made terms with the king at once; Owain gathered his followers and their belongings and fled to the mountains of Gwynedd, since there was no hiding place in Powys. Negotiations were soon opened, on the one hand between King Henry and Owain and on the other between Gruffydd and the commanders of the royal right wing. Owain seems to have obtained fairly easy terms, but Gruffydd, the chief threat in Henry's eyes, had to render homage and fealty in addition to paying a heavy fine. The power and resources of the English king so impressed him that he could never again be induced, even in a patriotic cause, to resort to force against the English crown.[130] New castles were built on the frontier, and Owain ap Cadwgan rose so high in the royal flavor that in September 1114 he accompanied the king to Normandy, returning with him to England in July 1115.[131]

Trouble had meanwhile been brewing in South Wales, and in 1116 it broke into open revolt. Gruffydd ap Rhys, the heir to the hegemony established by Rhys ap Tewdwr, had returned to Wales about 1113 after his years of exile in Ireland. Wandering from one princely court to another, he narrowly missed being handed over to King Henry by Gruffydd ap Cynan, who was determined that no act of his should jeopardize his relations with England. Crossing the bay of Cardigan, Gruffydd landed in South Wales, and in the spring of 1116 he attacked the castle of Narberth, which was captured and destroyed.[132] Heartened by this success, Gruffydd next attacked the castle of Llandovery in Cantref Bychan, held by Richard fitz Pons. But thanks to the skill of the Welsh castellan, Maredudd ap Rydderch ap Caradog, though the bailey was carried by the assailants, the keep held out until the Welsh withdrew. Swansea, a castle of Henry of Beaumont, earl of Warwick, was next singled out for attack, with the same results. Again the outworks were carried, but again the garrison made good its escape to the keep from which it could not be ejected by the ill-ordered assaults of Gruffydd's men.[133] These successes, though partial, aroused great enthusiasm among the South Welsh, and Gruffydd soon had a considerable armed following, though to call it an army would be misleading. The castle of Kidwelly was abandoned by William of London, and by now the rising had aroused the fears of the authorities, particularly for the safety of the castle of Carmarthen. It was decided to rotate command of the garrison among local chieftains who were out of sympathy with Gruffydd's revolt. Three of these—Maredudd of Cantref Bychan, Gruffydd's uncle Rydderch, and Owain ap Caradog—were designated castellans on a rotating basis, each to serve a two weeks' tour of duty.[134] The attack came while Owain was in command of the castle; and though the town and the castle bailey were overrun and put to the torch, and Owain himself was slain, the insurgents were repulsed in their assaults on the keep.[135]

Gruffydd's star was now at its zenith, and he led his unruly host into Ceredigion on a vast plundering raid. He attacked Blaen Porth Hodnant, but failed to take the castle.[136] Marching north into Penweddig, the insurgents stormed and burned Ystrad Peithyll, a stronghold of one Razo, the castellan of Earl Gilbert's castle at Aberystwyth. Then Gruffydd decided to attack Aberystwyth itself, but his inattention to even the rudiments of the military art allowed Razo to bring in reinforcements from the neighboring castle of Ystrad Meurig under cover of darkness. The next day Gruffydd postponed an assault until too late, and when it finally was delivered, lack of coordination among the attacking columns became an invitation to the Normans which the astute

Razo did not fail to exploit. Launching a counterattack from the castle, he easily put the Welsh host to flight.[137] This disaster marked the virtual end of the rebellion. Gruffydd's army dispersed, and he himself was compelled to seek refuge in the wilds of Cantref Mawr.

Before discussing the causes for the failure of the revolt, the fate of Owain ap Cadwgan of Powys is worth noting. When the rebellion appeared most formidable, the authorities used not only Norman troops but Welsh contingents as well. Owain and Llywarch of Arwystli were enlisted in the campaign against Gruffydd. After an obscure engagement near Carmarthen, in which Owain and Gerald of Pembroke were found fighting on the same side, Owain and a bodyguard of ninety men were retiring, laden with plunder. Suddenly they were set upon by a body of their onetime allies the Flemings of Dyfed, who also had some old scores to settle with Owain. In the ensuing scuffle, Owain was slain by the Flemish archers, and Gerald was avenged for the abduction of his wife seven years before.[138]

The causes for the failure of the revolt of Gruffydd ap Rhys are not difficult to discover. The movement from the very beginning lacked a purposeful objective, other than the vague one of liberating Deheubarth from Norman rule. That there was no plan of campaign indicates, of course, a lack of competent leadership. From the outset the rebellion was doomed because the insurgents were unable to capture the Norman castle keeps and their garrisons. The seeming victories were meaningless so long as these garrisons retained possession of the fortresses, from which lost territory could be reoccupied and new attacks could be launched against the rebels. Lack of generalship in turn fostered indiscipline in the ranks. The most elementary principles of security were ignored—as in the negligence that permitted reinforcements to enter Aberystwyth castle. The Welsh revolt of 1116 simply did not have the leadership and the perseverance to succeed.

The Normans, then, were left in almost undisputed possession of South Wales; as Lloyd remarks, at the end of the reign of Henry I scarcely a corner of Deheubarth was ruled by a native prince.[139] As in England after 1066, the typical seal of effective Norman occupation was the castle, and castles in Wales, although lacking the romantic connotations of castles in Spain, were much more of a reality. Pembroke was governed as an earldom, and included not only the original cantref of Penfro but also those of Rhos and Deugleddyf. The "county," if such it may be called, had its own sheriff; in 1130, he was one Hait, who accounted for £60 to the Exchequer.[140] Its organization was therefore probably more complex than that of the other marcher lordships. In addition to the castle at Pembroke, which the redoubtable Gerald held for most of the reign, strongholds were located at Carew, Manorbier, Haverford, Wiston (Castell Gwis), Nevern, and Emlyn (Cilgerran).[141] In Cardigan, which had come into the possession of Gilbert fitz Richard de Clare only in 1110, the new tenant constructed two castles to nail down his recent acquisition. The first of these was Cardigan (Dingeraint), built near the mouth of the Teifi, where Earl Roger had previously had a castle. This fortress commanded the river's tidal reaches, and also a bridge that gave access to Cemais and Dyfed. The second castle was at Aberystwyth, built on a site in the Ystwyth valley, a mile and a half south of the present town.[142] Other castles were built by Gilbert's tenants to insure the permanence of the Norman occupation. By 1114 Castell Gwalter (Llanfihangel Geneu'r Glyn) was in existence.[143] Additional strongholds were Humphrey's Castle (later known as Castel Hywel); Stephen's Castle, probably located at Lampeter, where the bridge over the Teifi is known as Pont Stephen; and an otherwise unidentified castle of Richard de la Mare in central Cardigan. There were also castles at Ystrad Peithyll, Ystrad Meurig, and Blaen Porth Hodnant, making Cardigan one of the most heavily fortified districts in all of South Wales.[144] Here again the building seem to have followed a systematic plan. J. G. Edwards has noted that there was at least one Norman castle in nine of the ten commotes of Cardigan, with a strong possibility that the tenth commote had one also. "One may argue, of course, that this distribution of Norman castles in Ceredigion was pure accident. Accidents, however, that happen seven or nine or ten times out of ten begin to look progressively less like accident, and more like design."[145]

Elsewhere in the south, the castle of Rhydygors seems to have been permanently abandoned early in the twelfth century, and the defense of eastern Dyfed came to be centered around the royal castle of Carmarthen at the head of navigation on the Towy. It is of some interest to note, in connection with Carmarthen, that the Welsh were already taking to Norman military practices. In 1130 one "Bledri the Welshman" was among the knights of the honor.[146] Norman influence had also penetrated Cantref Bychan. The leader of this enterprise seems to have been Richard fitz Pons, who crossed the mountains and before 1116 had built the castle of Llandovery.[147] Richard must have reached some accommodation with the local Welsh population; for during the revolt of 1116 the castellan at Llandovery was Maredudd ap Rhydderch ap Caradog. The commote of Cydweli passed into Norman hands at the death of Hywel ap Gronw in 1106. Shortly thereafter it was given by King Henry to his trusted minister, Bishop Roger of Salisbury, who built the castle of Kidwelly where the road to Carmarthen crossed the lesser Gwendraeth, and was still in his possession as late as July 1114, when his castellan Edmund witnessed one of his charters. By 1116, however, the castle and lordship had been transferred to Maurice of London. Gower, another of Hywel's possessions, had been given to Henry de Beaumont, earl of Warwick, who founded the castle of Swansea at the mouth of the Tawe. It soon attracted so considerable an English and Flemish settlement that the southern half of the district quite lost its Welsh character.[148]

In those parts of the march whose conquest had begun as early as the reign of William I, and had continued in that of William Rufus, the process of consolidation was well advanced. Philip de Braose held Radnor and Builth at the end of Henry's reign.[149] Between Radnor and Brecknock, Hugh Mortimer, who had succeeded his father Ralph in the lordship of Wigmore about 1104, seems to have done little beyond acquiring some hold on the valleys of the Ithon and Edw.[150] But in Brecknock, Bernard de Neuf-marché had been very active, and his lordship was organized on a completely feudal basis. The chief castle, Brecon, had early become a center of activity, civil and religious as well as military.[151] The castle of Talgarth likewise remained in the lord's hands. Bernard's chief tenants also had fortified their principal seats. In the valley of the Rhiangoll in the commote of Ystrad Yw Uchaf, Picard had built the castle of Tretower perhaps as early as 1093, to guard the pass over the mountains that separate the valleys of the Wye and the Usk.[152] Robert de Turbeville had a castle at Crickhowell (Crughywel), in the commote of Ystrad Yw Isaf, and William Revel held the castle of Hay (La Haie Taillée) on the upper Wye. This soon reverted to the demesne, and formed part of the dowry of Bernard's daughter Sibyl on her marriage to Miles of Gloucester. The lands between Brecon and Talgarth were held by Roger de Baskerville; and Walter Clifford, son of Richard fitz Pons, held possession of part of the commote of Cantref Selyf, with the *caput* of his honor at the castle of Bronllys on the Lynfi.[153]

The lordship of Glamorgan differed in several respects from that of Brecknock. The founder, Robert fitz Hamon, had centered his honor in the old Roman fort at Caerdyf, out of which rose his castle of Cardiff. The castle soon attracted settlers, and a flourishing borough grew up around it. Like Pembroke, Glamorgan was organized as a county with its own sheriff and county court. Moreover, much of the most fertile and desirable part of the region was retained by fitz Hamon in demesne. The castles of the honorial baronage were at Neath, Aberafan, Coity, Rhuthyn, Ogmore, Llanblethian, Penmark, Peterton on the Ely, and Newport. Glamorgan was perhaps unique in that a place in the feudal hierarchy was found for members of the dispossessed dynasty. Caradog, the son of the last Welsh ruler, Iestyn ap Gwrgant, became lord of Rhong Nedd ac Afan with its *caput* at the castle of Aberafan, and another son, Rhys ab Iestyn, became lord of the castle of Rhuthyn.[154] Farther to the east, Gwent presented an even more settled appearance. Here there was no paramount lord as in Brecknock or Glamorgan; nor were castles so numerous, since Gwent was no longer the first line of defense. Important strongholds had been erected at Chepstow, which during Henry's reign came into the hands of the Clares, and at Abergavenny, Caerleon, Monmouth, and Ewias Lacy.[155] South Wales during the latter part of the reign seemed to have become irrevocably Anglo-Norman. Norman castles and their garrisons studded the landscape and afforded protection to Norman, English, and Flemish colonists.

No Welsh prince of any significance ruled in the south. The old Welsh ecclesiastical organization was fast disappearing as Norman lords granted lands and churches to English or Norman foundations. The church was, indeed, no less a weapon of conquest in the hands of the Norman marchers than the castle or the mail-clad knight.[156]

While the Normans were thus consolidating their hold on South Wales, Gruffydd ap Cynan and his able sons Cadwallon, Owain, and Cadwaladr, having rebuilt the power of Gwynedd after the disasters of the late eleventh century, were beginning a deliberate if cautious policy of aggression aimed at ending the supremacy of Powys in north Welsh affairs. The great day of Powys had ended with the death of Owain ap Cadwgan in 1116; for, though his uncle Maredudd succeeded peacefully enough and remained lord of all Powys until his death in 1132, he was in no position to challenge effectively the growing power of Gwynedd.[157] Indeed, trapped between the Normans on one side and Gwynedd on the other, Maredudd was in an impossible position. He attempted to gain some elbow room at the expense of the earl of Chester, two of whose castles he captured and burned. But this only provoked King Henry to mount another expedition into Powys about midsummer of 1121. Forced to retreat to the mountains of Gwynedd for protection, Maredudd looked in vain to Gruffydd for support, and was finally compelled to purchase peace from the king with a fine of 10,000 cattle.[158] In the meantime Gwynedd itself was nibbling away at the western approaches to Chester. In 1118 Hywel ab Ithel, who as the client of Powys had ruled Rhos and Rhufoniog between the Conway and the Clwyd, became involved in a local fracas with the sons of Owain ab Edwin, ruler of Dyffryn Clwyd. The sons of Owain called in the Normans of Cheshire who still held Rhuddlan and possibly Degannwy; Hywel called on Powys for assistance, and Maredudd responded with a contingent of four hundred men. A bitter fight took place at Maes Maen Cymro, a mile northwest of Ruthin, but though Hywel and his allies were victorious, Hywel himself was mortally wounded and died six weeks later. Thus the tactical victory amounted to a strategic defeat for Maredudd of Powys, who was not strong enough to annex the two cantrefs outright to his

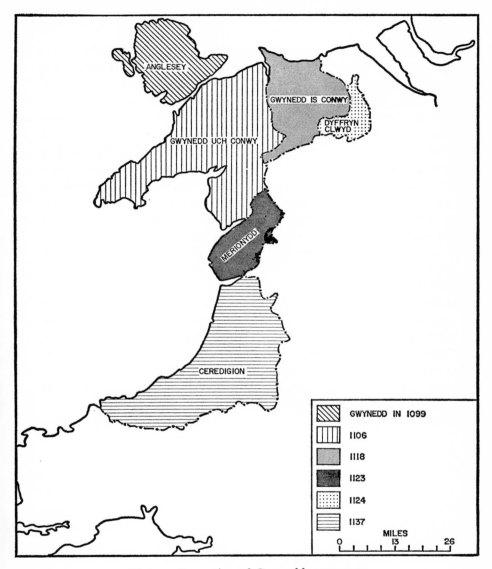

Map 12. Expansion of Gwynedd, 1099–1137

own dominions on the death of Hywel. The power vacuum was filled by Gwynedd, which occupied the territory,[159] and now had an excellent base for further expansion to the east.

The next thrust was southward against Meirionydd. Here Uchtred ab Edwin had made himself practically independent, and had built the first native Welsh castle of which there is notice at Cymmer, at the confluence of the rivers Wnion and Mawddach. But in 1116 Uchtred was driven out by a force from Powys under the command of Einon ap Cadwgan and Gruffydd ap Maredudd, and the castle was destroyed.[160] The occupation of Meirionydd by Powys did not last long, however; in 1123 Cadwaladr and Owain ap Gruffydd ejected the invaders, and Meririonydd was annexed to Gwynedd. This strategically important acquisition furnished Gwynedd with a staging area for any future offensive against Cardigan. In 1124 Cadwallon ap Gruffydd slew the rulers of Dyffryn Clwyd, and that cantref was probably annexed to Gwynedd; for only thus, as Lloyd notes, can the appearance of Cadwallon in the Dee valley some years later, and that of Owain before Mold in the next reign, be satisfactorily explained.[161] Cadwallon was slain in battle in 1132 while invading the Powysian commote of Nanheudwy, and for a time the expansion of Gwynedd was halted; but when Owain ap Gruffydd succeeded his father in 1137, the conquests of the three brothers gave him reason to be regarded as "the most powerful of Welsh princes and Gwynedd the chief state of Wales."[162]

Chapter 9

Warfare on the Marches of Wales, 1134-1189

AS the reign of Henry I drew to a close, there were increasing signs of unrest on the Welsh march. In 1134 a Welsh band struck across the Shropshire frontier from Powys, burned the castle of Cause, and "mercilessly cut off the heads of all the persons of both sexes whom they found within it." [1] And as soon as the strong hand of Henry I was removed, rebellion flared up all along the border. Scarcely had his successor Stephen been crowned than the Welsh were in arms. Oddly enough, it was in supposedly Norman-ized Brecknock that the rising originated. Hywel ap Maredudd, a Welsh magnate who had contrived to retain some authority, mustered an army and led it southeastward toward Gower, whose thriving Anglo-Norman communities were under the protection of the earls of Warwick. The local levy was summoned to meet the threat, and on 1 January 1136 a battle was fought somewhere between Loughor and Swansea, in which the Welsh were the victors, and in which some five hundred of the Anglo-Normans are alleged to have been slain.[2] This victory was a signal for a general rising throughout South Wales. The old warrior Gruffydd ap Rhys hurried north to Gwynedd to solicit aid in ejecting the Normans from Deheubarth, while his wife Gwenllian, herself the daughter of Gruffydd ap Cynan, assumed command of a Welsh column threatening the town and castle of Kidwelly. But a little to the north of the town her forces met a Norman army commanded by the lord of the place, Maurice of London, and were badly cut up. One of Gwenllian's sons was killed; another was taken prisoner on the field that is known to this day as Maes Gwenllian.[3]

This setback, however, did not impede the spread of the revolt, for an incident shortly occurred that heartened the Welsh and discouraged the Normans. On 15 April Richard fitz Gilbert de Clare, the lord of Cardigan, was returning from a trip to England, and halted at Abergavenny. The lord of the castle, Brian fitz Count, warned him of the disturbed state of the country, and offered an escort as far as Brecon. Richard rejected the offer, and proceeded on his journey. When the party reached the forested area of Coed Grwym, bordering on Gwent and Brecknock, Brian and his attendants turned back, while Richard with a few followers rode unarmed into the forest. As might be expected, they were riding straight into an ambush laid by the local Welsh led by Morgan ab Owain, a descendant of the native dynasty. Richard and his entire party were killed, and the news spread like wildfire.[4] Owain and Cadwaladr of Gwynedd, who for years had been waiting poised in Merionydd, seized their opportunity, now that the Normans were leaderless; and although Cardigan had never been part of Gwynedd, the men of the north poured across the frontier. It would appear, from the ease with which their castles fell into the hands of the Welsh, that the Normans for their part had been demoralized by the death of Richard fitz Gilbert. The strongholds of Walter de Bec at Llanfihangel Geneu'r Glyn, and of the de Clares at Aberystwyth, were stormed and burned. These successes persuaded many waverers to join the revolt; as the princes of Gwynedd led their army southward it was strengthened by the forces of Hywel ap Maredudd of Cantref Bychan, and Madog ab Idnerth of Rhwng Gwy a Hafren. Three more Norman castles in Cardigan soon fell—the thus far unlocated fortresses of Richard de la Mare, Dinerth, and Caerwedros.[5] By now the Welsh army was so encumbered with booty that a break in operations was necessary to dispose of it. Thus ended the opening phase of the campaign to recover Cardigan.

By the end of September Owain and Cadwaladr were again operating in Cardigan, and in addition to the magnates who had already joined them, they were now accompanied by Gruffydd ap Rhys. Men from every part of central Wales marched in an army that included both horse and foot; for, as Lloyd noted, "the Welsh had learned the arts of knighthood from their Norman masters and could put heavy cavalry in the field as well as the old national infantry." [6] Their objective was now the principal castle of the district, Cardigan itself. Were it to fall, the Normans would have little hope of retaining any part of the lordship. This the Normans also realized, and they made an extraordinary effort to hold it. Contingents from all over South Wales converged on the fortress above the Teifi. No overall commander of the Norman army is mentioned by the chroniclers, but the principal figures were Stephen, the constable of Cardigan; Robert fitz Martin, lord of neighboring Cemais; and William and Maurice, the sons of Gerald of Pembroke.[7] At the approach of the Welsh, during the second week in October 1136, a Norman army of perhaps 3,000 marched out of Cardigan and intercepted the enemy at Crug Mawr, two miles away. Unfortunately no detailed account of the action has survived, and it is impossible to reconstruct even a rudimentary order of battle for either side. The rather turgid Latin of the *Gesta* indicates that the Welsh were organized in three divisions which overlapped the flanks of the Norman army.[8] All that can be said with any certainty is that the ensuing fight was a bitter one, which ended with the total rout of the Normans. Not only were they driven from the field; under the relentless pressure of the Welsh, they could not reform or make an orderly withdrawal into the town. Many attempted to flee across the Teifi bridge in the hope of reaching Cemais; but the bridge, evidently overburdened by panic-stricken refugees, collapsed, and many who had escaped from the field of battle were drowned in a river already clogged with the bodies of slain men and horses. Those who reached the town perished even more miserably, for the victorious Welsh set it afire, and everyone in it fell victim to the flames. Only a remnant of the Norman host managed to take refuge in the castle, where they held out against the furious assaults of the Welsh. Although everything around it became Welsh again, the castle of Cardigan, since it could be supplied and reinforced by sea, for many years remained a solitary outpost of Norman power.[9]

The response of the crown and of the marcher lords themselves to the crushing defeat at Crug Mawr was surprisingly ineffectual. Miles of Gloucester did indeed lead a flying column from his castle of Brecon to rescue the widow of Richard fitz Gilbert, who was shut up in Cardigan castle.[10] This, however, was a deed of knight-errantry rather than a serious attempt to stem the tide of the rebellion. King Stephen commissioned Baldwin fitz Gilbert, a brother of the late lord, and provided him with a large sum of money, to raise an army to retrieve Cardigan for the Normans. Baldwin's force, said to have numbered five hundred knights and archers, advanced to Brecon, which was apparently to have been his forward base. But that is as far as he got. Alarmed by reports of the vast numbers of the enemy and the condition of the roads, which had all been blocked with felled trees, he delayed any advance until finally he ran out of cash, whereupon the expedition ignominiously broke up. The lord of Ewias Harold, Robert fitz Harold, was said to have assumed the offensive, but the account of the chronicler is so vague that it is impossible even to locate the scene of his exploits.[11] The marcher barons were in fact too engrossed with other matters to attend to the defense of the "colonies" strung out along the frontier, and it is small wonder that the king, noting their indifference, should have washed his hands of the whole problem. He decided, according to the author of the *Gesta,* to leave Wales to the Welsh in the expectation that they would wear themselves out in their usual fratricidal strife.[12] Matters did not, of course, work out so obligingly. Instead, the Welsh simply redoubled their assaults on the remaining Norman outposts in the west.

In 1137 Gruffydd ap Rhys launched an attack on Rhos in Dyfed that brought widespread devastation. Gruffydd's death soon afterward did not end the revolt.[13] For the third time Owain and Cadwaladr of Gwynedd invaded Cardigan, this time via the inland or eastern route; and as in the previous year, the demoralized Normans were unable to hold them back. The *Brut* continues a monotonous recital of castles seized and burned "by the sons of Gruffydd ap Cynan"—Ystrad Meurig, Pont Stephen, and Humphrey's Castle. With the exception of Cardigan castle itself, all of the old Ceredigion had now been reoccupied by the Welsh. Owain and Cadwaladr, riding the crest of victory, passed the Teifi, and captured the royal castle of Carmarthen.[14] This marked the southern limit of expansion for the princes of Gwynedd. Local ambitions proved stronger than devotion to a national cause, and the realistic and naturally cautious Owain was not to be drawn into adventures that would in the end merely dissipate the strength of his own principality. Therefore, instead of cooperating with the Welsh of Deheubarth in ejecting the Normans from Dyfed and Gower, he concentrated on the pacification of Cardigan and in effecting its absorption into Gwynedd.[15] In 1138 Owain and Cadwaladr made another attempt to reduce the stubborn Norman garrison in Cardigan castle, with the aid of Anarawd and Cadell ap Gruffydd. To block any attempt to reinforce the castle by sea, a squadron of fifteen Danish ships was hired to patrol the mouth of the Teifi. But again an obstinate defense withstood the attacks of the Welsh and their Danish mercenaries, and the campaign was abandoned.[16]

It is unfortunate that no coherent account of events in other parts of Wales has survived. From the scattered references that are available, it would appear that the fighting in western and southwestern Wales was by no means an isolated occurrence, although it is not always possible to determine precisely where and when it took place. John of Hexham, for example, lumped together under the year 1136 the death at the hands of the Welsh of Richard fitz Roger and Pain fitz John with the ambush and narrow escape of Earl Ranulf of Chester.[17] From other sources it can be determined that Pain, who was sheriff of Shropshire and Herefordshire, was slain on 10 July 1137 while pursuing a band of Welsh hostiles, thus throwing doubt on the accuracy of John's other statements. It is clear, however, that the revolt was general, and not confined to Deheubarth. On 3 March 1140 the castle of Bromfield near Wrexham was burned, probably by the Welsh of Powys.[18] The evidence is indirect, but the fact that Maelienydd had to be reconquered by Hugh Mortimer in 1144 points to an earlier Welsh occupation.[19] Despite the hold that Miles of Gloucester kept on Brecknock, great devastation was wrought, probably through the guerrilla activities of Hywel ap Maredudd. Another chieftain of the same name, Hywel ap Maredudd ap Rhyddarch, was equally active in Cantref Bychan, with the result that Walter Clifford, son of Richard fitz Pons, lost his hold on Llandovery. Even in Gwent, which had been under Norman control for half a century, native leaders of ability and initiative appeared. One such was Morgan ab Owain, who captured the castle of Usk, and who under cover of the general confusion—and of the Normans' preoccupation with English politics—also seized the one at Caerleon.[20]

Throughout 1138 the tension between King Stephen and the magnates continued to mount, and in the following year civil war broke out between the king and the partisans of the empress Mathilda.[21] Once again the Welsh had freedom of action. Royal interference was now impossible on two counts. The king has his hands more than full in dealing with the Angevin faction; and direct intervention in Welsh affairs was physically impossible since most of the marcher lords adhered to the cause of Mathilda. The impressive list of her supporters on the border included her half-brother, Earl Robert of Gloucester and lord of Glamorgan; Miles of Gloucester, lord of Brecknock and later earl of Hereford; Roger, earl of Warwick and lord of Gower; Brian fitz Count, lord of Abergavenny; Robert fitz Martin; William fitz Alan; Geoffrey Talbot; and Bishop Bernard of St. David's.[22] But although these men were able to preserve a regime of law and order in those areas still in Norman hands, for many years their chief energies were devoted to the factional warfare in England and the vain attempt to seat Mathilda on the throne of her father. Elsewhere on the march, powerful Norman lords played for their own advantage. Gilbert fitz Gilbert, a brother of the late lord of Cardigan, was at first a supporter of the king, who made him earl of Pembroke in 1138; later he changed sides. The most artful turncoat, however, was Earl Ranulf of Chester, whose shifts of allegiance have already been described. The total effect was that the marcher barons paid attention to border affairs only when there was no other business at hand; and that was seldom during the decade of the 1140's. Nine years elapsed from outbreak of the revolt to the first recorded important success by the Normans. In 1144 Hugh Mortimer reoccupied the cantref of Maelienydd, and in the following year Earl Gilbert finally took possession of his earldom and rebuilt the castle of Carmarthen.[23] Mutual distrust made cooperation between the crown and the barons of the march impossible, and when in 1144 the earl of Chester suggested a joint enterprise against the principality of Gwynedd, the king was advised—very properly, in view of the earl's past record—against putting himself in the power of Ranulf of Chester. Instead, Ranulf was seized and held a prisoner until he should agree to surrender certain of his castles. Probably because the king and the barons did nothing to relieve the pressure on Cheshire, the important border fortress of Mold fell to Owain Gwynedd before the end of the year.[24]

In the principality of Gwynedd, the death of Gruffydd ap Cynan in 1137 had brought to the throne one of the great figures of medieval Welsh history—Gruffydd's son Owain, usually known as Owain Gwynedd or Owain Fawr (the Great).[25] Unfortunately Owain had other troubles besides the Normans. One of these was his brother Cadwaladr, who frequently gave him as much difficulty as his enemies to the east. Owain has been characterized as "one of those exceptional characters in Welsh history who combined the best qualities of his race with a prudence, moderation, and statesmanship rarely to be found among his impetuous, violent, and quarrelsome countrymen."[26] Cadwaladr had none of these qualities. For a while, after the failure of the attempt on Cardigan in 1138, he dropped from sight. He next appeared on the scene as joint commander, with Madog ap Maredudd of Powys, of the Welsh mercenaries hired by the earl of Chester for the campaign that culminated on 2 February 1141 in the first Battle of Lincoln.[27] Although it is not recorded that these Welsh auxiliaries contributed to the decision, they took part in the pursuit, and joined—no doubt with glee—in sacking the prosperous city of Lincoln. This adventure can hardly have had the blessing of Owain, for it served only to strengthen the position of the marcher lords. Since he could not get along with his brother, Cadwaladr was ejected from Ceredigion; then the two princes made peace, and there was an uneasy truce until 1152, when Cadwaladr was driven from Gwynedd altogether. He spent five years' exile in England, during which he married Alice de Clare, probably a sister of Earl Gilbert of Hertford—an alliance that must have been regarded with suspicion by Owain.[28]

In the meantime, although internal problems also demanded his attention, Owain continued his pressure on the western borders of Cheshire. Whatever Earl Ranulf's motives in 1144, may have been, his appeal for help from the king was based on actual need. And as soon as the earl fell into Stephen's hands, his Welsh enemies made the most of the situation. An army from Powys promptly crossed the frontier and devastated Maelor Saesneg. On 3 September 1146 the invaders were met at Wick by a Cheshire force under the command of Robert of Mold, the hereditary steward of the earldom, and were defeated with heavy casualties.[29] But at the same time Robert's own castle of Mold was under siege by a column from Gwynedd, and before the end of the year it was captured and burned.[30]

As so frequently happened, the expansion of one Welsh principality now brought it into conflict with another—in this instance the conquests of Owain Gwynedd posed a threat to Powys, then ruled by Madog ap Maredudd. The occupation of Moldsdale (Ystrad Alun) by Gwynedd brought the frontier down to the commote of Ial, a district which in 1149 was also annexed by Owain, who then constructed the castle of Tomen y Rhodwydd at Buddugre.[31] Madog, like the other Welsh princes, had profited from the confusion of the times. The loser in the region was William fitz Alan, lord of Oswestry, as well as sheriff of Shropshire during the reign of Henry I. William, who adhered to the Angevin faction, became so engrossed in English affairs that he allowed the defenses of Oswestry to fall into disrepair—an open invitation to Madog, who in 1149 swooped down on the ill-defended castle, seized it, and at once repaired the defenses.[32] For the next few years the district was again Welsh, and one contemporary source—*The Dream of Rhonabwy*—spoke of Madog ap Maredudd as lord of Dudleston and of all the land between the Ceiriog and the Vyrnwy. Madog, an able and ambitious prince, was not likely to acquiesce in Owain's seizure of territory to which Powys had long maintained a claim. It seems likely that at this time Rhuddlan and the cantref of Tegeingl had also fallen to the prince of Gwynedd, and that these successes prompted Madog to act. In 1150 he invaded Owain's newly acquired territories, supported by a contingent of knights supplied by the earl of Chester, who was threatened no less than Madog by Owain's aggressive policies. The armies of Gwynedd and Powys met at

Coleshill, miles from the old Welsh frontier, and the men of Gwynedd had the victory.[33] This triumph gave Owain possession, for the time being, of Ial, Tegeingl, and Moldsdale; and in 1153 the accession of a six-year-old heir on the death of Earl Ranulf of Chester further strengthened the prince's position.[34] As Stephen's troubled reign drew to a close, Owain Gwynedd was undoubtedly the most powerful figure in Wales, and Gwynedd unquestionably had military pre-eminence. Its frontier marched with the Dee within sight of Chester itself, although Poole's assertion that the city was "almost within his grasp" seems an exaggeration.[35]

During this same interval the princes of South Wales, and in particular the sons of Gruffydd ap Rhys—Cadell, Maredudd, and Rhys—had been nearly as successful as Owain Gwynedd. Their sphere of activity was more circumscribed, for the Normans' hold on the south coast was more secure than that of the earl of Chester in the north. The most that the princes of Deheubarth could hope for was to strike a balance; they could not expect to regain all that had been lost since the Conqueror's time. Maelienydd—recovered by Hugh Mortimer in 1144—Brecknock, Glamorgan, Gwent, and Pembroke were irrevocably lost; but in the remainder of Deheubarth, in Dyfed, Cardigan, and Ystrad Tywi, the sons of Gruffydd had been more fortunate. From their base of operations in virtually inaccessible Cantref Mawr, attacks were launched upon the Norman castles and towns of the coastal plain, and in spite of stubborn if uncoordinated resistance, the colonists were split, being driven either eastward into English Gower, or westward into Pembroke and St. David's.[36]

Earl Gilbert of Pembroke apparently did not become a resident lord until about 1145, when he rebuilt the castle at Carmarthen that had been destroyed by the Welsh in 1137. Earl Gilbert also had an interest in recovering Cardigan, and as a base of operations he built a castle at or near Pencader in the commote of Mabudryd. But in 1146 the weakness of the Norman position was quickly revealed when the sons of Gruffydd—aided by Hywel ab Owain, who held southern Cardigan—swept down upon the new castle, carried it by storm, and put the garrison to the sword. They then recaptured Carmarthen and seized Llanstephan. Earl Gilbert's attempts to recapture these two fortresses ended in failure.

The Norman and Flemish colonists, under the command of William and Maurice fitz Gerald and William fitz Hai, made a determined effort to recover Llanstephan, whose loss left a gap in the defenses of South Wales. But the Welsh garrison, commanded by Maredudd ap Gruffydd, made an equally determined defense. The scaling ladders by which the attackers tried to enter the castle were thrown down into the ditch, and the Normans retired discomfited, leaving the Welsh in control of eastern Dyfed.[37]

In 1146 the Welsh also had a unique opportunity to profit from dissension among the colonists. A quarrel broke out between William fitz Gerald and Walter fitz Wigo, lord of Deugleddyf, and the half-Welsh William did not hesitate to seek assistance from the sons of Gruffydd and Hywel ab Owain—aid which the Welsh princes gladly gave. The allies destroyed Walter's castle at Wiston (Castell Gwis), and eliminated another barrier to the Welsh reoccupation of Dyfed. In 1150 Cadell thoroughly repaired the castle at Carmarthen, which he intended to make the administrative center of his expanding state, and in the same year he kept the Normans on the defensive by a raid through the commote of Kidwelly.[38] But Cadell was near the end of his active career. In 1151, while hunting in the forest of Coed Rhath, he was ambushed by a marauding party of knights and archers from the nearby Norman stronghold of Tenby, and left for dead. Although he survived, he never resumed his old position of leadership among the Welsh of Deheubarth. Eventually he took the cowl, and died a monk in 1175.[39] The transfer of leadership from Cadell to his brothers Maredudd and Rhys brought no loss of momentum. In 1151, using Kidwelly as an avenue of approach, they crossed the Loughor; and after destroying the castle of Aberllychwr, which commanded the river crossing, they harried the adjoining district mercilessly. With true strategic insight, the brothers kept the Normans off balance by striking in quick succession at widely separated localities. In 1153 Tenby was taken by a daring night escalade, which must have caused the men of Pembroke to look to their defenses. However, the Welsh were not able to exploit their advantage further in this direction. In May the sons of Gruffydd were testing the defenses of Glamorgan, now held by Earl William, the son of Robert of Gloucester, who had died in 1147. The castle of Aberafan, held by Caradog ab Iestyn, one of the Welsh tenants of the honor, was captured and razed on the same expedition.[40]

Another military problem that had to be settled by Maredudd and Rhys was the expulsion of Gwynedd from Cardigan. Although formerly part of Deheubarth, since 1136 it had been occupied by Gwynedd, and had been divided administratively into two parts. The Normans still clung tenaciously to their isolated post at Cardigan under Robert fitz Stephen, and another attempt on the castle in 1145 by Hywel and Cynan ab Owain had been successfully beaten off by the garrison.[41] Between 1150 and 1153 the occupation of Cardigan by Gwynedd was liquidated, as Maredudd and Rhys captured the castles of the district. Although this study is not primarily concerned with warfare among the Welsh states, it is interesting to note the important role that the castles were playing in this internecine warfare by the middle of the twelfth century. Some were reconditioned Norman castles, such as Humphrey's Castle (Castel Hywel), Ystrad Meurig, and Llanfihangel Geneu'r Glyn; others, like Pengwern and Llanrhystud, were certainly built by Welsh princes on Norman models.[42] Owain Gwynedd made no serious attempt to reconquer Cardigan —another indication of his wisdom, for it would have entailed a difficult campaign with a most uncertain outcome. The brothers Maredudd and Rhys were left in undisputed possession of Cardigan; and when Maredudd died in 1155, Rhys emerged unchallenged as the ruler of the independent South Welsh.[43]

The nineteen years of Stephen's reign had given an unparalleled opportunity to the Welsh, and to a large extent they had taken advantage of it. On every front the Normans had been pushed back, if not to the frontier of 1066, at least far enough to allow the Welsh some room for maneuver. But even when confronted with this chance, the fatal contentiousness of the Welsh worked against their success. Instead of uniting every resource in an effort to drive out the Normans, Owain Gwynedd and his sons found it necessary, or desirable, to fight his brother Cadwaladr and the prince of Powys. Maredudd and Rhys ap Gruffydd set about recovering Cardigan from Gwynedd instead of trying to eliminate the remaining Norman bases in

Pembroke. The accession of Henry II to an undisputed throne in 1154 ended the opportunity for the Welsh; and although some years were to pass before the full weight of the crown was to be felt again on the marches, there still remained bases from which a Norman counteroffensive could be mounted. Superficially the successes of Owain and the sons of Gruffydd appear brilliant; once analyzed, they become but a shadow of what they might have been.

Although there was no serious opposition to the accession of Henry II, a good many affairs called for his attention before the new king could devote much of it to Wales. Among these was an incipient rebellion on the march, where two important tenants, Earl Roger of Hereford and Hugh Mortimer of Wigmore, had even begun recruiting Welsh auxiliaries. Earl Roger submitted without a fight, but a regular campaign was required to perusade Hugh of his folly.[44] Other business, in England and on the Continent, kept the king occupied until 1157. Not until the Council of Northampton does any important decision on Welsh matters seem to have been reached. At this time a punitive expedition against Owain Gwynedd was resolved upon. The division among the Welsh princes was exploited, and a rather impressive group of these agreed to support the king—including Owain's renegade brother Cadwaladr, Madog ap Maredudd of Powys and his brother Iorwerth Coch, and Hywel of Arwystli. Knight service from the feudal tenants was demanded on a reduced scale in order that those mustered could serve in excess of the customary forty days. The missile arm consisted of archers from the Shropshire borders commanded by the sheriff, William fitz Alan. In addition to the normal logistical support, a fleet was collected at Pembroke to sail around Wales and support the army on its westward advance along the coast from its base at Chester.[45]

Owain, aided by his sons Dafydd and Cynan, met this threat by concentrating the major part of the forces of Gwynedd at Basingwerk (Dinas Basing), the northern terminus of Wat's Dike, astride the road from Chester to Rhuddlan, where the position was fortified.[46] To prevent the position at Basingwerk from being turned, the sons of Owain were posted with detachments in the forested high ground to the south.[47] And Henry, who was new to the business of border warfare, did in fact make the attempt to outflank the Welsh main body. While the mass of the English army marched west along the coast road, the king with a body of light-armed troops headed into the forest, beyond supporting distance of his own main body. The results were nearly disastrous for the English, who fell into an ambush laid by Dafydd and Cynan. The attack threw the English column into confusion, and in the fighting Robert de Courcy and Eustace fitz John, the hereditary constable of Chester, were slain. The king himself owed his life to Earl Robert of Hertford, but the rumor that he had been a casualty caused Henry of Essex, the hereditary constable of England, to throw down the royal standard and flee.[48] Although the English flanking column had been roughly handled, it accomplished its mission. The Welsh attack indeed gave Owain time to evacuate his prepared position and to fall back with his main body to the neighborhood of St. Asaph; but it ended all hope of a successful stand, and the morale of the Welsh must have suffered accordingly.[49] The royal army was now able to advance unopposed to Rhuddlan, which would serve admirably as an advanced base, whereupon the army of Gwynedd was pulled back even farther to the west.[50]

It was probably at this juncture that the king received news of the misadventures of his flotilla from Pembroke. It is difficult to understand the indiscipline of twelfth-century formations. It seems quite likely that the commander of the squadron was under orders to rendezvous with the army at some specific place, such as Rhuddlan or Degannwy. Instead, lured doubtless by the prospects of plunder, the fleet anchored in the harbor of Moelfre on Anglesey. A detachment of knights went ashore and plundered the vicinity, with little distinction between lay and ecclesiastical property—and foolishly remained there overnight. News of the landing spread rapidly over the island; during the hours of darkness the natives rushed to arms, and by dawn a considerable force had gathered. They attacked the landing party, and drove it back to the ships with heavy loss.[51]

Thus far victory and defeat had been evenly balanced. The success of the maneuver that had forced Owain out of his lines at Basingwerk without a major engagement, and of the unopposed reoccupation of Rhuddlan, was partly canceled by the check administered to the landing party on Anglesey. Moreover, Owain's main force was still intact. It is understandable, therefore, that Henry was willing to offer terms to avoid what might well have become a protracted and indecisive campaign. What is not so clear is why Owain accepted those terms when he still had considerable capacity for resistance. Lloyd's statement that the prince of Gwynedd was impressed by the might of the English king, and that his prudence and sagacity argued the need for purchasing a peace "which would give him time to consolidate his power," is not very convincing.[52]

Owain's forces had administered one notable check upon the invader; his own main army was in being and uncommitted, and the English had not yet reached the old frontiers of the principality. On the basis of previous experience it seems likely that had Owain continued his policy of withdrawal and harassment, the campaign of 1157 would have ended, like some of its predecessors, in the frustration of Henry's designs and the retreat of the English army to Chester. But whatever strategic advantages he possessed, Owain agreed to the demands of the English. He rendered homage to King Henry for his principality and gave hostages in pledge of his future good conduct; he agreed to restore his troublesome brother Cadwaladr to his possessions, and resigned all claims to Tegeingl.[53] Thus a campaign that could only be called a tactical stalemate ended in a decisive victory for the king; and well might the chronicler write, "Hoc anno subjugavit sibi rex Gualensis." [54] The English border was again advanced from the Dee to the Clwyd, and an advanced base was established at Rhuddlan; Basingwerk was also fortified. Owain might be expected to have his hands full, with the contentious Cadwaladr and his jealous neighbors in Powys. Indeed, before the end of the year the castle in Ial, built by Owain only eight years earlier, was attacked and destroyed by Iorwerth Coch.[55] For the next eight years Owain behaved in exemplary fashion, and King Henry was lulled into the false security of believing that he had settled the "Gwynedd question" for good. It was now the turn of Rhys ap Gruffydd to feel the power of the English crown.

Rhys, in the year following the humiliation of Gwynedd, found that he too would have either to abandon the aggressive policies that had served so well in Stephen's time, or else to face the consequences. But Rhys had none of Owain's caution and coolness. Intending at first to resist the king, he concentrated his forces in the fastnesses of Ystrad Tywi. But eventually less bellicose councils prevailed, and Rhys took the unusual step of going to England to throw himself on the king's mercy. Peace was made— but on Henry's terms, which meant enormous territorial concessions. In this instance, restoration of royal authority meant also the restoration of all the Norman colonists dispossessed since 1136, such as the Clares in Cardigan and the Cliffords in Cantref Bychan. Rhys's "principality of Deheubarth" was now reduced to the lordship of Cantref Mawr and a few enclaves surrounded by Norman lands.[56] The new order was not long in the making. By the beginning of June 1158, Earl Roger of Hertford was preparing to take over his father's inheritance after a lapse of twenty-two years. The strongholds lately garrisoned by Rhys—Humphrey's Castle (Castel Hywel), Ystrad Meurig, Llanrhystud, Dinerth, and Aberdovey—were now occupied by Roger's troops. Cantref Bychan, with its castle at Llandovery, was reoccupied by Walter Clifford. The Welsh did not take kindly to the return of the Anglo-Normans, and gave scant honor to the settlement of 1158. In the same year Einon ap Anarwd, a nephew of Rhys, sacked and destroyed Humphrey's Castle and slew its garrison.[57] When Rhys himself began hostile operations against both Earl Roger and Walter Clifford, his flagrant disregard of the settlement brought the king into South Wales post-haste, and Rhys again submitted to the royal authority. King Henry crossed the Channel in the middle of August, supposing that he left behind him a thoroughly cowed and submissive Wales.[58]

Of how mistaken he was, an incident that took place during 1158 in the supposedly quite Normanized honor of Glamorgan gave graphic demonstration. At this time the honorial lordship of Senghenydd, lying in the uplands between the Rhymney and the Taff, was held by one Ifor ap Meurig, a brother-in-law of Rhys ap Gruffydd. Ifor, a man of daring and resource, most adept at irregular warfare, was also a quarrelsome one. In a feud with his neighbors to the east, Morgan ab Owain, lord of Gwynllwg and

Caerleon, was waylaid and murdered in 1158.[59] This deed of violence brought Ifor no profit, since Morgan's brother Iorwerth succeeded him in the possession of Caerleon. Casting about for some new adventure, Ifor came up with a daring plan to kidnap Earl William of Gloucester, his wife, and his son from their own castle at Cardiff, and to hold them for ransom in the hills of Senghenydd. And this incredible plan was successfully carried out, with the aid of ladders, accomplices within the castle, and what must have been unusually lax arrangements for internal security. It is unknown what concessions Earl William was forced to grant before his release with his wife and son. In any event, the exploit shows that even among the feudalized Welsh of Glamorgan, something of the old spirit remained that could prove dangerous to the colonists in time of trouble.[60]

Henry's Welsh policy had been based on a complex balance of power all along the march. In the south the power of Rhys ap Gruffydd was apparently neutralized, if not completely nullified, by the return of the marchers and his own territorial losses. In the north the menace of Gwynedd was contained by the Normans of Chester and the Welsh of Powys, whose prince, Madog ap Maredudd, was closely allied to the English. To be sure, Madog had also had to make concessions, losing Oswestry to William fitz Alan, who was reinstated as sheriff of Shropshire in July 1155; but Madog found the English less of a threat to his position than his fellow Welshmen of Gwynedd, and he maintained the alliance faithfully until his death in 1160.[61] Then Henry's delicate balance began to disintegrate. Madog had no single heir to succeed him, and the unity of Powys disappeared as the principality was divided among five different princes. The end of political unity meant that unity of policy vanished likewise, for although the principal magnates, Owain Cyfeiliog and Iorwerth Coch, sometimes professed friendship with England, their usual policy was merely one of self-interest. At all events, Powys was no longer the threat to Gwynedd that it had been under the capable rule of Madog, and could no longer be so effective an instrument of English policy on the border.[62] As early as 1163, when Owain Cyfeiliog and Owain Fychan combined forces to capture and destroy the royal castle of Carreghofa, it was abundantly clear that one of the factors on which King Henry counted for the political and military stability of the marches had vanished.[63]

The prince of Gwynedd was not slow in taking advantage of the opportunity created by the death of Madog. Although his relations with the English government remained strictly correct, he was soon pursuing an aggressive policy toward fragmented Powys. By 1162 Owain had seized Cyfeiliog and its castle of Tafolwern, after a conflict with Hywel ab Ienef of Arwystli.[64] But if Owain kept to his agreement with King Henry, not so the volatile Rhys of Deheubarth. The second peace of 1158 lasted only a few months; by 1159, Rhys was again on a rampage in Dyfed. His siege of Carmarthen reduced the place to such straits that an army was mustered under Earl Reginald of Cornwall and marched to relieve it.[65] The siege was raised, and Rhys, checked for a time, retired to the fastnesses of Cantref Mawr. But the English apparently deemed that the time had come to make an end of Rhys altogether. The army that was recruited numbered five earls —Reginald of Cornwall, William of Gloucester, Roger of Hertford, Richard of Pembroke, and Patrick of Salisbury—among its commanders. Also present was a Welsh contingent from Gwynedd under the command of Owain's brother Cadwaladr, and of Hywel and Cynan ab Owain. The northern prince seems to have done more than was necessary to express his disapproval of the activities of the rebellious Rhys.[66] But for all the formidable array that mustered at Dinevor, the expedition was a fiasco. In the rough forested ground and on the treacherous moors of Cantref Mawr, Rhys was more than master of the situation. His positions were chosen with such skill that the enemy dared not risk an assault, and in the end the army of the five earls marched down the hills in complete ignominy. A face-saving truce was later arranged which permitted Rhys to demobilize his forces.[67]

For the next three years Rhys remained quiescent. In the north Owain Gwynedd pursued his policy of appeasement, even going so far as to turn fugitive Welsh princes over to the English king.[68] Then in 1162 Rhys again took up arms and captured the castle of Llandovery. That the crown for some years past had been at considerable expense on the fortifications of this castle, shows its importance in the scheme of border defense.[69] Its fall was apparently the last straw. Rhys's successes were due in part to the long absence of the king on the Continent; but in June 1163 Henry was once again in England, and within a short time he was on his way west to show that he meant business. The Cambrian annalist says that he marched "with the whole army of England and Wales." [70] He moved unopposed through Glamorgan and Gower, where Welsh irregulars were active, through Rhys's own sphere of influence; he passed through Carmarthen, crossed the defiles of the Gwili, and at last cornered his enemy at Pencader on the frontier of Cardigan. At a meeting between the king of England and the prince of Deheubarth, exactly what took place is not known, except that Rhys threw himself on the king's mercy and was carried back to England a prisoner. [71] Henry's return march was a show of force that took him through Cardigan, Maelienydd, and Radnor—with his princely captive as an exhibition of the folly of resistance to English might. On his return to England a decision had to be made as to the disposition of Cantref Mawr— whether to turn it over to the marchers or to set Rhys at liberty and permit him to return to his highland domain. Eventually the latter course was adopted, and on 1 July 1163 Rhys, along with Malcolm IV of Scotland and Owain of Gwynedd, rendered homage to the king at Woodstock. [72] Within a short time this stormy petrel of South Welsh history was back in his paternal home on the banks of the Towy. And once again it was not long before he found an excuse to repudiate the homage he had so recently sworn. The *casus belli,* on this occasion was that Earl Robert of Hertford had given protection to the murderer of Rhys's nephew Eunon, the crime presumably having been committed while Rhys was a prisoner in England. [73] On this pretext, Rhys launched a savage raid into Cardigan in 1164, destroying the principal castle of the commote of Mabwnion as well as one recently constructed at the mouth of the Rheidol— probably the second castle at Aberystwyth. [74] By the time Rhys had finished his work, little was left to the colonists in Cardigan save the town and castle of Cardigan itself. Within less than a year, all of Henry's work of 1163 had been more than undone. Resolutely, the king prepared for yet another expedition. A council at Northampton in October 1164 concurred in the levy of large numbers of infantry for service in Wales, and although numbers of the English tenants compounded their quotas for a money payment, others doubtless furnished the required number of troops, and the king used the money for the recruiting of mercenaries.[75] The Pipe Roll for the twelfth year of the reign (1165/1166) sheds interesting light on the preparations for the campaign. Some three hundred shields were made for mercenary troops at a cost of slightly over a shilling each. Ships were hired to transport grain from Worcester to Shrewsbury, the base of operations for the expedition. More significantly, nearly £115 was expended for services to Welsh princes, including Owain Cyfeiliog and Iorwerth Coch, among others—money that was wasted, as it turned out.[76]

But this time the Becket controversy had sharply divided public opinion in England. There can be little doubt that this division was what finally persuaded Owain Gwynedd, after years of appeasement, to become a Welsh patriot once again. And the decision of the prince of Gwynedd was the key to the entire military situation on the march. With both Rhys and Owain in the field, the lesser princes threw in their lot with what very nearly approached a national cause. Faced no longer with the relatively simple problem of running Rhys to earth, but with a rising of the entire Welsh people, Henry made preparations on a scale requisite to the threat. Troops were requisitioned or recruited from every part of the Angevin dominions and beyond—from England, Normandy, Flanders, Anjou, Poitou, Aquitaine, and Scotland, if the chronicler may be believed.[77] The tenants-in-chief mustered their knightly contingents as well as the foot "sergeants" demanded by the Council of Northampton. Mercenaries were hired; military supplies and commissary stores were forwarded to the staging area at Shrewsbury. By way of naval support, the king contracted for a Danish fleet from Dublin to create a diversion in the Welsh rear by harassing the coasts of Gwynedd.[78] To secure his own rear against attack, truces with the king of France and the count of Flanders were arranged during the spring of 1165. Returning about the middle of May from a hurried visit to the Continent, Henry found that hostilities had already been opened. A column from Gwynedd under the command of Dafydd ab

Owain had crossed the Clwydian hills into Tegeingl, momentarily depriving the English of the initiative. In addition to widespread plundering, the invaders had put the castles of Rhuddlan and Basingwerk in such jeopardy by their unexpected attack that the king abruptly had to alter his plans and hasten to their relief. Although he spent only a few days in the north, it is certain that the timetable for the start of the expedition was upset. Not until the end of July was the king back at Shrewsbury; somewhat later he was at Oswestry, putting the final touches on the preparations for the campaign.[79]

In the meantime the Welsh had not been idle. Faced with the greatest armament yet to be concentrated on the frontier, the princes exhibited a national solidarity for which there was no precedent in Welsh history. Apparently by unanimous consent the overall command was conferred on Owain Gwynedd, doubtless because the northern contribution in men was the largest; certainly his conduct of the campaign of 1157 was not such as to inspire confidence in his military judgment. With his brother Cadwaladr he concentrated the forces of Gwynedd at Corwen in the valley of the Edeyrnion—a sound strategic decision which put him on the flank of any English advance into Wales from Shrewsbury. At Corwen the army was joined by the contingents of the other principalities under their princes—Rhys of Deheubarth, Owain Cyfeiliog and Iorwerth Coch of Powys (despite the sums lavished on them by the English), and Cadwallon ap Madog and Einion Clud from the Welsh lands between the Wye and the Bristol channel. It was indeed a feat to have gathered so many Welsh princes together in a common case. And whatever the shortcomings of Owain Gwynedd as a military strategist, the unity of command contributed much to the outcome of the campaign.[80]

The English army moved out of Oswestry and crossed the frontier. It soon passed the cleared areas and found itself in the heavily forested valley of the Ceiriog. Here it had to contend not only with the physical difficulties of the terrain, but with Welsh irregulars who hung onto the flanks of the advancing army and inflicted numerous casualties with their harassing tactics. To counter this irritating though not particularly dangerous enemy, the king ordered that the passage be cleared of timber and undergrowth which afforded cover and concealment for the guerrillas. This was no doubt an effective measure, but it must have slowed the rate of march considerably. Across the valley the invading army began to climb the Berwyn range, which rises here to a height of nearly 2,000 feet, by a road still known as *Fford y Saeson*—the "English Road"—across a stretch of boggy moorland and heath leading down to the valley of the Dee.[81] In the open highlands the passage of the English army could be accomplished without harassment by irregulars, who were deprived of concealment. But the Welsh cause was now aided by a not unexpected ally—the weather. In a relatively dry August the Berwyn range, although troublesome to cross, presented no insuperable obstacle. But in August of 1165 it seems to have rained almost continually. The road became impassable, and the English army was forced to go into camp. As the rain continued, the camp became a morass, and the very size of the army now turned into a handicap. Not only was it too unwieldy to penetrate farther under such unfavorable conditions, but the logistical problem was insoluble. The continual rain had doubtless ruined many of the supplies carried with the army, and with the roads virtually impassable, additional supplies could not be forwarded in sufficient quantity from the advanced base at Oswestry. Food and forage were, of course, unobtainable on the bleak rain-soaked slopes of the Berwyns. King Henry was now forced to choose between the unpleasant alternatives of starvation or retreat. Reluctantly he chose the latter, and the frustrated English army slowly retraced its steps through the mud back to its base in Shropshire without ever having come to grips with the enemy. The king vented his wrath on his Welsh hostages, twenty-two of whom were blinded and castrated—including a son of Rhys and two sons of Owain. Henry hurried to Chester to see whether anything might yet be done to retrieve the disaster. But his last resort, the Danish fleet, was too small to attempt anything effective, and it was dismissed.[82]

There is perhaps no example in the military history of medieval England of an expedition so carefully planned in all its details that accomplished so little. Although Lloyd declares that the disaster was not accidental, it is hard not to agree with Henry's contemporary, Giraldus, concerning the reasons for its failure.[83]

The expedition of 1165 was not organized to campaign in Wales. Although some attention was paid to the recruitment of troops suitable for warfare in forest and mountains, there were obviously too many heavy contingents totally unsuited to fighting in Wales during a rainy August. At any rate, Henry regarded the defeat as final; he made no attempts in the following years to subdue the Welsh. Funds were expended on the garrisoning and provisioning of castles—Rhuddlan, Prestatyn, Mold, Chirk, Basingwerk, Whitchurch, Shrawardine, and Bishop's Castle—but these were defensive measures only, not preparations for a further offensive.[84] "Everything," as Lloyd has written, "goes to show that he looked on the Berwyn disaster as the grave of his Welsh ambitions." [85] And the debacle had come not through defeat in the open field, but through the vagaries of the weather—which did a better job probably, than the Welsh could have done themselves.

The Welsh concentration at Corwen broke up as soon as the threat of invasion was at an end, and each prince thereafter went his own way. Rhys ap Gruffydd marched south with the objective of finally clearing the Normans out of Cardigan. Almost the whole of the province was already in his hands except for the castle of Cardigan, which still held for Earl Roger by his castellan, Robert fitz Stephen. That stronghold fell at last on 1 November 1166 through the treachery of a Welsh priest, Rhygifarch. The garrison was allowed to march out with what amounted to the honors of war, but the castle was razed and the castellan, Robert, was imprisoned in chains where he languished for three years.[86] Shortly thereafter, the seizure by Rhys of the Carew fortress of Cilgerran put him in position to threaten the great castle of Emlyn. He was now master of Cardigan, as well as of Ystrad Tywi and a large part of Dyfed—a position that compared favorably with the one he had held at his first test of strength with Henry II. He had eliminated the Clares in Cardigan and the Cliffords in Cantref Bychan, and all attempts to evict him from his newly acquired territories had ended in failure. In 1166 an army of Normans and Flemings from Pembroke ravaged the commote of Iscoed and made two attempts to recapture Cilgerran, but Rhys was too strong to be ousted.[87] The debacle on the Berwyn slopes was having its repercussions all over Wales. The Welsh were encouraged to take the initiative on all fronts, and the Anglo-Normans had suffered a shock to both prestige and morale.

To the north Owain Gwynedd moved to take advantage of the situation, though, as might be expected, his actions were more cautious than those of the impetuous Rhys. His first objective was to eliminate the castles in Tegeingl that barred the advance of his frontier to the Dee. In 1166 Basingwerk was attacked and destroyed; and when, in November, a column commanded by the earls of Leicester and Essex was sent to rebuild the castle, the English were defeated and scattered by a sudden Welsh attack. No further attempt was made to refortify the site. In 1167 Owain laid siege to the fortress of Rhuddlan. In anticipation of an effort to relieve so important a castle, Owain appealed to Deheubarth for reinforcements, which Rhys willingly supplied. The siege dragged on for three months, while the Welsh persevered with unusual tenacity; at the end of the year with no relief in sight, the castle fell into the hands of Owain and was destroyed. With the capture of the nearby castle of Prestatyn, Owain was again master of Tegeingl, and the frontier of Gwynedd was once again advanced to the Dee.[88] The reduction of Rhuddlan and Prestatyn and the recovery of Tegeingl were the final military achievements of Owain Gwynedd, and the culminating success for the principality whose borders now extended from the Dovey to the Dee.[89]

While Rhys was expanding his dominions in the south at the expense of the Clares in Cardigan and Dyfed, and while Owain was pushing the boundaries of Gwynedd eastward at the expense of the earldom of Chester, both were meddling to their own advantage in the affairs of Powys. Once the "union of princes" had disintegrated, that unhappy principality was torn by dissension. Iorwerth Coch soon reverted to the English alliance, and was rewarded with the custody of the castle of Chirk as early as April 1166. This precipitated a war between Iorwerth and his nephews Owain ap Madog and Owain Cyfeiliog, who drove Iorwerth out of Mochnant and divided the region between themselves. But by the next year, 1167, Owain Cyfeiliog had renewed his English connection. This brought down on him the combined forces of Deheubarth and Gwynedd, acting, or so it was asserted, in the interests of Owain ap Madog. The commote of Caereinion with its castle was taken from Owain Cyfeiliog and given to Owain ap Madog. Owain Cyfeiliog then turned to his English friends, with whose assistance he recovered Caereinion; this seems to have cemented the alliance between him and the English, for thereafter he was usually on their side.[90] In truth, the princes of Powys were now in an impossible position, and they were probably correct in thinking that they had less to fear from the English, so long as they kept the peace, than from their powerful and rapacious neighbors in Gwynedd and Deheubarth.

But the era of Owain Gwynedd was nearly over. In 1168 he had sent an embassy to King Louis VII of France with an offer of assistance in the latter's war with Henry II. This was the old campaigner's final act of defiance toward the English king, for he died on 23 November 1170 and was buried near the high altar in the cathedral of Bangor.[91] Before the end of the year his sons had already fought one battle over the division of the inheritance. This led to the forcible elimination of Hywel by his half-brothers Dafydd and Rhodri. The remaining five brothers agreed for a time to partition the domains of Owain, and later those of their uncle Cadwaladr, who died in 1172. In 1173 the ambitions of Dafydd, who had come to terms with England, led to a renewal of the strife. He served Henry loyally in the revolt of 1173–1174; as a reward, in 1174 king's half-sister Emma, bastard daughter of Count Geoffrey of Anjou, became his wife. But his ambitions to reunite all of Gwynedd were more than he could carry out, and after 1176, when his brothers united against him, his domains were limited to the cantrefs east of the Conway. A rough balance was established among the princes, and was still operating at the death of Henry II.[92]

The death of Owain Gwynedd left Rhys ap Gruffydd of Deheubarth the unquestioned leader among the princes of Wales, a position of pre-eminence he occupied until his death some twenty years later. In a way the ascendancy of Deheubarth was a freak, the result of a unique set of conditions. The geography of South Wales was unfavorable to the permanent establishment of a strong native state. The country lay open to invasion on all sides; there were no such barriers as the Rhuddlan marshes or the cliffs of Penmaenmawr which guarded the approaches to Gwynedd. Cantref Mawr, in the center of South Wales, was wild and rugged enough to offer refuge to Welsh bands, but its very wildness prevented it from becoming the center of a viable territorial state. Deheubarth in the last part of the twelfth century was the personal creation of Rhys ap Gruffydd; but even his abilities, and his unquenchable energy and enthusiasm, might not have been of much avail had it not been for the existence of unusually favorable circumstances. Of these, the first was the quarrel of Henry II with Archbishop Becket, that culminated in the martyrdom of the latter in 1070. Although it is most certainly an exaggeration to say with Lloyd that the king was "so bereft of friends and reputation that the Welsh no longer had reason to fear his vengeance," his involvement in this and other matters made it impossible for Henry to deal singlemindedly with affairs on the border.[93] A second and more important circumstance, from the military point of view, was the Anglo-Norman conquest of Ireland. The history of that adventure falls outside the scope of this study; but its success had a bearing on the whole subsequent history of South Wales, for it upset the entire military balance of power in that region. "It would be no exaggeration to say that the exploits of Earl Richard and his followers was the making of Rhys as a prince of wide and firmly established authority." [94] In the first place, the pressure upon Rhys was removed as many of his most inveterate enemies were siphoned off by the Irish venture. In 1167 William fitz Godebert of Rhos departed; in 1169 he was joined by Robert fitz Stephen, the former castellan of Cardigan—whom Rhys had shrewdly let go after three years' imprisonment—together with Meilyr fitz Henry, Miles of St. David's, Robert of Barry, Maurice de Prendergast, Herve de Montmorenci, and Maurice fitz Gerald; and in 1170 Raymond the Fat, son of William fitz Gerald of Carew, and Strongbow himself, Earl Richard of Pembroke, crossed the Irish Sea to claim his royal bride.[95] Moreover, they took with them considerable numbers of men-at-arms and infantry. When the death of King Dermot in the spring of 1171 seemed to put the crown of Leinster within the grasp of the ambitious earl, the king had no choice but to intervene actively. There had been no royal sanction for the enterprise, and King Henry's displeasure was manifest when he received the news of Earl Richard's succession. A semi-independent marcher earl could by no means be allowed to become an independent king in Ireland. It requires only a little imagination to suppose that Henry was aware that many of the difficulties of his own position stemmed from that day in 1066 when a semi-independent duke of Normandy became an independent king of England.[96] In August 1171 Henry landed at Portsmouth; by early September he was at Newenham on the edge of the Forest of Dean, making final preparations for a march through South Wales to Milford Haven, where a fleet was being collected to transport him to Ireland. At this point Earl Richard saw the light and came to make his submission—at a price. At the same time, Rhys also met with the king and was granted the royal favor. In return the prince of Deheubarth promised to deliver twenty-four hostages as guarantees of his good behavior, and to make a payment of three hundred horses and four thousand cattle. The process had begun which was calculated to raise Rhys as a counterweight to the Anglo-Norman barons, and which within a short time was to make Rhys the principal agent of the crown in South Wales.[97]

In spite of the submission of Earl Richard at Newenham, the king marched through South Wales to Pembroke. Here he confirmed Rhys in all the lands he had recently won. There was no question this time of restoring the colonial families. In addition to his original holding of Cantef Mawr, Rhys was recognized as the legal possessor of Cardigan and Cantref Bychan, despite the claims of the houses of Clare and Clifford. Ystwyf and Efelffre on the south bank of the western Taf were to be his also, as well as the castle of Emlyn which Rhys had seized from William fitz Gerald in 1165.[98] As tangible evidence of his pre-eminent position, Rhys began, in the summer of 1171, to rebuild the castle of Aberteivi (Cardigan) as the military and administrative center of the principality. In 1172 he was created justiciar, probably as a legal recognition of his supremacy over the other princes of South Wales—a position well expressed by the popular title *yr Arglwydd Rhys*—"the Lord Rhys." [99]

But Rhys was much more than a Welsh prince in high favor with the king of England, or than an English stooge. He had become himself a marcher baron, and had the relationship persisted, the assimilation of Wales into England might have been achieved at far lower cost in men and money. As it was, the concord of the races depended almost entirely on the accord between King Henry and the Lord Rhys. When the rebellion of the Young King broke out in 1173, Rhys was prompt in sending his son Hywel to serve on the king's staff in Normandy.[100] In 1174 Rhys in person led a large contingent to the siege of Tutbury castle, which Earl William of Derby was holding against the king's deputies.[101] And when the revolt in England collapsed in July, about a thousand South Welsh troops were shipped across the Channel to augment Henry's continental forces in his war with Louis VII of France.[102] It might be said with justice that the tranquillity of Wales during the crisis of 1173-1174 and the active participation of Welsh troops in the suppression of the revolt were important factors in King Henry's ultimate triumph. It might also be said that Rhys, in supporting the king rather than attempting to make capital of the latter's difficulties, was playing a more intelligent role than any of his predecessors or successors. The survival of Wales, and of Welsh nationality, in the long run could not be achieved by indiscriminate resort to arms, for the two countries were not at all evenly matched in military or economic resources. These objectives could be won only by the cooperation of Welsh leaders with the English government, and this Rhys seems to have understood. In 1175 there were two conferences with the king—at Geddington and at Oxford—at which the Welsh princes rendered homage to Henry and recognized his overlordship. Lloyd's statement that this marked a truce in the long struggle between the two nationalities seems only partially true.[103] Poole's analysis is more nearly accurate concerning the attitude of the crown:

These councils illustrate the working of the new policy which had been adopted in 1171 towards Wales. It was a policy of peace, not one of war: of conciliation, not of destruction of Welsh independence. The king was content to leave the affairs on Wales in the hands of Welsh princes provided they remained loyal and recognized his suzerainty. On the whole it was a success. The country was relatively quiet during the later years of Henry's reign. The Welsh were not fighting against the English and not much among themselves. Not a few of them employed their military skill to their pecuniary advantage in the service of the Crown.[104]

The assertion that the Welsh were not fighting the English is, however, somewhat misleading. It is true that the major princes, those of Gwynedd, Powys, and Deheubarth, had adopted a peaceful policy toward the English crown. But some of the minor princes, particularly those in areas long considered pacified, stirred up considerable trouble in the 1170's and 1180's. These disorders are of interest because they illustrate on a small scale irregular military activity against an occupying power, as well as the difficulty experienced by the Lord Rhys in controlling the activities of the native magnates in his own bailiwick.

During the troubled times of Stephen the town and castle of Caerleon had been seized by a Welsh chieftain, the prince of Gwynllwg, in whose family it remained until 1171. On his march to Pembroke in that year King Henry dispossessed the current tenant, Iorwerth ab Owain, for undisclosed reasons. Lloyd's supposition that the king thought it improper for such an important castle to be in Welsh hands does not bear scrutiny in the light of his subsequent agreements with Rhys of Deheubarth.[105] Iorwerth, however, did not accept the royal judgment as final. Although the sources are not very revealing, it is reasonable to suppose that Iorwerth withdrew to the highlands of Gwynllwg and conducted his next operation from there. After waiting until the king and his army were well on their way to Pembroke, Iorwerth, with his sons Owain and Hywel and his nephew Morgan ap Seisyll of Upper Gwent, descended upon Caerleon and destroyed the town, although the castle had been provisioned against such an eventuality and was able to hold out. The contest continued despite the check, however, and in 1172 the king summoned Iorwerth to a conference at Newport in Monmouthshire for the purpose of airing his grievances. At this juncture Iorwerth's son Owain was murdered by the earl of Gloucester's men at Cardiff, and the negotiations were consequently broken off. The lord of Gwynllwg and his remaining son reverted to guerrilla warfare, and in the following year the revolt against the king gave them an unlooked-for opportunity. On 21 July Iorwerth launched a successful attack on the castle of Caerleon; in mid-August, a great raid conducted by Hywel on Nether Went carried to the very walls of Chepstow itself.[106] This was the chief success of the insurgents; for although the king returned to Normandy immediately after the suppression of the baronial revolt, steps were also taken to restore order in Gwent. Early in 1175 Iorwerth lost Caerleon, as well as the castle of Usk, which was betrayed to the men of Earl Richard of Pembroke and Striguil.[107] But the loss was only temporary; Caerleon was restored to Iorwerth through the good offices of the Lord Rhys at the Council of Gloucester (1175) and when Archbishop Baldwin made his journey through Wales in 1188, Usk was in the hands of Hywel ap Iorwerth.[108]

Brecknock and Upper Gwent, which might have been considered pacified, were also the scene of disorders. On 12 April 1175 Henry, the lord of these two districts, was killed in Gwent by Seisyll ap Dyfnal. Later that year the lordship passed by inheritance to William de Braose, also lord of Radnor and Builth, who for a generation and a half was to be prominent in the history of the march.[109] William played a perfidious role, which for many a year kept the border in a state of unrest that at times broke out into actual insurrection. In fact, he lost no time in putting himself at odds with the Welsh magnates of Gwent. He summoned the leading Welshmen of the district, including Seisyll ap Dyfnal, the slayer of Henry, and his son Geoffrey, to the castle of Abergavenny on the pretext of importing an official edict concerning the bearing of arms. There they were set upon and massacred without warning. At the same time, before news of the slaughter could spread, William dispatched a body of armed retainers to ravage Seisyll's lands. Seisyll's wife was taken captive, and his seven-year-old son was murdered before her eyes. Thus did William de Braose avenge the murder of his uncle. "The border warfare was at all times savage and unpitying, but it did not often witness perfidy and barbarity of this deep dye . . ."[110]

The massacre at Abergavenny was not forgotten, although the Gwentians were to wait seven years for a chance to avenge it. Finally, in 1182, the Welsh rose, led by the relatives of Seisyll, and besieged the castle of Abergavenny. The piping times of peace on the border had led to a neglect of the defenses; the castle ditch had been allowed to grow up with brush and undergrowth, and the assailants could advance under cover right up the walls. At dawn, when the vigilance of the constable's watch was at a low ebb, the insurgents broke into the castle, drove the garrison into the keep, and applied the torch. It was on this occasion, as Giraldus was to note a few years later; that Welsh arrows penetrated the oaken doors of the keep.[111] Hostilities did not cease with the destruction of Abergavenny castle. Sometime later, while William de Braose with the assistance of Ranulf Poer, the sheriff of Herefordshire and one of the principals in the massacre of 1175, was building a castle at Dingestow on the river Trothy, they were attacked by Welsh irregulars, again at dawn. The English were caught completely by surprise; in the ensuing fight Sheriff Ranulf was slain, and William de Braose barely escaped with his life. The timely arrival of Ranulf Glanville, the justiciar, with reinforcements saved the day, but the Welsh had won a considerable moral victory.[112]

Rhys thus had his difficulties in keeping the minor Welsh chieftains in check. Feuds that had gone on for generations were not to be put aside in a moment, and the conflict between Welshman and Anglo-Norman flared up periodically. At times native prince and Norman earl combined against another Welsh magnate, as in 1177, when Dafydd of Gwynedd aided Earl Hugh of Chester in the detachment of Maelor from Powys—though the conquest was not permanent. The prince of Deheubarth had trouble also with his male progeny, at least five of whom had reached maturity by the end of the reign and whose frequent escapades periodically had their father in hot water. Fortunately this was a problem that Henry II could well understand, and border incidents that might under other circumstances have precipitated hostilities were not permitted to undermine the royal policy of "peaceful coexistence." Where each side was determined to avoid a conflict, ways were found to do so.[113]

The most severe test of the cooperative relations between Henry and Rhys came in 1185, when a rising of the Welsh took place in Glamorgan, then administered by officials of the crown. The time, place, and leadership of the insurrection are uncertain, but Cardiff and Kenfig were burned, and Neath was so closely invested that it had to be relieved by sea. The level of military efficiency attained by the Welsh in the late twelfth century is indicated by their use of siege machinery, which was burned by the English when the besieging army retreated.[114] The determined effort to capture Neath points to Morgan ap Caradog ab Iestyn, lord of neighboring Rhwng Nedd ac Afan, as one of the leaders of the revolt.[115] The seriousness with which the crown regarded the rebellion is reflected in the Pipe Roll entries for the Exchequer year 1184/1185. Unusual expenses are recorded for South Wales, and particularly for Glamorgan. A total of £412 13s.4d. was disbursed for military purposes, by far the greater portion—£298 5s.—as wages to troops augmenting the garrisons of Neath, Newcastle Bridgend, Cardiff, Castleton, Kenfig, and Chepstow.[116] It is of interest to note that the erstwhile rebel, Hywel ab Iorwerth, lord of Caerleon, was now considered reliable enough to command stipendiary troops raised for the emergency.[117] Since most of these troops were raised for garrison duty, it is not surprising that they were mainly infantry, although mounted elements were stationed at Castleton and Chepstow.[118] Lesser sums were spent on provisions (£13 10s.), construction (£70 11s.3 1/2d.), and miscellaneous military items (£23 7s.1/2d.), including £8 19s.1/2d. for six ships to run arms and provisions into Neath.[119] Finally, £7 was paid out in compensation to individuals who had lost military equipment, presumably through enemy action. The justiciar, Ranulf Glanville, received £4 for one lorica and two hauberks lost at Neath, and Walter Luvel and John of Bath were paid £3 for two war horses. Either the royal claims agent was unusually tight-fisted, or at 30s. apiece these must have been sorry nags.[120]

The insurrection can scarcely have lasted beyond the summer of 1185, for few entries in the Pipe Roll for 1185/1186 can be construed as anything but ordinary military expenses for South Wales. The amity between King Henry and the Lord Rhys survived this crisis, and when the king died in 1189, the rulers of Wales were nearly all Welshmen. With the exception of Rhys himself, none of these was of outstanding character or ability; but mediocrity was sufficient under the political conditions then obtaining, for on the English side of the border a similar lack of talent prevailed. In the north, the palatine earldom of Chester was in the hands of the younger Ranulf, who had succeeded his father Earl Hugh in 1181. Because of his marriage, the center of his interests was on the Continent rather than on the march. Ellesmere was held by a native prince, Dafydd ab Owain. In Shropshire William fitz Allan II was lord of Oswestry and Clun; Montgomery was still in English hands, and the Mortimer lords of Wigmore exerted continual pressure on the princes of Maelienydd. To the south and west, William de Braose held the lordship not only of Brecknock but also of Builth, Radnor, and Upper Gwent, lands that pushed a huge salient into Welsh territory and formed an ever-present threat to Cardigan and Ystrad Tywi. However, William's harsh policies stirred up enough trouble among the Welsh of his own lordships to keep him fully occupied.[121] Pembroke and Glamorgan, the two great honors on the south coast, were still administered by the crown in 1189, and it was no part of royal policy at this stage to disturb the peaceful relations between the English government and the prince of Deheubarth.

Conditions were equally stable on the Welsh side of the border. In Gwynedd the balance of power that had been established in 1175 among the heirs of Owain Gwynedd was maintained. Powys was also still divided, but though there was constant armed bickering across the frontier, no permanent changes ensued. Likewise in Maelienydd, although incidents were frequent, no major conflict was allowed to develop.[122] The peace that generally reigned on the frontier at the death of Henry II was due in part, of course, to the royal policy of balancing the Welsh against the ambitious and potentially dangerous marcher lords. But the fact should not be ignored that the Welsh were themselves becoming more capable of resisting English aggression. It has been noted that the Welsh aristocracy had begun to adopt the heavy cavalry formations of their adversaries, while retaining the light-armed infantry so well adapted to rough forested terrain, as early as the second quarter of the twelfth century. By 1185 the Welsh were enough advanced in military technology to construct siege engines for the investment of Neath. And to an increasing extent the Welsh princes were relying on castles as centers of military and political authority. In 1188, when Giraldus accompanied Archbishop Baldwin on his mission through the country to preach the crusade, many of the castles at which they received hospitality were those of native Welsh magnates.[123] Some of these had been captured from the Normans; but others, such as Rhaiader-Gwy and Carn Madryn, had recently been built by the Welsh themselves.[124] This added, of course, to the military potential of the Welsh, and from then on increased the difficulty of reducing the principalities.

But though the military occupation of Wales was checked for the moment, and indeed had been thrust back at numerous points, the way for military and political conquest was being prepared by paramilitary means—namely the church, which ironically enough was better organized and in possession of a more efficient chain of command than any military organization of the day. From the very beginning, as noted elsewhere, the Norman settlers had made use of the church to secure the conquest. Though they were lavish in bestowing churches and tithes, and in setting up new monasteries, the beneficiaries were English, and particularly Norman, rather than Welsh establishments. In South Wales before 1135, this ecclesiastical imperialism aided immeasurably in helping the Normans to secure a firm foothold.[125] Equally important was the subjection of the four Welsh sees—St. David's, Bangor, Llandaff, and St. Asaph's—to Canterbury despite a spirited if somewhat fraudulent campaign to elevate St. David's to archiepiscopal rank. By 1143 all the Welsh bishoprics were occupied by Normans, or by clerics who had received their training under Norman influence and who gave canonical obedience to the archbishop of Canterbury.[126] With Norman bishops there came a reorganization of the cathedral clergy which destroyed the tradition and continuity of the Welsh church. These developments cannot be disregarded as factors in the conquest of Wales, and the final subjugation of the country may well be due less to the military than to the ecclesiastical conquest.

Chapter 10

Military Service and Military Manpower: The Knights

WELL over half a century has elapsed since J. H. Round produced his justly celebrated studies on the origins of English feudalism. Fully two generations of scholars have held up his theories and conclusions to detailed inspection, analysis, and criticism, but despite attacks on this or that point, the thesis so brilliantly developed in "The Introduction of Knight Service into England" has withstood all critical assaults and remains to this day the starting point for any discussion of Anglo-Norman military institutions and practices.[1] From the point of view of the military historian, Round's chief shortcoming was his undue emphasis upon the feudal aspects of military service, to the neglect of the nonfeudal or extrafeudal elements that were also conspicuous in all Anglo-Norman armies in the eleventh and twelfth centuries. But although both the old English militia or *fyrd,* and foreign mercenary bands, were frequently utilized by the Norman kings, the largest single reservoir of trained manpower consisted of the knights whom each tenant-in-chief was obliged to bring into the field at the king's summons.[2] The strength of each baronial contingent, which presumably had been specified by the king at the time the lands of the honor were granted, was usually some multiple of five.[3] All told, about 180 lay tenants were bound to provide military manpower; in addition, all the bishoprics—saving only those of Carlisle and the four Welsh sees, which then lay outside the conquered area—and many of the greater monasteries also held by knight service. Although the total potential down to the last knight will never be known, it was probably somewhere between 5,000 and 6,000 knights. How they were raised or maintained was a matter that interested the king only indirectly. So long as the tenant produced the required number of serviceable troops on demand, his handling of the personnel problem was, with few exceptions, left to his own devising. In the early days of the Conquest, when military operations were almost continuous, many knights were maintained in the lord's household; but as conditions became more settled it became increasingly likely that the knights were enfeoffed with land on condition of rendering military service, both in the field and in garrison at the lord's castle. It should be noted, however, that as late as the baronial inquest of 1166 there were still many tenants who retained a certain number of household knights.[4]

It was fashionable, not so long ago, to hold the knightly warrior up to ridicule; then it became popular to assert either that, at least in England, he was not a knight at all, but the lineal descendant of a Saxon militiaman whose knight service was but *fyrd* duty under another name, or that he was the substitute for a Danish *huscarle*.[5] More recently it has been argued that knight service itself was but a continuation of the old English five-hide military obligation, and that the Norman knight was really a *cniht*. Citing the grant of Gilbert Crispin, abbot of Westminster, to William Baynard, Richardson and Sayles assert that since William succeeded to the lands and rights of a thegn named Wulfric, "and since in return for the grant William is to do service as a knight, the inference is that Wulfric had also served as a knight." [6] Nothing of the sort is to be inferred, of course; it may be argued with equal logic that because knight service is specifically stated as a condition of the grant, William's predecessor had not been so bound.

But whatever his antecedents, the feudal knight was an important cog in the military machinery of the eleventh and twelfth centuries; and although Sidney Painter may have been guilty of some exaggeration in his summary of the achievements of European military feudalism, his opinion is worth quoting:

Feudal military organization was on the whole highly effective. The knights of Europe conquered vast territories from the Slavs, pressed the Moslems steadily back in Spain and drove them from Sicily, and established themselves at least temporarily in Palestine, Syria, the Byzantine lands, and Greece. As a defensive system feudalism was almost perfect. No organization ever devised could so quickly produce an effective military force wherever it was needed. The feudal army was essentially a militia, but a militia composed of the best soldiers of the day.[7]

Perhaps so strong an assertion was needed to put the accomplishments of the feudal knight in proper perspective.

It might be well to look at the incidence of knight service in England to see how the load was distributed among the tenants-in-chief. Unfortunately, little substantial evidence exists prior to the Pipe Rolls of Henry II, with their lists of scutage payments and feudal aids based on knight's fees, augmented, of course by the *cartae baronum* of 1166. Even this information is imprecise, and only an informed guess can be made as to the approximate number of knights required of the tenants *in capite* by William I. Since the number of ecclesiastical tenants owing knight service was smaller than that of the lay baronage, the military service due from church lands will be considered before the more complex and uncertain question of the basis for levying service among the lay tenants. Even the ecclesiastical fees are not entirely certain, for there was bickering between bishop and abbot on the one hand, and the crown on the other, as to the number of knights owed. Nevertheless, the totals arrived at are probably more accurate than any that can be worked out for the lay tenants.[8]

All the English bishoprics except Carlisle owed knight service, although the bishop of Rochester rendered his service to his ecclesiastical superior, the archbishop of Canterbury, instead of directly to the king.[9] The *servitia debita* of the bishops ran all the way from the sixty knights owed by the sees of **Canterbury,** Lincoln, Winchester, and probably Worcester, down to seven from the archbishopric of York and two from the bishopric of Chichester. The total from this source amounted to 466/456 knights.[10] In addition to this rather substantial contribution, twenty-two abbeys and two nunneries had quotas, totaling 298/ 293 knights.[11] This provided a total of 764/749 knights due from the ecclesiastical hierarchy; assuming the total *servitium debitum* of the kingdom to be about 6,000 knights, this accounts for nearly

13 per cent of the whole.[12] In all the argument over the basis on which these service quotas were fixed, very little notice has been taken of the military situation in England at the time they were presumably established. That this time was early is scarcely open to doubt, since the writ of William I to Abbot Aethelwig of Evesham, ordering him to report for duty with the five knights owed by the abbey, seems to date from about 1072.[13] Keeping in mind the early date of the establishment of the quotas, the distribution of military service can be accounted for. Although all the bishops held by knight service, a number of important pre-Conquest abbeys did not—the monasteries of Gloucester, Burton, Waltham, and Athelney, for example, and the nunneries of Barking and of St. Mary's, Winchester, all of which held of the king *in capite* at the time of the Domesday inquest, escaped military assessment.[14] Further, as Sanders has pointed out, all the religious houses holding by military service were in the south; the farthest north was Peterborough.[15] The south was, of course, the first part of the kingdom to come under Norman military control, and "it would seem that William, desirous of establishing his power over the southern part of the country, allotted military service to the religious houses before launching his attack on the more distant parts of England. Furthermore these twenty-four houses are the only ones in the country to owe military service to the crown." [16] This is indirect but convincing evidence for the early establishment of the military quotas.

Again, when the geographical distribution of the religious houses owing knight service is noted, it becomes evident that the area most in danger from foreign invasion—the southeast and east—was most heavily assessed. Of the four (or possibly five) ecclesiastical tenants having a *servitium debitum* of sixty knights, three were located in this part of the country—the archbishopric of Canterbury, the bishopric of Lincoln (Dorchester), and the abbey of Peterborough. Of four with a quota of forty knights, three were from eastern England—the bishoprics of Ely and Norwich, and the abbey of St. Edmund's. All told, of a total of 764 knights due from the church lands, 357 were from eastern prelates alone.[17] It seems clear that the quotas levied on ecclesiastical foundations were arbitrarily made to give the Normans military control over a newly conquered, not yet pacified country. In addition to providing a readily available military force at points of possible danger, it may well have been intended as a check on ecclesiastics whose loyalty to the new regime was uncertain. These considerations suggest that any attempt to determine a basis on which military service was allotted would be a fruitless enterprise. The basis was military expediency—no more, no less.

In recent years, efforts have been made to revive the thesis that the knight's fee contained five hides of land. But that thesis was effectively refuted by Round more than sixty years ago, and a few examples are sufficient to demonstrate its untenability. Hyde abbey's twenty knights represented the service of just under 300 hides, whereas Ramsey abbey owed but four knights for between 300 and 400 hides. Shaftesbury provided ten for 344 ½ hides, "while on the other hand the abbey of Tavistock, which appears in Domesday as holding not more than 30 hides was burdened with a *servicium* [*sic*] of no less than fifteen knights." [18] That the quotas for knight service were arbitrarily established cannot be gainsaid, and the exemption of some houses was just as arbitrary as the imposition of heavy obligations on others. "Each tenant-in-chief made what bargain he could with the king, who may on occasion have been induced to respect immunities granted by his Saxon predecessors, but who was doubtless in general influenced solely by immediate political considerations." [19] It might be added that military considerations were as important as the purely political.

Anyone who has read Edward Miller's masterful account of the Honor of St. Etheldreda cannot but be convinced that if the see of Ely is a representative example, the evolution of the military contingents of the ecclesiastical tenants occurred haphazardly and without much regard to system.[20] The *servitium debitum* of the abbot (later bishop) of Ely, forty knights, was due from nine private hundreds—the hundred and a half of Mitford in Norfolk, the five and a half hundreds of Wicklaw in Suffolk, and the two hundreds of the Isle of Ely—plus manors in six counties: Cambridge, Huntingdon, Hertford, Essex, Suffolk, and Norfolk.[21] This quota seems to have been established by 1072, for it is mentioned in connection with the Scottish expedition of that year. There was, at first, no attempt to settle the knights on the land; they were quartered in and about the monastery. This did not prove satisfactory, however, and there began a slow process of enfeoffment that is observable on other ecclesiastical estates—at Abingdon, Peterborough, Westminster, and Worcester.[22] By 1086 this process was well under way at Ely, and of twenty-one knights in Cambridgeshire, just over half had been put out on the land. Five fees were held directly of the bishop, six by honorial barons; ten remained still on the demesne.[23] But there was more to the process than simply providing landed tenements for a body of household knights. In the confusion of the years after 1066, many a knight simply took over a likely-looking piece of property regardless of ownership. Some of these knights are now nameless; others were men of power and influence, who held of the king *in capite,* but who nevertheless seized properties of the abbey for their own use.[24] Such proceedings were certainly not confined to the lands of the church of Ely; from the record of long-drawn-out legal processes, it appears in fact to have been rather common. In a review of J. A. Raftis's *The Estates of Ramsey Abbey,* Professor G. C. Homans writes: "After the Norman Conquest, for instance, the abbey could not prevent vagrant knights making themselves *de facto* if not *de jure* lords of some of its manors: they squatted, so to speak, on the lordships." [25] The problem was, of course, to convert de facto possession into a de jure military obligation, an extended process which led in the end to the creation of many more knights' fees than the number of knights owed the crown. At Ely the lands held by usurpers in fact "provided a major part of these 40 knights." [26] But it was not easy to establish the right of the abbots, and of their successors the bishops, to the military service of these fees. At Henry II's court at Windsor, "Roger Bigod recognized that he owed the service of six knights for land held of the bishop in Suffolk; and so closed a controversy which may go back to the Conqueror's time and which was still at issue in 1166." [27] Churchmen were, of course, at a disadvantage when it came to repossessing usurped lands, but they had recourse to the *curia regis.* The king seems to have solved the problem "by requiring the new Norman tenants to hold these lands of the church in question, so that the knight service for them would form part of the church's quota." [28] That this was not always easily done is clear from the difficulties encountered by the abbot of Abingdon in compelling his tenants to perform their military service. As late as the reign of Henry I, Abbot Faritus had to appeal to the crown to force recalcitrant vassals to fulfill their obligations.[29] One important aspect of the resumption of usurped lands, and the recognition by the usurper of the military service due, was the over-efeoffment of church lands. At Ely, the bishops had created fifty-six and one-half fees before 1135, and another sixteen and one-half between 1135 and 1166, bringing the total to seventy-three, although the *servitium debitum* of the bishopric was only forty. Although some of these excess fees represent rewards for services rendered, or were established for the benefit of relatives of the bishops, many of them doubtless came from the resumption of lands held by squatters.[30]

If there was no discernible system in the allocation of military service, there seems to have been equally little uniformity in the size of the knight's fee. Miss Chew demonstrates conclusively that although some similarity to the five-hide rule might be detected in the returns of the bishop of Salisbury and the abbot of Westminster in 1166, it can be detected nowhere else. At Shafterbury, St. Alban's, Abingdon, Malmesbury, Ramsey, and Peterborough there was no uniformity either among the abbeys or within the lands of the individual houses.[31] Even the two fees of the abbot of Middleton, who claimed that the service was imposed by Henry I, were held for two and two and a half hides.[32] "Clearly the process of sub-infeudation on individual fiefs was no more determined by the Saxon five-hide principle than was the Conqueror's assessment of the tenants-in-chief. In either case the determining factor was the caprice or the convenience of the lord." [33]

Among the lay tenants an equal diversity is to be found. The amount of military service due from each tenant *in capite* seems usually to have been set in round numbers "without any apparent relationship to the size or value of the holding." [34] But it is very difficult to find for the lay barons the same kind of evidence that has survived in ecclesiastical archives. At most, as Sanders points out, "some things seem to suggest that the Crown believed, in the thirteenth century, that the feudal military obligation of the lay tenants-in-chief had been fully organized by the first third of the twelfth century"; and Douglas asserts that the *servitia debita* was imposed by the king on the tenants-in-chief shortly after the Conquest.[35] But certain facts are ascertainable on the basis of isolated charters and the baronial *cartae* of 1166. One is that the lay tenants, in proportion, retained far more knights on demesne than did the church. The process of subinfeudation was slower in the Danelaw than elsewhere, for the likely reason, as Stenton suggests, that it was exposed to Danish attacks, and that many tenants must have kept their knights in their households on a standby basis.[36] But this phenomenon was by no means confined to the Danelaw. In Wiltshire, which certainly was not exposed to immediate danger, Walter Waleran, accounting for a *servitium* of twenty knights, reported eight still on the demesne.[37] In Devonshire, the honor of Totnes had seven knights on demesne; Robert of Stafford had enfeoffed fifty-one knights out of a quota of sixty, but still retained a household retinue of nine.[38] On the Welsh march, where fighting was chronic, much the same situation prevailed as in the Danelaw. Baderun of Monmouth, for example, had created ten fees, but the demesne was still responsible for the service of five knights; and Richard de Cormeilles had enfeoffed six and kept three on demesne.[39] In Norfolk, Hubert de Ria still had ten and one-sixth knights charged to the demesne in 1166.[40] But a larger percentage of the *servitium debitum* seems to have been retained as a permanent retinue by tenants-in-chief in the north. Walter de Aincourt, who owed the service of forty knights, had eleven on demesne; for Roger de Burun the corresponding figures were ten and four, for Hubert fitz Ralf thirty and ten, for Richard de Haia twenty and five, for Lambert of Scotney five and five, and for Robert fitz Hugh of Tattershall twelve and one-half and twelve and one-half.[41] Although these examples are not typical of England as a whole, they indicate that the creation of specific knights' fees was far from universal as late as the second half of the twelfth century.

Little is known of the household knight. Undoubtedly, although some were men who served a baronial court long and faithfully, others were doubtless vagrant adventurers of the class from which the mercenary bands were recruited. Their only distinction was their professional skill and their possession of the equipment for mounted service. The great survey often lumps the *milites* in with the villeins, bordars, and slaves. "Ibi xvii villani et unus miles et xii bordarii et i servus," although perhaps not characteristic, shows clearly that the knight had not yet achieved much in the way of status.[42] This may be one explanation for the disparate nature of the knight's fee about which so much argument has raged. It is very tempting to accept the formula "Quatuor virgate terra faciunt unam hidam et quinque hide faciunt unum militem," or the simple statement of Richard de Haia: "Et v carucatae faciunt j militem. . . ."[43] Unfortunately, there is no proof that any such uniformity ever existed, although it is quite easy to demonstrate exactly the reverse of lay fees as well as of ecclesiastical. In 1166 Lambert of Scotney held some twenty-six carucates of the king in chief. His *servitium debitum* was ten knights; five of these had been enfeoffed on sixteen carucates, and the ten-plus carucates of the demesne supported the other five.[44] The three virgates held by Nicholas fitz Harding's knights Baldwin and Hildebrand in Somerset cannot have supported them in unseemly luxury.[45]

Although it is estimated that the feudal levy would produce some 6,000 knights, for the eleventh and twelfth centuries the tactical organization of the host, once mustered, remains a matter of almost pure conjecture.[46] The high command was simple—usually the king himself. When the king was engaged in operations elsewhere, a special command was established. Not infrequently an ecclesiastic was named to this extraordinary command —as, for example, Bishop Wulfstan of Worcester was in the Severn valley in 1088, or as Archbishop Anselm was in southeastern England in 1095. If trouble arose during the king's absence on the Continent, the justiciar or his equivalent took command, as for example in 1075 and 1173. Regular commanders on the subordinate level seem not to have been appointed. The constables, of whom there appear to have been four, and likewise the marshals, were household officials from the very outset of the Norman regime in England, although they were never permitted to become the powerful military commanders they were in

France. The *Constitutio Domus Regis,* written shortly after the death of Henry I, records their prerogatives, but says very little about their duties.[47] The only military function assigned to these officers was command of the king's bodyguard of archers.[48] The names of the constables and marshals of the first three Norman kings are known. Some of these were important personages in their own right, and the constables derived additional significance from their command of the castles of Dover, Oxford, Gloucester, and Worcester, and their success in making these offices hereditary.[49] They also appear to have been responsible for the tactical organization of infantry and mounted contingents at the muster.[50] The Norman kings in general, however, were evidently determined not to permit their household officials to acquire too much power. "Even the constables, a Norman innovation, did not have much opportunity for aggrandizement, for their military duties were not those of commanders, as used to be thought, but rather those of quartermaster generals." [51] During the reign of Henry II, a rudimentary personal staff of knights made its appearance. Presumably this was under the direction of the constable—until the office was abolished in 1163—as a sort of personal chief of staff to the king.[52] Later, the seneschal seems to have taken over this role. These knights were members of the royal household, but their value to the crown was in the military, quasi-military, and diplomatic service which they rendered. "They took, often for long periods, those frontier sheriffdoms which had to be quasi-military, commanded the royal castles and went on diplomatic missions. . . . They are found as English sheriffs. In 1176, we are told, Henry took all the royal castles away from those who held them and gave them in charge to the Knights of his Household." [53] Beyond this it seems impossible to go, on the evidence now available. The command function was intensely personal, being centered in the king who usually commanded in person. He might delegate authority or command functions, but the small size of armies and the relative simplicity of tactics made anything like a permanent or professional staff unnecessary. Not until the reign of Henry II, with its centralizing tendencies in all aspects of government, was anything resembling even a personal staff to appear.

But if little is known of the command structure of the English feudal army, still less is known about its tactical organization, and that little is both obscure and controversial. Since it was not in being at all times, the feudal host was in a sense a militia or reserve force to be summoned in times of emergency. There was no question, at least at the beginning, of its liability to serve wherever and whenever the king might require.[54] Unfortunately, most of the evidence for any internal organization of the army comes from the late twelfth century at the very earliest, and it is of course hazardous to assume, even though military institutions have a way of persisting for long periods of time, that the practices of the 1190's were current fifty or seventy-five years earlier. Much of the argument centers about the theory advanced by Round that the military obligation of the Norman tenant-in-chief "was not determined by his holding, but was fixed in relation to, and expressed in terms of, the *constabularia* of ten knights, the unit of the feudal host. And I consequently hold that this military service was in no way derived or developed from that of the Anglo-Saxons, but was arbitrarily fixed by the king, from whom he received his fief, irrespectively both of its size and of all pre-existent arrangements." [55] Round notes that the *servitium debitum* of the feudal tenants "is almost invariably *a multiple of 5, if not of 10,*" and asserted, though not on the best authority, that service in Normandy was also based on a unit of five knights.[56] As proof that such a system prevailed in Norman England, Round cities evidence from the monastery of St. Edmund's that the forty knights of the abbot's *servitium debitum* were organized into four *constabularia* of ten knights, each unit serving three months' ward per year at Norwich.[57] Now the author of this information, Jocelin of Brakelond, was writing at the end of the twelfth century, when already the knights of St. Edmund's had converted their personal service to a money payment—at the ridiculous rate of 2s.5d., or 3s.—but a document of the early thirteenth century confirms the chronicler's use of the term constabulary, and even designates one member of each squad as the *constabularius,* or commander.[58] What is more important, these units of ten knights or constabularies can be projected back at least to 1145, when Stephen's charter to the abbot exempted the latter's knights from castle-guard at Norwich in quarterly contingents of ten knights each.[59] Round's thesis, a radical departure from the once accepted assumption as to the origins of knight service in England, soon became the canon. It was endorsed by Vinogradoff and confirmed by Haskins, who asserted that the tactical unit of five and ten knights was found both in Normandy and in Norman Italy and Sicily.[60] More recently, Sanders has contended that the reduced quotas demanded by King John in 1213–1214, and later in 1218 and 1229, "suggest that the size of the contingent which the king was demanding from great lords was influenced by the *constabularium* of 10 knights."[61] And although he avoids using the term *constabularium,* Smail agrees that the feudal contingent was specified when the lands were granted by the king, and that the quota was usually a multiple of twenty-five or ten.[62] But some reservations must be noted. Poole considers the terms *constabularium* and *constabularius* of too general an application to be of any real significance, and asserts that there is "no valid reason, therefore to identify the *constabularia* of the knights of St. Edmund's with the unit of the feudal host."[63] John, in his vitriolic attack—reminiscent of Round himself—on Round's thesis, concedes that the tactical unit may well have been the *constabularium* of ten knights, but contends that the Norman allocation of quotas by five and tens is merely an adaptation of the old English system for recruiting the *fyrd;* and Hollister seems sympathetic to this point of view.[64]

For the present argument it is immaterial whether or not the Norman knight was merely a thegn or a *cniht* with a foreign accent. The controversy over this point tends to obscure the real purpose of all institutional inquiry. William I was both a soldier and a statesman; but it should be re-emphasized that in allocating the quotas to his tenants-in-chief, he was thinking in military terms.[65] From reading John's pages one would suppose that the Saxons invented fives and tens, whereas any student of military history knows that the decimal system was a standard method not only of raising but of organizing troops, long before Hengist and Horsa grounded their longboats on Britain's pebbly beaches. Gideon's celebrated three hundred men were divided into three companies of one hundred each.[66] Thucydides noted that for the

Boeotian ships in the Trojan war as related by Homer, the complement was 120—exactly double the Worcester "shipfuls"— and that for the ships of Philocrates it was fifty—both divisible by five and ten.[67] Herodotus records that the army of Xerxes was organized in units of ten, one hundred, one thousand, and ten thousand men.[68] The Roman legions in the time of the Republic were divided into maniples of 60, and later of 120 men—again divisible by five and ten—and the Marian reforms replaced these with cohorts of six hundred men divided into six centuries.[69] Even more to the point is the composition of the legionary cavalry. Its three hundred men were organized into ten *turmae* of thirty men each, which in turn were divided into three *decuriones* of ten men each.[70] There is nothing peculiarly English about tactical units divisible by five, or ten, or both. Is it not at least conceivable that the Normans could have introduced a military system based on a *tactical* squadron of ten knights, which differed significantly from an English system that raised its troops in units of ten? Certainly the evidence points to a Norman system of knights' fees—when and if the tenants *in capite* got around to creating them—that bears relation not to any systematic hidation but to multiples of five and ten. And yet a serious scholar asserts in one place that "an original principle of one *miles* for five hides has been bent in course of time by beneficial or penal hidation," and in another that "units of thegnly service in Anglo-Saxon England must have sometimes 'contained' more or less than 5 hides." [71] An argument so lacking in clarity is difficult to follow.

To return to the *constabularium:* that there was such a unit at the end of the twelfth century is not open to doubt. Both Stenton and Poole cite numerous tenants during the reigns of Richard I and John who were fined because they or their men were not in their constabularies when they should have been.[72] But nowhere is there any indication of just what a constabulary was, how it was formed, or what relation it had to any larger tactical unit. Except for the evidence from St. Edmund's, a fog of uncertainty envelops the term. It can only be suggested that the *constabularium,* the squad of ten men, was the basic maneuver unit of the feudal army, and that possibly larger units could only be put together after the muster informed the commander of how many troops he actually had present for duty. There must also have been an intermediate tactical unit above the constabulary in any army numbering more than a few hundred men; but in the absence of any evidence to the contrary, it can only be surmised that this was improvised on the spot. So far as organization is concerned, the civic militia of London seems to have been more advanced than the feudal army.

There is very little to indicate any training beyond that which the individual knight received as a youth. Whether there was anything that might be called unit training is conjectural. Poole has suggested that in the twelfth century the tournament provided training for the knights,[73] but the tournament never became as popular in England as it did on the Continent, even though some English knights—of whom William Marshal is the most notable example—followed the tournament trail in the manner of today's professional golfer—and likewise made a good thing of it financially. At any rate, this sort of thing was probably true only of a small number of English knights.[74] Hollister reads into the bishop of Orkney's rhetorical statement before the Battle of the Standard, "In time of peace we prepare for war," the implication that the forty days' service in peacetime stated to be a knight's duty in John fitz Gilbert's charter, was utilized for training purposes.[75] But in all probability the soldier of the eleventh and twelfth centuries learned to fight in a unit by doing just that—which was, in fact, the way recruits were trained from classical times until less than a century ago. Until warfare became the highly specialized activity it is today, a period of training for recruits was not considered really necessary. In June 1863, during the Civil War in the United States, Major General William T. Sherman wrote to his superior, Major General U. S. Grant, that he hoped the newly enacted conscription law would fill up the depleted ranks of veteran regiments. On 19 June Grant forwarded the letter to President Abraham Lincoln with this endorsement: "A recruit added to them [the old regiments] would become an old soldier from the very contact before he was aware of it. . . . Taken in an economic view, one drafted man in an old regiment is worth three in a new one." [76] There were very few campaigning seasons after 1066 when fighting was not going on somewhere in England or on the Continent, and it is more than likely that knightly recruits were simply incorporated into existing units. Since they had already mastered the art of fighting on horseback they would, in General Grant's words, have become old soldiers before they were aware of it. This would be particularly true of a knight who fought—as undoubtedly most of them did—with members of his own baronial contingent. The simple tactics of the day could be absorbed in a short time, and the newcomer would have the advantage of learning how to live under field conditions—always the worst problem for a recruit—with the advice and help of comrades who were older or at least more experienced.

But the heyday of the feudal knight was a short one in England. By the beginning of the twelfth century, although kings continued to rely heavily on the contingents of the tenants-in-chief, various military, political, and economic factors led to payments of money in lieu of personal service in the field, and it is reasonably certain that some such system would have developed in the old English kingdom, whether or not military duty could be avoided by a money payment.[77] Although there has been much dispute concerning the development of scutage payments, on a few points all the disputants seem agreed. One of these is that the basis of all scutage rates was "the estimated cost of substitutes paid direct." [78] It is also unquestioned that the first known mention of scutage in the Anglo-Norman state is found in a document of 1100, in which Henry I exempted the priory of St. Pancras at Lewes from a long list of burdens, including scutage.[79] And although references to monetary payments in lieu of service in the field are infrequent during the first half of the twelfth century, there are nevertheless enough to indicate that such payments were nothing out of the ordinary.[80] It is also agreed that the crown and the tenants-in-chief both felt the need for a more efficient method for raising a field army than was possible through the operation of the feudal chain of command. Even in the best of circumstances, a tenant *in capite* must have had difficulty in putting his entire quota into the field at one time. Incapacity through illness or accident, not to mention minorities and superannuation among his own tenants, must have plagued him continually. The king, under such circumstances, could never be sure of a full response to a summons for military service. However, to provide against such contingencies, many tenants-in-chief seem to have enfeoffed more knights than were due the crown. This over-enfeoffment has frequently been re-garded as an attempt by the holders of the great honors to create private armies for the pursuit of their own ambitions.[81] But it is well established that on any given day a certain percentage of troops will be sick or otherwise unfit for duty, and some precau-tions had to be taken against the inevitable minorities and the debilities of age. Stenton and Hollister have hinted at this explanation for the over-enfeoffment of many fees, but it has never been seriously explored.[82] It is reasonable, however, to suppose that the tenants-in-chief had provided in this way for the mustering of full quotas on summons. If so, the king could have depended on very nearly the full *servitium debitum* when neces-sary.

But with the passage of time the failure of many baronial lines and the division of baronies among heiresses must have compli-cated enormously the problem of mustering the feudal host and of enforcing compliance with a summons. Many honors were split in half, or even into quarters or eighths, and a monetary payment was no doubt easier to collect from these fragmented fees than the actual service due.[83] On a lower level the fragmentation of the knight's fee must have presented an equally serious problem—though one of his own creation—to the baronial commander. About 1140, Earl Simon of Northampton granted to William his chamberlain three bovates and two tofts in Barton-on-Humber "per servitium xl partis unius militis." And during the reign of Henry II two bovates were held of Philip of Kyme as the sixteenth part of half a knight's fee. Just what service was expected of one-fortieth or one-thirty-second of a knight was not specified in these grants, and the whole matter was carried to extremes when Geoffrey of Keddington granted one-third of a bovate (two-thirds of a half-bovate) to be held of him and his heirs "for the hundredth part of the service of the fee of one knight for all services and exactions." [84] Obviously these grants were not for the purpose of providing military service. As Poole has pointed out, the holders of small parts of a knight's fee on some well-organized estate might agree to serve in rotation, but it could not be believed that the great mass of men who held fractional fees could render their service in this way. He notes, "As early as the reign of Henry I a charter records the grant of an estate in Warwickshire to be held 'by a third part of the service of one knight in such a way that he shall aquit his whole service by the yearly payment of twenty shillings.' . . . Knight service in respect of these small tenantry must always have been a matter of cash." [85] But although motives of economy and efficiency—as well as the desire of the military tenant to avoid hazardous duty—doubtless played a part in the development of scutage, the motives of the crown were almost certainly military; and it is likely that kings from Henry I onward encouraged the practice in order to provide funds which could be used to hire professionals, men whose services were not limited as to time and place so long as their pay was forthcoming. The role of the professional—or mercenary—soldier will be discussed shortly, but it should be noted here that he had none of the ties or traditions that bound him to a locality or a class. He was probably a more efficient soldier than the feudal tenant by knight service; and all monkish strictures to the contrary, he was likely to be better disciplined. In time the career soldier, by whatever name he might be called, was to dominate the battlefields of Europe until the advent of national armies late in the seventeenth century.

Until quite recently, the service for which payment of scutage provided an exemption was assumed to be a forty-day annual tour of duty. On the basis of both documentary and inferential evidence, however, this assumption has now been called into question. It can no longer be taken for granted that the feudal custom of Normandy was transferred intact to England, or that since it could be demonstrated that forty days' service was required in eleventh century Normandy, the practice in Norman England must have been identical.[86] As Stenton has noted, the best English evidence points to a different conclusion. As late as Stephen's reign John fitz Gilbert made a grant in Somersetshire to Hugh of Raleigh

. . . for the service of a knight "so defined that if there is war he shall find me an equipped knight for two months, and if there is peace, for 40 days, for such service as the knights of the barons of the land reasonably ought to do." The historical importance of this charter is greater than appears on the surface. John son of Gilbert had served Henry I and Stephen, and was to serve Henry II, as marshal. No one could speak with more authority about the proper duration of knight service. *The careful phrases of his charter may fairly be allowed the weight of an official definition.*[87]

Admittedly it is difficult to believe that the Conqueror could arbitrarily extend the annual tour of duty by fifty per cent, but again consideration must be given to the conditions existing in the early years of the Norman occupation. From 1066 to 1070, at the very least, sixty days' armed duty in wartime would have seemed quite reasonable; for many men, those years must have been a period of extended active duty with very little relief. When the time of consolidation began, and the old English militia was consolidated with the continentals who supplanted the native aristocracy, it may well have been possible to set a common period of service in wartime while retaining a period of forty days' active duty in peacetime.[88] The most convincing support that can be offered to the charter of John fitz Gilbert is that Henry I levied scutage as the rate of 30*s.* per knight's fee, which works out to precisely sixty days' service at 6*d. per diem.*[89] Although it can be demonstrated, as will appear later, that the sixty-day term did not apply universally to castle-guard service, there seems to be no other satisfactory explanation of the thirty-shilling rate. But if it is kept in mind that the eleventh and twelfth centuries were no more static than any others, and it would, perhaps, be more astonishing if conditions as to pay and length of service had not changed than if they had. It is certain that at the beginning of the twelfth century, and probably for some years thereafter, the annual term of field service in time of war, at any rate, was sixty days, and that at some time, probably during the middle years of the century, for reasons that are now unknown, it was reduced to forty days.[90] At the same time a steady inflation was raising the daily wage paid to a stipendiary knight, first to 8*d.* and later to 1*s.* Moreover, these rates were paid concurrently during the 1170's— that is, there was no abrupt change from one rate to another. In 1172/1173 the paid members of the garrison at Walton received a shilling a day, and at Porchester and elsewhere in the following year the rate seems to have been the same.[91] But in 1174/1175, when the crisis occasioned by the Young King's rebellion was over, the pay scale tended to revert to the earlier level, and the five knights who served for 146 days at Worcester were paid at the old rate of 8*d*.[92] Indeed, it is possible to find knights paid at either rate in the same castle during the same Exchequer year. At Northampton in 1172/1173 the Pipe Roll records payments to five knights for 35 days at the rate of 8*d*., and to ten knights for 139 days at 12*d*. per day.[93] And in the very same document that Hollister cites as evidence for the rise in pay, William fitz Peter is found serving for twenty days with four knights at the rate of 8*d*. per day.[94] As late as 1175, then, it was possible to hire knights at the rate of two marks on the fee for forty days' service. Most of these stipendiary knights seem to have been recruited to perform castle-guard service, and to the evolution of this aspect of the knightly obligation it is now necessary to turn.

The problems connected with the organization of castle-guard have been examined by some of the leading scholars of the twentieth century—J. H. Round, Sir Frank Stenton, and Sidney Painter.[95] It might, therefore, seem presumptuous to attempt a further analysis of this element of Anglo-Norman military practice, and indeed the following discussion is no more than an effort at synthesis, with some small shift in emphasis. The general characteristics of castle-guard service have been clearly outlined, so far as the evidence permits.

The feudal host, the expeditionary force (*expeditio*), was not, even in the warlike days of chivalry, always in being. It was only mustered when need arose and when fighting had to be done. Castles, on the other hand, had always to be kept in a state of preparedness. Garrison duty in the Norman period was probably a more serious call on the time and energies of the knightly class than service in the field.[96]

But it must also be remembered that the castle garrison was not composed entirely of knights—that many men held by sergeanty on condition of performing guard service.[97] Unfortunately, little of the information concerning military sergeanties is earlier than the thirteenth century; but there is no reason to suppose that the obligation of Richard fitz Nicholas, who held an acre of land in

Lametin (Cornwall) in 1210–1212, to serve for forty days in Launceston castle "cum sacco et lancea" was of recent imposition.[98] This would seem to be true of other documentary and charter evidence concerning military tenants of less than knightly rank, who in any normal garrison arrangement would undoubtedly have outnumbered their military and social superiors.[99] The evidence makes it fairly certain that several hundred castles were erected during the years immediately after 1066.[100] These castles had to be manned in time of peace as well as of war. By far the larger number were baronial castles, although a number of major fortresses were held by commanders appointed by the king. These latter required large garrisons; the problem of providing the requisite number of troops is one that will be considered later. Now, it will be seen at once that from a practical point of view the lords of castles faced a variety of problems. The lord of the honor of Richmond, with 187 1/4 knights, faced an entirely different situation in setting up his duty roster than did the lord of Harestan, near Horseley in Derbyshire, whose barony consisted of only ten fees, and who was also required to pull duty at Nottingham.[101] These examples doubtless represent extremes, with the vast majority of baronies falling somewhere in between. It is not surprising, then, that terms of castle-guard service show considerable variation. The thesis that a sixty-day term of service was uniform under the Norman kings, and changed to the traditional forty days only in the middle years of the twelfth century, breaks down when applied to garrison duty.[102] If it can be shown that the customary tour of duty at Richmond was sixty days—and there is abundant evidence on this score—it can as easily be demonstrated that the forty knights of St. Edmund's abbey served in groups of ten for ninety days each at Norwich castle.[103] Similarly the knights of the castle-guard at Hastings served a month thrice yearly.[104] At the other end of the scale, the abbot of Cerne in Dorset asserted, in responding to the baronial inquest of 1166, that his knights were required to make ward at Corfe castle for only thirty days a year.[105] Indeed, there is evidence that some sergeanties were held for much less than thirty days' ward per year.[106] Finally, it seems quite probable that there was not always uniform service within a single castle. At Dover, some knights apparently served only a month, while others were compelled to perform a thirty-day hitch two or three times a year.[107] The documentation for castle-guard duty is scanty, and if this wide variation is found within the meager sources, it is idle to contend that a uniform system existed. When no uniformity of service obtained among such important castles as Richmond, Norwich, Hastings, Dover, and Corfe, or within a first-class fortress like Dover, it seems probable that each tenant, at whatever level, scrambled about to make the best arrangements he could with his own tenants, and with his overlord, should he happen to owe ward to some major castle.

Although castle-guard must have been a universal obligation— or perhaps, indeed, because it was—references to it are surprisingly few. Painter has compiled a list of fifty-one English castles for which there seems clear evidence of ward duty either by knight service or by sergeanty.[108] Although Painter was dealing exclusively with knightly obligations, he missed some further examples, and the following can be added to the list: Brandon, Corfe, Durham, Ely (and perhaps Aldreth), Exeter, Newark, Nottingham, Pulford, and Trowbridge.[109] Evidence also exists of tenure by sergeanty in the castles of Denbigh, Hereford, Shrewsbury, Weston-Turville, Winchester, and York.[110] It might well be added that ward duty *per seriantiam* implies service *per loricam,* for, as Hollister observes, "sergeants did not fight in a separate army." [111] For the castles of Bishop's Stortford, Cambridge, Carmarthen, Ewias Harold, and Wark, the evidence is inconclusive as to whether reference is made to knight service, or service by sergeanty.[112] Altogether, then, there is evidence of ward service in seventy-two or seventy-three castles, a fairly representative number of both royal and baronial strongholds. For many of these, the garrisons must have been nominal in time of peace. It required nine knights' fees to provide a year's service for a single soldier in garrison on the basis of forty days' service, or six fees when the tour of duty was two months. As Painter remarks, "The average baron must have been forced to entrust the peacetime defense of his castle to the porter, the watchman, and one or two of his household knights while his tenants were bound to supply a more adequate force in time of war." [113] This undoubtedly is one reason why even in the twelfth century many tenants still retained knights charged to the demesne—as, for example, Roger de Buron of Hareston, or the Mowbray barony of Thirsk, which had a *servitium debitum* of sixty knights, all of whom had been enfeoffed by 1166, but which as late as 1144 still kept a retinue of household knights.[114] A castle so exposed to attack by the Scots as was Thirsk, required some provision for a permanent garrison.

But strategically placed baronial and royal castles required more adequate garrisons at all times than the ordinary baronial stronghold. To provide the necessary manpower, vast honors were created, known as *castellariae* or castleries. "In its broadest sense the word denoted a group of fees owing service at the castle from which it took its name by finding knights or sergeants for its defense, or by contributing money for this purpose." [115] In the narrower sense the castlery of Norman times was a compact fee—a territory that with little exaggeration might be called a military district, whose tenants were bound to the defense of a strategically important baronial castle. A number of such castleries are mentioned in *Domesday Book* and other early sources; the existence of one or two others may be inferred. For example, there is evidence that four of the five rapes of Sussex were castleries. Hastings and Lewes are specifically mentioned as such in *Domesday;* the castlery of Steyning (Bramber) is referred to in a monastic document to which Round assigns the date 1080/1108; and the castlery of Pevensey is noted in a charter of Stephen.[116] It would seem reasonable to suppose that the rape of Arundel with its castle also constituted a castlery, but of this there is no proof. In addition to Hastings and Lewes, *Domesday* also refers to the existence of similar military districts centered at Caerleon-on-Usk, Richard's Castle, Ewias Harold, Clifford, and Montgomery, on the Welsh march—a most likely place for such centers—and at Dudley in old Mercia, where there had been some resistance to the Conquest.[117] In the north the great castlery of Earl Alan is noted in more detail than the others; there is information that in his *castellatus* the earl had 199 manors of which his men held 133, and that elsewhere he had 43 manors of which his men held 10. In other words, a clear distinction was understood between the castlery, the compact fief later known as Richmondshire, and the estates held by Earl Alan or his tenants elsewhere.[118] Another such northern castlery was that at Clitheroe in Lancashire, which, although not mentioned by name, is referred to by *Domesday* as "the castlery of Roger the Poitevan." [119] That the de Lacy castle of Pontefract was early the center of a castlery, is shown by a grant of William II to Ilbert de Lacy "of the customs of the castlery of his castle" as he had them in the time of William I and Bishop Odo of Bayeux.[120]

It has been possible also, from indirect evidence, to infer the existence of another castlery of this type at Tutbury, located like Dudley, in the old Mercian kingdom. Tutbury castle was the *caput* of the fee of Henry de Ferrers in Derbyshire. The Ferrers fee was of considerable extent—some eighteen miles from east to west, and up to thirteen miles from north to south. From the lower course of the Derwent to the line of the Dove, Henry de Ferrers held some property in almost every village; in most of them he was the sole tenant-in-chief. Beyond the Dove the fee extended into Staffordshire, and was rounded off by a small cluster of manors in the vicinity of Tutbury itself, covering virtually all the lowland extending from the river to the slopes of Needwood forest. Nowhere does *Domesday* apply the term *castel- laria* to this extensive and compact holding, "but that it was recognized as such seems to be indicated by the name 'Castellae' attached in later days to a Derbyshire rural deanery which consisted almost entirely of parishes comprised within the boundaries of de Ferrers' fee." Before the Conquest these lands belonged to a great number of owners, and *Domesday* clearly indicates that they came into the hands of a single tenant only after 1066. Again, as is true of Earl Alan of Richmond, Henry de Ferrers' holdings were not confined to the military district that comprised his castlery; he was a tenant-in-chief in fourteen counties, although in some he held only an isolated manor or two.[121] By the time of Henry II, however, the term "castlery" was being used in a broader context. It might mean the whole group of fees which owed ward to a baronial or royal castle, or the group of baronies owing garrison duty at one of the great royal fortresses.[122] Although knowledge of the early Norman *castellariae* is severely limited, enough is known of their organization and location to conclude that they formed part of a kingdom-wide system of defense. They were located on sensitive frontiers, or in districts where unrest was chronic. The lands of the castlery were situated in close proximity to the castle in which the knights were required to serve. The development of the castlery is but another testimonial to the creative imagination brought to the problems of military government by William I.

For providing the necessary permanent garrisons at important royal castles, the services of a number of baronies were combined, and a regular rotation of duty was worked out. Such arrangements are known to have existed at Corfe, Dover, Exeter, Norwich, Lincoln, Newcastle-upon-Tyne, Northampton, Nottingham, Rochester, Rockingham, Salisbury, and Windsor.[123] This system obviously was devised in the early years of the Conquest, for the knights of the abbey of Abingdon owed ward to Windsor castle in the reign of William I.[124] This is the earliest reference to such an arrangement, but two other documents of the early twelfth century show that it was not new even then. In January (?) 1102, King Henry I alerted the "barons and vavassours owing ward to Rockingham castle" to repair to their posts on the summons of the castellan, Michael de Hanslope. A year later the king notified Geoffrey de Mandeville and the sergeants of Exeter castle "that Osbert the monk and the abbey of Tavistock be quit of castle-ward at Exeter for one knight." During the middle years of the reign the king released the abbey of St. Benet's Holme from castle-guard at Norwich.[125] Additional references come from the second quarter of the century. In 1130 the king, for a consideration of £1,000, released the knights of the bishop of Ely from the obligation of castle-guard at Norwich so that they might perform similar services for the bishop in the Isle of Ely.[126] And about 1133 the bishop of Lincoln was granted the right to withdraw a third of his knights from garrison duty at Lincoln so that he might assign them to keep guard at his castle of Newark.[127] But perhaps the most interesting document from this period, for the light it throws on the practices of the time, is a notification of Henry I to the men of the archbishop of Canterbury about 1129:

Henry king of the English to all the men of the archbishop of Canterbury, greeting. I grant that those of you shall do ward in Rochester castle whom the archbishop shall choose. And I command that the archbishop compel the other men who are not his men to do their ward to the extent which they ought by custom and right. And I grant the archbishop that lodging in the bailey of Rochester which was Geoffrey Talbot's.

Witness: The Chancellor   At London [128]

This document is of interest, first of all, because it shows that castle-guard was owed to Rochester "by custom and right" by men other than those of the archbishop of Canterbury, thus giving credence to later lists of the time of Henry II showing that five baronies provided men for the ward of the castle.[129] Secondly, it is worth noting that the king expected the archbishop to see to it that the duty was performed, though what method of coercion he could employ on a recalcitrant baron, other than the thunders of the church, is not specified. Later evidence from the *cartae* of 1166 shows that similar provisions existed for the ward of Salisbury castle. The bishop of Salisbury was said to owe the service of one knight; Earl Patrick owed twenty, and Walter Waleran, the lord of West Dean in Wiltshire, owed five.[130] The same returns show also that the abbot of Cerne owed 7 (10) knights to the garrison at Corfe.[131] From this evidence it would appear that the early thirteenth-century list of baronies owing ward to Newcastle-upon-Tyne dates from Henry II's resumption of the castle in 1157.[132] In like manner, the earliest list of baronies that had combined to provide a garrison for the great royal fortress at Dover dates from the reign of John. Nine baronies—including the constable's honor of Haughley in Essex, which alone contributed 56 or 57 knights—provided a duty roster of more than 170 knights.[133]

Before the twelfth century ended, the king and his tenants—and presumably their subtenants—had begun to commute castle-guard service into money payments for much the same reasons that scutage had been accepted at the beginning of the century. Improved economic conditions provided both knights and sergeants with the financial resources to buy out of personal service, and their interests were becoming less warlike and centered more and more on local issues. The process of converting garrison duty to an annual payment was first examined at length by Round, who believed that this commutation of service began in the reign of Henry II, when the knightly pay scale was set at 8*d.* per day, and he attempted to prove that knights seeking to escape the obligation of service in person were required to pay the amount necessary to hire a substitute. Round made his calculations on the evidence available for Dover and Windsor castles, on the assumption that the annual term of service was fifteen and thirty days respectively.[134] But it seems quite clear from the record that the annual tour of duty at Dover was thirty days, and then for only part of the garrison; and although the exact period of service for the components of the Windsor garrison is unknown, it would appear to have been forty days.[135] On the basis of this evidence Round's 8*d.* commutation rate becomes completely untenable, and a survey of ward payments at other castles confirms the suspicion that there was no uniformity of commutation. Although there are few castles at which the annual tour of duty and the rate of payment are known with certainty, it is possible to show that the money receipts in lieu of personal service were not sufficient to hire a substitute at any rate of pay suggested.[136] At Eye some fees, at least, paid half a mark (6*s.*8*d.*) for commutation of castle-ward.[137] At Rockingham the abbots of Peterborough were able to commute their service for 4*s.* per fee, and the same may be true of the tenants owing ward to Lincoln castle.[138] The commutation fee was 10*s.* at Dover, and apparently also at Wark and at Northampton.[139] At Newcastle-upon-Tyne and Alnwick the rate seems to have been one mark (13*s.*4*d.*) on the knight's fee.[140] At Windsor and Bamborough a knight paid 20*s.* to escape personal service.[141]

That commutation of ward duty was general cannot be doubted, for references to the practice are frequent from the late twelfth century onward. The real problem is to explain the diversity of the rates at which personal service was excused. It certainly cannot be maintained that garrison duty was usually commuted "at 6*d.* or 8*d.* for a day's service." [142] The 4*s.* rendered in lieu of service for the abbot of Peterborough's knights, even at the lower of the two rates, would have hired a substitute for precisely eight days, and even the munificent rate of 20*s.* paid by the warders of Windsor and Bamborough would pay a substitute for only the standard forty days' service. To me, Professor Painter's analysis of the problem and the logic of his conclusion appear faultless. What tends to be forgotten in dealing with this, as with many other problems concerning the Middle Ages, is that so many concepts that are regarded as essentially modern are not really new. Among these concepts is that of collective bargaining. Castle-guard, although probably onerous, or at least boring, was not in time of peace very dangerous. Certainly the dangers were not as great as those attending a campaign in Wales or France; and the expense was, of course, much less. Thus, although the crown tenants professed willingness to pay a standard sum to be relieved of field duty, the outcome of which might very well be doubtful, no such urgency attended castle-ward in peacetime.[143] Although in some instances garrison duty had to be performed at a distant castle, more frequently no great journey was involved. So there was nothing of importance to be gained by commuting ward service to a money payment. Indeed, the evidence suggests that tenants found it was cheaper to fulfill the obligation in person. For this reason, the king and barons had no bargaining position comparable to that enjoyed by the crown in the imposition of scutage. In haggling over terms the advantage lay with the tenant, and the less inconvenient the service the less the commutation payment. The knights of the honor of Richmond whose lands lay in Yorkshire compounded for a payment of half a mark (6s.8d.), while those whose lands lay farther away—some as far as Hertfordshire—were willing to go up to 10s. per annum.[144] It is very doubtful whether payments were ever on a scale sufficient to enable the holder of a castle to employ substitutes on a man-for-man basis. Even at the low rates for which the king and barons settled, there may have been a tendency for tenants to perform their service personally and to resist attempts at enforced commutation, as is reflected in Article 29 of *Magna Carta*.

No constable shall compel any knight to give money in lieu of castle-guard, when he is willing to perform it in his own person, or (if he cannot do it from any reasonable cause) then by another responsible man. . . .[145]

Some garrisons seem to have worked out a compromise with their superiors. Since the commander would rather have money in time of peace than go to the trouble of enforcing service, which must have been increasingly difficult as time went on, and since in wartime he needed the troops, it was quite possible to work out a system whereby the knights owing ward paid a commutation fee that enabled the castle to be garrisoned by a small number of hired knights in peacetime, whereas every knight who owed ward service reported for duty in time of war. Such a system seems to have been in effect at Devizes in Wiltshire. About twenty fees owed castle-guard here, with each fee owing forty days' service of one knight, or one sergeant for half a fee on a war footing. But in peacetime each fee paid 20s. or, for a half fee, 10s. The Hundred Rolls state that the castle could be held for 25 marks (£16 13s.4d.) per year, a sum well within the castle-guard payments which should have amounted to £20 a year, were they all collected.[146] For this sum it would be possible, depending on the going rate for knights, to provide a peacetime garrison variously of two knights and four sergeants, one knight and eight sergeants, or one knight and twelve sergeants—a force quite ample for routine duty. That this system was extensively used, at least in those castles in custody of the crown, is implied by a reference in the Hundred Rolls to "the castles of the lord king, that is . . . what wards are owed in time of peace and what in time of war." [147] Such an arrangement must have been satisfactory not only to the king, but to the lords of baronial castles as well. A small but reliable professional garrison kept the castle in time of peace, and during hostilities it was put on a war footing by calling up what amounted to an obligated reserve force. It is difficult to disagree with Painter's summary of the history of castle-guard service. The permanent garrisons of large baronial castles were provided under feudal arrangements for a century after 1066. Royal castles were garrisoned by contingents from baronies grouped together for that purpose. As internal conditions became more settled, garrisons at full strength became obviously less necessary, and as the lack of necessity became more obvious, it became more difficult to enforce castle-guard obligations.

As a result, the lord of a castle was inclined to commute his tenants' services in time of peace at the highest rate that he could persuade them to pay. With this money he could hire a small, reliable mercenary garrison. This process seems to have started during the reign of Henry II. At first, however, the king and his great barons probably continued to insist that their tenants perform their service in time of war.[148]

Thus the reign of Henry II, in relation to garrison service as well as that in the field, is notable for the increasing importance of the professional element in the armed forces. It ought not to be supposed that once hostilities had broken out the professional garrisons drew their pay and went home. In the revolt of 1173–1174, the small paid elements in many castles must have represented this hired contingent, whose continued service was necessary to stiffen the "reservists," many of whom had likely seen no active duty for a long time. The three "resident knights" who served at Cambridge, or the five knights at Yeldon, or even the five knights and sixteen sergeants at Newcastle-under-Lyme, cannot have represented the entire garrisons at these places during the emergency occasioned by the revolt.[149] Here can almost certainly be seen the paid soldiers who were the professional element in the many garrisons activated on the outbreak of hostilities. The crown could no longer rely entirely on amateurs or even semi-professionals; the stability of the monarchy was coming to depend to an ever-increasing degree on professional soldiers recruited and paid by the crown itself.

But the process by which this had come about had been a long one; and for many years after the Conquest, in spite of frequent if not customary resort to other sources of military manpower, it was the mailed knight on whom the Norman kings depended primarily. Unfortunately, little is known of the rank and file who made the military occupation of England effective. Although the holders of the great and of many of the lesser honors are real, and as it were three-dimensional persons—Odo of Bayeux and Urse d'Abitot, for example—their knights are for the most part nameless and faceless, mere statistics in *Domesday* and the occasional early charter. What their backgrounds were, where they had been trained—about these the military historian would like to know, but can only guess. That their origins were varied cannot be doubted. William's army at Hastings was recruited widely, and it included not only his own Norman tenants and their retainers, but Bretons and Flemings in considerable numbers, as well as adventurers from much of what is now France. Many were men of good family, perhaps the kin of some important lord. Others must have been landless soldiers of fortune on the make. Later, men from most parts of northern France are found settled on the land. Bretons were concentrated in Earl Alan's great honor of Richmond, but men from Brittany were also settled in Devonshire, Lincolnshire, Gloucestershire, Buckinghamshire, and Essex.[150] *Domesday Book* records tenants from Flanders, Boulogne, and Picardy, and the influx continued after the period of actual military occupation. New families were established by both William II and Henry I.[151] Most of the newcomers were of baronial status, although the Flemings settled in Pembroke by Henry I are clearly an exception, and not much light is thrown on the composition of the knightly class. All that can be surmised is that since the tenants-in-chief and the barons of their honors were of such diverse origins, their retainers must have been equally so. Finally, among the obviously continental names in *Domesday* can be found those of Englishmen or Scandinavians from the Danelaw, or men described obscurely as *milites anglici*.[152] There seems to be no reason why Englishmen in significant numbers should not have been assimilated into the knightly class, and it is perhaps surprising that more were not recorded as having done so. In Wales a generation or two later, Welshmen are found holding by knight service and serving as castellans in the fortresses of Norman overlords, or even holding castles in their own right in Norman territory.[153] That perhaps the English lacked the adaptability of the Welsh is a possibility raised by the unfortunate experiment of the archbishops of Canterbury in attempting to convert English administrative retainers (*drengs*) into knights. This seems to have occurred during Lanfranc's tenancy of the archiepiscopal see at the express command of William I.[154] Although the authority for this statement is late, confirmation is found in the celebrated dispute between Lanfranc's successor Archbishop Anselm and William II, who as early as 1094 were quarreling over the status of these very same English knights.[155] In a letter to Archbishop Hugh of Lyons, Anselm complained that as certain English knights died without heirs, William Rufus wanted to grant their lands to men of his own appointment; in fact, he had already begun to do so.

Apparently enough of them survived, however, to cause the archbishop more trouble when the feudal army was called out for the Welsh campaign of 1097. At the conclusion of this expedition the king wrote to Anselm about the Canterbury knights, complaining that "they were neither properly equipped nor were they suitable persons for warfare of that character. . . ." He further gave the archbishop notice that he might be impleaded on these charges before the royal *curia*.[156] As Stenton points out, there is no reason to believe that even though no love was lost between the king and the archbishop, William Rufus was merely inventing a charge to plague his ecclesiastical opponent. Whatever his shortcomings, all contemporaries agreed that the second William was a first-rate soldier. When, therefore, he accused the archbishop of sending untrained and ill-equipped men to the muster, the charges deserve serious consideration—especially in view of the Canterbury tradition of Lanfranc's coverted *drengs,* and Anselm's letter of 1094 to Archbishop Hugh.[157] The most unusual aspect of the whole affair is that Lanfranc's action should have been sanctioned by William I, the ablest commander of his day. He cannot but have known that the archbishop's *drengs* would be worthless as knights; the truth must have been that William could not ignore any source which could provide even the semblance of fighting men. "It was only when the danger of an English rebellion was over, when the kings of Cnut's house had accepted the inevitable, and the eldest line of King William's own descendants was extinct, that the military retinues of the barons ceased to be an essential factor in the defense of the land." [158]

Chapter 11

Military Service and Military Manpower: The Nonfeudal Elements

HAD the Conqueror's problems been limited to those involved in the military government of the kingdom, and to the suppression of native risings, his feudal resources would probably have been equal to the task. But as has been noted previously, throughout the first two decades of the Norman occupation there was the continued possibility of a full-scale Danish attack. That it never in fact took place does not lessen the reality of the danger, and it must have influenced the disposition of the military forces at William's command. In 1085, the Danish preparations appeared so alarming that the king recruited a formidable mercenary army, which he quartered on his English tenants.[1] In this emergency "the knight-service due to the king from his tenants in chief was obviously unequal to the defense of the land." [2] Indeed, according to Smail it was "doubtful if the military needs of English kings could ever have been met from feudal sources alone." [3] Although this statement is not applicable to those internal crises which seem to have been surmounted without recourse to nonfeudal auxiliaries, it is certain that the Conqueror had frequently to turn to extrafeudal sources of manpower. Even before the Norman landing at Pevensey, William had been obliged to fall back on the paid soldier so maligned and abhorred by all medieval writers. The mercenary was, nevertheless, an important though frequently undervalued supplement to the feudal army. J. O. Prestwich has done much to rescue the hired knight from his undeserved obscurity and to give him his rightful place in the military history of the eleventh and twelfth centuries.[4]

This valuable corrective must be accepted with some caution, however, for Prestwich's emphasis on the role of the mercenary conveys the impression that stipendiary troops were actually the principal military resource of the Norman kings, and that the feudal army played but a secondary part.[5]

The use of mercenary troops to augment the normal feudal contingents began with the expedition of 1066 itself. The resources of Normandy were inadequate for such a project as the proposed conquest of England. Although many of the additional troops recruited were doubtless volunteers, lured by the prospects of booty or of estates, others were mercenaries. Florence of Worcester and Guy of Amiens specifically mention categories of military specialists, such as archers and crossbowmen, in addition to the more conventional cavalry and infantry units, who were taken into the duke's service on a stipendiary basis.[6] The need for the services of mercenaries did not end with the defeat of Harold and William's coronation as king of England, although some were dismissed as early as March 1067 when the king returned to Normandy. The threat of native rebellion and foreign intervention raised military problems which could not have been handled successfully by the personal following of the king. Not until the suppression of the Yorkshire rising of 1069 and the completion of the Mercian campaign in the winter of 1069–1070 did William feel his position sufficiently secure to dismiss his mercenary forces.[7] Again in 1085, when a Danish invasion seemed imminent, William raised a large mercenary force on the Continent—chiefly French and Breton, both horse and foot—which he quartered on his tenants. At the close of the normal campaigning season the invasion had not materialized, and a part of this force was dismissed, the remainder being kept on foot until the following spring.[8] Although there is no direct reference to the use of mercenaries in England during the reign of William II, the Red King evidently did employ them, for William of Malmesbury noted that "military men flocked to him out of every province on this side of the mountains, whom he rewarded most generously." [9] In view of the rather extensive coverage of the revolt of 1088, it is doubtful whether stipendiary troops were extensively employed. The mustering of the *fyrd* received due attention, as well as the activities of the tenants who remained loyal to the king. Thus Prestwich's statement that there was "a seller's market for mercenaries in England" is hardly convincing.[10] It is more likely that, as usual, English money was paying for troops who would further the Red King's policies in Normandy. Indeed, much of Prestwich's argument depends upon the use of mercenaries by the Norman kings in their continental wars.

By the beginning of the twelfth century mercenary troops were being used not only by reigning princes, but by whatever magnates had the money to pay them. During the revolt of 1102 the most reliable element in Robert de Bellême's garrison at Bridgnorth was his four score stipendiary troops.[11] The ecclesiastical bias against mercenaries came mainly from their habitual failure to distinguish between lay and clerical property, and is clearly reflected in the chronicler's reference to their employment by Henry I. They were, he said, willing to enter any kind of conflict so long as the price was right.[12] Henry's employment of mercenaries is confirmed in the surviving Pipe Roll of the reign, which noted the expenditure of £14 5*s*.7 1/2*d*. in pay to the knights, sergeants, gatekeeper, and watchman at the castle of St. Briavels, and of £21 5*s*.10*d*. to one knight, ten sergeants, a gatekeeper, and a watchman in Roger de Mowbray's forfeited castle of Burton-in-Lonsdale.[13] The prejudice of the clerk of Malmesbury was even more apparent in his condemnations of the professional soldiers in Stephen's service:

Soldiers of all kinds, and light-armed troops were flocking to him [Stephen], chiefly from Flanders and Brittany. These were a most rapacious and violent race of men, who made no scruple at violating churchyards or pillaging a church. Moreover, they would not only drag men of the religious order from their horses, but they would also take them captive; and this was done, not just by foreign, but even by native soldiers. . . .[14]

But as Smail points out, the first Norman kings either did not or could not rely entirely on feudal sources of military manpower, and the use of stipendiary troops was a normal factor from the very outset of Norman rule in England. And although Stephen was following the practice of his predecessors, the disturbed state of the kingdom during much of his reign very naturally attracted mercenary bands and soldiers of fortune from all over western Europe. The employment of mercenaries, as suggested earlier, offered several advantages to the ruler who could afford their services. They were usually better trained than their feudal counterparts, and their length of service was limited only by the limits of their employer's ability to pay.[15] To a king in Stephen's position, faced with an active and strongly supported contender for the throne, it was but natural to rely on stipendiary troops who had no territorial stake in the outcome of the struggle, and who would not be so likely to connive with the opposition. It is not surprising, then, that Stephen relied to a great extent on mercenary contingents to bolster the never-too-loyal feudal service of his supporters. Even when his fortunes were at their lowest ebb, following his capture in the debacle of Lincoln, there is no indication that his hired troops deserted, or that his lieutenants were unable to pay them.

Stephen's dependence upon paid professionals was repeatedly noted by the chroniclers, all of whom condemned the practice. Even the author of the *Gesta*, who usually saw no wrong in the actions of his hero, deplored the depredations of the "savage crowd of barbarians who had swarmed to England in a body to serve as mercenaries."[16] Gervase of Canterbury singled out the Flemings in particular for their cruel ravages.[17] The Flemish mercenaries, both cavalry and infantry, were perhaps the main stipendiary force employed by Stephen, and their commander William of Ypres, became one of the king's ablest lieutenants and most trusted advisers.[18] He was in Stephen's employ as early as 1138 or 1139, and served the king faithfully until the latter's death in 1154. His position at court can be judged from that of his name in the list of witnesses to Stephen's second charter to Geoffrey de Mandeville in December 1141; it came immediately after the names of the earls. He was also present at the St. Albans court about the end of September 1143, when Earl Geoffrey was arrested and compelled to surrender his castles.[19] In all the important military engagements of the civil war William, characterized by Verbruggen as the first *condottiere,* was present with his Flemings.[20] The number of mounted men in William's band was estimated at three hundred by a Flemish chronicler—a not unreasonable figure, and one accepted by Verbruggen.[21] If William and his Flemings did not cover themselves with glory at Lincoln or at Wilton, they more than redeemed themselves by their steadfastness after Stephen's capture in 1141, and in their performance at the siege of Winchester and the subsequent rout of the Angevin army.[22]

Strangely enough, of all the foreign mercenary captains who must have served in England during the long years of civil strife, only William of Ypres and his relative, Robert fitz Hubert, are unmistakably mentioned by name. The Pharamus of Boulogne who also witnessed Stephen's second charter to Geoffrey de Mandeville, and whose ravages are noted as late as 1156, was a nephew of Queen Mathilda, and a minor landholder in Surrey.[23] Likewise, the men of Boulogne who in 1138 assisted the queen in the siege of Dover would seem to have been her tenants, rather than mercenaries.[24] Numerous references scattered through the chronicles point to the employment of mercenary troops. The "robbers, who collected enthusiastically" to the standard of Geoffrey de Mandeville in 1143 and 1144, were almost certainly mercenaries, and the author of the *Gesta* wrote that Earl Miles of Hereford needed a great deal of money to pay the knights he had recruited for service against the king.[25] There is also mention of what may be an early (1144) example of an English mercenary captain, one William of Dover:

. . . a man crafty and bold in warfare, relying on the support of the earl of Gloucester, came to the village named Cricklade, which is situated in a delightful spot abounding in resources of every kind, and with the greatest zeal built a castle which was inaccessible because of the barrier of water and marsh on every side, and with a large following of mercenary knights, also bands of archers, he made forays in every direction, ruthless and merciless; subduing the country far and wide on both banks of the Thames he committed the cruellest excesses against the king's adherents.[26]

Similarly the "garrison of plunderers" installed in the bishop of Winchester's castle of Downton (Wiltshire) in 1147/1148 by Earl Patrick of Salisbury may well have been mercenaries.[27] In view of the widespread employment of mercenaries, it is difficult to accept

Prestwich's contention that the civil war came about as a result of Stephen's inability to pay the mercenaries whose presence had enabled him to act with firmness and resolution through the first two years of his reign. He concluded that the disputed succession was a result of the civil war, not contrariwise, as has generally been believed.[28] All the evidence seems to indicate that Stephen was never at a loss for mercenary troops, and that he had the money to pay them. These bands were numerous, and were available to anyone who could offer sufficient pay or the prospects of plunder. At the very beginning of Stephen's reign, one of Henry I's janitors collected a motley force "tam rusticorum quam stipendiariorum militum," and ravaged the countryside until the king proceeded against him in person.[29] The king employed mercenaries first against the Welsh and later against the rebels; and he was by no means the only employer of the Flemings or Brabançons, as the record clearly shows. In 1140 Bishop Nigel of Ely hired "at his own expense, knights who were prepared for any crime. . . ."[30] Robert fitz Hubert, the kinsman of William of Ypres, was in the employ of the earl of Gloucester, and the siege of Winchester in 1141 was notable for the extraordinary number of foreigners that "had assembled from every quarter and was there in arms."[31] Now so far as is known, the financial resources of Angevin party did not equal those of the king; nor had it the opportunity, as Stephen did, to profit from the death of wealthy prelates. Yet the rebels were able to maintain their position in the Severn valley and, after capturing the king at Lincoln, to come within an ace of mastering the entire kingdom. Where did the Angevins find the money to pay the mercenaries they were employing as early as 1139?[32] Attempts to extract money from the church met with resistance, and in the restricted area controlled in the empress's name this could not have been a very lucrative source of income. A hint as to how the money was raised is to be found in the *Gesta* in reference to the administration of the area under Earl Robert's control.

Hoc autem illius dominium, pace et tranquiliatate ubique reformata, plurimum decorabat, excepto quod in castellis suis aedificandis operariorum exactionibus ab omnibus exigebat; et quotiens cum adversarius esset congrediendem, omnium sibi auxilia asciscebat, vel in militibus mittendis, vel in aeris descriptiones reddenda.[33]

Now in this context the "aeris descriptiones" can mean only one thing, namely that Earl Robert was levying scutage in those areas under his control; and it would be more than likely that Stephen raised revenue in the same manner. Although the statements of the chroniclers that many of Stephen's troubles from 1138 to 1140 stemmed from financial distress are too numerous to be ignored, there is believable evidence that the machinery of the central administration continued to function throughout Stephen's reign. Justice was administered in the area under his control, and in spite of Richard fitz Neal's comments, the Exchequer continued to function.[34] It can only be concluded that both parties to the civil strife during Stephen's reign employed stipendiary troops, both foreign and domestic, regularly and on a large scale, and that both sides resorted to devious methods to find the money to pay them.

That this was a regular practice can be inferred from the earliest years of the reign of Henry II, when stipendiary troops are known to have formed at least part of the garrisons of numerous royal castles. The dismissal of William of Ypres and his Flemings must be regarded as something in the nature of window dressing.[35] In 1157/1158 paid garrisons were occupying the castles of Norwich and Framlingham, which had been taken from William of Blois, King Stephen's son, and Hugh Bigod.[36] In succeeding years payments to knights and sergeants are recorded in Walton, Southampton, Dover, and Nottingham; although the sums spent are not large, they formed a significant part of the military budget in some years. In 1157/1158 the figure was £68. 10s.; in 1158/1159 it was £77. For the fiscal year 1159/1160, ten knights and four sergeants in Walton castle drew £126; stipendiary troops in Southampton and Dover were paid £82 8s.6d. in 1161/1162. In the tenth exchequer year of the reign (1163/1164), only £35 4s.7d. was disbursed for this purpose. In 1166/1167 the knights and sergeants at Walton and Dover received £73 19s.; from these entries it can be calculated that the daily wage of the knight was 8d., that of a sergeant 1d. In the fiscal year 1167/1168 the stipendiary garrisons in these two castles drew only £65 7s.6d.[37] It is perhaps worth noting that according to the account for 1166/1167, which is more than usually detailed, the service at Walton and Dover was performed between the end of April and the middle of October—the normal campaigning season of the twelfth century.[38] In the following year five knights at Dover were paid for duty between St. George's Day (23 April) and the feast of St. Luke the Evangelist (18 October).[39] During peacetime, then, it would seem that stipendiary troops were employed on a seasonal basis, and it might perhaps be suggested that these knights and sergeants were not mercenaries in the accepted sense of the word—that is, professional soldiers whose services went to whomever could meet the payroll—but were volunteers from the regular castle-guard contingents who accepted the "king's 8d." for extra duty. This then may very well have been, although proof is not likely to be forthcoming at this late date; but even so, these nameless individuals would seem to belong to the category of mercenaries in the strict definition of the term. They were certainly extrafeudal from the moment they began to draw a per diem from the Exchequer. Unfortunately, Boussard's brief monograph on mercenary service during the reign of Henry II made no use of the Pipe Rolls, the most detailed source of information on the employment of professional troops both in peace and in wartime. For example, the rolls show that for years before the Welsh rising of 1185, knights and sergeants were paid for duty at the border castles in the king's hands. Clun, Ruthin, Whitchurch, Carreghofa, Chester, Llandovery, Grosmont, Llantilio, Scenfrith, and Shrawardine are among the marcher fortresses having paid garrisons at one time or another.[40]

That the great revolt of 1173/1174 brought about an enormous increase in the use of paid soldiers, is reflected in the Pipe Rolls in those years and immediately afterward. But the rolls are more than a mere recital of payments to troops. They record the number and type of troops employed, their length of service, and rates of pay. Although no estimate of the total number of mercenaries employed during the conflict can be made, it is often possible to determine the composition of the garrison of a particular castle. For example, in 1173/1174 a hired contingent that was maintained at Newcastle-under-Lyme for 134 days consisted of five knights, six mounted sergeants, and ten foot soldiers.[41] All told, during the rebellion, stipendiary troops were serving in thirty-one castles, mostly in the Midlands and the eastern counties.[42] The extent to which paid soldiery was used may be seen from the payroll, which in 1172/1173 amounted to £825 11s.3d. for garrisons stationed in nineteen castles. In addition, stipendiary forces with the royal army besieging Leicester were paid £192 5s.4d.—which, together with pay to twenty knights whose duties are not specified, brought the total for the year to £1,037 16s.7d.[43] In the following year the cost of maintaining garrisons in twenty-six castles had risen to £1,980 7s., and the total pay to hired troops was £2,026 2s.10d.[44] Nor does this represent the total outlay; it can be shown that many of the troops must have had to wait for their pay. In 1174/1175, soldiers on active duty in five castles—Shrewsbury, Bridgnorth, Whitchurch, Warwick, and Worcester—were paid only £168 15s.5d., whereas the knights and sergeants who had been in the king's service during wartime received the great sum of £2,169 9s.10d., of which well over half—£1,228 16s.10d.—was charged against the revenues of the single county of York.[45]

Again the question arises: Were all these troops mercenaries, or were they men whose feudal obligation had expired and who continued to serve at the king's wages during the emergency? The evidence, though slight, seems to indicate that at least some of them were true professionals. The twenty *milites soldarii* in the garrison at Kenilworth, and a similar number at Lincoln, almost certainly were.[46] It would also seem probable that the "Henry de Chemesech, Derkino de Arra and other knights of the count of Boulogne" to whom £63 was paid, were mercenaries.[47] On the other hand, the sergeants of Shropshire who marched to Leicester under the command of the sheriff certainly were neither mercenaries nor feudal tenants performing their customary service.[48] Probably William fitz Peter and his four knights who served in the garrison at Warwick for twenty days at 8d. per day each, were feudal tenants who served at the king's wages. It would also appear that these local levies, recruited for the emergency, generally received lower wages than the mercenaries, whose usual pay seems to have been a shilling a day.[49]

The king, as has been seen, was not the only one to employ mercenary soldiers; his enemies did likewise. Earl Robert of Leicester's three thousand Flemings operated in East Anglia before they were annihilated at Fornham on 17 October 1173.[50] In the following year, mention is made of Flemish mercenaries employed by Earl Hugh of Norfolk and King William of Scotland. On 13 July a contingent of 500 Flemings, commanded by the count of Bar, landed at Hartlepool, but were dismissed at once by the bishop of Durham. It may be the effects of some of these soldiers that were accounted for by the sheriff of York in the Pipe Roll for 1174/1175.[51] The rebel garrison at Leicester seems also to have contained some of the foreign mercenaries, for in 1176 and 1177 the sheriff owed £22 for "Flemings who were in Leicester and are fled." [52]

As might be expected, stipendiary troops appear less frequently after the end of hostilities in 1174 and the subsequent destruction of many baronial strongholds. In the latter years of the reign, paid troops are usually found in castle garrisons on the marches, in places like Norham or Hereford, or in first-class fortresses such as the great new castle at Dover.[53] Throughout the century and a quarter that separated the Norman Conquest from the death of Henry II, the employment of mercenary troops had been an accepted practice rather than an expedient born of emergency. They were hired not only by kings, but also by rebellious tenants who could afford them. Although subsequent historians have been influenced against them by the strictures of the monkish chroniclers, it is a fairly safe guess that their soldierly qualities and the professional capabilities of their commanders at least equaled those of the feudal component, else their services would not have been in such great demand. Although, as Smail notes, the employment of mercenaries is associated with the development of scutage, the use of stipendiary troops began with the Conquest itself, and was not given up by English monarchs until the eighteenth century.[54] Even before the development of scutage, ways were found of raising money for hiring mercenary troops—

for example, William the Conqueror's levy of a Danegeld in 1084 at the unprecedented rate of 6s. on the hide.[55] By the end of the reign of Henry II the evolution that had begun in the old Conqueror's time was accelerating noticeably. Cavalry, which never had the all-importance claimed for it by its proponents, was becoming less significant. "The decline in the military value of the mounted force would cause the king to summon fewer knights, while scutage would be collected from others in order to pay mercenary troops." [56] Moreover, as Poole observes, the army was taking on a professional coloring, and even those English knights who participated in campaigns or served in garrisons were career men who fought for pay.[57]

Closely associated with the use of mercenary troops was the pseudo-feudal device known as the *fief-rente,* or money fief. Although in some instances, it was apparently designed to provide military service, there is no evidence that any of the military assistance guaranteed by the granting of such fiefs was ever required for operations in England. The entire subject has been treated with admirable thoroughness by Professor Lyon, and since the money fief has but limited application to England during the period covered by this study, a summary only seems necessary.[58] The money fief was an annual sum paid to an individual in return for some service, actual or contingent, and it should in no way be confused with the nonfeudal pay of mercenaries. In England, so far as can be determined, money fiefs were granted only by the king. And despite the feudal formulae, it is difficult to regard the money fief as anything other than a retainer. To expel a tenant from an ordinary fief, the feudal superior had to be in a position to use force; to end a money fief, he had merely to omit the payment. The analogy to a fief in land can be carried only so far.

Because of the efficient management of their finances both in England and in Normandy, the king-dukes had more ready cash at their disposal, and were able to "adapt money to feudal custom" far earlier than the French kings and Holy Roman Emperors.[59] But throughout the eleventh and twelfth century, the *fief-rente* in England appears to be a diplomatic instrument—a device intended to safeguard a position rather than actually to obtain military aid in time of war. This practice began, according to William of Malmesbury, in 1066, before the attack against England was launched. In return for homage, counsel, and military aid, Duke William granted to Count Baldwin V of Flanders a fief of 300 marks annually.[60] In this way William sought to neutralize Flanders during his absence, so as to forestall a possible incursion into Normandy. Baldwin and his successor seem to have received the annual payment until 1071, when Robert the Frisian usurped the comital throne and the Conqueror refused to recognize him. But in 1093 Robert and William II reached an understanding, and the fief was regranted.[61] When Henry I was seeking to strengthen his position on all fronts in view of the impending attack from Normandy by Duke Robert, and of probable trouble from Robert's supporters in England, the king hastened to renew the agreement with the Flemish count, and at Dover on 10 March 1101 they met and concluded an alliance. The terms stipulated that, saving his allegiance to the king of France, Robert would aid Henry in the defense of England, Normandy, and Maine with a thousand knights for an annual payment of £500.[62] As indicated in an earlier chapter, this alliance may very well have forced Duke Robert to look to the eastern defenses of Normandy, thus weakening of the forces available for the invasion of England. The alliance was renewed at Dover on 17 May 1110, with Count Robert promising to provide five hundred knights for Henry's service, in England if necessary, in return for a fief of 400 silver marks per annum.[63] There is no further mention of the fief during the remainder of Henry's reign or that of Stephen, but Lyon suspects that it continued to be paid until 1135, and that since Count Thierry remained on friendly terms with the empress, she may have paid it. However, in view of the financial straits to which the Angevin faction was sometimes reduced, this is pure speculation. One other money fief is known to have been granted by Henry I; probably in 1127/1128, 100 marks sterling were given to Baldwin IV, count of Hainaut, for unspecified services.[64]

From the fuller records of the reign of Henry II it is possible to obtain a more complete picture of the use of the money fief by the English kings. Payments to Count Thierry of Flanders are recorded from the very beginning of the reign; and although it is not certain whether they were part of the old fee of 400 marks, it seems likely that they were, for on 19 March 1163 the count met King Henry at Dover and the compact was renewed. In return for an annual payment of 400 marks, the Flemish count agreed to put a thousand knights into the field for the defense of England, Normandy, and Maine, saving only his allegiance to the king of France. Moreover, he agreed to have his knights ready within forty days of receipt of summons, and to assemble them at Flemish ports for transport as the king of England directed. At this same meeting, a number of the count's vassals acknowledged the military service due the king for their money fiefs. With these Henry, as befitted the most powerful monarch of his day—and the most feared—was fairly lavish. In 1166 a fief of £1,000 was conferred on Count Matthew of Boulogne; one of £500 was granted to Count Theobald of Blois, and in 1172 Baldwin V of Hainaut succeeded to the fief of 100 marks that his father had held, while six of his vassals received lesser grants.[65] When the younger Henry revolted in 1173 he outbid the king for the support of Count Philip of Flanders, who had succeeded his father in 1168, granting him a fief of £1,000 annually, plus the county of Kent and the castles of Dover and Rochester; Count Theobald was won over with the promise of a fief of £500 Angevin.[66] These shifts in allegiance had little effect on military operations in England, however. Count Matthew of Boulogne, who also supported the Young King, did indeed threaten to invade England, but when the justiciar, Richard de Lucy, prepared to defend the south coast, the count abandoned the attempt.[67] After the revolt had been crushed in 1174, a reconciliation took place between King Henry and Count Philip. In 1175 Philip agreed to give up any claim to the money fief granted him by the younger Henry, and again became the man of Henry II for a grant now advanced to 1,000 marks per annum. Payment appears to have been made regularly until the king's death in 1189.[68]

Thus the money fief played no significant role in the military history of England up to the death of Henry II. Large sums of English money had been paid to these princes for their services, but the purpose was to further the continental ambitions of the

English kings. Although this may have meant fewer calls for overseas service from the Anglo-Norman tenants, it is impossible to measure the effects of the money fief on the military history of the eleventh and twelfth centuries. The services of the troops provided by the Flemish alliance were never needed in England; and in more ways than one, it is probably a good thing that they were not. The treaty of 1101 stipulated that the knights, with three horses each, were to be picked up at Gravelines or Witsand in Henry's ships, transported to England, and returned to Flanders at the end of the campaign at the king's expense. Moreover, as long as the count and his men were in the king's service, Henry was to maintain them completely and make good all their losses in equipment and horses.[69] The treaties of 1110 and 1163 do not differ materially in their provisions. It seems probable that good mercenaries could have been hired as cheaply without the additional expense of the annual payment.

There remains one other source of military manpower—the defeated English population, which constituted potentially, at any rate, a reservoir of considerable importance. Recent scholarly writing on the transition from the "old" English kingdom to the "new" Norman monarchy has rightly stressed the continuity of many institutions. That continuity is not at all surprising, for English institutions were sometimes more efficient than those of the Norman duchy. As Lyon comments, the Norman rulers took a practical approach to the problems of government, and they never abolished a working institution.[70] One such institution was the English militia, the *fyrd,* which not only was a going concern at the time of the Conquest, but which continued to be so for more than a generation. It might be well at this point to determine just what the old English militiaman was not, for recently the novel argument has been advanced that the English *cniht* was in all essentials a knight who fought on horseback—even though supporting evidence is practically nonexistent.[71] The thesis rests on two assumptions: first, that the English army had cavalry capabilities; second, that the men recruited from the five-hide units were for this reason troopers, or *cnihts.* The contention that the English army of 1066 and earlier fought on horseback is comparatively recent, and rests almost entirely on Glover's acceptance of the account of Snorri Sturluson of the Battle of Stamford Bridge as reliable evidence for English tactics in the eleventh century.[72] Apart from this testimony, which is nearly two centuries removed from the event, Glover cites no instance of an English cavalry action other than Earl Ralf of Hereford's unfortunate experience in 1055—which Glover attempts to explain away by saying that the rough border terrain was not suitable for mounted action. Elsewhere he notes that English mounted troops are said to have participated in Welsh and Scottish campaigns, and that such troops were used in the pursuit of a flying enemy.[73] But nothing is said in any of these accounts about actual combat on horseback, and although it is not always safe to argue from silence, the long history of dragoon tactics certainly does not rule out the possibility, even the probability of an English army that rode to battle and dismounted to fight. It is indeed surprising that any thesis resting upon such slender evidence should have gained credence among reputable scholars. If Snorri is a dependable source for the Battle of Stamford Bridge, then Master Wace, who wrote within a century of Hastings, must also be considered a dependable source, and his account of the English palisade should be accepted without question. Better witnesses than Snorri will have to be produced before the concept of Saxon cavalry can be very convincing.

The second assumption, that the English soldier produced by the five-hide system of recruitment was a cavalryman, rests upon even slimmer evidence. To call him a *cniht* or a *thegn* does not make him one.[74] Hollister has shown conclusively that the five-hide soldier was not of the thegnly class, but was selected—usually on the basis of experience—and paid by the territorial unit that sent him to the host.[75] There is no reason to suppose that this obligation ceased after William became king of England; indeed, the well-known Berkshire entry in *Domesday* records that the five-hide units were still functioning in 1086.[76] Nor is there any reason to believe that the Englishmen who were called up by William Rufus in 1088, or the "peditum Anglicorum" who were summoned in 1094, were anything but the infantry of the *fyrd*, whether the term is used or not.[77] If they were not so recruited, it seems reasonable to ask how else some thousands of Englishmen might have been found who were available for military duty. Of course it will be argued that this presupposes a double obligation —that of providing knight service on the one hand, and on the other the old territorial obligation due from the five-hide units. Richardson and Sayles assume that this latter obligation is illusory —that the five-hide units produced knights, not infantrymen, and that, for example, the abbey of Abingdon had the quota on its Berkshire lands reduced by two-thirds, from one hundred to thirty knights.[78] Professor Hoyt has demonstrated quite convincingly that this is incorrect. Although the assessment of the abbey's Berkshire lands was reduced from 500 to 300 hides, the abbot was expected to put sixty infantrymen plus thirty knights into the field on summons—a reduction of a mere 10 per cent on the service due before 1066. There seems to have been no change in the abbey's obligation for its lands in Oxfordshire and Warwickshire.[79] Moreover, Hollister has proved conclusively that this double obligation existed on the lands of Peterborough, and that houses with no *servitia debita,* such as Thorney and Burton, did have a military obligation—which can only have been the old preConquest duty to supply a soldier for each five hides. Hollister does not take the final step and state that the double obligation existed, but the implication is obvious.[80] These calculations hold true for other religious houses whose hidation was greatly reduced after the Conquest. The benefit accruing therefrom was more apparent than real. Indeed, the so-called "Laws of Edward the Confessor," if they do actually reflect conditions during the reign of Henry I, confirm the existence of a double obligation.[81] What would be the purpose of surveying the arms of the rustics in the hundreds and wapentakes each year if there were no obligation for military service? The king's officials had better things to do with their time than to take meaningless inventories. It stands to reason that well into the twelfth century the old militia system was still in being. It seems most improbable that the purpose of this assize was to transfer the command of such forces "from the freeman's lord to the sheriff." [82] The commander of the shire-levies had always been the sheriff or some other representative of the king.[83] It ought to be evident that much of the current discussion of English military institutions in the eleventh and twelfth centuries fails to take into consideration the military as opposed to the institutional history of the period.

From the outset the *fyrd* played an important role in the military annals of Norman England. As early as 1067, the militia of Somersetshire, under Eadnoth the Staller, were called out to repel a raid from Ireland led by one of Harold's sons. In the engagement that followed, Eadnoth was slain and the *fyrd* suffered numerous casualties but drove the raiders back to their ships.[84] In the baronial revolt of 1088, and of 1101–1102, the *fyrd* was called out and made notable contributions to the victories of William II and Henry I over the feudal malcontents.[85] It was surely ironic that the English national levy should be an instrument in preserving the throne of its Norman conquerors. But that the *fyrd* was equal in importance to the feudal levy, as some scholars have suggested, is not borne out by the evidence. Although the *fyrd* participated in every important campaign through 1102, this participation was not decisive. It was called out because just such an infantry force was needed in the kind of war the Norman kings had to fight. It has already been emphasized that the baronial enemies of William II and Henry I, instead of risking a conflict in the open, took refuge in their castles. Thus it became necessary for the kings to resort to siege warfare, and for this an infantry force was necessary. The one most readily was, of course, the English militia. In the sieges of Tonbridge, Pevensey, and Rochester in 1088, and of Arundel and Bridgnorth in 1102, the *fyrd* played a significant role. Since the soldiers were paid by the localities in which they were raised, the king was spared the expense of hiring mercenary foot to do the job.[86]

In 1101 Henry I called out the *fyrd* to repel an expected invasion from Normandy, and personally took a hand in training it in anti-cavalry tactics.[87] This points to one of the weaknesses of the *fyrd* as a reliable reserve—its lack of adequate training. The knights had frequent opportunity for active duty, and there may have been a forty-day annual period of active duty for training in peacetime.[88] The militia went on active duty only in time of war, and had to learn on the job, as it were. This probably accounts for the decline in its importance during the twelfth century, and for the increasing reliance of Stephen and Henry II on mercenaries.[89] Henry's attempt in 1181 to revitalize the militia with the legislation of the Assize of Arms may have had an economic as well as a military purpose, since mercenary forces were expensive to maintain. Moreover, in an age of increasing specialization and professionalism, no monarch could rely on an untrained levy. Although the Assize of Arms made no provisions for training, it did attempt to ensure that each man had the military equipment suited to his economic status. Thus money, rather than land, was the basis of military obligation after 1181.[90]

The civic militia, which played so important a role in the military history of northern Italy and the Low Countries, had an English counterpart only in the city levy of London, which on occasion was called to service in times of domestic unrest. Nevertheless, the participation of the burgesses in military operations was not unknown; it dates, in fact, from the first days of the Conquest. Even before the Battle of Hastings, the men of Romney had defeated a Norman detachment, for which they were severely punished after the successful engagement of 14 October.[91] In 1068 the citizens of Exeter defended their town for more than two weeks against the Conquerer himself before surrendering, and in the following year these same townsmen stood a siege by English rebels from Devon and Cornwall.[92] The Pipe Rolls of the second and fourth years of Henry II carry the notation that "the burgesses of Bedford owe 20 marks of silver because they were in the castle against the king," and it may be supposed that during Henry's attack on the town and castle in 1153, some of the townsmen aided in the defense.[93] The reign of Stephen is notable, in fact, for its references to townsmen in arms. The citizens of Lincoln are mentioned repeatedly in this connection, most notably for their participation on the king's side in the disastrous battle of 2 February 1141. In Stephen's reign also there is a recorded attempt by the burgesses of Malmesbury to defend their walls against Duke Henry's mercenary infantry in 1153. The records, in the following reign, of the rebellion of 1173–1174, provide other instances of burgher participation in the conflicts of the day. At some time after 19 May 1174, the earl of Leicester's commander in Leicester castle, Ansket Mallory, conducted a raid against Northampton in which the burgesses of that town were defeated. It is not stated whether the townsmen were cut up outside the walls or not, but their inability to stand up to Mallory's troops laid the town open to plundering. Also mentioned as having taken part in the operations of this rebellion are the burgesses of London, Dunwich, and Nottingham.[94] These accounts contain no reference to the "burghal knights," and it may be assumed that if the *cnihtengilda* of the towns were actually fighting men, they cannot have been very important.[95]

The one city for which detailed information of the militia organization has survived is London. The composition of the civic levy has been admirably treated by Sir Frank Stenton, in an essay that ranks as a minor classic.[96] The Londoners had a warlike reputation, which they maintained even during the dark days of October–December 1066. It was a body of London men who attacked the cavalry covering the right wing of the Norman army as it wheeled westward below the city. Although they were defeated at Southwark, the aggressive spirit shown by the Londoners may well have influenced William's decision not to attempt a crossing of the Thames at this point. And although the accounts are confused, it seems likely that the burgesses did not submit until the Norman army was within sight of the city walls and some actual skirmishing had taken place.[97] During the periodic revolts that punctuated the reigns of the Conqueror and his sons, nothing is known of the participation, if any, of the city levy; but during the reign of Stephen it acted decisively in two campaigns on the king's behalf. In the summer of 1141, when that monarch was still a captive in Bristol castle, and his fortunes were at their lowest ebb, it was the London levy, nearly a thousand strong, together with the mercenary horse and foot of William of Ypres, that formed the nucleus of Queen Mathilda's army in the Winchester campaign. Following the Rout of Winchester, which resulted in the capture of Earl Robert of Gloucester and the eventual release of the king, the Londoners participated in the sack of Winchester together with other units of the royal army.[98] Four years later, the Londoners contributed to a victory that the contemporary chronicler, Henry of Huntingdon, regarded as the turning point in Stephen's career. This was the reduction of the castle of Faringdon in Berkshire, which severed the line of communications between the Angevin base in the Severn valley and its advanced outpost at Wallingford.[99]

The basic unit of the militia organization was the ward, of which there were probably twenty-four. In peacetime each ward was responsible for keeping watch within its boundaries; in time of war the levy of each ward, under the command of its alderman, was responsible for defending a section of the city wall.[100] When the civic levy was called upon to campaign outside of London, the command fell upon the lord of Baynard's Castle by customary right. Stenton accepts the Norman origin of a claim made by an early fourteenth-century descendant of the Norman lords of that castle:

. . . that in time of war he should come to the west door of St. Paul's, mounted, with eleven other knights, and there receive the banner of the city, that he should there direct the choice of a marshal for the city host, order the summoning of the commoners, and finally, in the priory of the Holy Trinity, Aldgate, choose two discreet men from each ward to keep the city safely.[101]

It requires very little imagination to picture the men of London to the number of almost a thousand, "magnificently equipped with helmets and coats of mail," the city standard flying at the head of the column, marching across old London bridge on their way to Winchester.[102]

Occasionally the chronicles of the eleventh and twelfth century contain a reference to military activity by the peasantry, but before the death of Henry II only one such reference is verifiable. In 1140 King Stephen had installed his son-in-law, Hervey of Brittany, as castellan at Devizes, a strategically located castle in Wiltshire; but the local population rose, apparently because of his oppressive rule, and Hervey was besieged in his castle by what the chronicler calls "a mob of plain peasants (*a simplici rusticorum plebe*)" until finally he surrendered the castle to the Angevins and fled the country in disgrace.[103] Such occurrences must have been very rare, although the English chronicler makes a similar statement in reference to the siege of Norwich during the revolt of Earl Ralph in 1075: ". . . But the castlemen who were in England, and the country people [*landfolc*] came against him. . . ."[104]

It cannot be certain whether the reference is to a real peasant rising, or to the mustering of the local *fyrd* for military service. It is also necessary to point out that in some instances countrymen of an intermediate status—between free and unfree —owed regular military service. Lennard has called attention to certain sokemen holding of the abbey of Peterborough in Northamptonshire and Leicestershire by servile tenure, who also served *cum militibus*.[105] But nowhere is there any evidence that the city militia or the general levy of the countryside played a role in post-Conquest military operations comparable to that of the *fyrd*.

The conclusions of this survey are inescapable. Raising an army in the eleventh and twelfth centuries was not simply a matter of summoning the tenants-in-chief to assemble with the knights of their honors. The military forces put into the field by the Anglo-Norman kings were recruited from a variety of sources. Gone is the illusion, so far as post-Conquest England is concerned, of a knightly monopoly of military service. And yet this newer picture of the real composition of the armies of the eleventh and twelfth centuries serves only to enhance the military reputation of the Conqueror and of his immediate successors. The combination of horse and foot, of archers and of spearmen and lancers, was far more flexible, tactically speaking, and could be more readily adapted to all conditions of terrain and enemy dispositions, than could formations composed entirely of squadrons of heavy cavalry.[106] In this adaptability and flexibility lies the explanation of the almost uniform success enjoyed by Anglo-Norman armies.

Notes

Introduction

[1] Charles Oman, *A History of the Art of War in the Middle Ages* (London, 1924); *A Muslim Manual of War,* ed. and tr. George T. Scanlon (Cairo, 1961), 3, 5; C. Warren Hollister, *Anglo-Saxon Military Institutions on the Eve of the Norman Conquest* (Oxford, 1962), 129–131.

[2] Oman, *Art of War,* I, 357, 360, 395, 399. Oman's credo is summed up in a single sentence: "The cavalry arm had the last word in all the battles of the twelfth and thirteenth centuries, except under abnormal circumstances" (*ibid.,* 402).

[3] R. C. Smail, "Art of War," in *Medieval England,* ed. Austin Lane Poole (rev. ed.; Oxford, 1958), I, 140.

[4] C. Warren Hollister, "The Norman Conquest and the Genesis of English Feudalism," *American Historical Review,* LXVI (1961), 663. The feudal contingents and the *fyrd,* plus such mercenaries as may have been employed, were certainly integrated under a single command. Unity of command is a cardinal principle of the military art, and there is no evidence that it was violated by the Conqueror or his sons. See Michael Powicke, *Military Obligation in Medieval England* (Oxford, 1962), 30.

[5] H. G. Richardson and G. O. Sayles, *The Governance of Mediaeval England from the Conquest to Magna Carta* (Edinburgh, 1963), 55, 61, 65, 71, 92. The contrary view is well expressed by David C. Douglas, *William the Conqueror* (Berkeley, 1964), 280: "Nevertheless, when all qualifications have been made, there can be no question that the destruction of one aristocracy in England and the substitution of another holding its lands by military tenure involved a revolutionary change."

[6] Richard Glover, "English Warfare in 1066," *English Historical Review,* LXVII (1952), 8–9.

[7] See the account of the Battle of Five Forks, 1 April 1865, between the dismounted cavalry of Major General Philip H. Sheridan and Confederate infantry units, in *The Blue and the Gray,* ed. Henry Steele Commager (New York, 1950), II, 1121–1122. The Federal cavalry was never a match for the Confederates in mounted fighting, but dismounted it was able to drive the best Confederate infantry.

[8] Giraldus Cambrensis, *Itinerarium Kambriae,* in Vol. VI, *Giraldi Cambrensis Opera,* ed. James F. Dimock (R.S.), (London, 1868), 220.

[9] Oman, *Art of War,* I, 270.

[10] Hans Delbrück, *Geschichte der Kriegskunst im Rahmen des Politische Geschichte* (Berlin, 1907–1921), I, 156–164.

[11] Oman, *Art of War,* I, 357.

[12] Sir Frank Stenton, *The First Century of English Feudalism, 1066–1166,* 2nd ed. (Oxford, 1961), 193; F. M. Stenton, *Anglo-Saxon England,* 2nd ed. (Oxford, 1947), 590–592, 601, 617.

[13] Stenton, *First Century,* 149; Douglas, *William the Conqueror,* 210, 244.

[14] Richardson and Sayles, *Governance of Mediaeval England,* 55–61.

[15] Stenton, *First Century,* 149.

[16] Sidney Painter, *Mediaeval Society* (Ithaca, N.Y., 1952), 7.

Chapter 1

[1] William of Potiers, *Gesta Guillielmi Ducis Normannorum et Regis Anglorum,* ed. Raymond Foreville (Paris, 1952), 160; William of Malmesbury, *De Gestis Regis Anglorum,* ed. William Stubbs (R.S.), (London, 1889), II, 299–300.

[2] William of Poitiers, 150.

[3] The figure of 60,000 given by William of Poitiers, 170, may be dismissed as a wild exaggeration. See Hans Delbrück, *Numbers in History* (London, 1913); Ferdinand Lot, *L'Art Militaire et les Armées au Moyen Age en Europe et dans le Proche Orient,* (Paris, 1946), I, 285; Oman, *Art of War,* I, 758; Major-General J. F. C. Fuller, *The Decisive Battles of the Western World,* (London, 1954–1956), I, 371; Lieutenant-Colonel Charles H. Lemmon, *The Field of Hastings* (St. Leonard-on-Sea, Sussex, 1956), 21. Oman's guess of 11,000 to 13,000 is almost certainly too large.

[4] *Florentius Wigorniensis Chronicon ex Chronicis,* ed. Benjamin Thorpe, (London, 1849), I, 227; William of Poitiers, 192. An admirable discussion of William's preparatory and staging operations is to be found in Douglas, *William the Conqueror,* 184–194.

[5] William of Poitiers, 160–162.

[6] For this and subsequent tidal data I am indebted to the Director of the Tidal Institute and Observatory of the University of Liverpool. A letter to the author dated 14 June 1963 contains this caveat: "It is difficult to say much about the accuracy of the values quoted. Over a thousand years changes may have taken place, particularly in the Somme estuary, which could affect the time of the tides. Because of this rather dubious value attached to the data available, fairly crude methods of tide prediction have been used. I should imagine that the times quoted are accurate to within half an hour either way, but errors of up to an hour would not surprise me."

[7] William of Poitiers, 160–162. Actually, low water occurred at approximately 10:45 P.M. (G.M.T.) and the transports must have been underway by this time. Letter, Tidal Institute and Observatory.

[8] Wace, *Le Roman de Rou et des Ducs de Normandie,* ed. H. Andresen, (Heilbronn, 1877–1879), II, 285; William of Jumièges, *Historia Northmannorum,* in *Patrologia Latina,* ed. J. P. Migne (Paris, 1882), CXLIX, 872; William John Corbett, "The Development of the Duchy of Normandy and the

Norman Conquest of England," in *The Cambridge Medieval History,* ed. J. R. Tanner *et al.* (Cambridge, 1943), XVI, v, 498; Fuller, *Decisive Battles,* I, 372. The lower figures might be more acceptable if it could be assumed that only a spearhead sailed on the night of the 27th, and that the remainder of the expedition was shuttled across the Channel only after a secure bridgehead had been established in the Pevensey-Hastings area. I am indebted for this suggestion to Professor Archibald Lewis of the Department of History at the University of Texas.

[9] *The Bayeux Tapestry,* gen. ed. Sir Frank Stenton (London, 1957), Pl. 43; William of Poitiers, 162.

[10] William of Poitiers, 164. Sunrise in mid-Channel on the morning of 28 September was at 6:17 A.M., Local Apparent Time. It was probably light enough to see an hour earlier. These and subsequent meteorological data have been furnished through the courtesy of the Superintendent, Her Majesty's Nautical Almanac Office, Royal Greenwich Observatory, Herstmonceux Castle, Hailsham, Sussex.

[11] *Widonis Carmen de Hastingae Proelio,* in *Scriptores Rerum Gestarum Willelmi Conquestores,* ed. J. A. Giles, London, 1845, 30–31; Letter, Tidal Institute and Observatory.

[12] Oman, *Art of War,* I, 355–358.

[13] For example, Stenton, *Anglo-Saxon England,* 583; Corbett, "Duchy of Normandy and Norman Conquest," 500.

[14] *The Anglo-Saxon Chronicle,* ed. Benjamin Thorpe, (R.S.) (London, 1861), I, 338; William of Jumièges, 872; Florence of Worcester, I, 227; *Bayeux Tapestry,* Pls. 43, 44, 45, 46.

[15] Ivan D. Margary, *Roman Roads in Britain* (London, 1955–1957), I, 64, 65.

[16] James A. Williamson, *The English Channel, A History* (Cleveland, 1959), 54, 77; I. D. Margary, *Roman Ways in the Weald* (London, 1949), 187; Lemmon, *Field of Hastings,* 33.

[17] William of Poitiers, 168.

[18] G. H. Rudkin, "Where did William Land?", *Sussex County Magazine,* II (1928), 60–63; Williamson, *English Channel,* 86

[19] Lemmon, *Field of Hastings,* 33. The Battle Abbey account might be interpreted to support this thesis; *Chronicon Monasterii de Bello,* ed. J. S. Brewer (London, 1846), 2–3.

[20] *Bayeux Tapestry,* Pls. 43, 45; William of Poitiers, 168; William of Jumièges, 872; *Anglo-Saxon Chronicle,* I, 338.

[21] *Bayeux Tapestry,* Pls. 46, 51; William of Jumièges, 872; William of Poitiers, 168; Florence of Worcester, I, 227; *Anglo-Saxon Chronicle,* I, 338. I must admit that this explanation is far from satisfactory. The probability seems entirely to support Colonel Lemmon's theory, but in the absence of any confirmatory evidence, the movement by sea cannot be stated as a fact. There would be no problem if it could be assumed that the transports shuttled back and forth across the Channel until the whole force had been landed.

[22] Williamson, *English Channel,* 76–79; Douglas, *William the Conqueror,* 196.

[23] Lieutenant-Colonel Alfred H. Burne, *The Battlefields of England* (London, 1950), 19; William of Malmesbury, *De Gestis Regum,* II, 300.

[24] As B. H. Liddell Hart put it: "In the West during the Middle Ages the spirit of feudal chivalry was inimical to military art, though the drab stupidity of its military course is lightened by a few bright gleams—no fewer perhaps, in proportion, than at any other period in history. The Normans provided some of the earliest gleams, and their descendants continued to illuminate the course of medieval warfare. The value they put on Norman blood led them to expend brains in substitution for it, with notable profit." *Strategy: The Indirect Approach* (New York, 1954), 75.

[25] *Bayeux Tapestry,* Pls. 47, 48, 49, 52.

[26] Guy of Amiens, 31–32; William of Poitiers, 180; *Chronicon de Bello,* 3; *Domesday Book: Liber Censualis Willelmi Primi,* ed. Abraham Furley and Henry Ellis (London, 1783–1816). The Domesday information is conveniently summed up in Francis Henry Baring, *Domesday Tables for the Counties of Surrey, Berkshire, Middlesex, Hertford, Buckingham, and Bedford and for the New Forest* (London, 1909), 207.

[27] Baring, *Domesday Tables,* 207. On the other hand, William of Malmesbury reports that Harold sent spies into the Norman camp; *De Gestis Regum,* II, 300–301. In this connection D. J. C. King suggests that the earthwork castle of Newenden, about ten miles from Battle, may have some affiliation with the Hastings campaign. King notes that "its total area is large, but its material is poor in the extreme—a sandy soil which has 'spread' badly, but has not apparently been revetted with stone or faced in clay as one usually finds where the local soil is unsuitable." D. J. C. King, letter to the author, dated 4 July 1964. It is possible that the site at Newenden represents an advanced outpost from which the Normans might hope to get early warning of an English advance.

[28] William of Poitiers, 170. Needless to say, this advice was ignored by William. There is also a notice in William of Malmesbury (*De Gestis Regum,* II, 301–302) that a priest, who may have been engaged in gathering intelligence, was sent to Harold with proposals that William must have known would be unacceptable.

[29] Margary, *Roman Roads,* I, 38–40.

[30] William of Poitiers, 180.

[31] William of Poitiers, 180.

[32] *Bayeux Tapestry,* Pls. 54, 55. Colonel Lemmon (*Field of Hastings,* 21) says, "It is unlikely that the Norman army was encamped on the low ground near the sea at Hastings; the advanced posts, at least, would have been about the Baldslow Ridge," which was some five miles from the English position. It seems most unlikely that the English army spent the night in carousal, as reported by William of Malmesbury, *De Gestis Regum,* II, 302.

[33] Letter, H.M. Nautical Almanac Office.

[34] *Bayeux Tapestry*, Pl. 56. The scout is identified as Vital, a vassal of Bishop Odo of Bayeux. Other Norman and English scouts are depicted on Pls. 57 and 58.

[35] Lemmon, *Field of Hastings*, 41. For another hypothesis see Burne, *Battlefields*, 27, 44–45.

[36] Lemmon, *Field of Hastings*, 41–42.

[37] *Bayeux Tapestry*, Pl. 59. Burne believes that William chose the first alternative. *Battlefields*, 27.

[38] William of Poitiers, 190, 192; Lemmon, *Field of Hastings*, 22–23, 41–42; Douglas, *William the Conqueror*, 199.

[39] Florence of Worcester, I, 227; Lemmon, *Field of Hastings*, 23.

[40] Lemmon, *Field of Hastings*, 23, map.

[41] *Ibid.*, 23–24; *Anglo-Saxon Chronicle*, I, 337, 338.

[42] Edward A. Freeman, *The History of the Norman Conquest of England* (Oxford, 1867–1879), II, 437–522; Major-General E. Renouard James, "The Battle of Hastings, 14th October, 1066," *Royal Engineers Journal*, v (1907), 18–34; Sir James Ramsey, *The Foundations of England* (Oxford, 1898), II, 14–36); Wilhelm Spatz, *Die Schlacht von Hastings*, (Berlin, 1896); Oman, *Art of War*, I, 152–166; Fuller, *Decisive Battles*, I, 360–384; Burne, *Battlefields*, 19–45; Lemmon, *Field of Hastings*.

[43] Colonel Burne writes in his forward to *The Field of Hastings*: "Colonel Lemmon is well qualified to write on the subject, for he lived for many years almost on the battlefield and came to know every inch of it." For this reason the present account follows, in the main, Colonel Lemmon's reconstruction. Anyone who has gone over the battlefield with *The Field of Hastings* in hand must have realized that it is the superlative guide. In reconstructing the progress of the battle, Colonel Lemmon's suppositions, based on his own experiences as a soldier, seem eminently plausible, and in William's place this author would have fought the action much as Colonel Lemmon believes the duke actually did.

[44] Burne, *Battlefields*, 25; Lemmon, *Field of Hastings*, 20, map. Lemmon's conjecture (*ibid.*, 40) that Harold's army was reinforced during the day is based on very slender evidence.

[45] Colonel Lemmon remarks: "On no other medieval battlefield, perhaps, is the commander's post so accurately pinpointed. The high altar of the Abbey church was built over the spot where Harold fell, which was where the ancient trackway from the coast crossed the Wasingate, a local track." *Field of Hastings*, 20. William of Malmesbury, *De Gestis Regum*, II, 326–327; *Chronicon de Bello*, 5.

[46] Burne, *Battlefields*, 25; Lemmon, *Field of Hastings*, 20. The latter estimates the number of huscarles at something over 2,000.

[47] Lemmon, *Field of Hastings*, 21. Although the huscarles apparently were mounted on nags during movement, they fought on foot in the traditional Scandinavian manner. William of Poitiers, 186; William of Malmesbury, *De Gestis Regum*, II, 302.

[48] William of Jumièges, 872; William of Poitiers, 166; William of Malmesbury, *De Gestis Regum,* II, 300; Florence of Worcester, I, 226; *Anglo-Saxon Chronicle,* I, 338–339. For an unbiased reconstruction of the Battle of Stamford Bridge, see F. W. Brooks, *The Battle of Stamford Bridge* (York, 1956).

[49] Burne, *Battlefields,* 21. Corbett's estimate is 2,000 knights and 3,000 other arms ("Duchy of Normandy and Norman Conquest," 498). Fuller, *Decisive Battles,* I, 372, accepts this estimate; Stenton, *Anglo-Saxon England,* 584, merely states that William's army was probably smaller than Harold's. More recently, H. G. Richardson and G. O. Sayles have declared "It is impossible to conceive how any force of knights in number approaching two thousand could be transported across the Channel and maintained in a state of efficiency." *The Governance of Mediaeval England* (Edinburgh, 1963), 84.

[50] C. W. C. Oman, *The Art of War in the Middle Ages, A.D. 378–1515,* ed. John H. Beeler (Ithaca, N.Y., 1953), 60.

[51] William of Poitiers, 188; Burne, *Battlefields,* 28; Lemmon, *Field of Hastings,* 24.

[52] William of Poitiers, 188; *Bayeux Tapestry,* Pls. 61, 62.

[53] In addition, the more rapid advance of the Bretons must have uncovered their right flank, for there is no evidence that an attempt was made to keep alignment. Of the opening phase of the battle Douglas writes that "both sides seem to have made abundant use of missile weapons which are not naturally to be associated with attacking cavalry or with defending infantry." *William the Conqueror,* 202. This is an unfortunate statement; examples to the contrary for both arms may be cited, from the horsed archers of the Scythians to the United States' infantry in Korea.

[54] William of Poitiers, 188–190; *Bayeux Tapestry,* Pls. 63, 66.

[55] Oman, *Art of War,* I, 161; Burne, *Battlefields,* 29; Ramsey, *Foundations of England,* II, 30–31; Freeman, *Norman Conquest,* III, 481–482.

[56] Lemmon, *Field of Hastings,* 43. This view is partially supported by Burne, *Battlefields,* 35.

[57] William of Poitiers, 190–192; *Bayeux Tapestry,* Pls. 67, 68.

[58] Burne, *Battlefields,* 30; Lemmon, *Field of Hastings,* 26–27. Colonel Burne suggests that the pause was necessary for replenishing stocks of missiles, for reorganizing units, and for staff consultations.

[59] It is hard to understand Lemmon's supposition (*Field of Hastings,* 27) that William's order to commit the mounted troops came as a surprise to his subordinate commanders. At this point the first two attacks had signally failed to shake the English line. Although he had probably planned to hold the cavalry for the pursuit, no other option was open at the moment. This must have been quite obvious. See Burne, *Battlefields,* 30–31.

[60] Lemmon, *Field of Hastings,* 27. William of Malmesbury asserts that the duke himself had three horses killed under him. *De Gestis Regum,* II, 303.

[61] William of Poitiers, 194; William of Malmesbury, *De Gestis Regum,* II, 302, 303; Burne, *Battlefields,* 42; Lemmon, *Field of Hastings,* 44; Brigadier Peter Young and John Adair, *Hastings to Culloden* (London, 1964), 15–16.

[62] Stenton, *Anglo-Saxon England*, 587; Young and Adair, 15–16. See also Oman, *Art of War*, I, 162; Fuller, *Decisive Battles*, I, 380; Hart, *Strategy*, 76; Douglas, *William the Conqueror*, 201, 203–204.

[63] Lemmon, *Field of Hastings*, 44. It should be noted, however, that Delbrück expressed doubts as to the "feigned flight" episode as long ago as 1907. Delbrück, *Geschichte der Kriegskunst*, III, 162.

[64] Edward Hall, *The Union of the Two Noble and Illustre Famelies of Lancaster and Yorke* (London, 1809), 300.

[65] W. M. Mackenzie, *The Battle of Bannockburn* (Glasgow, 1913), 69–85; Oman, *Art of War*, II, 93–97.

[66] If, as the Bayeux Tapestry suggests, Harold's brothers and chief lieutenants, Gyrth and Leofwine, were killed early in the day, a partial explanation of the failure of the command structure is possible. *Bayeux Tapestry*, Pl. 64. A similar suggestion is made by Douglas, *William the Conqueror*, 200.

[67] Lemmon, *Field of Hastings*, 28.

[68] On 14 October 1066 (O.S.), sunset at Battle was at 5:12 Local Apparent Time. Letter, H.M. Nautical Almanac Office.

[69] It would be interesting to know whether William, at this juncture, contemplated breaking off the action, as a lesser general would certainly have done. He might have got off with his cavalry, had a withdrawal been attempted, but the archers and infantry would surely have been sacrificed. Nor could any possible accretions from Normandy have offset the reinforcements which would have poured in to Harold's army after a successful stand at Hastings. It was neck or nothing with William, as he undoubtedly knew.

[70] If, as Colonel Burne maintains (*Battlefields*, 32), the archers were posted atop the hillock on the Norman left, this shot must have carried about 375 yards—an impossible distance for the short bow. The later long bow had an effective range of only 230–250 yards. Sir Ralph Payne-Gallway, "A Treatise on Turkish and other Oriental Bows," *The Crossbow* (London, 1958), 20. *Bayeux Tapestry*, Pl. 69; William of Malmesbury, *De Gestis Regum*, II, 303.

[71] *Chronicon de Bello*, 4, 5, 8; *Bayeux Tapestry*, Pls. 70, 71, 72; William of Malmesbury, *De Gestis Regum*, II, 303; *Anglo-Saxon Chronicle*, I, 337, 338.

[72] Guy of Amiens, 43; Florence of Worcester, I, 227; William of Malmesbury, *De Gestis Regum*, 303, 304.

[73] William of Poitiers, 200–202; *Bayeux Tapestry*, Pl. 73.

[74] William of Poitiers, 202; William of Jumièges, 872; *Chronicon de Bello*, 5; Ordericus Vitalis, II, 149–150; William of Malmesbury, *De Gestis Regum*, II, 303. The conflicting accounts of the chroniclers have led to equally conflicting versions by modern historians (compare Burne, *Battlefields*, 43, and Lemmon, *Field of Hastings*, 30, 45–49) as to the location and details of this incident. Practically speaking, these are so many words wasted, since the rearguard action at the Malfosse had no bearing at all on the battle which had already been lost and won.

[75] William of Poitiers, 202–204.

[76] Burne, *Battlefields,* 33.

[77] William of Malmesbury, *De Gestis Regum,* II, 307; Florence of Worcester, I, 227.

[78] William of Jumièges, 874; *Anglo-Saxon Chronicle,* I, 339; Florence of Worcester, I, 227. William of Malmesbury's statement that 15,000 Normans fell in the battle is a wild exaggeration. *De Gestis Regum,* II, 306.

[79] Guy of Amiens, 44; G. J. Turner, "William the Conqueror's March to London in 1066," *EHR,* XXVII (1912), 211; Fuller, *Decisive Battles,* I, 382.

[80] Baring, *Domesday Tables,* Appendix A, "On the Domesday Valuations with Special Reference to William's March from Hastings to London," 207–216; G. H. Fowler, "The Devastation of Befordshire and the Neighboring Counties in 1065 and 1066," *Archaeologia,* LXXII (1922), 41–50, are of inestimable value here. Baring states the problem well: "Attention was long ago called to the connexion between the movements of the two armies before the Battle of Hastings and the wasted lands in that rape mentioned in Domesday. . . . But the principle deserves to be carried farther and may well be applied to William's march on London. We know that he harried the country as he passed and Domesday gives us for most manors the value just before and just after the Conquest, so that we ought by these signs to be able to trace his footsteps. The attempt is worth making. . . ." Florence of Worcester (I, 228) notes in general the extent of the area devastated by the Normans. See also *Anglo-Saxon Chronicle,* I, 339.

[81] William of Poitiers, 210; Baring, *Domesday Tables,* 207.

[82] Baring, *Domesday Tables,* 207.

[83] There seems to be no doubt that Harold's fortress at Dover was a castle and not a *burh.* It is so described by William of Poitiers (210), Ordericus Vitalis (II, 153), and Guy of Amiens (44), and it seems to be the only known example of a purely English castle.

[84] Guy of Amiens, 44; William of Poitiers, 210.

[85] William of Poitiers, 212; Ordericus Vitalis, II, 153; Baring, *Domesday Tables,* 207–208.

[86] Ordericus Vitalis, II, 153; Guy of Amiens, 44.

[87] ". . . But amid the general destruction there were some notable exceptions. The archiepiscopal estates showed no loss. Were they spared to conciliate the church or to tempt the archbishop at a critical moment; or did the *post* and *quando receptum* of these entries refer not to 1067, but to a date after the deposition of Stigand in 1070 or his death in 1072?" Baring, *Domesday Tables,* 208.

[88] This is shown by comparing the depreciation figures for the Dover area and that of Canterbury. Baring, *Domesday Tables,* 207–208. Douglas's assertion (*William the Conqueror,* 205) that William was compelled to delay nearly a month in the vicinity of Canterbury is clearly impossible if the distances involved in his subsequent march are taken into account. The army included infantry as well as cavalry; it had to contend with the English autumn; and it had to forage for supplies as it marched.

[89] Baring, *Domesday Tables,* 208. A comparison between the route traced

out by Baring and the line of the Pilgrim's Way–North Downs Ridgeway compels the conclusion that the Norman line of march lay along this Romanized native track. See Margary, *Roman Ways in the Weald,* 259–262.

[90] Baring, *Domesday Tables,* 208, 209.

[91] William of Poitiers, 214, asserted that the flying column consisted of 500 knights, which must have been a considerable fraction of the mounted arm fit for duty. Baring, *Domesday Tables,* 209.

[92] William of Poitiers, 214.

[93] This interpretation of the Domesday figures, and of William's notice of an attack by the London militia, differs materially from that of Baring (*Domesday Tables,* 209) and Fuller (*Decisive Battles,* I, 382). Both assert that the raid was launched from Godstone, and that William continued his westward march while the operation was in progress. It seems contrary to what Colonel Burne himself calls "inherent military probability" that William would deliberately march away from so important a segment of his forces at this time. The suppositions that the operation was either a feint to pin down the Londoners while the army was marching across their front, or a dash to seize the city by surprise, if possible, are much more tenable from the military point of view.

[94] Baring, *Domesday Tables,* 209; also Fuller (*Decisive Battles,* I, 382), who follows Baring very closely here.

[95] Guy of Amiens, 45; Baring, *Domesday Tables,* 209.

[96] Baring, *Domesday Tables,* 209; Fuller, *Decisive Battles,* I, 382. This does not imply that no reinforcements had reached William before this time. Indeed, after the heavy losses that must have been incurred at Hastings, plus the normal wear and tear of a campaign in the late fall, it is difficult to believe that William could have got as far as the neighborhood of Winchester without replacements. Even before the end of October there had been an outbreak of dysentery (Ordericus Vitalis, II, 153), and the *Anglo-Saxon Chronicle* (I, 339) mentions the arrival of reinforcements. What probably happened was that as news of the Norman success at Hastings spread across northern France and the Low Countries, bands of adventurers hastened on their own initiative to get in on what appeared to be a good thing. With southern England cowed by the invading army, these soldiers of fortune would have had little difficulty in joining the army. The replacements from Chichester were numerous enough to leave a trail of destruction in their wake. Perhaps they were recruited, organized, and shipped by the regency in Normandy.

[97] Baring, *Domesday Tables,* 209, says "right wing," but the left wing is obviously meant.

[98] Baring, *Domesday Tables,* 209–210.

[99] Stenton, *Anglo-Saxon England,* 588; Fuller, *Decisive Battles,* I, 382. These conclusions are based on the statements of William of Jumièges (874) and William of Poitiers (216). A contrary view was expressed by Turner, "William the Conqueror's March," 209–225.

[100] William of Poitiers, 216.

[101] Fowler's assertion that William was at Wallingford "about the beginning of November ("Devastation of Bedforshire," 49) is impossible. It is known that William, after the battle, spent five days at Hastings and another eight at Dover, which would bring the date to 27 October without allowing for any time spent on the march. The line of march taken by the Norman army from Hastings to Wallingford works out to just under 220 miles. In the unlikely event that the advance averaged fifteen miles per day, the earliest date of arrival at Wallingford would be 10 November. But if, as would seem more likely, the daily average was around ten miles, William would not have been on the London side of the Thames until about 18 November.

[102] Stenton, *Anglo-Saxon England*, 589; Fowler, "Devastation of Bedfordshire," 43–44. The considerably simpler plan proposed by Fowler for the march from Wallingford to London seems much more realistic than the elaborate maneuvers suggested by Baring. The latter would soon have detached William's army of 5,000 to 7,000 men out of existence as an operational force.

[103] Fowler, "Devastation of Bedfordshire," 44. The left was probably strengthened to guard against any threat from the midland shires.

[104] Fowler, "Devastation of Bedfordshire," 44, 46.

[105] Florence of Worcester asserts (I, 228) that the earls Edwin and Morcar had returned north with their forces after the election of Edgar the Atheling.

[106] Fowler, "Devastation of Bedfordshire," 49.

[107] *Anglo-Saxon Chronicle*, I, 339; William of Poitiers, 216; Florence of Worcester, I, 229. It is now generally agreed that the surrender took place at Berkhamstead—see Stenton, *Anglo-Saxon England*, 589—although there is some logic in the argument that it occurred at Little Berkhamstead, some four miles south of Hertford. Fowler, "Devastation of Bedfordshire," 46; Baring, *Domesday Tables*, 212.

[108] *Anglo-Saxon Chronicle*, I, 339. Florence of Worcester, I, 228.

[109] William of Poitiers, 216. This is, of course, the principal argument for placing the site of the surrender of London at Little Berkhamstead, a point from which London can actually be seen. Fowler, "Devastation of Bedfordshire," 46.

[110] Guy of Amiens, 45–47.

[111] William of Jumièges, 874.

[112] William of Poitiers, 218. William of Malmesbury's account (*De Gestis Regum*, II, 307) of an enthusiastic welcome by the Londoners strikes a rather sour note.

[113] William of Poitiers, 220–222; William of Jumièges, 874; William of Malmesbury, *De Gestis Regum*, II, 307; Florence of Worcester, I, 228–229; *Anglo-Saxon Chronicle*, I, 337, 339.

[114] William of Poitiers, 236. Ordericus (II, 165) added that this castle, which must be considered the predecessor of the Tower, was completed "for defense against any outbreak by the fierce and numerous population."

[115] *Anglo-Saxon Chronicle,* I, 338.

[116] William of Poitiers, 204; William of Jumièges, 873; William of Malmesbury, *De Gestis Regum,* II, 301; Florence of Worcester, I, 227; *Anglo-Saxon Chronicle,* I, 337, 338. The Bayeux Tapestry seems to suggest that Gyrth and Leofwine were killed early in the battle. *Bayeux Tapestry,* Pl. 64.

[117] *Anglo-Saxon Chronicle,* I, 337; Stenton, *Anglo-Saxon England,* 583–584.

[118] Florence of Worcester, I, 227. See also William of Malmesbury, *De Gestis Regum,* II, 300; *Anglo-Saxon Chronicle,* I, 337.

[119] H. J. Hewitt, *The Black Prince's Expedition of 1355–1357* (Manchester, 1958), 46.

[120] Stenton, *Anglo-Saxon England,* 588; Fowler, "Devastation of Bedfordshire, 44.

[121] Baring, *Domesday Tables,* 216. This view opposes that of Sir Frank Stenton, who contends that William "began a movement on a large scale intended to isolate the city by the reduction of a broad belt of territory around it on either side of the Thames." *Anglo-Saxon England,* 585.

[122] Ordericus Vitalis, II, 184.

Chapter 2

[1] Ordericus Vitalis, II, 166.

[2] Stenton, *Anglo-Saxon England,* 591.

[3] *Regesta Regum Anglo-Normannorum (1066–1154),* ed. H. W. C. Davis, Charles Johnson, and H. A. Cronne (Oxford, 1913–   ), I, 3, 4. See also Richardson and Sayles, *The Governance of Mediaeval England,* 93.

[4] *Regesta,* I, 3,4; William of Malmesbury, *De Gestis Regum,* II, 351–352.

[5] William of Poitiers, 238.

[6] William of Poitiers, 238, 242–246; Ordericus Vitalis, II, 167; *Anglo-Saxon Chronicle,* I, 339, 340; Florence of Worcester, II, 1.

[7] *Anglo-Saxon Chronicle,* I, 339; William of Poitiers, 238–242; Florence of Worcester, II, 1. Hugh de Grantmesnil and Hugh de Montfort also remained in England. Douglas, *William the Conqueror,* 207.

[8] The view that *Guentae* (William of Poitiers, 238) refers to Norwich, which seems to have originated with Freeman (*Norman Conquest,* IV, 72) and has been perpetuated by Sir Frank Stenton (*Anglo-Saxon England,* 591), has been challenged; it seems highly probable that the reference is to the new castle at Winchester. Martin Biddle, M.A., F.S.A., Lecturer in Medieval Archaeology at the University of Exeter, conversation with the author, 8 April 1965.

[9] Stenton, *Anglo-Saxon England,* 601.

[10] *Anglo-Saxon Chronicle,* I, 339, 355; *Symeonis Monachi Opera Omnia,* ed. Thomas Arnold (R.S.), (London, 1882); II, 185; William of Poitiers, 238–240, 264; Florence of Worcester, II, 1.

[11] William of Poitiers, 264–266; William of Jumièges, 876.

[12] Ordericus Vitalis, II, 173–175; William of Jumièges, 876; William of Poitiers, 266–268.

[13] *Anglo-Saxon Chronicle,* I, 340; Florence of Worcester, II, 1–2.

[14] Ordericus Vitalis, II, 78; Florence of Worcester, II, 2.

[15] Ordericus Vitalis, II, 166.

[16] *Anglo-Saxon Chronicle,* I, 340; William of Malmesbury, *De Gestis Regum,* II, 307; Florence of Worcester, II, 2. (*William the Conqueror,* 213, 215) Douglas suggests that the Englishmen were mercenaries. It seems more likely that they were five-hide soldiers raised in those areas then under Norman control.

[17] Ordericus, Vitalis, II, 181.

[18] Douglas, *William the Conqueror,* 181–182, 213.

[19] *Ibid.,* 182–184.

[20] Ordericus Vitalis, II, 184; *Anglo-Saxon Chronicle,* I, 341–342.

[21] Ordericus Vitalis, II, 185; *Anglo-Saxon Chronicle,* I, 342. The *Chronicle* states that William built two castles at York, but the second was not erected until the following year. William of Malmesbury (*De Gestis Regum,* II, 307–308) also has condensed all the Yorkshire operations into one account. Florence of Worcester (II, 3) states that the garrison numbered 500 men, a suspiciously large figure.

[22] *Anglo-Saxon Chronicle,* I, 342; Ordericus Vitalis, II, 185.

[23] *Anglo-Saxon Chronicle,* I, 342; William of Malmesbury, *De Gestis Regum,* II, 312–313; Florence of Worcester, II, 3. For the location of the combat see *A Scottish Chronicle Known as the Chronicle of Holyrood,* ed. Marjorie Ogilvie Anderson and Alan Orr Anderson (Edinburgh, 1938), 108, n.5. Although it has been asserted that no example of a general call-up of the body of freemen is known between 1016 and 1138, it is very probable that the Somerset *fyrd* was called out on this occasion. The invaders were in sufficient strength to attempt the storm of Bristol, and a levy of some size must have been called out to check them. Richardson and Sayles, *Governance of Mediaeval England,* 52.

[24] *Anglo-Saxon Chronicle,* I, 342; Ordericus Vitalis, II, 189–190. A fleet of this size probably carried in excess of 500 fighting men.

[25] *Anglo-Saxon Chronicle,* I, 342; Ordericus Vitalis, II, 190; William of Jumièges, 877; Florence of Worcester, II, 3.

[26] *Anglo-Saxon Chronicle,* I, 342, 343.

[27] *Ibid.,* 342; Symeon of Durham, I, 98–99; *Chronicle of Holyrood,* 109. The statement of the English chronicler that Earl Robert's command was 900 strong is certainly an exaggeration; Ordericus Vitalis (II, 187) gives a figure of 500, which may be more nearly correct. However, 500 seems to be a favorite number with these writers. See also William of Jumièges, 876–877.

[28] Ordericus Vitalis, II, 187–188; *Anglo-Saxon Chronicle,* I, 342, 343. This shows as clearly as any incident in the Conquest, the rapidity with which a motte-and-bailey castle could be constructed.

[29] Ordericus Vitalis, 187–188.

[30] *Ibid.*, 190–192.

[31] Stenton, *Anglo-Saxon England*, 594; *Anglo-Saxon Chronicle*, I, 342, 343; Florence of Worcester, II, 3. Waltheof and Maerleswegen had earlier collaborated with the Normans.

[32] *William of Jumièges*, 877; William of Malmesbury, *De Gestis Regum*, II, 311–312; Florence of Worcester, II, 4. Florence's tally of 3,000 Norman casualties must be heavily discounted.

[33] *Anglo-Saxon Chronicle*, I, 342; Florence of Worcester, II, 4; Douglas, *William the Conqueror*, 218–219.

[34] Ordericus Vitalis, II, 192–193, 194.

[35] *Ibid.*, 194–195; Stenton, *Anglo-Saxon England*, 596. There is no mention of the fate of the covering force under the two Count Roberts.

[36] *Anglo-Saxon Chronicle*, I, 342, 343; Florence of Worcester, II, 4; Ordericus Vitalis, II, 195, 197.

[37] The most vivid account of the harrying of Yorkshire is to be found in Ordericus Vitalis, II, 196–107. Other accounts of these operations, which filled contemporaries with horror, are found in William of Malmesbury, *De Gestis Regum*, II, 308–309; *Anglo-Saxon Chronicle*, I, 342, 343; Hugh the Chantor, *The History of the Church of York*, 1066–1127, ed. and tr. Charles Johnson (London, 1961), 1. Refugees not only from Yorkshire, but from Cheshire, Shropshire, Staffordshire, and Derbyshire were given aid and shelter at the abbey of Evesham in Worcestershire. *Chronicon Abbatiae de Evesham ad Annum 1418*, ed. William Dunn Macray (London, 1863), 90–91. See also Florence of Worcester, II, 4.

[38] Hugh the Chantor, *History of the Church of York*, 3. Lanfranc must have been thinking of the day when William himself had been hallowed by Archbishop Aeldred of York.

[39] Ordericus Vitalis, II, 197, 198; *Anglo-Saxon Chronicle*, I, 342.

[40] Ordericus Vitalis, II, 193.

[41] *Ibid.* Although not expressly stated, in all probability the castle of Montacute was the objective of the attack.

[42] Ordericus Vitalis, II, 193–194.

[43] Margary, *Roman Roads in Britain*, II, 33–35, 98–99.

[44] Ordericus Vitalis, II, 193, 199.

[45] *Anglo-Saxon Chronicle*, I, 342.

[46] *The Chronicle of Hugh Candidus a Monk of Peterborough*, ed. W. T. Matthews (Oxford, 1949), 77; *Anglo-Saxon Chronicle*, I, 345; Ramsey, *Foundations of England*, II, 76–78

[47] Hugh Candidus, 77–79; *Anglo-Saxon Chronicle*, I, 345.

[48] Hugh Candidus, 80, 82; *Anglo-Saxon Chronicle*, I, 345–347; Florence of Worcester, II, 4. The arrival of Abbot Turold at Peterborough is dated by the English chronicler as 2 June.

[49] Ordericus Vitalis, II, 215–217; William of Malmesbury, *De Gestis Regum*, II, 311; *Anglo-Saxon Chronicle*, I, 346; Florence of Worcester, II, 8–9; *Liber Eliensis*, ed. E. O. Blake (London, 1962), 173.

[50] *Anglo-Saxon Chronicle,* I, 346. Ordericus Vitalis (II, 216) states that one of Edwin's own men betrayed him to the Normans.

[51] Florence of Worcester, II, 9; *Anglo-Saxon Chronicle,* I, 346, 347; *Liber Eliensis,* 173; *Henrici Archidiaconi Huntendunensis Historia Anglorum,* ed. Thomas Arnold (R.S.) (London, 1879), 205.

[52] *Liber Eliensis,* liv–lv.

[53] Ordericus Vitalis, II, 185.

[54] *Anglo-Saxon Chronicle,* I, 346; Henry of Huntingdon, 205; Florence of Worcester, II, 9; *Liber Eliensis,* 173.

[55] *Liber Eliensis,* lvii.

[56] *Gesta Herwardi Incliti Exulis et Militis,* in Vol. I, *Lestoire des Engles solum la translacion Maistre Geffrei Gaimar,* ed. Sir Thomas Duffus Hardy and Charles Trice Martin (R.S.) (London, 1888); *De Gestis Herwardi Saxonis,* Latin text transcribed by S. H. Miller, tr. W. D. Sweeting, supplement to *Fenland Notes and Queries,* III (1895–1897).

[57] *Gesta Herwardi,* Miller, Sweeting, 44, 45; Hardy, Martin, 377. A later passage states that "he caused also a large pile of wood and stones, and a heap of all kinds of timber; and he commanded all the fishermen of the province to come with their boats to 'Cotinglade,' so that they might transport what they had brought to the place, and with the materials construct mounds and hillocks on top of which they might fight." *Ibid.,* Miller, Sweeting, 55–56; Hardy, Martin, 388.

[58] *Liber Eliensis,* 185.

[59] *Gesta Herwardi,* Miller, Sweeting, 45; Hardy, Martin, 384; *Liber Eliensis,* 194.

[60] *Anglo-Saxon Chronicle,* I, 346, 347; Henry of Huntingdon, 205; Florence of Worcester, II, 9; *Liber Eliensis,* 189–190.

[61] *Liber Eliensis,* 174. Certainly the castle was in existence by 1082/87. *Ibid.,* 206.

[62] *The Chronicle of Melrose,* ed. Alan Orr Anderson and Marjorie Ogilvie Anderson (London, 1936), 27.

[63] Symeon of Durham, II, 200; Florence of Worcester, II, 9; *Anglo-Saxon Chronicle,* I, 346, 347; *Chronicle of Melrose,* 28.

[64] *Regesta,* I, 17; *Liber Eliensis,* 216–217. See also *Chronicon Monasterii de Abingdon,* ed. Joseph Stevenson (R.S.) (London, 1858), II, 9–10.

[65] *Anglo-Saxon Chronicle,* I, 351; Florence of Worcester, II, 13, *Chronicle of Melrose,* 28.

[66] The exact date of the king's return is not known, but he was in Normandy as late as 14 July. *Regesta,* I, 32.

[67] *Chron. Mon. de Abingdon,* II, 9–10; Symeon of Durham, II, 211; William of Malmesbury, *De Gestis Regum,* II, 309.

[68] Symeon of Durham, II, 211; *Monasticon Anglicanum,* ed. John Caley, Henry Ellis, Bulkeley Bandinel (London, 1817–1830), I, 236b.

[69] *Anglo-Saxon Chronicle,* I, 344, 345, 347, 348, 349.

[70] *Anglo-Saxon Chronicle*, I, 352; Florence of Worcester, II, 18. William of Malmesbury notes that Hugh the Great of France *cum illius commilitio* was one of the mercenary leaders engaged. *De Gestis Regum*, II, 317,319–320. For a most interesting account of the trials of a tenant-in-chief who had to maintain his knights on a war footing, see the *Vita Wulfstani of William of Malmesbury*, ed. Reginald R. Darlington (London, 1928), 55–56.

[71] Ordericus Vitalis, II, 262; William of Malmesbury, *De Gestis Regum*, II, 313–314; Florence of Worcester, II, 10–11.

[72] *Anglo-Saxon Chronicle*, I, 348,349; Florence of Worcester, II, 10. See also the letter of Archbishop Lanfranc of Canterbury to Earl Roger. *Lanfranci Opera Omnia*, ed. J. A. Giles (Oxford, 1844), I, 65.

[73] William of Malmesbury, *De Gestis Regum*, II, 314; Ordericus Vitalis, II, 262–263; Florence of Worcester, II, 11.

[74] *Anglo-Saxon Chronicle*, I, 348, 349. Whether the *landfolc* referred to here is the local *fyrd*, or a general peasant levy, is not clear.

[75] *Anglo-Saxon Chronicle*, I, 349; Lanfranc, *Opera*, I, 56; Florence of Worcester, II, 11.

[76] Anglo-Saxon Chronicle, I, 349; Ordericus Vitalis, II, 264; William of Malmesbury, *De Gestis Regum*, II, 314; Florence of Worcester, II, 11.

[77] J. H. Round, *Feudal England* (London, 1909), 292–293. There is no reason to doubt that the *servitia debita* was imposed by William I and did not evolve gradually. Powicke, *Military Obligation*, 29. For the opposite view see Richardson and Sayles, *Governance of Mediaeval England*, 62–66.

[78] Douglas, *William the Conqueror*, 217. His estimate of 84 castles in existence at the end of the eleventh century is, however, far too low.

[79] Oman, *Art of War*, II, 52.

[80] Oman, *Art of War*, II, 21; John H. Beeler, "Castles and Strategy in Norman and Early Angevin England," *Speculum*, XXXI (1956), 598.

[81] Oman, *Art of War*, II, 21; Ella S. Armitage, *The Early Norman Castles of the British Isles* (London, 1912), 85.

[82] This is well stated by Stenton, *First Century*, 193–194.

[83] This system was never put to a severe test in England, but on the marches of Wales there were many incidents of a similar nature.

[84] C. Warren Hollister, "The Irony of English Feudalism" *Journal of British Studies*, II (1963), 25.

[85] Armitage, *Early Norman Castles*, 83–84. These observations are, of course, at variance with the statement, previously quoted, that mottes in England were manorial rather than military in nature.

[86] Sidney Painter, "English Castles in the Early Middle Ages," *Speculum*, X (1935), 325–327. But in a conversation with the author a few months before his untimely death, Professor Painter conceded that while William probably could not tell a baron where to build a castle, he likely could tell him where he could not build it. See also Charles Homer Haskins, *Norman Institutions* (New York, 1960), 38, 60, 278. This is all the more credible in view of the restrictions imposed on castle-building by the so-called *Leges Henrici Primi*.

F. Liebermann, *Die Gesetze der Angelsachsen* (Halle, 1898–1916), I, 556, 558.

[87] Beeler, "Castles and Strategy," 594–595. A great majority of the motte-and-bailey castles which must have been built in the immediate post-Conquest years have no written history. The military historian must rely upon the archaeological surveys found in such publications as the Inventories of the Royal Commission on Historical Monuments and the chapters on Ancient Earthworks in the Victoria Histories of the counties of England. The following have been of especial value: by the Royal Commission on Historical Monuments, England: *An Inventory of the Historical Monuments in Buckinghamshire* (2 vols.; London, 1912–1913), *An Inventory of the Historical Monuments in Dorset* (London, 1952), *An Inventory of the Historical Monuments in Essex* (4 vols.; London, 1916–1923), *An Inventory of the Historical Monuments in Herefordshire* (3 vols.; London, 1931–1934), *An Inventory of the Historical Monuments in Hertfordshire* (London, 1911), *An Inventory of the Historical Monuments in Huntingdonshire* (London, 1926), *An Inventory of the Historical Monuments in Middlesex* (London, 1937), and *An Inventory of the Historical Monuments in Westmoreland* (London, 1936). See also the chapters on Ancient Earthworks in the following volumes of the *Victoria History of the Counties of England: Bedfordshire,* I (Westminster, 1904); *Berkshire,* I (Westminster, 1906); *Buckinghamshire,* II (Westminster, 1908); *Cornwall,* I (Westminster, 1906); *Cumberland,* I (Westminster, 1901); *Derby,* I (Westminster, 1905); *Devonshire,* I (Westminster, 1906); *Durham,* I (Westminster, 1905); *Essex,* I (Westminster, 1903); *Hereford,* I (Westminster, 1908); *Hertford,* II (Westminster, 1908); *Huntingdon,* I (Westminster, 1926); *Kent,* I (Westminster, 1908); *Lancaster,* II (Westminster, 1908); *Leicester,* I (Westminster, 1907); *Middlesex,* II (Westminster, 1911); *Northampton,* II (Westminster, 1906); *Nottingham,* I (Westminster, 1906); *Oxfordshire,* II (Westminster, 1907); *Rutland,* I (Westminster, 1908); *Shropshire,* I (Westminster, 1908); *Somerset,* II (Westminster, 1911); *Staffordshire,* I (Westminster, 1908); *Suffolk,* I (Westminster, 1911); *Surrey,* IV (Westminster, 1912); *Sussex,* I (Westminster, 1905); *Warwickshire,* I (Westminster, 1914); *Worcestershire,* IV (Westminster, 1924); *York,* II (Westminster, 1912).

[88] Two small mottes were located at South Mymms and Ruislip. *Historical Monuments Commission,* Middlesex, 95, 107–108.

[89] Painter, "English Castles," 326–327. A similar view is expressed by R. Allen Brown, *English Medieval Castles* (London, 1954), 192.

[90] Oman, *Art of War,* II, 22.

[91] Stenton, *First Century,* 193.

[92] Appendix A; see also Beeler, "Castles and Strategy," 581–601.

[93] Richardson and Sayles, *Governance of Mediaeval England,* 27,61. The authors have not so much as mentioned the castle and its significant role in the military history of Norman and Angevin England.

Chapter 3

[1] Stenton, *First Century*, 193.

[2] Ordericus Vitalis, III, 269–270; William of Malmesbury, *De Gestis Regum,* II, 360; Florence of Worcester, II, 21; Henry of Huntingdon, 214; *Anglo-Saxon Chronicle,* I, 356.

[3] *Anglo-Saxon Chronicle,* I, 356; William of Malmesbury, *De Gestis Regum,* II, 360–363; Ordericus Vitalis, III, 269; Florence of Worcester, II, 21.

[4] William of Malmesbury, *De Gestis Regum,* II, 360–363; Ordericus Vitalis, III, 270; Symeon of Durham, II, 215; *Anglo-Saxon Chronicle,* I, 356–357; Florence of Worcester, II, 21–22.

[5] Symeon of Durham, I, 171.

[6] Ordericus Vitalis, III, 270; *Anglo-Saxon Chronicle,* I, 356.

[7] *Anglo-Saxon Chronicle,* I, 356; Florence of Worcester, II, 22. Charles Wendell David, in *Robert Curthose, Duke of Normandy* (Cambridge, Mass., 1920), 46, suggests that the rebellion became open before the end of Lent; but this is difficult to reconcile with the positive statements in the *Chronicle* and Florence of Worcester.

[8] William of Malmesbury, *De Gestis Regum,* II, 361; Symeon of Durham, II, 215; *Anglo-Saxon Chronicle,* I, 357.

[9] Austin Lane Poole, *From Domesday Book to Magna Carta, 1087–1216,* 2nd ed. (Oxford 1955), 101; William of Malmesbury, *De Gestis Regum,* II, 361; Symeon of Durham, II, 215; *Anglo-Saxon Chronicle,* I, 356–357; Florence of Worcester, II, 24. The wording of Florence suggests the existence of a castle at Ilchester.

[10] Florence of Worcester, II, 24.

[11] Poole, *Domesday Book to Magna Carta,* 101; Ordericus Vitalis, III, 270–271; *Anglo-Saxon Chronicle,* I, 357; William of Malmesbury, *De Gestis Regum,* II, 361; Florence of Worcester, II, 24.

[12] Our only knowledge of this event comes from the notice of a gift of land made to the abbey of St. Peter of Gloucester by Bernard de Neuf-Marché. The document notes that "propter werram motam inter primates Angliae destructa est Gloucestria et ecclesia Sancti Petri." *Regesta,* I, 78.

[13] *Anglo-Saxon Chronicle,* I, 357; Ordericus Vitalis, III, 271–272; *Vita Wulfstani,* xiv, xxvii.

[14] Unfortunately the *Vita Wulfstani* throws no light on this important incident. It is a fairly safe guess, however, that the *Chronicle's* "men of his household" (*Anglo-Saxon Chronicle,* I, 357) refers to the bishop's knights. See also Symeon of Durham, II, 215; William of Malmesbury, *De Gestis Regum,* II, 361. The greatest amount of detail on this operation is to be found in Florence of Worcester (II, 24–26), but beyond the meager facts noted above, the worthy monk devotes most of his account to describing a miraculous paralysis that struck the attackers and made them fall an easy prey to the royalist defenders. If, in fact, Bishop Wulfstan was the author of the plan to

fall upon the rebels before they could cross the Severn, the trust of successive Norman kings in his military ability was well placed.

[15] William of Malmesbury, *De Gestis Regum*, II, 361; Poole, *Domesday Book to Magna Carta*, 100. It was on this occasion that William Rufus attempted to impose a quota of eighty knights on the bishopric of Ely instead of the forty which his father had demanded. *Liber Eliensis*, 218.

[16] Symeon of Durham, II, 216; *Anglo-Saxon Chronicle*, I, 357; William of Malmesbury, *De Gestis Regum*, II, 360.

[17] *Anglo-Saxon Chronicle*, I, 357; William of Malmesbury, *De Gestis Regum*, II, 360–361; Florence of Worcester, II, 23–24.

[18] David, *Robert Curthose*, 47–50; *Anglo-Saxon Chronicle*, I, 357; William of Malmesbury, *De Gestis Regum*, II, 362; Ordericus Vitalis, III, 272–273; Florence of Worcester, II, 22; Henry of Huntingdon, 215; Symeon of Durham, II, 216.

[19] *Anglo-Saxon Chronicle*, I, 357; William of Malmesbury, *De Gestis Regum*, II, 362; Florence of Worcester, II, 22–23.

[20] David, *Robert Curthose*, 49.

[21] William of Malmesbury, *De Gestis Regum*, II, 362; Symeon of Durham, II, 216; Florence of Worcester, II, 23; *Anglo-Saxon Chronicle*, I, 357. It is interesting to note that by 1088 the old English *cniht* is equated with the feudal horseman. See Stenton, *First Century*, 133.

[22] Symeon of Durham, II, 216; *Anglo-Saxon Chronicle*, I, 357.

[23] William of Malmesbury, *De Gestis Regum*, II, 362; Florence of Worcester, II, 24; *Anglo-Saxon Chronicle*, I, 357.

[24] *Anglo-Saxon Chronicle*, I, 357. See also Symeon of Durham, II, 216; William of Malmesbury, *De Gestis Regum*, II, 362–363; Henry of Huntingdon, 215.

[25] *Early Yorkshire Charters*, ed. William Farrer and C. T. Clay (Edinburgh, 1914–), VIII, 4,5.

[26] Symeon of Durham, II, 216; William of Malmesbury, *De Gestis Regum*, II, 362; *Anglo-Saxon Chronicle*, I, 357.

[27] Ordericus Vitalis (III, 272) states that the garrison numbered 500 men-at-arms, and William of Malmesbury writes that "almost all the young nobility of England were at Rochester." *De Gestis Regum*, II, 362. The former may not be far from the truth; the statement of William is probably an exaggeration. See also *Anglo-Saxon Chronicle*, I, 357–358.

[28] Ordericus Vitalis, III, 272; *Regesta*, I, 78, 79.

[29] Ordericus Vitalis, III, 273–278; William of Malmesbury, *De Gestis Regum*, II, 362; *Anglo-Saxon Chronicle*, I, 357–358; Poole, *Domesday Book to Magna Carta*, 102; David, *Robert Curthose*, 51.

[30] Ordericus Vitalis, III, 279; Symeon of Durham, II, 216.

[31] Symeon of Durham, I, 176–178; *Anglo-Saxon Chronicle*, I, 358; *Early Yorkshire Charters*, x, 1; Poole, *Domesday Book to Magna Carta*, 101–102; David, *Robert Curthose*, 46. The English chronicler asserts that Durham was surrendered only after it had stood a siege.

[32] Poole, *Domesday Book to Magna Carta,* 101.

[33] See Chapters VIII and IX.

[34] William of Malmesbury, *De Gestis Regum,* II, 365; Ordericus Vitalis, III, 394; *Anglo-Saxon Chronicle,* I, 359; Florence of Worcester, II, 28; Henry of Huntingdon, 216.

[35] Florence of Worcester, II, 28; Ordericus Vitalis, III, 366, 377, 381; William of Malmesbury, *De Gestis Regum,* II, 365.

[36] *Anglo-Saxon Chronicle,* I, 359; Ordericus Vitalis, III, 394; Florence of Worcester, II, 28.

[37] Symeon of Durham, I, 195; Florence of Worcester, II, 28; *Anglo-Saxon Chronicle,* I, 359.

[38] The account in Ordericus Vitalis (III, 394) is at variance with that found in those of the English chroniclers. *Anglo-Saxon Chronicle,* I, 359; Florence of Worcester, II, 28.

[39] *Anglo-Saxon Chronicle,* I, 359; Florence of Worcester, II, 28; Ordericus Vitalis, III, 394–396; William of Malmesbury, *De Gestis Regum,* II, 366.

[40] Florence of Worcester, II, 28.

[41] David, *Robert Curthose,* 68.

[42] Florence of Worcester, II, 29; *Anglo-Saxon Chronicle,* I, 359.

[43] *Anglo-Saxon Chronicle,* I, 359; Florence of Worcester, II, 30.

[44] Symeon of Durham, I, 140.

[45] *Anglo-Saxon Chronicle,* I, 359–360.

[46] *Ibid.,* I, 360–361. Although the figure 20,000 is no doubt an exaggeration, it proves that the old English military organization was still functioning efficiently nearly thirty years after the Conquest. For a dissenting view, see Richardson and Sayles, *Governance of Mediaeval England,* 54.

[47] Ramsey, *Foundations of England,* II, 199, 200; Poole, *Domesday Book to Magna Carta,* 109.

[48] Ordericus Vitalis, III, 406; William of Jumièges, 885.

[49] Florence of Worcester, II, 38–39; William of Malmesbury, *De Gestis Regum,* II, 372; *Lestoire des Engles solim la Translacion Maistre Geffrei Gaimar,* ed. Sir Thomas Duffus Hardy and Charles Trice Martin (R.S.) (London, 1888), I, 262; Ordericus Vitalis, III, 407; Symeon of Durham, II, 225–226; *Anglo-Saxon Chronicle,* I, 362; Reginald Lennard, *Rural England, 1086–1135* (Oxford, 1959), 69–70; Edward A. Freeman, *The Reign of William Rufus and the Accession of Henry the First* (Oxford, 1882), II, 41–69; Poole, *Domesday Book to Magna Carta,* 109–110; Ramsey, *Foundations of England,* II, 199–202.

[50] I. J. Sanders, *English Baronies, A Study of Their Origin and Descent, 1086–1327* (Oxford, 1960), 34, 119; *V. C. H. Oxfordshire,* II, 323–324; Lennard, *Rural England,* 69.

[51] Ordericus Vitalis, III, 411; Sanders, *Feudal Baronies,* 24, 95.

[52] Symeon of Durham, II, 225–226; Florence of Worcester, II, 38; *Anglo-Saxon Chronicle,* I, 361–362; Henry of Huntingdon, 218; Ordericus Vitalis,

III, 408; Geffrei Gaimar, I, 262; C. H. Hunter Blair, "The Early Castles of Northumberland," *Archaeologia Aeliana*, 4th ser., XXII (1944), 121, 151.

53 Florence of Worcester, II, 38; Symeon of Durham, II, 225; Poole, *Domesday Book to Magna Carta*, 109.

54 Ordericus Vitalis, III, 406–407.

55 *Regesta*, I, 93; *Anglo-Saxon Chronicle*, I, 361. Robert refused to attend, according to the English chronicler, because the king would not grant him a safe-conduct.

56 *Sancti Anselmi, Cantuariensis Archiepiscopi, Opera Omnia*, ed. Francis S. Schmitt (Edinburgh, 1946–1951), IV, 77–81.

57 There is no direct evidence for the participation of the *fyrd* in the campaign of 1095. The use of the term in the English chronicle simply means "army," but the known unreliability of many of the feudal contingents, the statement of Florence that William Rufus "assembled his army from every part of England," and the fact that in every other major campaign of the eleventh century the *fyrd* was employed, suggest that the militia was called out to aid in suppressing the Mowbray rebellion. *Anglo-Saxon Chronicle*, I, 361; Florence of Worcester, II, 38.

58 Ordericus Vitalis, III, 407–408.

59 Opinion is sharply divided on this point. Ramsey believed Newcastle was in the king's hands (*Foundations of England*, II, 200), and only one chronicler, the not always reliable Henry of Huntingdon (218) mentions the incident. However, Blair ("Early Castles of Northumberland," 119) states that the castle belonged to the earl, and it is impossible to ignore two notifications of William II given "at the siege of Newcastle." *Regesta*, I, 94. So it would seem that Freeman (*William Rufus*, II, 47) in this instance was right.

60 Florence of Worcester, II, 38; *Anglo-Saxon Chronicle*, I, 361; Henry of Huntingdon, 218; Symeon of Durham, II, 225–226.

61 Geffrei Gaimar, I, 262. It is unnecessary to invent a castle, as Freeman did (*William Rufus*, II, 48) to explain these references.

62 Ordericus Vitalis, III, 408; Florence of Worcester, II, 38; Henry of Huntingdon, 218; Symeon of Durham, II, 226; *Anglo-Saxon Chronicle*, I, 361–362; Geffrei Gaimar, I, 262.

63 Henry of Huntingdon, 218; Symeon of Durham, II, 226; Ordericus Vitalis, III, 408–409; Florence of Worcester, II, 38.

64 *Monasticon*, III, 303.

65 This incident is related in greater or less detail by a number of the chroniclers. The fullest accounts are those of Symeon of Durham (II, 226), and Florence of Worcester (II, 38). See also Ordericus Vitalis, III, 409; Henry of Huntingdon, 218; *Anglo-Saxon Chronicle*, I, 361–362. Geffrei Gaimar's statement that Robert fled by sea (I, 263) is not supported by any other evidence. Ramsey (*Foundations of England*, II, 201) for some unstated reason placed the scene of Robert's capture at Gilling in Yorkshire, nearly sixty miles south of Newcastle.

[66] Sextus Julius Frontinus, *The Stategems of War,* tr. Robert Scott (London, 1816), Book III, Ch. x, 233–235.

[67] *Anglo-Saxon Chronicle,* I, 362; Florence of Worcester, II, 39; Symeon of Durham, II, 226.

[68] Freeman, *William Rufus,* II, 54.

[69] William of Malmesbury, *De Gestis Regum,* II, 372–373; Florence of Worcester, II, 39; Symeon of Durham, II, 226; Henry of Huntingdon, 218; Geffrei Gaimar, I, 263; Ordericus Vitalis, III, 409; *Anglo-Saxon Chronicle,* I, 362.

[70] *Anglo-Saxon Chronicle,* I, 361. Fyrd used in this sense simply means "army" and not specifically the English levy. See note 57.

[71] Ordericus Vitalis, III, 407.

[72] Anselm, *Opera Omnia,* IV, 79.

[73] *Regesta,* I, 94–95; Sanders, *Feudal Baronies,* 12.

[74] Geffrei Gaimar, I, 261–262; *Anglo-Saxon Chronicle,* I, 362; Sanders, *Feudal Baronies,* 129.

[75] *Monasticon,* IV, 178; Ordericus Vitalis, IV, 32–33.

[76] *Anglo-Saxon Chronicle,* I, 363.

[77] William of Malmesbury, *De Gestis Regum,* II, 378–379.

[78] One of Henry's first acts after his coronation was to arrange for the return to England of Archbishop Anselm of Canterbury, who was living on the Continent in self-imposed exile. In a letter to the primate the king directed Anselm to return by way of Wissant in Flanders and to avoid Normandy. Anselm, *Opera Omnia,* IV, 109–110; William of Malmesbury, *De Gestis Regum,* II, 470; Florence of Worcester, II, 47; *Anglo-Saxon Chronicle,* I, 365.

[79] *Anglo-Saxon Chronicle,* I, 365–366; Florence of Worcester, II, 48; William of Malmesbury, *De Gestis Regum,* II, 471; Henry of Huntingdon, 234; Ordericus Vitalis, IV, 109.

[80] *Registrum Antiquissimum of Lincoln Cathedral,* ed. C. W. Foster (Lincoln Record Society, 1931–1937), I, 47.

[81] William of Malmesbury, *De Gestis Regum,* II, 471; Florence of Worcester, II, 48; *Annales Monasterii de Wintonia,* in *Annales Monastici,* ed. Henry Richards Luard (R.S.) (London, 1864–1869), II, 40.

[82] Ordericus Vitalis, IV, 103–104.

[83] William of Malmesbury, *De Gestis Regum,* II, 471, 473.

[84] *Eadmeri Historia Novorum in Anglia et Opuscula Duo de Vita Sancti Anselmi et Quibusdam Miraculis Ejus,* ed. Martin Rule (R.S.) (London, 1884), 126; *Anglo-Saxon Chronicle,* I, 365; Henry of Huntingdon, 233; Florence of Worcester, II, 49.

[85] *Foedera, Conventiones, Literae, etc.,* ed. Adam Clarke, J. Caley, J. Bayley, F. Holbrooke, J. W. Clarke, (London, 1816–1869), I, i, 7; *Regesta,* II, 7. See also J. F. Verbruggen, *Het Leger en de Vloot van de Graven van Vlaanderen vanaf het Onstaan tot in 1305* (Brussels, 1960), 68; F. L. Ganshof, R. Van Caenegem, and A. Verhulst, "Note sur le premier traité

anglo-flamand de Douvres," *Revue du Nord,* XL (1958), 245–257. Lot (*L'Art Militaire,* I, 130) expressed some doubt as to whether it would have been possible for the count to have honored this commitment, which he misdated 1103. The point is not whether the count had or did not have 1,000 *equites* to put at the disposal of the king of England, but that the threat of Flemish intervention in Normandy must surely have had some influence on the plans of Duke Robert. For the amount of the subsidy, see Poole, *Domesday Book to Magna Carta,* 118.

[86] *Anglo-Saxon Chronicle,* I, 365; *Annales Wintoniae,* 41; *Monasticon,* I, 242.

[87] It is very tempting to assign to this time a writ of Henry alerting the barons and vavasours who owed castle-guard at Rockingham. The editors of the *Regesta* (II, 17) tentatively date this document to January 1102; but early 1101, when Henry was preparing his defenses, seems more likely. Rockingham had been a royal castle from its foundation. *Domesday Book,* I, 220a, 1. See also Stenton, *First Century,* 20, 214, 284.

[88] Eadmer, 126; Florence of Worcester, II, 48.

[89] Florence of Worcester, II, 48–49; *Anglo-Saxon Chronicle,* I, 365; David, *Robert Curthose,* 130.

[90] The date is given as 24 June by William Farrer, *An Outline Itinerary of King Henry the First* (Oxford, n.d.), 9. See also *Anglo-Saxon Chronicle,* I, 365; Florence of Worcester, II, 48; Henry of Huntingdon, 233; William of Jumièges, 887; Eadmer, 126–127.

[91] *Annales Wintoniae,* 41. If the deductions of W. J. Corbett ("Duchy of Normandy and the Norman Conquest") with regard to the Conqueror's fleet are valid, Duke Robert's army may be put at just over 1,400 of all arms—not a large force with which to attempt the conquest of England, but then the duke was depending heavily on the support of the disaffected barons.

[92] Poole, *Domesday Book to Magna Carta,* 116; Florence of Worcester, II, 49.

[93] William of Malmesbury, *De Gestis Regum,* II, 472. This, one of the all too infrequent references to actual military training, is convincing proof that the English *fyrd* was an infantry force.

[94] *Anglo-Saxon Chronicle,* I, 365; Henry of Huntingdon, 233; Florence of Worcester, II, 48–49; Ordericus Vitalis, IV, 110; William of Malmesbury, *De Gestis Regum,* II, 471. Florence puts the landing date as *ca.* 1 August.

[95] *Anglo-Saxon Chronicle,* I, 365; Henry of Huntingdon, 233; *Liber Monasterii de Hyda. A Chronicle and Chartulary of Hyde Abbey Winchester,* ed. Edward Edwards (R.S.) (London, 1886), 305; William of Jumièges, 887.

[96] Ordericus Vitalis, IV, 210; Florence of Worcester, II, 49. Wace's statement (*Roman de Rou,* II, 440) that Robert abandoned the idea of attacking Winchester because the queen was in the town and in an advanced state of pregnancy, is too ridiculous to be taken seriously.

[97] Wace, *Roman de Rou,* II, 440–441.

[98] *Regesta*, II, 10–11; William of Malmesbury, *De Gestis Regum*, II, 472; Florence of Worcester, II, 49; *Anglo-Saxon Chronicle*, I, 365.

[99] Poole, *Domesday Book to Magna Carta*, 117; Armitage, *Early Norman Castles*, 264–265; Ordericus Vitalis, IV, 32–33; Florence of Worcester, II, 49; *Anglo-Saxon Chronicle*, I, 366; William of Malmesbury, *De Gestis Regum*, II, 472.

[100] *Brut y Tywysogion: or The Chronicle of the Princes*, ed. John Williams ab Ithel (R.S.) (London, 1860), 66–67; *Domesday Book*, I, 322a, 1.

[101] Ordericus Vitalis, IV, 169–170; Florence of Worcester, II, 50; Poole, *Domesday Book to Magna Carta*, 117; David, *Robert Curthose*, 139.

[102] *Anglo-Saxon Chronicle*, I, 366.

[103] Ordericus Vitalis, IV, 170; Florence of Worcester, II, 50.

[104] William of Malmesbury, *De Gestis Regum*, II, 472; Florence of Worcester, II, 49–50; Ordericus Vitalis, IV, 170–171; John Beeler, "Towards a Re-Evaluation of Medieval English Generalship," *Journal of British Studies*, III (1963), 2–4.

[105] Florence of Worcester, II, 50; *Brut*, 67, 69. Robert's Welsh vassals were Cadwgan, Iorweth, and Maredudd, the sons of Bleddyn. For their relations with Robert, see Sir John Edward Lloyd, *A History of Wales from the Earliest Times to the Edwardian Conquest*, (London, 1954), II, 412.

[106] Florence of Worcester, II, 50; *Anglo-Saxon Chronicle*, I, 366; Ordericus Vitalis, IV, 170.

[107] Florence of Worcester, II, 50.

[108] Ordericus Vitalis, IV, 170. The length of the siege argues strongly for the existence of a masonry castle at Arundel by this time.

[109] Ordericus Vitalis, IV, 171. The exact line of the king's march from Arundel to Tickhill is not known, nor is that of the subsequent march from Tickhill to Bridgnorth. The itinerary suggested in the *Regesta* (II, 19, 20, 22, 23) seems most unlikely.

[110] Florence of Worcester, II, 50; *Anglo-Saxon Chronicle*, I, 366.

[111] Ordericus Vitalis, IV, 173–174. William was a large landholder in Shropshire. Lloyd, *History of Wales*, II, 413.

[112] *Brut*, 71; Florence of Worcester, II, 50.

[113] Ordericus Vitalis, IV, 172–173, 174.

[114] *Ibid.*, 174–175; William of Malmesbury, *De Gestis Regum*, II, 472; *Anglo-Saxon Chronicle*, I, 366.

[115] Ordericus Vitalis, IV, 172–173, 175–176. This is one of the rare extant references to road construction in the twelfth century.

[116] William of Malmesbury, *De Gestis Regum*, II, 472–473; Ordericus Vitalis, IV, 176–178; Florence of Worcester, II, 50–51; *Anglo-Saxon Chronicle*, I, 366; *Brut*, 73; *Regesta*, II, 23.

[117] Florence of Worcester, II, 50; *Anglo-Saxon Chronicle*, I, 366.

[118] Ordericus Vitalis, IV, 174–175.

[119] Stenton, *First Century*, 197–198.

[120] *The Pipe Roll of 31 Henry I, Michaelmas 1130,* ed. Joseph Hunter (facsimile, ed. of 1833; London, 1929).

[121] Arundel, Bamborough, Belvoir, Brinklow, Burton-in-Lonsdale, Exeter, Gloucester, Kirkby Malzeard, Knaresborough, Norham, Northampton, Norwich, Pevensey, St. Briavels, Salisbury, Thirsk, Tickhill, Tower of London, and Wareham.

[122] *Pipe Roll, 31 Henry I,* 137–138.

[123] *Ibid.,* 42.

[124] *Ibid.,* 143, 144.

[125] *Ibid.,* 36, 78.

[126] *Ibid.,* 13, 35.

Chapter 4

[1] Ordericus Vitalis, v, 54–56; William of Jumièges, 907; *Anglo-Saxon Chronicle,* i, 381.

[2] A generation earlier, there would have been no question concerning the right of Earl Robert to succeed his father, whom he greatly resembled in ability. Concepts of morality had changed greatly since William the Bastard acceded to the Norman duchy.

[3] *The Chronicle of the Reigns of Stephen, Henry II and Richard I by Gervase, the Monk of Canterbury,* ed. William Stubbs (R.S.) (London, 1787), i, 94; *Anglo-Saxon Chronicle,* i, 381–382.

[4] *Gesta Stephani Regis Anglorum et Ducis Normannorum,* ed. and tr. K. R. Potter (London, 1955), 5; William of Malmesbury, *Historia Novella,* ed. and tr. K. R. Potter (London, 1955), 15.

[5] Ordericus Vitalis, v, 56; *Liber Eliensis,* 285; Henry of Huntingdon, 256–258; *The Chronicle of Richard Prior of Hexham,* in Vol. iii, *Chronicles of the Reigns of Stephen, Henry II, and Richard I,* ed. Richard Howlett (R.S.) (London, 1886), 144–145; Gervase of Canterbury, i, 94; *Historia Regum Symeonis Monachi Dunelmensis Continuata per Joannem Hagulstadensem,* in Vol. ii, *Symeonis Monachi Opera Omnia,* ed. Thomas Arnold (R.S.) (London, 1885), 286; Cont. Florence of Worcester, ii, 95; *Anglo-Saxon Chronicle,* ii, 382; *Gesta Stephani,* 8; William of Malmesbury, *Historia Novella,* 15–16.

[6] Henry of Huntingdon, 258; J. H. Round, *Geoffrey de Mandeville: A Study of the Anarchy* (London, 1892), 11. Included were Archbishop Thomas of Canterbury; the king's brother, Bishop Henry of Winchester; Roger, bishop of Salisbury; Hugh Bigod; and Miles of Gloucester, who was made hereditary constable of Gloucester and Brecon.

[7] Richard of Hexham, 145–146; John of Hexham, 287; William of Malmesbury, *Historia Novella,* 16; Henry of Huntingdon, 258–259.

[8] Richard of Hexham, 146; Henry of Huntingdon, 259.

[9] William of Malmesbury, *Historia Novella,* 17. Round puts the date of this meeting early in April (*Geoffrey de Mandeville,* 24).

[10] See the charter printed in Round, *Geoffrey de Mandeville,* 262–263.

Among those present on this occasion were the archbishops of Canterbury and Rouen, the bishops of Winchester, Salisbury, Lincoln, Ely, Norwich, Worcester, St. Davids, Evreux, Avranches, Hereford, Rochester, and Carlisle, and the earls of Gloucester, Warenne, Chester, and Warwick. Also signing were Robert de Vere, Miles of Gloucester, and Brian fitz Count as constables.

[11] *Henry of Huntingdon*, 259.

[12] *Ibid.; Gesta Stephani*, 20.

[13] *Anglo-Saxon Chronicle*, I, 382; *Gesta Stephani*, 20; Gervase of Canterbury, I, 95.

[14] Cont. Florence of Worcester, II, 96–97. *Gesta Stephani*, 21–28; Henry of Huntingdon, 259.

[15] *Gesta Stephani*, 27–28; Henry of Huntingdon, 259. Henry had only hard words for this lenient policy: ". . . he permitted the rebels to go without punishment, whereas if he had inflicted it, so many castles would not have been held against him."

[16] *Gesta Stephani*, 29; *Ancient Charters Royal and Private Prior to A.D. 1200*, ed. J. H. Round (London, 1888), 34–35. A charter of Stephen to Miles of Gloucester given at Farnham, may have been issued during Stephen's march to Southampton, according to Round.

[17] Henry of Huntingdon, 259; Richard of Hexham, 147; *Gesta Stephani*, 29–30.

[18] William of Malmesbury, *Historia Novella*, 21; *The Chronicle of Robert of Torigni (Robert de Monte)*, in Vol. IV, *Chronicles of the Reigns of Stephen, Henry II, and Richard I*, ed. Richard Howlett (R.S.) (London, 1889), 132–133; Henry of Huntingdon, 260; Ordericus Vitalis, V, 81, 91–92; *Anglo-Saxon Chronicle*, I, 382; Gervase of Canterbury, I, 101. Ordericus states that Stephen arrived in Normandy during the third week in March. This would put his arrival between 14 and 20 March, both dates inclusive. Robert and Ordericus state only that Stephen returned to England during Advent, which began 28 November; Gervase says more specifically that the king returned in December, and the archdeacon of Huntingdon says "on the very eve of Christmas."

[19] John of Hexham, 288; Donald Nicholl, *Thurstan, Archbishop of York (1114–1140)* (York, 1964), 218.

[20] Ordericus Vitalis, V, 92–93; *Liber Eliensis*, 286–287.

[21] *Gesta Stephani*, 31.

[22] The constableship of Bedford castle was hereditary in the Beauchamp family. Stephen wished to dispossess Miles, who was the heir of his father, or more probably of his uncle Robert, in favor of Hugh de Beaumont. Stenton, *First Century*, 237–238; *Gesta Stephani*, 32; Henry of Huntingdon, 260; Cont. Florence of Worcester, II, 102; Gervase of Canterbury, I, 101; Ordericus Vitalis, V, 103–104.

[23] Ordericus Vitalis, V, 104; *Gesta Stephani*, 32–33. A charter to Glastonbury abbey indicates that during the siege the king may have had his headquarters

at Gillingham, for it is given "apud Giltingtonam in obsidione Bedeford" (*Monasticon,* I, 37) . With less authority, Howlett puts Stephen's headquarters at Meppershall on the basis of a charter "apud Meperteshalam in obsidione." *Gesta Stephani Regis Anglorum,* in Vol. III, *Chronicles of the Reigns of Stephen, Henry II, and Richard I,* ed. Richard Howlett (R.S.) (London, 1886) , xxv. It is more likely that Miles de Beauchamp had garrisoned the motte-and-bailey at Meppershall as an outpost, and that the king was engaged in its reduction when the charter was issued.

[24] Richard of Hexham, 151; John of Hexham, 289; *Gesta Stephani,* 36.

[25] John of Hexham, 289; Richard of Hexham, 151–154; Cont. Florence of Worcester, II, 102.

[26] Richard of Hexham, 155; Cont. Florence of Worcester, II, 102. Richard puts the king's arrival in the north as early as 2 February, the Feast of the Purification of St. Mary. John of Hexham, 290, says only that the king arrived during Lent—which began on 16 February.

[27] The reason for Stephen's retreat is variously stated as due to the treachery of many of the English barons who were in league with the King of Scots (John of Hexham, 291) ; the refusal of the English troops to serve during Lent; and the exhaustion of supplies (Richard of Hexham, 155) . The latter reason is certainly the most convincing.

[28] John of Hexham, 291–292; Richard of Hexham, 155–158; Cont. Florence of Worcester, II, 112.

[29] Richard of Hexham, 159; J. Douglas Drummond, *Studien zur Kriegsgeschichite Englands im 12 Jahrhundert* (Berlin, 1905) , 58–60.

[30] Ailred of Rievaulx, *De Bello Standardi,* in Vol. III, *Chronicles of the Reigns of Stephen, Henry II, and Richard I,* ed. Richard Howlett (R.S.) (London, 1886) , 189–190.

[31] Richard of Hexham, 158, 159; Ramsey, *Foundations of England,* II, 367.

[32] Richard of Hexham, 159; Cont. Florence of Worcester, II, 111. The Continuator is rather confused in his chronology.

[33] *Historia Rerum Anglicarum of William of Newburgh,* in Vols. I and II, *Chronicles of the Reigns of Stephen, Henry II, and Richard I,* ed. Richard Howlett (R.S.) (London) , 1884–1885, I, 33; Richard of Hexham, 159; John of Hexham, 292.

[34] Richard of Hexham, 160.

[35] Ailred of Rievaulx, 181–182; Lieutenant-Colonel Alfred H. Burne, *More Battlefields of England* (London, 1952) , 96.

[36] John of Hexham, 292–295; Richard of Hexham, 159; Cont. Florence of Worcester, II, 111; William of Newburgh, I, 33; Ailred of Rievaulx, 182–183; Burne, *More Battlefields,* 96; Ramsey. *Foundations of England,* II, 367–368. For the role of the archbishop in these deliberations, see Nicholl, *Thurstan,* 221–223.

[37] *Historians of the Church of York,* ed. James Raine (R.S.) (London, 1879–1894) , III, 34–36; Richard of Hexham, 162; Ramsey, *Foundations of England,* II, 368; Richardson and Sayles. *Governance of Mediaeval England,* 75.

[38] Burne, *More Battlefields,* 96. Henry of Huntingdon, 261–265; John of Hexham, 292–295; Richard of Hexham, 163; Ramsey, *Foundations of England,* II, 368,369.

[39] Richard of Hexham, 161–162; Ailred of Rievaulx, 192–195; John of Hexham, 293–294.

[40] The Ferrers fee of Tutbury was due the service of 80 knights; the barony of Peak, held in 1138 by William Peverel II, answered for 43/44 knights in 1161 and 1162. Sanders, *Feudal Baronies,* 149, 136.

[41] Richard of Hexham, 162; Cont. Florence of Worcester, II, 111. Oman (*Art of War,* I, 391) assigned the command jointly to William of Aumale and Walter Espec, the sheriff of Yorkshire, but nowhere in the sources for the campaign is an overall commander mentioned. In view of the difficulties involved in organizing resistance in the first place, it would seem likely that matters of general policy were decided by a council of war in which, perhaps, Aumale and Espec had the most influential voices. The English chronicler mentions Aumale as the man "to whom the king had entrusted York." *Anglo-Saxon Chronicle,* I, 383.

[42] Richard of Hexham, 162: ". . . and passing the village of Northallerton, they arrived early in the morning at a plain distant from it by about two miles." Actually the battlefield is three miles from Northallerton. Burne, *More Battlefields,* 97.

[43] Cont. Florence of Worcester, II, 111.

[44] For a description of the battlefield, see Burne, *More Battlefields,* 97, 98–99. There is a map in C. B. R. Barrett, *Battles and Battlefields in England* (London, 1896), 34, but the troop dispositions must be ignored. For some inexplicable reason he has the Scots facing north and the English facing south. How the two armies got around each other is not explained, and there is no evidence to warrant this juxtaposition of the armies. There is a conjectural order of battle in Oman, *Art of War,* I, op. 400.

[45] Richard of Hexham, 163.

[46] Richard of Hexham, 163; Ailred of Rievaulx, 189; Cont. Florence of Worcester, II, 111. Colonel Burne does not mention these mounted men.

[47] The five modern accounts of the campaign and battle are all derived, of course, from the same contemporary sources: Barrett, *Battles and Battlefields,* 26–36; Ramsey, *Foundations of England,* II, 368–371; Oman, *Art of War,* I, 390–396; Burne, *More Battlefields,* 96–99; and from the Scottish point of view, R. L. Graeme Ritchie, *The Normans in Scotland* (Edinburgh, 1954), 258–268.

[48] Burne, *More Battlefields,* 97; Barrett, *Battles and Battlefields,* 31. Neither cites his authorities.

[49] Ramsey, *op. cit.,* II, 369. It is difficult to make much of this description. What, for example, is "a sort of rear rank"? Wisely, Ramsey did not try to put it down diagrammatically.

[50] Oman, *Art of War,* I, 391–392.

[51] Richard of Hexham, 163.

[52] *Ibid.*

[53] Ailred of Rievaulx, 189–190.

[54] Ailred of Rievaulx, 190.

[55] Richard of Hexham, 163; Ailred of Rievaulx, 190. Ritchie's account, following Ramsey (*Foundations of England,* II, 370), is impossible to reconcile with the authorities. *Normans in Scotland,* 297. Burne, *More Battlefields,* 97, is not much better. Indeed, this is not one of Burne's more convincing reconstructions.

[56] Oman, *Art of War,* I, op. 400. Barrett's projected order of battle (*Battles and Battlefields,* 34) also has the Scots aligned nearly in accordance with the authorities, although there seems to be no justification for his dividing right, center, and left into three lines each.

[57] Oman's comment that "neither side showed any tactical insight" scarcely does justice to King David's arrangements. *Art of War,* I, 391. That they did not produce victory does not prove the dispositions faulty.

[58] Richard of Hexham, 164; Ailred of Rievaulx, 196. Burne's assertion, *More Battlefields,* 97, that the Galwegians never reached the English line is contradicted by the evidence.

[59] Ailred of Rievaulx, 196,198. Only nineteen of two hundred knights escaped with their arms and armor according to the Continuator of Florence of Worcester, II, 112.

[60] Ailred of Rievaulx, 197.

[61] *Ibid.,* 198; Richard of Hexham, 164; Cont. Florence of Worcester, II, 112. The Continuator's statement that 10,000 Scots fell in the battle is a wild guess.

[62] Henry of Huntingdon, 264; Richard of Hexham, 165.

[63] Oman, *Art of War,* I, 395; Burne, *More Battlefields,* 99.

[64] At the feast of St. Michael, 29 September. Richard of Hexham, 165–167, 171–172; John of Hexham, 291–292; Cont. Florence of Worcester, II, 112–113. The latter account is not very accurate.

[65] In 1138 Easter fell on 17 April. Cont. Florence of Worcester, II, 105.

[66] Henry of Huntingdon, 261.

[67] Cont. Florence of Worcester, II, 105–106.

[68] *Ibid.,* 106–107; Ordericus Vitalis, V, 112.

[69] William of Malmesbury, *Historia Novella,* 23–24.

[70] *Annales de Wintonia,* 51.

[71] Ordericus Vitalis, V, 110; Henry of Huntingdon, 261.

[72] *Gesta Stephani,* 37, 45; Cont. Florence of Worcester, II, 108–109.

[73] Henry of Huntingdon, 261; Cont. Florence of Worcester, II, 110; Ordericus Vitalis, V, 111–113.

[74] Cont. Florence of Worcester, II, 110; Henry of Huntingdon, 261; Ordericus Vitalis, V, 110.

[75] Witness the plot which Geoffrey Talbot devised to seize Bath; his capture, and the scheme by which his release was effected. Henry of Huntingdon, 261; Cont. Florence of Worcester, II, 108–109; Ordericus Vitalis, V, 110; *Gesta Stephani,* 38–41.

[76] Ordericus Vitalis, v, 110–111; Henry of Huntingdon, 261.

[77] Round, *Geoffrey de Mandeville*, 23: "Attention should also perhaps be called to these repeated visits to Oxford. . . . For this its central position may doubtless partly account. . . . But it also represented for Stephen, as it were, a post of observation, commanding, in Bristol and Gloucester, the two strongholds of the opposition."

[78] Cont. Florence of Worcester, II, 109–110; *Gesta Stephani*, 43–44. There is also a suggestion that Stephen was advised to do this by his barons, with the implication that their loyalty was not above suspicion. Gervase of Canterbury, I, 104–105.

[79] *Gesta Stephani*, 45–46.

[80] Cont. Florence of Worcester, II, 110.

[81] See charter of Miles "apud Salopesbiriam in obsidione," Round, *Geoffrey de Mandeville*, 285.

[82] Ordericus Vitalis, v, 112–113; Cont. Florence of Worcester, II, 110; Henry of Huntingdon, 261.

[83] Ordericus Vitalis, v, 113.

[84] Cont. Florence of Worcester, II, 110.

[85] Ordericus Vitalis, v, 112.

[86] Henry of Huntingdon, 261.

[87] Gervase of Canterbury, I, 109.

[88] *Continuato Gemblacensis* to Sigebert of Gembloux, *Chronographia*, ed. Ludwig Conrad Bethmann, in Vol. VI, *Monumenta Germaniae Historica* (New York, 1963), 386.

[89] However, Leeds was either taken or retaken by the king *post Natali*, after which he departed for the north, according to Henry of Huntingdon, 265.

[90] Richard of Hexham, 177–178.

[91] John of Hexham, 300.

[92] Cont. Florence of Worcester, II, 115–116; Henry of Huntingdon, 265.

[93] William of Malmesbury, *Historia Novella*, 25.

[94] *Ibid.*, 27.

[95] *Ibid.*, 26; *Gesta Stephani*, 48.

[96] William of Malmesbury, *Historia Novella*, 26–27; Cont. Florence of Worcester, II, 107–108, 116; *Anglo-Saxon Chronicle*, I, 382; Henry of Huntingdon, 265; William of Newburgh, I, 35–36; John of Hexham, 301; *Gesta Stephani*, 51.

[97] Henry of Huntingdon, 265; Cont. Florence of Worcester, II, 108, 116; William of Malmesbury, *Historia Novella*, 27; William of Newburgh, I, 36; Ordericus Vitalis, v, 120–121; *Gesta Stephani*, 52; Gervase of Canterbury, I, 103–104. The *Gesta* states that Stephen also threatened to hang the chancellor, Roger le Poer.

[98] *Gesta Stephani*, 51; William of Malmesbury, *Historia Novella*, 27; Henry of Huntingdon, 266. The Continuator of Florence of Worcester notes that Stephen and his council later decreed that all castles and strongholds of a secular nature should come under royal jurisdiction. Cont. Florence of Worcester, II, 116.

[99] *Gesta Stephani,* 54–55. William of Malmesbury (*Historia Novella,* 37) places these events following the failure of the king to relieve Hereford in December. This is almost certainly incorrect.

[100] *Gesta Stephani,* 56. The chronology for the late summer of 1139 is quite confused in the accounts of the chroniclers. The most logical sequence is that Baldwin landed first at Wareham—perhaps as a diversionary operation—and that the landing of the empress and Earl Robert occurred later. There seems no other way of reconciling the conflicting accounts in the annals.

[101] Round (*Ancient Charters,* 39–41) dates as probably September 1139 a charter of Stephen to William, earl of Lincoln, given at Oxford.

[102] Gervase of Canterbury, I, 110; Cont. Florence of Worcester, II, 117; *Annales de Wintonia,* 51. Marlborough was a sensitive point, for the castle controlled the old Roman road northwest from Winchester to Gloucester and the Severn valley.

[103] Gervase of Canterbury, I, 110; Ordericus Vitalis, V, 121; Robert of Torigni, 137; Henry of Huntingdon, 266; *Gesta Stephani,* 58; Cont. Florence of Worcester, II, 117; William of Malmesbury, *Historia Novella,* 35; Round, *Geoffrey de Mandeville,* 280.

Chapter 5

[1] Robert of Torigni, 137; *Anglo-Saxon Chronicle,* I, 383; *Gesta Stephani,* 58–59; William of Malmesbury, *Historia Novella,* 35. The author of the *Gesta* attributed Earl Robert's escape to the treasonable connivance of the bishop of Winchester. William of Malmesbury put Robert's escort at a dozen men.

[2] Ordericus Vitalis, V, 121; *Gesta Stephani,* 58–59; Henry of Huntingdon, 266; John of Hexham, 302; Cont. Florence of Worcester, II, 117; William of Malmesbury, *Historia Novella,* 35. Ordericus ascribed this action to the carelessness and simplicity of the king. The anonymous author of the *Gesta* ascribed it to the treasonable designs of Stephen's brother, Bishop Henry; Henry of Huntingdon stated that the king "listening to perfidious council, or finding the castle too strong to be taken," allowed the empress to depart. John of Hexham tersely called it "an indiscreet simplicity of mind."

[3] *Gesta Stephani,* 59; Henry of Huntingdon, 266; John of Hexham, 302; Robert of Torigni, 137; Ordericus Vitalis, V, 122; Gervase of Canterbury, I, 110; Cont. Florence of Worcester, II, 117.

[4] John of Hexham, 302; *Gesta Stephani,* 60. Stenton accurately observed that "throughout the wars of Stephen's time, the course of events was influenced by the fact that Wallingford castle was held for the Empress by Brian fitz Count . . ." *First Century,* 236.

[5] Cont. Florence of Worcester, II, 117; *Gesta Stephani,* 60; William of Malmesbury, *Historia Novella,* 35.

[6] Cont. Florence of Worcester, II, 118; Gervase of Canterbury, I, 111; *Gesta Stephani,* 61.

[7] William of Malmesbury, *Historia Novella,* 36; *Gesta Stephani,* 62.

[8] *Gesta Stephani,* 62; Cont. Florence of Worcester, II, 118; Gervase of Canterbury, I, 111; William of Malmesbury, *Historia Novella,* 36.

[9] *Gesta Stephani,* 61,62,64; William of Malmesbury, *Historia Novella,* 36.

[10] *Gesta Stephani,* 64. Both Trowbridge and Devizes seem to have been neutralized by this move. The author of the *Gesta* remarked, doubtless with exaggeration, that "the mutual attack and incursion which they made on one another reduced the whole of the surrounding countryside to the state of a miserable desert."

[11] Cont. Florence of Worcester, II, 117–118; William of Malmesbury, *Historia Novella,* 35; Gervase of Canterbury, I, 110–111; *Gesta Stephani,* 63–64.

[12] *Gesta Stephani,* 62.

[13] Round, *Geoffrey de Mandeville,* 281.

[14] Gervase of Canterbury, I, 111. A vivid description of the sack is found in Cont. Florence of Worcester, II, 118–120.

[15] *Gesta Stephani,* 63; Cont. Florence of Worcester, II, 120, 123.

[16] *Gesta Stephani,* 63; John of Hexham, 302; William of Malmesbury, *Historia Novella,* 36.

[17] Cont. Florence of Worcester, II, 121; William of Malmesbury, *Historia Novella,* 36.

[18] Cont. Florence of Worcester, II, 121–122; Gervase of Canterbury, I, 112.

[19] Cont. Florence of Worcester, II, 122–123; Gervase of Canterbury, I, 112; *Gesta Stephani,* 65–67; *Liber Eliensis,* 314, 433.

[20] William of Malmesbury, *Historia Novella,* 44; Round, *Geoffrey de Mandeville,* 49.

[21] William of Malmesbury, *Historia Novella,* 42; *Gesta Stephani,* 67–69.

[22] The Continuator (II, 126–127) stated that the king was at Winchester during the spring, but his account is so garbled with a retelling of the events of the preceding November and December that it is impossible to unravel.

[23] William of Malmesbury, *Historia Novella,* 43–44; *Gesta Stephani,* 69–71; Cont. Florence of Worcester, II, 125–127.

[24] This unusual incident was recorded only in the *Gesta,* but the narrative is so circumstantial that there can be little doubt of its authenticity; *Gesta Stephani,* 71–72, 77.

[25] William of Malmesbury, *Historia Novella,* 42; Cont. Florence of Worcester, II, 127–128; *Gesta Stephani,* 72. William of Malmesbury adds that the rebels also recovered Sudely and Cerney during the summer, but this may be a rehash of the account of the campaign of the previous autumn.

[26] Cont. Florence of Worcester, II, 128–129; Gervase of Canterbury, I, 112. Ralph had commanded for the empress at Dudley in the preceding year. The Continuator noted that the expedition was a mixed force of horse and foot.

[27] William of Malmesbury, *Historia Novella,* 46–47. William's account of this affair is unusually biased in favor of the rebels.

[28] For these and subsequent details, see Ordericus Vitalis, v, 125. The idea of the soldiers of a medieval garrison engaging in sports is an intriguing one.

Is it possible to trace military athletic programs back to the twelfth century?

[29] *Ibid.*

[30] William of Malmesbury, *Historia Novella*, 47; *Gesta Stephani*, 73; Ordericus Vitalis, v, 125; Henry of Huntingdon, 268; William of Newburgh, I, 39; *Anglo-Saxon Chronicle*, I, 384. See also Kate Norgate, *England under the Angevin Kings*, (London, 1887), I, 315–316; Ramsey, *Foundations of England*, II, 397; Oman, *Art of War*, I, 396.

[31] The above account seems the most likely in view of the varying details furnished by the chroniclers. The *Gesta Stephani* (73) states that Ranulf escaped before the siege was established, and William of Malmesbury suggests that he escaped with the connivance of some of Stephen's army (*Historia Novella*, 47). See also *Anglo-Saxon Chronicle*, I, 384; John of Hexham, 307; Symeon of Durham, I, 161–162.

[32] Ordericus Vitalis, v, 125–126; *Gesta Stephani*, 73; William of Malmesbury, *Historia Novella*, 47; William of Newburgh, I, 39–40; Henry of Huntingdon, 268; John of Hexham, 307; *Anglo-Saxon Chronicle*, I, 384.

[33] Henry of Huntingdon, 268; *Gesta Stephani*, 73; Ordericus Vitalis, v, 127. For the identity of the Welsh mercenary captains see Lloyd, *History of Wales*, II, 489. Oman is certainly in error in speaking of the Welsh as having been raised by Robert of Gloucester (*Art of War*, I, 398), for the *Gesta* states specifically that these auxiliaries were brought into the field by Earl Ranulf; moreover, Gwynedd and Powys were in the sphere of influence of Cheshire rather than of Glamorgan.

[34] *Gesta Stephani*, 73; Ordericus Vitalis, v, 127; *Liber Eliensis*, 321.

[35] Norgate, *Angevin Kings*, I, 316. Ramsey (*Foundations of England*, II, 397) accepts this conjecture as probable.

[36] It seems to have escaped the notice of earlier writers that in a grant, tentatively dated July 1133, Henry I gave Bishop Alexander of Lincoln permission to build a bridge over the Trent at his castle of Newark. *Regesta*, II, 264. Hill, the historian of Lincoln, argued from William of Malmesbury's story that the army of the earls swam the flooded Trent, and that the bridge had not been built; but it seems more likely that William was confused on this point, J. W. F. Hill, *Mediaeval Lincoln* (Cambridge, 1948), 178; William of Malmesbury, *Historia Novella*, 48.

[37] William of Malmesbury, *Historia Novella*, 48.

[38] Henry of Huntingdon, 268.

[39] *Gesta Stephani*, 74. This seems to be the logical interpretation of the rather vague account of the chronicler. It should be noted that he mentions the dispersal of the covering force before the seizure of the ford. If this should be the correct order of events, Stephen's guard would have been on the wrong side of the Fossdyke. Had it been on the north bank, even a modest force could have held the ford against an enemy emerging from the icy water and the marshy ground, at least long enough for aid to be summoned.

[40] Norgate, *Angevin Kings*, I, 345–346.

[41] Ramsey (*Foundations of England*, II, 398–399) is somewhat uncertain as to how the guard at the ford was disposed of.

[42] Henry of Huntingdon, 268–271. The long speech attributed to Earl Robert is doubtless contrived, and seems to detail the opinions held by the Angevins of the king and his supporters.

[43] Ordericus Vitalis, v, 126–127; *Gesta Stephani*, 74.
Historia Novella, 48–49; Henry of Huntingdon, 271; John of Hexham, 307;

[44] Ordericus Vitalis, v, 127; *Gesta Stephani*, 74; William of Malmesbury, *Historia Novella*, 48–49; Henry of Huntingdon, 271; John of Hexham, 307; William of Newburgh, I, 40. Several of the chroniclers mention unfavorable omens foretelling the king's defeat and capture, but these were probably afterthoughts. In any event, Stephen seems to have been less superstitious than most of his contemporaries.

[45] Ramsey, *Foundations of England*, II, 398–399.

[46] Hill, *Mediaeval Lincoln*, 179.

[47] See Ramsey's suggested line of march in *Foundations of England*, II, op. 398.

[48] Norgate, *Angevin Kings*, I, 317,346; Oman, *Art of War*, I, 397.

[49] This can be inferred from the passage in the speech allegedly made by the earl of Gloucester: "There is one thing, however, brave nobles and soldiers all, which I want to impress upon your minds. There is no possibility of retreat over the marshes which you have just crossed with difficulty. Here, therefore, you must either conquer or die; for there is no safety in flight." Henry of Huntingdon, 269.

[50] Oman, *Art of War*, I, 397. This is Oman at his best. Hill (*Mediaeval Lincoln*, 179) refuses to decide as to the location on the grounds that no satisfactory evidence exists.

[51] Earl Waleran, who had served Stephen loyally since 1138, defected to the empress after the king's capture at Lincoln. He did not, however, become an active partisan, but retired to his Norman estates, and except for a brief visit in the winter of 1141–1142, there is no record of his ever having returned to England. G. H. White, "The Career of Waleran Count of Meulan and Earl of Worcester (1104–66)," *Transactions of the Royal Historical Society*, XVII (1934), 19–49.

[52] To state that "at the Battle of Lincoln in 1141 . . . all the royal troops fought on foot except for a small and ineffective band of mercenaries" does not seem warranted by the evidence. Hollister, "Irony of English Feudalism," 21. Ineffective the royal cavalry certainly was, but there is no suggestion that the mounted element was entirely mercenary in character, or that it constituted a minor element numerically. The wings of both armies remained mounted, and in all likelihood constituted a substantial fraction of the men under arms. Henry of Huntingdon, 272.

[53] Henry of Huntingdon, 269,271; John of Hexham, 308. The order of

battle suggested by Ramsey's plan is quite obviously impossible. *Foundations of England,* II op. 398. Oman seems to have the better of the argument here. *Art of War,* I, 397.

[54] Ordericus Vitalis, v, 127–128. See also Henry of Huntingdon, 271.

[55] Henry of Huntingdon, 272; Ordericus, v, 127; William of Newburgh, I, 40. Oman (*Art of War,* I, 398) takes the opposite view.

[56] Henry of Huntingdon, 271–273.

[57] Henry of Huntingdon, 268. See also Ordericus Vitalis, v, 127; Oman, *Art of War,* I, 398.

[58] Henry of Huntingdon, 273.

[59] William of Malmesbury, *Historia Novella,* 49.

[60] William of Malmesbury, *Historia Novella,* 49; *Gesta Stephani,* 74–75; Henry of Huntingdon, 273; Ordericus Vitalis, v, 128; William of Newburgh; I, 40; Symeon of Durham, I, 161–162; *Anglo-Saxon Chronicle,* I, 384; John of Hexham, 307–308.

[61] Henry of Huntingdon, 273–274; Ordericus Vitalis, v, 128. Henry states that William of Ypres, "as an experienced commander, seeing the impossibility of supporting the king, deferred his aid for better times." This was, as matters turned out, a very wise decision. Under the circumstances, William probably could not have prevented the king's capture. Thus the able mercenary remained at liberty to play a vital role in the summer campaign of 1141.

[62] Ordericus Vitalis, v, 129; John of Hexham, 308. Henry of Huntingdon, 273, has the sword–battle axe sequence reversed.

[63] John of Hexham, 308; Henry of Huntingdon, 274–275; William of Malmesbury, *Historia Novella,* 49; *Gesta Stephani,* 75; Ordericus Vitalis, v, 128; *Anglo-Saxon Chronicle,* I, 384.

[64] Ordericus Vitalis, v, 128; Henry of Huntingdon, 274.

[65] Henry of Huntingdon, 275. *Civitas ergo hostili lege direpta est . . .*

[66] Ordericus Vitalis, v, 129. The chronicler states that as many as 500 of the principal citizens perished in this manner, but the figure seems too high. William of Malmesbury callously dismisses the slaughter of the defeated infantry as "a result of the anger of the victors and without causing any grief to the vanquished, since it was they who by their instigation had given rise to this calamity." *Historia Novella,* 49.

[67] *Gesta Stephani,* 75; Ordericus Vitalis, v, 129; William of Malmesbury, *Historia Novella,* 49; Henry of Huntingdon, 275.

[68] Cont. Florence of Worcester, II, 129; *Anglo-Saxon Chronicle,* I, 384; *Gesta Stephani,* 75.

[69] Ramsey, *Foundations of England,* II, 401.

[70] Poole, *Domesday Book to Magna Carta,* 142.

[71] Oman, *Art of War,* I, 399.

[72] William of Malmesbury, *Historia Novella,* 50–51; *Gesta Stephani,* 76–77, 79; Cont. Florence of Worcester, II, 129–130; Gervase of Canterbury, I, 118–119.

[73] William of Malmesbury, *Historia Novella*, 51; *Gesta Stephani*, 77–78; Gervase of Canterbury, I, 118–119; Cont. Florence of Worcester, II, 130. Both Gervase and the Continuator suffer from bad chronology at this point.

[74] Cont. Florence of Worcester, II, 130; *Ancient Charters*, 41–42; William of Malmesbury, *Historia Novella*, 56.

[75] *Anglo Saxon Chronicle*, I, 384; Symeon of Durham, I, 145; Henry of Huntingdon, 275; William of Malmesbury, *Historia Novella*, 56; *Gesta Stephani*, 80–81,82–83; William of Newburgh, I, 41; Cont. Florence of Worcester, II, 131–133.

[76] Round, *Geoffrey de Mandeville*, 56; Cont. Florence of Worcester, II, 133; *Gesta Stephani*, 85. See also the charter in *Geoffrey de Mandeville*, 123–124.

[77] Charter in Round, *Geoffrey de Mandeville*, 93–95. R. H. C. Davis has attempted to show that both the charters issued by the empress to Geoffrey, as well as the charter of creation to Aubrey de Vere, date from the summer of 1141, and that the latter can be dated with some certainty before 1 August 1141. R. H. C. Davis, "Geoffrey de Mandeville Reconsidered," *English Historical Review*, LXXIX (1964), 299–307. The principal argument for changing the chronology established by Round for these charters is that two of the witnesses, Wido de Sable and Pagan de Clairvaux, are known to have been with the empress in England only during this period, and that "such a date would suit the general tenor of the charter and make sense of its reference to London." This latter argument is singularly unconvincing. Among other promises, the empress guarantees that she will not make peace with the Londoners "because they were his mortal enemies." And yet within a month of the alleged issuance of this charter, Geoffrey is to be found fighting side by side with these same "mortal enemies" against the empress at the blockade of Winchester. Geoffrey may not have been a "professional turncoat," but if Davis is correct, the earl was remarkably agile in transferring his allegiance from one side to the other. *Ibid.*, 306.

[78] *Ibid.*, 313–314; Stenton, *First Century*, 223.

[79] Round, *Geoffrey de Mandeville*, 65; John of Hexham, 308–309.

[80] *Gesta Stephani*, 83–84; William of Malmesbury, *Historia Novella*, 57–58. General accounts of the summer campaign will be found in Norgate, *Angevin Kings*, I, 324–328; Round, *Geoffrey de Mandeville*, 124–135; Ramsey; *Foundations of England*, II, 407–411.

[81] John of Hexham (310) is the only authority for the bishop's siege of the castle, but William of Malmesbury (*Historia Novella*, 58) records that Robert of Gloucester made a hurried trip to Winchester "to settle these disturbances if he could, but having accomplished nothing went back to Oxford . . ."

[82] William of Malmesbury, *Historia Novella*, 58; Henry of Huntingdon, 275. The assertion of the Continuator that the empress effected this concentration without the knowledge of the earl of Gloucester, can be dismissed as preposterous. Cont. Florence of Worcester, II, 133. The contention of the English chronicler that Bishop Henry promised to give up Winchester to the

empress, and so lured her army into a trap, finds no support in the other accounts. *Anglo-Saxon Chronicle*, I, 384.

[83] William of Malmesbury, *Historia Novella*, 59,67; *Gesta Stephani*, 84–85; John of Hexham, 310. De Mohun is described as earl of Dorset by the *Gesta*, but this is certainly an error, for he styles himself earl of Somerset in his charter to Bruton Priory. *Monasticon*, VI, 335. Although the narrative is none too clear at this point, the Continuator appears to state that numbers of mercenary troops were also in the employ of the empress. Cont. Florence of Worcester, II, 133.

[84] *Gesta Stephani*, 89.

[85] Round, *Geoffrey de Mandeville*, 125.

[86] *Gesta Stephani*, 84; Cont. Florence of Worcester, II, 133. William of Malmesbury's account is somewhat vague as to the initial sequence of events at Winchester. He states that after the empress occupied the castle, she sent for the bishop, but he put the messenger off with an ambiguous answer and then apparently made his escape. *Historia Novella*, 58.

[87] William of Malmesbury, *Historia Novella*, 58,60; Cont. Florence of Worcester, II, 133; John of Hexham, 310.

[88] Cont. Florence of Worcester, II, 133; William of Malmesbury, *Historia Novella*, 59; *Annales de Wintonia*, 52.

[89] *Annales Monasterii de Waverleia*, in Vol. II, *Annales Monastici*, ed. Henry Richards Luard (R.S.) (London, 1865), 229.

[90] *Gesta Stephani*, 84.

[91] Norgate, *Angevin Kings*, I, 325; Ramsey, *Foundations of England*, II, 407; Round, *Geoffrey de Mandeville*, 126. The map of Winchester in Norgate, I, op. 31, is more satisfactory for following operations than the sketch in Ramsey, II, 409.

[92] *Annales de Wintonia*, 51.

[93] Cont. Florence of Worcester, II, 133; *Annales de Wintonia*, 52; *Gesta Stephani*, 86; William of Malmesbury, *Historia Novella*, 59–60. The Continuator of Florence of Worcester doubtless exaggerates in stating that forty churches were destroyed in the conflagration. The chroniclers, as usual, deplored the deliberate burning of the town, attributing it to malicious and evil intent on the part of the bishop's garrison. They failed, almost invariably, to appreciate the military necessity which dictated such actions. Earl Robert, who is commended by William of Malmesbury for avoiding such measures, probably refrained not because of any humanitarian instincts but because no good purpose would be served by burning down the rest of the town—and the remaining houses were likely needed for quartering his troops.

[94] William of Malmesbury, *Historia Novella*, 58, 60; Henry of Huntingdon, 275; *Gesta Stephani*, 85.

[95] Henry of Huntingdon, 275; *Gesta Stephani*, 83; Ordericus Vitalis, V, 130.

[96] John of Hexham, 310.

[97] William of Malmesbury, *Historia Novella*, 59,67; Cont. Florence of Worcester, II, 134. Ramsey mistakenly identified Earl Gilbert as the earl of Pembroke. *Foundations of England*, II, 408.

[98] *Gesta Stephani*, 85,86; William of Malmesbury, *Historia Novella*, 59; Henry of Huntingdon, 275.

[99] Although the chroniclers and subsequent writers speak of a siege of the besiegers (Ramsey, *Foundations of England*, II, 410; Sidney Painter, "The Rout of Winchester," in *Feudalism and Liberty*, ed. Fred A. Cazel, Jr. [Baltimore, 1962], 157), it seems unlikely that a regular investment could have been undertaken. More probably the royalist army, encamped on the eastern side of the city, maintained a strict blockade of the roads over which any convoys might attempt to bring in supplies to the forces besieging the bishop's castle.

[100] That is, if there were actually two episcopal strongholds in the city. *Gesta Stephani*, 84.

[101] William of Malmesbury, *Historia Novella*, 59; *Gesta Stephani*, 86; John of Hexham, 310; Henry of Huntingdon, 275; Cont. Florence of Worcester, II, 134.

[102] *Anglo-Saxon Chronicle*, I, 384; John of Hexham, 310; *Gesta Stephani*, 86, 88.

[103] William of Malmesbury, *Historia Novella*, 59.

[104] *Gesta Stephani*, 87.

[105] *Ibid.* John of Hexham (310) reduces the size of the detachment to 200 men, and states that their mission was simply to bring in a convoy of provisions.

[106] *Gesta Stephani*, 87; William of Malmesbury, *Historia Novella*, 60; Cont. Florence of Worcester, II, 135; John of Hexham, 310. The account in the *Gesta*, with its vivid description of the confused fighting within the nunnery precincts, reads almost like the report of an eye witness. The late Sidney Painter endeavored to prove on the basis of an account in the early twelfth-century French biography *L'Histoire de Guillaume le Maréchal* (see "Rout of Winchester," *op. cit.*) that the Wherwell expedition was, in fact, an escort for the escape of the empress from Winchester. This incident is not mentioned by any of the contemporary chroniclers; the testimony of the *Histoire* has been refuted by Round (*Geoffrey de Mandeville*, 129–131), and Painter's theory was rejected by Poole (*Domesday Book to Magna Carta*, 144). Indeed, there are many reasons for distrusting the romantic tale in *L'Histoire de Guillaume le Maréchal*. Probably the most valid argument against sending the empress out of the city by this route is that of all the roads leading north or west from Winchester, this was the one most exposed to attack. If Earl Robert actually sent his sister out of Winchester via Wherwell, he must have been out of his mind. The merest glance at the map shows that a force retreating up the Winchester-Wherwell-Andover-Ludgershall road would be extremely vulnerable to attack from the queen's army, which was probably concentrated east of the town astride the London road.

Robert was a cautious, even a conservative general, and nothing in his record, past or future, would indicate that he would adopt so rash a scheme as this. The account in the *Gesta* is probably right. The expedition to Wherwell was intended only to open up a line of communication. Moreover, the successful establishment of a strong, fortified post at Wherwell *might* have enabled the main body to have gotten off from Winchester. To Painter's argument that no one in the queen's army would really have known the purpose of the Wherwell expedition, it may be replied that there was ample opportunity to find out why the detachment was at Wherwell, for a large portion of it was taken prisoner in the fight. A second reason for doubting the veracity of the story in the *Histoire* is its derivation. William Marshal left England for France *ca.* 1159, at the age of about thirteen. He does not seem to have returned to England until the death of his father, John the Marshal, in 1165. Therefore the stories of John's exploits in the Wherwell affair must have been told to the boy before he left for France. The *Histoire* was composed after William's death in 1219, although the author may have gathered some of his material much earlier. But the account of the Wherwell incident in the *Histoire* represents what the poet remembered of William Marshal's retelling of what his father had told him as much as half a century earlier. Sidney Painter, *William Marshal* (Baltimore, 1933), 17,25; Jessie Crosland, *William the Marshal* (London, 1962), 8. Soldiers' reports and tales are notoriously unreliable. See, for example, Joseph Bonaparte, *Mémoires et Correspondance*, ed. Baron A. du Carse, 2nd ed. (Paris, 1854), VI, 286; and Colonel W. A. Graham, *The Custer Myth* (Harrisburg, Pa., 1953), 267–278. John the Marshal's story had passed through the mouths of two old soldiers, and is not the sort of evidence that can be preferred to the contemporary accounts of the *Gesta Stephani* and John of Hexham.

[107] William of Malmesbury, *Historia Novella*, 60; *Gesta Stephani*, 87; John of Hexham, 310; Cont. Florence of Worcester, II, 134. The Continuator's account of a false truce proclaimed and then violated by Bishop Henry is mentioned by no other writer, and would seem to have been invented to put the bishop in a bad light. Round, *Geoffrey de Mandeville*, 132.

[108] William of Malmesbury, *Historia Novella*, 60, 61; *Gesta Stephani*, 88; Cont. Florence of Worcester, II, 134; Round, *Geoffrey de Mandeville*, 132, 133.

[109] Cont. Florence of Worcester, II, 134; *Gesta Stephani*, 89; William of Malmesbury, *Historia Novella*, 60–61.

[110] *Gesta Stephani*, 88.

[111] *Gesta Stephani*, 88–89; John of Hexham, 311; William of Malmesbury, *Historia Novella*, 60; Henry of Huntingdon, 275; Cont. Florence of Worcester, II, 135.

[112] William of Malmesbury, *Historia Novella*, 60, 67; Henry of Huntingdon, 275; *Anglo-Saxon Chronicle*, I, 384; *Annales de Wintonia*, 52; *Annales de Margan*, in Vol. I, *Annales Monastici*, ed. Henry Richards Luard (R.S.) (London, 1864), 14; *Annales de Waverleia*, 229; John of Hexham, 311; *Gesta*

Stephani, 88; Cont. Florence of Worcester, II, 134–135; William of Newburgh, I, 42.

[113] *Gesta Stephani*, 89; William of Newburgh, I, 42. The Londoners, being infantry, could not participate effectively in the running battle outside the city.

[114] Round, *Geoffrey de Mandeville*, 124–135. The campaign and rout of Winchester are either omitted or given merely a line or two by Oman and Delbrück, and by the later writers, Lot and Verbruggen. G. B. R. Barrett does not include it in his *Battles and Battlefields of England*, and Lt.-Col. Burne has not considered it in either *The Battlefields of England* or *More Battlefields of England*. Painter's article, "Rout of Winchester," is given over almost entirely to his attempt to prove the validity of the account of the fight at Wherwell in *L'Histoire de Guillaume le Maréchal*.

[115] If the Angevin army had been entirely mounted, and had moved by forced marches in an attempt to surprise Bishop Henry in Winchester, it might have departed Oxford as late as 29 July. The final episode of the campaign occurred on 14 September, forty-eight days later.

[116] Henry of Huntingdon, 275.

[117] William of Malmesbury, *Historia Novella*, 61–62; *Anglo-Saxon Chronicle*, I, 384; John of Hexham, 310; Henry of Huntingdon, 275; *Gesta Stephani*, 90; Cont. Florence of Worcester, II, 135–136.

[118] William of Malmesbury, *Historia Novella*, 62; Gervase of Canterbury, I, 123–124.

Chapter 6

[1] Symeon of Durham, I, 145–146; John of Hexham, 309.

[2] John of Hexham, 306–308. "Galcluit" has been tentatively identified with Gaultney Wood in Northamptonshire. *Early Yorkshire Charters*, IV, xxx.

[3] John of Hexham, 308.

[4] See charter in Round, *Geoffrey de Mandeville*, 142.

[5] Round, *Geoffrey de Mandeville*, 154; Poole, *Domesday Book to Magna Carta*, 155–156.

[6] Round, *Geoffrey de Mandeville*, 158, 159, 161–162.

[7] John of Hexham, 312; *Cal. Documents France*, 291.

[8] The king did not recover until Pentecost (7 June), and his protracted illness presented a great opportunity to his enemies.

[9] *Gesta Stephani*, 91–92.

[10] William of Malmesbury, *Historia Novella*, 71.

[11] This interesting charter is printed in Round, *Geoffrey de Mandeville*, 166–171. Round assigns this date to the second charter of the empress to Geoffrey de Mandeville (*Ibid.*, 165). This view is challenged by Davis ("Geoffrey de Mandeville," 306) chiefly on the ground that two of the witnesses attested no charters in England after the summer of 1141. But in the spring of 1142 active negotiations were going on between the Angevin party

in England and the count of Anjou. It is certainly not impossible that Wido de Sable and Pagan de Clairvaux were in England for the council held at Devizes on 21 June.

[12] *Ibid.,* 178–183.

[13] *Ancient Charters,* 43.

[14] William of Malmesbury, *Historia Novella,* 71–72; Robert of Torigni, 143.

[15] Beeler, "English Medieval Generalship," 6–7.

[16] William of Malmesbury, *Historia Novella,* 73.

[17] *Gesta Stephani,* 92; Round, *Geoffrey de Mandeville,* 197.

[18] *Gesta Stephani,* 93–94; *Anglo-Saxon Chronicle,* I, 384; John of Hexham, 317; William of Malmesbury, *Historia Novella,* 74, 76; Henry of Huntingdon, 276; Gervase of Canterbury, I, 124; William of Newburgh, I, 43. William of Malmesbury maintains, reasonably enough, that the king had more than a thousand knights in his army before Oxford castle.

[19] William of Malmesbury, *Historia Novella,* 75–76; *Gesta Stephani,* 95; Gervase of Canterbury, I, 123–124.

[20] *Gesta Stephani,* 94.

[21] William of Malmesbury, *Historia Novella,* 74, 76.

[22] *Gesta Stephani,* 94–96; John of Hexham, 317; William of Malmesbury, *Historia Novella,* 76, 77; *Anglo-Saxon Chronicle,* I, Gervase of Canterbury, I, 124–125.

[23] *Gesta Stephani,* 96.

[24] John of Hexham, 311–312.

[25] G. H. White, "King Stephen's Earldoms," *Transactions of the Royal Historical Society,* 4th ser., XIII (1930), 74.

[26] John of Hexham, 314; Symeon of Durham, I, 150–151, 152, 154, 163.

[27] John of Hexham, 314; William of Newburgh, I, 47.

[28] Gervase of Canterbury, I, 125; Henry of Huntingdon, 276; William of Newburgh, I, 42–43; *Gesta Stephani,* 96.

[29] *Gesta Stephani,* 98; Round, *Geoffrey de Mandeville,* 407. Gervase of Canterbury, I, 125, on the other hand states that Salisbury was controlled by the royalists.

[30] Gervase of Canterbury, I, 125–126; *Gesta Stephani,* 96–97; Henry of Huntingdon, 276: William of Newburgh, I, 42. The extraordinary vagueness of the chroniclers about the action at Wilton discourages any attempt at reconstruction.

[31] William of Newburgh, I, 42; Henry of Huntingdon, 276; *Gesta Stephani,* 98–99; Gervase of Canterbury, I, 126.

[32] Recently R. H. C. Davis ("Geoffrey de Mandeville," 306; "What Happened in Stephen's Reign, 1135–1154," *History,* XLIX [1964], 1–2) has attempted to show that Stephen was unjustified in arresting Earl Geoffrey. Even assuming that Davis's redating of the charters to the earl is correct, Geoffrey still had a record of desertions which must have raised suspicions in the king's mind.

[33] William of Newburgh, I, 44–45; *Gesta Stephani*, 108; Henry of Huntingdon, 276.

[34] *Gesta Stephani*, 108; John Beeler, "XIIth Century Guerilla Campaign," *Military Review*, XLII (1962), 39–46; Beeler, "Medieval English Generalship," 8–9.

[35] *Liber Eliensis*, 328, 329; Round, *Geoffrey de Mandeville*, 209.

[36] *Gesta Stephani*, 109; John of Hexham, 314–315; William of Newburgh, I, 45–46; Henry of Huntingdon, 276–277; *Liber de Antiquis Legibus*, ed. Thomas Stapleton (London, 1846), f.35; *Monasticon*, IV, 142; *Chronicon Abbatiae Rameseiensis*, ed. W. Dunn Macray (R.S.) (London, 1886), 329; *Liber Eliensis*, 328.

[37] *Regesta*, II, 189.

[38] *Gesta Stephani*, 108; William of Newburgh, I, 43.

[39] *Gesta Stephani*, 108; Sanders, *English Baronies*, 71.

[40] *Regesta*, II, 241; Edward Miller, *The Abbey and Bishopric of Ely* (Cambridge, 1951), 160–166; *Liber Eliensis*, 328.

[41] *Gesta Stephani*, 108; Gervase of Canterbury, I, 129.

[42] *Chronicon Abbatiae Rameseiensis*, 329–330; *Liber Eliensis*, 328.

[43] Round, *Geoffrey de Mandeville*, 211.

[44] *Gesta Stephani*, 108–109; *Monasticon*, IV, 142.

[45] *Domesday Book*, I, 189a; Ordericus Vitalis, II, 185.

[46] *Gesta Stephani*, 108–109.

[47] This raises the question of whether the castle was actually garrisoned in 1144. As late as 1173 the structure would still seem to have been of earth and timber and in need of repair. *The Great Roll of the Pipe for the Nineteenth Year of the Reign of King Henry the Second, 1172–73* (London, 1895), 157. It is certainly possible that castle had decayed and was untenable in 1144. On the other hand, Lethbridge suggests that Cambridge, Thetford, and Huntingdon were recommissioned at this time. T. C. Lethbridge, "Excavations at Burwell Castle, Cambridgeshire," *Proceedings of the Cambridge Antiquarian Society for 1934–35*, XXXVI (1936), 125.

[48] *Gesta Stephani*, 109; *Monasticon*, IV, 142; Round, *Geoffrey de Mandeville*, 212–213.

[49] William of Newburgh, I, 45; *Gesta Stephani*, 109.

[50] *Gesta Stephani*, 109.

[51] *Ibid.*, 109–110; Lethbridge, "Excavations at Burwell Castle," 125–126; *VCH Huntingdon*, I, 292.

[52] *Gesta Stephani*, 109.

[53] *Liber Eliensis*, 328.

[54] *Anglo-Saxon Chronicle*, I, 382–383.

[55] Another version has it that he was wounded while leading an assault in person, but it seems most unlikely that so seasoned a warrior would go into combat bareheaded, even on a hot August day. *Chronicon Abbatiae Rameseiensis*, 331, 332; Gervase of Canterbury, I, 128; *Gesta Stephani*, 110; *Monasticon*, IV, 142; Henry of Huntingdon, 276. Lethbridge ("Excavations at

Burwell Castle"; notes that Burwell as well as Rampton was never completed. D. J. C. King interprets this to indicate that Geoffrey's assault was successful. Letter, King to author dated 8 October 1962. Although this possibility cannot be entirely ruled out, the absence of any reference to the capture of the castle argues against it. The reports of Geoffrey's death were widespread, so that the capture of Burwell castle by the insurgents would hardly have gone unnoticed. It is just as probable that the unfinished castle of Burwell was pulled down during the general destruction of unlicensed or unnecessary castles at the end of Stephen's reign and the beginning of that of Henry II.

[56] Matthew Paris, *Historia Anglorum,* ed. Sir Frederick Madden (R.S.) (London, 1866–1869), II, 177; Round, *Geoffrey de Mandeville,* 221–222. King suggests, plausibly enough, that "Geoffrey's wound . . . was nothing much originally, but gangrened—a risk of war at all times, even in the antibiotic age, as well as in the days of the tough and resistant mediaeval body." Letter to author, 8 October 1962.

[57] Gervase of Canterbury, I, 129.

[58] *Gesta Stephani,* 98.

[59] *Ancient Charters,* 45–48; Round, *Geoffrey de Mandeville,* 233–234.

[60] Henry of Huntingdon, 277; William of Newburgh, I, 47–48.

[61] John of Hexham, 316; Symeon of Durham, I, 155, 157–160, 165.

[62] *Ancient Charters,* 48; *Gesta Stephani,* 113. An interesting sidelight on the period is thrown by the charter of the empress in which the borough and town of Malmesbury were granted to Humphrey de Bohun. Since Stephen's garrison occupied the castle at the time, Humphrey could scarcely have profited from the generosity of the empress unless he had been able to eject the king's troops.

[63] *Gesta Stephani,* 113–115.

[64] *Ibid.,* 116–117, 119. William had relinquished his command to go on crusade, and died in the Holy Land; Philip of Gloucester also grew tired of warfare and made the pilgrimage to Jerusalem. *Ibid.,* 118,126–127.

[65] *Gesta Stephani,* 119–121; Henry of Huntingdon, 278; William of Newburgh, I, 48–49.

[66] *Gesta Stephani,* 121–122. This is the first notice that Bedford was in the possession of the Angevin party.

[67] Henry of Huntingdon, 279; *Gesta Stephani,* 122; Gervase of Canterbury, I, 129–130; William of Newburgh, I, 49.

[68] *Gesta Stephani,* 122,128–130; John of Hexham, 324–325.

[69] John of Hexham, 325; William of Newburgh, I, 49; *Anglo-Saxon Chronicle,* I, 384; Henry of Huntingdon, 279; *Gesta Stephani,* 130–131. R. H. C. Davis cites the arrest of Earl Ranulf as another example of the king's shifty ways; but it is hard to believe that the earl, whose proffer of assistance was viewed askance by both sides during the Winchester campaign of 1141, was a model of probity. The indictment in the *Gesta* seems sufficient warrant for the earl's arrest. Davis, "What Happened in Stephen's Reign," 2–3.

[70] John of Hexham, 324; Henry of Huntingdon, 279; William of Newburgh, I, 49; *Gesta Stephani*, 132.

[71] *Gesta Stephani*, 133–135; *Ancient Charters*, 51. Earl Gilbert's three castles are not named, but Leeds and Tonbridge were probably two of them. Ramsey, *Foundations of England*, II, 429.

[72] *Gesta Stephani*, 135–138; *Monasticon*, I, 760; William of Newburgh, I, 70, 88; Gervase of Canterbury, I, 140–141; Poole, *Domesday Book to Magna Carta*, 148.

[73] *Gesta Stephani*, 139; *Annales de Margan*, 14.

[74] *Charters and Documents Illustrating the History of the Cathedral, City, and Diocese of Salisbury in the Twelfth and Thirteenth Centuries*, ed. W. H. Rich Jones and W. Dunn Macray (R.S.) (London, 1887), 32–33.

[75] Gervase of Canterbury, I, 133; *Anglo-Saxon Chronicle*, I, 384.

[76] Poole, *Domesday Book to Magna Carta*, 149.

[77] *Gesta Stephani*, 141. This castle had been built in 1138 by Bishop Henry. *Annales de Wintonia*, 51.

[78] *Gesta Stephani*, 141–142; John of Hexham, 322.

[79] With the recovery of the missing conclusion of the *Gesta Stephani*, every previous account of the final years of Stephen's reign became obsolete. The new material provided by this fortunate discovery makes it possible now to reconstruct with far greater accuracy the military history of the period from 1148 to the conclusion of Duke Henry's successful campaign in 1153.

[80] *Gesta Stephani*, XXII, 142; Gervase of Canterbury, I, 141; Robert of Torigni, 159; William of Newburgh, I, 70.

[81] *Gesta Stephani*, 142–143; Henry of Huntingdon, 282; John of Hexham, 324.

[82] *Ibid.*

[83] *Gesta Stephani*, 143–144. These events of 1149, and those following, are known for the first time from the recovered portions of the *Gesta*.

[84] *Ibid.*, 144,145. A better statement of the modern concept of total war would be difficult to find.

[85] *Gesta Stephani*, xxiii, 145.

[86] *Ibid.*, 146.

[87] *Ibid.*

[88] *Gesta Stephani*, 145–148.

[89] *Gesta Stephani*, 148; Gervase of Canterbury, I, 142.

[90] John of Hexham, 323.

[91] Henry of Huntingdon, 283.

[92] *Ibid.*, 282–283; *Gesta Stephani*, 151–152. The circumstantial detail provided in the *Gesta* points to the greater accuracy of this account.

[93] This document is quoted in full in Stenton, *First Century*, App. 48, 288.

[94] Snorri Sturluson, *Heimskringla*, tr. Samuel Lang, rev. Peter Foote (London, 1961). It seems strange that no English chronicler recorded a raid

of such proportions, for the kingdom was generally at peace, and there was not much civil strife to write about.

[95] *Gesta Stephani,* 150; Henry of Huntingdon, 284; Robert of Torigni, 173.

[96] Henry of Huntingdon, 284; Painter, *William Marshal,* 13–16. The account in the *Histoire de Guillaume le Maréchal* ought to be regarded with suspicion. So long a siege would hardly have escaped the notice of contemporary chroniclers.

[97] A fortified post had been established at Crowmarsh as early as 1145. Gervase of Canterbury, I, 130; *Gesta Stephani,* 150.

[98] *Gesta Stephani,* 150; Gervase of Canterbury, I, 154.

[99] Robert of Torigni, 174.

[100] *Gesta Stephani,* 150–151.

[101] *Gesta Stephani,* 151–152.

[102] William of Newburgh, I, 88; Robert of Torigni, 171; *Anglo-Saxon Chronicle,* I, 384–385.

[103] Gervase of Canterbury, I, 151; Robert of Torigni, 171.

[104] William of Newburgh, I, 88.

[105] *Calendar of Documents France,* 464–465.

[106] The itinerary developed by Potter in his introduction to the new edition of the *Gesta Stephani* (xxiii-xxix) has been followed in the main. See also Poole, *Domesday Book to Magna Carta,* 163–166.

[107] *Gesta Stephani,* xxvi.

[108] *Gesta Stephani,* 152–154; Henry of Huntingdon, 286.

[109] *Gesta Stephani,* 154; Henry of Huntingdon, 286; William of Newburgh, I, 89.

[110] Gervase of Canterbury, I, 152–153; Henry of Huntingdon, 287; *Gesta Stephani,* 154.

[111] *Gesta Stephani,* 154.

[112] *Ibid.,* xxvii. Potter suggests, on the basis of two charters in favor of the abbey of Evesham, neither having any indication of date or place issued, that Henry's line of march from Malmesbury to Gloucester took him through Evesham. But it is so far out of the way that such a route seems most unlikely.

[113] Robert of Torigni, 172; *Gesta Stephani,* 155.

[114] *Gesta Stephani,* xxvi, xxvii, 155.

[115] *Ibid.,* xxvii-xxviii,156.

[116] *Registrum Antiquissimum of Lincoln Cathedral,* I, 97–98; Round, *Geoffrey de Mandeville,* 418–419.

[117] *Gesta Stephani,* 156–157; Robert of Torigni, 172–173.

[118] Henry of Huntingdon, 287–288.

[119] *Gesta Stephani,* 157–158; Robert of Torigni, 174; Henry of Huntingdon, 288; *Anglo-Saxon Chronicle,* I, 384–385.

[120] Henry of Huntingdon, 288; William of Newburgh, I, 89; *Gesta Stephani,*

158. The author of the *Gesta* says that Eustace, disgruntled by the peaceful settlement at Wallingford, left his father, and died of grief within a few days. That this is erroneous is proved by the fact that Eustace witnessed his father's charter to Fountains Abbey at Ipswich. *Early Yorkshire Charters*, v, 348.

[121] Robert of Torigni, 176; Gervase of Canterbury, I, 155.

[122] Henry of Huntingdon, 288.

[123] *Gesta Stephani*, 155–156; William of Newburgh, I, 89; Henry of Huntingdon, 288; Robert of Torigni, 174. The *Gesta* mistakenly places this operation before the conclusion of the truce at Wallingford.

[124] A charter dated 31 August 1153 is given "in obsidione Stanfordiae." *Registrum Antiquissimum of Lincoln Cathedral*, I, 97. Henry of Huntingdon, 288; Robert of Torigni, 174; William of Newburgh, I, 89; *Gesta Stephani*, 156.

[125] William of Newburgh, I, 89–90; Henry of Huntingdon, 284.

[126] Poole, *Domesday Book to Magna Carta*, 164–165; Henry of Huntingdon, 289; Robert of Torigni, 177; *Early Yorkshire Charters*, VIII, 15–17; *Feodera*, I, I, 18; *Anglo-Saxon Chronicle*, I, 385.

[127] Robert of Torigni (177) gives the unlikely figure of 375 such castles, and Sidney Painter estimated the number in 1150 at some 1,200, a total which seems unjustifiably high. *A History of the Middle Ages, 284–1500* (New York, 1953), 179.

[128] Poole, *Domesday Book to Magna Carta*, 165–166; Henry of Huntingdon, 290.

[129] R. Allen Brown, H. M. Colvin, and A. J. Taylor, *The History of the King's Works: The Middle Ages* (London, 1963), I, 41.

[130] Oman, *Art of War*, I, 468.

[131] Stenton, *First Century*, 223.

[132] *Ibid.*, 202–205.

Chapter 7

[1] Gervase of Canterbury, I, 159.

[2] For details of Henry's early acts as king, see Poole, *Domesday Book to Magna Carta*, 321–322; J. H. Ramsey, *The Angevin Empire* (London, 1903), 4–6; Norgate, *Angevin Kings*, I, 428–430.

[3] William of Newburgh, I, 101–102; Gervase of Canterbury, I, 161; Robert of Torigni, 183,186; *Annales de Wintonia*, 55; *The Pipe Rolls of 2-3-4 Henry II*, ed. Joseph Hunter, (reprint of 1844 ed., London, 1930), 54,65, 101,102; *Annales Prioratus de Dunstaplia*, in Vol. III, *Annales Monastici*, ed. Henry Richards Luard (R.S.) (London, 1866), 17; *Annales Prioratus Wigornia*, in Vol. IV, *Annales Monastici*, ed. Henry Richards Luard (R.S.) (London, 1869), 380; *Radulfi de Diceto Decani Londoniensis Opera*, ed. William Stubbs (R.S.) (London, 1876), I, 301.

[4] Ramsey, *Angevin Empire,* 5; Norgate, *Angevin Kings,* I, 429; William of Newburgh, I, 103. Ramsey put the king's arrival in York at the beginning of February.

[5] Gervase of Canterbury, I, 161; Robert of Torigni, 183; Ralph Diceto, I, 301.

[6] Ramsey, *Angevin Empire,* 5; Norgate, *Angevin Kings,* I, 429.

[7] Gervase of Canterbury, I, 161; William of Newburgh, I, 105; Robert of Torigni, 184; *Chronicon Monasterii de Bello,* 75.

[8] Gervase of Canterbury, I, 162; Ramsey, *Angevin Empire,* 5.

[9] Robert of Torigni, 184; Gervase of Canterbury, I, 162.

[10] Gervase of Canterbury, I, 162; Robert of Torigni, 184; *Chronicon Monasterii de Bello,* 75. A charter of Henry to the monks of Fountains Abbey, given "in obsidione" at Bridgnorth, is witnessed by Archbishop Theobald, Archbishop Roger, Thomas the Chancellor, Earl Reginald of Cornwall, Earl Robert of Leicester, Earl Patrick of Salisbury, Eustace fitz John, and the constables, Henry of Essex and Richard de Humet. *Early Yorkshire Charters,* I, 73–74.

[11] Ramsey, *Angevin Empire,* 5. Farrer dates the charter cited above as May 1155.

[12] Gervase of Canterbury, I, 162; Robert of Torigni, 184.

[13] *Chronicon Monasterii de Bello,* 75. It was probably during the siege that the king had arrow shafts and engines sent to Bridgnorth. "Pipe Roll of 1 Henry II," in *The Red Book of the Exchequer,* ed. Hubert Hall (London, 1896), II, 658.

[14] Ramsey's account (*Angevin Empire,* 5) of the campaign is somewhat confused. All the chroniclers infer that Bridgnorth, where Hugh himself commanded, was the last rebel stronghold to fall. Robert of Torigni, 185; Gervase of Canterbury, I, 162; William of Newburgh, I, 105; *Chronicon Monasterii de Bello,* 75.

[15] Norgate, *Angevin Kings,* I, 430.

[16] Robert of Torigni, 192–193; Ramsey, *Angevin Empire,* 12; Norgate, *Angevin Kings,* I, 430.

[17] Robert of Torigni, 192; William of Newburgh, I, 105; Ralph Diceto, I, 302; *Chronicle of Holyrood,* 131.

[18] Poole, *Domesday Book to Magna Carta,* 154–157; *Herefordshire Domesday, circa 1160–1170,* ed. V. H. Galbraith and James Tate (London, 1950), xiv.

[19] Since the machinery of the Exchequer is known to have been functioning so soon after Henry's accession, it must have been maintained under Stephen, the records having been lost or destroyed. It would have been impossible to reinstitute this complex system in so short a time.

[20] *Pipe Roll 31 Henry I,* 137–138.

[21] *Pipe Roll 2–3–4 Henry II,* 52, 75, 107.

[22] *Ibid.,* 126, 155, 177.

[23] For 1155/1156 the only castles mentioned in the Pipe Roll were

Berkhamstead, Salisbury, Shrewsbury, Southampton, Winchester, and Wolvesey; for 1156/1157, Canterbury, Hereford, Norwich, Salisbury, Southampton, Stratton, Winchester, and Windsor. But in 1157–1158 the list includes Berkhamstead, Canterbury, Framlingham, Hereford, Norwich, Saffron Walden, Southampton, Stratton, Wark, Winchester, Windsor, and Worcester. In 1154 there were at least 245 baronial castles, as compared to 49 royal ones, according to R. A. Brown, "A List of the Castles," 1154–1216," *English Historical Review*, LXXIV (1959), 249. This list includes 327 royal and baronial fortresses in existence between these two dates.

[24] *Pipe Roll 2–3–4 Henry II*, 132.

[25] *Pipe Roll 5 Henry II* (London, 1884), 9.

[26] *Ibid.*, 13, 14.

[27] *Ibid.*, 29, 30, 31.

[28] *Ibid.*, 21, 53.

[29] *Pipe Roll 6 Henry II* (London, 1884), 26.

[30] *Ibid.*, 2.

[31] *Ibid.*, 54.

[32] *Ibid.*, 14, 56, 57.

[33] Armitage, *Early Norman Castles*, 367; *Pipe Roll 6 Henry II*, 7.

[34] *Pipe Roll 6 Henry II*, 12.

[35] *Pipe Roll 6 Henry II*, 7; *Pipe Roll 17 Henry II* (London, 1893), 112.

[36] *Pipe Roll 13 Henry II* (London, 1889), 77; *Pipe Roll 14 Henry II* (London, 1890), 117; *Pipe Roll 15 Henry II* (London, 1890), 143; *Pipe Roll 16 Henry II* (London, 1892), 59; *Pipe Roll 18 Henry II* (London, 1894), 3.

[37] *Pipe Roll 6 Henry II*, 27.

[38] *Pipe Roll 7 Henry II* (London, 1885), 39, 40; *Pipe Roll 8 Henry II* (London, 1885), 16; *Pipe Roll 9 Henry II* (London, 1886), 4; *Pipe Roll 10 Henry II* (London, 1886), 9; *Pipe Roll 11 Henry II* (London, 1887), 91; *Pipe Roll 13 Henry II*, 72; *Pipe Roll 14 Henry II*, 124; *Pipe Roll 15 Henry II*, 107; *Pipe Roll 17 Henry II*, 33.

[39] *Pipe Roll 11 Henry II*, 5.

[40] *Pipe Roll 12 Henry II* (London, 1888), 17, 35.

[41] Arundel, Canterbury, Carlisle, Colchester, Dover, Exeter, London, Norwich, Peak, Pevensey, Richmond, Rochester, Scarborough and Southampton.

[42] *Pipe Roll 15 Henry II*, 113.

[43] *Pipe Roll 17 Henry II*, 84.

[44] *Pipe Roll 18 Henry II*, 5.

[45] Bridgnorth, Bowes, Chilham, Newcastle-upon-Tyne, Nottingham, Orford, Scarborough, Wark, Winchester, and Windsor.

[46] *Pipe Roll 2–3–4 Henry II*, 177; *Pipe Roll 5 Henry II*, 13, 14; *Pipe Roll 6 Henry II*, 56, 57; *Pipe Roll 7 Henry II*, 23–25.

[47] John of Hexham, 315; William of Newburgh, I, 43.

[48] *Pipe Roll 5 Henry II*, 29, 30, 31; *Pipe Roll 6 Henry II*, 14; *Pipe Roll 7*

Henry II, 36; *Pipe Roll 8 Henry II*, 50; *Pipe Roll 9 Henry II*, 58; *Pipe Roll 10 Henry II*, 11, 12; *Pipe Roll 14 Henry II*, 79; *Pipe Roll 15 Henry II*, 31.

[49] *Pipe Roll 17 Henry II*, 63; *Pipe Roll 18 Henry II*, 55. In these two years £345 was spent on the keep at Bowes. *Pipe Roll 14 Henry II*, 169, 170, 173; *Pipe Roll 18 Henry II*, 66. Work at Newcastle amounted to £293 19s.8d.

[50] *Pipe Roll 14 Henry II*, 93, 94–95; *Pipe Roll 15 Henry II*, 107, 108, 110; *Pipe Roll 16 Henry II*, 132; *Pipe Roll 17 Henry II*, 32; *Pipe Roll 18 Henry II*, 110. In all £205 9s.2d. were spent on the castle at Bridgnorth.

[51] *Pipe Roll 17 Henry II*, 137; *Pipe Roll 18 Henry II*, 138.

[52] *Pipe Roll 17 Henry II*, 135. £10 of the revenue of the bishopric of Chichester, then in the king's hands, was spent on repairs for the castle at Arundel.

[53] *Pipe Roll 12 Henry II*, 130; *Pipe Roll 14 Henry II*, 188; *Pipe Roll 15 Henry II*, 150; *Pipe Roll 16 Henry II*, 25, 67, 70, 72, 74, 119, 125, 162; *Pipe Roll 17 Henry II*, 34, 40–41, 55, 126; *Pipe Roll 18 Henry II*, 16, 78, 84. The total amount for the work at Windsor was £241 12s.5d.

[54] *Pipe Roll 17 Henry II*, 50–51, 52; *Pipe Roll 18 Henry II*, 7. Work at Nottingham amounted to £675 12s.10d.

[55] *Pipe Roll 12 Henry II*, 17, 35; *Pipe Roll 13 Henry II*, 18, 33, 34, 35; *Pipe Roll 14 Henry II*, 15, 16; *Pipe Roll 15 Henry II*, 31, 94, 95; *Pipe Roll 16 Henry II*, 2–3; *Pipe Roll 17 Henry II*, 2; *Pipe Roll 18 Henry II*, 24.

[56] From 1167 to 1170, £132 3s.6d. were spent on Dover. *Pipe Roll 14 Henry II*, 209; *Pipe Roll 15 Henry II*, 161; *Pipe Roll 16 Henry II*, 156. In 1169/1170 and 1171/1172, £101 5s.2d. were charged to work at Exeter. *Pipe Roll 16 Henry II*, 98, 100; *Pipe Roll 18 Henry II*, 100. £110 was spent on the Tower of London in the thriteenth, fifteenth, and eighteenth years of the reign. *Pipe Roll 13 Henry II*, 1; *Pipe Roll 15 Henry II*, 129; *Pipe Roll 18 Henry II*, 141. Finally, £51 11s.3d. was spent at Richmond in 1171–1172. *Pipe Roll 18 Henry II*, 5.

[57] Bamborough, Berkhamstead, Caerleon, Ellesmere, Gloucester, Hastings, Hertford, Lydbury, Newark, Salisbury, Shrawardine, Shrewsbury, Stratton, and Whitchurch.

[58] See the accounts in Poole, *Domesday Book to Magna Carta*, 332–334; L. F. Salzman, *Henry II* (London, 1917), 125–129; John T. Appleby, *Henry II, the Vanquished King* (London, 1962), 194–195: Richard Barber, *Henry Plantagenet* (London, 1964), 160–170.

[59] *Gesta Regis Henrici Secundi Benedicti Abbatis,* ed. William Stubbs (R.S.) (London 1867), I, 45.

[60] *Ibid.; Chronica Magistri Rogeri de Houedene,* ed. William Stubbs (R.S.) (London, 1869), II, 47.

[61] *Gesta Regis*, I, 45, 48; *Ralph Diceto*, I, 371; Gervase of Canterbury, I, 243.

[62] *Gesta Regis*, I, 48.

[63] *Pipe Roll 21 Henry II* (London, 1897), 209, 212.

[64] *The Metrical Chronical of Jordan Fantosme,* in Vol. III. *Chronicles of the*

Reigns of Stephen, Henry II, and Richard I, ed. Richard Howlett (R.S.) (London, 1886), 338–339.

[65] *Gesta Regis,* I, 47.

[66] *Pipe Roll 19 Henry II* (London, 1895), 70, 117.

[67] *Ibid.,* 32–33, 113, 178, 178–179.

[68] *Ibid.,* 157, 167, 168.

[69] *Pipe Roll 19 Henry II,* 39.

[70] *Ibid.,* 32–33; *Pipe Roll 20 Henry II* (London, 1896), 54–55.

[71] *Pipe Roll 19 Henry II,* 117, 132, 162.

[72] *Ibid.,* 2, 23.

[73] *Ibid.,* 33.

[74] Ralph Diceto, I, 376; *Gesta Regis,* I, 58; William of Newburgh, I, 177.

[75] *Pipe Roll 19 Henry II,* 107–108, 156, 163, 173, 178.

[76] *Chronicle of Holyrood,* 153; *Chronicle of Melrose,* 40; Jordan Fantosme, 242–244, 258.

[77] Ralph Diceto, I, 376.

[78] Jordan Fantosme, 244–248; *Chronicle of Melrose,* 40.

[79] Ralph Diceto, I, 376; Jordan Fantosme, 248–252.

[80] Jordan Fantosme, 252–262; *Chronicle of Holyrood,* 153; *Chronicle of Melrose,* 40.

[81] William of Newburgh I, 177–178; *Gesta Regis,* I, 61; Roger of Hoveden, II, 54; Jordan Fantosme, 264–274; Ralph Diceto, I, 376; *Pipe Roll 19 Henry II,* 113.

[82] Roger of Hoveden, II, 54; Ralph Diceto, I, 376; Gervase of Canterbury, I, 246; Jordan Fantosme, 270; Cont. Florence of Worcester, II, 153. The Continuator gives the number as 3,000—a figure that may be inflated but is certainly not impossible, considering the magnitude of the revolt.

[83] Cont. Florence of Worcester, II, 153; *Gesta Regis,* I, 60; Roger of Hoveden, II, 54; Ralph Diceto, I, 377; Gervase of Canterbury, I, 246.

[84] The statement of Ralph Diceto (I, 377) that enmity between Earl Hugh and the countess of Leicester compelled this march should be viewed with suspicion. No explanation other than military necessity is required.

[85] Margary (*Roman Roads in Britain,* I, 231; see map at the end of volume) suggests that St. Edmundsbury may have been connected with the Icknield Way by a branch road.

[86] *Gesta Regis,* I, 62; Ralph Diceto, I, 377; Cont. Florence of Worcester, II, 153. Drummond (*Studien zur Kriegsgeschichte,* 71) comments: "3,000 nur weniger unmöglich als 10,000 ist." He gives no reasons for this conclusion.

[87] William of Newburgh, I, 178; Ralph Diceto, I, 376.

[88] *Gesta Regis,* I, 61; Roger of Hoveden, II, 55. Oman (*Art of War,* I, 401) dismisses the comital contribution as "a few loyalist knights." As a matter of fact, none of the current reconstructions is very satisfactory, mainly because the chroniclers failed to record the campaign in any detail. Probably the best of the lot is to be found in *Memorials of St. Edmund's Abbey,* ed. Thomas Arnold (R.S.) (London, 1890–1896), I, lviii-lix. Ramsey (*Angevin Empire,*

173–174) dismissed the entire action in four sentences. Miss Norgate's account (*Angevin Kings,* II, 149–151) does not consider all of the known factors. It might be noted in passing that there had never been a castle at St. Edmundsbury.

[89] Jordan Fantosme, 294.

[90] Oman, *Art of War,* I, 401; *Memorials of St. Edmund's Abbey,* I, lvii.

[91] Matthew Paris, *Historia Anglorum,* I, 381; Poole, *Domesday Book to Magna Carta,* 336; Verbruggen, *Het Leger en de Vloot van de Graven van Vlaanderen,* 123.

[92] *Gesta Regis,* I, 61.

[93] *Memorials of St. Edmund's Abbey,* I, lix.

[94] Jordan Fantosme, 294; Cont. Florence of Worcester, II, 153; *Gesta Regis,* I, 62; Roger of Hoveden, II, 55; William of Newburgh, I, 179; Ralph Diceto, I, 378.

[95] *Memorials of St. Edmund's Abbey,* I, 365. This is much more credible than the 10,000 casualties of the *Gesta Regis,* I, 62.

[96] Ralph Diceto, I, 378.

[97] Bolsover, Brackley, Bridgnorth, Colchester, Dover, Hastings, Kenilworth, Newcastle-under-Lyme, Newcastle-upon-Tyne, Northampton, Norwich, Nottingham, Orford, Peak, Prudhoe, Rockingham, Salisbury, Shrewsbury, Southampton, Stratton, Thetford, and Walton.

[98] *Pipe Roll 19 Henry II,* 33, 107–108, "In pay to ten knights for 139 days at the castle of Northampton, £69 10s." As will be seen, it was possible to hire knights at less than the shilling rate.

[99] Arundel, Berkhamstead, Bolsover, Canterbury, Carlisle, Chilham, Dover, Eye, Gloucester, Hastings, Hertford, Kenilworth, London, Newcastle-upon-Tyne, Norwich, Nottingham, Orford, Oxford, Peak, Salisbury, Walton, Warwick, Winchester, Windsor, and Worcester.

[100] Quartermaster stores laid in at London cost £151 16s.2d.; at Dover, £103 4s.11d.; at Berkhamstead, £86 13s.1d. This accounts for one-third of such expenses. *Pipe Roll 19, Henry II,* 21–22, 80–81, 87, 89, 183, 187–188.

[101] *Ibid.,* 13, 53, 56, 183.

[102] Bowes, £100; Childham, £152 5s.4d.; Dover, £162 4s.1d.; Newcastle-upon-Tyne, £167 14s.5d.; Nottingham, £140; Rochester, £111 16s.2d.; Windsor, £166 8s.6d. *Ibid.,* 2, 63, 68, 70, 80–81, 82–83, 84, 88–89, 91, 110, 173, 183.

[103] J. H. Round, Introduction to *Pipe Roll 19, Henry II,* xxiii.

[104] William of Newburgh, I, 181–192.

[105] William of Newburgh, I, 182; Jordan Fantosme, 316–325; *Gesta Regis,* I, 64–65; Roger of Hoveden, II, 60.

[106] Beeler, "Castles and Strategy," 599.

[107] William of Newburgh, I, 182; Jordan Fantosme, 324–331; *Gesta Regis,* I, 65; Roger of Hoveden, II, 60. Gospatric was later to repent of this hasty action, for after the war he was in mercy to the tune of 500 marks because "reddidit castellum regis de Appelbi regi Scottorum." Some twenty-five others

were also in mercy for sums ranging from 20*s.* to 40*m.* for the same offense. *Pipe Roll 22, Henry II* (London, 1904), 119–120.

[108] Jordan Fantosme, 244, 248, 300–311.

[109] For a rather sympathetic treatment of the role of Bishop Hugh in the rebellion, see G. V. Scammell, *Hugh du Puiset, Bishop of Durham* (Cambridge, 1956), 36–43.

[110] *Gesta Regis,* I, 65; Roger of Hoveden, II, 60; Jordan Fantosme, 252.

[111] Jordan Fantosme, 341–363; *Gesta Regis,* I, 65–66; William of Newburgh, I, 182–183; Gervase of Canterbury, I, 247; Roger of Hoveden, II, 60; *Chronicle of Melrose,* 41.

[112] Ralph Diceto, I, 384; *Gesta Regis,* I, 64, 68–69; Roger of Hoveden, II, 57–58.

[113] *Gesta Regis,* I, 67; Roger of Hoveden, II, 57, 63.

[114] *Pipe Role 20 Henry II,* 3, 29, 96, 118, 125, 138.

[115] *Gesta Regis,* I, 68, 69. Roger of Hoveden, II, 57–58. This is one of the numerous occasions in which a civic levy appears in the military history of twelfth century England.

[116] Roger of Hoveden, II, 58; William of Newburgh, I, 178; Ralph Diceto, I, 381; *Gesta Regis,* I, 68; Cont. Florence of Worcester, II, 153.

[117] *Gesta Regis,* I, 71; Roger of Hoveden, II, 59.

[118] Roger of Hoveden, II, 61–62; Gervase of Canterbury, I, 250; William of Newburgh, I, 187–190; Ralph Diceto, I, 383–384; Jordan Fantosme, 362; *Gesta Regis,* I, 72.

[119] William of Newburgh, I, 189–190; Roger of Hoveden, II, 63; Cont. Florence of Worcester, II, 154; *Gesta Regis,* I, 72; Jordan Fantosme, 368–370; Ralph Diceto, I, 383–384.

[120] William of Newburgh, I, 183–185; *Gesta Regis,* I, 66; Jordan Fantosme, 344–363; Cont. Florence of Worcester, II, 154; *Chronicle of Holyrood,* 155; *Chronicle of Melrose,* 41; Oman, *Art of War,* I, 400–401.

[121] Ralph Diceto, I, 384; William of Newburgh, I, 195; Roger of Hoveden, II, 64.

[122] *Pipe Roll 20 Henry II,* 38.

[123] Roger of Hoveden, II, 64; *Gesta Regis,* I, 73; Ralph Diceto, I, 384–385.

[124] Roger of Hoveden, II, 64–65; *Gesta Regis,* I, 73.

[125] Roger of Hoveden, II, 65; *Gesta Regis,* I, 73; Ralph Diceto, I, 384–385. As a reward for his services Rhys was given the castle of Emlyn in Cardiganshire. An English claimant, Odo fitz William, was granted an annuity of 100*s.* in the manor of Branton in return for surrendering his claim "to the land and castle of Emlyn which Rhys ap Gruffydd has." *Pipe Roll 20 Henry II,* 89.

[126] *Gesta Regis,* I, 73; Roger of Hoveden, II, 65; Ralph Diceto, I, 385; Jordan Fantosme, 372–375.

[127] *Gesta Regis,* I, 74; Ralph Diceto, I, 385; William of Newburgh, I, 195.

[128] *Pipe Roll 20 Henry II,* 112–113,116–117.

[129] *Ibid.,* 57, 139–140.

[130] *Pipe Roll 21 Henry II*, 131, 137, 183, 184; *Pipe Roll 22 Henry II* (London, 1904) , 16, 90, 136, 137, 140; *Pipe Roll 23 Henry II* (London, 1905) , 57, 82.

[131] Roger of Hoveden, II, 105. See also *Gesta Regis*, I, 124, 160; Ralph Diceto, I, 414. Brown ("A List of Castles," 253–254) doubts that Henry actually seized all of the approximately 250 baronial castles then in existence, but believes that he may have placed royal custodians in them. This action, "an essential part of confiscation but falling some way short of outright appropriation may well have been what happened."

[132] *Gesta Regis*, I, 93, 124, 161; Roger of Hoveden, II, 78.

[133] The Assize of Northampton was issued in January 1176. *Gesta Regis*, I, 110; Roger of Hoveden, II, 91.

[134] Assize of Northampton, Clause 11. This refers, of course, to castle-guard, and it is indeed unfortunate that the report which the justices were ordered to make has not survived.

[135] *Pipe Roll 21 Henry II*, 108; Cont. Florence of Worcester, II, 154.

[136] *Pipe Roll 20 Henry II*, 50. Henry is also known to have destroyed Allington (*Pipe Roll 21 Henry II*, 212) ; Bennington (*Pipe Roll 23 Henry II*, 144) ; Bungay (*Gesta Regis*, I, 127) ; Groby (*Gesta Regis*, I, 126; Ralph Diceto, I, 404; Roger of Hoveden, II, 101) ; Leicester (William of Newburgh, I, 197; Ralph Diceto, I, 404; Roger of Hoveden, II, 101; *Gesta Regis*, I, 126; *Pipe Roll 22 Henry II*, 179; *Pipe Roll 23 Henry II*, 29) ; Malzeard (Roger of Hoveden, II, 101; *Gesta Regis*, I, 126–127) ; Northallerton (Roger of Hoveden, II, 101) ; Saltwood (*Pipe Roll 21 Henry II*, 209) ; Thirsk (*Gesta Regis*, I, 126; Ralph Diceto, I, 404) ; Tutbury (Ralph Diceto, I, 404) ; Walton (*Ibid.; Pipe Roll 22 Henry II*, 60) ; Weston-Turville (*Pipe Roll 20 Henry II*, 82) . And as late as 1180 Adam Paynel was amerced 2 marks because the castle at Kinnardferry in the Isle of Axholme had not been properly demolished. *Early Yorkshire Charters*, VI, 264.

[137] This has been well summed up by Brown "A List of Castles," 256) , who believes there was "an Angevin castle-policy, consciously directed to the augmentation of royal power, chiefly at the expense of the baronage. That policy, moreover, has other complimentary features in the extensive fotification of royal castles undertaken by the kings of this period, and in the care with which they maintained an effective control over the castles in their hands."

[138] Stenton, *First Century*, 159.

[139] John E. Morris, *The Welsh Wars of Edward I* (Oxford, 1901) .

[140] Sidney Painter, *The Reign of King John* (Baltimore, 1949) .

[141] Stenton, *First Century*, 194.

[142] *Gesta Regis*, I, 134,160–161,178.

[143] R. Allen Brown, "Royal Castle-Building in England 1154–1216," *English Historical Review* LXX (1955) , 353–398.

[144] *Ibid.*, 379–383. *Pipe Roll 24 Henry II* (London, 1906) ; *Pipe Roll 25 Henry II* (London, 1907) ; *Pipe Roll 26 Henry II* (London, 1908) ; *Pipe Roll 27 Henry II* (London, 1909) ; *Pipe Roll 28 Henry II* (London, 1910) ; *Pipe*

Roll 29 Henry II (London, 1911); *Pipe Roll 30 Henry II* (London, 1912); *Pipe Roll 31 Henry II* (London, 1913); *Pipe Roll 32 Henry II* (London, 1914); *Pipe Role 33 Henry II* (London, 1915); *Pipe Roll 34 Henry II* (London, 1925); *Pipe Roll 1 Richard I, 1188–1189*, ed. Joseph Hunter (London, 1844). Since Henry II did not die until 6 July 1189, the greater part of the expenditure for the Exchequer year 1188/1189 must belong to his reign. The figures for nonmilitary construction do not include work lumped in with obviously military items, e.g. "work on the chamber and raising the wall and adding to the bailey enclosure, £140, by the king's writ," *P.R. 31 Henry II*, 110–111.

[145] These figures are derived entirely from the Pipe Rolls.

[146] *Pipe Roll 24 Henry II; Pipe Roll 34 Henry II.*

[147] Bridgnorth, Cardiff, Carmarthen, Chepstow, Eardisley, Emlyn, Ewias Lacy, Hereford, Llandaff (?), Llantilio (White Castle), Ludlow, Neath, Newcastle Bridgend, Pembroke, Skenfrith, Shrewsbury, Stratton, Swansea, Wilton (Here.), Woebley, and Worcester. *Pipe Roll 34 Henry II.*

[148] *Pipe Roll 33 Henry II.* The castles were Bridgnorth, Chepstow, Chester, Emlyn, Ewias Lacy, Hereford, Kington, Llantilio, Ludlow, Newcastle Bridgend, Pembroke, Skenfrith, Shrawardine, Shrewsbury, Stratton, Swansea, Woebley, and Worcester.

[149] See Chapters 8 and 9.

[150] Stenton, *First Century*, 194.

[151] A good description of the castle is to be found in C. A. Ralegh Radford, *Dover Castle* (Ministry of Works, London, 1956). The photograph on pp. 14–15 gives a spectacular view of Henry's masterpiece.

[152] Brown, "Royal Castle-Building," 390. The actual sum was £5,942. 5s. 111/2d.

[153] *Ibid.*, 357.

[154] Figures are from Brown, "Royal Castle-Building," 389–392. The castles on which these sums were spent are Arundel, Canterbury, Chilham, Dover, Exeter, Hastings, Rochester, Salisbury, Wallingford, Winchester, and Windsor. In addition, in the final twelve years of the reign, for example, small sums were spent on the upkeep of half a dozen other castles in the south—Carisbrooke, Dorchester, Launceston, Pevensey, Porchester, and Southampton. See *Pipe Roll 25 Henry II*, 109; *Pipe Roll 28 Henry II*, 82; *Pipe Roll 29 Henry II*, 72, 104; *Pipe Roll 30 Henry II*, 88; *Pipe Roll 31 Henry II*, 200; *Pipe Roll 32 Henry II*, 135; *Pipe Roll 33 Henry II*, 154, 158, 195; *Pipe Roll 34 Henry II*, 101, 148–149; *Pipe Roll 1 Richard I*, 111, 197.

[155] Brown, "Royal Castle-Building," 357, 376. Of the total expenditure of nearly £21,500, £11,372 3d. was spent on the major castles of these frontier areas, not counting lesser sums expended on other castles.

[156] *Ibid.*, 355–356. See Appendix C.

[157] . . . Cum ejusdem regni ossibus, id est munitionibus regiis." William of Newburgh, I, 331; Brown, "Royal Castle-Building," 361.

[158] *Gesta Regis*, I, 278–280; Roger of Hoveden, II, 260–263.

[159] *Gesta Regis,* 269–270.

[160] Titus Livius, *History of Rome,* ed. D. Spillan (London, 1889), I, 57–58. F. E. Adcock, *The Roman Art of War under the Republic* (Cambridge, Mass., 1940), 6, comments: "When the Roman Republic enters the light of history its army consists of legions of infantry levied from the citizens according to their ability to equip themselves, and a body of cavalry supplied by the best people which was tactically as much mounted infantry as cavalry in the strict sense . . ."

[161] *Gesta Regis,* I, 278; Roger of Hoveden, II, 263.

[162] *Gesta Regis,* I, 278–280; Roger of Hoveden, II, 260–263.

[163] *English Historical Documents,* II, 416; R. C. Smail, "Art of War," in *Medieval England,* ed. Austin Lane Poole, (Oxford, 1958), I, 139; Powicke, *Military Obligation,* 56.

[164] Paul Vinogradoff, *English Society in the Eleventh Century* (Oxford, 1908), 28–31. The conclusions of the earlier military historians have been buttressed by the recent studies of C. W. Hollister. See his "The Five-Hide Unit and the Old English Military Obligation," *Speculum,* XXXVI (1961), 64–65.

[165] Poole, *Domesday Book to Magna Carta,* 339, 369–370; Frank Barlow, *The Feudal Kingdom of England,* 1042–1216 (London, 1955), 321.

[166] Poole, *Domesday Book to Magna Carta,* 369–370.

[167] Arthur H. Noyes, *The Military Obligation in Mediaeval England* (Columbus, Ohio, 1930), 15.

[168] Smail, "Art of War," 137.

Chapter 8

[1] Herbert Murray Vaughan, "Wales," *Encyclopaedia Britannica,* 11th ed., XXVIII, 258.

[2] A. H. Williams, *An Introduction to the History of Wales* (Cardiff, 1949, I, 6; General Sir James Marshall-Cornwall, "The Military Geography of the Welsh Marches," *The Geographical Magazine,* XXX (1957), 1, Morris, *Welsh Wars of Edward I,* 8.

[3] Williams, *Introduction to the History of Wales,* I, 7; James F. Willard, "Inland Transportation in England during the Fourteenth Century," *Speculum,* I (1926), 374; Armitage, *Early Norman Castles,* 125; D. T. Williams, "Medieval Foreign Trade: Western Ports," in *An Historical Geography of England before* A.D. *1800,* ed. H. C. Darby (Cambridge, 1951), 289.

[4] Williams, *Introduction to the History of Wales,* I, 9; Marshall-Cornwall, "Military Geography," 1.

[5] Grace Simpson, *Britons and the Roman Army* (London, 1964), 5–6; Williams, *Introduction to the History of Wales,* I, 9.

[6] Margary, *Roman Roads in Britain,* II, 47–89.

[7] F. M. Stenton, "The Road System in Mediaeval England," *Economic History Review*, VII (1936) , 5, 9; Hewitt, *Black Prince's Expedition*, 17.

[8] Margary, *Roman Roads in Britain*, II, 79–82.

[9] E. Neaverson, *Medieval Castles in North Wales* (London, 1947) , 19. No road to Oswestry is known to Margary. See *Roman Roads in Britain*, II, 48.

[10] Margary, *Roman Roads in Britain*, II, 48; Stenton, "Road System in Medieval England," 9.

[11] Morris, *Welsh Wars of Edward I*, 10; Margary, *Roman Roads in Britain*, II, 48.

[12] Giraldus, *Itinerarium Kambriae*. The archbishop's itinerary was as follows: Radnor–Cruker Castle Hay–Llanddew–Brecknock–Abergavenny–Usk–Caerleon–Newport–Cardiff–Llandaff–Ewenny–Margam–Swansea–Kidwelly–Carmarthen–Haverfordwest–Camross–St. David's–St. Dogmael's–Cardigan–Cilgerran–Lampeter–Stratflur–Llandewi Brevi–Llanbadarn Fawr–Towyn–Llanvair–Nevyn–Carnarvon–Bangor–Rhuddlan–St. Asaph–Chester–Whitchurch–Oswestry–Shrewsbury–Wenlock–Bromfield–Ludlow–Leominster–Hereford.

[13] Vaughan, "Wales," 260.

[14] Giraldus Cambrensis, *Descriptio Kambriae*, in Vol. VI, *Giraldi Cambrensis Opera*, 200–201.

[15] *Ibid.*, 179–180; H. C. Darby, "The Economic Geography of England, A.D. 1000–1250," in Darby, *Historical Geography*, 204.

[16] Williams, *Introduction to the History of Wales*, I, 10; Morris, *Welsh Wars of Edward I*, 8–9; Poole, *Domesday Book to Magna Carta*, 284.

[17] Morris, *Welsh Wars of Edward I*, 8; Poole, *Domesday Book to Magna Carta*, 283–284.

[18] Morris, *Welsh Wars of Edward I*, 8.

[19] Poole, *Domesday Book to Magna Carta*, 284; Williams, *Introduction to the History of Wales*, I, 7.

[20] Poole, *Domesday Book to Magna Carta*, 284.

[21] *Ibid.;* Williams, *Introduction to the History of Wales*, I, 7.

[22] Morris, *Welsh Wars of Edward I*, 15.

[23] Giraldus, *Descriptio Kambriae*, 179.

[24] *Ibid.*, 177,180; Giraldus, *Itinerarium Kambriae*, 54. In the latter passage Giraldus cites a number of examples of the Gwentian prowess with the bow.

[25] Giraldus, *Descriptio Kambriae*, 209–210.

[26] *Ibid.*, 218. The most comprehensive listings of motte-and-bailey castles in Wales will be found in A. H. A. Hogg and D. J. C. King, "Early Castles in Wales and the Marches," *Archaeologia Cambrensis*, CXVII (1963) , 77–124. Other valuable lists are contained in the publications of The Royal Commission on Ancient and Historical Monuments in Wales and Monmouthshire. For titles, see bibliography, p. 464; also D. J. Cathcart King, "The Castles of Breconshire," *The Brecknock Society in Brycheiniog*, VII (1961) , 71–94; D. J. C. King, "The Castles of Cardiganshire," *Ceredigion*, 1956, 1–20.

[27] Giraldus, *Descriptio Kambriae*, 219.

[28] Giraldus, *Descriptio Kambriae*, 219–222.

[29] Gunther E. Rothenberg, *The Austrian Military Border in Croatia, 1522–1747* (Urbana, Ill., 1960), 27–39. This is not to assert that there was any "Welsh threat" in the twelfth century comparable to the Ottoman menace in the sixteenth; but the solution proposed by Giraldus was very similar to the practices adopted by the Austrians.

[30] *Anglo-Saxon Chronicle*, I, 315; Barlow, *Feudal Kingdom of England*, 61–62; Lloyd, *History of Wales*, II, 363.

[31] Symeon of Durham, II, 170; Florence of Worcester, I, 207; Barlow, *Feudal Kingdom of England*, 61; Lloyd, *History of Wales*, II, 363.

[32] *Anglo-Saxon Chronicle*, I, 316; Florence of Worcester, I, 207; Symeon of Durham, II, 168.

[33] Florence of Worcester, I, 213; *Anglo-Saxon Chronicle*, I, 324. These are the sole *contemporary* references to Englishmen fighting on horseback.

[34] *Anglo-Saxon Chronicle*, I, 324–326; Florence of Worcester, I, 213; *Annales Cambriae*, ed. John Williams ab Ithel (R.S.) (London, 1860), 25; *Brut y Tywysogion*, 42.

[35] *Anglo-Saxon Chronicle*, I, 326; Florence of Worcester, I, 213–214.

[36] Lloyd, *History of Wales*, II, 373.

[37] *Anglo-Saxon Chronicle*, I, 340; Florence of Worcester, II, 1–2.

[38] Lloyd, *History of Wales*, II, 374.

[39] Ordericus Vitalis, II, 193, 198–199; Florence of Worcester, II, 7.

[40] For example, Round assigns to the reign of William I the gift by Wihenoc and his nephew William of the land and church of Monmouth, and the tithes, near their castle of Monmouth, to St. Florent of Sanmur. *Calendar of Documents France*, 406–407.

[41] *Annales Cambriae*, 26; Lloyd, *History of Wales*, II, 375–376.

[42] Lloyd, *History of Wales*, II, 374.

[43] Ordericus Vitalis, II, 262–264; *Anglo-Saxon Chronicle*, I, 348–349; William of Malmesbury, *De Gestis Regum*, II, 314; *Regesta*, I, 20–21; Lanfranc, *Opera*, I, 64–66.

[44] Lloyd, *History of Wales*, II, 376.

[45] *Ibid.*, 381–382.

[46] Lloyd, *History of Wales*, II, 381–382.

[47] Lloyd, *History of Wales*, II, 383–385.

[48] *Annales Cambriae*, 26.

[49] Lloyd, *History of Wales*, II, 389,390. The establishment of the Normans at Montgomery provided what may be an example of a planned defensive system. D. J. C. King notes that a number of earthwork castles in the vicinity of Montgomery are of a similar type. These mottes are small but tall. He continues: "I am inclined to conclude that the Montgomery group shows the impress of a master plan—presumably that of Earl Roger himself . . . The Montgomery sites are tidily arranged, each by a hamlet or former hamlet, so their great numbers are not the result of shifting." Letter, to author, 4 July 1964.

[50] *Annales Cambriae,* 28; *Anglo-Saxon Chronicle,* I, 351; *Annales de Wintonia,* 32.

[51] Lloyd, *History of Wales,* II, 393–394.

[52] *Anglo-Saxon Chronicle,* I, 355.

[53] *Domesday Book,* I, 269a,1–2; Ordericus Vitalis, III, 283.

[54] *Domesday Book,* I, 269a,2; Lloyd, *History of Wales,* II, 387.

[55] *Domesday Book* I, 269a,2.

[56] Lloyd, *History of Wales,* II, 387–388.

[57] Stenton, *Anglo-Saxon England,* 607.

[58] *Domesday Book,* I, 253a1, 253b1, 254a1, 258b1.

[59] The building of Cardiff castle is ascribed to the year 1080 by the *Brut y Tywysogion,* 50, and the gift to Battle Abbey of "the church of St. John the Evangelist lying beyond the fortifications of his castle of Brecknock" by Bernard de Neuf-marché is referred to the reign of William I. *Chronicon Monasterii de Bello,* 34.

[60] *Domesday Book,* I, 162a1, 180a2, 180b2, 183a2, 183b1, 184a1, 185a2, 185b1, 186a1, 186b2.

[61] Lloyd, *History of Wales,* II, 395.

[62] *Herefordshire Domesday,* 101.

[63] Lloyd, *History of Wales,* II, 395–396.

[64] *Domesday Book,* I, 179a2; Lloyd, *History of Wales,* II, 392–393, 394; Poole, *Domesday Book to Magna Carta,* 287.

[65] Lloyd, *History of Wales,* II, 394.

[66] Armitage, *Early Norman Castles,* 94–95; Marshall-Cornwall, "Military Geography," 7–9.

[67] George Ormerod, *The History of the County Palatine and City of Chester,* rev. Thomas Helsby, (London, 1882) ; *Hist. Mon. Com. Herefordshire; VCH Hereford; VCH Shropshire.*

[68] *Hist. Mon. Com. Herefordshire,* I, 57, 152, 225, 245; II, 68, 170, 195; II, 9, 27, 29, 33, 45, 47, 49, 59, 192; *VCH Hereford,* I, 224–233, 236; Marshall-Cornwall, "Military Geography," 8.

[69] F. M. Stenton, in *Hist. Mon. Com., Herefordshire,* III, lxi.

[70] There seems to be no other explanation for the 74 castles in Shropshire and the 87 in Herefordshire. Cheshire and Gloucestershire, the other two border counties, have yet to be properly surveyed. See Appendix A.

[71] *Supra,* Chapter 3.

[72] Ordericus Vitalis, III, 270–271; William of Malmesbury, *De Gestis Regum,* II, 361; *Anglo-Saxon Chronicle,* I, 356.

[73] Ordericus Vitalis, III, 270.

[74] *Regesta,* I, 78.

[75] *Anglo-Saxon Chronicle,* I, 356–357; Florence of Worcester II, 189–191; Ordericus Vitalis, III, 270–271; William of Malmesbury, *De Gestis Regum,* II, 361; *Vita Wulfstani,* xxvii; Symeon of Durham, II, 215.

[76] Ordericus Vitalis, III, 280, 283–286, 288–289.

[77] Lloyd, *History of Wales,* II, 392.

[78] Symeon of Durham, II, 224; *Brut y Tywysogion*, 60.

[79] Lloyd, *History of Wales*, II, 392.

[80] *Ibid.*, 403.

[81] William of Malmesbury, *De Gestis Regum*, II, 376; *Annales de Margan*, 6; *Anglo-Saxon Chronicle*, I, 361.

[82] William of Malmesbury, *De Gestis Regum*, II, 376; Lloyd, *History of Wales*, II, 404.

[83] Lloyd, *History of Wales*, II, 398.

[84] *Annales Cambriae*, 29; Ordericus Vitalis, III, 43–44; Florence of Worcester, II, 31; Lloyd, *History of Wales*, II, 398. Lloyd hints at treachery, but both Ordericus and Florence specifically speak of a battle, whereas the Cambrian annals merely state that Rhys was killed by the French of Brecknock.

[85] Lloyd, *History of Wales*, II, 398–399; Ordericus Vitalis, III, 43–44.

[86] *Annales Cambriae*, 29; Lloyd, *History of Wales*, II, 400–401.

[87] Giraldus, *Itinerarium Kambriae*, 89–91.

[88] Lloyd, *History of Wales*, II, 401–402.

[89] *Ibid.*; Morris, *Welsh Wars of Edward I*, 10–11.

[90] Lloyd, *History of Wales*, II, 402–403.

[91] *Annales Cambriae*, 29–30; *Brut y Tywysogion*, 56; Florence of Worcester, II, 35.

[92] *Anglo-Saxon Chronicle*, I, 362; Symeon of Durham, II, 226; Florence of Worcester, II, 38–39.

[93] *Anglo-Saxon Chronicle*, I, 362; *Annales Cambriae*, 30; Symeon of Durham, II, 226; Florence of Worcester, II, 39.

[94] Lloyd, *History of Wales*, II, 405.

[95] *Anglo-Saxon Chronicle*, I, 362.

[96] William of Malmesbury, *De Gestis Regum*, II, 365.

[97] *Anglo-Saxon Chronicle*, I, 362; Symeon of Durham, II, 226; Florence of Worcester, II, 39; *Annales Cambriae*, 30.

[98] Symeon of Durham, II, 226; Florence of Worcester, II, 40; Ordericus Vitalis, III, 411; Sanders, *English Baronies*, 95.

[99] *Annales Cambriae*, 30; *Brut y Tywysogion*, 58; Lloyd, *History of Wales*, II, 406.

[100] *Annales Cambriae*, 30; *Anglo-Saxon Chronicle*, I, 363; Lloyd, *History of Wales*, II, 407.

[101] *Annales Cambriae*, 30; *Brut Y Tywysogion*, 58.

[102] Giradlus, *Itinerarium Kambriae*, 89–91. Giraldus was writing as a partisan; and old soldiers' stories must be discounted to a large extent. Nevertheless, what he wrote was accounted credible in the late twelfth century—that is, the stories of the conduct of the garrison of Pembroke in 1096 did not seem unbelievable in the 1180's. If Giraldus can be believed, Gerald of Windsor, the castellan of Pembroke, was an eleventh century *beau ideal*. When some knightly members of the garrison, despairing of success, tried to escape by sea, the attempt was thwarted by Gerald, the culprits were brought back, and their fiefs were bestowed on their squires. On another

occasion he had the last four flitches of bacon in the commissariat cut up and tossed into the Welsh camp to give the impression that the garrison was amply supplied with food. Again, he wrote to Arnulf de Montgomery, his feudal superior, a letter stating that Pembroke could hold out for four months without relief, and allowed it to fall into the hands of Bishop Wilfred of St. David's, who was at least sympathetic to the Welsh cause.

[103] Lloyd, *History of Wales*, II, 407.

[104] *Brut y Tywysogion*, 58, 60; *Annales Cambriae*, 30.

[105] *Anglo-Saxon Chronicle*, I, 363; *Annales Cambriae*, 30–31; Florence of Worcester, II, 40–41. Lloyd asserts that the castles built by order of Rufus "must have had some effect on the situation." *History of Wales*, II, 408. But from the Chronicler's statement it seems more likely that these castles were for defense of the border, rather than bases for offensive operations against the Welsh.

[106] Lloyd, *History of Wales*, II, 408.

[107] *Annales Cambriae*, 31; Lloyd, *History of Wales*, II, 409.

[108] William of Malmesbury, *De Gestis Regum*, II, 376; *Anglo-Saxon Chronicle*, I, 364; Ordericus Vitalis, IV, 30–32; *Annales de Margan*, 6; *Annales Cambriae*, 31; Florence of Worcester, II, 41–42.

[109] *Annales de Margan*, 6; *Annales Cambriae*, 31; William of Malmesbury, *De Gestis Regum*, II, 376; Florence of Worcester, II, 42. The assertion by William and Florence that the earls prevented Magnus from effecting a landing on the mainland does not seem to be very accurate.

[110] Lloyd, *History of Wales*, II, 410.

[111] *Annales Cambriae*, 31–32; Lloyd, *History of Wales*, II, 410–411.

[112] Ordericus Vitalis, IV, 32–33.

[113] Florence of Worcester, II, 49.

[114] Lloyd, *History of Wales*, II, 400.

[115] *Annales Cambriae*, 32–33.

[116] For the role of the Welsh in the revolt of 1102 see Ordericus Vitalis, IV, 173; William of Malmesbury, *De Gestis Regum*, II, 472; Florence of Worcester, II, 50; *Annales Cambriae*, 33; Lloyd, *History of Wales*, II, 412–413.

[117] Ordericus Vitalis, IV, 176–177; William of Malmesbury, *De Gestis Regum*, II, 472–473; *Brut y Tywysogion*, 66–72; *Annales Cambriae*, 33; Florence of Worcester, II, 50–51.

[118] Lloyd, *History of Wales*, II, 414.

[119] *Brut y Tywysogion*, 76; Lloyd, *History of Wales*, II, 415.

[120] *Annales Cambriae*, 33; *Brut y Tywysogion*, 76.

[121] William of Malmesbury, *De Gestis Regum*, II, 365–366; Florence of Worcester, II, 64; *Annales Cambriae*, 33–34.

[122] Lloyd, *History of Wales*, II, 425; William of Malmesbury, *De Gestis Regum*, II, 366.

[123] Lloyd, *History of Wales*, II, 411, 417–421.

[124] *Brut y Tywysogion*, 82, 84; *Annales Cambriae*, 35. There is some doubt

as to the identity of Cenarth Bychan. Armitage (*Early Norman Castles*, 278) seems to think that it was identical with Pembroke—clearly an impossibility, since the *Brut* records its foundation *sub anno* 1106 (1108). Lloyd tentatively identifies it with Cilgerran, or Emlyn on the banks of the Teifi. *History of Wales*, II, 418. Neither identification can be proven.

[125] *Annales Cambriae*, 35; Lloyd, *History of Wales*, II, 420–421, 426; Morris, *Welsh Wars of Edward I*, 12–13.

[126] Lloyd, *History of Wales*, II, 421.

[127] *Ibid.*, 416, 421, 462–463; Florence of Worcester, II, 67.

[128] From the charters and notifications emanating from Castle Holgate, and from the testators, it seems clear that the whole apparatus of government had been transferred to this Shropshire fortress. Among the witnesses to the king's acts were Ranulf the Chancellor, Gilbert d'Aquila, Hamo the Dapifer, William d'Albini, Pain Peverel, and William Peverel of Dover. *The Cartae Antiquae Rolls*, ed. Lionel Landon (London, 1939), 29, 30; *Regesta*, II, 115, 116.

[129] *Anglo-Saxon Chronicle*, I, 370; *Annales Wintonia*, 44; *Annales de Margan*, 9; *Annales Cambriae*, 35; *Brut y Tywysogion*, 114; William of Malmesbury, *De Gestis Regum*, II, 477–478; Lloyd, *History of Wales*, II, 463.

[130] Lloyd, *History of Wales*, II, 421, 463–464.

[131] *Anglo-Saxon Chronicle*, I, 370; *Annales Wintonia*, 44; *Annales Cambriae*, 35.

[132] *Annales Cambriae*, 36; *Brut y Tywysogion*, 122; Florence of Worcester, II, 68–69.

[133] *Brut y Tywysogion*, 122.

[134] Lloyd, *History of Wales*, II, 434. This sounds remarkably like castle-guard service.

[135] *Brut y Tywysogion*, 136–138.

[136] Lloyd, *History of Wales*, II, 434.

[137] *Brut y Tywysogion*, 130–134; *Annales Cambriae*, 36.

[138] *Brut y Tywysogion*, 136–138; *Annales Cambriae*, 36.

[139] Lloyd, *History of Wales*, II, 423.

[140] *Pipe Roll 31 Henry I*, 136.

[141] Lloyd, *History of Wales*, II, 423–425.

[142] *Brut y Tywysogion*, 104; Lloyd, *History of Wales*, II, 426.

[143] *Regesta*, II, 113.

[144] *Brut y Tywysogion*, 158; Lloyd, *History of Wales*, II, 427.

[145] J. G. Edwards, "The Normans and the Welsh March," *Proceedings of the British Academy*, XLII (1956), 167.

[146] *Pipe Roll 31 Henry I*, 89.

[147] *Brut y Tywysogion*, 122; *Monasticon*, III, 448.

[148] *Regesta*, II, 114; Lloyd, *History of Wales*, II, 429–430.

[149] Giraldus, *Itinerarium Kambriae*, 16.

[150] Lloyd, *History of Wales*, II, 436.

[151] Before his death *ca.* 1125 Brecon possessed a parish church outside the

walls of the castle which Bernard gave to Battle abbey. *Chronicon Monasterii de Bello*, 34; *Monasticon*, III, 244.

[152] Sir Charles Oman, *Castles* (London, 1926), 152, 172.

[153] *Regesta*, II, 162; Lloyd, *History of Wales*, II, 437–438.

[154] Lloyd, *History of Wales*, II, 439–442; *Monasticon*, V, 259.

[155] *Calendar of Documents, France*, 408, 413; *Regesta*, II, 62–63; Lloyd *History of Wales*, II, 442–443.

[156] Numerous examples could be cited: for example, a confirmation by Henry I of the grant by Robert fitz Hamon of the parish church of Cardiff and the chapel of the castle to Tewkesbury abbey (*Regesta*, II, 73); the grant of Hugh fitz William to the monks of St. Peter's abbey, Gloucester, of the church of St. David with the chapel of the Blessed Mary in his castle of Kilpeck (*Monasticon*, I, 548); confirmation by Henry I of the gift by Hamelin de Ballou to St. Vincent of Le Mans of the chapel of Abergavenny castle (*Regesta*, II, 62–63).

[157] Lloyd, *History of Wales*, II, 422, 464–465.

[158] Symeon of Durham, II, 263; *Anglo-Saxon Chronicle*, I, 373; Cont. Florence of Worcester, II, 76; *Annales Cambriae*, 37.

[159] Lloyd, *History of Wales*, II, 465–466.

[160] *Brut y Tywysogion*, 140.

[161] Lloyd, *History of Wales*, II, 467.

[162] *Ibid.*, 467–468.

Chapter 9

[1] Ordericus Vitalis, V, 43.

[2] This figure is suspiciously large, for it seems unlikely that Gower alone could have mustered 500 men, and certainly they were not all killed in battle. Cont. Florence of Worcester, II, 97; Poole, *Domesday Book to Magna Carta*, 290–291; Lloyd, *History of Wales*, II, 470.

[3] Lloyd, *History of Wales*, II, 470.

[4] *Annales Cambriae*, 40; *Gesta Stephani*, 10–11; Cont. Florence of Worcester, II, 97.

[5] *Brut y Tywysogion*, 158; *Annales Cambriae*, 40.

[6] Lloyd, *History of Wales*, II, 472. He went on to add that the mounted contingent consisted of "many hundreds of well-armed horsemen," a statement that is surely open to question.

[7] *Annales Cambriae*, 40.

[8] *Gesta Stephani*, 11: ". . . in tres se terribilis turmas ordinate et bellicose diviserunt . . . ex tribus partibus perlustrantes in fugam miserunt . . ." The *Gesta* also states that the contingents, horse and foot, that marched to the aid of Cardigan numbered 3,000, a not impossible figure.

[9] *Annales Cambriae*, 40; *Annales de Margan*, 13–14; Cont. Florence of Worcester, II, 97; *Gesta Stephani*, 11.

[10] *Gesta Stephani,* 11–12.

[11] *Ibid.,* 12–13; Lloyd, *History of Wales,* II, 474–475.

[12] *Gesta Stephani,* 13–14.

[13] *Annales de Margan,* 14; *Annales Cambriae,* 40.

[14] *Brut y Tywysogion,* 162; *Annales Cambriae,* 40–41.

[15] Lloyd, *History of Wales,* II, 476.

[16] *Annales Cambriae,* 41.

[17] John of Hexham, 287.

[18] Cont. Florence of Worcester, II, 98; Lloyd, *History of Wales,* II, 476–477.

[19] *Brut y Tywysogion,* 166; *Monasticon,* VI, 349.

[20] Ordericus Vitalis, V, 110; Lloyd, *History of Wales,* II, 477–478.

[21] *Supra,* Chapter 5.

[22] Lloyd, *History of Wales,* II, 478. At the beginning of the revolt against King Stephen, the marcher strongholds of Shrewsbury, Ludlow, Hereford, Overton, Woebley, Abergavenny, and Usk were in the hands of his enemies. *Gesta Stephani,* 69; William of Malmesbury, *Historia Novella,* 36; *Monasticon,* III, 623; John of Hexham, 302; *Ancient Charters,* 43, 48; Ordericus Vitalis, V, 110–113; Cont. Florence of Worcester, II, 106–107, 110, 115–116; Henry of Huntingdon, 261, 265.

[23] *Brut y Tywysogion,* 166; *Annales Cambriae,* 43; *Monasticon,* VI, 349.

[24] *Brut y Tywysogion,* 172; Lloyd, *History of Wales,* II, 479–480.

[25] This Owain ap Gruffydd must be distinguished from another contemporary prince of the same name—Owain ap Gruffydd ap Maredudd. One is usually known as Owain Gwynedd, the other as Owain Cyfeiliog. Lloyd, *History of Wales,* II, 487.

[26] Poole, *Domesday Book to Magna Carta,* 291.

[27] *Supra,* Chapter 5.

[28] Lloyd, *History of Wales,* II, 489–492; *Brut y Tywysogion,* 164, 174; *Annales Cambriae,* 44.

[29] Lloyd, *History of Wales,* II, 492.

[30] *Brut y Tywysogion,* 172.

[31] *Brut y Tywysogion,* 176; *Annales Cambriae,* 44.

[32] *Brut y Tywysogion,* 176.

[33] Lloyd, *History of Wales,* II, 494.

[34] Lloyd, *History of Wales,* II, 494; *Annales Cambriae,* 45.

[35] Poole, *Domesday Book to Magna Carta,* 491.

[36] Lloyd, *History of Wales,* II, 500–501.

[37] *Brut y Tywysogion,* 166, 168; *Annales Cambriae,* 43.

[38] *Brut y Tywysogion,* 172–174, 178; *Annales Cambriae,* 43, 44, 45.

[39] *Annales Cambriae,* 45; Lloyd, *History of Wales,* II, 502–503.

[40] *Annales Cambriae,* 45; *Brut y Tywysogion,* 180, 182.

[41] Lloyd, *History of Wales,* II, 504.

[42] *Brut y Tywysogion,* 176–180; *Annales Cambriae,* 45.

[43] Lloyd, *History of Wales,* II, 505.

[44] *Supra,* Chapter 7.

[45] Lloyd, *History of Wales,* II, 496, 497; *Annales Cambriae,* 46.

[46] *Annales Cambriae,* 46.

[47] Lloyd, *History of Wales,* II, 497.

[48] *Annales Cambriae,* 46–47; *Annales Monasterii de Osenia, in* Vol. IV, *Annales Monastici,* ed. Henry Richards Luard (R.S.) (London, 1869), 30; *The Chronicle of Jocelin of Brakelond,* ed. and tr. H. E. Butler (London, 1951), 70.

[49] *Annales Cambriae,* 46–47; *Brut y Tywysogion,* 184–186. Lloyd's interpretation (*History of Wales,* II, 498) is not very convincing. If the English column rejoined its main body in front of Owain's prepared position, there seems to be no real explanation for the Welsh withdrawal. If, on the other hand, King Henry actually had outflanked the defenses of Basingwerk, Owain had no choice but to retreat or be taken in the rear. This view is supported by D. J. C. King, letter to the author dated 8 October 1962.

[50] *Annales Cambriae,* 47.

[51] *Annales Cambriae,* 47; Lloyd, *History of Wales,* II, 498–499.

[52] Lloyd, *History of Wales,* II, 499; Poole, *Domesday Book to Magna Carta,* 293.

[53] *Annales Cambriae,* 47; Lloyd, *History of Wales,* II, 499–500.

[54] *Annales Wintoniae,* 56. See also *Annales Cambriae,* 47; *Annales de Osenia,* 30; *Annales de Theokesberia, in* Vol. I, *Annales Monastici,* ed. Henry Richards Luard (R.S.) (London, 1864), 48.

[55] *Brut y Tywysogion,* 188.

[56] Lloyd, *History of Wales,* II, 506; *Annales Cambriae,* 47.

[57] *Brut y Tywysogion,* 190, 192; *Annales Cambriae,* 47–48.

[58] Lloyd, *History of Wales,* II, 507.

[59] *Annales Cambriae,* 47; Lloyd, *History of Wales,* II, 507.

[60] Giraldus, *Itinerarium Kambriae,* 63–64; *Annales de Margan,* 15.

[61] *Annales Cambriae,* 48; Lloyd, *History of Wales,* II, 508.

[62] Lloyd, *History of Wales,* II, 509.

[63] *Brut y Tywysogion,* 196.

[64] *Ibid.*

[65] *Brut y Tywysogion,* 192; *Annales Cambriae,* 48.

[66] *Annales Cambriae,* 48.

[67] *Brut y Tywysogion,* 190; *Annales Cambriae,* 48. No overall commander is mentioned for this campaign. If the command was shared jointly by the five earls, the failure of the expedition becomes more understandable.

[68] *Annales Cambriae,* 49.

[69] *Brut y Tywysogion,* 190; *Annales Cambriae,* 49; *Red Book of the Exchequer,* II, 692; *Pipe Roll 6 Henry II,* 23, 30; *Pipe Roll 7 Henry II,* 22.

[70] *Annales Cambriae,* 49.

[71] *Annales Cambriae,* 49; *Annales de Margan,* 15.

[72] Lloyd, *History of Wales,* II, 513.

[73] *Ibid.,* 513–514; *Annales Cambriae,* 49.

[74] *Brut y Tywysogion*, 198; *Annales Cambriae*, 49–50.

[75] *Pipe Roll 12 Henry II*, 84, 85, 94–95, 101, 103. The commutation seems to have been at the rate of 15s.3d. per sergeant. Among those commuting their quotas were the bishops of Ely, Bath, and Winchester, the abbot of Abingdon, and Earl Reginald of Cornwall.

[76] *Ibid.*, 59, 81, 131.

[77] *Annales Cambriae*, 50.

[78] Lloyd's translation of *servientium* as "serving man" is not very apt. *History of Wales*, II, 515.

[79] *Annales Cambriae*, 50; *Annales de Margan*, 15; Lloyd, *History of Wales*, II, 515–516.

[80] *Annales Cambriae*, 50; Lloyd, *History of Wales*, II, 516.

[81] Lloyd, *History of Wales*, II, 516–517; *Annales Cambriae*, 50.

[82] Lloyd, *History of Wales*, II, 517–518; *Annales Cambriae*, 50.

[83] *Ibid.*, 518; Giraldus, *Descriptio Kambriae*, 219–220.

[84] *Pipe Roll 12 Henry II*, 59, 67; *Pipe Roll 13 Henry II*, 72, 77, 140, 160.

[85] Lloyd, *History of Wales*, II, 518.

[86] *Annales Cambriae*, 50; *Brut y Tywysogion*, 202.

[87] *Brut y Tywysogion*, 202, 204; *Annales Cambriae*, 51; Lloyd, *History of Wales*, II, 519.

[88] *Brut y Tywysogion*, 204, 206; Lloyd, *History of Wales*, II, 519.

[89] Lloyd, *History of Wales*, II, 520.

[90] *Brut y Tywysogion*, 204; *Annales Cambriae*, 51.

[91] *Annales Cambriae*, 53; Lloyd, *History of Wales*, II, 522.

[92] Lloyd, *History of Wales*, II, 549–552, 564–565.

[93] Lloyd, *History of Wales*, II, 536.

[94] *Ibid.*, 537.

[95] *Ibid.*, 538–539; *Annales Cambriae*, 52–53.

[96] Morris, *Welsh Wars of Edward I*, 18–19; Lloyd, *History of Wales*, II, 539.

[97] Lloyd, *History of Wales*, II, 540; *Brut y Tywysogion*, 212.

[98] Lloyd, *History of Wales*, II, 541–542; *Annales Cambriae*, 53. For many years the Pipe Rolls carried the entry: "£20 to Odo fitz William fitz Gerald in Branton for his claim to the castle and land of Emlyn which Rhys ap Gruffydd has." *Pipe Roll 28 Henry II*, 27.

[99] *Brut y Tywysogion*, 212; Giraldus, *Itinerarium Kambriae*, 80–81; *Descriptio Kambriae*, 172.

[100] Lloyd, *History of Wales*, II, 544.

[101] Ralph Diceto, I, 384.

[102] Lloyd, *History of Wales*, II, 544.

[103] Lloyd, *History of Wales*, II, 552–554.

[104] Poole, *Domesday Book to Magna Carta*.

[105] Lloyd, *History of Wales*, II, 540.

[106] *Brut y Tywysogion*, 212, 222.

[107] Lloyd, *History of Wales*, II, 546.

[108] *Ibid.*; Giraldus, *Itinerarium Kambriae*, 60–61.

[109] Lloyd, *History of Wales*, II, 547.

[110] Lloyd, *History of Wales*, II, 548; *Annales Cambriae*, 54; *Brut y Tywysogion*, 226.

[111] Giraldus, *Itinerarium Kambriae*, 49–52; Lloyd, *History of Wales*, II, 568.

[112] Giraldus, *Itinerarium Kambriae*, 47–48.

[113] Lloyd, *History of Wales*, II, 565, 567, 568–569.

[114] *Ibid.*, 571; *Annales de Margan*, 17–18.

[115] Lloyd, *History of Wales*, II, 572. It is interesting to note that at least two of the tenants of the honor of Glamorgan forfeited their lands when they failed to answer "the summons of the justiciar to rescue the earl's castle of Neath." *Pipe Roll 30 Henry II*, 111–112.

[116] *Pipe Roll 31 Henry II*, 6, 7, 8, 10.

[117] *Ibid.*, 7.

[118] *Ibid.*, 7, 10. The vagueness of the Pipe Roll entries makes it impossible to calculate with any exactness the number of troops raised to suppress the revolt. The roll mentions 656 infantry and 49 cavalry, but there is no way of determining whether or not the indivduals represented by these figures were counted more than once. Furthermore, some entries specify neither the number of troops nor the length of service for which payment is made. "In allowances to the sergeants resident in the castles of Neath, Kenfig, and Newcastle, £22 19s.4d., by the king's writ," (*ibid.*, 8) is not very enlightening.

[119] *Ibid.*, 6.

[120] *Pipe Roll 31 Henry II*, 7. Possibly, also, war horses in the twelfth century were not the expensive steeds they later became. Compare, however, the seeming value attached to the *dextrarius* about 1160 in the transfer of lands between Geoffrey and John Ridel. *Documents Illustrative of the Social and Economic History of the Danelaw*, ed. F. M. Stenton (London, 1920), 337–338.

[121] Lloyd, *History of Wales*, II, 570–571.

[122] *Ibid.*, 564–566.

[123] Giraldus, *Itinerarium Kambriae*, 18, 60–61, 80–81, 122, 123, 137; *Descriptio Kambriae*, 172, 176

[124] Native Welsh castles were to be found in Cardigan, Carmarthenshire, Denbigh, Merioneth, Montgomery, and Radnor. Armitage, *Early Norman Castles*, 299–300, 300, 301, 394, 388–389; *Hist. Mon. Com., Carmarthen*, 107–108; Neaverson, *Mediaeval Castles in North Wales*, 19–21; *Hist. Mon. Com., Denbigh*, 83, 174; *Hist. Mon. Com., Merioneth*, 18, 85, 96, 179; *Hist. Mon. Com., Montgomery*, 65; *Hist. Mon. Com., Radnor*, 137–138.

[125] Lloyd, *History of Wales*, II, 430–433, 436–437, 443–446. In a typical document, dated 28 August 1098 by Round, Arnulf de Montgomery, son of Earl Roger, gave to the brethren of the Abbey of St. Martin of Sees, in free alms forever, the church of St. Nicholas at Pembroke, a castle of his. *Calendar of Documents, France*, 237–238.

[126] Lloyd, *History of Wales*, II, 447–461, 485.

Chapter 10

[1] J. H. Round, "The Introduction of Knight Service into England," in *Feudal England,* 225–314. To distinguish between "knight service" and "military service" as Richardson and Sayles (*Governance of Mediaeval England,* 68) have attempted to do is merely to quibble. Among medieval scholars the terms have been interchangeable for the better part of a century.

[2] Powicke, *Military Obligation,* 28.

[3] Douglas writes (*William the Conqueror,* 276) : "Despite arguments to the contrary, it would seem that there is as yet insufficient evidence to disturb the belief that the allocation of these quotas was an innovation introduced into England by the first Norman king, and one which owed little or nothing to Anglo-Saxon precedent."

[4] *Ibid.,* 274–275; Smail, "Art of War," 136–137.

[5] Hollister, "The Norman Conquest and the Genesis of English Feudalism," 662–663; Eric John, *Land Tenure in Early England* (Leicester, 1960), 160–161.

[6] Richardson and Sayles, *Governance of Mediaeval England,* 101. The text of the charter is printed in J. Armitage Robinson, *Gilbert Crispin Abbot of Westminster* (Cambridge, 1911), 38.

[7] Painter, *Mediaeval Society,* 100.

[8] On the other hand, Douglas argues that the original assessments can be ascertained with some confidence from the 1166 returns, which themselves accurately reflected conditions prevailing before 1135. *William the Conqueror,* 281.

[9] Round, *Feudal England,* 250. The bishopric of Carlisle was not created until the reign of Henry I.

[10] The other bishoprics were obligated as follows: 40—Ely and Norwich; 32—Salisbury; 25—Exeter (including Chapelry of Bosham) ; 20—Bath and Wells, and London; 15—Coventry and Lichfield, and Hereford; 10—Durham. Helena M. Chew, *The English Ecclesiastical Tenants-in-Chief and Knight Service* (Oxford, 1932), 4. The number of knights due depends on whether the bishop of Worcester or the crown had the right figure. *Pipe Roll 2 Henry II,* 63.

[11] The monastic quotas were as follows: 60—Peterborough; 40—Glastonbury and St. Edmund's; 20—Hyde; 15—St. Augustine's Canterbury, Tavistock, and Westminster; 10—Coventry; 10 or 7—Shaftesbury; 6—St. Alban's; 5—Evesham and Wilton; 4—Ramsey; 3—St. Benet's Holme and Malmesbury; 3 or 2—Cerne and Pershore; 2—Middleton, Sherburne, and Winchcombe; 1—Abbotsbury and Michelney. Chew, *Ecclesiastical Tenants-in-Chief,* 5.

[12] Round (*Feudal England,* 252) calculates that 784 knights were due from the church fiefs.

[13] *Ibid.,* 304. Douglas (*William the Conqueror,* 325) asserts that these

assessments were imposed upon the English bishoprics and monasteries in or shortly after 1070.

[14] Chew, *Ecclesiastical Tenants-in-Chief,* 8.

[15] I. J. Sanders, *Feudal Military Service in England* (Oxford, 1956), 17.

[16] *Ibid.,* 18.

[17] The archbishopric of Canterbury, 60; bishopric of Lincoln, 60; abbey of Peterborough, 60; bishopric of Ely, 40; bishopric of Norwich, 40; abbey of St. Edmund's, 40; bishopric of London, 20; abbey of Westminster, 15; St. Augustine's abbey, Canterbury, 15; Ramsey abbey, 4; abbey of St. Benet's, Holme, 3.

[18] Chew, *Ecclesiastical Tenants-in-Chief,* 6; Round, *Feudal England,* 293. A notable recent attempt to link the pre-Conquest system for raising troops and the Norman quotas is to be found in John's *Land Tenure in Early England,* but reviews of this work by Dorothy Whitelock in *American Historical Review,* LXVI (1961), 1009–1010, and by Robert S. Hoyt in *Speculum,* XXXVI (1962), 663–665, and the letters of Mr. John and Professor Whitelock in *American Historical Review,* LXVII (1962), 582–584, indicate that many of his conclusions are open to serious question.

[19] Chew, *Ecclesiastical Tenants-in-Chief,* 8; Douglas, *William the Conqueror,* 273; Richardson and Sayles, *Governance of Mediaeval England,* 69.

[20] Miller, *Abbey and Bishopric of Ely,* 154–156, 164–167.

[21] *Ibid.,* opp. 76.

[22] *Chron. Monasterii de Abingdon,* II, 3; Round, *Feudal England,* 300; Chew, *Ecclesiastical Tenants-in-Chief,* 114. The conduct of the knights, which perhaps had a great deal to do with their enfeoffment, is described in *Vita Wulfstani,* 46, 99. Even so, Bishop Wulfstan enfeoffed only 37 1/2 knights out of a total *servitium debitum* of 60 (or 50). *Ibid.,* XLIII.

[23] Miller, *Abbey and Bishopric of Ely,* 58, 187.

[24] Miller, *Abbey and Bishopric of Ely,* 176.

[25] George C. Homans, review of J. Ambrose Raftis, *The Estates of Ramsey Abbey,* in *Speculum,* XXXIII (1958), 563.

[26] Miller, *Abbey and Bishopric of Ely,* 166.

[27] *Ibid.,* 173; *Red Book of the Exchequer,* I, 364.

[28] Lennard, *Rural England,* 52.

[29] *Chron. Monasterii de Abingdon,* II, 90, 91, 92, 128, 129, 135; *Regesta,* II, 48.

[30] *Red Book of the Exchequer,* I, 363–366; Miller, *Abbey and Bishopric of Ely,* 166–167.

[31] Chew, *Ecclesiastical Tenants-in-Chief,* 121–122.

[32] *Red Book of the Exchequer,* I, 210.

[33] Chew, *Ecclesiastical Tenants-in-Chief,* 122.

[34] Poole, *Domesday Book to Magna Carta,* 12–13; Doulgas, *William the Conqueror,* 273.

[35] Sanders, *Feudal Military Service,* 18; Douglas, *William the Conqueror,* 274.

[36] Stenton, *First Century,* 139.

[37] *Red Book of the Exchequer,* I, 241–242.

[38] *Ibid.,* 258, 264–265.

[39] *Ibid.,* I, 280–281, 285–286.

[40] *Ibid.,* I, 401.

[41] *Ibid.,* I, 380–381, 342, 343–344, 390–391, 385–386, 388–390.

[42] *Domesday Book,* I, 210. See Stenton, *First Century,* 140–145 for an admirable discussion of the landless knight.

[43] Poole, *Domesday Book to Magna Carta,* 14–15; *Red Book of the Exchequer,* I, 390.

[44] *Red Book of the Exchequer,* I, 385.

[45] *Red Book of the Exchequer,* I, 230. This sort of information seems to have been ignored by Richardson and Sayles. *Governance of Mediaeval England,* 95–98.

[46] Smail, "Art of War," 137. Round estimated that "the whole *servitium debitum,* clerical and lay, of England can scarcely have exceeded, if indeed it reached, 5,000 knights." *Feudal England,* 292. Poole is more cautious: "The feudal army was never large. Although the usually accepted estimate of about 5,000 is almost certainly too low, it can scarcely ever have exceeded 7,000 knights; and it may but rarely have been mustered at its full strength." *Domesday Book to Magna Carta,* 15.

[47] *Red Book of the Exchequer,* III, 807–813.

[48] *Ibid.,* 813; Poole, *Domesday Book to Magna Carta,* 9. This royal guard is mentioned by the Continuator of Florence of Worcester, II, 93.

[49] *Regesta,* I, xxvi–xxvii; II, xv–xvii.

[50] Powicke, *Military Obligation,* 30, 34.

[51] S. B. Chrimes, *An Introduction to the Administrative History of Mediaeval England* (New York, 1952), 24.

[52] Henry of Essex forfeited the constableship with the honor of Rayleigh for his alleged treasonable conduct at the battle near Basingwerk. The office was revived about 1173, when Humphrey de Bohun held the office, but it lapsed with his death. *Pipe Roll 20 Henry II,* 51.

[53] J. E. A. Jolliffe, *Angevin Kingship* (London, 1955), 211.

[54] Stenton, *First Century,* 178.

[55] Round, *Feudal England,* 261.

[56] *Ibid.,* 259, 260.

[57] *Chronicle of Jocelin of Brakelond,* 99–100.

[58] Austin Lane Poole, *Obligations of Society in the XII and XIII Centuries* (Oxford, 1946), 48–49.

[59] *Monasticon,* III, 153b; Saltman, *Theobald,* 252. It should be noted, however, that the abbot was never able to make this exemption stick.

[60] Vinogradoff, *English Society in the Eleventh Century,* 43; Haskins, *Norman Institutions,* 23–24.

[61] Sanders, *Feudal Military Service,* 68.

[62] Smail, "Art of War," 136.

[63] Poole, *Obligations of Society,* 50.

[64] John, *Land Tenure in Early England,* 149–154; Hollister, "The Norman Conquest and English Feudalism," 644.

[65] Douglas remarks: "The feudal policy of the Conqueror was thus a response to immediate military need. The Anglo-Norman polity became an aristocracy organized for war. Only as such was it enabled to survive." *William the Conqueror,* 273.

[66] Judges 7:16.

[67] Thucydides, *Peloponnesian War,* tr. R. Crawley (New York, 1934), 7.

[68] Herodotus, *The Persian Wars,* tr. George Rawlinson (New York, 1942), 578.

[69] Adcock, *The Roman Art of War,* 8; H. M. D. Parker, *The Roman Legions* (New York, 1958), 11, 14, 27, 30.

[70] Parker, *Roman Legions,* 14.

[71] John, *Land Tenure in Early England,* 148–149.

[72] Stenton, *First Century,* 180; Poole, *Obligations of Society,* 50.

[73] Poole, *Domesday Book to Magna Carta,* 25.

[74] For William Marshal's career, see Painter, *William Marshal.*

[75] Hollister, "Military Service," 42.

[76] Letter, Grant to Lincoln, 19 June 1863, with enclosed letter, Sherman to Grant, *Official Records,* Series III, iii, 386–388.

[77] C. Warren Hollister, "The Significance of Scutage Rates in Eleventh and Twelfth-Century England," *English Historical Review,* LXXV (1960), 584–588. This in turn involves the argument as to whether such expedients as scutage and the money fief were feudal or not. The basic question here is what can be defined as feudal, and as Professor Hoyt has well stated, "If feudalism be understood to be essentially and above all a 'system' of tenures supporting military service, and if every other kind of arrangement by which rulers or lords obtained military service is understood to be 'non-feudal' or even 'anti-feudal,' then it could reasonably be argued that medieval European society was never feudal—at least not completely or 'perfectly' feudal. Or alternatively the beginning of the decline of feudalism might be pushed back to the years just following the battle of Tours in 733." Robert S. Hoyt, "The Iron Age of English Feudalism," *Journal of British Studies,* II (1963), 27–28.

[78] Round, *Feudal England,* 271.

[79] *Regesta,* II, 6; W. A. Morris, "A Mention of Scutage in the Year 1100," *English Historical Review,* XXXVI (1921), 45–46.

[80] Stenton, *First Century,* 180–185.

[81] Ramsey, *Angevin Empire,* 80; Douglas, *William the Conqueror,* 282; Richardson and Sayles, *Governance of Mediaeval England,* 99.

[82] Stenton, *First Century,* 193; Hollister, "Knights of Peterborough," 426. A random check of statistics for the Civil War in the United States (1861–1865) revealed that the number of men present for duty in comparison with those carried on the official rolls varied from 62.2% to 80.5%. *Official Records,* Series III, i, 775; Series III, ii, 957. Statistical evidence of this sort can be developed for any war during which regular strength returns were made. How

such problems were dealt with in the fifteenth century is shown at length in R. A. Newhall, *Muster and Review* (Cambridge, Mass., 1940).

[83] See "Chart of Service" in Sanders, *Feudal Military Service*, 139–154.

[84] *Danelaw Charters*, 40, 347, 390.

[85] Poole, *Domesday Book to Magna Carta*, 17.

[86] Haskins, *Norman Institutions*, 20, 21.

[87] Stenton, *First Century*, 177–178.

[88] C. Warren Hollister, "The Annual Term of Military Service in Medieval England," *Medievalia et Humanistica*, XIII (1960), 42; Hollister, "Scutage Rates," 583–584. It must be added that Hollister's citation from Henry of Huntingdon ". . . *vos in pace armis exercemini, ut in bello casus belli dubios non sentiatis,*" is not very convincing proof of the existence of a forty-day annual training period. My own opinion is that the field and garrison aspects of knight service were tied together in some way that has yet to be fully explored. That there was a connection is clear from the later claims that knights who performed their regular garrison duty were not obligated for service in the field, and that a tenant was not bound to furnish so large a contingent for field duty as for garrison service. Sanders, *Feudal Military Service*, 45–49. In all probability the peacetime service was performed in garrison, for other than Bishop Ralph's statement, no evidence has been produced to show that anything like routine unit exercises were practiced by knights and sergeants. This double obligation also goes far to explain the continued reliance on mercenaries. The feudal levy, even at maximum strength, could not at one and the same time provide a field army and garrisons for some hundreds of castles.

[89] There seems no doubt that Hollister's arguments are valid on this point. "Scutage Rates," 581–582; Powicke, *Military Obligation*, 33. Stenton's handling of this question (*First Century*, 181–183) is uncharacteristically vague, and Poole (*Domesday Book to Magna Carta*, 16–17) evades the issue altogether.

[90] This may conceivably have occurred during Stephen's reign, but Hollister's suggestion ("Military Service," 45) that the barons extracted such a concession from the monarch is not borne out by any contemporary evidence, and it seems most unlikely that the reduction of military service by a third would have escaped the notice of every English chronicler of the eleventh and twelfth centuries.

[91] *Pipe Roll 19 Henry II*, 30–31; *Pipe Roll 20 Henry II*, 63, 96, 125, 139.

[92] *Pipe Roll 21 Henry II*, 127–128. Hollister fails to note this in "Scutage Rates," 586.

[93] *Pipe Roll 19 Henry II*, 32–33.

[94] *Pipe Roll 20 Henry II*, 139.

[95] J. H. Round, "Castle-Guard," *Archaeological Journal*, LIX (1902), 2nd ser., IX, 144–159; Sir Frank Stenton, "Castles and Castle-Guard," Chapter VI in *First Century of English Feudalism*, 192–217; Sidney Painter, "Castle-

Guard," *American Historical Review*, XL (1935), 450–459; reprinted in *Feudalism and Liberty*, ed. Fred A. Cazel, Jr. (Baltimore, 1961), 144–156.

[96] Poole, *Domesday Book to Magna Carta*, 18.

[97] Stenton, *First Century*, 206–209.

[98] *Red Book of the Exchequer*, II, 540. That there was nothing consistent about the terms of military tenure among the sergeants is graphically illustrated by the preceding entry, stating that John de Pencoit, who held an acre and a half, was bound to serve but fifteen days.

[99] Stenton, *First Century*, 206.

[100] Beeler, "Castles and Strategy," 597–598; Hollister, *Anglo-Saxon Institutions*, 141. Stenton (*First Century*, 201) argued that "the essential facts which point to an earlier origin than this [i.e. Stephen's reign] for the majority of motte-and-bailey castles are the large scale on which they tend to be planned and the evidence of deliberation of design which most of them show. A highly developed castle of this type . . . could not have been raised under the conditions which were inevitable in a time of feudal anarchy." This argument misses the point. The real reason for assuming that most of the motte-and-bailey castles were constructed shortly after the Conquest is military necessity —Colonel Burne's "inherent military probability."

[101] *Early Yorkshire Charters*, V, 2; *Red Book of the Exchequer*, I, 342. Roger de Buron, the lord of the honor in 1166, had enfeoffed six knights and retained four on the demesne. Stenton, *First Century*, 215.

[102] Hollister, "Annual Term of Military Service," 40–47; "Significance of Scutage Rates," 580–581.

[103] At Richmond the service year was divided into six parts, beginning with August–September. The numbers of knights assigned for each of the two-month periods are 32, 30, 26, 29, 27, and 30 respectively, which shows some attempt at equalizing service throughout the year. *Early Yorkshire Charters*, V, 2; *Calendar of Miscellaneous Inquisitions*, (London, 1916–   ), I, 168–169. Before 1139 Stephen quit-claimed the obligation of St. Edmund's to provide 40 knights for castle-guard at Norwich in quarterly details of 10 knights each. A confirmation of Stephen's charter was issued by Archbishop Theobald between 1139 and 1145. *Monasticon*, III, 153; Saltman, *Theobald*, 252.

[104] *Red Book of the Exchequer*, II, 622–623; Painter, "Castle-Guard," 146–147.

[105] *Red Book of the Exchequer*, I, 212.

[106] Service of less than 40 days was perhaps more common than Hollister seems to think ("Annual Term of Military Service," 43). A messuage in Broghton was held of the king in chief by castle-guard service at Montgomery for fifteen days in time of war (*Calendar of Miscellaneous Inquisitions*, I, 185). In 1210–1212 John of Pencoit owed fifteen days ward at Launceston (*Red Book of the Exchequer*, II, 540); at Shrewsbury in 1212 Adam de Leton owed ward of 8 days at his own expense, and if he had to serve longer, at the king's expense (*The Book of Fees*, ed. H. C. Maxwell Lyte, [London,

1921–1931], II, 145) ; and certain tenements at Denbigh were held by the service "of finding for the ward of Denbigh castle in time of war two armed horsemen for four days, or one for 8 days . . ." (*Calendar of Miscellaneous Inquisitions,* II, 280). It is perhaps significant that in two of these examples no mention is made of peacetime service.

[107] *Red Book of the Exchequer,* II, 706–712; Round, "Castle-Guard," 152; Painter, "Castle-Guard," 147.

[108] Aldford, Alnwick, Arundel, Bamburgh, Banbury, Baynard, Belvoir, Brecknock, Canterbury, Chester, Clifford, Clun, Corsham, Devizes, Dodleston, Dover, Eye, Farnham, Framlingham, Hastings, Hedingham, Kington, Knockin, Lancaster, Launceston, Lydbury, Lincoln, Montgomery, Newcastle-upon-Tyne, Northampton, Norwich, Peak, Pevensey, Plympton, Prudhoe, Richmond, Rochester, Rockingham, Salisbury, Shrawardine, Skipsea, Skipton, Stogursey, Tickhill, Trematon, Wallingford, Warwick, Wem, Whitchurch, Wigmore, and Windsor. Painter, "Castle-Guard," 145.

[109] Stenton, *First Century,* 211, 212, 215; Sanders, *Feudal Military Service,* 41, 45, 46; *Red Book of the Exchequer,* I, 212; *Regesta,* II, 33, 241, 264, 274, 381; R. B. Pugh, "Great Chalfield," in *VCH Wiltshire,* VII, 62–63.

[110] *Calendar of Miscellaneous Inquisitions,* II, 280; *Book of Fees,* I, 101, 343; II, 145; *Red Book of the Exchequer,* II, 454, 460, 467, 492–493, 511; Stenton, *First Century,* 208.

[111] Hollister, "Military Service," 43.

[112] *Calendar of Miscellaneous Inquisitions,* I, 43, 241, 291–292, 495; *Brut,* 124–126.

[113] Painter, "Castle-Guard," 146.

[114] *Red Book of the Exchequer,* I, 420; *Monasticon,* V, 350.

[115] Stenton, *First Century,* 194.

[116] *Domesday Book,* I, 18a; II, 163b; *Calendar of Documents France,* 4–5, 511.

[117] *Domesday Book,* I, 185b, 185, 184, 183, 253b, 177.

[118] *Ibid.,* I, 381; *Early Yorkshire Charters,* III, 124; Stenton, *First Century,* 194–195.

[119] *Domesday Book,* I, 332a.

[120] *Regesta,* II, 402.

[121] Lennard, *Rural England,* 32–33.

[122] Stenton, *First Century,* 196,215; Sanders, *Feudal Military Service,* 45.

[123] Painter, "Castle-Guard," 146–149; Stenton, *First Century,* 215.

[124] *Chron. Monasterii de Abingdon,* II, 3.

[125] *Regesta,* II, 33, 168, 563.

[126] *Ibid.,* 241; *Pipe Roll 31 Henry I,* 44; *Liber Eliensis,* 254.

[127] *Regesta,* II, 264; *Monasticon,* VI, 1277.

[128] *Regesta,* II, 231. Latin text, 367.

[129] Stenton, *First Century,* 213.

[130] *Red Book of the Exchequer*, I, 236, 240.

[131] *Ibid.*, 212.

[132] *Ibid.*, II, 606.

[133] *Red Book of the Exchequer*, II, 613–618.

[134] Round, "Castle-Guard," 149, 151–152.

[135] *Red Book of the Exchequer*, II, 706–712; Painter, "Castle-Guard," 151.

[136] Painter, "Castle-Guard," 153.

[137] *Calendar of Miscellaneous Inquisitions*, I, 422. Painter ("Castle-Guard," 153) is in error here. The manor of Dullingswirth was held by Roger Bigod, *except* one half a knight's fee which was held of the honor of Richmond, and rendered 40 pence yearly for the ward of Eye castle.

[138] *Calendar of Miscellaneous Inquisitions*, I, 505; *Danelaw Charters*, 400.

[139] *Calendar of Miscellaneous Inquisitions*, I, 375, 395; II, 494.

[140] *Ibid.*, I, 256; *Red Book of the Exchequer*, II, 712–713.

[141] *Red Book of the Exchequer*, II, 716–717, 607.

[142] Poole, *Domesday Book to Magna Carta*, 18.

[143] The Exchequer accounts testify eloquently to the difficulty of collecting scutage payments. Many of the accounts ran on for years.

[144] *Calendar of Inquisitions Post Mortem* (London, 1904–   ), II, 210–221.

[145] *Magna Carta*, with notes by Faith Thompson, Senate Doc. No. 180, 81st Congress, 2nd Session (Washington, 1950), 10.

[146] *Rotuli Hundredorum*, ed. W. Illingworth and J. Caley (London, 1812–1818), II, 236.

[147] *Rotuli Hundredorum*, II, 68.

[148] Painter, "Castle-Guard," 155–156. He might have added that enforcement of service also became more difficult as a result of the division of baronies and the fragmentation of the knight's fee.

[149] *Pipe Roll 20 Henry II*, 63, 55, 94.

[150] *Early Yorkshire Charters*, V, 11–12; Stenton, *First Century*, 26.

[151] Stenton, *First Century*, 28–29.

[152] *Domesday Book*, I, 62b, 130a; Powicke, *Military Obligation*, 28.

[153] *Pipe Roll 31 Henry I*, 89; *Brut*, 124–126; Giraldus, *Itinerarium Kambriae*, 60–61.

[154] Stenton, *First Century*, 146–148.

[155] Anselm, *Opera*, IV, 59; Norman F. Cantor, *Church, Kingship and Lay Investiture in England, 1089–1135* (Princeton, N.J., 1958), 73.

[156] Eadmer, *Historia Novorum*, 78; *Vita Anselmi*, 377. Perhaps Anselm had recourse to such as the "knights" of Canterbury who were the ruling members of the chapmen's gild. Richardson and Sayles, *Governance of Mediaeval England*, 56, 80.

[157] Stenton, *First Century*, 148–149.

[158] *Ibid.*, 144.

Chapter 11

[1] *Anglo-Saxon Chronicle,* I, 352.

[2] Stenton, *First Century,* 151.

[3] Smail, "Art of War," 137.

[4] J. O. Prestwich, "War and Finance in the Anglo-Norman State," *Transactions of the Royal Historical Society,* 5th ser., IV, 19–43.

[5] This view has been adopted in its entirety by Richardson and Sayles, *Governance of Mediaeval England,* 54,72,75.

[6] Florence of Worcester, I, 227; Guy of Amiens, 37; J. Boussard, *Les Mercenaires à XII Siecle, Henri II Plantagenet et les Origines de L'Armée de Métier* (Paris, 1947), 5. Another study of the use of mercenaries in the twelfth century completely ignores their use in England during the reigns of Stephen and Henry II. Herbert Grundmann, "Rotten und Brabanzonen: Soldnerheere im 12. Jahrhundert," *Deutsches Archiv für Geschichte des Mittelalters,* V (1941–1942), 419–492.

[7] Ordericus Vitalis, II, 167, 199.

[8] *Anglo-Saxon Chronicle,* I, 352; *Annales de Wintonia,* 34.

[9] William of Malmesbury, *De Gestis Regum,* II, 368, 379.

[10] Prestwich, "War and Finance," 26.

[11] Ordericus Vitalis, IV, 172–173, 174–175.

[12] William of Malmesbury, *De Gestis Regum,* II, 478.

[13] *Pipe Roll 31 Henry I,* 76, 138. This early use of paid garrisons seems to have escaped the notice of Richardson and Sayles, *Governance of Mediaeval England,* 73 (n.6).

[14] William of Malmesbury, *Historia Novella,* 17.

[15] Smail, "Art of War," 137–138.

[16] *Gesta Stephani,* 102.

[17] Gervase of Canterbury, I, 110–111.

[18] *Ibid.,* 105. For William's career see Verbruggen, *Het Leger . . . van de Graven van Vlaanderen,* 56, 82, 122, 149; Galbert of Bruges, *The Murder of Charles the Good, Count of Flanders,* tr. J. B. Ross (New York, 1959), 15, 134, 277.

[19] Round, *Geoffrey de Mandeville,* 140–144, 202–203; Davis, "Geoffrey de Mandeville," 300.

[20] Verbruggen, *Het Leger . . . van de Graven van Vlaanderen,* 8.

[21] *Ibid.,* 69. It would be interesting to know the ratio of horse to foot in the contingent, but all that can be ascertained with certainty is that both arms were represented. That the Flemings were still in the field in 1154 is testimony both to William's ability as a commander and to the efficient operation of Stephen's exchequer.

[22] Henry of Huntingdon, 275, 280–281; John of Hexham, 309–310; William of Malmesbury, *Historia Novella,* 58–61; *Gesta Stephani,* 86–89; Cont.

Florence of Worcester, II, 133–134; William of Newburgh, I, 41–42; Gervase of Canterbury, I, 125–126.

[23] Symeon of Durham, II, 310; *Pipe Roll 2 Henry II,* 15; Round, *Geoffrey de Mandeville,* 147.

[24] Round, *Geoffrey de Mandeville,* 2.

[25] *Gesta Stephani,* 104–105, 108.

[26] *Ibid.,* 113.

[27] *Ibid.,* 141.

[28] Prestwich, "War and Finance," 37–43.

[29] *Gesta Stephani,* 4–5.

[30] *Ibid.,* 10,12,65.

[31] *Ibid.,* 69, 86; William of Malmesbury, *Historia Novella,* 36; Cont. Florence of Worcester, II, 133.

[32] Cont. Florence of Worcester, II, 118.

[33] *Gesta Stephani,* 99.

[34] *De Necessariis Observantiis Scaccarii Dialogus,* ed. and tr. Charles Johnson (London, 1950), 50; Henry of Huntingdon, 267; William of Malmesbury, *Historia Novella,* 20, 42; William of Newburgh, I, 33; *Gesta Stephani,* 53, 79; Poole, *Domesday Book to Magna Carta,* 155–156. If exchequer practice had been so nearly forgotten during the troubled time of Stephen, would not the knightly quotas due the crown equally have been forgotten? Richardson and Sayles, *Governance of Mediaeval England,* 89, 166.

[35] Gervase of Canterbury, I, 161; Powicke, *Military Obligation,* 49.

[36] *Pipe Roll 4 Henry II,* 126.

[37] *Ibid.; Pipe Roll 5 Henry II,* 9, 62; *Pipe Roll 6 Henry II,* 2; *Pipe Roll 7 Henry II,* 56, 61; *Pipe Roll 10 Henry II,* 34, 61; *Pipe Roll 13 Henry II,* 208; *Pipe Roll 14 Henry II,* 210, 221–222, 232.

[38] *Pipe Roll 13 Henry II,* 208. Between the feasts of St. Mark the Evangelist (25 April) and St. Luke the Evangelist (18 October).

[39] *Pipe Roll 14 Henry II,* 221–222.

[40] *Pipe Roll 6 Henry II,* 7, 26, 27; *Pipe Roll 7 Henry II,* 22, 38; *Pipe Roll 9 Henry II,* 7; *Pipe Roll 14 Henry II,* 124; *Pipe Roll 15 Henry II,* 107; *Pipe Roll 16 Henry II,* 134; *Pipe Roll 17 Henry II,* 33; *Pipe Roll 18 Henry II,* 110.

[41] *Pipe Roll 20 Henry II,* 94.

[42] Brackley, Whitchurch, Hastings, Nottingham, Bolsover, Peak, Colchester, Southampton, Berkhamstead, Norwich, Northampton, Newcastle-upon-Tyne, Prudhoe, Newcastle-under-Lyme, Orford, Walton, Kenilworth, Salisbury, "castle of Roger of Powys," Cambridge, Worcester, Warwick, Wark, Lincoln, Leicester, Canterbury, Hertford, Winchester, Porchester, Windsor, and Yeldon.

[43] The castles were Brackley, Whitchurch, Hastings, Nottingham, Bolsover, Peak, Colchester, Southampton, Berkhamstead, Norwich, Northampton, New-

castle-upon-Tyne, Prudhoe, Newcastle-under-Lyme, Orford, Walton, Kenil-worth, Salisbury, and the "castle of Roger of Powys." *Pipe Roll 19 Henry II,* 22, 25, 28–29, 30–31, 32–33, 53, 58, 70, 97, 101–102, 107–109, 113, 118–121, 129–130, 132, 173, 174, 177, 178–179, 183.

[44] Whitchurch, Hastings, Nottingham, Bolsover, Peak, Colchester, South-ampton, Norwich, Northampton, Newcastle-under-Lyme, Orford, Walton, Kenilworth, Salisbury, Cambridge, Worcester, Warwick, Wark, Lincoln, Leicester, Canterbury, Hertford, Winchester, Porchester, Windsor, and Yel-don. *Pipe Roll 20 Henry II,* 2, 9, 14, 26, 29, 34, 37–38, 51–52, 54–57, 59, 63, 67, 73, 94, 96, 105, 107–108, 111, 117, 125, 138–140, 142–144.

[45] *Pipe Roll 21 Henry II,* 4, 6, 36–37, 39, 91, 107, 127–128, 164–173.

[46] *Pipe Roll 20 Henry II,* 96, 139–140.

[47] *Pipe Roll 21 Henry II,* 107.

[48] *Pipe Roll 19 Henry II,* 107–108.

[49] *Pipe Roll 20 Henry II,* 96, 139–140.

[50] Florence of Worcester, II, 153; Ralph Diceto, I, 377–378; Gervase of Canterbury, I, 246; Verbruggen, *Het Leger . . . van de Graven van Vlaan-deren,* 123.

[51] *Gesta Regis,* I, 67, 68; Roger of Hoveden, II, 64; William of Newburgh, I, 181–182; Jordan Fantosme, 344–363; *Annales de Wintonia,* 61; *Pipe Roll 21 Henry II,* 172.

[52] *Pipe Roll 22 Henry II,* 184; *Pipe Roll 23 Henry II,* 29.

[53] See, for example, *Pipe Roll 22 Henry II,* 57, 61–62; also *28 Henry II,* 21; *31 Henry II,* 128, 143, 223–225; *34 Henry II,* 9; *1 Richard I,* 8, 232.

[54] Smail, "Art of War," 138–139; Sanders, *Feudal Military Service,* 51.

[55] Poole, *Domesday Book to Magna Carta,* 110.

[56] Sanders, *Feudal Military Service,* 51.

[57] Poole, *Domesday Book to Magna Carta,* 27.

[58] Bryce D. Lyon, *From Fief to Indenture* (Cambridge, Mass., 1957) ; "The Money Fief under the English Kings, 1066–1485," *English Historical Review,* LXVI (1951), 161–193; Powicke, *Military Obligation,* 27; Richardson and Sayles, *Governance of Mediaeval England,* 73.

[59] Lyon, *Fief to Indenture,* 32–33.

[60] William of Malmesbury, *De Gestis Regum,* II, 478–479.

[61] Lyon, *Fief to Indenture,* 33.

[62] Rymer, *Foedera,* I, i, 7; *Regesta,* II, 7. Lyon is almost certainly incorrect in assigning this treaty to 1103. Of the witnesses, William Giffard had ceased to be chancellor by 3 September 1101, and Arnulf de Montgomery had been exiled in 1102 for his share in the revolt of Robert de Bellême. Ganshof, Van Caenegem, and Verhulst, "Note sur le premier traité anglo-flamand de Douvres," 246.

[63] Rymer, *Foedera,* I, i, 6.

[64] Lyon, *Fief to Indenture,* 35.

[65] Rymer, *Foedera,* I, i, 22–23; Lyon, *Fief to Indenture,* 35–36.

[66] *Gesta Regis,* I, 44–45; Roger of Hoveden, II, 46–47, 63–64, 72.

[67] Gervase of Canterbury, I, 203.

[68] *Gesta Regis,* I, 83, 246–247; Roger of Hoveden, II, 72.

[69] Rymer, *Foedera,* I, i, 7.

[70] Bryce Lyon, *A Constitutional and Legal History of Medieval England* (New York, 1960), 103. The subject of English participation in post-Conquest wars is well analyzed by Powicke, *Military Obligation,* 37–47.

[71] Richardson and Sayles, *The Governance of Mediaeval England,* 55–61. This argument is not concerned with the social or economic status of either *cniht* or knight, but with his military capabilities, and nowhere is there convincing evidence that the English fought on horseback. Harold's "knights," as Richardson and Sayles would have it, are not depicted in fighting gear in the Bayeux tapestry. It should also be noted that the only Englishman shown mounted and in armor is Harold himself, and in neither scene is he represented in combat. *Bayeux Tapestry,* Pls. 28, 58; Glover, "English Warfare," 5; Douglas, *William the Conqueror,* 278.

[72] An excellent refutation of Glover's thesis is D. G. Millar, "The Anglo-Saxon Cavalry Reconsidered," an unpublished study, Stanford University, 1963. It may be noted in passing that even Sir Walter Scott knew that the Saxons did not fight on horseback. *Ivanhoe,* Ch. VIII.

[73] Glover, "English Warfare," 9.

[74] Richardson and Sayles, *Governance of Mediaeval England,* 54,60. That the English word *cniht,* rather than the French *chivaler,* became the common word for the mounted warrior (knight) need not be a cause for surprise. One is reminded of the English settlers in eastern North America who named one of the indigenous birds (*Turdus migratorius*) a robin although it bore only a vague similarity in size, shape, or coloration to the English robin (*Erithacus rubecula*).

[75] Hollister, *Anglo-Saxon Military Institutions,* 38–84; Richardson and Sayles, *Governance of Mediaeval England,* 101. Certainly there is no evidence that the military representative of the five-hide unit himself held five hides. C. Warren Hollister, "The Knights of Peterborough and the Anglo-Saxon Fyrd," *English Historical Review,* LXXII (1962), 421.

[76] *Domesday Book,* I, 56b.

[77] *Anglo-Saxon Chronicle,* I, 360–361; Florence of Worcester, II, 35; Henry of Huntingdon, 217.

[78] Richardson and Sayles, *Governance of Mediaeval England,* 67.

[79] Robert S. Hoyt, "The Abingdon Fee in 1086," a paper delivered at the Annual Meeting of the Pacific Coast Branch of the American Historical Association, San Francisco, California, 29 September 1963; Letter, Robert S. Hoyt to author, dated 12 November 1963.

[80] Hollister, "Knights of Peterborough," 418, 420–421, 428, 431–432.

[81] Lieberman, *Gesetze der Angelsachsen,* I, 656; Richardson and Sayles, *Governance of Mediaeval England,* 75–76.

[82] Richardson and Sayles, *Governance of Mediaeval England,* 76.

[83] William Alfred Morris, *The Constitutional History of England to 1216*

(New York, 1930) , 165; Lyon, *Constitutional and Legal History of Medieval England,* 169.

[84] *Anglo-Saxon Chronicle,* I, 342. Professor Hollister suggests, "It is certain that many of the *milites* of *Domesday Book* were not knights but fyrd soldiers" ("Knights of Peterborough," 430) .

[85] But to say that "within five years of the Conquest itself the native English were the most faithful and vigorous supporters of the Norman monarchy" is to stretch a point. Hollister, "Irony of English Feudalism," 17.

[86] In view of the statement of William of Malmesbury, it is not impossible that Rufus hired mercenaries in 1088, but no mention is made of them in accounts of operations. *De Gestis Regum,* II, 368.

[87] *Ibid.,* 472.

[88] Poole, *Domesday Book to Magna Carta;* Hollister, "Military Service," 42.

[89] Powicke, *Military Obligation,* 46.

[90] *Gesta Regis,* I, 278–280; Roger of Hoveden, II, 260–263; *English Historical Documents,* II, 416–417; Poole, *Domesday Book to Magna Carta,* 339.

[91] William of Poitiers, 210.

[92] Ordericus Vitalis, II, 179–181,193–194.

[93] *Pipe Roll 2 Henry II,* 22; *P. R. 4 Henry II,* 139.

[94] *Gesta Regis,* 68, 69; Jordan Fantosme, 278, 298.

[95] Richardson and Sayles, *Governance of Mediaeval England,* 56–57.

[96] Sir Frank Stenton, "Norman London," in *Social Life in Early England,* ed. Geoffrey Barraclough (London, 1960) , 179–207.

[97] William of Poitiers, 214–216, 218–220; Guy of Amiens, 45–47.

[98] *Gesta Stephani,* 85, 89; Round, *Geoffrey de Mandeville,* 119, 127–128.

[99] Henry of Huntingdon, 278; William of Newburgh, I, 48–49; Stenton, "Norman London," 185.

[100] Stenton, "Norman London," 185.

[101] *Ibid.*

[102] *Gesta Stephani,* 85.

[103] *Gesta Stephani,* 72, 77.

[104] *Anglo-Saxon Chronicle,* I, 348, 349.

[105] Hugh Candidus, 165; *Chronicon Petroburgense,* ed. Thomas Stapleton (London, 1849) , 169,172,173; Lennard, *Rural England,* 228, 381.

[106] Douglas, *William the Conqueror,* 278.

Appendix A

Castles in England and Wales, 1052-1189

I. England

THIS list, although probably incomplete, includes the names of all castles for which there is evidence, documentary or archaeological, of their existence prior to the death of Henry II in 1189. Included also are castles considered by specialists to have been built before that date.

Castle	Type	Earliest mention or conjectural date of construction	Authority
BEDFORDSHIRE			
Bedford	motte-and-bailey	1137	*Gesta Stephani,* 31
Bletsoe	motte-and-bailey		
Clophill (Cainhoe)	motte-and-bailey		
Eaton Socon	motte-and-bailey		
Flitwick	motte-and-bailey		
Great Barford (nr.)	motte-and-bailey		
Higham Gobion	motte-and-bailey		
Meppershall	motte-and-bailey	1137/38	*Monasticon,* IV, 216
Odell	motte-and-bailey		
Ridgemount (Seg-enhoe)	motte-and-bailey		
Risinghoe	motte	1180/1200	*Wardon Cartulary,* Beds. Rec. Soc., XIII, 125
Sandye Place	motte-and-bailey		
Sutton Park	motte-and-bailey		
Tempsford (?)	motte-and-bailey		

Castle	Type	Earliest mention or conjectural date of construction	Authority
BEDFORDSHIRE (cont.)			
Thurleigh	motte-and-bailey		
Toddington	motte-and-bailey		
Totternhoe	motte-and-bailey		
Yeldon	motte-and-bailey	1173/74	*Pipe Roll 20 Henry II,* 55
BERKSHIRE			
Abingdon	motte	1142	Wm. of Malmes., *Hist. Nov.,* 77
Brightwell	motte-and-bailey	1152	Robert of Torigni, 174
Faringdon	motte-and-bailey	1145	Wm. of Newburgh, I, 48–49
Hinton Waldrist	motte-and-bailey		
Newbury	no data	1152	Henry of Hunt., 284
Reading	motte-and-bailey	1152	Robert of Torigni, 174
South Moreton	motte		
Wallingford	motte-and-bailey	1087	*Domesday Bk.,* I, 56a
Windsor	motte-and-bailey	1066/70	*Regesta,* I, 13
BUCKINGHAMSHIRE			
Bradwell	motte-and-bailey	T.R.W I	
Buckingham	motte-and-bailey		*Gesta Herewardi,* 70
Castle Hill (Wing Parish)	motte		
Castle Thorpe	motte-and-bailey		
Cublington	motte		
Cymbeline's Mount (Ellesborough Par.)	motte-and-bailey		
Desborough Castle (?)	motte-and-bailey		
Drayton Parslow	motte		
Hanslope	motte-and-bailey		
High Wycombe	motte-and-bailey		
Hoggeston Mound	motte-and-bailey		
Lavendon	motte-and-bailey		
Little Kimble	motte-and-bailey		
Ludgershall	motte-and-bailey		
Missenden	motte-and-bailey		
Newport	motte		

Castle	Type	Earliest mention or conjectural date of construction	Authority
BUCKINGHAMSHIRE (cont.)			
Princes Risborough	motte-and-bailey		
Saunderton	motte-and-bailey		
Shenley Church End	motte-and-bailey		
Stantonbury	motte-and-bailey		
Weston Turville	motte-and-bailey	1173/74	*Pipe Roll 20 Henry II*, 82
Whitchurch	motte-and-bailey		
Wolverton	motte-and-bailey		
CAMBRIDGESHIRE AND THE ISLE OF ELY			
Aldreth	no data	T.R.W I	*Liber Eliensis*, 194
Benwick	no data	1143	*Liber Eliensis*, 328
Burne	no data	T.R.W I	*Monasticon*, VI, 86
Burwell	no data	1144	Gervase of Cant., I, 128
Cambridge	motte-and-bailey	1068	Ordericus, II, 185
Castle Camps	motte		
Ely	motte-and-bailey	1071	*Liber Eliensis*, 174
Fordham	no data	1143	*Liber Eliensis*, 328
Knapwell	motte-and-bailey		
Rampton	motte-and-bailey		
Wisbeach	motte-and-bailey	1071	Rog. Wendover, I, 339
CHESHIRE			
Aldford	motte-and-bailey		
Castle Field (near Macclesfield)	motte		
Chester	motte-and-bailey	1070	Ordericus, II, 198–199
Dodleston	motte-and-bailey		
Dunham	motte	1173	*Gesta Regis*, I, 48
Frodsham	no data		
Halton	no data	T.R.W I	*Monasticon*, VI, 315
Kinderton	motte-and-bailey		
Malpas	motte		
Northwich	motte	derelict T.R.R I	*Harl. MSS.* 2074, 189
Peele Castle	motte-and-bailey		
Pulford	motte-and-bailey		
Runcorn	motte (?)		
Shipbrook	motte		
Shocklach	motte-and-bailey		

Castle	Type	Earliest mention or conjectural date of construction	Authority
CHESHIRE (cont.)			
Shotwick	motte-and-bailey		
Stockport	no data	1173	*Gesta Regis*, I, 48
Torkington	motte		
Ullersford	motte		
Ullerwood	no data	1173	*Gesta Regis*, I, 48
CORNWALL			
Boscastle	no data		
Bossiney	motte-and-bailey		
Kilkhampton	motte-and-bailey		
Launceston	motte-and-bailey	1087	*Domesday Bk.*, I, 121b
Liskeard	no data		
Restormel	motte		
Tintagel	promontory castle		
Trematon	motte-and-bailey	1087	*Domesday Bk.*, I, 122a
Truro	motte-and-bailey		
CUMBERLAND			
Beaumont (**Castle** Green)	motte		
Borough Hill (nr. Braystones)	motte-and-bailey		
Brampton Mote (nr. Irthington)	motte		
Carlisle	no data	1092	*Anglo-Saxon Chron.*, I, 359
Castle Sowerby	no data	1186/87	*Pipe Roll 33 Henry II*, 95
Cockermouth	no data		
Denton Hall	motte-and-bailey		
Downhall	motte-and-bailey		
Egremont	no data		
Frizington	motte-and-bailey		
Headswood	motte-and-bailey		
High Mains	motte-and-bailey		
Holm Cultram	motte-and-bailey		
Ivy Hill	motte		
Liddell	motte-and-bailey	1174	Roger of Hoveden, II, 60
Maryport	motte-and-bailey		
Over Denton	motte-and-bailey		
Peel (nr. Lorton)	motte		

Castle	Type	Earliest mention or conjectural date of construction	Authority
CUMBERLAND (cont.)			
St. John's	motte-and-bailey		
Scaleby	motte-and-bailey		
Weary Hall (nr. Whitehall)	motte		
Whitehall	motte		
Wodabank	motte		
DERBYSHIRE			
Bakewell	motte-and-bailey		
Bolsover	natural cliff	1172/73	*Pipe Roll 19 Henry II,* 174
Bretby	motte-and-bailey		
Castle Wood (nr. So. Normanton)	motte-and-bailey		
Duffield	motte-and-bailey	1173	*Gesta Regis,* I, 48
Gresley	motte		
Holmesfield	motte		
Hope Church	motte		
Horsley Castle (Harestan)	motte		
Morley	motte		
Morley Moor	motte		
Peak	natural site	1087	*Domesday Bk.,* I, 276a
Pinxton	motte-and-bailey		
Tapton	motte		
DEVONSHIRE			
Bampton	motte-and-bailey	1136	Henry of Hunt., 259
Barnstaple	motte	T.R.W I/W II	*Monasticon,* V, 197
Berry Pomeroy	motte-and-bailey		
Blackawton	motte		
Bridestowe	motte-and-bailey		
Bridport	no data	1149	*Gesta Stephani,* 147
Buckerell	motte-and-bailey		
Buckfastleigh (Hembury Castle)	motte-and-bailey		
Bushy Knap	motte		
Croft Castle	motte		
Durpley	motte-and-bailey		
Exeter	motte	1068	Ordericus, II, 179–181

Castle	Type	Earliest mention or conjectural date of construction	Authority
DEVONSHIRE (cont.)			
Gidleigh	no data		
Hembury Fort	motte-and-bailey		
Highweek	motte-and-bailey		
Holwell Castle	motte-and-bailey		
Loddiswell	motte-and-bailey		
Loxhore	motte		
Lydford	motte		
Milton Damerel	motte-and-bailey		
North Tawton	motte		
Okehampton	motte-and-bailey	1087	*Domesday Bk.*, I, 105b
Plympton	motte-and-bailey	1136	*Gesta Stephani*, 23–24
Tiverton	no data		
Totnes	motte-and-bailey	T.R.W I	*Monasticon*, IV, 630
Wembworthy	motte-and-bailey		
DORSETSHIRE			
Bow and Arrow (Rufus Castle)	no data	1142	Wm. of Malmes., *Hist. Nov.*, 76
Corfe	motte-and-bailey	1087	*Domesday Bk.*, I, 78b
Dorchester	no data	1138	*Ann. Winton.*, 51
East Chelborough	motte-and-bailey		
Lulworth	no data	1142	Wm. of Malmes., *Hist. Nov.*, 76
Marshwood	motte-and-bailey		
Powerstock	motte-and-bailey		
Sherborne	masonry	1122 (?)	*Regesta*, II, 172
Wareham	motte-and-bailey	1113	*Anglo-Saxon Chron.*, I, 370
Wimborne	no data	1138	*Ann. Winton.*, 51
DURHAM			
Barnard	motte	1123/33	*Regesta*, II, 287
Bishopton	motte-and-bailey	1143	Symeon of Dur., I, 150–151
Blackwell	motte-and-bailey		
Castle Eden	no data	1143/52	*E.Y.C.*, II, 2–3
Durham	motte	1072	Symeon of Dur., II, 200
Merrington	fortified church	1144	Symeon of Dur., I, 158
Middleton St. George	motte		

Castle	Type	Earliest mention or conjectural date of construction	Authority
DURHAM (cont.)			
Thornlaw	no data	1143	Symeon of Dur., I, 164–165
The Yoden	motte-and-bailey		
ESSEX			
Barking	motte-and-bailey (?)		
Berden	motte		
Birch Castle	motte		
Canfield	motte-and-bailey		
Chrishall	motte		
Clavering (Robert's Castle?)	motte-and-bailey	1052 (?)	Anglo-Saxon Chron., I, 321
Colchester	masonry	1100/02	Regesta, II, 18
Elmdon	motte		
Great Easton	motte-and-bailey		
Hedingham	motte-and-bailey	T.R.H II	Monasticon, IV, 437
Latton	motte		
Mount Bures	motte-and-bailey		
Navestock	motte-and-bailey		
Ongar	motte-and-bailey	1156 (?)	Chron. Mon. Bello, 84
Orsett	motte-and-bailey		
Pleshy	motte-and-bailey	1143	Henry of Hunt., 276
Purleigh	motte-and-bailey		
Raleigh	motte-and-bailey	1087	Domesday Bk., II, 43b
Rickling	motte-and-bailey		
Saffron Walden	motte-and-bailey	1139	Ann. de Waverleia, 227
Stansted Montfichet	motte-and-bailey		
Stebbing Mount	motte		
Willingale Doe	motte-and-bailey		
GLOUCESTERSHIRE			
Berkeley	motte	1087	Domesday Bk., I, 163a
Bristol	no data	1088	Anglo-Saxon Chron., I, 356–357
Cerney	no data	1139	Gesta Stephani, 62
Cirencester	no data	1142	Gesta Stephani, 91
Dursley	no data	1149	Gesta Stephani, 143, 144
English Bicknor	motte-and-bailey		
Gloucester	motte-and-bailey	1087	Domesday Bk., I, 162a
Hailes	no data	1140/50	Lanaboc . . . de Winchelcumba, I, 65

Castle	Type	Earliest mention or conjectural date of construction	Authority
GLOUCESTERSHIRE (cont.)			
Lydney	motte		
St. Briavels	no data	1130	*Pipe Roll 31 Henry I,* 76
Sudeley	no data	1139	Cont. Flor. Worc., II, 120
Tetbury	no data	1144	*Gesta Stephani,* 114
Winchcomb	motte	1139	*Gesta Stephani,* 63
HAMPSHIRE AND THE ISLE OF WIGHT			
Bishop's Waltham	masonry	1138	*Ann. Winton.,* 51
Carisbrooke	motte-and-bailey	1087	*Domesday Bk.,* I, 52b
Christchurch	motte	1147	*Gesta Stephani,* 140
Hursley (?)	masonry		
"Lidelea"	no data	1147	*Gesta Stephani,* 138
Merdon	motte-and-bailey	1138	*Ann. Winton.,* 51
Odiham	masonry		
Old Basing	motte-and-bailey	T.R.H I	*Monasticon,* VI, 1014
Porchester	motte-and-bailey	1153	Charter in Round, *Commune of London,* 82
Southampton	no data	1153	*Foedera,* I, i, 18
Winchester	motte-and-bailey	1067	Ordericus, II, 166–167
Wolvesey	masonry	1138	*Ann. Winton.,* 51
HEREFORDSHIRE			
Almely	motte-and-bailey		
Ashton Castle Tump	motte		
Aston Tump	motte-and-bailey		
Bacton	motte-and-bailey		
Brampton	motte-and-bailey		
Bredwardine	motte-and-bailey		
Breinton	motte-and-bailey		
Buckton	motte		
Buckton Tump	motte		
Camp Wood Tump	motte		
Castle Frome	motte-and-bailey		
Chanstone	motte-and-bailey		
Clifford	motte-and-bailey	1087	*Domesday Bk.,* I, 183a
Combe Tump	motte		
Cusop Castle	motte		
Cwmm Mound	motte		

Castle	Type	Earliest mention or conjectural date of construction	Authority
HEREFORDSHIRE (cont.)			
Didley Court Farm	motte-and-bailey		
Dilwyn	motte-and-bailey		
Dinmore	motte		
Dorstone	motte-and-bailey		
Downton-on-the-Rock	motte		
Eardisland Mounts	motte		
Eardisley	motte-and-bailey	1183	*Pipe Roll 29 Henry II*, 111
Eccleswall	motte-and-bailey		
Edvin Ralph	motte-and-bailey		
Ewias Harold (Pentecost's Castle)	motte-and-bailey	1052	Symeon of Dur., II, 170
Goodrich	no data	1101/02	*Cal. Docs. Fr.*, 408
Hereford	motte-and-bailey	1055	*Brut*, 42/43
Hereford Cathedral Close	siege castle	1140	*Gesta Stephani*, 72
Hereford Beacon	motte-and-bailey		
Howton Mound	motte		
Huntingdon	motte-and-bailey		
Kentchurch	motte-and-bailey		
Kilpeck	motte-and-bailey	1134	*Monasticon*, I, 548
Kingsland	motte-and-bailey		
Kington	motte	1186/87	*Pipe Roll 33 Henry II*, 131
Kington Rural	motte-and-bailey		
Layster's Tump	motte-and-bailey		
Lenmore	motte		
Lingen	motte-and-bailey		
Lingen Tump	motte-and-bailey		
Little Hengoed	motte		
Little Hereford	motte-and-bailey		
Llancillo	motte-and-bailey		
Longtown (Ewias Lacy)	motte-and-bailey	1087	*Domesday Bk.*, I, 184a
Lower Court	motte		
Lower Hergest Castle Twts	motte-and-bailey		
Lower Pedwardine	motte-and-bailey		
Lower Pont-Hendre	motte-and-bailey		
Lyonshall Castle	motte-and-bailey		
Madley Mound	motte-and-bailey		

Castle	Type	Earliest mention or conjectural date of construction	Authority
HEREFORDSHIRE (cont.)			
Mansell Lacy	motte		
Michaelchurch Escley	motte-and-bailey		
Moccas	motte-and-bailey		
Mortimer's Castle	motte-and-bailey	1153	*Foedera*, I, i, 18
Mouse Castle	motte-and-bailey		
Much Dewchurch	motte-and-bailey		
Mynydd-Brith	motte-and-bailey		
Nant-y-Bar	motte		
Newton Tump	motte-and-bailey		
Old Castleton	motte-and-bailey		
Oldcastle Twt	motte-and-bailey		
Orcop	motte-and-bailey		
Pembridge Mound	motte		
Richard's Castle	motte-and-bailey	1052	*Anglo-Saxon Chron.*, I, 316
Rowlstone Mount	motte-and-bailey		
St. Devereux	motte		
St. Weonard's Tump	motte		
Shobdon Court Mount	motte		
Snodhill	motte-and-bailey		
Soller's Hope	motte		
Stapleton	motte-and-bailey		
Staunton-on-Arrow	motte-and-bailey		
Thruxton Tump	motte-and-bailey		
Tregate Castle Farm	motte-and-bailey		
Tretire Castle	motte-and-bailey		
Turnastone	motte		
Turret Castle	motte-and-bailey		
Urishay Castle	motte-and-bailey		
Vowchurch Tump	motte-and-bailey		
Wacton Mound	motte		
Walford Tump	motte		
Waltersone Mound	motte-and-bailey		
Wigmore	motte-and-bailey	1087	*Domesday Bk.*, I, 180a
Wilton	no data	1187/88	*Pipe Roll 34 Henry II*, 210
Woebley	motte-and-bailey	1138	Cont. Flor. Worc., II, 106
Woodville Mount	motte		

Castle	Type	Earliest mention or conjectural date of construction	Authority
HERTFORDSHIRE			
Anstey	motte-and-bailey		
Bennington	motte-and-bailey	1176/77	*Pipe Roll 23 Henry II,* 144
Berkhamstead	motte-and-bailey	T.R.W I	*Monasticon,* VI, 2, 1090
Brent Pelham	motte		
Chelsing	motte		
Great Wymondley	motte-and-bailey		
Hertford	motte-and-bailey	1170/71	*Pipe Roll 17 Henry II,* 118–119
Little Wymondley	motte-and-bailey		
Pirton	motte-and-bailey		
Reed	motte-and-bailey		
Sandon Mount	motte		
Stortford	motte-and-bailey	1085/87	*Regesta,* I, 72–73
Therfield	motte-and-bailey		
Walkern	motte-and-bailey		
HUNTINGDONSHIRE			
Boughton-in-Southoe	no data	1140/1153	*Add. Chart.,* 11,233
Chesterton Mound	motte		
Great Staughton	motte-and-bailey		
Huntingdon	motte-and-bailey	1068	Ordericus, II, 185
Kimbolton	motte-and-bailey		
Ramsey	motte-and-bailey (?)	1143	Henry of Hunt., 276–277
Sapley	motte-and-bailey		
Wood Walton	motte-and-bailey		
KENT			
Allington	motte-and-bailey	1174/75	*Pipe Roll 21 Henry II,* 212
Binbury Castle	motte-and-bailey		
Brenchley	motte		
Canterbury	motte-and-bailey (?)	1087	*Domesday Bk.,* I, 2a
Castle Toll (nr. Newenden)	motte-and-bailey		
Chilham	motte-and-bailey	1170/71	*Pipe Roll 17 Henry II,* 137
Dover	motte-and-bailey	1066	Wm. of Poitiers, 210
Eynsford	masonry		
Folkestone	motte-and-bailey	1095	*Monasticon,* IV, 674b

Castle	Type	Earliest mention or conjectural date of construction	Authority
KENT (cont.)			
Frittenden	motte		
Hunton	motte-and-bailey (?)		
Ightham	motte		
Leeds	fortified island	1138	Ordericus, v, 112
Leybourne	motte-and-bailey		
Rochester	motte-and-bailey	1087	*Domesday Book, I, 2b*
Saltwood	motte-and-bailey	1174/75	*Pipe Roll 21 Henry II,* 209
Selling	motte		
Stockbury	motte-and-bailey		
Swanscombe	motte		
Thurnham (Goddard's Castle)	motte-and-bailey		
Tonbridge	motte-and-bailey	1088	*Anglo-Saxon Chron.,* I, 357
Tonge Castle	motte		
Wouldham	motte		
LANCASHIRE			
Aldingham	motte-and-bailey		
Arkholme-with-Cawood	motte		
Bury	motte		
Clitheroe	motte-and-bailey	1087	*Domesday Bk., I, 332a*
Halton	motte-and-bailey		
Hornby	motte-and-bailey		
Lancaster	motte-and-bailey		
Manchester	no data	1183/84	*Pipe Roll 30 Henry II,* 23
Melling	motte-and-bailey		
Merhull	motte-and-bailey		
Newton-in-Makerfield	motte-and-bailey		
Pennington	motte		
Penwortham	motte-and-bailey	1087	*Domesday Bk., I, 270a*
Preston	motte-and-bailey		
Rochdale (Castleton)	motte-and-bailey		
Warrington	motte-and-bailey		
West Derby	motte-and-bailey		
Whittington	motte-and-bailey		

Castle	Type	Earliest mention or conjectural date of construction	Authority
LEICESTERSHIRE			
Belvoir	motte-and-bailey	T.R.W I	*Monasticon,* III, 288
Donnington	motte-and-bailey		
Earl Shilton	motte-and-bailey		
Gilmorton	motte-and-bailey		
Groby	motte-and-bailey	1173	*Gesta Regis,* I, 48
Hallaton	motte-and-bailey		
Hinckley	motte		
Leicester	motte-and-bailey	1088	Wm. of Malmes., *De Gestis Regum,* II, 361
Mountsorrel	no data	1148/53	*Lansdowne MS.* 415, f.41
Ratcliffe Culey	motte		
Ravenstone	no data	1148/53	*Cott. MS Nero C* III, f.178
Scraptoft	motte		
Shackerstone	motte-and-bailey		
Whitwick	motte-and-bailey	1148/53	*Cott. MS. Nero C* III, f.178
LINCOLNSHIRE			
Barrow upon Humber	no data	1189	*Monasticon,* VI, 327
Barton-on-Humber	no data	T.R.S or H II	*Monasticon,* I, 631
Bitham	motte-and-bailey	1087 (?)	*Domesday Bk.,* I, 360b
Bolingbroke	motte-and-bailey		
Bourne	motte-and-bailey	1092 (?)	*Monasticon,* VI, 87a
Carlton	motte-and-bailey		
Folkingham	motte-and-bailey		
Gainsborough	no data	1142	Charter in Round, *Geoffrey de Mandeville,* 159
Goxhill	no data	1143/47	*Danelaw Charters,* 167
Kinnard Ferry (Axholme)	motte-and-bailey	1173	*Gesta Regis,* I, 48
Lincoln	motte-and-bailey	1068	*Anglo-Saxon Chron.,* I, 342
Partney	no data	1141/42	E.Y.C., X, 114–115
Sleaford	no data	1139	Henry of Hunt., 266
Stamford-on-the Welland	motte	1087	*Domesday Bk.,* I, 366b

Castle	Type	Earliest mention or conjectural date of construction	Authority
LINCOLNSHIRE (cont.)			
Swineshead	no data	1185/86	*Pipe Roll 32 Henry II*, 81
Thorngate	no data	1141	*Reg. Antiq. of Linc. Cath.*, I, 61–62
Torkesey	motte		
Welbourne	no data	1158 (?)	*Add. Chart.* 6,038
MIDDLESEX			
Baynard's Castle	no data	1111	*Monasticon*, VI, 147
Hillingdon	motte-and-bailey		
London (the Tower)	masonry	1067	Wm. of Poitiers, 236
Montfichet's Castle	no data	1135	Hugh of Flavigny, 495–496
Ruislip	motte-and-bailey		
South Mymms	motte-and-bailey		
MONMOUTHSHIRE			
Abergavenny	motte-and-bailey	1087/1100	*Cal. Docs. Fr.*, 367–368
Caerleon	motte-and-bailey	1087	*Domesday Bk.*, I, 185b
Caerwent	no data		
Caldicot	motte-and-bailey	*ca.* 1150	*Liber Land.*, 44
Castleton	motte	1184/85	*Pipe Roll 31 Henry II*, 6
Chepstow	masonry	1087	*Domesday Bk.*, I, 162a
Dingestow	motte-and-bailey	1176 (?)	*Itin. Kamb.*, 47–48
Dinham	no data	*ca.* 1150	*Liber Landav.*, 44
Grosmont	motte-and-bailey	1162/63	*Pipe Roll 9 Henry II*, 7
Monmouth	motte	1087	*Domesday Bk.*, I, 180b
Newport	no data	1184/85	*Pipe Roll 31 Henry II*, 7
Scenfrith	motte-and-bailey	1162/63	*Pipe Roll 9 Henry II*, 7
Usk	no data	1138	Ordericus, V, 110
White Castle (Llantilio)	no data	1162/63	*Pipe Roll 9 Henry II*, 7
NORFOLK			
Buckenham	motte-and-bailey		
Castle Acre	motte-and-bailey	1085 (?)	*E.Y.C.*, VIII, 4, 5
Castle Rising	motte-and-bailey		
Denton	motte-and-bailey		

Castle	Type	Earliest mention or conjectural date of construction	Authority
NORFOLK (cont.)			
Norwich	motte-and-bailey	1075	*Anglo-Saxon Chron.*, I, 348
Old Buckenham	motte-and-bailey	T.R.S.	*Monasticon*, VI, 419
Thetford	motte	1103/04 (?)	*Monasticon*, V, 150
Weeting	no data		
Wormegay	motte-and-bailey		
NORTHAMPTONSHIRE			
Alderton	motte		
Brackley	motte-and-bailey (?)	1172/73	*Pipe Roll 19 Henry II*, 70
Cransley	motte		
Culworth Castle	motte		
Earl's Barton	motte		
Farthingstone	motte-and-bailey		
Fortheringhay	motte-and-bailey		
Gaultney ("Galclint")	motte (?)	1140	John of Hexham, II, 306
Lilbourne Castle	motte-and-bailey		
Little Houghton	motte		
Long Buckby	motte-and-bailey		
Northampton	motte-and-bailey	1130	*Pipe Roll 31 Henry I*, 135
Peterborough	motte	1069/98	Hugh Candidus, 86
Preston Capes	motte	T.R.W. I or W. II	*Monasticon*, V, 178
Rockingham	motte-and-bailey	1087	*Domesday Bk.*, I, 220a
Sibbertoft Castle Yard	motte-and-bailey		
Sulgrave Castle	motte		
Towcester	motte		
Wollaston Castle	motte		
NORTHUMBERLAND			
Alnwick	motte-and-bailey	1136	Ric. of Hexham, 145
Bamburgh	natural site	1070	Symeon of Dur., II, 191
Bellingham	motte-and-bailey		
Bolam	motte-and-bailey		
Bothal	motte-and-bailey		
Elsdon	motte-and-bailey		
Fenham	motte-and-bailey		

Castle	Type	Earliest mention or conjectural date of construction	Authority
NORTHUMBERLAND (cont.)			
Gunnerton	motte-and-bailey		
Haltwhistle	motte		
Harbottle	motte-and-bailey	1174	Roger of Hoveden, II, 60
Lowick	motte-and-bailey		
Lucker	motte-and-bailey		
Mitford	motte-and-bailey	1138	Rich. of Hexham, 158
Morpeth	motte-and-bailey	1095	Geoffrey Gaimar, I, 262
Newcastle-upon-Tyne	motte-and-bailey	1080	Symeon of Dur., II, 211
Norham	motte-and-bailey	1121	Symeon of Dur., II, 260
Prudhoe	motte-and-bailey (?)	1172/73	*Pipe Roll 19 Henry II*, 113
Rothbury	motte		
Shipley	motte-and-bailey		
Simonburn	motte-and-bailey		
South Middleton	motte-and-bailey		
Tynemouth	motte-and-bailey	1095	*Anglo-Saxon Chron.*, I, 361
Wark-upon-Tweed	motte-and-bailey	1136	Richard of Hexham, 145
Wark-upon-Tyne	motte-and-bailey		
Warkworth	motte-and-bailey	1174	Roger of Hovenden, II, 60
Wooler	motte-and-bailey		
NOTTINGHAMSHIRE			
Annesley	motte-and-bailey		
Aslockton	motte-and-bailey		
Bothamsall	motte		
Cuckney	no data	T.R.S.	*Monasticon*, VI, 873
Egmanton	motte-and-bailey		
Lambley	motte		
Laxton (Lexington)	motte-and-bailey		
Lowdham	motte		
Newark-on-Trent	no data	1123/33	*Regesta*, II, 264
Nottingham	motte-and-bailey	1068	*Anglo-Saxon Chron.*, I, 342
Worksop	motte-and-bailey		

Castle	Type	Earliest mention or conjectural date of construction	Authority
OXFORDSHIRE			
Ascot-under-Wych-wood	motte-and-bailey	*ante* T.R.H. II	*Cart. Mon. St. Frideswide*, II, 242
Bampton	fortified church	1142	*Gesta Stephani*, 92
Banbury	motte-and-bailey	1146	*Cartae Antiquae*, I, 195–197
Beaumont Castle	motte-and-bailey		
Chipping Norton	motte-and-bailey		
Crowmarsh	motte-and-bailey	1146	Gervase of Cant., I, 130
Dedington	motte-and-bailey		
Middleton	motte-and-bailey		
Oxford	motte-and-bailey	1072	*Monasticon*, VI, 251–253
Radcot	no data	1142	*Gesta Stephani*, 91
Swerford	motte-and-bailey		
Woodstock	no data	1142	*Gesta Stephani*, 91
RUTLANDSHIRE			
Beaumont Chase	motte-and-bailey		
Burley	motte-and-bailey		
Pilton	motte		
SHROPSHIRE			
Abberbury	motte-and-bailey		
Bettws-y-Crwyn	motte-and-bailey		
Bicton Mound	motte		
Binewston	motte		
Bishop's Castle (Lydbury)	motte-and-bailey	1166/67	*Pipe Roll 13 Henry II*, 77
Bridgnorth	masonry	1098/99	Ordericus, IV, 32–33
Broadward Hall Mound	motte		
Brocton	motte-and-bailey		
Brompton and Rhiston	motte-and-bailey		
Bryn	no data	1138	Ordericus, V, 111
Bucknell	motte		
Caynham	motte-and-bailey		
Castell Brogyntyn	motte		
Castell Bryn Amlwg	motte		
Castle Bank	motte-and-bailey		

Castle	Type	Earliest mention or conjectural date of construction	Authority
SHROPSHIRE (cont.)			
Castle Holgate	motte-and-bailey	1087	*Domesday Bk.*, I, 258b
Caus	motte-and-bailey	1134	Ordericus, v, 43
Charlton Castle	motte-and-bailey		
Church Stretton	motte-and-bailey	1156/57	*Pipe Roll 3 Henry II*, 88
Cleobury	no data	1155	Gervase of Cant., I, 162
Clun	motte-and-bailey	1146	*Cal. Docs. Fr.*, 403
Clungunford	motte		
Colebatch	motte		
Corfton Mount	motte-and-bailey		
Ellesmere Mount	motte-and-bailey	1138	Ordericus, v, 111
Great Ness	motte		
Hardwick Mount	motte-and-bailey		
Hawcock's Mount	motte		
Hisland Mount	motte		
Hockleton	motte-and-bailey		
Hodnet	motte-and-bailey		
Hopton Castle	motte-and-bailey		
Kinnerley	motte-and-bailey		
Knockyn	motte-and-bailey	1164/65	*Pipe Roll 11 Henry II*, 91
Lady House	motte		
Leebotwood	no data	1172	Harl. MS, 3868 (after Hogg and King)
Lee Brockhurst	motte		
Linley Mound	motte		
Little Ness	motte-and-bailey		
Little Stretton	motte		
Lower Down	motte		
Ludlow	motte-and-bailey	1137	Henry of Hunt., 261
Lydbury North	motte		
Lydham Castle	motte-and-bailey		
Marton	motte-and-bailey		
Middlehope	motte-and-bailey		
More Castle	motte-and-bailey		
Oakland's Mount	motte		
Oldbury	motte-and-bailey		
Old Quatford	motte-and-bailey	1087	*Domesday Bk.*, I, 254a
Oswestry	motte-and-bailey	1087	*Domesday Bk.*, I, 253b
Pontesbury	motte		
Prees	motte		

Castle	Type	Earliest mention or conjectural date of construction	Authority
SHROPSHIRE (cont.)			
Pulverbach	motte-and-bailey		
Rabbit Berries	motte		
Rushbury	motte		
Shrawardine	no data	1165/66	*Pipe Roll 12 Henry II,* 59
Shrewsbury	motte-and-bailey	1069	Ordericus, II, 193
Smethcott	motte-and-bailey		
Stanton Lacy	motte-and-bailey		
Stapleton	motte		
Upper Gwarthlow	motte		
Wem	motte		
West Felton	motte		
Weston	motte		
Whitchurch	motte-and-bailey	1160/61	*Pipe Roll 7 Henry II,* 20
Whittington	motte-and-bailey	1138	Ordericus, V, 111
Wilderley Hall	motte-and-bailey		
Wilmington	motte-and-bailey		
Wollaston Mount	motte-and-bailey		
Woolstaston	motte		
Worthen	motte		
Wortherton	motte		
Yockleton Mount	motte		
SOMERSETSHIRE			
Ballands	motte-and-bailey		
Bath	no data	1138	Con. Flor. Worc., II, 108–109
Bridgewater	no data		
Bury	motte-and-bailey		
Castle Cary	no data	1138	*Ann. de Waverleia,* 226
Castle Neroche	motte-and-bailey		
Castle Orchard	motte-and-bailey		
Charlton Musgrove	motte		
Culverhay Castle	motte-and-bailey		
Downend	motte-and-bailey		
Dunster	motte-and-bailey	1087	*Domesday Bk.,* I, 95b
Glastonbury	motte-and-bailey		
Harptree	no data	1138	*Gesta Stephani*
Ilchester	no data	1088	Flor. Worc., II, 24
Locking	motte-and-bailey		

Castle	Type	Earliest mention or conjectural date of construction	Authority
SOMERSETSHIRE (cont.)			
Montacute	motte-and-bailey	1069	Ordericus, II, 193
Stogursey	motte-and-bailey		
Stowey Castle	motte-and-bailey	*ante* 1155	*Cal. Chart. Rolls*, II, 363
Taunton	motte-and-bailey	1138	*Ann. Winton.*, 51
Walton in Gordano	motte		
STAFFORDSHIRE			
Alton	no data	1176	*Monasticon*, v, 662
Burton	motte-and-bailey	1087	*Domesday Bk.*, I, 248b
Chartley Castle	motte-and-bailey		
Dudley	motte-and-bailey	1087	*Domesday Bk.*, I, 177a
Heighley	motte		
Lichfield	no data	1129	*Monasticon*, VI, 1241a
Newcastle-under-Lyme	motte	1154/55	*Red Bk. Exch.*, II, 652
Stafford	motte-and-bailey	1070	Ordericus, II, 199
Trentham	no data	1168/69	*Pipe Roll 15 Henry II*, 72
Tutbury	motte-and-bailey	1070	Ordericus, II, 222
SUFFOLK			
"Ambli"	no data	T.R.S	Joc. of Brakelond, 138
Brampton	motte		
Bungay	motte-and-bailey	1140	*Ann. de Waverleia*, 228
Burgh	motte		
Burgh Castle	motte		
Clare	motte-and-bailey	1090	*Monasticon*, VI, 1659
Combs	motte		
Denham	motte-and-bailey		
Eye	motte-and-bailey	1087	*Domesday Bk.*, II, 378b
Framlingham	motte-and-bailey	1157/58	*Pipe Roll 4 Henry II*, 126
Freckenham	no data		
Great Ashfield	motte		
Groton	motte		
Haughley (Haganet)	motte-and-bailey	1173	Gervase of Cant., I, 246
Hunston	motte		
Ilketshall St. John	motte-and-bailey		
Ipswich	no data	1153	Henry of Hunt., 288

Castle	Type	Earliest mention or conjectural date of construction	Authority
SUFFOLK (cont.)			
Lidgate Castle	motte-and-bailey		
Lindsey Castle	motte-and-bailey	T.R.S	Joc. of Brakelond, 138
Milden Castle	motte-and-bailey	T.R.S	Joc. of Brakelond, 138
Offton Castle	motte		
Orford	motte-and-bailey	1165/66	*Pipe Roll 12 Henry II,* 17
Otley	motte-and-bailey		
Walton	no data	1158/59	*Pipe Roll 5 Henry II,* 9
SURREY			
Abinger	motte		
Blenchingley	motte-and-bailey		
Farnham	motte-and-bailey	1138	*Ann. Winton.,* 51
Guildford	motte-and-bailey	1141 (?)	Wm. of Malmes., *Hist. Nov.,* 57–58
Oxted	motte		
Reigate	motte-and-bailey		
Thunderfield	motte-and-bailey		
Walton-on-the-Hill	motte		
SUSSEX			
Arundel	motte-and-bailey	1087	*Domesday Bk.,* I, 23a
Bramber	motte-and-bailey	1073	*Cal. Docs. Fr.,* 405
Burghlow	motte-and-bailey		
Chichester	motte-and-bailey	1173/74	*Pipe Roll 20 Henry II,* 118
Edburton	motte-and-bailey		
Hartfield	motte-and-bailey		
Hastings	motte-and-bailey	1066	*Anglo-Saxon Chron.,* I, 338
Knepp	motte-and-bailey		
Lewes	motte-and-bailey	1077/78	*Monasticon,* v, 12a
Park Mount	motte		
Pevensey	motte-and-bailey	1066	Wm. of Poitiers, 168
Verdley	motte		
WARWICKSHIRE			
Ansley	no data		
Beaudesert	motte-and-bailey	1141	Charter in Round, *Geoffrey de Mandeville,* 65

Castle	Type	Earliest mention or conjectural date of construction	Authority
WARWICKSHIRE (cont.)			
Beausale	no data		
Brailes	motte-and-bailey		
Brandon	water defenses	T.R.S	Charter in Stenton, *First Century*, 211–212
Brinklow	motte-and-bailey	1130	*Pipe Roll 31 Henry I*, 138
Castle Bromwich	motte-and-bailey		
Churchover	motte		
Coleshill	no data		
Coventry	no data	1147	*Gesta Stephani*, 132
Fillongley	motte-and-bailey		
Hartshill	motte-and-bailey		
Hatton	no data	1151/57	*Cal. Docs. Fr.*, 412
Henley-in-Arden	motte		
Kenilworth	motte-and-bailey	1122	*Monasticon*, VI, 220–221
Kineton	motte-and-bailey		
Old Fillongley	motte-and-bailey		
Oversley	no data	1140	*Monasticon*, IV, 175
Rugby	no data		
Seckington	motte-and-bailey		
Solihull	motte		
Tamworth	motte-and-bailey	1141	Charter in Stenton, *First Century*, 225
Tanworth	no data		
Warwick	motte-and-bailey	1068	Ordericus, II, 184
WESTMORELAND			
Appleby	motte-and-bailey	1130	*Pipe Roll 31 Henry I*, 143
Brough	no data	1174	Wm. of Newburgh, I, 182
Brougham	no data		
Castle Howe	motte-and-bailey		
Cockpit Hill	motte		
Kendal	motte		
Lower Greenhow	motte-and-bailey		
Pendragon	masonry		
Tebay	motte-and-bailey		

Castle	Type	Earliest mention or conjectural date of construction	Authority
WILTSHIRE			
Burton	no data	1147	*Gesta Stephani,* 132
Calne	no data		
Cricklade	no data	1144	*Gesta Stephani,* 113
Devizes	motte-and-bailey	1138	*Ann. Winton.,* 51
Downton	no data	1138	*Ann. Winton.,* 51
Ludgershall	no data	1138	*Ann. Winton.,* 51
Malmesbury	no data	1138	*Ann. Winton.,* 51
Marlborough	no data	1137/38	*Ancient Charters,* 36–38
Mere	motte		
Salisbury	motte-and-bailey	1069/70	*Regesta,* I, 13
Trowbridge	motte-and-bailey	1139	Wm. of Malmes., *Hist. Nov.,* 36
Wilton	converted nunnery	1143	Gervase of Cant., I, 125–126
WORCHESTERSHIRE			
Bengeworth	no data	1149/59	*Chron. de Evesham,* 100
Castlemorton	motte-and-bailey		
Elmley	motte-and-bailey		
Ham Castle	motte-and-bailey		
Leigh	motte-and-bailey		
Tenbury Castle	motte		
Worcester	motte-and-bailey	1088	*Anglo-Saxon Chron.,* I, 357
YORKSHIRE			
Ailcy Hill	motte		
Aldbrough	motte-and-bailey	1115	*Monasticon,* VI, 1020
Almondbury	motte-and-bailey	1142/54	*E.Y.C.,* III, 146
Aughton	motte-and-bailey		
Bardsey	motte-and-bailey		
Barwick-in-Elmet	motte-and-bailey	1142/54	*E.Y.C.,* III, 146
Beacon Hill	motte		
Boroughbridge	no data	1175	*Rot. Claus.,* I, 57
Bowes	no data	1170/71	*Pipe Roll 17 Henry II,* 63
Bridlington	converted monastery	1144	Wm. of Newburgh, I, 47
Burton-in-Lonsdale	motte-and-bailey	1130	*Pipe Roll 31 Henry I,* 138

Castle	Type	Earliest mention or conjectural date of construction	Authority
YORKSHIRE (cont.)			
Castle Bailey	motte-and-bailey		
Castlehaugh (Gisburn)	motte		
Catterick	motte-and-bailey		
Conisbrough	motte-and-bailey	1174/78	*E.Y.C.*, VIII, 251
Cotherstone	motte		
Cottingham	no data	T.R.S	*E.Y.C.*, IX, 5
Crake	motte-and-bailey		
Cropton	motte-and-bailey		
Cropton Castle	motte-and-bailey		
Drax	no data	1154	Wm. of Newburgh, I, 94
Driffield	motte-and-bailey		
Flamborough	no data	1180/93 (?)	*E.Y.C.*, II, 254
Gilling	motte		
Haverah Park	motte		
Helmsley	masonry		
Hode	no data	*post* 1145	*Monasticon*, VI, 320
Hunmanby	motte-and-bailey		
Hunsingore	motte		
Hutton Conyers	motte-and-bailey (?)	1140	*E.Y.C.*, IV, 90
Kildale	motte		
Killerby	motte-and-bailey		
Kippax	motte-and-bailey		
Kirkby	no data	1123/25	*E.Y.C.*, III, 180
Knaresborough	no data	1130 (?)	*Pipe Roll 31 Henry I*, 31
Langthwaite	motte-and-bailey		
Laughton-en-le-Morthen	motte-and-bailey		
Levington	motte		
Lockington	motte-and-bailey		
Malton	motte	1138	Richard of Hexham, 165
Malzeard	no data	1130	*Pipe Roll 31 Henry I*, 137
Mexborough	motte-and-bailey		
Middleham	motte-and-bailey		
Mirfield	motte-and-bailey		
Montferrand	no data	T.R.S	*Chron. de Melsa*, I, 106
Mulgrave	motte	T.R.W I	*Monasticon*, I, 410

Castle	Type	Earliest mention or conjectural date of construction	Authority
Northallerton	motte-and-bailey	1142	Symeon of Dur., I, 148
Paullholme	motte		
Pickering	motte-and-bailey	1179/80	*Pipe Roll 26 Henry II*, 75
Pickhill	motte-and-bailey		
Pontefract	motte-and-bailey	1087	*Domesday Bk.*, I, 373b
Rastrick	motte		
Richmond	no data	1087	*Domesday Bk.*, I, 381a
Rougemont	motte-and-bailey		
Sandal	motte-and-bailey		
Scarborough	no data	1155	Wm. of Newburgh, I, 104
Sedburgh	motte-and-bailey		
Selby	no data	1143/53	*Coucher Bk. of Selby*, I, 33
Sheffield	no data	1183/84	*Pipe Roll 30 Henry II*, 100
Sheriff Hutton	motte-and-bailey	1140	John of Hexham, 306
Skelton	motte	T.R.W I	*Monasticon*, VI, 267
Skipsea	motte-and-bailey	T.R.W I	*Monasticon*, V, 393
Skipton	no data	1130/40	*E.Y.C.*, VII, 288
Sprotbrough	motte		
Swine	motte		
Tadcaster	motte-and-bailey		
Thirsk	motte-and-bailey	1130	*Pipe Roll 31 Henry I*, 138
Thorne	motte		
Tickhill	motte-and-bailey	1102	Ordericus, IV, 171
Topcliffe	motte-and-bailey	1174	Roger of Hoveden, II, 59
Wakefield	motte-and-bailey	1174/78	*E.Y.C.*, VIII, 114
Wheldrake	no data	1150	John of Hexham, 323
Whitwood	motte-and-bailey		
Whorlton	motte-and-bailey		
Yafforth	motte	T.R.H II	*E.Y.C.*, V, 292
York	motte-and-bailey	1068	Ordericus, II, 185

SCOTS BORDER

Castle	Type	Earliest mention	Authority
Berwick-on-Tweed	no data	1175	Roger of Wendover, I, 104
Roxburgh	no data	1175	Roger of Wendover, I, 104

Castle	Type	Earliest mention or conjectural date of construction	Authority
UNIDENTIFIED			
"Aldewich"		1185/86	*Pipe Roll 32 Henry II,* 82
"Caperun"		1155/56	*Pipe Roll 2 Henry II,* 51
"Crast"		1173/74	*Pipe Roll 20 Henry II,* 55
"Gaittecastellum"		1161/67	*E.Y.C.,* I, 441
Silva		1147	*Gesta Stephani,* 138
Veteri castello de Dena		*ante* 1154	*Monasticon,* V, 590

II. Wales

THE problem of listing the Welsh castles is compounded by the fact that motte-and-bailey castles continued to be erected until long after the death of Henry II. For this reason, only those castles for which there is documentary evidence or that are considered by a specialist to have existed prior to 1189, have been included. Many sites will of course be obviated by this limitation. The report of the Commission on Ancient and Historical Monuments for Pembrokeshire alone, for example, lists thirty-six castles in addition to those named below.

Castle	Type	Earliest mention or conjectural date of construction	Authority
ANGLESEY			
Aber Lleiniog	motte	1094	Sym. of Durham, II, 224
BRECKNOCKSHIRE			
Blaen Lyfni	motte		
Brecon (Aber-honddu)	motte-and-bailey	T.R.W II	Ordericus, III, 43–44
Bronllys	motte-and-bailey	1188	*Itin. Kamb.,* 31
Builth	motte-and-bailey	1070	*Ann. Cambriae,* 52
Crickhowell	motte		
Hay (Tregelli)	motte-and-bailey	1121	*Ancient Chart.,* 8
Peel of Talgarth	motte-and-bailey		

Castle	Type	Earliest mention or conjectural date of construction	Authority
BRECKNOCKSHIRE (cont.)			
Trecastle	motte-and-bailey		
Tretower	motte-and-bailey		
Waynards Castle	no data	*ca.* 1150	*Monasticon,* III, 265
CARDIGANSHIRE			
Aberdovey	motte	1155	*Brut,* 184/85
Aberystwyth (Llan-badarn)	motte	1107	*Brut,* 104/05
Blaen Porth	no data	1116	*Brut,* 128/29
Caerwedros	motte	1137	*Brut,* 158/59
Cardigan (Aber-teifi)	motte	1136	*Gesta Stephani,* 11
Castel Abereinion	no data	1168	*Ann. Camb.,* 52
Castel Rhos (Llan-rhystyd)	motte-and-bailey	1148	*Brut,* 176/77
Castell Flemys	no data	1184	*Monasticon,* V, 632
Castle of Richard de La Mare	no data	1136	*Brut,* 158/59
Chastel Gwalter (Llanfihangel)	motte-and-bailey	1114	*Regesta,* II, 113
Dinerth	motte	1137	*Brut,* 158/59
Emlyn	motte	1173/74	*Pipe Roll 20 Henry II,* 89
Humphrey's Castle	motte	1138	*Brut,* 162/63
Pont-y-Stuffan	motte	1138	*Brut,* 162/63
Ystrad-Meuric	motte-and-bailey	1116	*Brut,* 130/31
Ystrad Peithyll	motte-and-bailey	1116	*Brut,* 130/31
CARMARTHENSHIRE			
Abercavwy	no data	1116	*Brut,* 126/27
Allt Cunedda	motte-and-bailey		
Allt-y-Ferin	motte-and-bailey		
Carmarthen	motte	1116	*Brut,* 124/25–126/27
Castell Aber Tav	motte-and-bailey	1116	*Brut,* 126/27
Dinevor (Din-weiler)	motte-and-bailey	1145	*Brut,* 168/69
Kidwelly	no data	1114	*Regesta,* II, 114
Laugharne	no data	1116	*Brut,* 126/27
Llandovery	motte-and-bailey	1116	*Brut,* 122/23
Llanstephen	motte-and-bailey	1145	*Brut,* 168/69
Pencader	motte-and-bailey		
Rhyd y Gors	no data	1094	*Brut,* 56/57
Ystrad Cyngen (St. Clears)	motte-and-bailey	1154	*Brut,* 182/83

Castle	Type	Earliest mention or conjectural date of construction	Authority
CARNARVONSHIRE			
Aber (Abermenai, Bangor)	motte	*ca.* 1090	*Hist. of Gruffydd,* 133
Carnarvon	motte-and-bailey	1188	*Itin. Kambriae,* 124
Diganwy	motte	1088 (?)	Ordericus, III, 283–284
Dolwyddelan	no data		
DENBIGHSHIRE			
Chirk	motte-and-bailey	1164/65	*Pipe Roll 11 Henry II,* 90
Erddig	motte		
Llanarmon	motte-and-bailey		
Llangwm	motte-and-bailey		
Ruthin	motte-and-bailey	1160/61	*Pipe Roll 7 Henry II,* 40
Tomen y Rhodwydd	motte-and-bailey	1149	*Brut,* 176/77
Voelas	motte-and-bailey		
Wrexham	motte-and-bailey	1160/61	*Pipe Roll 7 Henry II,* 35
FLINTSHIRE			
Basingwerk	motte-and-bailey	1165/66	*Pipe Roll 12 Henry II,* 67
Hawarden	motte	1173 (?)	*Gesta Regis,* I, 48–49
Hodesley	motte-and-bailey	1160/61	*Pipe Roll 7 Henry II,* 35
Holywell	motte-and-bailey		
Leeswood	motte-and-bailey		
Mold	motte-and-bailey	1147	*Brut,* 172/73
Overton	no data	1138	Ordericus, V, 111
Prestatyn	motte-and-bailey	1165/66	*Pipe Roll 12 Henry II,* 67
Rhuddlan	motte	1087	*Domesday Bk.,* I, 269a
Tyddyn	motte-and-bailey		
GLAMORGANSHIRE			
Aberavon	motte	1152	*Brut,* 182/83
Bridgend	no data	1184/85	*Pipe Roll 31 Henry II,* 5
Cardiff	motte-and-bailey	1082	*Brut,* 50/51
Castleton	no data	1186/87	*Pipe Roll 33 Henry II,* 134
Coity	motte-and-bailey		

Castle	Type	Earliest mention or conjectural date of construction	Authority
GLAMORGANSHIRE (cont.)			
Kenfig	motte-and-bailey	1183/84	*Pipe Roll 30 Henry II*, 60
Llandaff	no data	1187/88	*Pipe Roll 34 Henry II*, 9
Loughor	motte	1150	*Brut*, 180/81
Neath	no data	T.R.H I	*Monasticon*, v, 259a
Ogmore	motte-and-bailey	1116	*Brut*, 126/27
Old Castle Camp	motte-and-bailey		
Oystermouth	motte-and-bailey		
Penrice	motte-and-bailey		
Ruperra	motte		
St. Donat's	no data		
Swansea	motte	1116	*Brut*, 122/23
Woebley	motte		
MERIONETHSHIRE			
Aber Ia (Deutrait)	no data	1188	*Itin. Kambriae.*, 123
Carrog Mount	motte-and-bailey		
Castell Gronw	motte-and-bailey		
Castell Prysor	motte-and-bailey		
Cymmer	motte	1116	*Brut*, 140/41
Cynfael	motte	1146	*Brut*, 174/75
Dernio (Edernion)	motte-and-bailey	1159/60	*Pipe Roll 6 Henry II*, 26
Gwerclas	motte-and-bailey		
Gwyddewern	motte-and-bailey		
Hendwr	motte-and-bailey		
Llanfor	motte-and-bailey		
Llangar	motte-and-bailey		
Tomen-y-Bala	motte-and-bailey		
Tomen-y-Mur	motte	1115	*Brut*, 114/15
Ucheldre	motte-and-bailey		
MONTGOMERYSHIRE			
Caereinon	motte	1155	*Brut*, 184/85
Carreghofa	motte	1098	Flor. of Worc., II, 49
Hen Domen	motte-and-bailey		
Lady's Mount	motte-and-bailey		
Montgomery	motte-and-bailey	1087	*Domesday Bk.*, I, 253b 254a
Powis	motte-and-bailey		

Castle	Type	Earliest mention or conjectural date of construction	Authority
MONTGOMERYSHIRE (cont.)			
Rhyd yr Onen	motte-and-bailey		
Tafolwern	motte-and-bailey	1163	*Brut*, 196/97
PEMBROKESHIRE			
Carew	motte-and-bailey		
Castell	motte-and-bailey		
Cilgerran	motte	1107	*Brut*, 104/05
Haverfordwest	motte	1188	*Itin. Kambriae*, 109
Little Cenarth	no data	1107	*Brut*, 82/83
Little Newcastle	motte-and-bailey		
Llawhadon	motte-and-bailey	1188	*Itin. Kambriae*, 172
Manorbier	motte-and-bailey	1188	*Itin. Kambriae*, 92–93
Narberth	motte-and-bailey	1116	*Brut*, 122/23
Nevern	motte-and-bailey	1188	*Itin. Kambriae*, 111–112
Pembroke	motte-and-bailey	1094	*Brut*, 56/57
Pointz	motte		
Tenby	no data	1152	*Brut*, 182/83
Wiston	motte-and-bailey	1148	*Brut*, 172/73
RADNORSHIRE			
Castell Colwyn	motte-and-bailey	1143	*Brut*, 166/67
Crug Eryr	motte-and-bailey	1188	*Itin. Kambriae*, 16
Cwm Aron	motte-and-bailey	1143	*Brut*, 166/67
Dinytha	motte-and-bailey	*ca.* 1100	*Monasticon*, VI, i, 349
Knighton	motte	1181/82	*Pipe Roll 28 Henry II*, 11
Old Radnor	motte-and-bailey	T.R.H I	*Itin. Kambriae*, 16
Pains Castle	motte-and-bailey		
Rhyader Gwy	motte-and-bailey	1177	*Brut*, 230/31
UNIDENTIFIED			
"Carn Madryn"		1188	*Itin. Kambriae*, 123
Castle Teirtut		*ca.* 1150	*Liber Landav.*, 134

A Chronological List of Castles Built Before 1189, Acccording to Documentary Evidence

I. England

PRE-CONQUEST TO 1066

Clavering (Robert's Castle?, Essex)	1052	*Anglo-Saxon Chron.*, I, 321
Dover (Kent)	1066	Wm. of Poitiers, 210
Ewias Harold (Pentecost's Castle, Here.)	1052	Symeon of Dur., II, 170
Hereford (Here.)	1055	*Brut*, 42/43
Richard's Castle (Here.)	1052	*Anglo-Saxon Chron.*, I, 316

WILLIAM I (1066–1087)

Aldreth (Cambs.)		*Liber Eliensis*, 194
Arundel (Sussex)	1087	*Domesday Bk.*, I, 23a
Bamburgh (Northumb.)	1070	Symeon of Dur., II, 191
Barnstaple (Devon)		*Monasticon*, V, 197
Belvoir (Leics.)		*Monasticon*, III, 288
Berkeley (Glos.)	1087	*Domesday Bk.*, I, 163a
Berkhamstead (Herts.)		*Monasticon*, VI, 2, 1090
Bitham (Lincs.)	(?) 1087	*Domesday Bk.*, I, 360b
Bramber (Sussex)	1073	*Cal. Docs. Fr.*, 405
Buckingham (Bucks.)		*Gesta Herewardi*, 70
Burne (Cambs.)		*Monasticon*, VI, 86
Burton (Staffs.)	1087	*Domesday Bk.*, I, 248b
Cambridge (Cambs.)	1068	Ordericus, II, 185
Canterbury (Kent)	1087	*Domesday Bk.*, I, 2a
Carisbrooke (I.O.W.)	1087	*Domesday Bk.*, I, 52b
Castellum Waynardi		*Monasticon*, III, 265
Castle Acre (Norf.)	ca. 1085	*E.Y.C.*, VIII, 4, 5

Castle Holgate (Salop)	1087	*Domesday Bk.,* I, 258b
Chepstow (Mon.)	1087	*Domesday Bk.,* I, 162a
Chester (Cheshire)	1070	Ordericus, II, 198–199
Clifford (Here.)	1087	*Domesday Bk.,* I, 183a
Clitheroe (Lancs.)	1087	*Domesday Bk.,* I, 322a
Corfe (Dorset)	1087	*Domesday Bk.,* I, 78b
Dudley (Staffs.)	1087	*Domesday Bk.,* I, 177a
Dunster (Somerset)	1087	*Domesday Bk.,* I, 95b
Durham (Dur.)	1072	Symeon of Dur., II, 200
Ely (Cambs.)	1071	*Liber Eliensis,* 174
Exeter (Devon)	1068	Ordericus, II, 179–181
Eye (Suff.)	1087	*Domesday Bk.,* II, 378b
Gloucester (Glos.)	1087	*Domesday Bk.,* I, 162a
Halton (Cheshire)		*Monasticon,* VI, 315
Hastings (Sussex)	1066	*Anglo-Saxon Chron.,* I, 338
Huntingdon (Hunts.)	1068	Ordericus, II, 185
Launceston (Corn.)	1087	*Domesday Bk.,* I, 121b
Lewes (Sussex)	1077/78	*Monasticon,* V, 12a
Lincoln (Lincs.)	1068	*Anglo-Saxon Chron.,* I, 342
London (Middlesex)	1067	Wm. of Poitiers, 236
Longtown (Ewias Lacy, Here.)	1087	*Domesday Bk.,* I, 184a
Monmouth (Mon.)	1087	*Domesday Bk.,* I, 180b
Montacute (Somerset)	1069	Ordericus, II, 193
Mulgrave (Yorks.)		*Monasticon,* I, 410
Newcastle-upon-Tyne (Northumb.)	1080	Symeon of Dur., II, 211
Norwich (Norf.)	1075	*Anglo-Saxon Chron.,* I, 348
Nottingham (Notts.)	1068	*Anglo-Saxon Chron.,* I, 342
Okehampton (Devon)	1087	*Domesday Bk.,* I, 105b
Old Quatford (Salop)	1087	*Domesday Bk.,* I, 254a
Oswestry (Salop)	1087	*Domesday Bk.,* I, 253b
Oxford (Oxon.)	1072	*Monasticon,* VI, 251–253
Peak (Derby)	1087	*Domesday Bk.,* I, 276a
Penwortham (Lancs.)	1087	*Domesday Bk.,* I, 270a
Peterborough (Northants.)	1069/98	Hugh Candidus, 86
Pevensey (Sussex)	1066	Wm. of Poitiers, 168
Pontefract (Yorks.)	1087	*Domesday Bk.,* I, 373b
Preston Capes (Northants.)		*Monasticon,* V, 178
Raleigh (Essex)	1087	*Domesday Bk.,* II, 43b
Richmond (Yorks.)	1087	*Domesday Bk.,* I, 381a
Rochester (Kent)	1087	*Domesday Bk.,* I, 2b
Rockingham (Northants.)	1087	*Domesday Bk.,* I, 22a

Salisbury (Wilts.)	1069/70	*Regesta*, I, 13
Shrewsbury (Salop)	1069	Ordericus, II, 193
Skelton (Yorks.)		*Monasticon*, VI, 267
Skipsea (Yorks.)		*Monasticon*, V, 393
Stafford (Staffs.)	1070	Ordericus, II, 199
Stamford-on-the-Welland (Lincs.)	1087	*Domesday Bk.*, I, 366b
Stortford (Herts.)	1085/87	*Regesta*, I, 72–73
Totnes (Devon)		*Monasticon*, IV, 630
Trematon (Corn.)	1087	*Domesday Bk.*, I, 122a
Tutbury (Staffs.)	1070	Ordericus, II, 222
Wallingford (Berks.)	1087	*Domesday Bk.*, I, 56a
Warwick (War.)	1068	Ordericus, II, 184
Wigmore (Here.)	1087	*Domesday Bk.*, I, 180a
Winchester (Hants.)	1067	Ordericus, II, 166–167
Windsor (Berks.)	1066/70	*Regesta*, I, 13
Wisbeach (Cambs.)	1071	Roger of Wendover, I, 339
York (Yorks.)	1068	Ordericus, II, 185

WILLIAM II (1087–1100)

Abergavenny (Mon.)	1087/1100	*Cal. Docs. Fr.*, 367–368
Bourne (Lincs.)	(?) 1092	*Monasticon*, VI, 87a
Bridgnorth (Salop)	1098/99	Ordericus, IV, 32–33
Bristol (Glos.)	1088	*Anglo-Saxon Chron.*, I, 356–57
Carlisle (Cumb.)	1092	*Anglo-Saxon Chron.*, I, 359
Clare (Suff.)	1090	*Monasticon*, VI, 1659
Folkestone (Kent)	1095	*Monasticon.* IV, 674
Ilchester (Somerset)	1088	Flor. of Worc., II, 24
Leicester (Leics.)	1088	Wm. of Malmes., *De. Gestis Regum*, II, 361
Morpeth (Northumb.)	1095	Geoffrey Gaimar, I, 262
Tonbridge (Kent)	1088	*Anglo-Saxon Chron.*, I, 357
Tynemouth (Northumb.)	1095	*Anglo-Saxon Chron.*, I, 361
Worcester (Worc.)	1088	*Anglo-Saxon Chron.*, I, 357

HENRY I (1100–1135)

Aldbrough (Yorks.)	1115	*Monasticon*, VI, 1020
Appleby (Westmore.)	1130	*Pipe Roll 31 Henry I*, 143
Barnard (Durham)	1123/33	*Regesta*, II, 287

Baynards Castle (Middlesex)	1111	*Monasticon,* VI, 147
Brinklow (War.)	1130	*Pipe Roll 31 Henry I,* 138
Burton-in-Lonsdale (Yorks.)	1130	*Pipe Roll 31 Henry I,* 138
Caus (Salop)	1134	Ordericus, V, 43
Colchester (Essex)	1100/02	*Regesta,* II, 18
Goodrich (Here.)	1101/02	*Cal. Docs. Fr.,* 408
Kenilworth (War.)	1122	*Monasticon,* VI, 220–221
Kilpeck (Here.)	1134	*Monasticon,* I, 548
Kirkby (Yorks.)	1123/25	*E.Y.C.,* III, 180
Knaresborough (Yorks.)	1130 (?)	*Pipe Roll 31 Henry I,* 31
Lichfield (Staffs.)	1128	*Monasticon,* VI, 1241
Malzeard (Yorks.)	1130	*Pipe Roll 31 Henry I,* 137
Newark-on-Trent (Notts.)	1123/33	*Regesta,* II, 264
Norham (Northmub.)	1121	Symeon of Dur., II, 260
Northampton (Northants.)	1130	*Pipe Roll 31 Henry I,* 135
Old Basing (Hants.)		*Monasticon,* VI, 1014
St. Briavel's (Glos.)	1130	*Pipe Roll 31 Henry I,* 76
Sherborne (Dorset)	1122 (?)	*Regesta,* II, 172
Skipton (Yorks.)	1131/40	*E.Y.C.,* VII, 288
Thetford (Norf.)	ca. 1103/04	*Monasticon,* V, 150
Thirsk (Yorks.)	1130	*Pipe Roll 31 Henry I,* 138
Tickhill (Yorks.)	1102	Ordericus, IV, 171
Wareham (Dorset)	1113	*Anglo-Saxon Chron.,* I, 370

STEPHEN (1135–1154)

Abingdon (Berks.)	1142	Wm. of Malmes., *Hist. Nov.,* 77
Almondbury (Yorks.)	1142/54	*E.Y.C.,* III, 146
Alnwick (Northumb.)	1136	Richard of Hexham, 145
"Ambli" (Norf.)		Joc. of Brakelond, 138
Ascot-under-Wychwood (Oxon.)	ante	*Cart. Mon. St. Frideswide,* II, 242

T.R.H II

Bampton (Devon)	1136	Henry of Hunt., 259
Bampton (Oxon.)	1142	*Gesta Stephani,* 92
Banbury (Oxon.)	1146	*Cartae Antiquae,* I, 195–97

Barton-on-Humber (Lincs.)		*Monasticon,* I, 631
Barwick-in-Elmet (Yorks.)	1142/54	*E.Y.C.,* III, 146
Bath (Somerset)	1138	Cont. Flor. of Worc., II, 108–109
Beaudesert (War.)	1141	Charter in Round, *Geoffrey de Mandeville,* 65
Bedford (Beds.)	1137	*Gesta Stephani,* 31
Bengeworth (Worc.)	1149/59	*Chron. Abb. de Evesham,* 100
Benwick (Cambs.)	1143	*Liber Eliensis,* 328
Bishop's Waltham (Hants.)	1138	*Ann. Winton.,* 51
Bishopton (Dur.)	1143	Symeon of Dur., I, 150–151
Boughton-in-Southoe (Hunts.)	1140/53	*Add. Charters,* 11 233
Bow and Arrow (Rufus's Castle, Dorset)	1142	Wm. of Malmes., *Hist. Nov.,* 76
Brandon (War.)		Charter in Stenton, *First Century,* 211–212
Bridlington (Yorks.)	1144	Wm. of Newburgh, I, 47
Bridport (Devon)	1149	*Gesta Stephani,* 147
Brightwell (Berks.)	1152	Robert of Torigni, 174
Bryn (Salop)	1138	Ordericus, V, 111
Bungay (Suff.)	1140	*Ann. de Waverleia,* 228
Burton (Wilts.)	1147	*Gesta Stephani,* 132
Burwell (Cambs.)	1144	Gervase of Cant., I, 128
Castle Cary (Somerset)	1138	*Ann. de Waverleia,* 226
Castle Eden (Dur.)	1143/52	*E.Y.C.,* II, 2–3
Cerney (Glos.)	1139	*Gesta Stephani,* 62
Christchurch (Hants.)	1147	*Gesta Stephani*
Cirencester (Glos.)	1142	*Gesta Stephani*
Cottingham (Yorks.)		*E.Y.C.,* IX, 5
Coventry (War.)	1147	*Gesta Stephani,* 132
Cricklade (Wilts.)	1144	*Gesta Stephani,* 113
Crowmarsh (Oxon.)	1146	Gervase of Cant., I, 130
Cuckney (Notts.)		*Monasticon,* VI, 873
Dena, veteri castello de	*ante* 1154	*Monasticon,* V, 590
Devizes (Wilts.)	1138	*Ann. Winton.,* 51
Dorchester (Dorset)	1138	*Ann. Winton.,* 51
Downton (Wilts.)	1138	*Ann. Winton.,* 51
Drax (Yorks.)	1154	Wm. of Newburgh, I, 94
Dursley (Glos.)	1149	*Gesta Stephani,* 143–144
Ellesmere Mount (Salop)	1138	Ordericus, V, 111

Faringdon (Berks.)	1145	Wm. of Newburgh, I, 48–49
Farnham (Surrey)	1138	*Ann. Winton.,* 51
Fordham (Cambs.)	1143	*Liber Eliensis,* 328
Gainsborough (Lincs.)	1142	Charter in Round, *Geoffrey de Mandeville,* 159
Gaultney ("Galclint", Northants.)	1140	John of Hexham, II, 306
Goxhill (Lincs.)	1143/47	*Danelaw Charters,* 167
Guildford (Surrey)	1141	Wm. of Malmes., *Hist. Nov.,* 57–58
Hailes (Glos.)	1140/50	*Lanaboc . . . de Winchelcumbe,* I, 65
Harptree (Somerset)	1138	*Gesta Stephani,* 45
Hatton (War.)	1151/57	*Cal. Docs. Fr.,* 412
Hode (Yorks.)	*post* 1145	*Monasticon,* VI, 320
Hutton Conyers (Yorks.)	1140	*E.Y.C.,* IV, 90
Ipswich (Suff.)	1153	Henry of Hunt., 288
Leeds (Kent)	1138	Ordericus, V, 112
"Lidelea" (Hants.)	1138	*Gesta Stephani,* 138
Lindsey Castle (Suff.)		Joc. of Brakelond, 138
Ludgershall (Wilts.)	1138	*Ann. Winton.,* 51
Ludlow (Salop)	1137	Henry of Hunt., 261
Lulworth (Dorset)	1142	Wm. of Malmes., *Hist. Nov.,* 76
Malmesbury (Wilts.)	1138	*Ann. Winton.,* 51
Malton (Yorks.)	1138	Richard of Hexham, 165
Marlborough (Wilts.)	1137/38	*Ancient Charters,* 36–38
Meppershall (Beds.)	1137/38	*Monasticon,* IV, 216
Merdon (Hants.)	1138	*Ann. Winton.,* 51
Merrington (Dur.)	1144	Symeon of Dur., I, 158
Milden Castle (Suff.)		Joc. of Brakelond, 138
Mitford (Northumb.)	1138	Richard of Hexham, 158
Montferrand (Yorks.)		*Chron. de Melsa,* I, 106
Montfichet's Castle (Middlesex)	*ante* 1136	*Add. MS.* 14 252 in Bateson, "London Municipal Col.," *EHR,* XVII, 485–486
Mortimer's Castle (Here.)	1153	*Foedera,* I, i, 18
Mountsorrel (Leics.)	1148/53	*Lansdowne MS.* 415, f.41
Newbury (Berks.)	1152	Henry of Hunt., 284

Northallerton (Yorks.)	1142	Symeon of Dur., I, 148
Old Buckenham (Norf.)		*Monasticon*, VI, 419
Oversley (War.)	1140	*Monasticon*, IV, 175
Partney (Lincs.)	1141/42	E.Y.C., X, 114–115
Pleshy (Essex)	1143	Henry of Hunt., 276
Plympton (Devon)	1136	*Gesta Stephani*, 23–24
Porchester (Hants.)	1153	Charter in Round, *Commune of London*, 82
Radcot (Oxon.)	1142	*Gesta Stephani*, 91
Ramsey (Hunts.)	1143	Henry of Hunt., 276–277
Ravenstone (Leics.)	1148/53	*Cott. MS. Nero C*, III, f 178
Reading (Berks.)	1152	Robt. of Torigni, 174
Saffron Walden (Essex)	1139	*Ann. de Waverleia*, 227
Selby (Yorks.)	1143/53	*Coucher Bk. of Selby*, I, 33
Sheriff Hutton (Yorks.)	1140	John of Hexham, 306
Silva	1147	*Gesta Stephani*, 138
Sleaford (Lincs.)	1139	Henry of Hunt., 266
Southampton (Hants.)	1153	*Foedera*, I, i, 18
Sudeley (Glos.)	1139	Cont. Flor. of Worc., II, 120
Tamworth (War.)	1141	Charter in Stenton, *First Century*, 225
Taunton (Somerset)	1138	*Ann. Winton.*, 51
Tetbury (Glos.)	1144	*Gesta Stephani*
Thorngate (Lincs.)	1141	*Reg. Antiq. of Linc. Cath.*, I, 61–62
Thornlaw (Dur.)	1143	Symeon of Dur., I, 164–165
Trowbridge (Wilts.)	1139	Wm. of Malmes., *Hist. Nov.*, 36
Usk (Mon.)	1138	Ordericus, V, 110
Wark-upon-Tweed (Northumb.)	1136	Richard of Hexham, 145
Weobley (Here.)	1138	Cont. Flor. of Worc., II, 106
Wheldrake (Yorks.)	1150	John of Hexham, 323
Whittington (Salop)	1138	Ordericus, V, 111
Whitwick (Leics.)	1148/53	*Cott. MS Nero C*, III, f.178
Wilton (Wilts.)	1143	Gervase of Cant., I, 125–126

Wimbourne (Dorset)	1138	*Ann. Winton.,* 51
Winchcomb (Glos.)	1139	*Gesta Stephani,* 63
Wolvesey (Hants.)	1138	*Ann. Winton.,* 51
Woodstock (Oxon.)	1142	*Gesta Stephani,* 91

HENRY II (1154–1189)

"Aldewich"	1185/86	*Pipe Roll 32 Henry II,* 82
Allington (Kent)	1174/75	*Pipe Roll 21 Henry II,* 212
Alton (Staffs.)	1176	*Monasticon,* v, 662
Barrow-upon-Humber (Lincs.)	1189	*Monasticon,* vi, 327
Bennington (Herts.)	1176/77	*Pipe Roll 23 Henry II,* 144
Berwick-on-Tweed	1175	Roger of Wendover, i, 104
Bishop's Castle (Lydbury, Salop)	1166/67	*Pipe Roll 13 Henry II,* 77
Bolsover (Derby)	1172/73	*Pipe Roll 19 Henry II,* 174
Boroughbridge (Yorks.)	1175	*Rot. Claus.,* i, 57f
Bowes (Yorks.)	1170/71	*Pipe Roll 17 Henry II,* 63
Brackley (Northants.)	1172/73	*Pipe Roll 19 Henry II,* 70
Brough (Westmore.)	1174	Wm. of Newburgh, i, 182
"Caperun"	1155/56	*Pipe Roll 2 Henry II,* 51
Castle Sowerby (Cumb.)	1186/87	*Pipe Roll 33 Henry II,* 95
Castleton (Mon.)	1184/85	*Pipe Roll 31 Henry II,* 6
Chichester (Sussex)	1173/74	*Pipe Roll 20 Henry II,* 118
Chilham (Kent)	1170/71	*Pipe Roll 17 Henry II,* 137
Church Stretton (Salop)	1156/57	*Pipe Roll 3 Henry II,* 88
Cleobury (Salop)	1155	Gervase of Cant., i, 162
Conisborough (Yorks.)	1174/78	*E.Y.C.,* viii, 251
"Craft"	1173/74	*Pipe Roll 20 Henry II,* 55
Dingestow (Mon.)	ca. 1176	*Itin. Kambriae,* 47–48
Duffield (Derby)	1173	*Gesta Regis,* i, 48

Dunham (Cheshire)	1173	*Gesta Regis*, I, 48
Eardisley (Here.)	1182/83	*Pipe Roll 29 Henry II,* 111
Flamborough (Yorks.)	ca. 1180/93	*E.Y.C.*, II, 254
Framlingham (Suff.)	1157/58	*Pipe Roll 4 Henry II,* 126
"Gaittecastellum"	1161/67	*E.Y.C.*, I, 441
Groby (Leics.)	1173	*Gesta Regis,* I, 48
Grosmont (Mon.)	1162/63	*Pipe Roll 9 Henry II,* 7
Harbottle (Northumb.)	1174	Roger of Hoveden, II, 60
Haughley (Suff.)	1173	Gervase of Cant., I, 246
Hedingham (Essex)		*Monasticon,* IV, 437
Hertford (Herts.)	1170/71	*Pipe Roll 17 Henry II,* 118–119
Kington (Here.)	1186/87	*Pipe Roll 33 Henry II,* 131
Kinnard Ferry (Axholme, Lincs.)	1173	*Gesta Regis*, I, 48
Liddell (Cumb.)	1174	Roger of Hoveden, II, 60
Manchester (Lancs.)	1183/84	Pipe Roll 30 Henry II, 23
Newcastle-under-Lyme (Stafs.)	1154/55	*Red Bk. of the Exch.,* II, 652
Newport (Mon.)	1184/85	*Pipe Roll 31 Henry II,* 7
Northwich (Cheshire)	derelict T.R.R I	Harl. MS., 2 074, 189
Ongar (Essex)	1156	*Chron. Mon. de Bello,* 83
Orford (Suff.)	1165/66	*Pipe Roll 12 Henry II,* 17
Pickering (Yorks.)	1179/80	*Pipe Roll 26 Henry II,* 75
Prudhoe (Northumb.)	1172/73	*Pipe Roll 19 Henry II,* 113
Risinghoe (Beds.)	1180/1200	*Warden Cart.,* 125
Roxburgh (Rox.)	1175	Roger of Wendover, I, 104
Saltwood (Kent)	1174/75	*Pipe Roll 21 Henry II,* 209
Scarborough (Yorks.)	1155	Wm. of Newburgh, I, 104
Sheffield (Yorks.)	1183/84	*Pipe Roll 30 Henry II,* 100

Shrawardine (Salop)	1165/66	*Pipe Roll 12 Henry II,* 59
Skenfrith (Mon.)	1162/63	*Pipe Roll 9 Henry II,* 7
Stockport (Cheshire)	1173	*Gesta Regis,* I, 48
Stowey Castle (Somerset)	*ante* 1155	*Cal. Charter Rolls,* II, 363
Swineshead (Lincs.)	1185/86	*Pipe Roll 32 Henry II,* 81
Topcliffe (Yorks.)	1174	Roger of Hoveden, II, 59
Trentham (Staffs.)	1168/69	*Pipe Roll 15 Henry II,* 72
Ullerwood (Cheshire)	1173	*Gesta Regis,* I, 48
Wakefield (Yorks.)	1174/78	*E.Y.C.,* VIII, 114
Walton (Suff.)	1158/59	*Pipe Roll 5 Henry II,* 9
Warkworth (Northumb.)	1174	Roger of Hoveden, II, 60
Welbourne (Lincs.)	*ca.* 1158	*Add. Charters,* 6 038
Weston Turville (Bucks.)	1173/74	*Pipe Roll 20 Henry II,* 82
Whitchurch (Salop)	1160/61	*Pipe Roll 7 Henry II,* 20
White Castle (Llantilio, Mon.)	1162/63	*Pipe Roll 9 Henry II,* 7
Wilton (Here.)	1187/88	*Pipe Roll 34 Henry II,* 210
Yafforth (Yorks.)		*E.Y.C.,* v, 292
Yeldon (Beds.)	1173/74	*Pipe Roll 20 Henry II,* 55

II. Wales

WILLIAM I (1066–1087)

Cardiff (Glam.)	1082	*Brut,* 50/51
Montgomery (Mont.)	1087	*Domesday Bk.,* I, 253b., 254a
Rhuddlan (Flint)	1087	*Domesday Bk.,* I, 269a

WILLIAM II (1087–1100)

Aber Lleiniog (Anglesey)	1094	Symeon of Dur., II, 224
Brecon (Aberhonddu, Brecknock)		Ordericus, III, 43–44
Carreghofa (Mont.)	1098	Flor. of Worc., II, 49
Diganwy (Carn.)	*ca.* 1088	Ordericus, III, 283–384
Pembroke (Pemb.)	1094	*Brut,* 56/57
Rhyd y Gors	1094	*Brut,* 56/57

HENRY I (1100–1135)

Abercavwy (Carm.)	1116	*Brut,* 126/127
Aberystwyth (Llanbadarn, Card.)	1107	*Brut,* 104/05
Carmarthen (Carm.)	1116	*Brut,* 124/25–126/27
Castell Aber Tav (Carm.)	1116	*Brut,* 126/27
Chastell Gwalter (Llanfihangel, Card.)	1114	*Regesta,* II, 113
Cilgerran (Pemb.)	1107	*Brut,* 104/05
Cymmer (Merion.)	1116	*Brut,* 140/41
Dynetha (Radnor)	*ca.* 1100	*Monasticon,* VI, i, 349
Hay (Tregelli, Brecknock)	1121	*Ancient Charters,* 8
Kidwelly (Carm.)	1114	*Regesta,* II, 114
Laugharne (Carm.)	1116	*Brut,* 126/27
Little Cenarth (Pemb.)	1107	*Brut,* 82/83
Llandovery (Carm.)	1116	*Brut,* 122/23
Narberth (Pemb.)	1116	*Brut,* 122/23
Neath (Glam.)		*Monasticon,* V, 259
Ogmore (Glam.)	1116	*Brut,* 126/127
Old Radnor		*Itin. Kambriae,* 16
Swansea (Glam.)	1116	*Brut,* 122/23
Tomen-y-Mur (Merion.)	1111	*Brut,* 114/15
Ystrad-Meuric (Card.)	1116	*Brut,* 130/31
Ystrad Peithyll (Card.)	1116	*Brut,* 130/31

STEPHEN (1135–1154)

Aberavon (Glam.)	1152	*Brut,* 182/83
Caerwedros (Card.)	1137	*Brut,* 158/59
Cardigan (Aberteifi, Card.)	1136	*Gesta Stephani,* 11
Castell Colwyn (Radnor)	1143	*Brut,* 166/67
Castel Rhos (Llanrhystyd, Card.)	1148	*Brut,* 176/77
Castle of Richard de la Mare (Card.)	1136	*Brut,* 158/59
Castle Teirtut	*ca.* 1150	*Liber Landav.,* 134
Cwm Aron (Radnor)	1143	*Brut,* 166/67
Cynfael (Merion.)	1146	*Brut,* 174/75
Dinerth (Card.)	1137	*Brut,* 158/59
Dinevor (Dinweiler, Carm.)	1145	*Brut,* 168/69
Humphrey's Castle (Card.)	1138	*Brut,* 162/63
Llanstephan (Carm.)	1145	*Brut,* 168/69
Loughor (Glam.)	1150	*Brut,* 180/81
Mold (Flint)	1147	*Brut,* 172/73
Overton (Flint)	1138	*Ordericus,* V, 111
Pont-y-Stuffan (Card.)	1138	*Brut,* 162/63
Tenby (Pemb.)	1152	*Brut,* 182/83
Tomen-y-Rhodwydd (Denbigh)	1149	*Brut,* 176/77
Waynard's Castle (Brecknock)	*ca.* 1150	*Monasticon,* III, 265

Wiston (Pemb.)	1148	*Brut,* 172/73
Ystrad Cyngen (Carm.)	1154	*Brut,* 192/93

HENRY II (1154–1189)

Aberdovey (Card.)	1155	*Brut,* 184/85
Basingwerk (Flint)	1165/66	*Pipe Roll 12 Henry II,* 67
Bridgend (Glam.)	1184/85	*Pipe Roll 31 Henry II,* 5
Bronllys (Brecknock)	1188	*Itin. Kambriae,* 31
Builth (Brecknock)	1170	*Ann. Cambriae,* 52
Caereinion (Mont.)	1155	*Brut,* 184/85
Carnarvon (Carn.)	1188	*Itin. Kambriae,* 124
"Carn Madryn"	1188	*Itin. Kambriae,* 123
Castell Flemys (Card.)	1184	*Monasticon,* v, 632
Castleton (Glam.)	1186/87	*Pipe Roll 33 Henry II,* 134
Chirk (Denbigh)	1164/65	*Pipe Roll 11 Henry II,* 90
Crug Eryr (Radnor)	1188	*Itin. Kambriae,* 16
Dernio (Merion.)	1159/60	*Pipe Roll 6 Henry II,* 26
"Deutrait" (Aber Ia, Merion.)	1188	*Itin. Kambriae,* 123
Emlyn (Card.)	1173/74	*Pipe Roll 20 Henry II,* 89
Haverfordwest (Pemb.)	1188	*Itin. Kambriae,* 109
Hawarden (Flint)	1173 (?)	*Gesta Regis,* I, 48–49
Kenfig (Glam.)	1183/84	*Pipe Roll 30 Henry II,* 60
Knighton (Radnor)	1181/82	*Pipe Roll 28 Henry II,* 11
Llandaff (Glam.) (?)	1187/88	*Pipe Roll 34 Henry II,* 9
Llawhadon (Pemb.)	1188	*Itin. Kambriae,* 172
Manorbier (Pemb.)	1188	*Itin. Kambriae,* 92–93
Nevern (Pemb.)	1188	*Itin. Kambriae,* 111–112
Prestatyn (Flint)	1165/66	*Pipe Roll 12 Henry II,* 67
Rhyader Gwy (Radnor)	1177	*Brut,* 230/31
Ruthin (Denbigh)	1160/61	*Pipe Roll 7 Henry II,* 40
Tafolwern (Mont.)	1163	*Brut,* 196/97
Wrexham (Denbigh)	1160/61	*Pipe Roll 7 Henry II,* 35

Appendix C

Castles Mentioned in the Pipe Rolls of Henry II and in That of the First Year of Richard I (1154–1189)

Castle	1	2	3	4	5	6	7	8	9	10	11	12	13	14	15	16	17	18	19	20	21	22	23	24	25	26	27	28	29	30	31	32	33	34	1
Aldreth																			x																
Allington																					x														
Alnwick																																x	x	x	x
Appleby																						x													
Arundel																			x						x	x	x	x		x			x	x	x
Bamburgh										x				x		x													x						
Basingwerk												x																							
Bedford																										x			x					x	
Bennington																							x												
Berkeley																	x																		
Berkhamstead				x		x		x										x	x							x	x	x		x	x				
Bolsover																		x	x	x															
Bourne (Lincs.)																								x	x	x	x	x							
Bowes																	x	x	x	x				x								x	x	x	

Appendix C (continued)

	1	2	3	4	5	6	7	8	9	10	11	12	13	14	15	16	17	18	19	20	21	22	23	24	25	26	27	28	29	30	31	32	33	34	1
Brackley	x																																		
Bridgnorth														x	x	x	x	x	x	x	x	x	x	x	x	x	x	x	x	x	x	x	x	x	x
Bristol														x							x							x	x	x	x	x			
Brough																					x														
Caerleon																		x			x														
Cambridge				x	x														x	x															
Canterbury						x									x		x	x	x	x	x			x	x		x	x	x	x	x		x	x	x
Cardiff																					x			x						x	x			x	
Carisbrooke													x												x										
Carlisle																			x					x		x	x	x	x	x	x	x	x	x	x
Carmarthen					x																			x											
Carreghofa						x	x	x																											
Castle Sowerby																															x		x	x	
Castleton																															x				
Chepstow																			x											x				x	
Chester						x																										x	x		
Chichester																				x															x

	1	34	33	32	31	30	29	28	27	26	25	24	23	22	21	20	19	18	17	16	15	14	13	12	11	10	9	8	7	6	5	4	3	2	1
Chilham															×		×	×	×																
Chirk															×							×		×	×										
Clun																										×	×	×	×	×					
Colchester							×	×		×			×			×	×																		
Corfe								×																											
"Craſi"																																			
Cwm Aron								×																											
Dernio																														×					
Devizes																×																			
Dorchester				×										×																					
Dover		×	×	×	×	×	×	×	×	×	×	×	×		×	×	×	×	×	×	×			×	×	×		×	×	×	×				×
Eardisley		×	×		×	×	×																												
Ellesmere																		×																	
Emlyn		×	×	×	×	×	×	×	×	×	×	×		×																					×
Ewias Lacy			×	×																															
Exeter									×		×		×			×																			
Eye		×	×	×			×	×			×	×				×	×	×																	×
Framlingham				×										×	×																				

Appendix C (continued)

	1	2	3	4	5	6	7	8	9	10	11	12	13	14	15	16	17	18	19	20	21	22	23	24	25	26	27	28	29	30	31	32	33	34	1
"Givelden"																				×															
Gloucester										×									×	×															
Grosmont									×																				×	×		×			
Guildford																				×															
Harbottle																					×														
Hastings							×						×				×	×	×	×															×
Hereford		×	×	×													×	×	×	×				×	×	×	×	×	×				×	×	
Hertford							×								×		×	×	×	×				×				×	×	×			×		
Hodesley							×	×																											
Huntingdon																				×															
Kenfig																														×	×				
Kenilworth																			×	×							×	×	×	×	×	×	×	×	×
Kington																																	×		
Knighton																												×							
Launceston																						×	×					×							
Leicester																				×										×	×	×	×	×	×
Lincoln																				×									×	×	×	×	×	×	×

	1	2	3	4	5	6	7	8	9	10	11	12	13	14	15	16	17	18	19	20	21	22	23	24	25	26	27	28	29	30	31	32	33	34	1
Llandaff (?)																																			
Llantilio									×																						×	×	×	×	×
London												×			×			×	×	×	×	×		×			×	×	×	×	×	×	×	×	×
Ludlow	×												×	×	×	×	×	×	×			×	×	×	×	×	×	×	×	×	×	×	×		×
Lydbury																				×															
Malmesbury																																			
Malton																																		×	
Manchester																						×								×		×	×		
Marlborough																						×	×							×					
Mountsorrel																													×						
Munhalt												×																							
Neath																												×	×	×	×			×	
Newark																	×	×																	
Newcastle-Bridgend																															×		×	×	
Newcastle-under-Lyme																			×	×															
Newcastle-upon-Tyne																		×	×	×	×	×	×	×	×	×	×	×	×	×	×	×	×	×	×
Newport (Mon.)																														×					

Appendix C (continued)

	1	2	3	4	5	6	7	8	9	10	11	12	13	14	15	16	17	18	19	20	21	22	23	24	25	26	27	28	29	30	31	32	33	34
Norham																					×										×	×	×	×
Northampton			×																×	×	×	×	×	×	×		×	×	×	×			×	
Norwich			×	×			×							×			×	×	×	×	×	×								×			×	
Nottingham												×	×	×	×	×	×	×	×	×	×	×	×	×	×	×	×	×	×	×	×	×	×	×
Orford												×	×	×								×					×		×					×
Overton					×	×								×																				
Oxford	×					×											×		×	×		×	×	×	×	×	×	×	×	×	×	×	×	×
Peak																										×				×	×			×
Pembroke																											×				×		×	
Pevensey							×					×														×				×				
Pickering																										×			×			×		
Porchester																				×				×					×					
Prestatyn											×																		×					
Prudhoe																		×	×															
Raleigh														×					×								×			×				
Rhuddlan											×	×	×																×			×		
Richmond																		×			×								×		×	×	×	
Rochester													×				×		×		×							×	×	×	×	×	×	

	1	34	33	32	31	30	29	28	27	26	25	24	23	22	21	20	19	18	17	16	15	14	13	12	11	10	9	8	7	6	5	4	3	2	1
Rockingham	×	×	×	×	×	×	×	×	×	×	×	×			×	×	×			×															
Ruthin																										×	×	×	×	×					
Saffron Walden																																×			
St. Briavels																											×	×	×	×					
Salisbury	×	×	×	×	×	×	×	×			×	×	×	×	×	×	×		×		×	×	×	×											×
Saltwood					×																						×								
Scarborough		×													×						×	×				×					×				
Scenfrith							×																				×								
Sheffield			×	×	×																														
Shrawardine				×														×	×																
Shrewsbury						×													×					×					×	×	×	×	×	×	
Southampton							×															×	×	×				×	×	×	×	×	×	×	
Stortford																									×	×									
Stretton	×	×	×	×	×	×	×	×	×	×	×	×	×	×	×	×	×	×	×	×	×	×	×	×		×	×	×		×	×	×	×		
Swansea		×	×																																
Swineshead																																		×	
Thetford																	×																		
Tickhill	×	×	×	×				×		×	×											×													

Appendix C (continued)

	1	2	3	4	5	6	7	8	9	10	11	12	13	14	15	16	17	18	19	20	21	22	23	24	25	26	27	28	29	30	31	32	33	34	1
Topcliffe																					x														
Trentham															x																				
Usk																				x															
Wallingford																			x	x					x				x						
Walton										x			x	x								x													
Wark				x	x	x	x													x		x													
Warwick					x	x	x																												
Weston-Turville				x	x																														
Whitchurch						x		x	x	x	x		x	x			x		x	x	x														
Whittington											x			x																					
Wilton (Here.)															x																				
Winchester		x	x	x	x									x	x	x	x	x	x	x	x		x	x	x	x	x	x	x	x	x	x	x	x	x
Windsor			x	x												x	x	x				x	x	x	x		x	x	x	x		x	x	x	
Wisbeach								x											x																
Woebley																																	x	x	
Wolvesey			x																																
Worcester		x		x									x								x			x	x	x		x	x	x	x	x	x	x	x
Wrexham							x																												
York																			x														x	x	x

Bibliography

I. Official Records, Charters, Laws, Source Collections, and Similar Documents

Ancient Charters, Royal and Private prior to A.D. 1200, ed. J. H. Round. London, 1888.

Bonaparte, Joseph. *Mémoires et Correspondance,* ed. Baron A. du Carse. 2nd ed. 10 vols. Paris, 1854.

Calendar of Charter Rolls. 6 vols. London, 1903–1927.

Calendar of Documents Preserved in France Illustrative of the History of Great Britain and Ireland, ed. J. H. Round. London, 1899.

Calendar of Inquisitions Post Mortem (First series). 14 vols. London, 1904– .

Calendar of Miscellaneous Inquisitions. 4 vols. London, 1916– .

The Cartae Antiquae Rolls, 1–10, ed. Lionel Landon. London, 1939.

Cartulary of the Cistercian Abbey of Old Wardon, ed. G. H. Fowler. (Beds. Hist. Rec. Soc., XIII.) 1930.

Cartulary of the Monastery of St. Frideswide, ed. S. R. Wigram. 2 vols. (Oxford Hist. Soc., XXVIII, XXXI.) 1895–1896.

Charters and Documents Illustrating the History of the Cathedral, City, and Diocese of Salisbury in the Twelfth and Thirteenth Centuries, ed. W. Rich Jones and W. Dunn Macray (R.S.). London, 1891.

Documents Illustrative of the Social and Economic History of the Danelaw, ed. F. M. Stenton. London, 1920.

Domesday Book: Liber Censualis Willelmi Primi, ed. Abraham Furley and Henry Ellis. 4 vols. London, 1783–1816.

Early Yorkshire Charters, ed. William Farrer and C. T. Clay. 10 vols. and index. Edinburgh, 1914– .

English Historical Documents, 1042–1189, ed. David C. Douglas and George W. Greenaway. London, 1953.

Foedera, Conventiones, Litterae et Cuiusque Genera inter Reges An-

447

gliae et Alios Quosius Imperatores, Reges, Pontifices, Princeps, vel Comunitates ab Ingressu Gulielmi in Angliam A.D. 1066 ad Nostra usque Tempora, ed. Adam Clarke, J. Caley, J. Bayley, F. Holbrooke, J. W. Clarke. New ed., 4 vols. in 7. London, 1816–1869.

Frontinus, Sextus Julius. *The Strategems of War,* tr. Robert Scott. London, 1816.

Die Gesetze der Angelsachsen, ed. F. Liebermann. 3 vols. Halle, 1898–1916.

Herefordshire Domesday, circa 1160–1170, ed. V. H. Galbraith and James Tait. London, 1950.

Landboc sive Registrum Monasterii de Winchelcumba, ed. D. Royce. 2 vols. Exeter, 1892–1903.

Lanfranci Opera Omnia, ed. J. A. Giles. 2 vols. Oxford, 1844.

Liber de Antiquis Legibus, ed. Thomas Stapleton. London, 1846.

Liber Feodorum: The Book of Fees commonly called Testa de Nevill, ed. H. C. Maxwell Lyte. 3 vols. London, 1921–1931.

"A London Municipal Collection of the Reign of John," ed. Mary Bateson, *English Historical Review,* XVII (1902), 480–511, 707–730.

Magna Carta, with notes by Faith Thompson (Senate Doc. No. 180, 81st Congress, 2nd Session). Washington, 1950.

Memorials of St. Edmund's Abbey, ed. Thomas Arnold (R.S.). 3 vols. London, 1890–1896.

Monasticon Anglicanum, ed. John Caley, Henry Ellis, and Bulkeley Bandinel. 6 vols. in 8. London, 1817–1830.

A Muslim Manual of War, being the Tafrīj al-Kurūb fi Tadbīr al-Hurūb by 'Umar ibn Ibrahim al-Awsī al-Ansarī, ed. and tr. George T. Scanlon. Cairo, 1961.

De Necessariis Observantiis Scaccarii Dialogus qui Vulgo Dicitur Dialogus de Scaccario, ed. and tr. Charles Johnson. London, 1950.

The Pipe Roll of 31 Henry I, Michaelmas 1130, ed. Joseph Hunter (Facsimile of 1833 ed.). London, 1929.

The Great Roll of the Pipe for the Second, Third and Fourth Years of the Reign of King Henry the Second, A.D. 1155, 1156, 1157, 1158, ed. Joseph Hunter (Facsimile of 1844 ed.). London, 1930.

The Great Rolls of the Pipe for the Fifth to the Thirty-fourth Years of the Reign of King Henry the Second. 30 vols. London, 1884–1925.

The Great Roll of the Pipe for the First Year of the Reign of King Richard the First, 1188–1189, ed. Joseph Hunter. London, 1844.

Recueil des Actes de Henri II, Roi d'Angleterre et Duc de Normandie Concernant les Provinces Françaises et les Affaires de France, ed. Victor Leopold de Lisle and E. Berger. 4 vols. Paris, 1909–1927.

The Red Book of the Exchequer, ed. Hubert Hall (R.S.). 3 vols. London, 1896.

Regesta Anglo-Normannorum (1066–1154), ed. H. W. C. Davis, Charles Johnson, and H. A. Cronne. 2 vols. Oxford, 1913– .

Registrum Antiquissimum of Lincoln Cathedral, ed. C. W. Foster. 4 vols. (Linc. Rec. Soc., vols., 27, 28, 29, 32) Lincoln, 1931–1937.

Rotuli Hundredorum, ed. W. Illingworth and J. Caley. 2 vols. London, 1812–1818.

Rotuli Litterarum Clausarum in Turri Londinensi Asservati, ed. T. D. Hardy. 2 vols. London, 1833–1844.

Sancti Anselmi, Cantuariensis Archiepiscopi Opera Omnia, ed. Francis S. Schmitt. 5 vols. Edinburgh, 1946–1951.

Sources of English Constitutional History, ed. and tr. Carl Stephenson and Frederick George Marcham. New York, 1937.

War of the Rebellion: A Compilation of the Official Records of the Union and Confederate Armies. 130 vols. Washington, 1880–1901.

II. Narrative Sources

Ailred of Rievaulx, *De Bello Standardi,* in Vol. III, *Chronicles of the Reigns of Stephen, Henry II and Richard I,* ed. Richard Howlett (R.S.). London, 1886.

The Anglo-Saxon Chronicle According to the Several Original Authorities, ed. Benjamin Thorpe (R.S.). 2 vols. London, 1861.

Annales Cambriae, ed. John Williams ab Ithel (R.S.). London, 1860.

Annales de Margan, in Vol. I, *Annales Monastici,* ed. Henry Richards Luard (R.S.). London, 1864.

Annales de Theokesberia, in Vol. I, *Annales Monastici,* ed. Henry Richards Luard (R.S.). London, 1864.

Annales Monasterii de Oseneia, in Vol. IV, *Annales Monastici,* ed. Henry Richards Luard (R.S.). London, 1869.

Annales Monasterii de Waverleia, in Vol. II, *Annales Monastici,* ed. Henry Richards Luard (R.S.). London, 1865.

Annales Monasterii de Wintonia, in Vol. II, *Annales Monastici,* ed. Henry Richards Luard (R.S.). London, 1865.

Annales Prioratus de Dunstaplia, in Vol. III, *Annales Monastici,* ed. Henry Richards Luard (R.S.). London, 1866.

Annales Prioratus de Wigornia, in Vol. IV, *Annales Monastici,* ed. Henry Richards Luard (R.S.). London, 1869.

The Bayeux Tapestry, ed. Sir Frank Stenton. London, 1957.

Brut y Tywysogion; or the Chronicle of the Princes, ed. John Williams ab Ithel (R.S.) . London, 1860.

The Chronicle of Melrose, ed. Alan Orr Anderson and Marjorie Ogilvie Anderson (Studies in Economics and Political Science, No. 100, London School of Economics and Political Science) . London, 1936.

Chronicon Abbatiae de Evesham ad Annum 1418, ed. William Dunn Macray (R.S.) . London, 1863.

Chronicon Abbatiae Rameseiensis, ed. W. Dunn Macray (R.S.) . London, 1886.

Chronicon Monasterii de Abingdon, ed. Joseph Stevenson (R.S.) . 2 vols. London, 1858.

Chronicon Monasterii de Bello, ed. J. S. Brewer. London, 1846.

Chronicon Petroburgense, ed. Thomas Stapleton. London, 1849.

Continuato Gemblacensis to Sigeberti Gemblacensis Chronographia, ed. Ludwig Conrad Bethmann, in Vol. VI, *Monumenta Germaniae Historica.* New York, 1963.

Eadmeri Historia Novorum in Anglia et Opuscula Duo de Vita Sancti Anselmi et Quibusdam Miraculis Ejus, ed. Martin Rule (R.S.) . London, 1884.

Florence of Worcester. *Chronicon ex Chronicis,* ed. Benjamin Thorpe. 2 vols. London, 1849.

Galbert of Bruges. *The Murder of Charles the Good, Count of Flanders,* tr. J. B. Ross. New York, 1949.

Geoffrey Gaimar. *Lestoire des Engles solum la Translacion Maistre Geffrei Gaimar,* ed. Sir Thomas Duffus Hardy and Charles Trice Martin (R.S.) . 2 vols. London, 1888.

Gervase of Canterbury, The Chronicle of the Reigns of Stephen, Henry II and Richard I by Gervase, the Monk of Canterbury, ed. William Stubbs (R.S.) . 2 vols. London, 1879.

Gesta Herwardi Incliti Exulis et Militis, in Vol. I, *Lestoire des Engles solum la Translacion Maistre Geffrei Gaimar,* ed. Sir Thomas Duffus Hardy and Charles Trice Martin (R.S.) . London, 1888.

De Gestis Herwardi Saxonis, ed. S. H. Miller, tr. W. D. Sweeting; supplement to *Fenland Notes and Queries,* III (1895–1897) . Peterborough, 1895.

Gesta Regis Henrici Secundi Benedicti Abbatis, ed. William Stubbs (R.S.) . 2 vols. London, 1867.

Gesta Stephani Regis Anglorum, in Vol. III, *Chronicles of the Reigns of Stephen, Henry II and Richard I,* ed. Richard Howlett (R.S.) . London, 1886.

Gesta Stephani Regis Anglorum et Ducis Normannorum, ed. and tr. K. R. Potter. London, 1955.

Giraldus Cambrensis. *Descriptio Kambriae,* in Vol. vi, *Giraldi Cambrensis Opera,* ed. James F. Dimock (R.S.). London, 1868.

———. *Itinerarium Kambriae,* in Vol. vi, *Giraldi Cambrensis Opera,* ed. James F. Dimock (R.S.). London, 1868.

Guy of Amiens. *Widonis Carmen de Hastingae Proelio,* in *Scriptores Rerum Gestarum Willelmi Conquestatoris,* ed. J. A. Giles. London, 1845.

Hall, Edward. *Chronicle Containing the History of England.* London, 1809.

Henry of Huntingdon. *Henrici Archidiaconi Huntendunensis Historia Anglorum,* ed. Thomas Arnold (R.S.). London, 1879.

Herodotus. *The Persian Wars,* tr. George Rawlinson. New York, 1942.

Historians of the Church of York, ed. James Raine (R.S.). 3 vols. London, 1879–1894.

History of Gruffydd ap Cynan, ed. and tr. Arthur Jones. Manchester, 1910.

Holy Bible, Authorized Version.

Hugh Candidus. *The Chronicle of Hugh Candidus a Monk of Peterborough,* ed. W. T. Matthews. Oxford, 1949.

Hugh the Chantor. *The History of the Church of York, 1066–1127,* ed. and tr. Charles Johnson. London, 1961.

Jocelin of Brakelond. *The Chronicle of Jocelin of Brakelond,* ed. and tr. H. E. Butler. London, 1951.

John of Hexham. *Historia Regum Symeonis Monachi Dunelmensis continuata Der Joannem Hagulstadensem,* in Vol. ii, *Symeonis Monachi Opera Omnia,* ed. Thomas Arnold (R.S.). London, 1885.

Jordan Fantosme. *The Metrical Chronicle of Jordan Fantosme,* in vol. iii, *Chronicles of the Reigns of Stephen, Henry II and Richard I,* ed. Richard Howlett (R.S.). London, 1886.

Liber Eliensis, ed. E. O. Blake (Camden Third Series, xcii). London, 1962.

Liber Landaviensis, ed. William J. Rees. Llandovery, 1840.

Liber Monasterii de Hyda. A Chronicle and Chartulary of Hyde Abbey, Winchester, 455–1023, ed. Edward Edwards (R.S.). London, 1866.

Livius, Titus. *History of Rome,* ed. D. Spillman. 4 vols. London, 1889.

Matthew Paris. *Historia Anglorum (Historia Minor),* ed. Sir Frederick Madden (R.S.). 3 vols. London, 1866–1869.

Ordericus Vitalis. *Historica Ecclesiastica,* ed. August le Prevost. 5 vols. Paris, 1838–1855.

Ralph Diceto. *Radulfi de Diceto Decani Lundonensis Opera Historica,* ed. William Stubbs (R.S.). 2 vols. London, 1876.

Richard of Hexham, *The Chronicle of Richard, Prior of Hexham,* in Vol. III, *Chronicles of the Reigns of Stephen, Henry II and Richard I,* ed. Richard Howlett (R.S.). London, 1886.

Robert of Torigni. *The Chronicle of Robert of Torigni,* in Vol. IV, *Chronicles of the Reigns of Stephen, Henry II and Richard I,* ed. Richard Howlett (R.S.). London, 1889.

Roger of Hoveden. *Chronica Magistri Rogeri de Houedene,* ed. William Stubbs (R.S.). 4 vols. London, 1868–1871.

A Scottish Chronicle Known as the Chronicle of Holyrood, ed. Marjorie Ogilvie Anderson and Alan Orr Anderson (Publications of the Scottish History Soc., 3rd. Ser., xxx). Edinburgh, 1938.

Snorri Sturluson. *Heimskringla: Sagas of the Norse Kings,* tr. Samuel Lang and Peter Foote. London, 1961.

Symeon of Durham. *Symeonis Monachi Opera Omnia,* ed. Thomas Arnold (R.S.). 2 vols. London, 1882.

Thucydides. *The Peloponnesian War,* tr. R. Crawley. New York, 1934.

Wace. *Maistre Wace's le Roman de Rou et des Ducs de Normandie,* ed. Hugo Andresen. 2 vols. Heilbronn, 1877–1879.

William of Jumièges. *Willelmi Calculi Gemmeticensis Monachi Historiae Northmannorum,* in Vol. CXLIX, *Patrologia Cursus Completus, Series Latina,* ed. J. P. Migne. Paris, 1882.

William of Malmesbury. *De Gestis Regum Anglorum,* ed. William Stubbs (R.S.). 2 vols. London, 1889.

——. *Historia Novella,* ed. and tr. K. R. Potter. London, 1955.

——. *Vita Wulfstani,* ed. Reginald R. Darlington (Camden Soc., XL). London, 1928.

——. *Willelmi Malmesbiriensis de Gestis Pontificum Anglorum,* ed. N. E. S. A. Hamilton (R.S.). London, 1870.

William of Newburgh. *Historia Rerum Anglicarum of William of Newburgh,* in Vols. I and II of *Chronicles of the Reigns of Stephen, Henry II and Richard I,* ed. Richard Howlett (R.S.). London, 1884–1885.

William of Poitiers. *Gesta Guillelmi Ducis Normannorum et Regis Anglorum,* ed. Raymonde Foreville. Paris, 1952.

III. Secondary Works

Adcock, F. E. *The Roman Art of War under the Republic.* Cambridge, Mass., 1940.

Allcroft, A. Hadrian. *Earthworks of England*. London, 1908.

——. "The First Castle of William de Warenne," *Archaeological Journal*, LXXIV (1917), 36–78.

Appleby, John T. *Henry II, the Vanquished King*. London, 1962.

Armitage, Ella S. *The Early Norman Castles of the British Isles*. London, 1912.

——. "The Early Norman Castles in England," *English Historical Review*, XIX (1904), 209–245, 417–455.

——. "Anglo-Saxon Burhs and Early Norman Castles," *Proc. Soc. Antiq. Scotland*, XXXIV, 260–288.

Astley, H. J. Dukinfield. "Mediaeval Colchester—Town, Castle, and Abbey, from MSS. in the British Museum," *Transactions of the Essex Archaeological Society*, New Series, VIII (1903), 117–138.

Baddeley, St. Clair. "Berkeley Castle," *Transactions of the Bristol and Gloucester Archaeological Society*, XLVIII (1926), 133–180.

——. "St. Briavel's Castle (*Ledeney Parva*)," *Transactions of the Bristol and Gloucester Archaeological Society*, XLIII (1921), 79–84.

Baker, R. S. "Yeldon Castle in Bedfordshire," *Associated Architectural Societies Reports*, XVI, Pt. 2 (1882), 251–264.

Baldwin, F. J. *The Scutage and Knight Service in England*. Chicago, 1897.

Barber, Richard. *Henry Plantagenet*. London, 1964.

Barbier, Paul. *The Age of Owain Gwynedd*. London, 1908.

Baring, Francis Henry. *Domesday Tables for the Counties of Surrey, Berkshire, Middlesex, Hertford, Buckingham, and Bedford and for the New Forest*. London, 1909.

——. "The Battle Field of Hastings," *English Historical Review*, XX (1905), 65–70.

——. "The Malfosse at the Battle of Hastings," *English Historical Review*, XXII (1907), 69.

——. "Hastings Castle 1050–1100," *Sussex Archaeological Collections*, LVII (1915), 119–135.

Barlow, Frank. *The Feudal Kingdom of England, 1042–1216*. London, 1955.

Barrett, C. R. B. *Battles and Battlefields in England*. London, 1896.

Bartelot, R. Grosvenor. "The Vanished Mediaeval Castles of Dorset," *Proceedings of the Dorset Natural History and Archaeological Society*, LXVI (1944), 65–75.

Bates, Cadwallader J. "The Border Holds of Northumbria," *Archaeologia Aeliana*, 2nd ser., I, 1921.

Batty, R. E. "Historic Sketch of Pontefract Castle," *Associated Architectural Societies Reports,* II (1852–1853), 90–104.

Bazeley, William. "Berkeley Castle," *Journal of the British Archaeological Association,* New series, XVIII (1912), 211–219.

———. "Sudeley Castle," *Journal of the British Archaeological Association,* New series, XIX (1913), 55–61.

Beeler, John H. "Castles and Strategy in Norman and Early Angevin England," *Speculum,* XXXXI (1956), 581–601.

———. "XIIth Century Guerilla Campaign," *Military Review,* XLII (1962), 39–46.

———. "Towards a Re-Evaluation of Medieval English Generalship," *Journal of British Studies,* III (1963), 1–10.

———. "The Composition of Anglo-Norman Armies, *Speculum,* XXXIX (1965), 398–414.

Belloc, Hilaire. *Warfare in England.* London, n.d.

Berkeley, The Earl of. "Berkeley Castle," *Transactions of the Bristol and Gloucester Archaeological Society,* XLIX (1927), 183–194.

Bigge, H. E. "Historical and Architectural Notices of Rockingham Castle," *Associated Architectural Societies Reports,* XI, Pt. 1 (1871), 109–118.

Blair, C. H. Hunter. "Norham Castle," *Proceedings of the Society of Antiquaries of Newcastle upon Tyne,* 4th series, III (1927), 46–53.

———. "The Early Castles of Northumbria," *Archaeologia Aeliana,* 4th series, XXII (1944), 116–170.

———. "Baronys and Knights of Northumberland A.D. 1166–c. A.D. 1266," *Archaeologia Aeliana,* 4th series, XXX (1952), 1–56.

Bond, Brian. "Some Attractions and Pitfalls of Military History," *Military Review,* XLV (1965), 87–96.

Bosanquet, Robert C. "Excavations at Dunstanburgh Castle," *Archaeologia Aeliana,* 4th series, XIII (1936), 279–292.

Boussard, Jacques. *Les Mercenaires au XIIe Siècle: Henri Plantagenet et les Origines de l'Armée de Métier.* Paris, 1947.

———. *Le Gouvernement d'Henri II Plantagenet.* Paris, 1956.

Brakspear, Harold. "Dudley Castle," *Archaeological Journal,* 2nd series, XXI (1914), 1–24.

Braun, Hugh. *The English Castle,* 2nd ed., rev. London, 1943.

———. "Earthwork Castles," *Journal of the British Archaeological Association,* 3rd series, I (1937), 128–156.

———. "Some Notes on Bungay Castle," *Proceedings of the Suffolk Institute of Archaeology and Natural History,* XXII, Pt. 1 (1935), 109–119.

———. "Bungay Castle: Report on the Excavations," *Proceedings of the*

Suffolk Institute of Archaeology and Natural History, xxii, pt. 2 (1936), 201–233.

——. "The Keep of Bungay Castle in Suffolk," *Journal of the British Archaeological Association,* 3rd series, i (1937), 157–167.

——. "Notes on Newark Castle," *Transactions of the Thoroton Society,* xxxix (1936), 53–91.

Brook, Sir Thomas. "Castle Hill, Almondbury," *Yorkshire Archaeological and Topographical Journal,* xvi (1901), 241–247.

Brooks, F. W. *The Battle of Stamford Bridge.* York, 1956.

Brown, R. Allen. *English Medieval Castles.* London, 1954.

——. "Royal Castle-Building in England 1154–1216," *English Historical Review,* lxx (1955), 353–398.

——. "A List of the Castles, 1154–1216," *English Historical Review,* lxxiv (1959), 249–280.

——, H. M. Colvin, and A. J. Taylor. *The History of the King's Works: The Middle Ages.* 2 vols. London, 1963.

Browne, A. L. "Robert de Todeni and His Heirs," *Transactions of the Bristol and Gloucester Archaeological Society,* lii (1930), 103–112.

Bugden, W. "Pevensey Castle Guard and Endlewick Rents," *Sussex Archaeological Collections,* lxxvi (1935), 115–134.

Burne, Lt.-Col. Alfred H. *The Battlefields of England.* London, 1950.

——. *More Battlefields of England.* London, 1952.

Cantor, Norman F. *Church, Kingship, and Lay Investiture in England, 1089–1135.* Princeton, 1958.

Casey, D. A. "Lydney Castle," *Antiquaries Journal,* xi (1931), 240–261.

Chadwick, S. J. "Excavations on the Site of Almondbury Castle," *Yorkshire Archaeological and Topographical Journal,* xv (1898–1899), 118–119.

Chew, Helena M. *The Ecclesiastical Tenants-in-Chief and Knight Service.* Oxford, 1932.

Chrimes, S. B. *An Introduction to the Administrative History of Mediaeval England.* New York, 1952.

Christy, Miller. "The Excavations of Foundations on the Castle Keep at Pleshy," *Transactions of the Essex Archaeological Society,* New series, xvi (1923), 190–204.

Clapham, A. W. "An Early Hall at Chilham Castle, Kent," *Antiquaries Journal,* viii (1928), 350–353.

Clark, George T. *Mediaeval Military Architecture in England.* 2 vols. London, 1884.

Clephan, R. Coltman. "Notes on Roman and Medieval Engines of War," *Archaeologia Aeliana,* xxiv (1902), 69–114.

Cokayne's Complete Peerage of England, Scotland, Ireland, Great

Britain, and the United Kingdom, ed. V. Gibbs et al. 13 vols. London, 1910–1959.

Collingwood, W. G. "Pre-Norman Remains," in Vol. I, *The Victoria History of the County of Cumberland,* ed. James Wilson. Westminster, 1901.

——. "Three More Ancient Castles of Kendal," *Transactions of the Cumberland and Westmoreland Antiquarian and Archaeological Society,* New series, VIII (1908), 97–112.

Compton, C. H. "The Castle of Dunstanburgh," *Journal of the British Archaeological Association,* New series, IX (1903), 111–116.

Conway, Agnes E. "The Owners of Allington Castle, Maidstone, (1086–1279)," *Archaeologia Cantiana,* XXIX (1911), 1–39.

Conway, W. Martin. "Allington Castle," *Archaeologia Cantiana,* XXVIII (1909), 337–362.

——. "Leeds Castle," *Archaeological Journal,* LXXXII (1925), 259.

Corbett, John Stuart. "Caerphilly Castle," *Transactions of the Bristol and Gloucester Archaeological Society,* XXXI (1908), 261–269.

Corbett, William John. "The Development of the Duchy of Normandy and the Norman Conquest of England," in *The Cambridge Mediaeval History,* ed. J. R. Tanner et al. V. 16. Cambridge, 1943.

Cronne, H. A. "The Honour of Lancaster in Stephen's Reign," *English Historical Review,* L (1935), 670–680.

Crosland, Jessie, *William the Marshal, the Last Great Feudal Baron.* London, 1962.

Cruden, Stewart. *The Scottish Castle.* London, 1960.

Currey, P. H. "Bolsover Castle," *Journal of the Derbyshire Archaeological and Natural History Society,* XXXVIII (1916), 1–28.

Curwen, John F. "Brough Castle," *Transactions of the Cumberland and Westmoreland Antiquarian and Archaeological Society,* New series, IX (1909), 177–191.

——. "Brougham Castle," *Transactions of the Cumberland and Westmoreland Antiquarian and Archaeological Society,* New series, XXII (1922), 143–157.

Darby, H. C. "The Economic Geography of England, A.D. 1000–1250," in *An Historical Geography of England before A.D. 1800,* ed. H. C. Darby. Cambridge, 1951.

D'Auvergne, Edmund B. *The Castles of England.* London, 1907.

David, Charles Wendell. *Robert Curthose, Duke of Normandy.* Cambridge, Mass., 1920.

Davis, G. R. C. *Medieval Cartularies of Great Britain, A Short Catalogue.* London, 1958.

Davis, H. W. C. "The Anarchy of Stephen's Reign," *English Historical Review*, XVIII (1903), 630–641.

——. "Henry of Blois and Brian Fitz-Count," *English Historical Review*, XXV (1910), 297–303.

Davis, R. H. C. "Geoffrey de Mandeville Reconsidered," *English Historical Review*, LXXIX (1964), 294–307.

——. "What Happened in Stephen's Reign, 1135–54," *History*, XLIV (1964), 1–12.

Dawson, C. *History of Hastings Castle*. 2 vols. London, 1909.

Delbrück, Hans. *Geschichte der Kriegskunst im Rahmen des Politische Geschichte*. 6 vols. Berlin, 1907–1921.

——. *Numbers in History*. London, 1913.

The Dictionary of National Biography, ed. Leslie Stephen and Sidney Lee. 63 vols. London, 1885–1900.

The Domesday Geography of Eastern England, ed. H. C. Darby. Cambridge, 1952.

The Domesday Geography of Midland England, ed. H. C. Darby and I. B. Terrett. Cambridge, 1954.

The Domesday Geography of Northern England, ed. H. C. Darby and I. S. Maxwell. Cambridge, 1962.

The Domesday Geography of Southeast England, ed. H. C. Darby and Eila M. J. Campbell. Cambridge, 1962.

Douglas, David C. *William the Conqueror*. Berkeley, 1964.

——. "The Norman Conquest and English Feudalism," *Economic History Review*, IX (1939), 128–143.

Drummond, J. Douglas. *Studien zur Kriegsgeschichte Englands im 12 Jahrhundert*. Berlin, 1905.

Edwards, J. G. "The Normans and the Welsh March," *Proceedings of the British Academy*, XLII (1956), 155–177.

Eyton, R. W. *Court, Household, and Itinerary of King Henry II*. London, 1878.

Farrer, William. *Honours and Knight's Fees*. 3 vols. London and Manchester, 1923–1925.

——. *An Outline Itinerary of King Henry the First*. Oxford, n.d.

——. "The Sheriffs of Lincolnshire and Yorkshire, 1066–1130," *English Historical Review*, XXX (1915), 277–285.

Fishwick, Henry. "The Old Castles of Lancashire," *Transactions of the Lancashire and Cheshire Antiquarian Society*, XIX (1901), 45–76.

Fowler, G. H. "The Devastation of Bedfordshire and the Neighboring Counties in 1065 and 1066," *Archaeologia*, LXXII (1922), 41–50.

Fowler, H. "Berkhamstead Castle," *Transactions of the St. Albans Architectural and Archaeological Society* (1890–1891) , 17–28.

——. "Someries Castle," *Transactions of the St. Albans Architectural and Archaeological Society* (1889) , 31–45.

Freeman, Edward A. *The History of the Norman Conquest of England.* 6 vols. Oxford, 1867–1879.

——. *The Reign of William Rufus and the Accession of Henry the First.* 2 vols. Oxford, 1882.

Fuller, Maj.-Gen. J. F. C. *The Decisive Battles of the Western World.* 3 vols. London, 1954–1956.

Ganshof, F. L., R. van Caenegem, and A. Verhulst. "Note sur le premier traité anglo-flamand de Douvres," *Revue du Nord,* xl (1958) , 245–257.

Glover, Richard. "English Warfare in 1066," *English Historical Review,* lxvii (1952) , 1–18.

Gould, I. Chalkley. "Bures Mount," *Transactions of the Essex Archaeological Society,* New series, ix (1906) , 20–21.

——. "Great Easton Mount," *Transactions of the Essex Archaeological Society,* New Series, viii (1903) , 324–326.

——. "The Castle of Ongar," *Transactions of the Essex Archaeological Society,* New series, vii (1900) , 137–141.

——. "Rickling Mount," *Transactions of the Essex Archaeological Society,* New series, ix (1906) , 377–379.

Graham, T. H. B. "Six Extinct Cumberland Castles," *Transactions of the Cumberland and Westmoreland Antiquarian and Archaeological Society,* New series, ix (1909) , 209–224.

——. "Extinct Cumberland Castles," *Transactions of the Cumberland and Westmoreland Antiquarian and Archaeological Society,* New series, x (1910) , 102–117.

——. "Extinct Cumberland Castles, III," *Transactions of the Cumberland and Westmoreland Antiquarian and Archaeological Society,* New series, xi (1911) , 233–259.

Graham, Col. W. A. *The Custer Myth.* Harrisburg, Pa., 1953.

Grundmann, Herbert. "Rotten und Brabanzonen: Soldner-Heere im 12. Jahrhundert," *Deutsches-Archiv für Geschichte des Mittelalters,* v (1941–1942) , 419–492.

Hadcock, R. Neville. "A Map of Mediaeval Northumberland and Durham," *Archaeologia Aeliana,* 4th series, xvi (1939) , 148–218.

Hamp, Wilfrid J. "Denbigh Castle," *Y Cymmrodor,* xxxvi (1926) , 65–120.

——. "The Castle of Ewloe and the Welsh Castle Plan," *Y Cymmrodor*, XXXIX (1928), 4–19.

Hardman, F. W. "Castleguard Service of Dover Castle," *Archaeologia Cantiana*, XLIX (1937), 96–107.

Hart, B. H. Liddell. *Strategy: The Indirect Approach*. New York, 1954.

Harvey, Alfred. *The Castles and Walled Towns of England*. London, 1911.

Harvey, John H. *English Mediaeval Architects: A Biographical Dictionary Down to 1550*. Boston, 1954.

——. "Side-Lights on Kenilworth Castle," *Archaeological Journal*, CI (1944), 91–107.

Haskins, Charles Homer. *Norman Institutions*. New York, 1960.

Hewitt, H. J. *The Black Prince's Expedition of 1355–1357*. Manchester, 1958.

Hill, J. W. F. *Mediaeval Lincoln*. Cambridge, 1948.

——. "Lincoln Castle," *Archaeological Journal*, CIII (1947), 157–159.

Hogg, A. H. A., and D. J. C. King. "Early Castles in Wales and the Marches," *Archaeologia Cambrensis*, CXVII (1963), 77–124.

Hollings, Marjory. "The Survival of the Five Hide Unit in the Western Midlands," *English Historical Review*, LXIII (1948), 453–487.

Hollister, C. Warren. *Anglo-Saxon Military Institutions on the Eve of the Norman Conquest*. Oxford, 1962.

——. "The Annual Term of Military Service in Medieval England," *Medievalia et Humanistica*, XIII (1960), 40–47.

——. "The Significance of Scutage Rates in Eleventh- and Twelfth-Century England," *English Historical Review*, LXXV (1960), 577–588.

——. "The Five-Hide Unit and the Old English Military Obligation," *Speculum*, XXXVI (1961), 61–74.

——. "The Norman Conquest and the Genesis of English Feudalism," *American Historical Review*, LXVI (1961), 641–663.

——. "The Knights of Peterborough and the Anglo-Saxon Fyrd," *English Historical Review*, LXXVII (1962), 417–436.

——. "The Irony of English Feudalism," *Journal of British Studies*, II (1963), 1–26.

Holt, J. C. "Feudalism Revisited," *Economic History Review*, 2nd series, XIV (1961), 333–340.

Homans, George C. review of J. Ambrose Raftis, *The Estates of Ramsey Abbey*, *Speculum*, XXXIII (1958), 562–564.

Hope, W. H. St. John. *Windsor Castle*. 2 vols. London, 1913.

——. "English Fortresses and Castles of the Tenth and Eleventh Centuries," *Archaeological Journal*, LX (1903), 72–90.

——. "The Norman Origin of Cambridge Castle," *Proceedings of the Cambridge Antiquarian Society*, XLVII (1905–1906), 324–345.

——. "The Castle of Ludlow," *Archaeologia*, LXI (1908), 257–328.

Howard, Michael. "The Use and Abuse of Military History," *Military Review*, XLII (1962), 8–10.

Hoyt, Robert S. *The Royal Demesne in English Constitutional History: 1066–1272*. Ithaca, N.Y., 1950.

——. Review of Eric John, *Land Tenure in Early England*, *Speculum*, XXXVI (1961), 663–665.

——. "The Iron Age of English Feudalism," *Journal of British Studies*, II (1963), 27–30.

Jähns, M. *Handbuch einer Geschichte des Kriegswesen von der Urzeit bis zur Renaissance*. 2 vols. Leipzig, 1878–1880.

James, Maj.-Gen. E. Renouard. "The Battle of Hastings, 14th October 1066," *The Royal Engineers Journal*, V (1907), 18–34.

John, Eric. *Land Tenure in Early England*. Leicester, 1960.

Jolliffe, J. E. A. *Angevin Kingship*, London, 1955.

Jones, W. T. "Chronological Order of Different Portions of Durham Castle," *Archaeological Journal*, LXXXII (1925), 226–227.

Kelly, Amy. *Eleanor of Aquitaine and the Four Kings*. Cambridge, Mass., 1950.

King, D. J. C. "Bow and Arrow Castle, Portland," *Proceedings of the Dorset Natural History and Archaeological Society*, LXIX (1947), 65–67.

——. "The Castles of Cardiganshire," *Ceredigion*, 1956, 1–20.

——. "The Castles of Breconshire," *The Brecknock Society in Brycheiniog*, VII (1961), 71–94.

Kirke, Henry. "Peverel's Castle in the Peake," *Journal of the Derbyshire Archaeological and Natural History Society*, XXVIII (1906), 134–146.

Knowles, W. H. "The Castle of Newcastle-upon-Tyne," *Archaeologia Aeliana*, 4th series, II (1926), 1–51.

Köhler, G. *Die Entwickelung des Kriegswesen und der Kriegführung in der Ritterzeit von Mitte des 11. Jahrhundert bis zu den Hussitenkriegen*. 3 vols. Breslau, 1886–1890.

Krieg von Hochfelden, G. H. *Geschichte der Militar-Architektur in Deutschland*. Stuttgart, 1859.

Leeds, Edward T. "An Adulterine Castle on Faringdon Clump, Berkshire," *Antiquaries Journal*, XVI (1936), 165–178.

——. "An Adulterine Castle on Faringdon Clump, Berkshire (Second Report)," *Antiquaries Journal,* XVII (1937), 294–298.

Lemmon, Lieut.-Col. Charles H. *The Field of Hastings,* St. Leonards-on-Sea, 1956.

Lennard, Reginald. *Rural England, 1086–1135.* Oxford, 1959.

Lethbridge, T. C. "Excavations at Burwell Castle, Cambridgeshire," *Cambridge Antiquarian Society Proceedings for 1934–35,* XXXVI (1936), 121–123.

Lipson, E. *The Economic History of England.* I: *The Middle Ages.* 11th ed. London, 1956.

Lloyd, Sir John Edward. *A History of Wales from the Earliest Times to the Edwardian Conquest,* 3rd ed. 2 vols. London, 1954.

Lot, Ferdinand. *L'Art Militaire et les Armées au Moyen Age en Europe et dans le Proche Orient.* 2 vols. Paris, 1946.

Lyon, Bryce. *From Fief to Indenture: The Transition from Feudal to Non-Feudal Contract in Western Europe.* Cambridge, Mass., 1957.

——. *A Constitutional and Legal History of Medieval England.* New York, 1960.

——. "The Money Fief under the English Kings, 1066–1485," *English Historical Review,* LXXI (1951), 161–193.

Mackenzie, Sir J. D. *The Castles of England, their Story and Structure.* 2 vols. New York, 1896.

Mackenzie, W. Mackay. *The Battle of Bannockburn: A Study in Mediaeval Warfare.* Glasgow, 1913.

——. *The Mediaeval Castle in Scotland.* London, 1927.

Macpherson, E. R., and E. G. J. Amos. "The Norman Waterworks in the Keep of Dover Castle," *Archaeologia Cantiana,* XLIII (1931), 173–186.

Maitland, F. W. *Domesday Book and Beyond: Three Essays in the Early History of England.* London, 1960.

Malden, Henry Elliot. "Blechingley Castle and the de Clares," *Surrey Archaeological Collections,* XV (1900), 17–26.

——. "The Shell Keep at Guildford Castle," *Surrey Archaeological Collections,* XVI (1901), 28–34.

Margary, Ivan D. *Roman Ways in the Weald.* London, 1949.

——. *Roman Roads in Britain.* 2 vols. London, 1955–1957.

Marshall-Cornwall, General Sir James. "The Military Geography of the Welsh Marches," *Geographical Magazine,* XXX (1957), 1–12.

Miller, Edward. *The Abbey and Bishopric of Ely.* Cambridge, 1951.

Morris, John E. *The Welsh Wars of Edward I.* Oxford, 1901.

———. "The Assessment of Knight Service in Bedfordshire," *Bedfordshire Historical Record Society,* v (1920), 1–26.

Morris, William Alfred. *The Medieval English Sheriff to 1300.* London, 1927.

———. *The Constitutional History of England to 1216.* New York, 1930.

———. "The Office of Sheriff in the Early Norman Period," *English Historical Review,* xxxiii (1918), 145–175.

———. "A Mention of Scutage in the Year 1100," *English Historical Review,* xxxvi (1921), 45–46.

Neaverson, E. *Mediaeval Castles in North Wales.* London, 1947.

Newhall, R. A. *Muster and Review, A Problem of English Military Administration 1420–1440.* Cambridge, Mass., 1940.

Nicholl, Donald. *Thurstan, Archbishop of York (1114–1140).* York, 1964.

Nicholl, Lewis D. *The Normans in Glamorgan, Gower, and Kidweli.* Cardiff, 1936.

Norgate, Kate. *England under the Angevin Kings.* 2 vols. London, 1887.

Northumberland County History Committee. *A History of Northumberland.* 15 vols. London, 1893–1940.

Noyes, Arthur H. *The Military Obligation in Mediaeval England with Especial Reference to Commissions of Array.* Columbus, 1930.

Oman, Sir Charles W. C. *A History of the Art of War in the Middle Ages.* 2 vols. London, 1924.

———. *Castles.* London, 1926.

———. *The Art of War in the Middle Ages, A.D. 378–1515,* rev. and ed. John H. Beeler. Ithaca, N.Y., 1953.

O'Neil, Bryan H. St. J. "The Castle of Caereinon," *Montgomeryshire Collections,* xliv (1935), 39–44.

———. "A Note on the Date of Clifford's Tower, York," *Archaeological Journal,* xci (1934), 296–300.

———. "Finds from Coity, Ogmore, Grosmont, and White Castles," *Antiquaries Journal,* xv (1935), 320–335.

———. "Criccieth Castle, Caernarvonshire," *Archaeologia Cambrensis,* xcviii (1944), 1–51.

———. "The Castle and Borough of Llanidloes," *Montgomeryshire Collections,* xliii (1934), 47–65.

Ormerod, George. *The History of the County Palatine and City of Chester,* rev. and enlarged by Thomas Helsby. 2d ed. 3 vols. London, 1882.

Painter, Sidney. *William Marshal, Knight-Errant, Baron, and Regent of England.* Baltimore, 1933.

——. *Studies in the History of the English Feudal Barony.* Baltimore, 1943.

——. *The Reign of King John.* Baltimore, 1949.

——. *Mediaeval Society.* Ithaca, N.Y., 1952.

——. *A History of the Middle Ages, 284–1500.* New York, 1953.

——. "Castle-Guard," *American Historical Review,* XL (1935), 450–459.

——. "English Castles in the Early Middle Ages," *Speculum,* X (1935), 321–332.

——. "The Rout of Winchester," in *Feudalism and Liberty,* ed. Fred A. Cazel, Jr. Baltimore, 1961.

Parker, H. M. D. *The Roman Legions.* New York, 1958.

Payne-Gallway, Sir Ralph. *The Crossbow.* London, 1958.

Pearson, J. Moreton. "Powis Castle," *Montgomery Society Year Book for 1936–37,* (1936), 7–11.

Pelham, R. A. "The Gough Map," *Geographical Journal,* LXXXI (1933), 34.

Pitt-Rivers, Major-General Augustus H. L. F. "Excavations at Caesar's Camp near Folkestone, conducted in June and July, 1878," *Archaeologia,* XLVII (1883), 429–465.

Poole, Austin Lane. *Obligations of Society in the XII and XIII Centuries.* Oxford, 1946.

——. *From Domesday Book to Magna Carta 1087–1216.* 2nd ed. Oxford, 1955.

——. "Henry Plantagenet's Early Visits to England," *English Historical Review,* XLVII (1932), 447–452.

Powicke, Michael. *Military Obligation in Mediaeval England.* Oxford, 1962.

Preston, Arthur E. "A Moated Mound at Abingdon, Berks," *Antiquaries Journal,* XIV (1934), 417–421.

Prestwich, J. O. "War and Finance in the Anglo-Norman State," *Transactions of the Royal Historical Society,* 5th ser., IV, 19–43.

Pryce, T. Davies. "Earthworks of the Moated Mound Type," *Journal of the British Archaeological Association,* XII (1906), 231–268.

——, and Ella Armitage. "The Alleged Norman Origin of 'Castles' in England," *English Historical Review,* XX (1905), 703–718.

Pugh, R. B. "Great Chalfield," in Vol. VII, *The Victoria History of the County of Wilts.* London, 1953.

Radford, C. A. Ralegh. *Dover Castle.* London, 1956.

——. "Tintagel: The Castle and Celtic Monastery, Interim Report," *Antiquaries Journal,* XV (1935), 401–419.

Raftis, J. Ambrose. *The Estates of Ramsey Abbey.* Toronto, 1957.

Ramsay, Sir James H. *The Foundations of England.* 2 vols. Oxford, 1898.

——. *The Angevin Empire.* London, 1903.

——. "The Strength of English Armies in the Middle Ages," *English Historical Review,* XXIX (1914), 221–227.

Richardson, H. G., and G. O. Sayles. *The Governance of Mediaeval England from the Conquest to Magna Carta.* Edinburgh, 1963.

Ritchie, R. L. Graeme. *The Normans in Scotland.* Edinburgh, 1954.

Roberts, R. A. "Orford Castle," *Journal of the British Archaeological Association,* New series, XXXVI (1930), 33–58.

Robinson, J. Armitage. *Gilbert Crispin Abbot of Westminster.* Cambridge, 1911.

Rodd, Lord Rennell of. "Aids to the Domesday Geography of North-West Hereford," *Geographical Journal,* CXX (1954), 458–467.

Rössler, Oskar. *Kaisarin Mathilde, Mutter Heinrichs von Anjou, und das Zeitalter der Anarchie in England.* Berlin, 1896.

Rothenberg, Gunther Eric. *The Austrian Military Border in Croatia, 1522–1747.* Urbana, Ill., 1960.

Round, J. Horace. *The Commune of London and Other Studies.* Westminster, 1899.

——. *Feudal England.* London, 1909.

——. *Geoffrey de Mandeville: A Study of the Anarchy.* London, 1892.

——. "English Castles," *Quarterly Review,* CLXXIX (1894), 27–51.

——. "The Castles of the Conquest," *Archaeologia,* LVII (1902), 313–340.

——. "Castle-Guard," *Archaeological Journal,* 2nd ser., IX, (1902) 144–159.

——. "The Early Sheriffs of Norfolk," *English Historical Review,* XXXV (1920), 481–496.

——. "The Chronology of Henry II's Charters," *Archaeological Journal,* 2nd series, XIV (1907) 63–79.

——. "King Stephen and the Earl of Chester," *English Historical Review,* X (1895), 87–91.

The Royal Commission on Ancient and Historical Monuments in Wales and Monmouthshire. *An Inventory of the Ancient Monuments in Anglesey.* London, 1937.

——. *An Inventory of the Ancient Monuments in Caernarvonshire.* London, 1956.

The Royal Commission on Ancient and Historical Monuments and Constructions in Wales and Monmouthshire. *An Inventory of the Ancient Monuments in Wales and Monmouthshire.* 7 vols. London, 1911–1925.

Royal Commission on Historical Monuments—England. *An Inventory of the Historical Monuments in Buckinghamshire,* 2 vols. London, 1912–1913.

——. *An Inventory of the Historical Monuments in Dorset.* London, 1952.

——. *An Inventory of the Historical Monuments in Essex,* 4 vols. London, 1916–1923.

——. *An Inventory of the Historical Monuments in Herefordshire.* 3 vols. London, 1931–1934.

——. *An Inventory of the Historical Monuments in Hertfordshire.* London, 1911.

——. *An Inventory of the Historical Monuments in Huntingdonshire.* London, 1926.

——. *An Inventory of the Historical Monuments in Middlesex.* London, 1937.

——. *An Inventory of the Historical Monuments in Westmoreland.* London, 1935.

Rudkin, E. H. "Where did William Land?" *Sussex County Magazine,* II (1928), 60–63.

Rutter, J. A. "Moated Mounds," *The Antiquary,* XXXVIII (1902), 239–241, 271–275.

St. Joseph, J. D. "Castles of Northumberland from the Air," *Archaeologia Aeliana,* 4th series, XXVIII (1950), 7–17.

Salter, H. E. *Map of Mediaeval Oxford.* Oxford, 1934.

——. "The Death of Henry of Blois, Bishop of Winchester," *English Historical Review,* XXXVII (1922), 79–80.

Saltman, Avrom. *Theobald Archbishop of Canterbury.* London, 1956.

Salzmann, L. F. *Henry II.* London, 1917.

Sanders, I. J. *Feudal Military Service in England.* Oxford, 1956.

——. *English Baronies, A Study of their Origin and Descent, 1086–1327.* Oxford, 1960.

Scammell, G. V. *Hugh du Puiset, Bishop of Durham.* Cambridge, 1956.

Scott, Forrest S. "Earl Waltheof of Northumbria," *Archaeologia Aeliana,* 4th series, XXX (1952), 149–215.

Simpson, Grace. *Britons and the Roman Army.* London, 1964.

Simpson, W. Douglas. *Castles from the Air.* London, 1949.

——. "The Castles of Dudley and Ashby-de-la-Zouche," *Archaeological Journal,* XCVI (1939), 142–158.

——. "Dunstanburgh Castle," *Archaeologia Aeliana,* 4th series, XVI (1939), 31–42.

——. "Further Notes on Dunstanburgh Castle," *Archaeologia Aeliana,* 4th series, XXVII (1949), 1–28.

———. "Flint Castle," *Archaeologia Cambrensis,* xcv (1940) , 20–26.

———. "Tonbridge Castle," *Journal of the British Archaeological Association,* 3rd series, v (1940) , 63–72.

Smail, R. C. "Art of War," in Vol. I *Medieval England,* ed. Austin Lane Poole. London, 1958.

Smith, Frederick R. *The Historical Archietcture of Britain.* London, 1935.

South Mymms Castle Excavation Committee. "A Norman Mound and Bailey Castle," *Transactions of the London and Middlesex Archaeological Society,* New series, vii (1934) , 175–179.

Spatz, Wilhelm. *Die Schlacht von Hastings.* Berlin, 1896.

Spence, Joseph E. "The Development of the Castle," *Ancient Monuments Society Yearbook and Proceedings for 1935–1936* (1936) , 47–57.

Spencer, J. Houghton. "Structural Notes on Taunton Castle," *Proceedings of the Somerset Archaeological and Natural History Society,* lvi (1910) , 38–49.

Stenton, Sir Frank M. *Anglo-Saxon England.* 2nd ed. Oxford, 1947.

———. *The First Century of English Feudalism, 1066–1166.* 2nd ed. Oxford, 1961.

———. "The Road System in Mediaeval England," *Economic History Review,* vii (1936) , 1–21.

———. "Norman London," in *Social Life in Early England,* ed. Geoffrey Barraclough. London, 1960.

———. "The Development of the Castle in England and Wales," in *Social Life in Early England,* ed. Geoffrey Barraclough. London (1960) , 96–123.

Stephenson, Carl. "Feudalism and its Antecedents in England," *American Historical Review,* xlviii (1943) , 245–265.

Stewart-Brown, R. "The End of the Norman Earldom of Chester," *English Historical Review,* xxxv (1920) , 26–53.

Stone, Percy G. "A Vanished Castle. An Attempt to Reconstruct the Castle of Southampton from Observation, Analogy, and Documentary Evidence," *Hampshire Field Club Papers and Proceedings,* xii (1934) , 241–270.

Thompson, A. H. *Military Architecture in England during the Middle Ages.* London, 1912.

———. "Military Architecture," Ch. 22, in Vol. vi, *Cambridge Mediaeval History.* New York, 1936.

———. "The Art of War to 1400," Ch. 23, in Vol. vi, *Cambridge Mediaeval History.* New York, 1936.

Thornber, W. "The Castle Hill of Penwortham," *Transactions of the Historical Society of Lancashire and Cheshire,* IX (1856–1857), 61–76.

Toy, Sidney. *The Castles of Great Britain.* London, 1953.

——. *Castles: A Short History of Fortifications from 1600 B.C. to A.D. 1600.* London, 1939.

——. *A History of Fortification from 3000 B.C. to A.D. 1700.* London, 1955.

——. "The Town and Castle of Conway," *Archaeologia,* LXXXVI (1937), 163–194.

Turner, G. J. "William the Conqueror's March to London in 1066," *English Historical Review,* XVII (1912), 209–225.

Turner, T. Hudson, and J. H. Parker. *Some Account of Domestic Architecture in England.* 3 vols. in 4. Oxford, 1851–1859.

Varah, W. E. "Ancient Humber Ferries and the Roads they Served," *Notes and Queries,* CLXVIII (1935), 418–419.

Vaughan, Herbert Murray. "Wales," *Encyclopaedia Britannica,* 11th ed., XXVIII, 258–268.

Verbruggen, J. F. *De Krijgskunst in West-Europa in de Middeleeuwen (IXe tot Begin XIVe Eeuw).* Brussels, 1954.

——. *Het Leger en de Vloot van de Graven van Vlaanderen vanaf het Onstaan tot in 1305.* Brussels, 1960.

Victoria Histories of the Counties of England. Westminster and London, 1901– . Chapters entitled "Ancient Earthworks" as follows:

Armitage, Ella S., and Duncan Montgomerie. *York,* Vol. II. 1912.

Bothamley, C. H. *Somerset,* Vol. II. 1911.

Clinch, George, *Buckingham,* Vol. II. 1908.

——. *Sussex,* Vol. I. 1905.

—— and Duncan Montgomerie. *Surrey,* Vol. IV. 1912.

Cornish, J. B. *Cornwall,* Vol. I. 1906.

Cowper, H. Swainson. *Lancaster,* Vol. II, 1908.

Cox, J. C. *Derby,* Vol. I. 1905.

Downman, E. A. *Northampton,* Vol. II. 1906.

Goddard, A. R. *Bedford,* Vol. I. 1904.

Gould, I. Chalkley. *Durham,* Vol. I. 1905.

——. *Essex,* Vol. I. 1903.

——. *Hereford,* Vol. I. 1908.

——. *Kent,* Vol. I, 1908.

Ladds, S. Inskip. *Huntingdon,* Vol. I. 1926.

Lynam, Charles. *Stafford,* Vol. I, 1908.

Montgomerie, D. H. *Hertford,* Vol. II. 1908.

———. *Worcester,* Vol. IV. 1924.
Peake, Harold T. E. *Berks,* Vol. I. 1906.
Potts, William. *Oxford,* Vol. II. 1907.
Stevenson, W. *Nottingham,* Vol. I. 1906.
Wall, J. Charles. *Devon,* Vol. I. 1907.
———. *Leicester,* Vol. I. 1907.
———. *Middlesex,* Vol. II. 1911.
———. *Rutland,* Vol. I. 1908.
———. *Shropshire,* Vol. I. 1908.
———. *Suffolk,* Vol. I. 1911.
Willoughby, Gardner. *Lancaster,* Vol. II. 1908.
———. *Warwick,* Vol. I. 1904.
Vinogradoff, Paul. *English Society in the Eleventh Century.* Oxford, 1908.
Viollet-le-Duc, E. *Dictionnaire Raisonné de l'Architecture Française du XIe au XVIe Siècle.* 10 vols. Paris, 1854.
———. *Essai sur l'Architecture Militaire au Moyen Age.* Paris, 1854.
Vivian-Neal, A. W., and H. St. George Gray. "Materials for the History of Taunton Castle," *Proceedings of the Somerset Archaeological and Natural History Society,* LXXXVI (1940), 45–78.
Westell, W. Percival. "Sandon Mount, Hertfordshire: Its Site, Excavations and Problems," *Transactions of the St. Albans and Hertfordshire Architectural and Archaeological Society for 1934* (1935), 173–183.
Wheatley, S. W. "Boley Hill, Rochester," *Archaeologia Cantiana,* XXXIX (1927), 159–164.
———. "Boley Hill, Rochester," *Archaeologia Cantiana,* XLI (1929), 127–142.
White, G. H. "King Stephen's Earldoms," *Transactions of the Royal Historical Society,* 4th series, XIII (1930), 51–82.
———. "The Career of Waleran Count of Meulan and Earl of Worcester (1104–66)," *Transactions of the Royal Historical Society,* 4th series, XVII (1934), 19–49.
White, Herbert M. "Excavations in Castle Hill, Burton in Lonsdale," *The Antiquary,* XLI (1905), 411–418.
White, Lynn, Jr. *Medieval Technology and Social Change.* Oxford, 1962.
———. "Technology and Invention in the Middle Ages," *Speculum,* XV (1940), 141–160.
Whitelock, Dorothy. Review of Eric John, *Land Tenure in Early England, American Historical Review,* LXVI (1961), 1009–1010.

Whiting, C. E. "The Castle of Durham in the Middle Ages," *Archaeologia Aeliana,* 4th series, x (1933), 123–132.

Whitley, H. Michell. "Totnes Castle and Walled Town," *Transactions of the Devonshire Association,* 3rd series, VIII (1916), 189–198.

———. "Truro Castle," *Devon and Cornwall Notes and Queries,* XIII (1924–1925), 40–42.

Willard, James F. "Inland Transportation in England during the Fourteenth Century," *Speculum,* I (1926), 361–374.

Williams, A. H. *An Introduction to the History of Wales.* 2 vols. Cardiff, 1949.

Williams, D. T. "Medieval Foreign Trade: Western Ports," in *An Historical Geography of England before A.D. 1800,* ed. H. C. Darby. Cambridge, 1951.

Williamson, James A. *The English Channel, A History.* Cleveland, 1959.

Young, Brigadier Peter, and John Adair. *Hastings to Culloden,* London, 1964.

IV. Unpublished Papers and Letters

Hoyt, Robert S. "The Abingdon Fee in 1086," A paper read at the Annual Meeting of the Pacific Coast Branch of the American Historical Association, San Francisco, 29 August 1963.

Letter to author from John H. Barry for the Superintendent, Her Majesty's Nautical Almanac Office, Royal Greenwich Observatory, Herstmonceux Castle, Hailsham, Sussex, dated 16 May 1963.

Letter to author from D. J. C. King, F.S.A., Clevedon, Somerset, dated 8 October 1962.

Letter to author from D. J. C. King, F.S.A., Clevedon, Somerset, dated 4 July 1964.

Letter to author from J. R. Rossiter, Director, University of Liverpool Tidal Institute and Observatory, Birkenhead, Cheshire, dated 14 June 1963.

Millar, D. G. "The Anglo-Saxon Cavalry Reconsidered," an unpublished study, Department of History, Stanford University, 1963.

Index

471